# About the Cover Image

**Alfredo Ramos Martínez, _La India de las Floripondias_, ca. 1932** In this painting by the Mexican painter and muralist Alfredo Ramos Martínez (1871–1946), an indigenous woman holding an agave and standing in front of trumpet flower trees gazes at the viewer. Trained in Mexico and Paris, Ramos Martínez opened new types of art schools in Mexico in the 1910s and 1920s before moving to Los Angeles, where he spent the rest of his career. Known for his colorful and sympathetic paintings of indigenous people, Ramos Martínez painted large wall murals as well as works on paper and canvas. Mural painting, often with social and political messages, was an important art form in Mexico, and it inspired artists in other parts of the Americas, including the United States.

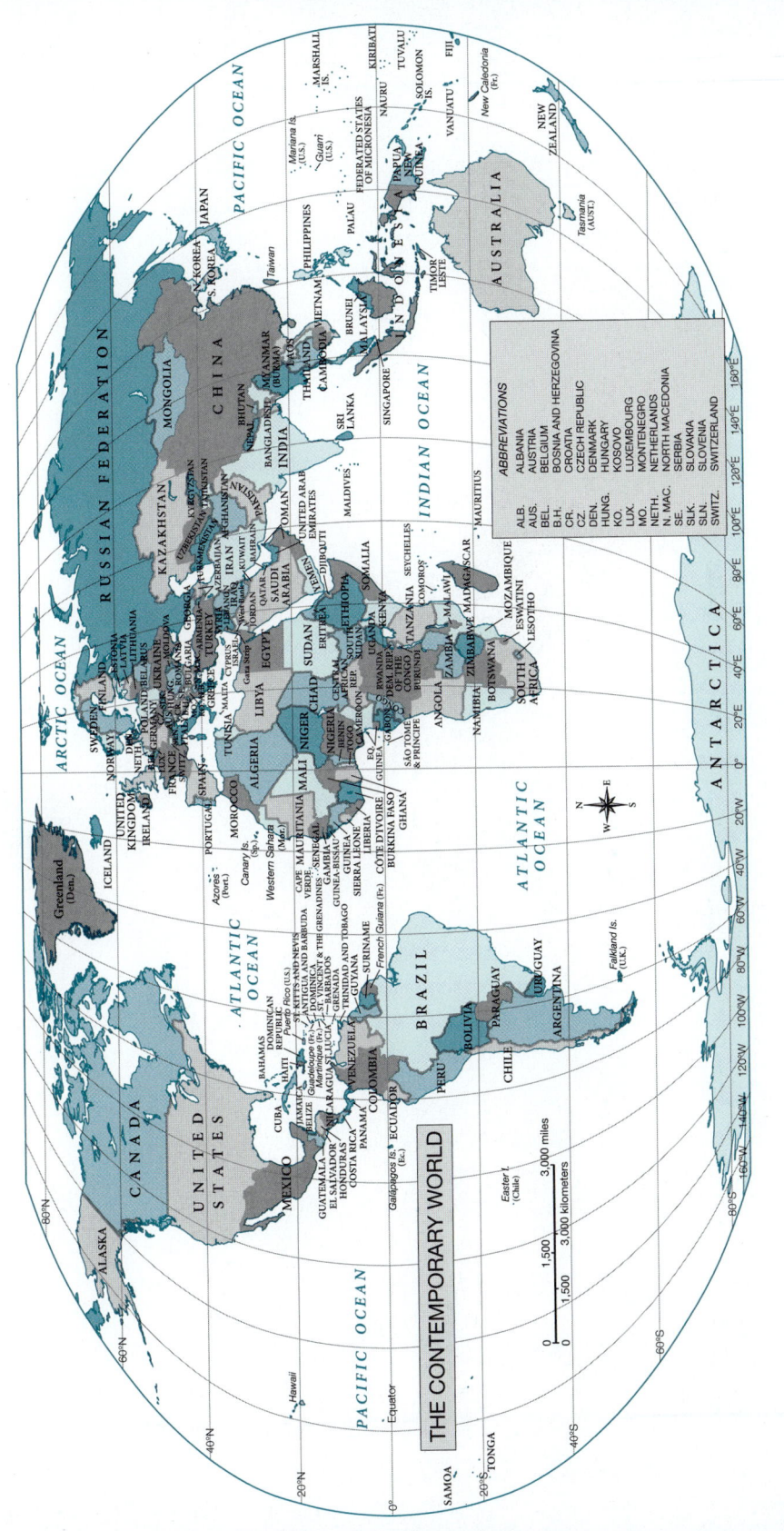

THE CONTEMPORARY WORLD

PACIFIC OCEAN

Equator – 0°

20°N

40°N

Tropic of Cancer

60°N

Arctic Circle

80°N

PACIFIC OCEAN

ASIA

GOBI

Yellow R. (Huang He)

Yangtze R.

URAL MTS.

HIMALAYA MTS.

Ganges R.

Bay of Bengal

South China Sea

20°S

40°S

60°S

80°S

AUSTRALIA

INDIAN OCEAN

Tropic of Capricorn

Arabian Sea

ARABIAN DESERT

Nile R.

Zambezi R.

Congo R.

AFRICA

KALAHARI DESERT

Niger R.

SAHARA

Mediterranean Sea

EUROPE

ALPS

0°

20°E

40°E

60°E

80°E

100°E

120°E

140°E

160°E

Ob R.

Volga R.

ATLANTIC OCEAN

20°W

40°W

60°W

80°W

100°W

120°W

140°W

160°W

NORTH AMERICA

ROCKY MTS.

APPALACHIAN MTS.

Mississippi R.

Gulf of Mexico

Caribbean Sea

SOUTH AMERICA

Amazon R.

ANDES MTS.

PACIFIC OCEAN

Antarctic Circle

N
E
W
S

0    1,000    2,000    3,000 miles

0  1,000  2,000  3,000 kilometers

**Vegetation zones**

Tundra
Northern forest
Temperate forest
Temperate grassland
Desert and dry shrub
Mediterranean shrub
Mountain grassland
Tropical grassland and savanna
Tropical forest
Permanent ice cover

VALUE EDITION

# A History of World Societies

**Twelfth Edition**

## Volume 2: Since 1450

**Merry E. Wiesner-Hanks**
*University of Wisconsin–Milwaukee*

**Patricia Buckley Ebrey**
*University of Washington*

**Roger B. Beck**
*Eastern Illinois University*

**Jerry Dávila**
*University of Illinois at Urbana-Champaign*

**Clare Haru Crowston**
*University of Illinois at Urbana-Champaign*

**John P. McKay**
*University of Illinois at Urbana-Champaign*

bedford/st.martin's
Macmillan Learning

Boston | New York

*Vice President:* Leasa Burton
*Senior Program Director:* Michael Rosenberg
*Senior Executive Program Manager:* William J. Lombardo
*Director of Content Development:* Jane Knetzger
*Senior Development Editor:* Leah R. Strauss
*Assistant Editor:* Julia Bell
*Director of Media Editorial:* Adam Whitehurst
*Media Editor:* Mollie Chandler
*Senior Marketing Manager:* Melissa Rodriguez
*Senior Director, Content Management Enhancement:* Tracey Kuehn
*Senior Managing Editor:* Michael Granger
*Executive Content Project Manager:* Christina M. Horn
*Assistant Content Project Manager:* Natalie Jones
*Senior Workflow Project Manager:* Jennifer Wetzel
*Production Supervisor:* Brianna Lester
*Director of Design, Content Management:* Diana Blume
*Interior Design:* Lumina Datamatics, Inc.
*Cover Design:* William Boardman
*Cartographer:* Mapping Specialists, Ltd.
*Director of Rights and Permissions:* Hilary Newman
*Text Permissions Manager, Lumina Datamatics, Inc.:* Elaine Kosta
*Executive Permissions Editor:* Robin Fadool
*Photo Researcher:* Bruce Carson
*Director of Digital Production:* Keri deManigold
*Executive Media Project Manager:* Michelle Camisa
*Copy Editor:* Susan Zorn
*Indexers:* Leoni Z. McVey, Rebecca McCorkle
*Composition:* Lumina Datamatics, Inc.
*Cover Image:* © The Alfredo Ramos Martínez Research Project/Christie's Images/
   Bridgeman Images
*Printing and Binding:* LSC Communications

Library of Congress Control Number: 2020942198

ISBN: 978-1-319-24454-5 (Combined Edition)
ISBN: 978-1-319-30406-5 (Volume 1)
ISBN: 978-1-319-30409-6 (Loose-leaf Edition, Volume 1)
ISBN: 978-1-319-30407-2 (Volume 2)
ISBN: 9781-319-30411-9 (Loose-leaf Edition, Volume 2)

Printed in the United States of America.
1  2  3  4  5  6      25  24  23  22  21  20

**ACKNOWLEDGMENTS**

*Acknowledgments and copyrights appear on the same page as the text and art selections they cover; these acknowledgments and copyrights constitute an extension of the copyright page.*

*For information, write:* Bedford/St. Martin's, 75 Arlington Street, Boston, MA 02116

# Preface
## Why This Book This Way

We are pleased to publish the Value Edition of *A History of World Societies,* Twelfth Edition. The Value Edition provides the social and cultural focus, comprehensive regional organization, and global perspective that have long been hallmarks of *A History of World Societies* in a two-color, trade-sized format at a low price. Featuring the unabridged narrative of the twelfth edition of the comprehensive parent text and select images, maps, and pedagogical tools, the Value Edition incorporates the latest and best scholarship in the field in an accessible, student-friendly manner. Each of the authors on our collaborative team is a regional expert who has deep experience in teaching world history and who brings insights into the text from the classroom, as well as from new secondary works and his or her own research in archives and libraries. The pedagogical tools of the Value Edition—both print and digital—have been carefully designed to help students think historically and master the material.

## The Story of *A History of World Societies*

In this age of global connections, with their influence on the economy, migration patterns, popular culture, disease, and climate change, among other aspects of life, the study of world history is more vital and urgent than ever before. An understanding of the broad sweep of the human past helps us comprehend today's dramatic changes and enduring continuities. People now migrate enormous distances and establish new lives far from their places of birth, yet migration has been a constant in history since the first humans walked out of Africa. Satellites and cell phones now link nearly every inch of the planet, yet the expansion of communication networks is a process that is thousands of years old. Children who speak different languages at home now sit side by side in schools and learn from one another, yet intercultural encounters have long been a source of innovation, transformation, and, at times, unfortunately, conflict.

This book is designed for twenty-first-century students who will spend their lives on this small interconnected planet and for whom an understanding of only local or national history will no longer be sufficient. We believe that the study of world history in a broad and comparative context is an exciting, important, and highly practical pursuit. It is our conviction, based on considerable experience in introducing large numbers of students to world history, that a book reflecting current trends in scholarship can excite readers and inspire an enduring interest in the long human experience.

Our strategy has been twofold. First, we have made social, cultural, and environmental history the core elements of our narrative. We know that engaging students' interest in the past is often a challenge, but we also know that the emphasis on individual experience connects with students and makes the past vivid and accessible. We seek to re-create the lives of ordinary people in appealing human terms and also to highlight the interplay between men's and women's lived experiences and the ways they reflect on these to create meaning. Thus, in addition to foundational works of philosophy and literature, we include popular songs and stories. We present objects along with texts as important sources for studying history, and this has allowed us to incorporate the growing emphasis on material culture in the work of many historians. People from all walks of life commented on (and complained about) the weather, discussed changing harvests and declines in animal and fish stocks, and contemplated the relationship of humans to nature. Thus integrating our new environmental theme with the existing social and cultural themes was not difficult. At the same time, we have been mindful of the need to give great economic, political, and intellectual developments the attention they deserve. We want to give individual students and instructors an integrated perspective so that they can pursue—on their own or in the classroom—the themes and questions that they find particularly exciting and significant.

Second, we have made every effort to strike an effective global and regional balance. The whole world interacts today, and to understand the interactions and what they mean for today's citizens, we must study the whole world's history. Thus we have adopted a comprehensive regional organization with a global perspective that is clear and manageable for students. For example, Chapter 7 introduces students in depth to East Asia, and at the same time the chapter highlights the cultural connections that occurred via the Silk Road and the spread of Buddhism. We study all geographical areas, conscious of the separate histories of many parts of the world, particularly in the earliest millennia of human development. We also stress the links among cultures, political units, and economic systems, for these connections have made the world what it is today. We make comparisons and connections across time as well as space, for understanding the unfolding of the human story in time is the central task of history. We further students' understanding of these connections with the addition of timelines in each chapter that put regional developments into a global context.

## Primary Sources for Historical Thinking

For those who are using LaunchPad, *A History of World Societies* offers an extensive program of primary source assignments to help students master a number of key learning outcomes, among them **critical thinking, historical thinking, analytical thinking**, and **argumentation**, as well as learning about the **diversity of world cultures**. In this twelfth edition, every chapter includes **Think Like a Historian**, which typically groups five or six textual or visual sources around a central question, with additional questions to guide students' analysis of the evidence and a "Put It All Together" assignment that asks them to synthesize the sources with what they have learned in class and use the evidence to create an argument. Topics include "Slavery in Roman and Germanic Society" (Chapter 8), "When and Why Did Foot Binding Begin?" (Chapter 12), "Forced Relocation of Armenians to Persia" (Chapter 17), "The Rights of Which Men?" (Chapter 22), and "The Relationships Between People and Epidemics" (Chapter 33).

To encourage comparisons, we have sharpened the focus of the **Compare Viewpoints** feature, which provides students with perspectives from two people on a key issue, sometimes within one culture and sometimes from two different cultures. This feature offers a pair of primary documents on a topic that illuminates the human experience, allowing us to provide more concrete examples of differences in the ways people thought. Anyone teaching world history has to emphasize larger trends and developments, but students sometimes get the wrong impression that everyone in a society thought alike. We hope that teachers can use these passages to get students thinking about diversity both within and across societies. The 33 Compare Viewpoints assignments — one in each chapter — introduce students to working with sources, encourage critical analysis, and extend the narrative while giving voice to the people of the past. Each includes a brief introduction and questions for analysis. Carefully chosen for accessibility, each pair of documents presents views on a diverse range of topics, such as "Calendar Megaliths in Egypt and England" (Chapter 1), "Roman and Chinese Officials Confront Natural Disasters" (Chapter 6), "The Muslim Conquest of Spain" (Chapter 9), "Aztec and Spanish Views on Christian Conversion in New Spain" (Chapter 16), "Jean-Jacques Rousseau and Mary Wollstonecraft on Women's Nature" (Chapter 19), and "Gandhi and Mao on Revolutionary Means" (Chapter 29).

A third type of original source feature, **Analyze Visual Evidence** and **Analyze Written Evidence** (one of each in each chapter), features an individual visual or written source that is longer and more substantial than those in other features and is chosen to extend and illuminate a major historical issue, with headnotes and questions that help students understand the source and connect it to the rest of the chapter. Selected for their interest and carefully integrated into their historical context, these in-depth examinations of sources provide firsthand encounters with people of the past and should, we believe, help students "hear" and "see" the past. Topics include "The Teachings of Confucius" (Chapter 4); "Orthodox Icon of Jesus" (Chapter 8); "The Court of the Lions at the Alhambra" (Chapter 9); "Woodcuts from Agricola's *De re metallica*" (Chapter 15); "Control of Locusts" (Chapter 21); "*Rain, Steam, and Speed—the Great Western Railway*" (Chapter 23); "Reyita Castillo Bueno on Slavery and Freedom in Cuba" (Chapter 27); "C. L. R. James on Pan-African Liberation" (Chapter 31); "A Member of China's Red Guards on Democratic Reform" (Chapter 32); and "A Brazilian Band on Globalization" (Chapter 33).

Taken together, the primary source features in the LaunchPad for this book offer the tools for building historical skills, including **chronological reasoning, explaining causation, evaluating context,** and **assessing perspective.** The suggestions for essays based on the primary sources encourage students to further expand their skills as they use their knowledge to develop historical arguments and write historical analyses. In LaunchPad these features are each accompanied by autograded questions that test students on their basic understanding of the sources so instructors can ensure that students read the sources, quickly identify and help students who may be struggling, and focus more class time on thoughtful discussion and instruction. (For more on LaunchPad, see below.)

In addition, our **primary source documents collection,** *Sources of World Societies,* includes written and visual sources, many chosen by the authors of the textbook, that closely align the readings with the chapter topics and themes of this edition. The documents are available in a fully assignable and assessable electronic format within each chapter in LaunchPad, and the multiple-choice questions — now accompanying each source — measure comprehension and hold students accountable for their reading.

Finally, the **Bedford Document Collections** provide a flexible repository of discovery-oriented primary source projects ready to assign. These primary source projects are available in a low-cost, easy-to-use digital format or can be combined with other course materials in Bedford Select to create an affordable, personalized print product. Each curated project poses a historical question and guides students through analysis of the sources. Examples include "The Silk Road: Travel and Trade in Premodern Inner Asia"; "The Spread of Christianity in the Sixteenth and Early Seventeenth Centuries"; "The Singapore Mutiny of 1915: Understanding World War I from a Global Perspective"; and "Living Through Perestroika: The Soviet Union in Upheaval, 1985–1991."

## Updates to the Narrative

This edition is enhanced by the incorporation of new scholarship and subject areas that immerse students in the dynamic and ongoing work of history. Along with the **addition of material on the environment and science-based evidence throughout**, updates to the twelfth edition include a revised section on human evolution to fit with newest scholarship (Chapter 1); a thorough chapter revision to include more discussion of the reasons for Roman success, the incorporation of conquered peoples as citizens, the continued role of elites, the organization of the army, and the importance of cultural blending (Chapter 6); a significant chapter revision, including more on the actual practices of Islam (Chapter 9); revised discussions of the Incas, religion in the Americas, and crop domestication (Chapter 11); revision of the section on the Black Death to incorporate new scholarship (Chapter 14); new section on weaponry and mining (Chapter 15); expanded coverage of the Indian Ocean trade and new section on ideas about race (Chapter 16); more discussion of Sufism and updated material on shifting trade routes (Chapter 17); more thorough discussion of the Little Ice Age, the fiscal-military state, and Poland-Lithuania (Chapter 18); revised analyses of the Scientific Revolution and the Enlightenment (Chapter 19); new material on gunpowder weapons and ocean fishing and whaling (Chapter 21); new discussion of settler colonialism and its impacts (Chapter 27); revised discussions of Korean and Vietnamese independence and war (Chapter 31); a new section exploring human rights and liberation movements (Chapter 32); and coverage of recent global events including the COVID-19 pandemic (Chapter 33). In terms of chapter organization, our own teaching and discussion with colleagues led us to reverse the chapter order of Chapters 12 and 13. Chapter 12: States and Cultures in East Asia, 800–1400, is now followed by Chapter 13: Cultural Exchange in Central and Southern Asia, 300–1400, to fit better with the more common course organization.

## Student Engagement with Biography

In our years of teaching world history, we have often noted that students come alive when they encounter stories about real people in the past. To give students using the LaunchPad a chance to see the past through ordinary people's lives, each chapter includes one of the popular **Individuals in Society** biographical essays, each of which offers a brief study of an individual or group, informing students about the societies in which the individuals lived. This feature grew out of our long-standing focus on people's lives and the varieties of historical experience, and we believe that readers will empathize with these human beings who themselves were seeking to define their own identities. The spotlighting of individuals, both famous and obscure, perpetuates the book's continued attention to cultural and intellectual developments, highlights human agency, and reflects changing interests within the historical profession as well as the development of "micro-history." New biographical essays include "King Taharqa, Ruler of Kush and Egypt" (Chapter 2); "Li Bing, Water-Works Expert" (Chapter 4); "King Ezana, Christian Ruler of Aksum" (Chapter 10); "Bana, Romance Writer" (Chapter 13); "Leonardo da Vinci, Artist, Inventor, Genius" (Chapter 15); "Vincent Ogé, Free Man of Color and Revolutionary" (Chapter 22); "George Sand, Novelist Who Defied Gender Roles" (Chapter 24); "Nawal El Saadawi, Public Health Advocate in Egypt" (Chapter 31); and "Anani Dzidzienyo, Scholar of the African Diaspora" (Chapter 32).

## Geographic Literacy

We recognize students' difficulties with geography, and the new edition retains our **Map the Past map activities** in LaunchPad. Included in each chapter, these activities ask students to analyze a map and make connections to the larger processes discussed in the narrative, giving them valuable practice in reading and interpreting maps. In LaunchPad, these maps come with new assignable activities. Throughout the textbook and online in LaunchPad, nearly **100 full-size maps** illustrate major developments in the chapters. In addition, **75 spot maps** are embedded in the narrative to show specific areas under discussion.

## Chronological Literacy in a Global Context

The increased attention to global connections and comparisons that marks this edition can also be seen in timelines at the end of each chapter. Along with graphically displaying major events and developments from the chapter, they also include key developments in other regions with cross-references to the chapters in which they are discussed. These comparisons situate events in the global story and help students identify similarities and differences among regions and societies.

## Helping Students Understand the Narrative

We know firsthand and take seriously the challenges students face in understanding, retaining, and mastering so much material that is often unfamiliar. With the goal of making this the most student-centered edition yet, we continued to enhance the book's pedagogy on many fronts. To focus students' reading, each chapter opens with a chapter preview with focus questions keyed to the main chapter headings. These questions are repeated within the chapter and again in the "Chapter Review" section at the end of each chapter that provides helpful guidance for reviewing key topics. "Chapter Review" also includes "Make Comparisons and Connections" questions that prompt students to assess larger developments across chapters, thus allowing them to develop skills in evaluating change and continuity, making comparisons, and analyzing context and causation.

Within the narrative, a chapter summary reinforces key chapter events and ideas for students. This is followed by the chapter-closing **Make Connections, Look**

**Ahead** feature, which synthesizes main developments and makes connections and comparisons between countries and regions to explain how events relate to larger global processes, such as the influence of the Silk Road, the effects of the transatlantic slave trade, and the ramifications of colonialism. This feature also serves as a bridge to subsequent chapters.

**Key terms** are bolded in the text, defined in the margin, and listed in the "Chapter Review" section to promote clarity and comprehension, and **phonetic spellings**—increased in this edition—are located directly after terms that readers are likely to find hard to pronounce. A **Glossary of Key Terms** can be found at the end of the book.

The high-quality art and map program has been thoroughly revised and features **hundreds of contemporaneous illustrations**. To make the past tangible, and as an extension of our attention to cultural history, we include numerous artifacts—from weapons and armor to dishes, furnishings, and figurines. As in earlier editions, all illustrations have been carefully selected to complement the text, and all include captions that inform students while encouraging them to read the text more deeply. **Numerous high-quality full-size maps** illustrate major developments in the narrative, and helpful spot maps are embedded in the narrative to locate areas under discussion.

## Helping Instructors Teach with Digital Resources

For instructors who want a basic autograded tool that will ensure that students read the narrative before they come to class, mobile-ready and accessible **Achieve Read & Practice for *A History of World Societies*** offers an exceptionally easy-to-use option at a value-based price. This simple product pairs the Value Edition e-book—a two-color narrative-only text (no boxed features or sources and reduced number of visuals)—with the power of **LearningCurve** quizzing, all in a format that is mobile-friendly, allowing students to read and take quizzes on the reading using the device of their choosing.

For instructors who want an e-book with a full suite of primary sources and autograded assessments for the narrative and sources, *A History of World Societies* is offered in Macmillan's premier learning platform, **LaunchPad**, an intuitive, interactive e-book and course space with a comprehensive set of options for engaging and assessing students. Available packaged with the print text or at a low price when used alone, LaunchPad grants students and teachers access to a wealth of online tools and resources built specifically for our text to enhance reading comprehension and promote in-depth study. LaunchPad's course space and interactive e-book are ready to use as is, or they can be edited and customized with the instructor's own materials and assigned right away.

Developed with extensive feedback from history instructors and students, **LaunchPad for *A History of World Societies*** includes the complete narrative of the print book; the companion reader, *Sources of World Societies*; and **LearningCurve**, an adaptive learning tool designed to get students to read before they come to class. With new **source-based questions in the test bank and in LearningCurve**, instructors now have more ways to test students on their understanding of sources and narratives in the book.

This edition of LaunchPad also includes **Guided Reading Exercises** that prompt students to be active readers of the chapter narrative and autograded **primary source quizzes** to test comprehension of written and visual sources. These features, plus **additional primary source documents, video sources and tools for making video assignments, map activities, flashcards, and customizable test banks**, make LaunchPad the premium platform for instructors who want a multifaceted teaching tool for enlivening their courses and accessing their students.

These learning platforms have not changed the central mission of the book but seek to enhance it by reaching students wherever they are in their learning and give instructors new ways to invigorate their courses. To learn more about the benefits of LearningCurve, LaunchPad, and Achieve Read & Practice, see the "Versions and Supplements" section on page xvii.

## Acknowledgments

It is a pleasure to thank the many instructors who critiqued the book in preparation for this revision: Kevin M. Brady, Tidewater Community College; Curt Cardwell, Drake University; A. H. Chamberlin, Virginia Western Community College; Thomas C. Doumaux, Pitt Community College; Steven C. Eames, Saint Anselm College; Joseph S. Freedman, Alabama State University; Robin Hermann, University of Louisiana at Lafayette; Benjamin Hurwitz, La Salle University; John O. Hyland, Christopher Newport University; Brian C. Johnson, Kilgore College; Barry E. Lee, Morehouse College; Rebecca Lindsay, Utah Valley University; Lise Namikas, Baton Rouge Community College; Kristen Post Walton, Salisbury University; Martina Saltamacchia, University of Nebraska at Omaha; Michael Bland Simmons, Auburn University; Michael F. Strmiska, SUNY–Orange (Orange County Community College); Joel Van Amberg, Tusculum University–Greenville; Godfrey Vincent, Tuskegee University; and Jill Young, Fort Valley State University.

It is also a pleasure to thank the many editors who have assisted us over the years, first at Houghton Mifflin and now at Bedford/St. Martin's (Macmillan Learning). At Bedford/St. Martin's, these include senior development editor Leah Strauss, senior program manager William J. Lombardo, senior program director Michael Rosenberg, executive content project manager Christina Horn, assistant project manager Natalie Jones, media editor Mollie Chandler, assistant editor Julia Bell, and photo researcher Bruce Carson. Other key contributors were text permissions editor Elaine Kosta, photo permissions editor Robin Fadool, copy editor Susan Zorn, proofreader Leslie Hoy, indexers Leoni McVey and Rebecca McCorkle, and cover designer William Boardman.

Many of our colleagues at the University of Illinois, the University of Washington, the University of Wisconsin–Milwaukee, and Eastern Illinois University continue to provide information and stimulation, often without even knowing it. We thank them for it. The authors recognize John P. McKay, Bennett D. Hill, and John Buckler, the founding authors of this textbook, whose vision set a new standard for world history textbooks. The authors also thank the many students over the years with whom we have used earlier editions of this book. Their reactions and opinions helped shape our revisions to this edition, and we hope it remains worthy of the ultimate praise they bestowed, that it is "not boring like most textbooks." Merry Wiesner-Hanks would, as always, like to thank her husband, Neil, without whom work on this project would not be possible. Patricia Ebrey thanks her husband, Tom. Clare Haru Crowston thanks her husband, Ali, and her children, Lili, Reza, and Kian, who are a joyous reminder of the vitality of life that we try to showcase in this book. Roger Beck thanks Ann for supporting him through six editions now, and for sharing his love of history. He is also grateful to the World History Association for all past, present, and future contributions to his understanding of world history. Jerry Dávila thanks Liv, Ellen, and Alex, who are reminders of why history matters.

Each of us has benefited from the criticism of his or her coauthors, although each of us assumes responsibility for what he or she has written. Merry Wiesner-Hanks has written and revised Chapters 1, 2, 5, 6, 8, 9, 14, and 15; Patricia Buckley Ebrey has written and revised Chapters 3, 4, 7, 12, 13, 21, and 26; Roger B. Beck has written and revised Chapters 10, 20, 25, and 28–30; Clare Haru Crowston has written and revised Chapters 16–19 and 22–24; and Jerry Dávila has written and revised Chapters 11, 27, and 31–33.

MERRY E. WIESNER-HANKS

PATRICIA BUCKLEY EBREY

ROGER B. BECK

JERRY DÁVILA

CLARE HARU CROWSTON

# Versions and Supplements

Adopters of *A History of World Societies* and their students have access to abundant print and digital resources and tools, the acclaimed *Bedford Series in History and Culture* volumes, and much more. The LaunchPad course space for *A History of World Societies* provides access to the narrative as well as a wealth of primary sources and other features, along with assignment and assessment opportunities at the ready. Achieve Read & Practice supplies adaptive quizzing and our mobile, accessible Value Edition e-book in one easy-to-use, affordable product. Both products also include a downloadable e-book for reading offline. See below for more information, visit the book's catalog site at **macmillanlearning.com**, or contact your local Bedford/St. Martin's sales representative.

## Get the Right Version for Your Class

To accommodate different course lengths and course budgets, *A History of World Societies* is available in several different versions and formats to best suit your course needs. The comprehensive *A History of World Societies* includes a full-color art program and a robust set of features. *A History of World Societies*, Concise Edition, also provides the unabridged narrative, with a streamlined art and feature program in full color, at a lower price. *A History of World Societies*, Value Edition, offers a trade-sized two-color option with the unabridged narrative and selected art and maps at a steeper discount. The Value Edition is also offered at the lowest price point in loose-leaf format, and all of these versions are available as e-books. To get the best value of all, package a new comprehensive or Concise print book with LaunchPad or a Value version with Achieve Read & Practice at a discount. LaunchPad users get a print version for easy portability with an interactive e-book for the full-feature text and course space, along with LearningCurve and loads of additional assignment and assessment options; Achieve Read & Practice users get a print version with a mobile, interactive Value Edition e-book plus LearningCurve adaptive quizzing in one exceptionally affordable, easy-to-use product.

- **Combined Volume** (Chapters 1–33): available in paperback comprehensive version, Concise Edition, Value Edition, loose-leaf, and e-book formats and in LaunchPad and Achieve Read & Practice
- **Volume 1: To 1600** (Chapters 1–16): available in paperback comprehensive version, Concise Edition, Value Edition, loose-leaf, and e-book formats and in LaunchPad and Achieve Read & Practice
- **Volume 2: Since 1450** (Chapters 16–33): available in paperback comprehensive version, Concise Edition, Value Edition, loose-leaf, and e-book formats and in LaunchPad and Achieve Read & Practice

As noted below, any of these volumes can be packaged with additional titles for a discount. To get ISBNs for discount packages, visit **macmillanlearning.com** or contact your Bedford/St. Martin's representative.

## Achieve READ & PRACTICE Assign Achieve Read & Practice So Your Students Can Read and Study Wherever They Go

Available to your students at an inexpensive price or for packaging with Value Edition survey books at no additional charge, Achieve Read & Practice is Bedford/St. Martin's most affordable digital solution for history courses. Intuitive and easy to use for students and instructors alike, Achieve Read & Practice is ready to use as is and can be assigned quickly. Achieve Read & Practice for *A History of World Societies* includes the Value Edition interactive e-book, a downloadable e-book for reading offline, LearningCurve adaptive quizzing, assignment tools, and a gradebook. All this is built with an intuitive interface that can be read on mobile devices and is fully accessible, easily integrates with course management systems, and is available at a discounted price so anyone can use it. Instructors can set due dates for reading assignments and LearningCurve quizzes in just a few clicks, making it a simple and affordable way to engage students with the narrative and hold students accountable for course reading so they will come to class better prepared. For more information, visit **macmillanlearning.com/ReadandPractice**, or to arrange a demo or class test, contact us at **historymktg@macmillan.com**.

## LearningCurve macmillan learning Assign LearningCurve So Your Students Come to Class Prepared

Students using LaunchPad receive access to LearningCurve for *A History of World Societies*. Assigning LearningCurve in place of reading quizzes is easy for instructors, and the reporting features help instructors track overall class trends and spot topics that are giving students trouble so they can adjust their lectures and class activities. This online learning tool is popular with students because it was designed to help them rehearse content at their own pace in a nonthreatening, game-like environment. The feedback for wrong answers provides instructional coaching and sends students back to the book for review. Students answer as many questions as necessary to reach a target score, with repeated chances to revisit material they haven't mastered. When LearningCurve is assigned, students come to class better prepared.

## LaunchPad macmillan learning Assign LaunchPad—an Assessment-Ready Interactive E-book and Course Space

Available for discount purchase on its own or for packaging with new survey books at no additional charge, LaunchPad is a breakthrough solution for history courses. Intuitive and easy to use for students and instructors alike, LaunchPad is ready to use as is and can be edited, customized with your own material, and assigned quickly. LaunchPad for *A History of World Societies* includes Bedford/St. Martin's high-quality content all in one place, including the full interactive e-book and the companion reader *Sources of World Societies*, a downloadable e-book for reading offline, plus LearningCurve formative quizzing, guided reading activities designed to help students read actively for key concepts, autograded quizzes for each primary source, and chapter summative quizzes. Through a wealth of formative and summative assessments, including the adaptive learning program of LearningCurve (see the full description ahead), students gain confidence and get into their reading before class. These features, plus additional primary source documents, video sources and tools for making video assignments, map activities, flashcards, and customizable test banks integrated into each chapter for instructor use, make LaunchPad an invaluable asset for any instructor.

LaunchPad easily integrates with course management systems, and with fast ways to build assignments, rearrange chapters, and add new pages, sections, or links, it lets teachers build the courses they want to teach and hold students accountable. For more information, visit **launchpadworks.com** or to arrange a demo or class test, contact us at **historymktg@macmillan.com.**

## Tailor Your Text to Match Your Course with Bedford Select for History

Create the ideal textbook for your course with only the chapters you need. Starting from the Value Edition version of the text, you can delete and rearrange chapters, select chapters of primary sources from *Sources of World Societies*, and add additional primary sources, curated skills tutorials, or your own original content to create just the book you're looking for. With Bedford Select, students pay only for material that will be assigned in the course, and nothing more. It is easy to build your customized textbook, without compromising the quality and affordability you've come to expect from Bedford/St. Martin's. For more information, talk to your Bedford/St. Martin's representative or visit **macmillanlearning.com/bedfordselect.**

## iClicker iClicker, Active Learning Simplified

iClicker offers simple, flexible tools to help you give students a voice and facilitate active learning in the classroom. Students can participate with the devices they already bring to class using our iClicker Reef mobile apps (which work with smartphones, tablets, or laptops) or iClicker remotes. iClicker Reef access cards can also be packaged with LaunchPad or your textbook at a significant savings for your students. To learn more, talk to your Macmillan Learning (Bedford/St. Martin's) representative or visit **www.iclicker.com.**

## Take Advantage of Instructor Resources

Bedford/St. Martin's has developed a rich array of teaching resources for this book and for this course. They range from lecture and presentation materials and assessment tools to course management options. Most can be found in LaunchPad or can be downloaded or ordered at **macmillanlearning.com.**

**Instructor's Resource Manual.** The instructor's manual offers both experienced and first-time instructors tools for presenting textbook material in engaging ways. It includes content learning objectives, annotated chapter outlines, and strategies for teaching with the textbook, plus suggestions on how to get the most out of LearningCurve and a survival guide for first-time teaching assistants.

**Guide to Changing Editions.** Designed to facilitate an instructor's transition from the previous edition of *A History of World Societies* to this new edition, this guide presents an overview of major changes as well as of changes in each chapter.

**Online Test Bank.** The test bank includes a mix of fresh, carefully crafted multiple-choice, matching, short-answer, and essay questions for each chapter. Many of the multiple-choice questions feature a map, an image, or a primary source excerpt as the prompt. All questions appear in Microsoft Word format and in easy-to-use test bank software that allows instructors to add, edit, re-sequence, filter by question type or learning objective, and print questions and answers. Instructors can also export questions into a variety of course management systems.

*The Bedford Lecture Kit*: **Lecture Outlines, Maps, and Images.** Look good and save time with *The Bedford Lecture Kit*. These presentation materials include fully customizable multimedia presentations built around chapter outlines that are embedded with maps, figures, and images from the textbook and are supplemented by more detailed instructor notes on key points and concepts.

## Print, Digital, and Custom Options for More Choice and Value

For information on free packages and discounts up to 50%, visit **macmillanlearning .com**, or contact your local Bedford/St. Martin's sales representative.

*Sources of World Societies,* Twelfth Edition. This primary source collection provides a revised selection of sources to accompany *A History of World Societies. Sources of World Societies* provides a broad selection of 165 primary source documents and images as well as editorial apparatuses to help students understand the sources. Each chapter contains five written and visual sources and includes a selection of sources dedicated to varied viewpoints on a specific topic. This companion reader is an exceptional value for students and offers plenty of assignment options for instructors. Available free when packaged with the print text and included in the LaunchPad e-book with autograded quizzes for each source. Also available on its own as a down-loadable e-book.

**Bedford Select for History.** Create the ideal textbook for your course with only the chapters you need. Starting from a Value Edition history text, you can rearrange chapters, delete unnecessary chapters, select chapters of primary sources from the companion reader and add primary source document projects from the Bedford Document Collections, or choose to improve your students' historical thinking skills with the Bedford Tutorials for History. In addition, you can add your own original content to create just the book you're looking for. With Bedford Select, students pay only for material that will be assigned in the course, and nothing more. Order your textbook every semester, or modify from one term to the next. It is easy to build your customized textbook, without compromising the quality and affordability you've come to expect from Bedford/St. Martin's.

**Bedford Document Collections.** These affordable, brief document projects provide 5 to 7 primary sources, an introduction, historical background, and other peda-gogical features. Each curated project—designed for use in a single class period and written by a historian about a favorite topic—poses a historical question and guides students through analysis of the sources. Document collections in world history include "The Silk Road: Travel and Trade in Premodern Inner Asia"; "The Spread of Christianity in the Sixteenth and Early Seventeenth Centuries"; "The Singapore Mutiny of 1915: Understanding World War I from a Global Perspective"; and "Living Through Perestroika: The Soviet Union in Upheaval, 1985–1991." These primary source projects are available in a low-cost, easy-to-use digital format or can be combined with other course materials in Bedford Select to create an affordable, personalized print product.

**Bedford Tutorials for History.** Designed to customize textbooks with resources relevant to individual courses, this collection of over a dozen brief units, each roughly 16 pages long and loaded with examples, guides students through basic skills such as using historical evidence effectively, working with primary sources, taking effective notes, avoiding plagiarism and citing sources, achieving the Texas student learning outcomes, and more. Up to two tutorials can be added to a Bedford/St. Martin's history survey title at no additional charge, freeing you to spend your class time focusing on content and interpretation. For more information and the full list of Bedford Tutorials for History, visit **macmillanlearning.com/historytutorials**.

**The Bedford Series in History and Culture.** More than 100 titles in this highly praised series combine first-rate scholarship, historical narrative, and important primary documents for undergraduate courses. Each book is brief, inexpensive, and focused on a specific topic or period. Recently published titles include *Apartheid in South Africa: A Brief History with Documents* by David M. Gordon; *Politics and Society in Japan's Meiji Restoration: A Brief History with Documents* by Anne Walthall and M. William Steele; and *The Congo Free State and the New Imperialism: A Brief History with Documents* by Kevin Grant. For a complete list of titles, visit **macmillanlearning.com**. Package discounts are available.

**Trade Books.** Titles published by sister companies Hill and Wang; Farrar, Straus and Giroux; Henry Holt and Company; St. Martin's Press; Picador; and Palgrave Macmillan are available at a 50% discount when packaged with Bedford/St. Martin's textbooks. For more information, visit **macmillanlearning.com/tradeup**.

*A Pocket Guide to Writing in History.* Updated to reflect changes made in the 2017 *Chicago Manual of Style* revision, this portable and affordable reference tool by Mary Lynn Rampolla provides reading, writing, and research advice useful to students in all history courses. Concise yet comprehensive advice on approaching typical history assignments, developing critical reading skills, writing effective history papers, conducting research, using and documenting sources, and avoiding plagiarism—enhanced with practical tips and examples throughout—has made this slim reference a bestseller. Package discounts are available.

*A Student's Guide to History.* This complete guide to success in any history course provides the practical help students need to be successful. In addition to introducing students to the nature of the discipline, author Jules Benjamin teaches a wide range of skills from preparing for exams to approaching common writing assignments, and explains the research and documentation process with plentiful examples. Package discounts are available.

# Brief Contents

# Contents

## CHAPTER 23

## The Revolution in Energy and Industry, 1760–1850   585

## CHAPTER 24

## Ideologies of Change in Europe, 1815–1914   612

# Maps, Figures, and Tables

# Introduction
## The Origins of Modern World Societies

The origins of modern societies lie deep in the past. World historians increasingly begin their exploration of the human past millions of years ago, when humans evolved from a primate ancestor in eastern Africa. Humans migrated out of Africa in several waves, walking along coasts and over land, eventually spreading across much of the earth. Their tools were initially multipurpose sharpened stones and sticks, but gradually they invented more specialized tools that enabled them to obtain food more easily, make clothing, build shelters, and decorate their surroundings. Environmental changes, such as the advance and retreat of the glaciers, shaped life dramatically.

## The Earliest Human Societies, to 2500 B.C.E.

Studying the physical remains of the past, scholars constructed a model of time and gave labels to eras according to the primary materials out of which tools that survived were made. (Constructing models of time is called "periodization.") Thus the earliest human era became the Stone Age, the next era the Bronze Age, and the next the Iron Age. They further divided the *Stone* Age into the Old Stone Age, or Paleolithic, during which people used stone, bone, and other natural products to make tools and obtained food largely by foraging, that is, by gathering plant products, trapping or catching small animals and birds, and hunting larger prey. This was followed by the New Stone Age, or Neolithic, which saw the beginning of agricultural and animal domestication. People around the world adopted agriculture at various times, and some never did, but the transition between the Paleolithic and the Neolithic is usually set at about 9000 B.C.E., the point at which agriculture was first developed.

In the Paleolithic period, people lived in small groups of related individuals, moving through the landscape in the search for food. Most had few material possessions, and social and gender hierarchies were probably much less pronounced than they would become later. Beginning around 50,000 B.C.E. people in many parts of the world began to decorate their surroundings and the objects they made, often with vivid representations of animals and people, and sometimes with symbols. These, and careful burials of the dead, suggest that people had developed ideas about supernatural or spiritual forces beyond the visible material world.

Beginning about 9000 B.C.E. people living in the Near East, and then elsewhere, began to plant seeds as well as gather wild crops, raise certain animals instead of hunt them, and selectively breed both plants and animals to make them more useful to humans. This domestication of plants and animals, called the Agricultural Revolution, was the most important change in human history. Crop raising began as horticulture, in which people—often women—used hand tools to plant and harvest. Animal domestication began with sheep and goats, which were often herded from place to place so that they could eat the available vegetation, an economic system called pastoralism. The domestication of large animals such as cattle and water buffalo led to plow agriculture, through which humans could raise much more food. Agriculture required more labor than did foraging, but it allowed the human population to grow far more quickly.

The division of labor that plow agriculture required led to growing social hierarchies between those who could afford the new tools and products and those who could not. These were reinforced over generations as children inherited goods and status from their parents, and as social norms and laws were developed that led members of the elite to marry one another. Plow agriculture also strengthened differentiation based on gender; men became more associated with the world beyond the household and women with the domestic realm. Neolithic agricultural communities developed technologies to meet their needs, including pottery, cloth-weaving, and wheeled vehicles, and they often traded with one another for products that they could not obtain locally. In some parts of the world, production and trade included copper and bronze, although most tools continued to be made of stone, bone, and wood. Religious ideas came to reflect the new agricultural society, with fertility as the most important goal and the gods, like humans, arranged in a hierarchy.

Although today's complex world seems very different from that of the earliest human societies, some aspects of life in the Neolithic, and even the Paleolithic, were very slow to change. Foraging, horticulture, pastoralism, and agriculture have been the primary economic activities of most people throughout the entire history of the world. Though today there are only a few foraging groups in very isolated areas, there are significant numbers of horticulturalists and pastoralists, and their numbers were much greater just a century ago. At that point the vast majority of the world's people still made their living directly through agriculture. The social patterns set in early agricultural societies — with most of the population farming the land, and a small number of elite who lived off their labor — lasted for millennia.

## The Ancient World, 3500 B.C.E.–500 C.E.

Ten thousand years ago, humans were living in most parts of the planet. They had designed technologies to meet the challenges presented by deep forests and jungles, steep mountains, and blistering deserts. As the climate changed, they adapted, building boats to cross channels created by melting glaciers, and finding new sources of food when old sources were no longer plentiful. In some places the new sources included domesticated plants and animals, which allowed people to live much more closely to one another than they had as foragers.

That proximity created opportunities, as larger groups of people pooled their knowledge to deal with life's challenges, but it also created problems. Human history from that point on can be seen as a response to these opportunities, challenges, and conflicts. As small villages grew into cities, people continued to develop technologies and systems to handle new issues. They created structures of governance based on something beyond the kin group to control their more complex societies, along with military forces and taxation systems to support the structures of governance. In some places they invented writing to record taxes, inventories, and payments, and they later put writing to other uses, including the preservation of stories, traditions, and history.

Writing, first developed around 3000 B.C.E., was perhaps the most important of the new technologies. Written sources provide a wider range of information about past societies than is available from physical evidence alone, which means that we know much more about the societies that left written records than about those that did not. Writing was developed to meet the needs of the more complex urban societies that are often referred to as civilizations, and particularly to meet the needs of the state, a new structure of governance distinct from tribes and kinship groups. In states, a small share of the population is able to coerce resources out of everyone else, and leaders gain and maintain power through organized violence, bureaucracies, systems of taxation, and written laws. These laws generally created more elaborate social and gender hierarchies.

## Mesopotamia and Egypt

States first developed in Mesopotamia, the land between the Euphrates and Tigris Rivers. Starting in the southern part of Mesopotamia known as Sumeria, sustained agriculture reliant on irrigation resulted in larger populations, a division of labor, and the growth of cities. Priests and rulers invented ways to control and organize these complex societies, including armies, taxation systems, and cuneiform writing. Conquerors from the north unified Mesopotamian city-states into larger empires and spread Mesopotamian culture over a large area. The most significant of these was the Babylonian empire, which under King Hammurabi in 1790 B.C.E. developed a written code of law and expanded trade connections.

During the third millennium B.C.E., a period known as the Old Kingdom, Egypt grew into a cohesive state under a single ruler in the valley of the Nile, which provided rich farmland and an avenue of communication. The Egyptians developed powerful beliefs in life after death, and the focal point of religious and political life was the pharaoh, a god-king who commanded the wealth, resources, and people of Egypt. For long stretches of history Egypt was prosperous and secure in the fertile Nile Valley, although at times various groups migrated in seeking better lives or invaded and conquered. Often the newcomers adopted aspects of Egyptian religion, art, and politics, and the Egyptians adopted aspects of the newcomers' cultures, such as the Hyksos's techniques for making and casting bronze. During the period known as the New Kingdom (ca. 1550–1070 B.C.E.), warrior-pharaohs expanded their power beyond the Nile Valley and created the first Egyptian empire, during which they first fought and then allied with the iron-using Hittites. After the collapse of the New Kingdom, the Nubian rulers of Kush conquered Egypt, and another group, the Phoenicians, came to dominate trade in the Mediterranean, spreading a letter alphabet.

For several centuries after the collapse of New Kingdom Egypt, a Semitic people known as the Hebrews or the Israelites controlled a small state on the western end of the Fertile Crescent. Their most important legacy was not political, but rather a new form of religious belief, Judaism, based on the worship of a single all-powerful god. The Hebrews wrote down their religious ideas, traditions, laws, advice literature, prayers, hymns, history, and prophecies in a series of books, which came to define the Hebrews as a people. This group of books, the Hebrew Bible, describes the Covenant between God and the Hebrew people and sets out laws and traditions that structured Hebrew society and family life. Reverence for these written texts was passed from Judaism to the other Western monotheistic religions that grew from it, Christianity and Islam.

In the ninth century B.C.E. the Assyrians began a rise to power from northern Mesopotamia, creating an empire by means of often brutal military conquest. Assyria's success was also due to sophisticated, farsighted, and effective military tactics, technical skills, and organization. From a base in what is now southern Iran, the Persians established an even larger empire, developing effective institutions of government and building roads. Though conquerors, the Persians, unlike the Assyrians, usually respected their subjects and allowed them to practice their native customs, traditions, and religions. Around 600 B.C.E. a new religion based on the teachings of the prophet Zoroaster grew in Persia. This religion emphasized the individual's responsibility to choose between good and evil.

## The Greeks

The people of ancient Greece developed a culture that fundamentally shaped the civilization of the western part of Eurasia. The Greeks were the first in the Mediterranean and neighboring areas to explore most of the philosophical questions that still concern thinkers today. Going beyond mythmaking, the Greeks strove to understand the world in logical, rational terms. The result was the birth of philosophy and science, subjects as important to many Greeks as religion. Drawing on their day-by-day experiences, the Greeks also developed the concept of politics, and their contributions to literature still fertilize intellectual life today.

The history of the Greeks is divided into two broad periods: the Hellenic, roughly the time between the founding of the first complex societies in the area that is now the Greek islands and mainland, about 3500 B.C.E., and the rise of the kingdom of Macedonia in the north of Greece in 338 B.C.E.; and the Hellenistic, the years from the reign of Alexander the Great (336–323 B.C.E.) through the spread of Greek culture from Spain to India (ca. 100 B.C.E.). During the Hellenic period Greeks developed a distinctive form of city-state known as the polis and made lasting cultural and intellectual achievements. During the Hellenistic period Macedonian and Greek armies defeated the Persian Empire and built new cities and kingdoms. During their conquests they blended their ideas and traditions with those of the societies they encountered, creating a vibrant culture.

In its earliest history, Greece's mountainous terrain and lack of navigable rivers led to political fragmentation. The Greeks developed the independent city-state, known as the polis, in which individuals governed themselves without elaborate political machinery. The two most important poleis were Sparta and Athens, which formed new social and political structures. Sparta created a military state in which men remained in the army most of their lives and women concentrated on raising healthy soldiers. After much social conflict, Athens created a democracy in which male citizens both voted for their leaders and had a direct voice in an assembly. As was the case in all democracies in ancient Greece, women, slaves, and outsiders could not be citizens.

In the classical period, between 500 and 336 B.C.E., Greek civilization reached its highest peak in politics, thought, and art, even as it engaged in violent conflicts. The Greeks successfully defended themselves from Persian invasions but nearly destroyed themselves in the Peloponnesian War, which pitted Sparta and its allies against Athens and its allies. In the last half of the fifth century B.C.E. the brilliant Athenian leader Pericles turned Athens into the showplace of Greece by sponsoring the construction of temples and other buildings. In other artistic developments, wealthy Athenians paid for theater performances in which dramatists used their art in attempts to portray, understand, and resolve life's basic conflicts. This period also saw the rise of philosophy, and Socrates, Plato, and Aristotle began a broad examination of the universe and the place of humans in it.

In the middle of the fourth century B.C.E. the Greek city-states were conquered by King Philip II and his son Alexander, rulers of Macedonia to the north of Greece. A brilliant military leader, Alexander conquered the entire Persian Empire, along with many territories to the east of Persia. He also founded new cities in which Greek and local populations mixed. His successors continued to build cities and colonies, which became powerful instruments in the spread of Greek culture and in the blending of Greek traditions and ideas with those of other peoples. The mixing of peoples in the Hellenistic era influenced religion, philosophy, and science. In the scholarly realm, advances were made in mathematics, astronomy, and mechanical design.

The Greek world was largely conquered by the Romans, and the various Hellenistic monarchies became part of the Roman Empire. In cultural terms the lines of conquest were reversed: The Romans derived their alphabet from the Greek alphabet, though they changed the letters somewhat. Roman statuary was modeled on Greek and was often made by Greek sculptors, who found ready customers among wealthy Romans. The major Roman gods and goddesses were largely the same as the Greek ones, though they had different names.

The influence of the ancient Greeks was not limited to the Romans. Art and thought in northern India was shaped by the blending of Greek and Buddhist traditions. European thinkers and writers made conscious attempts to return to classical ideals in art, literature, and philosophy during the Renaissance. In America political leaders from the Revolutionary era on decided that important government buildings should be modeled on the Parthenon and other temples, complete with marble statuary of their own heroes.

## The Romans

Like the Persians and the Macedonians, the Romans conquered vast territories. Their singular achievement lay in their ability to incorporate conquered peoples into the Roman system. Roman history is usually divided into two periods. The first is the republic (509–27 B.C.E.), the age in which Rome grew from a small group of cities in the middle of the Italian peninsula to a state that ruled much of the Mediterranean. The second period is the empire (27 B.C.E.–476 C.E.), in which the vast Roman territories were ruled by an emperor together with the Senate and other elites.

In its earliest development, Roman culture was influenced by the Etruscans, people who established permanent settlements in northern and central Italy. The Roman alphabet, toga, gladiatorial combat, paved roads, and urban drainage systems all came from the Etruscans. The city of Rome appears to have been originally ruled by kings. Sometime in the sixth century B.C.E. a group of aristocrats revolted against these kings and established a government in which the main institution of power was the Senate, an assembly of aristocrats. Rome thereby became a republic and expanded its territory in Italy through military conquests and alliances. Social conflict between aristocrats (patricians) and ordinary people (plebeians) led to a slight broadening of political rights.

In a series of wars the Romans conquered the Mediterranean, creating an overseas empire that brought them enormous power and wealth. Yet social unrest came in the wake of the war, opening unprecedented opportunities for ambitious generals who wanted to rule Rome like an empire. Civil war ensued, and it appeared as if the great politician and general Julius Caesar would emerge victorious, but he was assassinated by a group of senators. After his assassination and another period of civil war, his grandnephew Augustus finally restored peace and order to Rome, and transformed the government into one in which he held increasing amounts of power.

Augustus's success in creating solid political institutions was tested by the ineptness of some leaders who followed him, but later in the first century C.E. Rome entered a period of political stability, prosperity, and relative peace that lasted until the end of the second century C.E. During this period, later dubbed the *pax Romana*, the city of Rome became the magnificent capital of the empire. The Roman provinces and frontiers also saw extensive prosperity in the second century through the growth of agriculture, trade, and industry, among other factors. As the Roman Empire expanded eastward from Europe, it met opposition, yet even during the fighting, commerce among the Romans and peoples who lived in central and southern Asia thrived along a series of trade routes.

One of the most significant developments during the time of Augustus was the beginning of Christianity. Christianity was a religion created by the followers of Jesus of Nazareth (ca. 3 B.C.E.–29 C.E.), a Jewish man who taught that belief in his divinity led to eternal life. His followers spread their belief across the Roman Empire, transforming Christianity from a Jewish sect into a new religion. Christian groups were informal at first, but by the second century they began to develop hierarchical institutions modeled on those of Rome. At first many pagans in the Roman Empire misunderstood Christian practices and rites, and as a result Christians suffered sporadic persecution under certain Roman emperors. Gradually, however, tensions between pagans and Christians lessened, particularly as Christianity modified its teachings to make them more acceptable to wealthy and educated Romans.

In terms of politics and economics, the prosperity of the Roman Empire in the second century C.E. gave way to a period of civil war, barbarian invasions, and conflict with foreign armies in the third century. These disrupted agriculture, trade, and production and damaged the flow of taxes and troops. At the close of the third century the emperor Diocletian ended the period of chaos, in part because he recognized that the empire had become too great for one man to handle. He therefore divided it into a western and an eastern half. Diocletian and his successor, Constantine, also took rigid control of the struggling economy, but their efforts were not successful. Free tenant farmers lost control of their lands, exchanging them for security that landlords offered against barbarians and other threats. Meanwhile, tolerance of Christianity grew, and Constantine legalized the practice of the religion throughout the empire. The symbol of all the changes in the empire became the establishment of its new capital, Constantinople, the New Rome.

From the third century onward the Western Roman Empire slowly disintegrated. The last Roman emperor in the West, Romulus Augustus, was deposed by the

Ostrogothic chieftain Odoacer (OH-duh-way-suhr) in 476, but much of the empire had come under the rule of various barbarian tribes long before this. Thus despite the efforts of emperors and other leaders, by the fifth century the Western Roman Empire no longer existed, a development that scholars who focus on Europe have long seen as one of the great turning points in history.

## India

The vast subcontinent of India, protected from outsiders by the towering Himalayan Mountains to the north and by oceans on its other borders, witnessed the development of several early civilizations, primarily in the richly cultivated valley of the Indus River, which flows about 1,980 miles before reaching the ocean. Only in the northwest—the area between modern Afghanistan and Pakistan—was India accessible to invasion. The northwest was also the area of the earliest civilization in India, the Harappan, which built large cities mostly of brick. After the decline of this civilization, the Aryans, a nomadic Indo-European people, entered India by way of the Khyber Pass around 1500 B.C.E. They were able to establish dominance over large areas, including the eastern regions of the Ganges River. By 500 B.C.E. the Aryans ruled a number of large kingdoms in which cities were the centers of culture. The period of Aryan rule saw the evolution of a caste system designed to denote birth or descent and to distinguish Aryan from non-Aryan and rulers from the ruled. The four groups, or castes, that emerged—the *Brahmin* (priests), the *Kshatriya* (warriors), the *Vaishya* (peasants), and the *Shudra* (serfs)—became the dominant features of Indian society. Persons without a place in the hierarchical strata or who lost their caste status because of some violation of ritual were *outcastes*.

Through the Khyber Pass in 513 B.C.E. the Persian king Darius I entered India and conquered the Indus Valley. The Persians introduced political administration and coin-minting techniques, and they brought India into commercial and cultural contact with the sophisticated ancient Middle East. From the Persians the Indians adopted the Aramaic language and script, which they adapted to their needs and languages. In 326 B.C.E. the Macedonian king Alexander the Great invaded the Indus Valley, but his conquests had no lasting effect. Under Ashoka (r. 269–232 B.C.E.), ancient India's greatest ruler, India enjoyed peace and stability, but from 180 B.C.E. to 200 C.E. the region suffered repeated foreign invasions. There was no dominant unifying state, and regional cultures flourished. In the northwest rulers such as the Shakas and Kushans came from outside India.

Ancient India's most enduring legacies are the three great religions that flowered in the sixth and fifth centuries B.C.E.: Hinduism, Jainism, and Buddhism. One of the modern world's largest religions, Hinduism holds that the Vedas—hymns in praise of the Aryan gods—are sacred revelations and that these revelations prescribe the caste system. Religiously and philosophically diverse, Hinduism assures believers that there are many legitimate ways to worship Brahman, the supreme principle of life. India's best-loved hymn, the *Bhagavad Gita*, guides Hindus in a pattern of life in the world and of release from it.

Jainism derives from the teachings of the great thinker Vardhamana Mahavira (ca. 540–468 B.C.E.), who held that only an ascetic life leads to bliss and that all life is too sacred to be destroyed. Nonviolence is a cardinal principle of Jainism. Thus a Jain who wishes to do the least violence to life turns to vegetarianism.

Mahavira's contemporary, Siddhartha Gautama (ca. 563–483 B.C.E.), better known as the Buddha, was so deeply distressed by human suffering that he abandoned his Hindu beliefs in a search for ultimate enlightenment. Meditation alone, he maintained, brought total enlightenment in which everything is understood. Buddha developed the "Eightfold Path," a series of steps of meditation that could lead to *nirvana*, a state of happiness attained by the extinction of self and human desires. Buddha opposed all religious dogmatism and insisted that anyone, regardless of sex or class, could achieve enlightenment. He attracted many followers, and although Buddhism split into several branches after his death, Buddhist teachings spread throughout India to China, Japan, Korea, and Vietnam. Buddhism remains one of the great Asian religions and in recent times has attracted adherents in the West.

## China

Chinese civilization, which developed initially along the Huang He (Yellow) River, was much farther away from the ancient Middle East than India and had much less in the way of contact with other early civilizations. Still, the Shang Dynasty (ca. 1200 B.C.E.) shared features of other early civilizations, such as bronze technology, cities, and writing. The writing system China developed, with separate symbols for each word, had no connection to the writing systems of other parts of Eurasia and became a key feature of Chinese culture.

The Chinese always looked back on the Zhou period (ca. 1000–256 B.C.E.) as their classical age, when social and political ideas were perfected. After a few centuries, political unity was lost, and China consisted of many states, large and small, that made alliances with each other but also frequently fought each other. Political disorder seems to have stimulated philosophy, and this became the period when "one hundred schools of thought contended." Compared to Indian religious speculation, Chinese thinkers were more secular than religious in outlook. Interested primarily in social and economic problems, they sought universal rules of human conduct from the level of the family up to that of the state. Ancient China witnessed the development of Confucianism, Daoism, and Legalism, philosophies that profoundly influenced subsequent Chinese society and culture.

Confucius (551–479 B.C.E.) was interested in orderly and stable human relationships, and he focused on the proper duties and behavior of the individual. Confucius considered the family the basic unit in society. Within the family, male was superior to female and age to youth. If order was to exist in society, he taught, it must start at the level of the family. Those who help the king govern should be gentlemen, by which he meant men who exhibited the virtues of loyalty, sincerity, deference, generosity, and commitment. Only gentlemanly conduct, which involved a virtuous and ethical life, would lead to well-run government and peaceful conditions in society at large. Self-discipline, courtesy to others, punctiliousness in service to the state, and justice to the people are the obligations and behaviors expected of Confucian gentlemen. Confucius minimized the importance of class distinctions and taught that men of humble birth could achieve a high level of conduct and become gentlemen through education and self-discipline. The fundamental ingredient in the evolution of the Chinese civil service, Confucianism continued to shape Chinese government up to the twentieth century.

Daoism treated the problems of government very differently. In its two surviving books, *Laozi* and *Zhuangzi*, each named after a Daoist master, earnest efforts to perfect society were ridiculed. Daoism maintained that people would be happier only if they abandoned the world and reverted to simpler ways. Daoists insisted that the best government is the least active government. Public works and government services require higher taxes, which lead to unhappiness and popular resistance. According to the Daoists, the people should be kept materially satisfied and uneducated. A philosophy of consolation, Daoism was especially popular among those who were frustrated by the political system.

Legalism is the name given to a number of related political theories originating in the third century B.C.E. The founders of Legalism proposed pragmatic solutions to the problems of government, exalted the power of the state, and favored an authoritarian ruler who would root out dissent. They argued that laws should be made known, the penalties for infractions should be clear and harsh, and the laws and penalties should apply to everyone in society, even the close relatives of the ruler. Though Legalism seemed too harsh to many, it did contribute to the Chinese system of centralized bureaucratic rule.

In the third century B.C.E. the state of Qin adopted Legalism and then set out to defeat all the other states, thus unifying China. The Qin government attempted to achieve uniformity at many levels, standardizing weights and measures, writing systems, and laws. It even tried to do away with ideas it disapproved of by collecting and burning books. The new dynasty was called *Qin*, from which the Western term "China" derives. Under the Qin Dynasty and its successor, the Han, China achieved political and social stability and economic prosperity. On its northern border, however, Qin and Han faced tough military opponents in the Xiongnu, pastoralists who excelled at horsemanship.

The period of the Han Dynasty (206 B.C.E.–220 C.E.) witnessed notable intellectual achievements. First, many of the books that had been burned by the Qin were reconstructed from memory or hidden copies. These texts came to be known as the *Confucian Classics*. Scholars piously studied the books and worked to make them widely accessible as standards of moral behavior. Second, historical writing developed. The historian Sima Qian (145–ca. 85 B.C.E.) produced the *Records of the Grand Historian*, a massive and comprehensive survey of earlier Chinese civilization. These two sets of writings left a permanent mark on Chinese thought and peoples.

## The Islamic World, 600–1400

One of the most important developments in world history — whose consequences redound to our own day — was the rise and remarkable expansion of Islam in the early Middle Ages. Muhammad (ca. 570–632), a devout merchant of Mecca in present-day Saudi Arabia, called on his followers to return to God. Even before Muhammad's death his teachings spread through Arabia, uniting the tribes there. Within two centuries his followers controlled Syria, Palestine, Egypt, Iraq, Iran, northern India, Spain, and southern France, and his beliefs were carried eastward across Central Asia to the borders of China. In the ninth, tenth, and eleventh centuries the Muslims created a brilliant civilization centered at Baghdad in Iraq and Córdoba in Spain.

Muhammad believed that God sent him messages or revelations. These were later collected and published as the Qur'an, from an Arabic word meaning "reading" or "recitation." On the basis of God's revelations to him, Muhammad preached a strictly monotheistic faith based on the principle of the absolute unity and omnipotence of God. His followers came to call themselves Muslims, a word meaning "those who comply with God's will." The religion itself came to be called Islam, which means "submission to God." Muhammad described himself as the successor both of the Jewish patriarch Abraham and of Christ, and he asserted that his teachings replaced theirs. He invited and won converts from Judaism and Christianity.

Muhammad's followers carried their religion to the east and west by military conquest. Their rapid expansion was made possible by their own economic needs, the political weaknesses of their enemies, a strong military organization, and the practice of establishing army camps in newly conquered territories. Islam blended with local traditions in ways that made it broadly appealing to many ethnic and social groups.

At the same time that Islam expanded, it also split. Opposition arose to several of the individuals chosen to be caliphs, or successors to the Prophet Muhammad, which coalesced around Ali, Muhammad's cousin and son-in-law, who was chosen as the fourth leader in 656. Ali's supporters began to assert that Muhammad had designated Ali as imam, or leader, and that any leader who was not a descendant of Ali was a usurper. These supporters of Ali—termed Shi'a or Shi'ites from Arabic terms meaning "supporters" or "partisans" of Ali—saw Ali and subsequent imams as the divinely inspired leaders of the whole community. The larger body of Muslims—termed Sunnis, a word derived from Sunna, the practices of the community derived from Muhammad's example—accepted the first elections and saw the first caliphs as proper political leaders. This schism within Islam continues today. Sufism, an ascetic movement within Islam that sought a direct and mystical union with God, drew many followers from all classes.

Long-distance trade and commerce, which permitted further expansion of the Muslim faith, played a prominent role in the Islamic world, in contrast to the limited position it held in the heavily agricultural medieval West. The Black and Caspian Seas, the Volga River giving access deep into Russia, the Arabian Sea and the Indian Ocean, and to a lesser extent the Mediterranean Sea were the great commercial waterways of the Islamic world. Goods circulated freely over them. Muslims introduced new crops and agricultural techniques in many areas, and they invented capitalist commercial tools such as the bill of exchange, the check, and the joint stock company, which later spread to other parts of the world.

Long-distance trade brought the wealth that supported a gracious and sophisticated culture in the cities of the Muslim world. Baghdad in Iraq and Córdoba in Spain, whose streets were thronged with a kaleidoscope of races, creeds, customs, and cultures and whose many shops offered goods from all over the world, stand out as superb examples of cosmopolitan Muslim civilization. Baghdad and Córdoba were also great intellectual centers where Muslim scholars made advances in mathematics, medicine, and philosophy. The Arabs translated many ancient Greek texts by writers such as Plato and Aristotle. When, beginning in the ninth century, those texts were translated from Arabic into Latin, they came to play an important part in the formation of medieval European scientific, medical, and philosophical thought. Modern scholars consider Muslim civilization in the period from about 900 to 1200 among the most brilliant in the world's history.

# Asia, 300–1400

Between about 300 and 1400 the various societies of Asia continued to evolve their own distinct social, political, and religious institutions. Also in these years momentous changes swept across Asia. Buddhism spread from India to Central Asia, China, Korea, Japan, Southeast Asia, and Tibet. Turkic peoples in inner and western Asia converted to Islam, and one group of these conquered much of the Indian subcontinent. China, under the Tang and Song Dynasties, experienced a golden age. The first Japanese state was established. The Mongols formed a confederation of the tribes of the steppes of Inner Asia that had extraordinary success in conquering cities from Korea and China to Persia, Baghdad, and Russia. These centuries witnessed cultural developments that have molded and influenced later Asian societies.

## India

Under the Gupta kings, who ruled from around 320 to 500, India enjoyed a great cultural flowering. Interest in Sanskrit literature—the literature of the Aryans—led to the preservation of much Sanskrit poetry. A distinctly Indian drama appeared, and India's greatest poet, Kalidasa (ca. 380–450), like Shakespeare, blended poetry and drama. Mathematicians arrived at the concept of zero, essential for higher mathematics, and scientific thinkers wrestled with the concept of gravitation.

The Gupta kings succeeded in uniting much of the subcontinent. They also succeeded in repulsing an invasion by the Huns, but the effort exhausted the dynasty. After 600 India reverted to the pattern of strong local kingdoms in frequent conflict. Between 600 and 1400, India suffered repeated invasion as waves of steppe peoples swept down through the northwest corridor. The most successful were Turkic conquerors from the area of modern Afghanistan, who held power in Delhi for three centuries and managed to turn back the Mongols. By around 1400 India was as politically splintered as it had been before Gupta rule. Under the Delhi sultanate Islam became dominant in the Indus Valley (modern Pakistan). Elsewhere Hinduism resisted Islam.

One other development had a lasting effect on Indian society: the proliferation and hardening of the caste system. Early Indian society had been divided into four major groups. After the fall of the Guptas, further subdivisions arose, reflecting differences of profession, trade, tribal or racial affiliation, religious belief, and even place of residence. By 800 India had more than three thousand castes, each with its own rules and governing body. As India was politically divided, the castes served to fragment it socially.

## China

Scholars consider the period between 580 and 1200, which saw the rule of Tang and Song Dynasties, as China's golden age. In religion, political administration, agricultural productivity, and art, Chinese society attained a remarkable level of achievement. This era was followed by the rise of the Mongols, who in time engulfed China.

Merchants and travelers from India introduced Buddhism to China from the first century C.E. on. Scholars, rulers, the middle classes, and the poor all found appealing concepts in Buddhist teachings, and the new faith won many adherents.

China distilled Buddhism to meet its own needs, and Buddhism gained a place next to Confucianism and Daoism in Chinese life.

The Tang Dynasty, which some historians consider the greatest in Chinese history, built a state bureaucracy, the political sophistication of which was unequaled until recent times. Tang emperors subdivided the imperial administration into departments of military organization, maintenance and supply of the army, foreign affairs, justice, education, finance, building, and transportation. To staff this vast administration, an imperial civil service developed in which education, talent, and merit could lead to high office, wealth, and prestige. So effective was the Tang civil service and so deeply rooted did it become in Chinese society that it lasted until the twentieth century.

Under the Song Dynasty (960–1279), greatly expanded agricultural productivity, combined with advances in the technology of coal and iron and efficient water transport, supported a population of 100 million. (By contrast, Europe did not reach this figure until the late eighteenth century.) Greater urbanization followed in China. Political stability and economic growth fostered technological innovation, the greatest being the invention of printing. Tang craftsmen invented the art of carving words and pictures into wooden blocks, inking the blocks, and then pressing them onto paper. The invention of movable type followed in the eleventh century. As would happen in Europe in the fifteenth century, the invention of printing lowered the price and increased the availability of books and contributed to the spread of literacy. Printing led to the use of paper money, replacing bulky copper coinage, and to developments in banking. The highly creative Tang and Song periods also witnessed the invention of gunpowder, originally used for fireworks, and the abacus, which permitted the quick computation of complicated sums. In the creation of a large collection of fine poetry and prose, and in the manufacture of porcelain of superb quality and delicate balance, the Tang and Song periods revealed an extraordinary literary and artistic flowering.

Shipbuilding advanced, and large ships were used both for war and for trade. Trade expanded as Japan and Korea eagerly imported Chinese silks and porcelains. The Muslims shipped Chinese goods across the Indian Ocean to East African and Middle Eastern markets. Southern China participated in a commercial network that stretched from Japan to the Mediterranean.

The thirteenth century witnessed the violent and amazingly fast creation of the Mongol Empire, the largest continuous land empire in world history. The Mongols were a steppe nomadic people in north-central Asia who had fought largely among themselves until about 1200. Their extraordinary expansion was the result of a shortage of pasture land for their sheep, goats, and cattle, and the rise of a great warrior-leader, Chinggis Khan (1162–1227), who united the steppe peoples and led them to conquer and absorb one neighbor after another. Building a vast army of loyal followers to whom he displayed great generosity, and using a policy of terror as a weapon of war, Chinggis swept across Central Asia into northern China. In 1215, he burned Beijing, and many Chinese governors quickly submitted. Chinggis then turned westward and destroyed the Persian Empire, massacring hundreds of thousands of people. Under Chinggis's sons, the Mongols won control of Kievan Russia and Moscow, looted cities in Poland and Hungary, and established the Khanate of the Golden Horde. Chinggis's grandson Khubilai (r. 1260–1294) completed the conquest of

China and overran Korea. The Mongols viewed China as their most important conquest; Mongol rule extended over most of East Asia, which they called the Great Khanate. They even invaded, but did not conquer, Japan. The Chinese called the period of Mongol rule the Yuan Dynasty. In 1368 Hungwu, the first emperor of the Ming Dynasty, restored Chinese rule.

## Japan

The chain of islands that constitutes Japan entered written history only in sporadic references in Chinese writings, the most reliable set down in 297 C.E. Because the land of Japan is rugged, lacking navigable waterways, and because perhaps only 20 percent of it is arable, political unification by land proved difficult until modern times. The Inland Sea served both as the readiest means of communication and as a rich source of food; the Japanese have traditionally relied on fish and other marine products as important parts of their diet.

Early Japan was divided into numerous political units, each under the control of a particular clan, a large group of families claiming descent from a common ancestor and worshipping a common deity. In the third century C.E. the Yamato clan gained control of the fertile area south of modern Kyoto near Osaka Bay and subordinated many other clans. The Yamato chieftain proclaimed himself emperor and assigned specific duties and functions to subordinate chieftains. The Yamato established their chief shrine in the eastern part (where the sun-goddess could catch the first rays of the rising sun) of Honshu, the largest of Japan's four main islands. Around this shrine local clan cults sprang up, giving rise to a native religion that the Japanese called Shinto, the "Way of the Gods." Shinto became a unifying force and protector of the nation.

Through Korea two significant Chinese influences entered Japan and profoundly influenced Japanese culture: the Chinese system of writing and record keeping, and Buddhism. Under Prince Shotoku (574–622), talented young Japanese were sent to Tang China to learn Chinese methods of administration and Chinese Buddhism. They returned to Japan to share and enforce what they had learned. The Nara era of Japanese history (710–794), so called after Japan's first capital city, north of modern Osaka, was characterized by the steady importation of Chinese ideas and methods. Buddhist monasteries became both religious and political centers, supporting Yamato rule.

Perhaps because Buddhist temples had too much power in Nara, in 794 the imperial family removed the capital to Heian (modern Kyoto), where it remained until 1867. A strong reaction against Buddhism and Chinese influences followed, symbolized by the severance of relations with China in 838. The eclipse of Chinese influences liberated Japanese artistic and cultural forces, and a new Japanese style of art and architecture appeared. In writing, Japanese scholars produced two syllabaries, sets of phonetic signs that stand for syllables instead of whole words or letters. Unshackled from Chinese forms, Japanese writers created their own literary styles and modes of expression. The writing of history and poetry flowered, and the Japanese produced their first novel, *The Tale of Genji*, a classic of court life by the court lady Lady Murasaki written over several years (ca. 1000–1010).

The later Heian period witnessed the breakdown of central authority as aristocrats struggled to free themselves from imperial control. In 1156 civil war among the leaders of the great clans erupted. By 1192 the Minamato clan had defeated all opposition. Its leader Yoritomo (1147–1199) became *shogun*, or general-in-chief. Thus began the Kamakura Shogunate, which lasted from 1185 until 1333.

In addition to the powerful shogun, a dominant figure in the new society was the *samurai*, the warrior who by the twelfth century exercised civil, judicial, and military power over the peasants who worked the land. The samurai held his land in exchange for his promise to fight for a stronger lord. In a violent society strikingly similar to that of western Europe in the early Middle Ages, the Japanese samurai, like the French knight, constituted the ruling class at the local level. Civil war among the emperor, the leading families, and the samurai erupted again in 1331. In 1338 one of the most important military leaders, Ashikaga Takauji, defeated the emperor and established the Ashikaga Shogunate, which lasted until 1573. Meanwhile, the samurai remained the significant social figure.

By 1400 the continents of Africa, Asia, and Europe experienced considerable cultural contact with one another. Chinese silks passed across the Great Silk Road to southwestern Asia and Europe. The religious ideals of Buddhism spread from India to China and Korea. The expansion of Islam across northern Africa and into the Iberian Peninsula, down the east coast of Africa, across Central Asia and into northern India, and through the Malay Archipelago led to rich commercial contacts. Religious and philosophical ideas, artistic and architectural models, and scientific and medical learning flowed across these international trade routes. The centuries that witnessed the European religious-military-imperialistic expeditions to the Middle East known as the Crusades (ca. 1100–1300) led to the slow filtering of Muslim (and ancient Greek) medical and architectural knowledge to Europe. By way of Islam, features of Chinese technology, such as paper manufacture, and nautical information, such as the compass and the astrolabe, reached Europe.

## African Societies and Kingdoms, 1000 B.C.E.–1500 C.E.

Africa is a huge continent with many different climatic zones and diverse geography. The peoples of Africa are as diverse as the topography. Groups relying on herd animals developed in the drier, disease-free steppe regions well suited to domesticated animals, while agricultural settlements developed in the wetter savanna regions. In the tropical forests of central Africa and arid zones of southern Africa, hunter-gatherers dominated. Along the coasts and by lakes and rivers grew maritime communities whose inhabitants relied on fishing and trade for their livelihood.

Agriculture began very early in Africa. Knowledge of plant cultivation arrived in the Nile Delta in Egypt about the fifth millennium B.C.E. Settled agriculture then traveled down the Nile Valley and moved west across the Sahel to the central and western Sudan. Early societies across the western Sudan were profoundly affected as they switched from hunting and gathering in small bands to form settled farming communities. Populations increased significantly in this rich savanna zone that was ideally suited for grain production. Blood kinship brought together families in communities governed by chiefs or local councils. Animistic religions that recognized ancestral and nature spirits developed. The nature spirits were thought to dwell in nearby streams, forests, mountains, or caves.

Settled agriculture developed independently in West Africa. From there it spread to the equatorial forests. The spread of agriculture was related to the expansion of Bantu-speaking peoples, who originated in the Benue region, the borderlands of modern Cameroon and Nigeria. In the second millennium B.C.E. they began to spread south and east into the forest zone of equatorial Africa, eventually spreading across all of central and southern Africa. Possessing iron tools and weapons, domesticated livestock, and a knowledge of settled agriculture, these Bantu-speakers assimilated, killed, or drove away all the previous inhabitants of these regions.

Lines of trade and communication linked many parts of Africa with each other and with other parts of the world. The peoples of North Africa were closely connected with the Middle Eastern and European civilizations of the Mediterranean basin. Similarly, the peoples of the Swahili coast of East Africa participated in trade with Arabia, the Persian Gulf, India, China, and the Malay Archipelago.

Between 700 and 900, a network of caravan routes running south from the Mediterranean coast across the Sahara to the Sudan developed. Arab-Berber merchants exchanged manufactured goods for African gold, ivory, gum, and slaves from the West African savanna. The most essential component in the trans-Saharan trade was the camel. The camel made it possible for great loads to be hauled across vast stretches of hot, dry desert. The Berbers of North Africa endured these long treks south and then north again across the Sahara. To control this trade they fashioned camel saddles that gave them great political and military advantage. The primary items of trade were salt from the north and gold from the south, although textiles, fruit, ivory, kola nuts, gum, beads, and other goods were also prized by one side or the other. Enslaved West Africans, males and females, were also traded north to slave markets in Morocco, Algiers, Tripoli, and Cairo.

The trans-Saharan trade had three important effects on West African society. First, it stimulated gold mining. Second, it increased the demand for West Africa's second most important commodity, slaves. Third, the trans-Saharan trade stimulated the development of large urban centers in West Africa, such as Gao, Timbuktu, Koumbi Saleh, Sijilmasa, and Jenne. In the period after 700 it had a fourth major effect, introducing Islam to West African society. Conversion led to the involvement of Muslims in African governments, bringing efficient techniques of statecraft and advanced scientific knowledge and engineering skills. Between the ninth and fifteenth centuries, Islam greatly accelerated the development of the African kingdoms. Through the trans-Saharan trade, Africans living in the Sahel zone of West Africa became part of the larger world of Islam.

The period from 800 to 1450 witnessed the flowering of several powerful African states. In the western Sudan, the large empires of Ghana (ca. 900–1100) and Mali (ca. 1200–1450) arose. Each had an elaborate royal court, a massive state bureaucracy, a sizable army, a sophisticated judicial system, and a strong gold industry. The fame of Ghana rested on gold, and when the fabulously rich Mali king Mansa Musa (r. ca. 1312–1337), a devout Muslim, made a pilgrimage to Mecca, his entourage included one hundred elephants, each carrying one hundred pounds of gold.

Mali's strength resulted from two fundamental assets. First, its strong agricultural and commercial base provided for a large population and enormous wealth. Second, Mali had two rulers, Sundiata and Mansa Musa, who combined military success with exceptionally creative personalities. The city of Timbuktu developed into a great center of scholarship and learning. Architects, astronomers, poets, lawyers, mathematicians, and theologians flocked there. Intermarriage between Arab and North African Muslim intellectuals and traders and local women brought into being a group of racially mixed people. The necessity of living together harmoniously, the traditional awareness of diverse cultures, and the cosmopolitan atmosphere of Timbuktu all contributed to a rare degree of racial toleration and understanding.

Meanwhile, the East African coast gave rise to powerful city-states such as Kilwa, Mombasa, and Mogadishu, which maintained a rich maritime trade with India, China, and the Muslim cities of the Middle East. Like the western Sudan, the East African cities were much affected by Muslim influences. Like East Africa, South Africa was made up of city-states, chief among them Great Zimbabwe, which flourished between the eleventh and fifteenth centuries. Located at the southernmost reach of the Indian Ocean trade network, these city-states exchanged their gold for the riches of Arabia and Asia. Somewhat more isolated, the kingdom of Aksum in Ethiopia utilized its access to the Red Sea to trade north to the Mediterranean and south to the Indian Ocean.

The East African city-states and the kingdoms of the western Sudan were part of the world of Islam. Arabian merchants brought Islam with them as they settled along the East African coast, and Berber traders brought Islam to West Africa. Differing from its neighbors, Ethiopia was a unique enclave of Christianity in the midst of Islamic societies. The Bantu-speaking peoples of Great Zimbabwe were neither Islamic nor Christian, but practiced indigenous forms of worship such as animism.

## The Americas, 2500 B.C.E.–1500 C.E.

The first humans settled in the Americas between 40,000 and 15,000 B.C.E., after emigrating from Asia. The melting of glaciers 13,000 to 11,000 years ago separated the Americas from Afroeurasia, and the Eastern and Western Hemispheres developed in isolation from one another. There were many parallels, however: In both hemispheres people initially gathered and hunted their food, and then some groups began to plant crops, adapting plants that were native to the areas they settled. Techniques of plant domestication spread, allowing for population growth. In certain parts of both hemispheres, efficient production and transportation of food supplies led to the growth of cities and to larger political entities such as states and empires.

In the Americas, all the highly varied environments, from polar tundra to tropical rain forests, came to support human settlement. About 8000 B.C.E. people in some parts of the Americas began raising crops as well as gathering wild produce. Maize became the most important crop, with knowledge about its cultivation spreading from Mesoamerica — present-day Mexico and Central America — into North and South America.

Agricultural advancement led to an increase in population, which allowed for greater concentrations of people and the creation of the first urban societies. Towns dependent on agriculture flourished in certain parts of North and South America. Some groups in North America began to build large earthwork mounds; others in Mesoamerica and South America practiced irrigation. The Olmecs created the first society with cities in Mesoamerica, with large ceremonial buildings, an elaborate calendar, and a symbolic writing.

The urban culture of the Olmecs and other Mesoamerican peoples influenced subsequent societies. Especially in what became known as the classical era (300–900 C.E.), various groups developed large states centered on cities, with high levels of technological and intellectual achievement. Of these, the Maya were the longest-lasting, creating a complex written language, multiple-crop milpas (fields) and raised beds for agriculture, roads connecting population centers, trading practices that built unity among Maya communities as well as wealth, and striking art. Peoples living in North America built communities that were smaller than those in Mesoamerica, but many also used irrigation techniques to enhance agricultural production and continued to build earthwork mounds for religious purposes.

In Mesoamerica, the Mexica built a unified culture based on the heritage of earlier societies and distinguished by achievements in engineering, sculpture, and architecture, including the streets, canals, public squares, and aqueduct of Tenochtitlan, the most spectacular and one of the largest cities in the world in 1500. In Mexica society, religion was the dynamic factor that transformed other aspects of the culture: economic security, social mobility, education, and especially war. War was an article of religious faith, providing riches and land, sacrificial victims for ceremonies honoring the gods, laborers, and warriors who created an empire, later called the Aztec Empire. Aztec society was hierarchical, with nobles and priests having special privileges.

In the Andes, Inca achievements built on those of cultures that preceded theirs, including the Moche and Chavín civilizations. Moche, Chavín, and Inca cultures made their home in the valleys along the Peruvian coast and in the Andean highlands, cultivating food crops and cotton. The Incas, who began as a small militaristic group, eventually created the largest empire in South America in the fifteenth century and conquered surrounding groups. Their far-flung empire stretched along the Andes and was kept together by a system of roads, along which moved armies and administrators. The Incas achieved imperial unification by imposing their gods on conquered peoples, forcing local chieftains to participate in the central bureaucracy, and pursuing a policy of colonization. The imperial expansion that increased the Incas' strength also caused stress. Andean society was dominated by clan groups, and Inca measures to disrupt these groups and move people great distances created resentment.

# Europe, 500–1500

In the fifteenth century, scholars in Europe began the practice of dividing European history into different periods. They called the time of Greece and Rome the ancient or classical era, and the thousand-year period between the fall of the Western Roman Empire and their own day the Middle Ages. This three-part division — ancient, medieval, and modern — has been very influential, even in areas beyond Europe.

## The Middle Ages

The transition from ancient to medieval was a slow process, not a single event. The main human agent of change in late antiquity was the migration of groups the Romans labeled "barbarians" throughout much of Europe and western Asia, migration spurred in part by climate instability. The barbarians brought different social, political, and economic structures with them. Although Greco-Roman art and architecture still adorned the land and people continued to travel on Roman roads, the roads were rarely maintained, and travel itself was much less secure than during the empire. Merchants no longer traded over long distances, so people's access to goods produced outside their local area plummeted. There was intermarriage and cultural assimilation among Romans and barbarians, but there was also violence and great physical destruction.

The Eastern Roman Empire, called the Byzantine Empire, did not fall to barbarian invasions. During the sixth and seventh centuries the Byzantine Empire survived waves of attacks, owing to effective military leadership and to fortifications around Constantinople. Byzantium protected the cultural heritage of Greco-Roman civilization and then passed it on. The Byzantine Empire lasted until 1453, nearly a millennium longer than the Roman Empire in the West. Byzantine emperors organized and preserved Roman law, and because of the Byzantines many masterpieces of ancient Greek literature survived to influence the intellectual life of the modern world. In mathematics and science, the Byzantines passed Greco-Roman learning on to the Arabs.

Along with Byzantium, the Christian Church was an important agent of continuity in the transition from ancient to medieval in Europe, north Africa, and western Asia. Christianity gained the support of the fourth-century emperors and gradually adopted the Roman system of hierarchical organization. The church possessed able administrators and leaders whose skills were tested in the chaotic environment of the end of the Roman Empire in the West. Bishops expanded their activities, and in the fifth century the bishops of Rome, taking the title "pope," began to stress their supremacy over other Christian communities. Monasteries offered opportunities for individuals to develop deeper spiritual devotion and also provided a model of Christian living, methods that advanced agricultural development, and places for education and learning. Missionaries and church officials spread Christianity within and far beyond the borders of what had been the Roman Empire, transforming a small sect into the most important and wealthiest institution in Europe, North Africa, and the eastern Mediterranean.

Christian thinkers reinterpreted the classics in a Christian sense, incorporating elements of Greek and Roman philosophy and of various pagan religious groups into Christian teachings. Missionaries and priests helped pagan and illiterate peoples to understand and become more accepting of Christianity by preaching the basic teachings of the religion, stressing similarities between pagan customs and beliefs and those of Christianity, and introducing the ritual of penance and the veneration of saints.

Barbarian society was hierarchical, with a warrior-elite, free people, and slaves. The basic social unit was the tribe, made up of kin groups formed by patriarchal families. In late antiquity, barbarian elites blended with Roman ones, and controlling land and the people who lived on it became the most important marker of elite status. Family groups lived in small agriculture-based villages, where there were great differences in wealth and status. Most barbarian kingdoms were weak and short-lived, though the kingdom of the Franks was relatively more unified and powerful. Rulers first in the Merovingian dynasty of the fifth century, and then in the Carolingian of the eighth century, used military victories, strategic marriage alliances, and the help of the church to enhance their authority.

The Frankish kingdom broke down in the late ninth century, and continental Europe was fractured politically. No European political power was strong enough to put up effective resistance to external attack, which came from many directions. Vikings from Scandinavia carried out raids for plunder along the coasts and rivers of Europe and traveled as far as Iceland, Greenland, North America, and Russia. In many places they set up permanent states, as did the Magyars, who came into central Europe from the east. From the south came Muslims, who conquered Sicily and drove northward into Italy. All these invasions as well as civil wars weakened the power of kings, and local nobles became the strongest powers against external threats. They established a new form of decentralized government, later known as feudalism, similar to that of Japan in the era of the samurai. Common people turned to nobles for protection, paying with their land, labor, and freedom.

Beginning in the last half of the tenth century, the invasions that had contributed to European fragmentation gradually ended, and domestic disorder slowly subsided. Feudal rulers began to develop new institutions of law and government that enabled them to assert their power over lesser lords and the general population. Centralized states slowly crystallized, first in western Europe in the eleventh century, and then in eastern and northern Europe. An era of relative stability and prosperity followed, generally known as the "High Middle Ages," which lasted until climate change and disease brought calamity in the fourteenth century.

At the same time that rulers expanded their authority, energetic popes built their power within the Western Christian Church. They asserted their superiority over kings and emperors, though these moves were sometimes challenged by those secular rulers. Monasteries continued to be important places of learning and devotion, and new religious orders were founded. Meanwhile, Christianity expanded into Europe's northern and eastern regions, and Christian rulers expanded their holdings in Muslim Spain. On a more personal scale, religion structured people's daily lives and the yearly calendar.

A papal call to retake the holy city of Jerusalem from the Muslims led to nearly two centuries of warfare between Christians and Muslims. Christian warriors, clergy, and settlers moved in all directions from western and central Europe, so that through conquest and colonization border regions were gradually incorporated into a more uniform European culture. The enormous popular response to the pope's call reveals the influence of the papacy and the new sense that war against the church's enemies was a duty of nobles. The Crusades were initially successful, and small Christian states were established in the Middle East. They did not last very long, however, and other effects of the Crusades were disastrous: Jewish communities in Europe were regularly attacked; relations between the Western and Eastern Christian Churches were poisoned by the Crusaders' attack on Constantinople; and Christian-Muslim relations became more uniformly hostile than they had been earlier.

For most people, the High Middle Ages did not bring dramatic change. The vast majority of medieval Europeans were rural peasants who lived in small villages and worked their own and their lords' land. Peasants led hard lives, and most were bound to the land, although there were some opportunities for social mobility. Nobles were a tiny fraction of the total population, but they exerted great power over all aspects of life. Aristocratic values and attitudes, often called chivalry, shaded all aspects of medieval culture. Medieval towns and cities grew initially as trading centers and recruited people from the countryside with the promise of greater freedom and new possibilities. They also became centers of production, and merchants and artisans formed guilds to protect their livelihoods. Not everyone in medieval towns and cities shared in the prosperity, however; many residents lived hand-to-mouth on low wages.

The towns that became centers of trade and production in the High Middle Ages also developed into cultural and intellectual centers. Trade brought in new ideas as well as merchandise, and in many cities a new type of educational institution — the university — emerged from cathedral and municipal schools. Universities developed theological, legal, and medical courses of study based on classical models and provided trained officials for the new government and church bureaucracies. People also wanted permanent visible representations of their piety, and church and city leaders supported the building of churches and cathedrals as symbols of their Christian faith and their civic pride. Cathedrals grew larger and more sumptuous, with high towers, soaring arches, and exquisite stained-glass windows in a style known as Gothic. New types of vernacular literature arose in which poems, songs, and stories were written down in local dialects.

In the fourteenth century the prosperity of the High Middle Ages ended. The northern hemisphere entered into a period of colder and wetter weather that climatologists label the "Little Ice Age," which they can trace through both natural and human records. Its effects were dramatic and disastrous, including famine and disease. One of these diseases, the Black Death, caused enormous population losses and had social, psychological, and economic consequences. Additional difficulties included the Hundred Years' War between England and France, which devastated much of the French countryside and bankrupted England; a schism among rival popes that weakened the Western Christian Church; and peasant and worker frustrations that exploded in uprisings. These revolts were usually crushed, though noble landlords were not always successful in reasserting their rights to labor services instead of cash rents.

## The Renaissance

While Europe suffered greatly in the fourteenth century, a new culture was beginning to emerge in southern Europe. First in Italy and then elsewhere scholars, writers, and artists thought that they were living in a new golden age, later termed the Renaissance, French for "rebirth." The word *renaissance* was used initially to describe art that seemed to recapture, or perhaps even surpass, the glories of the classical past, and then came to be used for many aspects of life of the period. The new attitude diffused slowly out of Italy, with the result that the Renaissance "happened" at different times in different parts of Europe.

The Renaissance was characterized by self-conscious awareness among fourteenth- and fifteenth-century Italians, particularly scholars and writers known as humanists, that they were living in a new era. Key to this attitude was a serious interest in the Latin classics, a belief in individual potential, and a more secular attitude toward life. Humanists opened schools to train boys and young men for active lives of public service, but they had doubts about whether humanist education was appropriate for women. As humanism spread to northern Europe, religious concerns became more pronounced, and Christian humanists set out plans for the reform of church and society. Their ideas were spread to a much wider audience than those of early humanists as a result of the development of the printing press with movable metal type, which revolutionized communication. Interest in the classical past and in the individual shaped Renaissance art in terms of style and subject matter. Also important to Renaissance art were the wealthy patrons who helped fund it.

Social hierarchies in the Renaissance developed new features that contributed to the modern social hierarchies of race, class, and gender. The distinction between free people and slaves was one such hierarchy. Although slavery in Europe was not limited to Africans during the Renaissance, increasing numbers of black Africans entered Europe as slaves to supplement the labor force, and black skin color was increasingly viewed as a mark of inferiority. In terms of class, the medieval hierarchy of orders based on function in society intermingled with a new hierarchy that created a new social elite whose status was based on wealth. In regard to gender, the Renaissance debate about women led many to discuss women's nature and proper role in society, a discussion sharpened by the presence of a number of ruling queens in this era. Nevertheless, women continued to lag behind men in social status and earnings.

During the Renaissance the feudal monarchies of medieval Europe gradually evolved into nation-states. Beginning in the fifteenth century rulers in western Europe used aggressive methods to build up their governments, reducing violence, curbing unruly nobles, and establishing domestic order. They emphasized royal majesty and royal sovereignty and insisted on the respect and loyalty of all subjects. War and diplomacy were important ways that states increased their power, and so was marriage. Because almost all of Europe was ruled by hereditary dynasties, claiming and holding resources involved shrewd marital alliances.

The Renaissance is often seen as a radical change, but it contained many elements of continuity as well. Artists and humanists looked back to the classical era for inspiration, and political leaders played important roles in cultural developments, just as they had for centuries in Europe and other parts of the world. The Renaissance was also closely connected with European exploration and colonization, which you will study in depth in Chapter 16 of this text. Renaissance monarchs paid for the expeditions' ships, crews, and supplies, expecting a large share of any profits gained and increasingly viewing overseas territory as essential to a strong state. The desire for fame, wealth, and power that was central to the Renaissance was thus key to the European voyages and to colonial ventures as well.

# 16

# The Acceleration of Global Contact

## 1450–1600

### CHAPTER PREVIEW

**The Afro-Eurasian Trade World**
- What was the Afro-Eurasian trade world prior to the era of European exploration?

**The European Voyages of Discovery**
- How and why did Europeans undertake ambitious voyages of expansion?

**Conquest and Settlement**
- What was the impact of Iberian conquest and settlement on the peoples and ecologies of the Americas?

**The Era of Global Contact**
- How was the era of global contact shaped by new commodities, commercial empires, and forced migrations?

**Changing Attitudes and Beliefs**
- How did new encounters shape cultural attitudes and beliefs in Europe and the rest of the world?

**BEFORE 1500 EUROPEANS WERE RELATIVELY MARGINAL PLAYERS** in a centuries-old trading system centered on the Indian Ocean that linked Africa, Asia, and Europe. In this vibrant Afro-Eurasian trading world, Arab, Persian, Indian, African, and Chinese merchants competed for trade in spices, silks, and other goods. A century later, by 1550, the Portuguese search for better access to African gold and Asian trade goods had led to a new overseas empire in the Indian Ocean, and Spanish explorers had accidentally discovered the Western Hemisphere. Through violent conquest, the Iberian powers established large-scale colonies in the Americas, and northern European powers soon followed their example. The era of European expansion had begun, creating new political systems and forms of economic exchange as well as cultural assimilation, conversion, and resistance. This age of encounters laid the foundations for the modern world.

# The Afro-Eurasian Trade World

### What was the Afro-Eurasian trade world prior to the era of European exploration?

During the Middle Ages, a type of world economy, known as the Afro-Eurasian trade world, linked the products, people, and ideas of Africa, Europe, and Asia. This trade world was centered on the Indian Ocean, where monsoon winds generated seasonal rhythms of travel. Over time, Indian Ocean trade was facilitated by the spread of Islam, which provided a common legal system, language, and faith, and also by the economic growth and political unification of China. Italian merchants served as middlemen who brought Eastern luxury goods to western Europe.

## The Trade World of the Indian Ocean

Covering 20 percent of the earth's total ocean area, the Indian Ocean is the globe's third-largest waterway (after the Pacific and Atlantic). Moderate and predictable monsoon winds blow from the northeast between November and January; rougher winds blow from the south and southwest between April and August. By following the alternating directions of the monsoons, sailors profited from constantly favorable winds to maximize the speed of travel. In the fifteenth century, Arab navigator Ibn Majid published a book listing well-known trade routes in the Indian Ocean and the times of year when travel to and from different port cities was possible.

From the seventh through the fourteenth centuries, the volume and integration of Indian Ocean trade steadily increased, encouraged by two factors: the spread of Islam through much of the Indian Ocean world and the political unification and economic growth of China. Starting in the mid-seventh century, and eventually favored by the political stability and cultural unity of the Abbasid caliphate, Muslim Arab and Persian merchants expanded along the coast of East Africa and across the Indian Ocean to western India. A few centuries later, economic growth under the Song Dynasties (960–1279) enabled the Chinese to enter the Indian Ocean trade. Then, in the following Mongol era (1279–1368), Mongol emperors safeguarded the Silk Road overland trade routes through Central Asia and strengthened China's connections to the Indian Ocean world. The Venetian merchant Marco Polo's tales of his travels from 1271 to 1295 praised the splendors of the khan's court and the city of Hangzhou, which he described as "the finest and noblest in the world" in which "the number and wealth of the merchants, and the amount of goods that passed through their hands, was so enormous that no man could form a just estimate thereof."[1]

After the Mongols fell to the Ming Dynasty in 1368, China entered a new period of agricultural and commercial expansion, population growth, and urbanization (see "Ming China" in Chapter 21). The Ming emperor dispatched Admiral Zheng He (JEHNG HUH) on a remarkable series of naval expeditions that traveled the oceanic web as far as Aden in the Red Sea. From 1405 to 1433, each of his seven expeditions

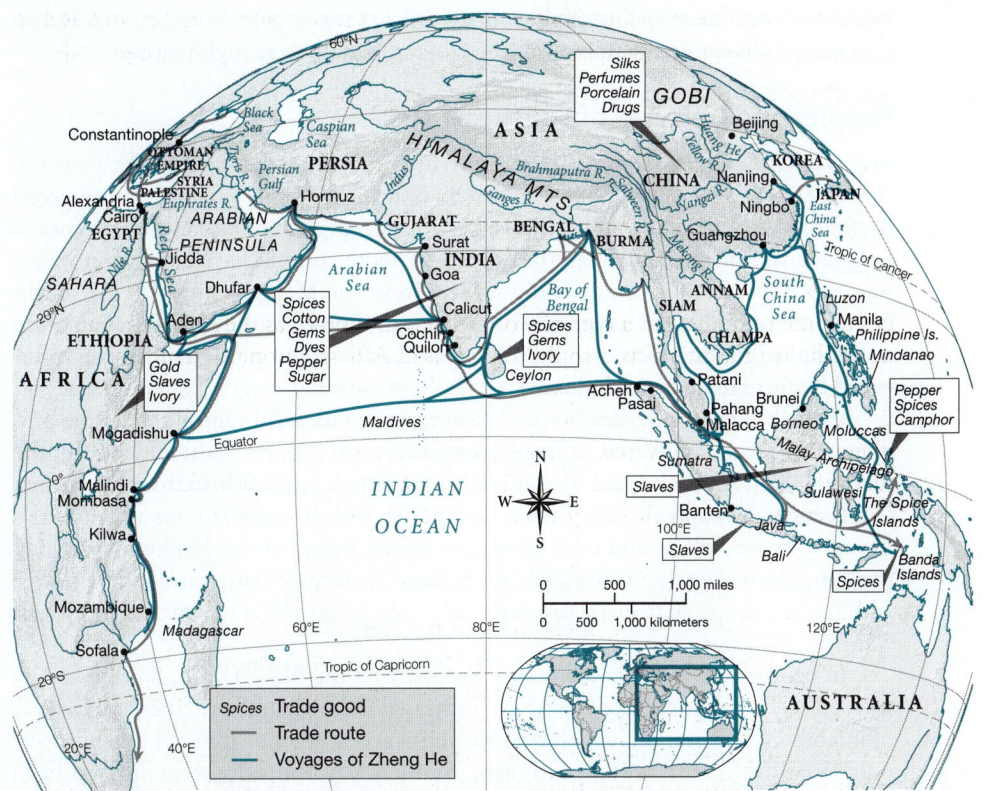

**MAP 16.1   The Fifteenth-Century Afro-Eurasian Trading World**
After a period of decline following the Black Death and the Mongol invasions, trade revived in the fifteenth century. Muslim merchants dominated trade, linking ports in East Africa and the Red Sea with those in India and the Malay Archipelago. The Chinese admiral Zheng He followed the most important Indian Ocean trade routes on his voyages (1405–1433), hoping to impose Ming dominance of trade and tribute.

involved hundreds of ships and more than twenty thousand men. After the deaths of Zheng He and the emperor, the voyages ceased, but Chinese overseas traders continued vigorous activity in the South China Sea and throughout the Indian Ocean.

Shaped by monsoon patterns, Indian Ocean trade moved through three overlapping geographic circuits. The western zone, dominated by Arab traders, linked the east coast of Africa and the Arabian peninsula to the southwestern Malabar coast of India. The opposite extreme was a predominantly Chinese trade zone focused on the South China Sea that linked China to the busy trading posts of Southeast Asia (Map 16.1). The central zone of Indian Ocean trade linked the Indian subcontinent, and in particular the southeastern Coromandel coast, to Southeast Asia across the Bay of Bengal. Muslim Arab and Persian merchants who circumnavigated India on their way to trade in the South China Sea established trading posts along the southern coasts of east and west India, and cities such as Calicut and Quilon became thriving commercial centers. India was also an important contributor of goods to the world trading system. Most of the world's pepper was grown in India, and Indian cotton and silk textiles, mainly from the Gujarat region, were highly prized.

## Peoples and Cultures of Southeast Asia

Just as environmental factors dictated the rhythms of Indian Ocean trade, they also shaped common ways of life and culture in Southeast Asia, a vast region composed of the northern mainland and a series of archipelagoes to the south and east. Since at least the first millennium B.C.E., the peoples of Southeast Asia have engaged in water-borne commerce. With trade came settlers from the Malay Peninsula (the southern extremity of the Asian continent), India, and China, resulting in the widespread adoption of Hinduism and Buddhism as well as forms of monarchical rule influenced by these religious traditions.

Water brought trade, settlers, and culture; it also played a central role in the production of food. Cultivated in irrigated terraces, rice formed the staple food of the diet. The long coastlines and many rivers provided plentiful fish, crabs, and shrimp, and fishing served as the chief male occupation. With mountainous uplands and low-lying coastal plains and river basins, the region harbored rich biodiversity, allowing Southeast Asians to domesticate a large variety of fruits and other crops. Indigenous crops that were to play a key role in global trade included cloves, nutmeg, and sugarcane.

In comparison to India, China, or Europe after the Black Death, Southeast Asia was sparsely populated. People were concentrated in low-lying port cities and in areas of intense rice cultivation, which became political centers. The forested uplands were only loosely affiliated to state authority. Another way Southeast Asia differed from India, China, and Europe was the higher status of women, which was associated with their primary role in planting and harvesting rice. At marriage, which typically occurred around age twenty, the groom paid the bride a sum of money called **bride wealth**, which remained under her control. This practice was in sharp contrast to the Chinese, Indian, and European dowry, which came under the husband's control. Property was administered jointly, and family lineage was traced through both the maternal and paternal lines. All children, regardless of gender, inherited equally.

Respect for women carried over to the commercial sphere. Women participated in business as partners and independent entrepreneurs. When Portuguese and Dutch men settled in the region and married local women, their wives continued to play important roles in trade and commerce.

In contrast to most parts of the world other than Africa, Southeast Asian peoples also had an accepting attitude toward premarital sexual activity. Divorce carried no social stigma and was easily attainable by either partner if a pair proved incompatible.

## Muslim Influences and African Trade

From its capital in Baghdad, the Abbasid caliphate (750–1258) controlled an enormous region reaching from Spain to the western borders of China, including the Red Sea and the Persian Gulf, the two major waterways linking the Indian Ocean trade world to the Mediterranean. The political stability endowed by the caliphate, along with the shared language of Arabic and the common legal system and culture of Islam, fostered economic prosperity and peaceful commercial relations.

On the east coast of Africa, Muslim traders established Swahili-speaking city-states that engaged directly in the Indian Ocean trade, exchanging ivory, rhinoceros horn, tortoise shells, and slaves for textiles, spices, cowrie shells, porcelain, and other goods. Cities such as Kilwa, Malindi, and Mogadishu were famed for their prosperity. From these bases and from ports like Aden on the Red Sea and Hormuz on the Persian Gulf, Arab, Persian, and Jewish traders traveled even farther across the trade routes of the Indian Ocean to China and Southeast Asia.

After the Abbasids fell to the Mongols, the Mamluk rulers of Egypt proclaimed a new caliphate. Until its defeat by the Ottomans in 1517, the Mamluk empire was one of the most powerful polities on the continent. Its capital, Cairo, was a center of Islamic learning and religious authority as well as a major hub for goods moving between the Indian Ocean trade world and the Mediterranean.

West Africa also played an important role in world trade. In the fifteenth century the western part of the Sudan region and the Akan (AH-kahn) peoples living near present-day Ghana were major suppliers of gold. Transported across the Sahara by camel caravans, the gold was sold in ports along the Mediterranean. Inland nations that sat astride the north-south caravan routes grew wealthy from this trade. In the mid-thirteenth century the kingdom of Mali became an important player in the overland trade route, gaining prestige from its ruler Mansa Musa's fabulous pilgrimage to Mecca in 1324–1325. Desire to gain direct access to African gold motivated the initial Portuguese incursions into Africa.

**Mansa Musa** This detail from the *Catalan Atlas* of 1375, a world map created for the Catalan king, depicts a king of Mali, Mansa Musa, who was legendary for his wealth in gold. European desires for direct access to the trade in sub-Saharan gold helped inspire Portuguese exploration of the west coast of Africa in the fifteenth century. (From *The Catalan Atlas*, 1375, by Abraham Cresques/Bibliothèque Nationale, Paris, France/Getty images)

## Genoese and Venetian Middlemen

In the late Middle Ages, the Italian city-states of Venice and Genoa controlled European trade with the East. In 1304 Venice established formal relations with the Mamluk sultan, allowing Venetian merchants to purchase goods in Cairo for re-export throughout Europe. Venetians funded these purchases through trade in European woolen cloth and metal goods, as well as through shipping and trade in firearms and slaves.

Venice's ancient trading rival was Genoa. By 1270 Genoa dominated the northern route to Asia through the Black Sea. From then until the fourteenth century the Genoese expanded their trade routes as far as Persia and the Far East. In the fifteenth century, with Venice claiming victory in the spice trade, the Genoese shifted focus from trade to finance and from the Black Sea to the western Mediterranean. When Spanish and Portuguese voyages began to explore the western Atlantic, Genoese merchants, navigators, and financiers provided their skills and capital to the Iberian monarchs.

A major element of Italian trade was slavery. Merchants purchased slaves in the Balkans and the Black Sea region. After the loss of the Black Sea trade routes to the Ottomans, the Genoese sought new supplies of slaves in the West, eventually seizing or buying and selling the Guanches (indigenous peoples from the Canary Islands), Muslim prisoners and Jewish refugees from Spain, and, by the early 1500s, both sub-Saharan and Berber Africans. With the growth of Spanish colonies in the New World, Genoese and Venetian merchants became important players in the Atlantic slave trade.

# The European Voyages of Discovery

## How and why did Europeans undertake ambitious voyages of expansion?

Europe was by no means isolated before the voyages of exploration and the "discovery" of the New World. Italian merchants traded actively for West African gold and Indian Ocean luxury goods, but trade through intermediaries was slow and expensive. In the first decades of the fifteenth century, new European players entered the scene with novel technology, eager to spread Christianity and to find direct access to trade. First Portuguese and then Spanish expeditions undertook long-distance voyages that helped create the modern world, with immense consequences for their own continent and the rest of the planet.

## Causes of European Expansion

European expansion had multiple causes. The first was economic. By the middle of the fifteenth century Europe was experiencing a revival of population and economic activity after the lows of the Black Death. This revival created renewed demand for luxuries, especially spices, from the East. Introduced by the Crusaders in the twelfth century, spices such as pepper, nutmeg, cinnamon, and cloves added variety to the monotonous European diet and were also used as incense for religious rituals and as perfumes, medicines, and dyes in daily life. Like other imported luxury goods, they demonstrated the wealth and sophistication of the social elite.

Religious fervor and the crusading spirit were the second important catalyst for expansion. Just seven months separated Isabella and Ferdinand's conquest of the emirate of Granada, the last Muslim state on the Iberian Peninsula, and Columbus's departure across the Atlantic. Overseas exploration thus transferred the militaristic religious fervor of the reconquista (reconquest) to new territories. With conquest, Iberians brought the attitudes and administrative practices developed during the reconquista to the New World. **Conquistadors** (kohn-KEES-tuh-dorz) (Spanish for "conqueror") fully expected to be rewarded with land, titles, and power over conquered peoples, just as the leaders of the reconquista had been.

Competition among European powers for the prestige and profit of overseas exploration was a third factor encouraging the steady stream of expeditions that began in the late fifteenth century. Once the profits from Portuguese expansion became evident, first the Spanish and then other European powers vied for direct access to global trade. This competition enabled merchants to gain legal authorization and financial support for their expeditions.

The small number of Europeans who could read provided a rapt audience for tales of fantastic places and unknown peoples. One of the most popular books of the time was the fourteenth-century text *The Travels of Sir John Mandeville*, which purported to be a firsthand account of the author's travels in the Middle East, India, and China.

## Technology and the Rise of Exploration

In the quest to open new trade routes, the Portuguese were pioneers in seeking technological improvements in shipbuilding, weaponry, and navigation. Medieval European seagoing vessels consisted of single-masted sailing ships or galleys propelled by oars. Though adequate for short journeys that hugged the shoreline, such vessels were incapable of long-distance journeys or high-volume trade. In the fifteenth century the Portuguese developed the **caravel**, a two- or three-masted sailing ship. Its multiple sails and sternpost rudder made the caravel a more maneuverable vessel that required fewer crewmen to operate. The Portuguese were also the first to fit their ships with cannon, a key military advantage.

This period also saw great strides in cartography. Around 1410 a Latin translation reintroduced western Europeans to **Ptolemy's *Geography***. Written in the second century, the work synthesized the geographical knowledge of the classical world. It represented a major improvement over medieval cartography because it depicted the world as round and introduced latitude and longitude markings, but it also contained significant errors. Unaware of the Americas, Ptolemy showed the world as much smaller than it is, so that Asia appeared not very much to the west of Europe.

Navigational aids also improved. Originating in China, the magnetic compass was brought to the West in the late Middle Ages. By using the compass to determine their direction and estimate their speed of travel, mariners could track the course of a ship's voyage. In the late fifteenth century, Portuguese scholars devised a new technique of "celestial reckoning" that involved using the astrolabe, an instrument invented by the ancient Greeks, to determine the position of the stars. Commissioned by Portuguese king John II, a group of astronomers in the 1480s showed that mariners could determine their latitude at sea by using a specially designed astrolabe to determine the altitude of the polestar or the sun, and by consulting tables of these bodies' movements. This was a crucial step forward in maritime navigational techniques.

Much of the new technology that Europeans used on their voyages was borrowed from the East. Gunpowder, the compass, and the sternpost rudder were Chinese inventions. The triangular lateen sail, which allowed caravels to tack against the wind, was a product of the Indian Ocean trade world. Advances in cartography and navigation also drew on rich traditions of Jewish and Arab mathematical and astronomical learning. In exploring new territories, European sailors thus called on techniques and knowledge developed over centuries in China, the Muslim world, and trading centers along the Indian Ocean.

**Portuguese Mariner's Bronze Astrolabe, 1555** Between 1500 and 1635 over nine hundred ships sailed from Portugal to ports on the Indian Ocean, in annual fleets composed of five to ten ships. Portuguese sailors used astrolabes, such as the bronze example shown here, to accurately plot their positon. (Granger)

## The Portuguese in Africa and Asia

Established during the reconquista in the mid-thirteenth century, the kingdom of Portugal had a long Atlantic coastline that favored maritime activity. By the end of the thirteenth century Portuguese merchants were trading fish, salt, and wine to ports in northern England and the Mediterranean. Nature favored the Portuguese: winds blowing along their coast offered passage to Africa, its Atlantic islands, and, ultimately, Brazil. Once they had mastered the secret to sailing against the wind to return to Europe (by sailing farther west to catch winds from the southwest), they were poised to pioneer Atlantic exploration.

In the early phases of Portuguese exploration, Prince Henry (1394–1460), a younger son of the king, played a leading role. A nineteenth-century scholar dubbed Henry "the Navigator" because of his support for Portuguese voyages of discovery. In 1415, Henry participated in Portugal's conquest of the port of Ceuta (sa-OO-tah), a major outlet for West African gold. Inspired by this victory, in the 1420s, under Henry's direction, the Portuguese began to settle the Atlantic islands of Madeira (ca. 1420) and the Azores (1427). In 1443 they founded their first African commercial settlement at Arguin on the West African coast.

By the time of Henry's death in 1460, his support for exploration had resulted in thriving sugar plantations on the Atlantic islands, the first arrival of enslaved Africans in Portugal, and new access to African gold. These achievements, which heralded a new phase of European exploitation of non-European peoples, places, and goods, were fully approved by the Catholic Church. In 1454, Pope Nicholas V issued a bull reiterating the rights of the Portuguese Crown to conquer and enslave non-Christians and recognizing Portuguese possession of territories in West Africa.

To consolidate their position in west African trade, the Portuguese established fortified trading posts, called factories, on the gold-rich Guinea coast (Map 16.2). By 1500 Portugal controlled the flow of African gold to Europe. In contrast to the Spanish, who later conquered the Americas, the Portuguese did not establish large settlements in West Africa and were unable to transform the lives and religious beliefs of people beyond their coastal holdings. Instead they pursued easier and faster profits by seeking entry to existing trading systems. For the first century of their relations, African rulers were equal partners with the Portuguese, benefiting from their experienced armies and European vulnerability to tropical diseases.

In 1488 Bartholomew Diaz (ca. 1451–1500) rounded the Cape of Good Hope at the southern tip of Africa (see Map 16.2), but poor conditions forced him to turn back. A decade later Vasco da Gama (ca. 1469–1524), commanding a fleet in search of a sea route to India, finally succeeded in rounding the Cape. With the help of a

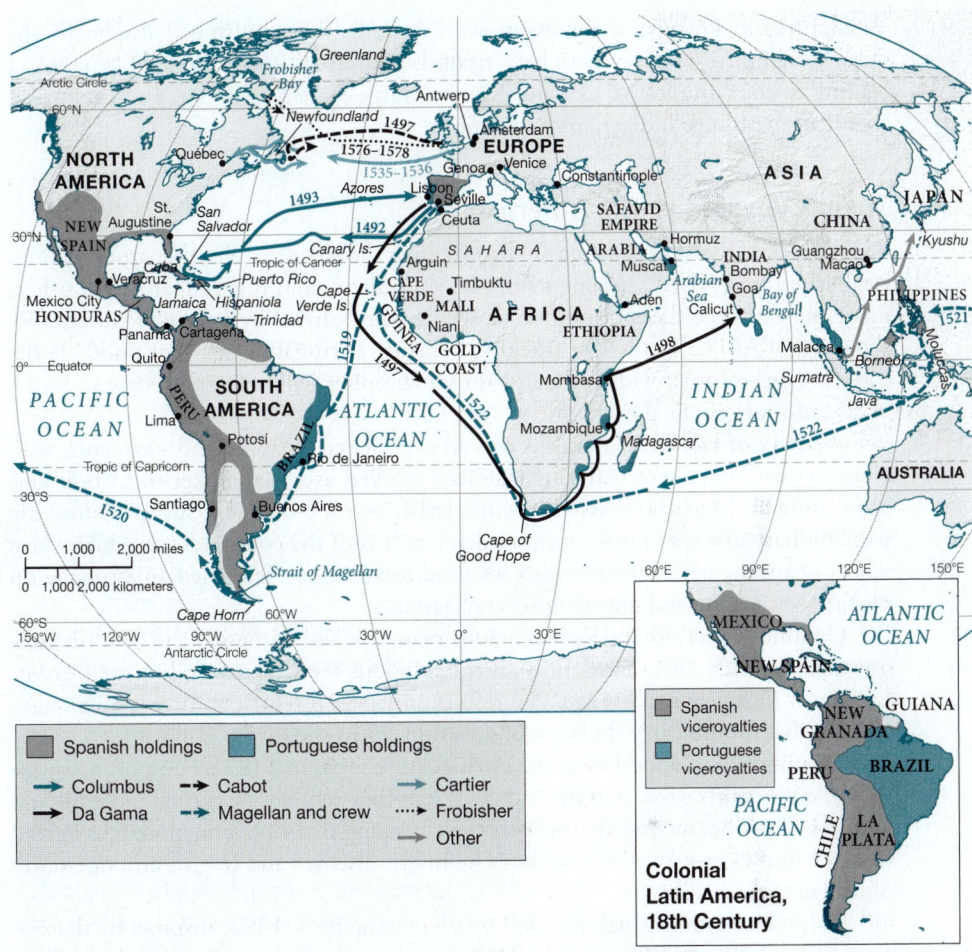

**MAP 16.2  Overseas Exploration and Conquest in the Fifteenth and Sixteenth Centuries**
The voyages of discovery marked a dramatic new phase in the centuries-old migrations of European peoples.
This map depicts the voyages of the most significant European explorers of the period.

local pilot with experience in Indian Ocean trade, da Gama reached the port of
Calicut in India. He returned to Lisbon with spices and Indian cloth, thus proving
it was possible to conduct direct trade with Asia. Thereafter, a Portuguese convoy
set out for passage around the Cape every March.

Lisbon became the entrance port for Asian goods into Europe, but this was not
accomplished without a fight. From 1500 to 1515 the Portuguese used a combination of bombardment and diplomatic treaties to establish trading factories at Goa,
Malacca, Calicut, and Hormuz, thereby laying the foundation for a Portuguese trading empire. The acquisition of port cities and their trade routes brought riches to
Portugal, but, as in Africa, the Portuguese had limited impact on the lives and religious faith of peoples beyond coastal holdings.

Spurred by Portuguese success in overseas trade, the Spanish had also begun the quest for empire. Theirs was to be a second, entirely different mode of expansion, leading to the conquest of existing empires, large-scale settlement, and the forced assimilation of huge indigenous populations.

## Spain's Voyages to the Americas

Christopher Columbus was not the first to cross the Atlantic. Ninth-century Vikings established short-lived settlements in Newfoundland, and it is probable that others made the voyage, either on purpose or accidentally, carried by westward currents off the coast of Africa. In the late fifteenth century, Portugal's control of trade via the eastern Cape route provided impetus for Christopher Columbus's attempt to find a westward route across the Atlantic to Asia.

A native of Genoa, Columbus was an experienced seaman and navigator, with close ties to Portuguese seafaring. He had worked as a mapmaker in Lisbon and spent time on Madeira, where his wife's father was a prominent sugar planter. He was familiar with *portolans*—written descriptions of the courses along which ships sailed—and the use of the compass for dead reckoning. (He carried an astrolabe on his first voyage, but did not use it for navigation.)

Columbus was also a deeply religious man. He had witnessed the Spanish conquest of Granada and shared fully in the religious fervor surrounding that event. Like most Europeans of his age, Columbus understood Christianity as a missionary religion that should carry the hope of salvation across the earth.

Columbus first appealed to the Portuguese Crown in 1483 to support a voyage to find a westward passage to the Indies. When they refused, he turned to Ferdinand and Isabella of Spain, and finally won their backing in 1492. The monarchs agreed to make him viceroy over any territory he might discover and to give him one-tenth of its material rewards.

Columbus and his small fleet left Spain on August 3, 1492. Inspired by the stories of Mandeville and Marco Polo, Columbus dreamed of reaching the court of the Mongol emperor, the Great Khan, not realizing that the Mongols had fallen to the Ming Dynasty in 1368. Based on Ptolemy's *Geography* and other texts, he expected to pass the islands of Japan and then land on the east coast of China. On October 12 Columbus landed in the Bahamas, which he christened San Salvador and claimed for the Spanish Crown. In a letter to Ferdinand and Isabella on his return to Spain, Columbus described the natives as handsome, peaceful, and primitive. Believing he was somewhere off the east coast of Japan, in what he considered the Indies, he called them "Indians," a name that was later applied to all inhabitants of the Americas. Columbus concluded that they would make good slaves and could quickly be converted to Christianity.

Scholars have identified the inhabitants of the islands as the Taino (TIGH-noh) people. Columbus then sailed southwest, landing on Cuba on October 28. Deciding that he must be on the mainland of China near the city of Quinsay (now Hangzhou), he dispatched a small landing party to locate the city. The landing party found only small villages. This disappointment led Columbus to abandon his aim to meet the Great Khan and focus instead on finding gold or other resources. In early December he landed on an island, called Ayti by its Taino inhabitants, that he renamed Hispaniola.

The sight of Taino people on Hispaniola wearing gold ornaments suggested that gold was available in the region. In January, he headed back to Spain to report on his discovery.

On his second voyage, Columbus took control of Hispaniola and enslaved its indigenous peoples. On this and subsequent voyages, he brought settlers for the new Spanish territories, along with agricultural seed and livestock. However, Columbus's poor governing skills soon sparked revolt among the settlers on Hispaniola. He was forced to Spain, and a royal governor assumed control of the colony.

## Spain "Discovers" the Pacific

Columbus never realized the scope of his achievement: that he had found a vast continent unknown to Europeans, except for the fleeting Viking presence centuries earlier. The Florentine navigator Amerigo Vespucci (veh-SPOO-chee) (1454–1512) realized what Columbus had not. Writing about his own discoveries on the coast of modern-day Venezuela, Vespucci stated: "Those new regions which we found and explored with the fleet . . . we may rightly call a New World." This letter was the first document to describe America as a continent separate from Asia. In recognition of Amerigo's bold claim, the continent was named for him.

Upon Columbus's return from the first voyage, Isabella and Ferdinand appealed to Spanish-born Pope Alexander VI for support in claiming the newly discovered territories. The pope proposed drawing an imaginary line down the Atlantic, giving Spain possession of all lands discovered to the west of the line and Portugal everything to the east. He enjoined both powers to carry the Christian faith to these newly discovered lands and peoples. The **Treaty of Tordesillas** (tor-duh-SEE-yuhs) negotiated between Spain and Portugal in 1494 retained the pope's idea but moved the line further west as a concession to the Portuguese. This arbitrary division worked in Portugal's favor when in 1500 an expedition led by Pedro Álvares Cabral, en route to India, landed on the coast of Brazil, which Cabral claimed as Portuguese territory. (Because the line was imagined to extend around the globe, it meant that the Philippine Islands would eventually end up in Spanish control.)

The search for profits determined the direction of Spanish exploration. Because its revenue from Hispaniola and other Caribbean islands was insignificant compared to Portugal's enormous riches from the Asian spice trade, Spain renewed the search for a western passage to Asia. In 1519 Charles I of Spain (who was also Holy Roman emperor Charles V) commissioned Ferdinand Magellan (1480–1521) to find a direct sea route to Asia. Magellan sailed southwest across the Atlantic to Brazil, and eventually located the strait off the southern tip of South America that now bears his name (see Map 16.2). After passing through the strait into the Pacific Ocean in 1520, his fleet sailed north up the west coast of South America and then headed west into the Pacific.

Terrible storms, disease, starvation, and violence devastated the expedition. Magellan himself was killed in a skirmish in the Philippines, and only one of the five ships that began the expedition made it back to Spain. This ship returned home in 1522 with only eighteen men aboard, having traveled from the east by way of the Indian Ocean, the Cape of Good Hope, and the Atlantic. The voyage—the first to circumnavigate the globe—had taken close to three years.

Despite the losses, this voyage revolutionized Europeans' understanding of the world by demonstrating the vastness of the Pacific. The earth was clearly much larger than shown on Ptolemy's map. Magellan's expedition also forced Spain's rulers to rethink their plans for overseas commerce and territorial expansion. The westward passage to the Indies was too long and dangerous for commercial purposes. Thus Spain soon abandoned the attempt to oust Portugal from the Eastern spice trade and concentrated on exploiting its New World territories.

## Early Exploration by Northern European Powers

Shortly following Columbus's voyages, northern European nations entered the competition for a northwest passage to the Indies. In 1497 John Cabot (ca. 1450–1499), a Venetian merchant commissioned by the English Crown, landed on Newfoundland. The next year he returned and explored the New England coast. These forays proved futile, and at that time the English established no permanent colonies in the territories they explored.

News of the riches of Mexico and Peru later inspired the English to renew their efforts, this time in the extreme north. Between 1576 and 1578 Martin Frobisher (ca. 1535–1594) made three voyages in and around the Canadian bay that now bears his name. Frobisher brought a quantity of ore back to England, but it proved to be worthless.

Early French exploration of the Atlantic was equally frustrating. Between 1534 and 1541 Frenchman Jacques Cartier (1491–1557) made several voyages and explored the St. Lawrence River of Canada, searching for a passage to the wealth of Asia. When this hope proved vain, the French turned to a new source of profit within Canada itself: trade in beavers and other furs. As had the Portuguese in Asia, French traders bartered with local peoples whom they largely treated as autonomous and equal partners. French fishermen also competed with the Spanish and English for the schools of cod they found in the Atlantic waters around Newfoundland.

# Conquest and Settlement

## What was the impact of Iberian conquest and settlement on the peoples and states of the Americas?

Before Columbus's arrival, the Americas were inhabited by thousands of groups of indigenous peoples with distinct languages and cultures. These groups ranged from hunter-gatherer tribes organized into tribal confederations to settled agriculturalists to large-scale empires containing large cities and towns. The best estimate is that the peoples of the Americas numbered between 50 and 65 million in 1492. These numbers were decimated, and the lives of survivors radically altered, by the arrival of Europeans.

## Spanish Conquest of the Aztec and Inca Empires

The first two decades after Columbus's arrival in the New World saw Spanish settlement of Hispaniola, Cuba, Puerto Rico, and other Caribbean islands. Based on rumors of a wealthy mainland civilization, the Spanish governor in Cuba sponsored expeditions to the Yucatán coast of the Gulf of Mexico, including one in 1519 under the command of Hernán Cortés (1485–1547), a Spanish nobleman with considerable experience as an imperial administrator. Cortés and a party of several hundred Spaniards as well as enslaved Taino and African people landed on the Mexican coast on April 21, 1519. His camp soon received visits by delegations of Aztec leaders bearing gifts and news of their great emperor.

The **Aztec Empire**, formed in the early fifteenth century through an alliance of the Mexica people with other peoples in the Valley of Mexico, had expanded rapidly through conquest. At the time of the Spanish arrival, Moctezuma II (r. 1502–1520) ruled an empire of several million inhabitants from his capital at Tenochtitlan (tay-nawch-TEET-lahn), now Mexico City. The Aztec Empire was a highly organized state, with specialized law courts, advanced astronomy, mathematics, and engineering. Its cities featured urban plazas dominated by massive temple pyramids and with bustling markets selling jade, obsidian, and cacao supplied by regional trade networks. A hereditary nobility dominated the army, priesthood, and state bureaucracy and reaped the gains from the agricultural labor of the common people. The Aztec state practiced constant warfare against neighboring peoples to secure captives for religious sacrifices and laborers for agricultural and building projects. Once conquered, subject tribes paid continual tribute to the empire through their local chiefs.

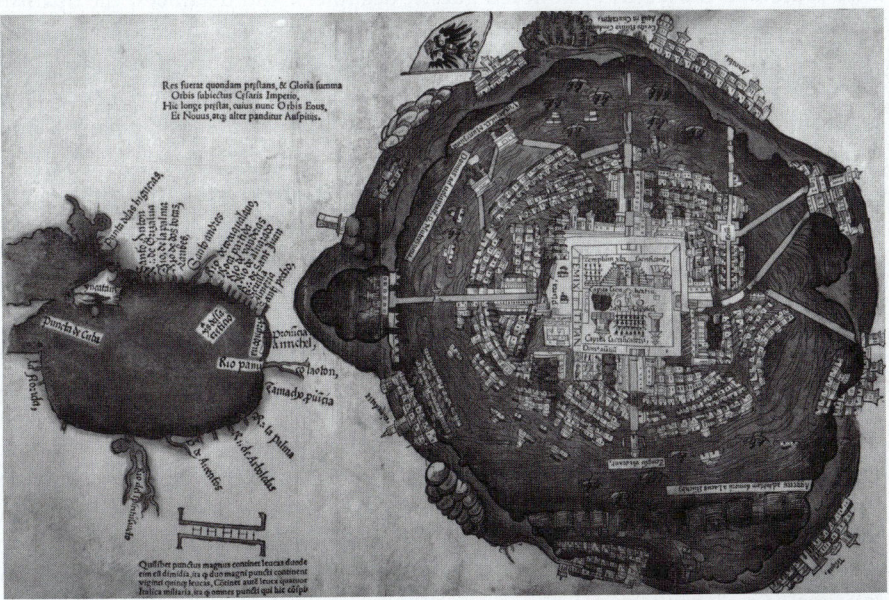

**The Aztec Capital of Tenochtitlan** This woodcut map was published in 1524 along with Cortés's letters describing the conquest of the Aztecs. As it shows, Tenochtitlan occupied an island and was laid out in concentric circles. The administrative and religious buildings were at the heart of the city, which was surrounded by residential quarters. Cortés himself marveled at the city in his letters: "The city is as large as Seville or Cordoba. . . . There are bridges, very large, strong, and well constructed, so that, over many, ten horsemen can ride abreast. . . . The city has many squares where markets are held. . . . There is one square . . . where there are daily more than sixty thousand souls, buying and selling. In the service and manners of its people, their fashion of living was almost the same as in Spain, with just as much harmony and order." (Newberry Library, Chicago/Bridgeman Images)

The brutal nature of Aztec rule provided an opening for Cortés. Within weeks of his arrival, Cortés acquired translators who provided information on the empire and its weaknesses. In September 1519, after initial hostilities in which many Spaniards died, Cortés formed an alliance with Tlaxcala (tlah- SKAH- lah), an independent city-state that had successfully resisted incorporation into the Aztec Empire.

In October a combined Spanish-Tlaxcalan force marched to the city of Cholula, which had recently switched loyalties from Tlaxcala to the Aztec Empire, and massacred many thousands of inhabitants, including women and children. Impressed by this display of ruthless power, other groups joined Cortés's alliance against Aztec rule. In November 1519, these combined forces marched on Tenochtitlan.

Historians have long debated Moctezuma's response to the arrival of the Spanish. Despite the fact that Cortés was allied with his enemies, the emperor refrained from attacking the Spaniards and instead welcomed Cortés and approximately 250 Spanish followers into Tenochtitlan. Cortés later claimed that at this meeting the emperor, inspired by prophecies of the Spaniards' arrival, agreed to become a vassal of the Spanish king. Although impossible for historians to verify, Cortés and later Spanish colonists used this claim to legitimate violence against any who resisted their rule.

After spending more than seven months in the city, in an ambiguous position that combined the status of honored guests, occupiers, and detainees, the Spanish seized Moctezuma as a hostage. During the ensuing attacks and counterattacks, Moctezuma was killed. The city's population rose up against the Spaniards, who fled with heavy losses. In May 1521 the Spanish-Tlaxcalan alliance assaulted Tenochtitlan a second time, leading an army of approximately one thousand Spanish and seventy-five thousand Mesoamerican warriors.[2]

The fall of the Aztec capital in late summer 1521 was hard-won and greatly facilitated by the effects of smallpox, which had devastated the besieged population of the city. After establishing a new capital in the ruins of Tenochtitlan, Cortés and other conquistadors began the systematic conquest of Mexico, a decades-long and brutal process.

More remarkable than the defeat of the Aztecs was the fall of the remote **Inca Empire** in Peru. Living in a settlement perched more than 9,800 feet above sea level, the Incas were not in contact with the Mesoamerican civilization of the Aztecs. In 1438, the hereditary ruler of the Incas had himself crowned emperor and embarked on a successful campaign of conquest. At its greatest extent, the empire extended to the frontier of present-day Ecuador and Colombia in the north and to present-day Chile in the south, an area containing some 16 million people and 350,000 square miles.

Ruled from the capital city of Cuzco (KOOS-ko), the empire was divided into four major regions, each region into provinces, and each province into districts. Officials at each level used the extensive network of roads to transmit information and orders. While the Aztecs used a system of glyphs for writing, the Incas had devised a complex system of colored and knotted cords, called khipus, for administrative bookkeeping.

By the time of the Spanish invasion, however, the Inca Empire had been weakened by a civil war over succession and an epidemic of disease, probably smallpox, spread through trade with groups in contact with Europeans. The Spanish conquistador Francisco Pizarro (ca. 1475–1541) landed on the northern coast of Peru on May 13, 1532, the very day the Inca leader Atahualpa (ah-tuh-WAHL-puh) won control of the empire. As Pizarro advanced across the Andes toward Cuzco, Atahualpa was also heading there for his coronation.

Like Moctezuma in Mexico, Atahualpa sent envoys to greet the Spanish. His plan was to lure them into a trap, seize their horses and ablest men for his army, and execute the rest. With an army of some forty thousand men stationed nearby, Atahualpa seems to have felt he had little to fear. Instead the Spaniards ambushed and captured him, extorted an enormous ransom in gold, and then executed him on trumped-up charges in 1533. The Spanish then marched on to Cuzco, profiting, as with the Aztecs, from internal conflicts to form alliances with local peoples. When Cuzco fell in 1533, the Spanish plundered the empire's wealth in gold and silver.

As with the Aztec Empire, the fall of the imperial capital did not immediately end hostilities. Warfare between Spanish and Inca forces continued to the 1570s. During this period, civil war broke out among Spanish settlers vying for power.

For centuries students have wondered how it was possible for several hundred Spanish conquistadors to defeat powerful empires commanding large armies, vast wealth, and millions of inhabitants. This question is based on a mistaken understanding of the conquest as the quick work of Spaniards acting alone, ideas that were spread in the aftermath by the conquistadors themselves. Instead, historians now emphasize that the defeat of the Aztec and Inca Empires was a long process enabled by divisions within the empires, which produced many native allies willing to fight alongside the Spanish. Spanish steel swords, guns, horses, and dogs bestowed military advantages, but these tools of war were limited in number and effectiveness in the environmental conditions of the Americas. Perhaps the most important factor was the devastating impact of contagious diseases among the indigenous population, which swept through the Aztec and Inca Empires at the time of the conquest.

## Portuguese Brazil

Unlike Mesoamerica or the Andes, the territory of Brazil contained no urban empires but instead had roughly 2.5 million nomadic and settled people divided into small tribes and many different language groups. In 1500 the Portuguese Crown named Pedro Álvares Cabral commander of a fleet headed for the spice trade of the Indies. En route, the fleet sailed far to the west, claiming the coast where they accidentally landed for Portugal under the terms of the Treaty of Tordesillas. The Portuguese soon undertook a profitable trade with local people in brazilwood, a valued source of red dye, which inspired the name of the new colony.

In the 1520s Portuguese settlers brought sugarcane production to Brazil. They initially used enslaved indigenous laborers on sugar plantations, but the rapid decline in the indigenous population soon led to the use of forcibly transported Africans. In Brazil the Portuguese thus created a new form of colonization in the Americas: large plantations worked by enslaved people. This model of slave-worked sugar plantations would spread throughout the Caribbean in the seventeenth century.

## Colonial Administration

While early conquest and settlement were conducted largely by private initiatives, the Portuguese and Spanish governments soon assumed more direct control. Both Portugal and Spain required all merchandise from their American colonies to travel through a single port, where it could be taxed and then transported elsewhere in Europe. They ruled conquered peoples through a combination of European and indigenous institutions and practices.

In 1482, King John II of Portugal established a royal trading house in Lisbon to handle gold and other goods being extracted from Africa. After the Portuguese expanded into the Indian Ocean spice trade, it was named the Casa da India (House of the Indies). Through the Casa, the Crown exercised a monopoly over the export of European goods and the import and distribution of spices and precious metals. It charged taxes on all other incoming goods. The Casa also established a viceroy in the Indian city of Goa to administer Portuguese trading posts and naval forces in Africa and Asia.

To secure the vast expanse of Brazil, in the 1530s the Portuguese implemented a distinctive system of rule called **captaincies**, in which hereditary grants of land were given to nobles and loyal officials who bore the costs of settling and administering their territories. Over time, the Crown secured greater power over the captaincies, appointing royal governors to act as administrators. The captaincy of Bahia was the site of the capital, Salvador, home to the governor general and other royal officials.

Spain adopted a similar system for overseas trade. In 1503 the Spanish granted the port of Seville a monopoly over all traffic to the New World and established the House of Trade to oversee economic matters. In 1523 Spain created the Royal and Supreme Council of the Indies, with authority over all colonial affairs subject to approval by the king.

By the end of the sixteenth century the Spanish had successfully overcome most indigenous groups and expanded their territory throughout modern-day Mexico, the southwestern United States, and Central and South America. In Mesoamerica and the Andes, the Spanish had taken over the cities and tribute systems of the Aztecs and the Incas, leaving in place well-established cities and towns, but redirecting tribute payments toward the Crown. Through laws and regulations, the Spanish Crown strove to maintain two separate populations, a "Spanish Republic" and an "Indian Republic," with distinct rights and duties for each group.

The Spanish Crown divided its New World possessions initially into two **viceroyalties**, or administrative divisions: New Spain, created in 1535; and Peru, created in 1542. In the eighteenth century two new viceroyalties, New Granada and La Plata, were created (see Map 16.2).

Within each territory, the viceroy, or imperial governor, exercised broad military and civil authority. The viceroy presided over the *audiencia* (ow-dee-EHN-see-ah), a board of judges that served as his advisory council and the highest judicial body. As in Spain, settlement in the Americas was centered on cities and towns. In each city, the municipal council, or *cabildo*, exercised local authority. Women were denied participation in public life, a familiar pattern from both Spain and precolonial indigenous society.

## Economic Exploitation of the Indigenous Population

From the first decades of settlement, the Spanish made use of the **encomienda system**, by which the Crown granted the conquerors the right to force groups of Native Americans to perform labor and to demand tribute from them in exchange

chalchicueyca

**Spanish Exploitation of Indigenous Labor** This image depicts Spanish conquistadors supervising indigenous laborers as they carry arms along the steep road from Veracruz to Tlaxcala in 1520. It was part of a larger painting, produced in the postconquest era and known as the *Lienzo de Tlaxcala*, that tells the story of the alliance between the Tlaxcala kingdom and the Spanish and their defeat of the Aztec Empire. (Sarin Images/Granger)

for providing food and shelter. The encomiendas (en-ko-me-EN-duhz) were also intended as a means to organize indigenous people for missionary work and Christian conversion. This system was first used in Hispaniola to work gold fields and then in Mexico for agricultural labor and, when silver was discovered in the 1540s, for silver mining.

A 1512 Spanish law authorizing the use of encomiendas called for indigenous people to be treated fairly, but in practice the system led to terrible abuses, including overwork, beatings, and sexual violence. King Charles I responded to complaints in 1542 with the New Laws, which set limits on the authority of encomienda holders, including their ability to transmit their privileges to heirs. The New Laws recognized indigenous people who accepted Christianity and Spanish rule as free subjects of the Spanish Crown. The New Laws provoked a revolt in Peru among encomienda holders, and the laws were little enforced throughout Spanish territories. Nonetheless, the Crown gradually gained control over encomiendas in central areas of the empire and required indigenous people to pay tributes in cash, rather than in labor.

In the second half of the sixteenth century, in response to persistent abuses in the encomiendas and a growing shortage of indigenous workers, royal officials gradually established a new government-run system of forced labor, called *repartimiento* in New Spain and *mita* in Peru. Administrators assigned a certain percentage of the inhabitants of native communities to labor for a set period each year in public works, mining, agriculture, and other tasks.

Spanish systems for exploiting the labor of indigenous peoples were both a cause of and a response to the disastrous decline in their population that began soon after the arrival of Europeans. Some indigenous people died as a direct result of the violence of conquest and the disruption of agriculture and trade caused by warfare. The most important cause of death, however, was infectious disease.

Colonial administrators responded to this population decline by forcibly combining dwindling indigenous communities into new settlements and imposing the rigors of the encomienda and the repartimiento. By the end of the sixteenth century the search for fresh sources of labor had given birth to the new tragedy of the Atlantic slave trade.

## Patterns of Settlement

The century after the discovery of silver in 1545 marked the high point of Iberian immigration to the Americas. Although the first migrants were men, soon whole families began to cross the Atlantic, and the European population began to increase through natural reproduction. By 1600 American-born Europeans, called *Creoles*, outnumbered immigrants.

Iberian settlement was predominantly urban in nature. Spaniards settled into the cities and towns of the former Aztec and Inca Empires as the native population dwindled through death and flight. They also established new cities in which settlers were quick to develop urban institutions familiar to them from Spain: city squares, churches, schools, and universities.

Despite the growing number of Europeans and the rapid decline of the indigenous population, Europeans remained a small minority of the total inhabitants of the Americas. Iberians had sexual relationships with native women, leading to the growth of a substantial population of mixed Iberian and Indian descent known as *mestizos* (meh-STEE-zohz). The large-scale arrival of enslaved Africans, starting in Brazil in the mid-sixteenth century, added new ethnic and racial dimensions to the population.

# The Era of Global Contact

**How was the era of global contact shaped by new commodities, commercial empires, and forced migrations?**

The centuries-old Afro-Eurasian trade world was forever changed by the European voyages of discovery and their aftermath. For the first time, a truly global economy emerged in the sixteenth and seventeenth centuries, and it forged new links among far-flung peoples, cultures, and societies. The ancient civilizations of Europe, Africa, the Americas, and Asia confronted each other in new and rapidly evolving ways. Those confrontations often took the form of conquest, forced migration, and brutal exploitation. They also contributed to cultural exchange, ecological transformation, and new patterns of life.

## Population Loss and the Ecological Impacts of Contact

Contact between the Old and New Worlds had profound ecological ramifications. In particular, the travel of people and goods led to an exchange of animals, plants, and diseases, a complex process known as the **Columbian exchange**. Everywhere they settled, the Spanish and Portuguese brought and raised wheat. Grapes and olives imported from Spain did well in parts of Peru and Chile. Perhaps the most significant introduction to the diet of Native Americans came via the meat and milk of the livestock that the early conquistadors brought with them, including cattle, sheep, and goats. The horse enabled both the Spanish conquerors and indigenous populations to travel faster and farther and to transport heavy loads more easily.

In turn, Europeans returned home with food crops that became central elements of their diet and eventually of many parts of the world. Crops originating in the Americas included tomatoes, squash, pumpkins, peppers, and many varieties of beans, as well as tobacco. One of the most important of such crops was maize (corn). By the late seventeenth century maize had become a staple in Spain, Portugal, southern France, and Italy, and in the eighteenth century it became one of the chief foods of southeastern Europe and southern China. Even more valuable was the nutritious white potato, which slowly spread from west to east, contributing everywhere to a rise in population.

While the exchange of foods was a great benefit to cultures across the world, the introduction of European pathogens to the New World had a disastrous impact on the native population. In Europe infectious diseases like smallpox, measles, and influenza—originally spread through contact with domestic animals—killed many people each year. Given the size of the population and the frequency of outbreaks, in most of Europe these diseases were experienced in childhood, and survivors carried immunity or resistance. Prior to contact with Europeans, indigenous peoples of the New World suffered from insect-borne diseases and some infectious ones, but their lack of domestic livestock spared them the host of highly infectious Old World diseases. The arrival of Europeans spread these microbes among a totally unprepared population, and they fell victim in vast numbers.

Overall, the indigenous population declined by as much as 90 percent or more, but with important regional variations. In general, densely populated urban centers were worse hit than rural areas, and tropical, low-lying regions suffered more than cooler, higher-altitude ones. The world after Columbus was thus profoundly transformed by disease as well as by trade and colonization.

## Sugar and Early Transatlantic Slavery

Throughout the Middle Ages, slavery was deeply entrenched in the Mediterranean. The constant warfare of the reconquista had supplied captive Muslims for domestic slavery in Iberia, but the success of these wars meant that the number of captives had greatly dwindled by the mid-fifteenth century.

As Portuguese explorers began their voyages along the western coast of Africa in the 1440s, one of the first commodities they sought was slaves. While the first slaves were simply seized by small raiding parties, Portuguese merchants soon found that it was easier and more profitable to trade with African leaders, who were accustomed to dealing in enslaved people captured through warfare with neighboring powers. In 1483 the Portuguese established an alliance with the kingdom of Kongo. The royal family eventually converted to Christianity, and Portuguese merchants intermarried with Kongolese women, creating a permanent Afro-Portuguese community. From 1490 to 1530 Portuguese traders brought between three hundred and two thousand enslaved Africans to Portugal each year.

In this stage of European expansion, the history of slavery became intertwined with the history of sugar. In the Middle Ages, sugarcane — native to the South Pacific — was brought to Mediterranean islands. Population increases and greater prosperity in the fifteenth century led to increasing demand for sugar. The establishment of sugar plantations on the Canary and Madeira Islands in the fifteenth century after Iberian colonization testifies to this demand.

Sugar was a particularly difficult crop to produce for profit, requiring constant, arduous labor. The invention of roller mills to crush the cane more efficiently meant that yields could be significantly augmented, but only if a sufficient labor force was found to supply the mills. Plantation owners solved their labor problem by forcing first native islanders and then transported Africans to perform the backbreaking work.

The transatlantic slave trade that would ultimately result in the forced transport of over 12 million people began in 1518, when Spanish king Charles I authorized traders to bring enslaved Africans to the Americas. The Portuguese brought the first enslaved people to Brazil around 1550. After its founding in 1621, the Dutch West India Company forcibly transported thousands of Africans to Brazil and the Caribbean, mostly to work on sugar plantations. In the late seventeenth century, with the chartering of the Royal African Company, the English entered the slave trade.

Before 1700, when slavers decided it was better business to improve conditions for the captives, some 20 percent of enslaved people died on the voyage across the Atlantic.[3] The most common cause of death was dysentery induced by poor-quality food and water, lack of sanitation, and intense crowding. On sugar plantations, death rates among enslaved people from illness and exhaustion were extremely high.

## Spanish Silver and Its Economic Effects

In 1545, at an altitude of fifteen thousand feet, the Spanish discovered an extraordinary source of silver at Potosí (poh-toh-SEE) (in present-day Bolivia) in unsettled territory captured from the Inca Empire. By 1550 Potosí yielded perhaps 60 percent of all the silver mined in the world. From Potosí and the mines at Zacatecas (za-kuh-TAY-kuhs) and Guanajuato (gwah-nah-HWAH-toh) in Mexico, huge quantities of precious metals poured forth.

Mining became the most important industry in the colonies. Millions of indigenous laborers suffered brutal conditions and death in the silver mines. Demand for new sources of labor for the mines also contributed to the intensification of the African slave trade. Profits for the Spanish Crown were immense. The Crown claimed the quinto, one-fifth of all precious metals mined in South America, which represented 25 percent of its total income. Between 1503 and 1650, 35 million pounds of silver and over 600,000 pounds of gold entered Seville's port.

Spain's immense profits from silver paid for the tremendous expansion of its empire and for the large armies that defended it. However, the easy flow of money had the unanticipated effect of dampening economic innovation. It also exacerbated the rising inflation Spain was already experiencing in the mid-sixteenth century due to population growth and stagnant production. Only after 1600, when the population declined, did prices slowly stabilize. Nevertheless, King Philip II and his successors were forced to write off the state debt several times between 1550 and 1650, thereby undermining confidence in the government and further weakening the economy.

Philip II paid his armies and foreign debts with silver bullion, and thus Spanish inflation was transmitted to the rest of Europe. Between 1560 and 1600 prices in most parts of Europe doubled and in some cases quadrupled. Because money bought less, people who lived on fixed incomes, such as nobles, were badly hurt. Those who owed fixed sums of money, such as the middle class, prospered because in a time of rising prices, debts lessened in value each year. Food costs rose most sharply, and the poor fared worst of all.

In many ways, though, it was not Spain but China that controlled the world trade in silver. The Chinese demanded silver for their products and for the payment of imperial taxes. China was thus the main buyer of world silver, absorbing half the world's production. The silver market drove world trade, with New Spain and Japan acting as major sources of the supply of silver and China dominating demand. The world trade in silver is one of the best examples of the new global economy that emerged in this period.

## The Birth of the Global Economy

With Europeans' discovery of the Americas and their exploration of the Pacific, the entire world was linked for the first time in history by oceanic trade. The opening of that trade brought into being three successive commercial empires: the Portuguese, the Spanish, and the Dutch.

In the sixteenth century the Portuguese controlled the sea route to India (Map 16.3). From their bases at Goa on the Arabian Sea and at Malacca on the Malay Peninsula, ships carried goods to the Portuguese settlement at Macao. From Macao Portuguese ships loaded with Chinese silks and porcelains sailed to Japan and the Philippines, where Chinese goods were exchanged for Spanish silver from New Spain. Throughout Asia the Portuguese traded in enslaved people, some of whom were brought all the way across the Pacific to Mexico. Returning to Portugal, they brought Asian spices that had been purchased with textiles produced in India and with gold and ivory from East Africa. From their colony in Brazil they shipped sugar produced by enslaved Africans whom they had forcibly transported across the Atlantic.

Coming to empire a few decades later than the Portuguese, the Spanish were determined to claim their place in world trade. The Spanish Empire in the New World was basically land based, but across the Pacific the Spaniards built a seaborne empire centered at Manila in the Philippines. Established in 1571, the city of Manila served as the transpacific link between Spanish America and China. In Manila Spanish traders used silver from American mines to purchase Chinese silk for European markets.

In the seventeenth century the Dutch challenged the Spanish and Portuguese empires. The Dutch East India Company was founded in 1602 with the stated intention of capturing the spice trade from the Portuguese. Drawing on their commercial wealth and long experience in European trade, the Dutch emerged by the end of the century as the most powerful worldwide seaborne trading power (see "The Dutch Trading Empire" in Chapter 18).

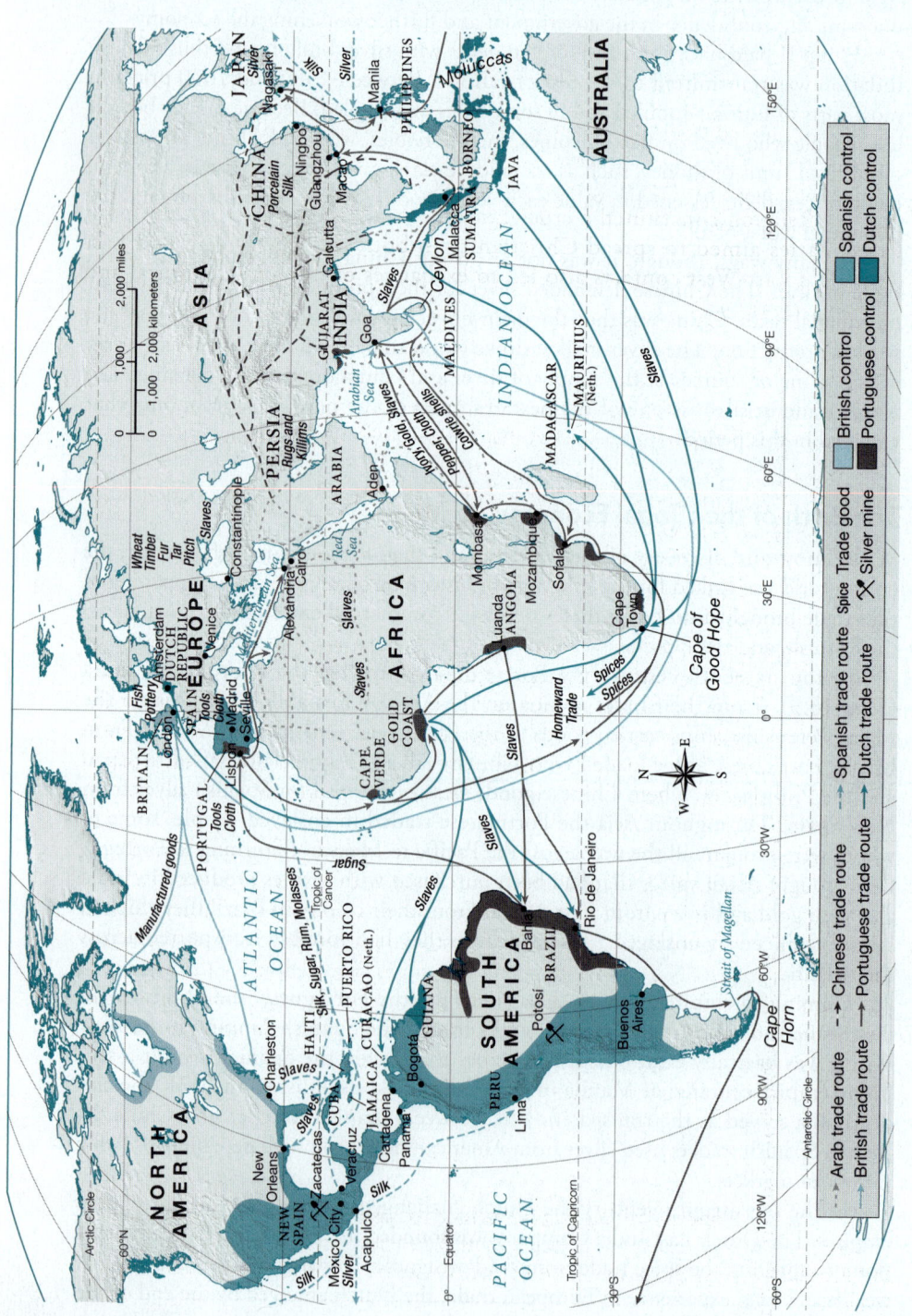

# Changing Attitudes and Beliefs

**How did new encounters shape cultural attitudes and beliefs in Europe and the rest of the world?**

The age of overseas expansion heightened Europeans' contacts with the rest of the world. These contacts gave birth to new ideas about the inherent superiority or inferiority of different groups of people, increasingly conceived as distinct "races." Religion constituted a crucial means of cultural contact, as European missionaries aimed to spread Christianity in both the New World and East Asia. The East-West contacts also led to exchanges of influential cultural and scientific ideas.

## Religious Conversion

Christian conversion was one of the most important justifications for European expansion. Jesuit missionaries were active in Japan and China in the sixteenth and seventeenth centuries, until authorities banned their teachings. The first missionaries to the New World accompanied Columbus on his second voyage, and more than 2,500 Franciscans, Dominicans, Jesuits, and other friars crossed the Atlantic in the following century. Colonial powers built convents, churches, and cathedrals for converted indigenous people and European settlers, and established religious courts to police correct beliefs and morals.

To stamp out old beliefs, colonial authorities destroyed shrines and objects of religious worship. They harshly persecuted men and women who continued to practice traditional spiritual rituals and imposed European Christian norms of family life, especially monogamous marriage, on indigenous people. While many resisted these efforts, over time a larger number accepted Christianity. It is estimated that missionaries had baptized between 4 and 9 million indigenous people in New Spain by the mid-1530s.[4]

Christian conversation was an ambiguous and complex process involving cultural exchanges that impacted both sides. Catholic friars were among the first Europeans to seek an understanding of native cultures and languages as part of their effort to render Christianity comprehensible to indigenous people. In Mexico they not only learned the Nahuatl language, but also taught it to non-Nahuatl-speaking groups to create a shared language for Christian teaching. In translating Christianity, missionaries, working in partnership with indigenous converts, adapted it to the symbols and ritual objects of pre-existing cultures and beliefs, thereby creating distinctive New World forms of Catholicism.

**< MAP 16.3　Seaborne Trading Empires in the Sixteenth and Seventeenth Centuries**
By the mid-seventeenth century trade linked all parts of the world except for Australia. Notice that trade in slaves was not confined to the Atlantic but involved almost all parts of the world.

## European Debates About Indigenous Peoples

Iberian exploitation of the native population of the Americas began from the moment of Columbus's arrival in 1492. Denunciations of this abuse by Catholic missionaries, however, quickly followed, inspiring vociferous debates in both Europe and the colonies about the nature of indigenous peoples and how they should be treated. Bartolomé de Las Casas (1474–1566), a Dominican friar and former encomienda holder, was one of the earliest and most outspoken critics of the brutal treatment inflicted on indigenous peoples.

Mounting criticism in Spain led King Charles I to assemble a group of church-men and lawyers to debate the issue in 1550 in the city of Valladolid. One side of the **Valladolid debate**, led by Juan Ginés de Sepúlveda, argued that conquest and forc-ible conversion were both necessary and justified to save indigenous people from the horrors of human sacrifice and idolatry. To counter these arguments, Las Casas and his supporters depicted indigenous people as rational and innocent children, who deserved protection and tutelage.

While the debate did not end exploitation of indigenous people, the Crown did use it to justify limiting the rights of settlers and increasing legal protections for indigenous communities. In 1573, Philip II issued detailed laws regulating how new towns should be established and administered and how Spanish settlers should interact with indigenous populations. The impact of these laws can still be seen in Mexico's colonial towns, which are laid out as grids around a central plaza.

## New Ideas About Race

European conquest and settlement led to the emergence of new ideas about "race" as a form of human identity. In medieval Spain and Portugal, sharp distinctions were drawn between supposedly "pure-blooded" Christians, on the one hand, and Jews and conversos, people of Jewish origins who had converted to Christianity, on the other. In the fifteenth century, Iberian rulers issued discriminatory laws against conversos as well as against Muslims and their descendants. Feeling that conversion could not erase the taint of heretical belief, they came to see Christian faith as a type of inherited identity that was passed through the blood.

The idea of "purity of blood" changed when Iberians conquered the Americas. The colonial population included people of European, indigenous, and (after the introduction of the transatlantic slave trade) African descent. Spanish colonizers came to believe that the indigenous people of the Americas were free from the taint of unbelief because they had never been exposed to Christianity. Accordingly, the ideology of "purity of blood" they brought from Iberia could more easily incorporate indigenous populations; by contrast, Africans—viewed as having refused the mes-sage of Christ that was preached in the Old World—were seen as impure, as much on the grounds of religious difference as physical characteristics.

Despite later efforts by colonial officials to segregate Europeans, Native Americans, and people of African descent, racial mixing began as soon as the first conquista-dors arrived in the Americas. A complex system of racial classification, known as castas in Spanish America, emerged to refer to different proportions of European, indigenous, and African parentage. Spanish concerns about religious purity were thus transformed in the colonial context into concerns about racial bloodlines, with "pure" Spanish blood occupying the summit of the racial hierarchy and mixtures of European, indigenous and African descent ranked in descending order. These concerns put childbirth and reproduction at the center of anxieties about racial mixing, heightening scrutiny of women's sexual activities.

All European colonies in the New World, including later French and English settlements, drew racial distinctions between Europeans, indigenous people, and those of African descent. With its immense slave-based plantation agriculture system, large indigenous population, and relatively low Portuguese immigration, Brazil developed a particularly complex racial and ethnic mosaic.

# Chapter Summary

Prior to Columbus's voyages, centuries-old trade routes linked the peoples and products of Africa, Asia, and Europe. As the economy and population recovered from the Black Death, Europeans began to seek more direct and profitable access to the Afro-Eurasian trade world. Technological innovations, many borrowed from the East, enabled explorers to undertake ever more ambitious voyages.

In the aftermath of conquest, the Portuguese and Spanish established new forms of governance to dominate indigenous peoples and exploit their labor. The arrival of Europeans brought enormous population losses to native communities, primarily through the spread of infectious diseases. Disease was one element of the Columbian exchange, a complex transfer of germs, plants, and animals between the Old and New Worlds that helped create the first truly global economy. Tragically, a major component of global trade was the transatlantic slave trade, in which Europeans forcibly transported Africans to labor in the sugar plantations and silver mines of the New World. European nations vied for supremacy in global trade, with early Portuguese success in Asia being challenged first by the Spanish and then by the Dutch.

Increased contact with the outside world led Europeans to develop new ideas about cultural and racial differences. Debates occurred in Spain and its colonies over the treatment of the indigenous peoples of the Americas, and new ideas about racial inequality emerged. Religion was a key means of cultural contact, as European missionaries aimed to spread Christianity in the New World.

## NOTES

1. Marco Polo, *The Book of Ser Marco Polo, the Venetian: Concerning the Kingdoms and Marvels of the East*, vol. 2, trans. and ed. Colonel Sir Henry Yule (London: John Murray, 1903), pp. 185–186.
2. Thomas Benjamin, *The Atlantic World: Europeans, Africans, Indians and Their Shared History, 1400–1900* (Cambridge: Cambridge University Press, 2009), p. 141.
3. Herbert S. Klein, "Profits and the Causes of Mortality," in *The Atlantic Slave Trade*, ed. David Northrup (Lexington, Mass.: D. C. Heath, 1994), p. 116.
4. David Carrasco, *The Oxford Encyclopedia of Mesoamerican Cultures* (Oxford: Oxford University Press, 2001), p. 208.

## MAKE CONNECTIONS  LOOK AHEAD

Just three years separated Martin Luther's attack on the Catholic Church in 1517 and Ferdinand Magellan's discovery of the Pacific Ocean in 1520. Within a few short years western Europeans' religious unity and notions of terrestrial geography were shattered. In the ensuing decades Europeans struggled to come to terms with religious differences between Protestants and Catholics at home and with the multitudes of new peoples and places they encountered abroad. While some Europeans were positively inspired by this new diversity, more often the result was suffering and violence. Europeans endured decades of religious civil war, and indigenous peoples overseas underwent massive population losses as a result of European warfare, disease, and exploitation. Religious leaders condoned the transatlantic slave trade that brought suffering and death to millions as well as the conquest of Native American land and the subjugation of indigenous people.

Even as the voyages of discovery introduced new forms of diversity to European culture, they also played a role in state centralization and consolidation. Henceforth, competition to gain overseas colonies became an integral part of European politics. While Spain's enormous profits from conquest ultimately led to a weakening of its power, over time the Netherlands, England, and France used profits from colonial trade to help build modernized, centralized states.

Two crucial consequences emerged from this era of expansion. The first was the creation of enduring contacts among five of the seven continents of the globe—Europe, Asia, Africa, North America, and South America. From the sixteenth century onward, the peoples of the world were increasingly entwined in new forms of economic, social, and cultural exchange. The second was the growth of European power. Europeans gradually asserted control over the Americas and over existing trade networks in Asia and Africa. Although China remained the world's most powerful economy until at least 1800, the beginnings of European dominance had emerged.

# Chapter 16 Review

## IDENTIFY KEY TERMS

**Identify and explain the significance of each item below.**

bride wealth (p. 386)

conquistador (p. 388)

caravel (p. 389)

Ptolemy's *Geography* (p. 389)

Treaty of Tordesillas (p. 393)

Aztec Empire (p. 395)

Inca Empire (p. 396)

captaincies (p. 398)

viceroyalties (p. 398)

encomienda system (p. 398)

Columbian exchange (p. 400)

Valladolid debate (p. 406)

## REVIEW THE MAIN IDEAS

**Answer the focus questions from each section of the chapter.**

1. What was the Afro-Eurasian trade world prior to the era of European exploration? (p. 384)

2. How and why did Europeans undertake ambitious voyages of expansion? (p. 388)

3. What was the impact of Iberian conquest and settlement on the peoples and ecologies of the Americas? (p. 394)

4. How was the era of global contact shaped by new commodities, commercial empires, and forced migrations? (p. 400)

5. How did new encounters shape cultural attitudes and beliefs in Europe and the rest of the world? (p. 405)

## MAKE COMPARISONS AND CONNECTIONS

**Analyze the larger developments and continuities within and across chapters.**

1. If Europe was at the periphery of the global trading system prior to 1492, what role did Europeans play by the middle of the sixteenth century? What had changed? What had not?

2. How does the spread of Christianity in the aftermath of European conquest in the New World compare with the earlier spread of Christianity under the Roman Empire (Chapter 6) and the spread of Buddhism (Chapter 7) and Islam (Chapters 9, 10, 13)?

3. How did European expansion in the period covered in this chapter draw on earlier patterns of trade and migration in Africa (Chapter 10) and Asia (Chapters 12, 13)?

4. To what extent did the European voyages of expansion and conquest inaugurate an era of global history? Did this era represent the birth of "globalization"? Why or why not?

## CHRONOLOGY

| | |
|---|---|
| **1368–1644** | • Ming Dynasty in China (Ch. 21) |
| **1405–1433** | • Zheng He's naval expeditions |
| **1443** | • Portuguese establish first African trading post at Arguin |
| **1453** | • Ottoman conquest of Constantinople (Ch. 17) |
| **ca. 1464–1591** | • Songhai kingdom dominates the western Sudan (Ch. 20) |
| **1467–1600** | • Period of civil war in Japan (Ch. 21) |
| **1492** | • Columbus lands on San Salvador |
| **1494** | • Treaty of Tordesillas ratified |
| **1518** | • Atlantic slave trade begins |
| **1519–1522** | • Magellan's expedition circumnavigates the world |
| **1521** | • Cortés conquers Aztec Empire |
| **1533** | • Pizarro conquers Inca Empire |
| **1556–1605** | • Reign of Akbar in Mughal Empire (Ch. 17) |
| **1571** | • Spanish establish port of Manila in the Philippines |
| **1602** | • Dutch East India Company founded |

# 17

# The Islamic World Powers

## 1300–1800

**AFTER THE DECLINE OF THE MONGOL EMPIRE IN THE MID-FOURTEENTH** century, powerful new Islamic states emerged in south and west Eurasia. By the sixteenth century the Ottoman Empire, in Anatolia and the Balkans; the Safavid (SAH-fah-vid) Empire in Persia; and the Mughal (MOO-guhl) Empire in India controlled vast territories from West Africa to Central Asia, from the Balkans to the Bay of Bengal.

Lasting more than six centuries (1299–1922), the Ottoman Empire was one of the largest, best-organized, and most enduring political entities in world history. In Persia (now Iran) the Safavid Dynasty created a Shi'a state and presided over a brilliant culture. In India the Mughal leader Babur and

411

his successors gained control of much of the Indian subcontinent. Mughal rule inaugurated a period of administrative reorganization in India and the flowering of intellectual and architectural creativity.

Although these three dynasties were rivals and sometimes waged war against one another, the empires they built shared important characteristics and challenges, including the Muslim faith and Turco-Mongol origins, as well as common military, political, and cultural trends. In contrast to contemporary European states, they accepted a high degree of religious diversity among their subject peoples, although all three moved toward greater religious orthodoxy over time. Merchants, poets, philosophers, artists, and military advisers moved relatively easily across their political boundaries, building strong cultural connections among the empires.

# The Islamic Empires: The Ottomans, Safavids, and Mughals

**How were the major Islamic empires established, and what forms of government did they set up?**

Before the Mongols arrived in Central Asia and Persia, groups of nomadic Turkish-speaking tribes from the region of modern Mongolia had moved west and gained control over key territories from Anatolia to Delhi in north India. Later, under the empire created by Chinggis Khan and its successor khanates, Mongols who moved into Central Asia and Persia adopted the language and culture of the Turkic peoples they conquered, creating a blended Turco-Mongolian cultural tradition.

In the late fourteenth century, Turco-Mongol leader Amir Timur (1336–1405), also called Tamerlane, attempted to rebuild the Mongol Empire, claiming legitimacy both through his marriage to a descendant of Chinggis Khan and through his self-portrayal as a defender of Islam and patron of Sufi mystics. From his base in Samarkand, he built an empire that reached into India and through Persia to the Black Sea. After his death, his sons and grandson fought one another for succession, and by 1450 his empire was in rapid decline.

The three empires studied in this chapter emerged into world history with the waning of Mongol power, sharing a common Turco-Mongolian heritage and Muslim religion, as well as a shared influence from Persian language and culture. Confronted with common environmental, political, and administrative challenges, they adopted some of the same solutions for governing large, heterogeneous empires.

## Environmental Challenges

To varying degrees, the Islamic powers shared common environmental challenges — lack of water, recurrent plagues of infectious disease, and, in the sixteenth and seventeenth centuries, a long period of unusually cool climate. Because water was scarce in the region, the population tended to cluster around cities located at oases, which were linked by networks of trade caravans. The Iranian Plateau (home of the Persian Safavid Empire) was particularly constrained by environmental conditions. It was a landlocked territory composed of arid basins surrounded by high mountain ranges, with uninhabited salt deserts in the east. These constraints meant that food production and natural resources were limited, and the population of Safavid Persia remained small compared to its rivals.

The Ottomans and Mughals occupied more varied and fertile terrain and had much larger populations, but they experienced environmental challenges of their own. Given the central position they occupied on world trading routes, infectious diseases arrived regularly through the movement of caravans and ships carrying people, goods, and fleas. Islamic theology interpreted plague, like earthquakes and other natural disasters, as a manifestation of the will of God, a belief shared by Christian authorities. While historians used to believe that these ideas produced an attitude of fatalism in Muslim lands that prevented efforts to avoid contagion, more recent research suggests that, in practice, many Muslims fled plague-stricken cities for the safety of rural areas, just as European Christians did. Compared to Christian states, the Ottomans were slower to develop comprehensive quarantine policies, for reasons that are not yet well understood.

The three empires also suffered from the period of cool climate that affected much of the globe in the sixteenth and seventeenth centuries, which historians have dubbed the "Little Ice Age" (see "The Little Ice Age and the Black Death" in Chapter 14). Drought, crop failure, and famine contributed to social unrest and political decline, especially in the Ottoman Empire.

## The Expansion of the Ottoman Empire

The **Ottomans** took their name from Osman (r. 1299–1326), the chief of a band of seminomadic Turkic people that had migrated into western Anatolia while the Mongols still held Persia. The Ottomans gradually expanded at the expense of other small Turkic states and the Byzantine Empire (Map 17.1). Although temporarily slowed by defeat at the hands of Timur in 1402, they quickly reasserted themselves after Timur's death in 1405.

Osman's campaigns were intended to subdue, not to destroy. The Ottomans built their empire by absorbing the Muslims of Anatolia and by becoming the protector of the Orthodox Church and millions of Orthodox Christians in Anatolia and the Balkans. A series of victories between 1326 and the mid-1350s made the Ottomans masters of the Balkans. After these victories, they made slaves of many captives and trained them as soldiers. These troops were outfitted with the new gunpowder weapons and artillery and trained to use them effectively.

In 1453, during the reign of Sultan Mehmet II (r. 1451–1481), the Ottomans conquered Constantinople and its small surrounding territory, all that remained of the once mighty Byzantine Empire. Ottoman **sultans** (supreme political and military rulers) henceforth considered themselves successors to both the Byzantine and Seljuk Turk emperors. In the sixteenth century they continued to expand through the Middle East and into North Africa.

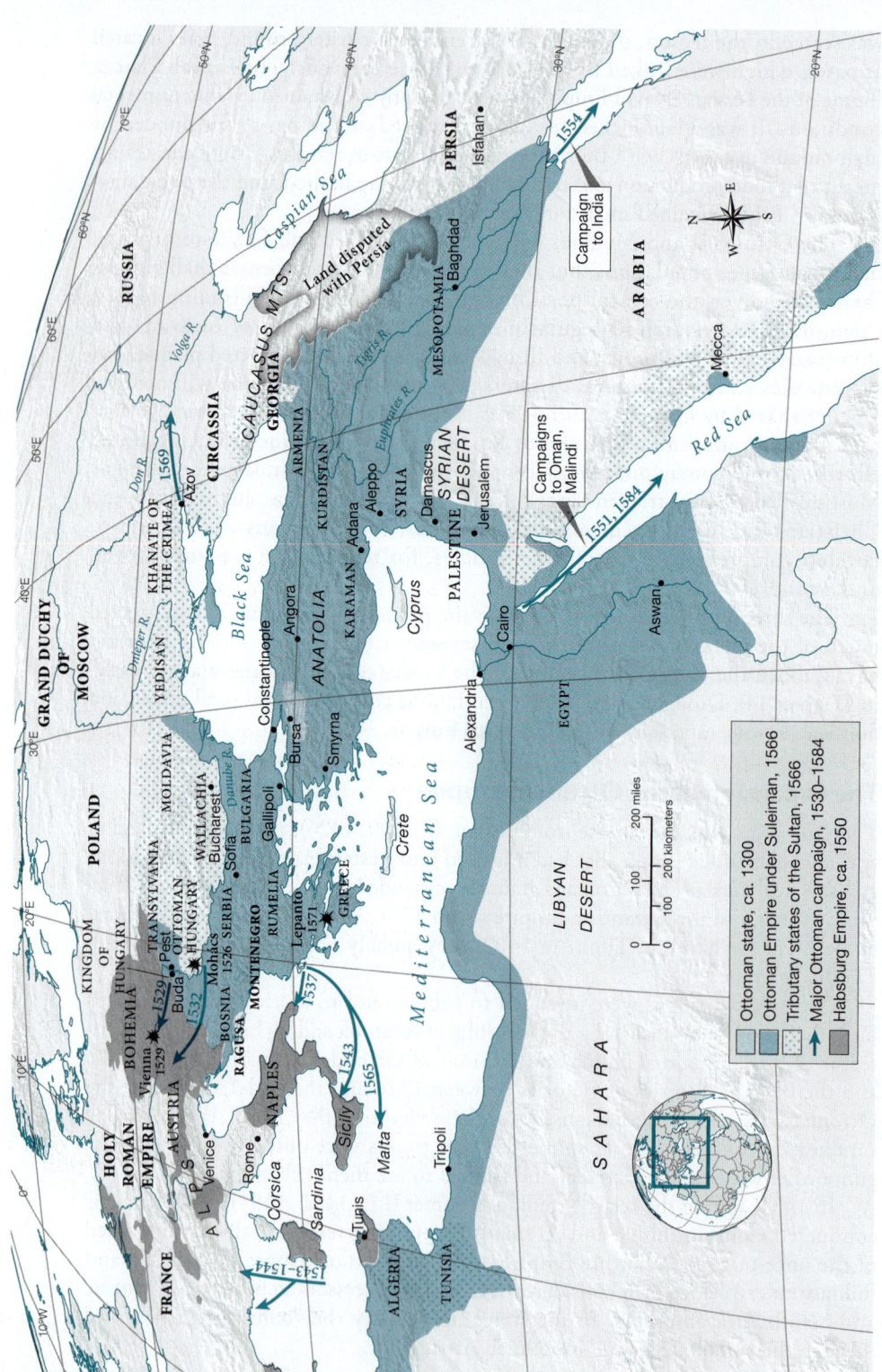

RUSSIA

*Caspian Sea*

CAUCASUS MTS.

Land disputed
with Persia

PERSIA
Isfahan

Baghdad

MESOPOTAMIA

*Tigris R.*

*Euphrates R.*

ARABIA

1554

Campaign
to India

N
W E
S

*Red Sea*

Mecca

GEORGIA

ARMENIA

KURDISTAN

SYRIA
Aleppo
Adana
Damascus
Jerusalem

SYRIAN DESERT

PALESTINE

Campaigns
to Oman,
Malindi

1551, 1584

CIRCASSIA

*Volga R.*

*Don R.*

KHANATE OF
THE CRIMEA
1569
Azov

YEDISAN

*Dnieper R.*

*Black Sea*

Constantinople

Angora

ANATOLIA

KARAMAN

Cyprus

Bursa
Smyrna

Cairo

Aswan

Alexandria

EGYPT

GRAND DUCHY
OF
MOSCOW

POLAND

KINGDOM
OF
HUNGARY

TRANSYLVANIA

MOLDAVIA

WALLACHIA
Bucharest

*Danube R.*

BULGARIA
Sofia

RUMELIA

BOSNIA
SERBIA
MONTENEGRO
RAGUSA

Gallipoli

GREECE
Lepanto
1571

Crete

*Mediterranean Sea*

BOHEMIA

Vienna
1529
1529
Pest
Buda
1532
Mohács
1526
OTTOMAN
HUNGARY

AUSTRIA

A L P S

Venice

Rome

NAPLES

Corsica

Sardinia

HOLY
ROMAN
EMPIRE

FRANCE

1337

1543

1565

Sicily

Malta

Tripoli

Tunis

ALGERIA

TUNISIA

1543–1544

S A H A R A

LIBYAN
DESERT

200 miles
200 kilometers
0    100    200
0    100    200

Ottoman state, ca. 1300

Ottoman Empire under Suleiman, 1566

Tributary states of the Sultan, 1566

Major Ottoman campaign, 1530–1584

Habsburg Empire, ca. 1550

To begin the transformation of Constantinople into an Ottoman capital, Mehmet sponsored the building of mosques, markets, fountains, baths, and other public facilities, and ordered the military-political elite to do so as well. To make up for population losses from war, he transplanted inhabitants of other territories to the city, granting them tax remissions and possession of empty houses. He wanted them to start businesses, make Constantinople prosperous, and transform it into a microcosm of the empire.

Gunpowder, which was invented by the Chinese and adapted to artillery use by the Europeans, played an influential role in the expansion of the Ottoman state. After mastering this technology, the Ottomans used it to gain control of shipping in the eastern Mediterranean and to eliminate the Portuguese from the Red Sea. In 1514, under the superb military leadership of Selim (r. 1512–1520), the Ottomans turned the Safavids back from Anatolia. When the Ottomans acquired Syria and Palestine (1516) and Egypt (1517), they gained control of the holy cities of Islam. Before long the Ottomans had extended their rule across North Africa to Tunisia and Algeria. For the next four centuries a majority of Arabs lived under Ottoman rule.

The Ottomans also made incursions into Europe. In 1526 Suleiman I (r. 1520–1566) crushed the Hungarians at Mohács. Most of the Hungarian army was killed and the king drowned while escaping the battlefield. Three years later the Ottomans unsuccessfully besieged the Habsburg capital of Vienna. In the late sixteenth century, under Suleiman's descendants, the empire reached its widest geographical extent (see Map 17.1).

From the late fourteenth to the early seventeenth centuries, the Ottoman Empire and other Islamic powers were keenly involved in European politics. In 1525 Francis I of France and Suleiman struck an alliance to prevent Habsburg domination of Europe. The Habsburg emperor Charles V retaliated by seeking an alliance with Safavid Persia. Suleiman renewed the French agreement with Francis's son, Henry II (r. 1547–1559), and this accord became the cornerstone of Ottoman policy in western Europe. Ottoman pressure contributed to the official recognition of Lutheran Protestants at the Peace of Augsburg in 1555 and the consolidation of the national monarchy in France.

Though usually victorious on land, the Ottomans did not enjoy complete dominion on the seas. In the mid-sixteenth century, they failed to wrest control of the Persian Gulf from the Portuguese, although they continued to hold Yemen and the Red Sea, thereby maintaining an outlet for Indian Ocean trade. Competition with the Habsburgs for control of the Mediterranean led the Ottomans to conquer Cyprus in 1571 and to settle thousands of Turks from Anatolia there. In response, Pope Pius V organized a Holy League against the Ottomans, which won a victory in 1571 at Lepanto off the west coast of Greece with a squadron of more than two hundred Spanish, Venetian, and papal galleys. Still, the Ottomans remained supreme on land and quickly rebuilt their entire fleet.

> **MAP 17.1  The Ottoman Empire at Its Height, 1566**
The Ottomans, like their great rivals the Habsburgs, rose to rule a vast dynastic empire encompassing many different peoples and ethnic groups. The army and the bureaucracy served to unite the disparate territories into a single state.

**Persian Cavalry Fighting Turkish Soldiers**   Shah Abbas (r. 1587–1629) created the first Safavid standing army, composed of enslaved prisoners of war and their descendants. In 1623, he deployed this army against the Ottomans, in the last of a series of wars between the two powers that had begun a century earlier. Shah Abbas succeeded in recapturing Baghdad and other territories previously lost to the Ottomans; however, the treaty that ended the war in 1639 favored the larger and wealthier Ottoman Empire.   (PHAS/Getty Images)

To the east, war with Safavid Persia occupied the sultans' attention throughout the sixteenth and well into the seventeenth century. Several issues lay at the root of the long and exhausting conflict: religious antagonism between the Sunni Ottomans and the Shi'a Persians, competition to expand geographically and economically at each other's expense, and rival European alliances. Finally, in 1638 the Ottomans recaptured Baghdad (which they had originally taken in 1534); the following year the treaty of Kasr-i-Shirin established a permanent border between the two powers.

## Landholding, Slavery, and Imperial Administration

Given its early foundation, Ottoman institutions were fully formed during the fifteenth century, more than a century earlier than for the Safavids or Mughals. In the Ottoman state, all authority flowed from the sultan to his public servants: provincial governors, military generals, heads of treasuries, and **viziers** (chief assistants to sultans). The power of the Ottoman central government was sustained through the training of enslaved youths. Slaves were captured in battle; purchased from Spain, North Africa, and Venice; or drafted through the system known as **devshirme**, by which the sultan's agents took a set number of boys every three years from Christian families in the Balkans. (The devshirme system did not apply to girls; instead, enslaved girls and women entered the empire as prisoners of war and through the slave trade.) The slave boys were converted to Islam and trained for service in the palace, the administration, and the army. The brightest 10 percent entered the palace school, where they learned to read and write Arabic, Ottoman Turkish, and Persian in preparation for administrative jobs. Other boys were sent to Turkish farms, where they acquired physical toughness in preparation for military service. Known as **janissaries** (Turkish for "new soldiers"), they formed the elite army corps, which successfully adapted to the use of firearms. The devshirme system enabled the Ottomans to apply merit-based recruitment to create a highly effective military and administrative elite.

The Ottoman ruling class included people of varied ethnic origins who rose through the bureaucratic and military ranks, many beginning as the sultan's slaves. In return for their services to the sultan, they held landed estates for the duration of their lives. Because all property belonged to the sultan and reverted to him on the holder's death, Ottoman elites, unlike their European counterparts, did not have a local base independent of the ruler. The Ottomans ruled their more distant lands, such as those in North Africa, relatively lightly. Governors of distant provinces collected taxes and maintained trade routes, but their control did not penetrate deeply into the countryside.

Whereas most European dynasties practiced primogeniture, or inheritance by the eldest son, the Ottomans, as well as the Safavids and Mughals, followed the Mongol practice of having a ruler's male children compete for the throne. From about 1500 on, Ottoman sultans did not contract legal marriages but had children with enslaved **concubines**. When one of the sultan's concubines delivered a boy, she raised him until the age of ten or eleven. Then the child was given a province to govern under his mother's supervision. This had the benefit of providing practical governing experience to the sons—any one of whom might inherit the throne—and preventing concubines from exerting too much power over the sultan.

Slave concubinage paralleled the Ottoman use of slave soldiers and slave viziers. All held positions entirely at the sultan's pleasure, owed loyalty solely to him, and were thus more reliable than a hereditary nobility. Great social prestige, as well as the opportunity to acquire power and wealth, was attached to being a slave of the imperial household.

Suleiman I was known to his subjects as "The Lawgiver" because he reformed and codified Ottoman law. Suleiman ordered Lütfi Paşa (d. 1562), a poet and juridical scholar of slave origin, to draw up a new general code of laws that prescribed penalties for routine criminal acts such as robbery, adultery, and murder. It also sought to reduce bureaucratic and financial corruption, such as foreign merchants' payment of bribes to avoid customs duties, imprisonment without trial, and promotion in the provincial administration because of favoritism rather than ability. The legal code also introduced the idea of balanced government budgets. The head of the religious establishment was given the task of reconciling sultanic law with Islamic law.

Suleiman also drastically altered dynastic succession practices and court life by marrying his favorite concubine and maintaining all of his children and concubines in the royal palace. This change, which became permanent, gave women in the royal household greater influence over politics, a development traditionally associated with a long-term decline of the sultan's authority.

## The Safavid Empire in Persia

With the eclipse of Timur's empire after 1450, Persia was controlled by Turkic rulers, with no single one dominant until 1501, when fourteen-year-old Isma'il (1487–1524) led an army to capture Tabriz and declared himself **shah** (Persian word for "king").

The strength of the early **Safavid** state (Map 17.2) rested on three crucial features. First, the state utilized the skills of urban bureaucrats and made them an essential part of the civil machinery of government. Second, it secured the loyalty and military support of nomadic Turkic tribesmen known as **Qizilbash** (KIH-zihl-bahsh) (a Turkish word meaning "redheads" that was used because of the red hats they wore). In return for the vast grazing lands granted to them, the Qizilbash supplied the shah with troops.

The third source of Safavid strength was the Shi'a branch of Islam, which became the compulsory religion of the empire. The Shi'a believed that leadership among Muslims rightfully belonged to the Prophet Muhammad's descendants. Because Isma'il claimed descent from a line of twelve infallible imams (leaders) beginning

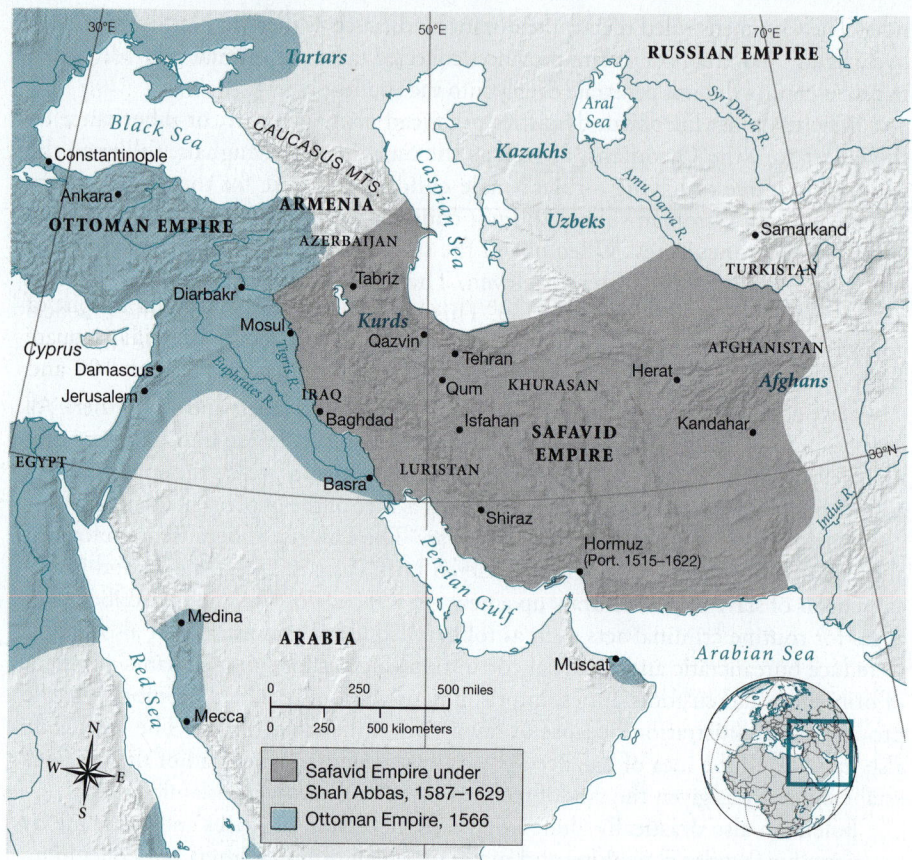

**MAP 17.2 The Safavid Empire, 1587–1629**
In the late sixteenth century the power of the Safavid kingdom of Persia rested on its strong military force, its Shi'a Muslim faith, and its extraordinarily rich trade in rugs and pottery. Many of the cities on the map, such as Tabriz, Qum, and Shiraz, were great rug-weaving centers.

with Ali (Muhammad's cousin and son-in-law), he was officially regarded as their representative on earth. Isma'il recruited Shi'a scholars to instruct and guide his people, and he persecuted and exiled Sunni **ulama** (religious scholars who interpret the Qur'an and the Sunna, the deeds and sayings of Muhammad). To this day, Iran remains the only Muslim state in which Shi'ism is the official religion.

Safavid power reached its height under Shah Abbas (r. 1587–1629), who moved the capital from Qazvin to Isfahan. His military achievements, support for trade and commerce, and endowment of the arts earned him the epithet "the Great." In the military realm he adopted the Ottoman practice of building an army of slaves, primarily captives from the Caucasus, and used them as a counterweight to the Qizilbash, whom he considered a threat. He also increased the use of gunpowder weapons and made alliances with European powers against the Ottomans and Portuguese. In his campaigns against the Ottomans, Shah Abbas captured Baghdad, Mosul, and Diyarbakir in Mesopotamia (see Map 17.2).

Conflict between the Ottomans and the Safavids was not an even match. The Safavids did not have as many people or as much wealth as the Ottomans and continually had to defend against encroachments on their western border. Still, they were able to ally with some of the Turks in Ottoman lands who felt that their government had shifted too far from its nomadic roots. After Shah Abbas, Safavid power was sapped by civil war between tribal factions vying for control of the court.

## The Mughal Empire in India

Of the three great Islamic empires of the early modern world, the **Mughal** Empire of India was the largest, wealthiest, and most populous. Extending over 1.2 million square miles at the end of the seventeenth century, with a population between 100 and 150 million, and with fabulous wealth and resources, the Mughal Empire surpassed the other two by a wide margin. In the sixteenth century only the Ming Dynasty in China could compare.

In 1504 Babur (r. 1483–1530), a Turco-Mongolian ruler forced out of a small territory in Central Asia, captured Kabul and established a kingdom in Afghanistan, under the patronage of the Safavids. A descendant of Chinggis Khan and Timur, Babur moved southward in search of resources to restore his fortunes. In 1526, with a force of only twelve thousand men, Babur defeated the sultan of Delhi at Panipat. Babur's capture of the cities of Agra and Delhi, key fortresses of the north, paved the way for further conquests in northern India. Although many of his soldiers wished to return to Afghanistan with their spoils, Babur decided to stay in India.

A gifted writer, Babur wrote an autobiography in Turkish that recounts his military campaigns, describes places and people he encountered, and shows his wide-ranging interests in everything from fruit and swimming to a Turkish general who excelled at leapfrog. Babur's son Humayun (r. 1530–1540 and 1555–1556) briefly lost Mughal territories in India and Afghanistan, the only gap in more than three hundred centuries of Mughal rule. After temporary exile in Persia, Humayun reconquered the lost territories, setting the stage for the reign of his son Akbar (r. 1556–1605), which may well have been the greatest in the history of India.

A boy of thirteen when he succeeded to the throne, Akbar pursued expansionist policies. Under his dynamic leadership, the Mughal state took definitive form and encompassed most of the subcontinent north of the Godavari River. The once-independent states of northern India were forced into a centralized political system under the sole authority of the Mughal emperor. Henceforth, the Mughals became the model for Islamic sultanates in the Indian Ocean and Southeast Asia.[1]

By the late sixteenth century, the Mughals had adopted Persian as the language of state affairs and intellectual life. To govern the vast and diverse empire, composed of a majority of non-Muslims, Akbar developed a complex administrative bureaucracy that was centered on four co-equal departments: finance; the army and intelligence; the judiciary and religious patronage; and the imperial household, whose jurisdiction included roads, bridges, and infrastructure throughout the empire. Under Akbar's Hindu finance minister, Raja Todar Mal, a uniform system of taxes was put in place. In the provinces imperial governors were appointed by and responsible solely to the emperor.

Whereas the Ottoman sultans and Safavid shahs made extensive use of slaves acquired from non-Muslim lands for military and administrative positions, Akbar used the services of royal princes, nobles, and warrior-aristocrats from the subjugated territories. Rather than supplanting local elites, the Mughals relied on them to collect taxes and provide administration. Ambitious provincials were able to integrate the Mughal power structure by adopting the Persian language and culture, even if they did not convert to Islam.

Akbar's descendants extended the Mughal Empire further. His son Jahangir (r. 1605–1628) consolidated Mughal rule in Bengal. Jahangir's son Shah Jahan (r. 1628–1658) launched fresh territorial expansion. Faced with dangerous revolts by the Muslims in Ahmadnagar and the resistance of the newly arrived Portuguese in Bengal, Shah Jahan not only crushed this opposition but also strengthened his northwestern frontier. Shah Jahan's son Aurangzeb (r. 1658–1707), unwilling to wait for his father to die, deposed him and confined him for years in a small cell. A devout Muslim, as well as a skillful general and a clever diplomat, Aurangzeb ruled more of India than did any previous Mughal emperor, having extended the realm deeper into south India. His reign, however, also marked the beginning of the empire's decline. In the south resistance to Mughal rule led to major uprisings, and his efforts to appease the south only served to alienate his northern provinces. As the eighteenth century progressed, revenue from outlying provinces diminished greatly and central control diminished.

# Religious Developments

**How did religious beliefs and practices evolve, and how did they affect non-Muslims?**

The Ottoman, Safavid, and Mughal Dynasties dominated the Muslim world at the time of its greatest growth since the first period of Arab conquest, sharing a common basis of legitimacy in models of Islamic rule that originated with the Abbasid caliphate (750–1258). And yet, more Muslims lived beyond the borders of the three Islamic empires than within them, and the two largest, the Ottomans and the Mughals, were majority non-Muslim states. One of the most important characteristics of these Islamic empires was the diversity of their populations and the extent to which their rulers accommodated religious and cultural difference.

Although we have come to associate these empires with distinct and opposing forms of Islam, these differences should be seen as a product of the long-term rivalry among the empires rather than as an inherent characteristic of them. Modern divisions in the Muslim world are thus one important legacy of the early modern empires studied in this chapter.

## Religious Legitimacy and Orthodoxy

The rulers of all three empires drew legitimacy from Islam and from traditions of combining religious and political authority established in the Abbasid caliphate. The ruler was sent by God to establish peace and justice on earth; his followers owed him religious devotion as well as political obedience. For example, Shah Isma'il I, the founder of the Safavid Dynasty, descended from Sufi mystics and rose to power after being recognized as a holy figure by his followers. Under Akbar, Mughal elites of all faiths were considered both servants and religious disciples of the emperor. Rulers of the Islamic powers combined this religious authority with more secular claims on power, in particular the legacy of universal empire inherited from the Roman, Byzantine, and Mongol Empires.

In their early years, the Islamic empires were characterized by a high degree of religious openness and experimentation. Only over time, and as a result of the fierce competition among them, did the distinction between Sunnism and Shi'ism emerge as defining characteristics of the empires. This development can be seen as parallel to the way differences between Catholicism and Protestantism in Europe were shaped by intracontinental struggles for power and legitimacy.[2]

The rivalry between Ottomans and Safavids thus inspired efforts to define and enforce religious orthodoxy on both sides. For the Safavids this entailed suppressing Sunnis and Sufi movements and enshrining Shi'ism as central to the identity of the state. The original Qizilbash warriors came to be seen as politically disruptive, in part because of their association with Sufism. For their part, the Ottomans claimed their opposition to heretical Shi'ism as a central pillar of their rule. The Mughal emperor Aurangzeb, in the second half of the seventeenth century, also adopted stricter forms of Sunnism, breaking with the more open attitude of his predecessors.

## Sufism

The mystical and ascetic strain of Islam known as Sufism was influential for all three empires. Sufism originated in the early years of Islam in response to the increasing worldliness of the expanding Muslim community. To move closer to God, Sufis engaged in dance, music, and prayer. Sufi fraternities thrived throughout the Muslim world in this era, particularly in Safavid Persia. Adherence to Sufism persisted, even when the states tried to impose what they saw as more orthodox religious practice.

In India Sufi orders also influenced non-Muslims. The mystical Bhakti movement among Hindus involved dances, poems, and songs reminiscent of Sufi practice. The development of the new religion of the Sikhs (SEEKS) was also influenced by Sufis. The Sikhs traced themselves back to a teacher in the sixteenth century who argued that God did not distinguish between Muslims and Hindus but saw everyone as his children. Sikhs rejected the caste system (division of society into hereditary groups) and forbade alcohol and tobacco, and men did not cut their hair, covering it instead with a turban. The Sikh movement was most successful in northwest India, where Sikh men armed themselves to defend their communities.

## Non-Muslims Under Muslim Rule

Drawing on Qur'anic teachings, Muslims had long practiced a religious tolerance unknown in Christian Europe. Muslim rulers for the most part guaranteed the lives and property of Christians and Jews in exchange for their promise of obedience and the payment of a poll tax. In the case of the Ottomans, this tolerance extended not only to the Christians and Jews who had been living under Muslim rule for centuries but also to Serbs, Bosnians, Croats, and other Orthodox Christians in the newly conquered Balkans. In 1454 Rabbi Isaac Sarfati sent a letter to Jews in central and eastern Europe, urging them to move to Turkey because of the favorable treatment there. A massive migration to Ottoman lands followed. When Ferdinand and Isabella of Spain expelled the Jews in 1492 and later, many migrated to the Ottoman Empire.

The Safavid authorities made efforts to convert Armenian Christians in the Caucasus, and many seem to have embraced Islam, some more willingly than others. Nevertheless, the Armenian Christian Church retained its vitality, and under the Safavids Armenian Christians were prominent merchants in long-distance trade.

Babur and his successors acquired even more non-Muslim subjects with their conquests in India, which included not only Hindus but also substantial numbers of Jains, Zoroastrians, Christians, and Sikhs. Over time, the number of Indians who converted to Islam increased, but the Mughal rulers did not force conversion. Akbar went the furthest in promoting Muslim-Hindu accommodation. He celebrated important Hindu festivals, such as Diwali, the festival of lights, and he wore his uncut hair in a turban as a concession to Indian practice. Akbar also married a number of Hindu princesses as a means to consolidate alliances with Hindu rulers, one of whom became the mother of his heir, Jahangir. Eventually, Hindus totaled 30 percent of the imperial bureaucracy, a contrast to both the Ottoman and the Safavid states, where non-Muslim subjects were tolerated but not accepted in positions of power and authority.

Some of Akbar's successors, above all Aurangzeb, were less tolerant of religious diversity. Aurangzeb appointed censors of public morals in important cities to enforce Islamic laws against gambling, prostitution, and the use of alcohol and narcotics. He forbade sati—the self-immolation of widows on their husbands' funeral pyres—and the castration of boys to be sold as eunuchs. He also abolished taxes not authorized by Islamic law and required Hindus to pay higher customs duties than Muslims. Aurangzeb's attempts proved highly unpopular and aroused resistance that weakened Mughal rule.

# Cultural Flowering

**What cultural advances occurred under the Ottoman, Safavid, and Mughal Empires?**

The three Islamic empires presided over the most important period of cultural achievement in the Muslim world since the golden age of the Abbasid caliphate. This extraordinary artistic and intellectual flowering drew on the strong influence of Persian culture on Turkic groups from the tenth century on. It encompassed everything from carpetmaking to architecture and gardening, from geography and astronomy to medicine. At the same time, new religious practices (and conflicts) emerged, and people found new outlets for socializing and exchanging ideas. Artistic and intellectual advances spread from region to region, encouraged by the travels of diplomats, merchants, and scholars. This exchange was also aided by shared languages, especially Arabic, Turkish, and Persian. Arabic was a lingua franca of the entire region because of its centrality in Islam. Persian was the major language of the Safavid domains and was used by elites in Mughal India. In Ottoman lands both Persian and Arabic were literary languages, but Turkish slowly became the lingua franca of the realm.

## The Arts

The art of carpetmaking was shared by all three empires. Carpet designs and weaving techniques demonstrated both cultural integration and local distinctiveness. Turkic migrants carried their weaving traditions with them as they moved but also readily adopted new motifs, especially from Persia. Shah Abbas was determined to improve

Persia's export trade and built the small cottage business of carpet weaving into a national industry. In the capital city of Isfahan alone, factories employed more than twenty-five thousand weavers who produced woolen carpets, brocades, and silks of brilliant color, design, and quality. Women and children were often employed as weavers, especially of the most expensive rugs, because their smaller hands could tie tinier knots.

Another art that spread from Persia to both Ottoman and Mughal lands was miniature painting, especially for book illustration. Miniature paintings and carpets both featured naturalistic depictions of lotus blossoms, peonies, chrysanthemums, tulips, carnations, birds, and even dragons.

## City and Palace Building

In all three empires strong rulers built capital cities and imperial palaces as visible expressions of dynastic majesty. Suleiman I used his fabulous wealth and thousands of servants to adorn Istanbul with palaces, mosques, schools, and libraries. The building of hospitals, roads, and bridges and the reconstruction of the water systems of the great pilgrimage sites at Mecca and Jerusalem benefited his subjects. Safavid Persia and Mughal India produced rulers with similar ambitions.

The greatest builder under the Ottomans was Mimar Sinan (1491–1588), a Greek-born devshirme recruit who rose to become imperial architect under Suleiman. A contemporary of Michelangelo, Sinan designed 312 public buildings, including mosques, schools, hospitals, public baths, palaces, and burial chapels. His masterpieces, the Shehzade and Suleimaniye Mosques in Istanbul, were designed to maximize the space under the dome.

Shah Abbas made his capital, Isfahan, the jewel of the Safavid Empire. In the center of the city, in front of the palace and the main royal mosque complex, he built a public square that served as a major marketplace for splendid rugs, pottery and fine china, metalwork of exceptionally high quality, and silks and velvets of stunning weave and design. A city of perhaps 750,000 people, Isfahan also contained 162 mosques, 48 schools where future members of the ulama learned the sacred Muslim sciences, 273 public baths, and the vast imperial palace. Private houses had their own garden courts, and public gardens, pools, and parks adorned the wide streets.

Among the Mughal emperors, Shah Jahan had the most sophisticated interest in architecture. In 1639 he decided to found a new capital city at Delhi. In the design and layout of the buildings, Persian traditions predominated. The walled palace-fortress alone extended over 125 acres. Built partly of red sandstone, partly of marble, it included private chambers for the emperor; mansions for the wives, widows, and concubines of the imperial household; huge audience rooms for the conduct of public business; baths; and vast gardens filled with flowers, trees, and thirty silver fountains spraying water. In 1650, with living quarters for guards, military officials, merchants, dancing girls, scholars, and hordes of cooks and servants, the palace-fortress housed fifty-seven thousand people. It also boasted a covered public bazaar.

Shah Jahan's most enduring monument is the Taj Mahal. Between 1631 and 1648 twenty thousand workers toiled over the construction of this memorial in Agra to Shah Jahan's favorite wife, who died giving birth to their fourteenth child. One of the most beautiful structures in the world, the Taj Mahal is both an expression of love and a superb architectural blending of Islamic and Indian culture.

**Two Masterpieces of Islamic Architecture** Istanbul's Suleimaniye Mosque, designed by Sinan and commissioned by Suleiman I, was finished in 1557. Its interior (below) is especially spacious. The Taj Mahal (left), built about a century later in Agra in northern India, is perhaps the finest example of Mughal architecture. Its white marble exterior is decorated with Arabic inscriptions and floral designs. (Taj Mahal: mazzur/Getty Images; mosque: Murat Tander/AGE Fotostock)

## Gardens

Many of the architectural masterpieces of this age had splendid gardens attached to them. Gardens represented a distinctive and highly developed feature of Persian culture. They commonly were walled, with a pool in the center and geometrically laid-out flowering plants, especially roses. Identified with paradise in Islamic tradition, gardens served not only as centers of prayer and meditation but also as places of leisure and revelry.

After the incorporation of Persia into the caliphate in the seventh century, formal gardening spread west and east through the Islamic world, as illustrated by the magnificent gardens of Muslim Spain, southern Italy, and, later, southeastern Europe. When Babur established the Mughal Dynasty in India, he adapted the Persian garden to the warmer southern climate. Gardens were laid out near palaces, mosques, shrines, and mausoleums, including the Taj Mahal, which had four water channels symbolizing the four rivers of paradise.

Gardens, of course, are seasonal. To remind themselves of paradise during the cold winter months, rulers, city people, and nomads ordered Persian carpets, most of which feature floral patterns and have formal garden designs.

## Intellectual Advances

Between 1400 and 1800 the intellectual life of the Islamic empires developed in many directions. Particularly notable were advances in mathematics, geography, astronomy, and medicine. Building on the knowledge of earlier Islamic writers and stimulated by Ottoman naval power, the geographer and cartographer Piri Reis created the *Book of the Sea* (1521), which contained 129 chapters, each with a map incorporating all Islamic (and Western) knowledge of the seas and navigation and describing harbors, tides, dangerous rocks and shores, and storm areas. In the field of astronomy, Takiyuddin Mehmet (1521–1585) built an observatory at Istanbul. His *Instruments of the Observatory* catalogued astronomical instruments and described an astronomical clock that fixed the location of heavenly bodies with greater precision than ever before. There were also advances in medicine. Under Suleiman the imperial palace itself became a center of medical science, and the large number of hospitals established in Istanbul and throughout the empire testifies to his support for medical research and his concern for the sick.

Viewing the Qur'an as the literal word of God, Muslim culture accorded special reverence to books and the written word. Scribes occupied a respected social position, and their beautiful calligraphy, along with accompanying miniature paintings, made books valuable and cherished possessions. For these religious and aesthetic reasons, and because of opposition from organizations of scribes who sought to defend their economic livelihood, the Islamic states were slow adopters of the printing press. The first press in the Ottoman Empire was founded in 1493 by Sephardic Jews fleeing expulsion from Spain, who received permission to print works in Hebrew for their fellow Jews. During the sixteenth and seventeenth centuries, additional groups of Jews, Armenians, and Greeks established presses and printed in their own languages. In 1727, an Ottoman court administrator opened a press, which was the first officially sanctioned press for a Muslim audience in the Muslim world. Printing was similarly slow to spread in the Mughal Empire, although Jesuit missionaries printed Bibles in Indian languages beginning in the 1550s.

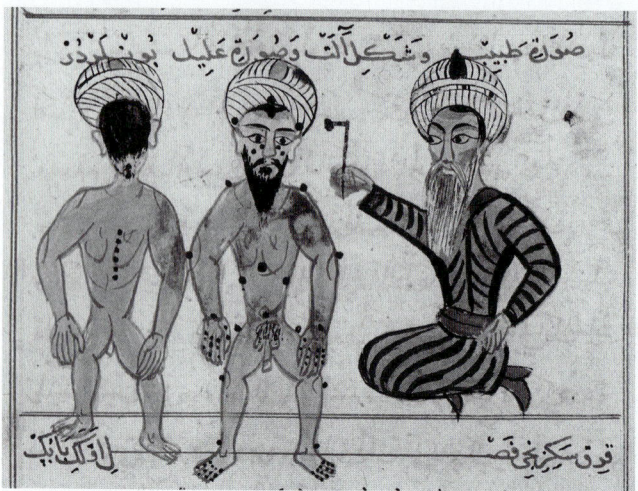

**Illustrated Medical Manual** The Turkish physician Serafeddin Sabuncuoglu (1385–1470) wrote a treatise of surgery in Turkish, with illustrations, in 1465. This page shows a physician cauterizing leprosy lesions. (Bibliothèque Nationale, Paris, France/© Archives Charmet/ Bridgeman Images)

# New Patterns of Trade and European Penetration

## How were the Islamic empires affected by new trade goods and patterns of trade?

Despite the incursion of Europeans into Indian Ocean trade, Turkish, Persian, and Indian merchants remained very active as long-distance traders into the eighteenth century and opened up many new routes themselves. The introduction of novel foods and stimulants, including goods imported from the New World, fostered new forms of public life. By 1800 the population of India was about 190 million, that of Safavid lands about 8 million, and that of Ottoman lands about 24 million. (By comparison, China's population stood at about 300 million in 1800 and Russia's at about 35 million.)

## New Forms of Consumption

In the early modern period, the Islamic empires were enmeshed in emerging global trade networks that stimulated the exchange of new products and the formation of new habits of consumption. Introduced in the mid-fifteenth century, coffee spread quickly throughout the Islamic world. Arab writers trace the origins of coffee drinking to Sufis in Yemen who sought a trancelike concentration on God and found that coffee helped them stay awake. Before long, coffee was being used as a business lubricant—an extension of hospitality to a potential buyer in a shop. Merchants carried the Yemenite practice to Mecca in about 1490. From Mecca, where pilgrims were introduced to it, coffee drinking spread to Egypt and Syria. In 1555 two Syrians opened a coffeehouse in Istanbul. Coffee and coffeehouses spread to Europe in the seventeenth century.

While coffee was indigenous to the Islamic world, other important new products came to the region as a result of the Columbian exchange that brought foods, stimulants, and other goods from the Americas. In addition to maize, chocolate, and peppers, one of the most popular of these goods was tobacco, which spread quickly. Opium, a product of East Asia, also grew in popularity during this period.

Coffeehouses, where patrons consumed both coffee and tobacco, provided a place for conversation and male sociability. But they also encountered opposition: some people argued that coffee and tobacco were intoxicating, making them analogous to wine, which was prohibited to Muslims, and others asserted that political discussion in coffeehouses could lead to sedition. On the other hand, trade in the new goods was a major source of profit that local notables sought to control. Although debate over the morality of coffeehouses continued, their eventual acceptance represented a revolution in Islamic life because socializing was no longer confined to the home.

## The Impact of Gunpowder

While traditional military weapons and tactics remained paramount, especially heavy mounted cavalry, the Islamic powers were early adopters of gunpowder weapons, another important new commodity in global trade. The Ottoman janissary corps was the first military unit to carry firearms, and it used artillery in its successful siege of Constantinople in 1453.

Ottoman adoption of firearms set off an arms race that revolutionized global diplomatic and trade relations. Beaten in battle by the Ottomans in the 1520s, the Safavids formed trade relations with Portugal and Venice to obtain arms. Meanwhile, the expansion of Portuguese power led rulers across the Indian Ocean trade world to seek military technology from foreign powers. In the 1530s, the emir of Zeyla (in modern-day Somalia) became a tributary of the Ottomans to acquire gunpowder weapons and military experts. In 1566, Ottoman sultan Selim II sent soldiers, weapons, and gunpowder to support the sultan of Aceh against the Portuguese in Southeast Asia in exchange for pearls and precious stones.

## European Trade in Asia and the Islamic Powers' Response

During the seventeenth century, the Dutch gradually replaced the Portuguese as the dominant trading power in the Indian Ocean. Over time, however, the British and French exerted increasing influence in South Asia. The British East India Company, formed in 1600, gained important commercial concessions from Mughal emperor Jahangir in 1619. By 1700 the company had founded the cities that became Madras and Calcutta (today called Chennai and Kolkata) and had taken over Bombay (today Mumbai), which had been a Portuguese possession (Map 17.3). Profits grew even larger after 1700, when the company began to trade with China.

The shifting trade patterns associated with European colonial expansion brought no direct benefit to the Ottomans and the Safavids, whose merchants could now be bypassed by Europeans seeking goods from India, Southeast Asia, or China. Yet merchants from these Islamic empires proved adaptable, finding ways to benefit from the new trade networks. In the case of India, the appearance of European traders led to a rapid increase in overall trade, helping Indian merchants and the Indian economy. Some Indian merchants in Calcutta and Bombay, for instance, made gigantic

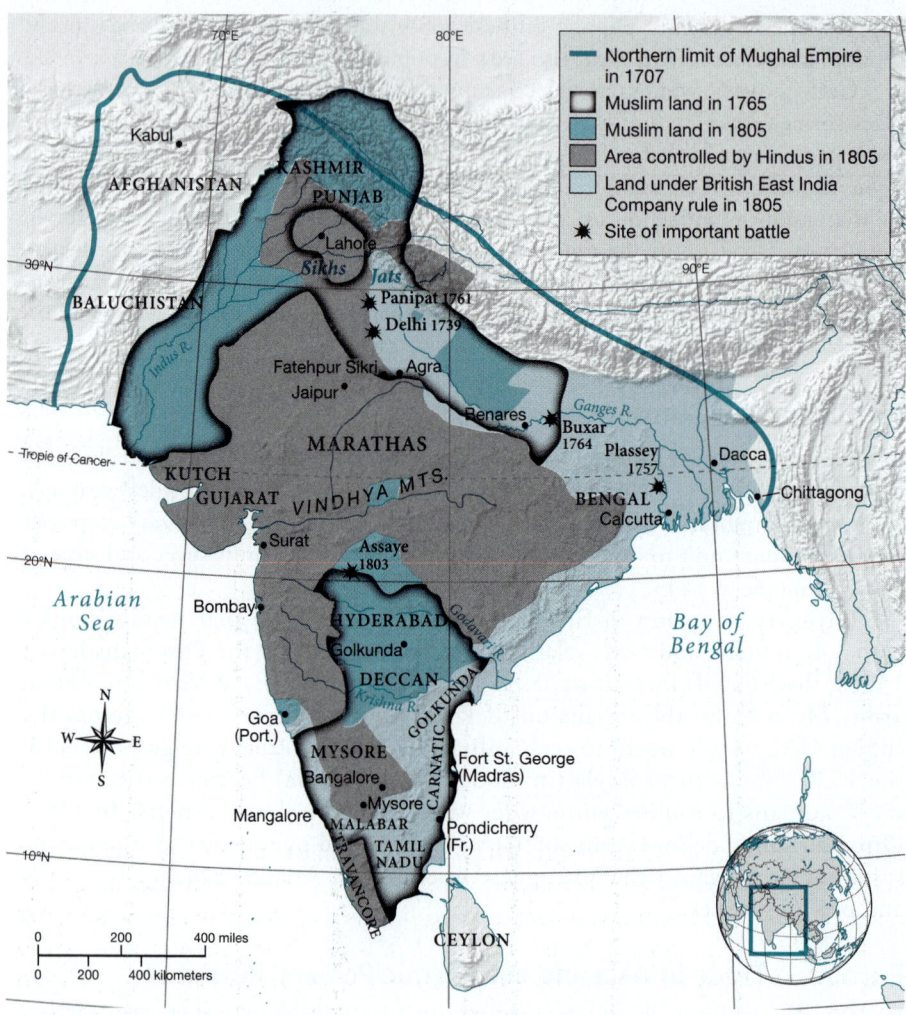

**MAP 17.3   India, 1707–1805**
In the eighteenth century Mughal power gradually yielded to the Hindu Marathas and to the British East India Company.

fortunes from trade with Europeans. Block-printed cotton cloth, produced by arti-sans working at home, was India's chief export.

Within India the demand for cotton cloth, as well as for food crops, was so great that Akbar had to launch a wide-scale road-building campaign to facilitate commercial transportation. From the Indian region of Gujarat, Indian merchant bankers shipped their cloth worldwide: across the Indian Ocean to Aden and the Muslim-controlled cities on the east coast of Africa; across the Arabian Sea to Muscat and Hormuz and up the Persian Gulf to the cities of Persia; up the Red Sea to the Mediterranean; by sea also to Malacca, Indonesia, China, and Japan; by land across Africa to Ghana on the west coast; and to Astrakhan, Poland, Moscow, and even

Russian cities on the distant Volga River. Indian businessmen had branch offices in many of these places, and all this activity produced fabulous wealth for some Indian merchants. Indian merchants were often devout Hindus, Muslims, Buddhists, or Jains, evidence that undermines the argument of some Western writers, notably Karl Marx (see "The Birth of Socialism" in Chapter 24), that religion retarded Asia's economic development.

Throughout Muslim lands both Jews and Christians were active in commerce. A particularly interesting case involves Armenian Christians in the sixteenth to eighteenth centuries. Armenian merchants had been trading from their base in Armenia for centuries and were especially known for their trade in Persian silk. When the Portuguese first appeared on the western coast of India in 1498 and began to settle in south India, they found many Armenian merchant communities already there. A few decades later Akbar invited Armenians to settle in his new capital, Agra. In 1603 Shah Abbas captured much of Armenia, taking it from the Ottomans, and forced the Armenians to move more deeply into Persia.

Armenian merchant networks stretched from Venice and Amsterdam in western Europe, Moscow in Russia, and Ottoman-controlled Aleppo and Smyrna to all the major trading cities of India and even regions farther east, including Guangzhou in southern China and Manila in the Philippines. Many Armenian communities in these cities became substantial centers, built churches, and recruited priests. Using couriers, these Armenian merchants sent long letters describing the trade environment and the prices that could be realized for given goods.

## From the British East India Company to the British Empire in India

Britain's presence in India began with the British East India Company and its desire to profit from trade. Managers of the company in London discouraged all unnecessary expenses and financial risks and thus opposed missionary activities or interference in local Indian politics. Nevertheless, the company responded to political instability in India in the early eighteenth century by extending political control. When warlords appeared or an uprising occurred, people from the surrounding countryside flocked into the company's factory-forts, which gradually came to exercise political authority over the territories around them. The company's factories evolved into defensive installations manned by small garrisons of native troops—known as **sepoys**—trained in Western military weapons and tactics.

Britain eventually became the dominant foreign presence in India, despite challenges from the French. From 1740 to 1763 Britain and France were engaged in a tremendous global struggle, and India, like North America in the Seven Years' War (see Chapter 22), became a battlefield and a prize. The French won land battles, but English sea power proved decisive by preventing the landing of French reinforcements. The Treaty of Paris of 1763 recognized British control of much of India, marking the beginning of the British Empire in India.

How was Britain to govern so large a territory? Eventually, the East India Company was pushed out of its governing role because the English Parliament believed it was corrupt. The Regulating Act of 1773 created the office of governor general to exercise political authority over the territory controlled by the company. The East India Company Act of 1784 required that the governor general be chosen from outside the company, and it made company directors subject to parliamentary supervision.

Implementation of these reforms fell to three successive governors: Warren Hastings (r. 1774–1785), Lord Charles Cornwallis (r. 1786–1794), and the marquess Richard Wellesley (r. 1797–1805). Hastings sought allies among Indian rulers wishing to escape Mughal authority, laid the foundations for the first Indian civil service, abolished tolls to facilitate internal trade, placed the salt and opium trades under government control, and planned a codification of Muslim and Hindu laws. Cornwallis introduced the British style of property relations, in which the rents of tenant farmers supported the landlords. Wellesley was victorious over local rulers who resisted British rule, vastly extending British influence in India. Like most nineteenth-century British governors of India, Wellesley believed that British rule strongly benefited the Indians. With supreme condescension, he wrote that British power should be established over the Indian princes in order "to deprive them of the means of prosecuting any measure or of forming any confederacy hazardous to the security of the British empire, and to enable us to preserve the tranquility of India by exercising a general control over the restless spirit of ambition and violence which is characteristic of every Asiatic government."[3]

# Political Decline

**What common factors led to the decline of central power in the Islamic empires in the seventeenth and eighteenth centuries?**

By the end of the eighteenth century all three of the major Islamic empires were on the defensive and losing territory (Map 17.4). They faced some common problems — succession crises, financial strain, and loss of military superiority — but their circumstances differed in significant ways as well, with the Ottomans proving the most resilient and longest lasting of the three.

In all three empires fiscal difficulties contributed to strain on the state. A long period of peace in the late sixteenth century and again in the mid-eighteenth century, as well as a decline in the frequency of visits of the plague, led to a doubling of the population. Increased population, coupled with the "Little Ice Age" of the mid-seventeenth century, meant that the land could not sustain so many people, nor could the towns provide jobs for the thousands of agricultural workers who fled to them. The return of demobilized soldiers aggravated the problem. Inflation, famine, and widespread uprisings resulted. Power was seized by local notables and military strongmen at the expense of central government officials.

The first to fall was the Safavid Empire. Persia did not have the revenue base to maintain the sort of standing armies that the Ottomans and the Mughals had. Decline in the strength of the army encouraged increased foreign aggression. In 1722 the Afghans invaded from the east, seized Isfahan, and were able to repulse an Ottoman invasion from the west. In Isfahan thousands of officials and members of the shah's family were executed. In the following century no leaders emerged capable of reuniting all of Persia. In this political vacuum, Shi'a religious institutions grew stronger.

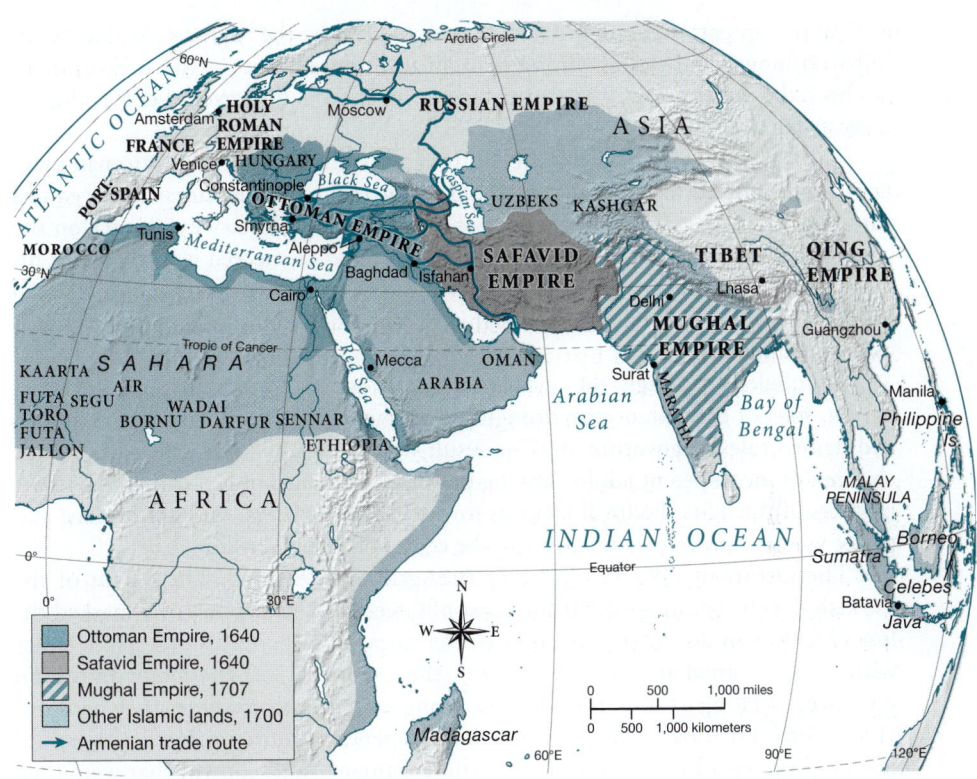

**MAP 17.4   The Muslim World, ca. 1700**
The three great Islamic empires were adjacent to each other and of similar physical size. Many of their other neighbors were Muslim as well.

In Mughal India the practice of letting heirs fight for the throne persisted, leading to frequent struggles over succession, but also to strong rulers. Yet military challenges proved daunting there as well. After defeating his father and brothers, Aurangzeb made it his goal to conquer the south. The stiffest opposition came from the Marathas, a militant Hindu group centered in the western Deccan. From 1681 until his death in 1707, Aurangzeb led repeated sorties through the Deccan. He took many forts and won several battles, but total destruction of the Maratha bands eluded him.

Aurangzeb's death led to thirteen years of succession struggles, shattering the empire. His eighteenth-century successors were less successful than the Ottomans in making the dynasty the focus of loyalty. Mughal provincial governors began to rule independently, giving only minimal allegiance to the throne at Delhi. Meanwhile, the Marathas pressed steadily northward, constituting the gravest threat to Mughal authority. Threats also came from the west. In 1739 the Persian adventurer Nadir Shah invaded India, defeated the Mughal army, looted Delhi, and, after massacring the populace, carried off a huge amount of treasure. Constant skirmishes between the Afghans and the Marathas for control of the Punjab and northern India ended in 1761 at Panipat, where the Marathas were crushed by the Afghans. At that point, India no longer had a state strong enough to impose order on the subcontinent or check the penetration of the British. Not until 1857, however, did the Mughal Dynasty come to a formal end.

The Ottoman Empire also suffered from poor leadership. Early Ottoman practice had guaranteed that the sultans would be forceful men. The sultan's sons gained administrative experience as governors of provinces and military experience on the battlefield. After the sultan died, any son who wanted to succeed had to contest his brothers to claim the throne, after which the new sultan would have his defeated brothers executed. Although bloody, this system led to the succession of capable, determined men.

After Suleiman's reign, the tradition was abandoned. To prevent threats of usurpation, sons of the sultan were brought up in the harem, confined there as adults, and denied roles in government. The result was a series of rulers who were minor children or incompetent adults, leaving power in the hands of high officials and the mothers of the heirs. Political factions formed around viziers, military leaders, and palace women, leading to instability at the center of imperial rule.

The Ottoman Empire's military strength also declined. The defeat of the Turkish fleet by the Spanish off the coast of Greece at Lepanto in 1571 marked the loss of Ottoman dominance in the Mediterranean. By the terms of a peace treaty with Austria signed at Karlowitz (1699), the Ottomans lost the major European provinces of Hungary and Transylvania, along with the tax revenues they had provided. Also, Ottoman armies, which were depending more on mercenaries, did not keep up with the innovations in drill, command, and control that were then transforming European armies. From the late seventeenth century on, Ottoman armies began losing wars and territory along both northern and eastern borders. In 1774 the empire lost the lands on the northern bank of the Black Sea to Russia. In North Africa the local governors came to act more independently, sometimes starting hereditary dynasties.

These challenges reduced the military and political strength of the Ottomans, but the empire managed to adjust to changing conditions and persisted until the first decades of the twentieth century. One reason for this long-term resiliency, compared to the Mughals and the Safavids, was the greater degree of control the imperial government exercised over provincial administration and tax collecting, which prevented the collapse of central control.

## Chapter Summary

After the decline of the Mongols in Central Asia and Persia, many small Turkic-ruled states emerged in the region from Anatolia through Afghanistan. Three of them went on to establish large empires: the Ottomans in Anatolia, the Safavids in Persia, and the Mughals in India. In the Ottoman Empire, all authority flowed from the sultan to his public servants: provincial governors, police officers, military generals, heads of treasuries, and viziers. In Persia in 1501, a fourteen-year-old military leader with Turkic origins declared himself shah. The strength of this Safavid state rested in part on the skills of urban bureaucrats, who were vital to the civil machinery of government. Babur, from his base in Afghanistan, founded the Mughal Empire in India, and his grandson Akbar extended Mughal rule far into India. Whereas the Ottoman sultans and Safavid shahs used slaves acquired from non-Muslim lands for military and administrative positions, Akbar relied on the services of royal princes, nobles, and warrior-aristocrats. All three empires quickly adapted to new gunpowder technologies.

Each of the three Islamic empires presided over an extraordinary artistic and intellectual flowering in everything from carpetmaking and book illustration to architecture and gardening, from geography and astronomy to medicine. Each of these empires drew legitimacy from its support for Islam. There were, however, key differences: the Ottomans and Mughals supported the Sunni tradition, the Safavids the Shi'a tradition.

The three Islamic empires all had a substantial number of non-Muslim subjects. The Ottomans ruled over the Balkans, where most of the people were Christian, and Muslims in India were greatly outnumbered by Hindus.

European exploration opened new trade routes and enabled Europeans to trade directly with India and China, bypassing Muslim intermediaries in the Middle East. Within India British merchants increased their political control in politically unstable areas, leading before the end of the eighteenth century to a vast colonial empire in India.

By the end of the eighteenth century, all three of the major Islamic empires were losing territory. The first to fall was the Safavid Empire. From the late seventeenth century on, Ottoman armies began losing wars along the northern and eastern borders, resulting in substantial loss of territory. Military challenges proved daunting in Mughal India as well. In all three empires, as central power declined, local notables and military strongmen seized power.

## NOTES

1. S. Subrahmanyam, "A Tale of Three Empires: Mughals, Ottomans, and Habsburgs in a Comparative Context," *Common Knowledge* 12, no. 1 (Winter 2006): 66–92.
2. Giancarlo Casale, "The Islamic Empires of the Early Modern World," in *The Construction of a Global World, 1400–1800 CE*, Part 1: *Foundations*, ed. Jerry H. Bentley, Sanjay Subrahmanyam, and Merry E. Wiesner-Hanks (Cambridge: Cambridge University Press, 2015), pp. 334–336.
3. Quoted in W. Bingham, H. Conroy, and F. W. Iklé, *A History of Asia*, vol. 2 (Boston: Allyn and Bacon, 1967), p. 74.

## MAKE CONNECTIONS LOOK AHEAD

From 1300 to 1800 and from North Africa to India, Islamic civilization thrived under three dynastic houses: the Ottomans, the Safavids, and the Mughals. All three empires had a period of expansion when territory was enlarged, followed by a high point politically and culturally and later a period of contraction, when territories broke away. Two of the empires had large non-Muslim populations. India, even under Mughal rule, remained a predominantly Hindu land, and the Ottomans, in the process of conquering the Balkans, acquired a population that was largely Greek Orthodox Christian. Though all three states supported Islam, the Safavids took Shi'a teachings as orthodox, while the other two favored Sunni teachings. At the cultural level, the borders of these three states were porous, and people, ideas, art motifs, languages, and trade flowed back and forth.

In East Asia the fifteenth through eighteenth centuries also saw the creation of strong, prosperous, and expanding states, though in the case of China (under the Qing Dynasty) and Japan (under the Tokugawa Shogunate) the eighteenth century was a cultural high point, not a period of decline. The Qing emperors were Manchus, from the region northeast of China proper, reminiscent of the Mughals, who began in Afghanistan. As in the Islamic lands, during these centuries the presence of European powers became an issue in East Asia, though the details were quite different. Although one of the commodities that the British most wanted was the tea produced in China, Britain did not extend political control in China the way it did in India. Japan managed to refuse entry to most European traders after finding their presence and their support for missionary activity disturbing. Chapter 21 takes up these developments in East Asia.

In the next three chapters the focus is on two other regions of the world, Europe and Africa. To fully understand what Britain was doing in India requires more background on what was happening in Europe from 1500 to 1800, a period when religious differences were causing strife between European states that were at the same time beginning to build overseas empires. By the eighteenth century the Scientific Revolution and the Enlightenment were having a major impact on people's lives in Europe, and the slave trade was tying Europe to both Africa and the Americas.

# Chapter 17 Review

## IDENTIFY KEY TERMS

**Identify and explain the significance of each item below.**

| | |
|---|---|
| Ottomans (p. 413) | shah (p. 417) |
| sultan (p. 413) | Safavid (p. 417) |
| viziers (p. 416) | Qizilbash (p. 417) |
| devshirme (p. 416) | ulama (p. 418) |
| janissaries (p. 416) | Mughal (p. 419) |
| concubine (p. 417) | sepoys (p. 429) |

## REVIEW THE MAIN IDEAS

**Answer the focus questions from each section of the chapter.**

1. How were the major Islamic empires established, and what forms of government did they set up? (p. 412)

2. How did religious beliefs and practices evolve, and how did they affect non-Muslims? (p. 420)

3. What cultural advances occurred under the Ottoman, Safavid, and Mughal Empires? (p. 422)

4. How were the Islamic empires affected by new trade goods and patterns of trade? (p. 426)

5. What common factors led to the decline of central power in the Islamic empires in the seventeenth and eighteenth centuries? (p. 430)

## MAKE COMPARISONS AND CONNECTIONS

**Analyze the larger developments and continuities within and across chapters.**

1. In what sense were the states of the Ottomans, Safavids, and Mughals empires rather than large states? Do all three equally deserve the term *empire*? Why or why not?

2. How did the expansion of European presence in the Indian Ocean after 1450 impinge on the societies and economies of each of the Islamic empires?

3. What made it possible for Islamic rulers to tolerate more religious difference than European Christian rulers of the same period did?

## CHRONOLOGY

| | |
|---|---|
| **1299–1326** | • Reign of Osman, founder of the Ottoman Dynasty |
| **1299–1922** | • Ottoman Empire |
| **1336–1405** | • Life of Timur |
| **ca. 1350–1520** | • Italian Renaissance (Ch. 15) |
| **1368–1644** | • Ming Dynasty in China (Ch. 21) |
| **1405–1433** | • Zheng He's naval expeditions (Ch. 21) |
| **ca. 1428–1521** | • Aztec Empire dominates Mesoamerica (Ch. 11) |
| **ca. 1438–1532** | • Inca Empire dominates the Andes (Ch. 11) |
| **ca. mid-1400s** | • Coffeehouses become center of Islamic male social life |
| **1453** | • Ottoman conquest of Constantinople |
| **ca. 1464–1591** | • Songhai kingdom dominates the western Sudan (Ch. 20) |
| **1492** | • Columbus lands on San Salvador (Ch. 16) |
| **1501–1722** | • Safavid Empire in Persia |
| **1517** | • Luther's Ninety-five Theses (Ch. 15) |
| **1520–1566** | • Reign of Ottoman sultan Suleiman I |
| **1526–1857** | • Mughal Empire in India |
| **1556–1605** | • Reign of Akbar in Mughal Empire |
| **1631–1648** | • Construction of Taj Mahal under Shah Jahan in India |
| **ca. 1690–1789** | • European Enlightenment (Ch. 19) |
| **1763** | • Treaty of Paris recognizes British control over much of India |

# 18

# European Power and Expansion

## 1500–1750

**THE TWO CENTURIES THAT OPENED THE EARLY MODERN ERA WITNESSED** crisis and transformation in Europe. What one historian has described as the long European "struggle for stability" originated with conflicts sparked by the Protestant and Catholic Reformations in the early sixteenth century and continued with economic and social breakdown into the late seventeenth century.[1] To consolidate their domestic authority and compete with rival states, European rulers greatly increased the size of their armies. This required taxing subjects more heavily and implementing bureaucratic forms of government.

By the end of the seventeenth century, a more powerful centralized state had emerged, which historians have termed the fiscal-military state.

The growth of state power within Europe raised a series of questions: Who held supreme power? What made it legitimate? Conflicts over these questions led to rebellions and at times outright civil war. The result was a wide variety of political systems across Europe, ranging from absolutism to republicanism and, by the end of the seventeenth century, constitutional monarchy.

One important catalyst for state formation was competition over territory. As for the Islamic powers discussed in Chapter 17, this was a period of imperial expansion among European states. While Russia resembled the Islamic powers in creating a massive contiguous land empire, England, France, and the Netherlands vied with Spain for overseas territory in Asia and the Americas. This was a distinctive moment in world history, when exchange within and among empires produced constant movement of people, goods, and culture, with no one region or empire able to dominate the others entirely.

# The Protestant and Catholic Reformations

**How did the Protestant and Catholic Reformations change power structures in Europe and shape European colonial expansion?**

As a result of a movement of religious reform known as the **Protestant Reformation**, Western Christendom broke into many divisions in the sixteenth century. This splintering happened not only for religious reasons but also because of political and social factors. Religious transformation provided a source of power for many rulers and shaped European colonial expansion.

## The Protestant Reformation

In early-sixteenth-century western Europe, calls for reform in the church came from many quarters, both within and outside the church. Critics of the church concentrated their attacks on clerical immorality, ignorance, and absenteeism. Charges of immorality were aimed at priests who were drunkards, neglected the rule of celibacy, gambled, or indulged in fancy dress. Charges of ignorance applied to barely literate priests who delivered poor-quality sermons.

In regard to absenteeism, many clerics, especially higher ecclesiastics, held several benefices (offices) simultaneously, but seldom visited the communities served by the benefices. Instead they collected revenues from their benefices and hired a poor priest to fulfill their spiritual duties.

There was also local resentment of clerical privileges and immunities. Priests, monks, and nuns were exempt from civic responsibilities, such as defending the city and paying taxes. Yet religious orders frequently held large amounts of urban property. City governments were increasingly determined to integrate the clergy into civic life. This brought city leaders into opposition with bishops and the papacy, which for centuries had stressed the independence of the church from lay control.

This range of complaints helps explain why the ideas of Martin Luther (1483–1546), a priest and professor of theology from the German University of Wittenberg, found a ready audience. Luther and other Protestants—the word comes from a "protest" drawn up by a group of reforming princes in 1529—developed a new understanding of Christian doctrine in which salvation came through God's grace by faith alone and religious authority rested solely in the Bible. These ideas directly contradicted the teachings of the Catholic Church, but they were attractive to educated people and urban residents, and they spread rapidly through preaching, hymns, and the printing press.

Luther lived in the Holy Roman Empire, a loose collection of largely independent states in which the emperor had far less authority than did the monarchs of western Europe. The Habsburg emperor, Charles V, was a staunch supporter of Catholicism, but the ruler of the state in which Luther lived protected the reformer. Although Luther appeared before Charles V when he was summoned, he was not arrested and continued to preach and write.

Luther's ideas appealed to the local rulers of the empire for a variety of reasons. Though Germany was not a nation, people did have an understanding of being German because of their language and traditions. Luther frequently used the phrase "we Germans" in his attacks on the papacy, and his appeal to national feeling influenced many rulers. Also, while some German rulers were sincerely attracted to Lutheran ideas, material considerations swayed many others. The adoption of Protestantism would allow them to confiscate church properties. Thus many political authorities in the empire used the religious issue to extend their power and to enhance their independence from the emperor. Luther worked closely with political authorities, viewing them as fully justified in reforming the church in their territories. Thus, just as in the Ottoman and Safavid Empires, rulers drew their legitimacy in part from their support for religion. By 1530 many parts of the Holy Roman Empire and Scandinavia had broken with the Catholic Church.

In England the issue of the royal succession triggered that country's break with Rome, and a Protestant Church was established during the 1530s under King Henry VIII (r. 1509–1547) and reaffirmed under his daughter Elizabeth I (r. 1558–1603). Church officials were required to sign an oath of loyalty to the monarch, and people were required to attend services at the state church, which became known as the Anglican Church.

Protestant ideas also spread into France, the Netherlands, Scotland, and eastern Europe. In all these areas, a second generation of reformers built on earlier ideas to develop their own theology and plans for institutional change. The most important of the second-generation reformers was the Frenchman John Calvin (1509–1564), who reformed the city of Geneva, Switzerland. Calvin believed that God was absolutely sovereign and omnipotent and that humans had no free will. Thus men and women could not actively work to achieve salvation, because God had decided at the beginning of time who would be saved and who damned, a theological principle called predestination.

The church in Geneva served as the model for the Presbyterian Church in Scotland, the Huguenot (HYOO-guh-naht) Church in France, and the Puritan Churches in England and New England. Calvinism became the compelling force in international Protestantism, first in Europe and then in many Dutch and English colonies around the world. Calvinism was also the dominant form of Protestantism in France (Map 18.1).

## The Catholic Reformation

In response to the Protestant Reformation, by the 1530s the papacy was leading a movement for reform within the Roman Catholic Church. Pope Paul III (pontificate 1534–1549) established the Supreme Sacred Congregation of the Roman and

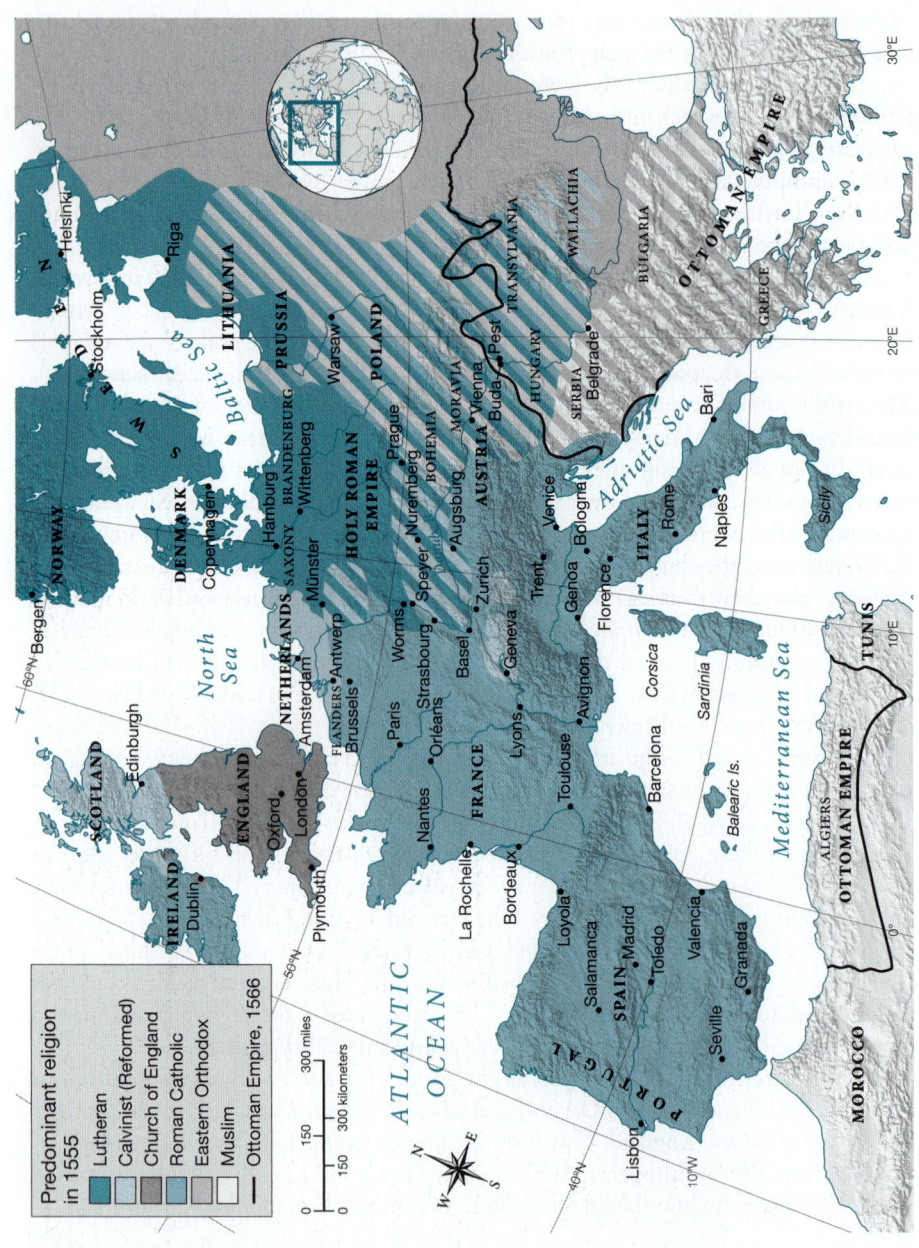

Universal Inquisition, often called the Holy Office, with judicial authority over all Catholics and the power to imprison and execute. He also called a general council of the church, which met intermittently from 1545 to 1563 at the city of Trent. The Council of Trent laid a solid basis for the spiritual renewal of the Catholic Church. It gave equal validity to the Scriptures and to tradition as sources of religious truth and tackled problems that had disillusioned many Christians. Bishops were required to live in their dioceses and to establish a seminary for educating and training clergy. Finally, it placed great emphasis on preaching to and instructing the laity. For four centuries the Council of Trent served as the basis for Roman Catholic faith, organization, and practice.

Just as seminaries provided education, so did new religious orders, which aimed to raise the moral and intellectual level of the clergy and people. The Ursuline (UHR-suh-luhn) order of nuns, founded by Angela Merici (1474–1540), attained enormous prestige for its education of women.

Another important new order was the Society of Jesus, or **Jesuits**. Founded by Ignatius Loyola (1491–1556) in 1540, this order played a powerful international role in strengthening Catholicism in Europe and spreading the faith around the world. Recruited primarily from wealthy merchant and professional families, the Society of Jesus developed into a highly centralized organization. It established well-run schools to educate the sons of the nobility as well as the poor. The Jesuits achieved phenomenal success for the papacy and the reformed Catholic Church, carrying Christianity to South and Central America, India, and Japan before 1550 and to Brazil, North America, and the Congo in the seventeenth century. Also, as confessors and spiritual directors to kings, Jesuits exerted great political influence.

## Religious Violence

Religious differences led to riots, civil wars, and international conflicts in Europe during the sixteenth century. In the Holy Roman Empire fighting began in 1546. The empire was a confederation of hundreds of principalities, independent cities, duchies, and other polities loosely united under an elected emperor. The initial success of Emperor Charles V led to French intervention on the side of the Protestants, lest the emperor acquire even more power. In 1555 Charles agreed to the Peace of Augsburg, which officially recognized Lutheranism and ended religious war in Germany for many decades. Under this treaty, the political authority in each territory of the Holy Roman Empire was permitted to decide whether the territory would be Catholic or Lutheran. His hope of uniting his empire under a single church dashed, Charles V abdicated in 1556, transferring power over his Spanish and Dutch holdings to his son Philip II and his imperial power to his brother Ferdinand.

**< MAP 18.1  Religious Divisions, ca. 1555**
In the mid-sixteenth century, much of Europe remained Catholic. The Peace of Augsburg (1555) allowed the ruler of each territory in the Holy Roman Empire to determine the religion of its people. The northern territories of the empire became Lutheran, as did Scandinavia, while much of the southern empire remained Catholic. Sizable Calvinist populations existed in Scotland, the Netherlands, and central Europe. Eastern Europe was dominated by Orthodox Christianity, and the Ottoman Empire to the south and southeast was Muslim.

In France armed clashes between Catholic royalists and Calvinist antiroyalists occurred in many parts of the country. A savage Catholic attack on Calvinists in Paris on August 24, 1572 — Saint Bartholomew's Day — occurred at the marriage of the king's sister Margaret of Valois to the Protestant Henry of Navarre. The Saint Bartholomew's Day massacre initiated a civil war that dragged on for fifteen years, destroying agriculture and commercial life in many areas.

In the Netherlands the movement for church reform developed into a struggle for Dutch independence. In the 1560s Spanish authorities attempted to suppress Calvinist worship and raised taxes. Civil war broke out from 1568 to 1578 between Catholics and Protestants in the Netherlands and between the provinces of the Netherlands and Spain. Eventually the ten southern provinces came under the control of the Spanish Habsburg forces. The seven northern provinces, led by Holland, formed the Union of Utrecht (United Provinces of the Netherlands) and in 1581 declared their independence from Spain. The north was Protestant, and the south remained Catholic. Hostilities continued until 1609, when Spain agreed to a truce that recognized the independence of the northern provinces.

The era of religious wars was also the time of the most extensive witch persecutions in European history, with between 100,000 and 200,000 people officially tried for witchcraft in the sixteenth and seventeenth centuries. Both Protestants and Catholics persecuted accused witches, with church officials and secular authorities acting together. The heightened sense of God's power and divine wrath in the Reformation era was an important factor in the witch-hunts, as were new demonological ideas, legal procedures involving torture, and neighborhood tensions. Though the gender balance of the accused varied widely in different parts of Europe, between 75 and 85 percent of those tried and executed were women, whom some demonologists viewed as weaker and so more likely to give in to the Devil.

# Seventeenth-Century Crisis and Rebuilding

**What were the common crises and achievements of seventeenth-century European states?**

Historians often refer to the seventeenth century as an "age of crisis" because Europe was challenged by population losses, economic decline, and social and political unrest. These difficulties were partially due to climate changes that reduced agricultural productivity. But they also resulted from military competition among European powers, the religious divides of the Reformations, increased taxation, and industrial stagnation. Peasants and the urban poor were especially hard hit by the economic problems, and they frequently rioted against high food prices.

The atmosphere of crisis encouraged governments to take emergency measures to restore order, measures that they successfully turned into long-term reforms that strengthened the power of the state. In the long run, European states proved increasingly able to impose their will on the populace.

## The Social Order and Peasant Life

Peasants occupied the lower tiers of a society organized in hierarchical levels. In much of Europe, the monarch occupied the summit and was celebrated as a semidivine being chosen by God to embody the state. The clergy generally constituted the first order of society, due to its sacred role interceding with God on behalf of its flocks. Next came nobles, whose privileged status derived from their ancient bloodlines and leadership in battle. Many prosperous mercantile families had bought their way into the nobility through service to the monarchy in the fifteenth and sixteenth centuries, and they constituted a second tier of nobles. Those lower on the social scale, the peasants and artisans who formed the vast majority of the population, were expected to show deference to their betters. This was the "Great Chain of Being" that linked the Christian God to his entire creation in a series of ranked groups.

In addition to being rigidly hierarchical, European societies were patriarchal. Religious and secular law commanded a man's wife, children, servants, and apprentices to respect and obey him. Fathers were entitled to use physical violence, imprisonment, and other forceful measures to impose their authority. These powers were balanced by expectations that a good father would care benevolently for his dependents.

In the seventeenth century most Europeans lived in the countryside, as was the case in most parts of the world. In western Europe a small number of peasants owned enough land to feed themselves and possessed the livestock and plows necessary to work their land. These independent farmers were leaders of the peasant village. Below them were small landowners and tenant farmers who did not have enough land to be self-sufficient. At the bottom were villagers who worked as dependent laborers and servants. Private landowning among peasants was a distinguishing feature of western Europe. In central and eastern Europe the vast majority of peasants toiled as serfs for noble landowners.

## Environmental, Economic, and Social Crises

In the seventeenth century a period of colder and more variable climate afflicted much of the globe. Dubbed the "Little Ice Age" by historians, this period of cold weather, accompanied by both too much rain and episodes of severe drought, resulted in shorter growing seasons with lower yields. A bad harvest created food shortages; a series of bad harvests could lead to famine. Recurrent famines significantly diminished the population of Europe and Asia in this period, through reduced fertility, increased susceptibility to disease, and outright starvation.

Industry also suffered. In Europe the output of woolen textiles, the most important industrial sector, declined sharply. Food prices were high, wages stagnated, and unemployment soared. This economic crisis was not universal: it struck various regions at different times and to different degrees. In the middle decades of the century, for example, Spain, France, Germany, and the British Isles all experienced great economic difficulties, as did the Ottoman Empire and China, but these years were the golden age of the Netherlands (see "The Dutch Republic"). Japan also emerged relatively unscathed, as did South Asia and the Americas.

The urban poor and peasants were the hardest hit. When the price of bread rose beyond their capacity to pay, they frequently expressed their anger by rioting. Women often led these actions, since their role as mothers gave them some impunity in authorities' eyes. Historians have used the term **moral economy** for this vision of a world in which community needs predominate over competition and profit and in which necessary goods should thus be sold at a fair price.

During the middle years of the seventeenth century, harsh conditions transformed neighborhood bread riots into armed uprisings across much of Europe. Popular revolts

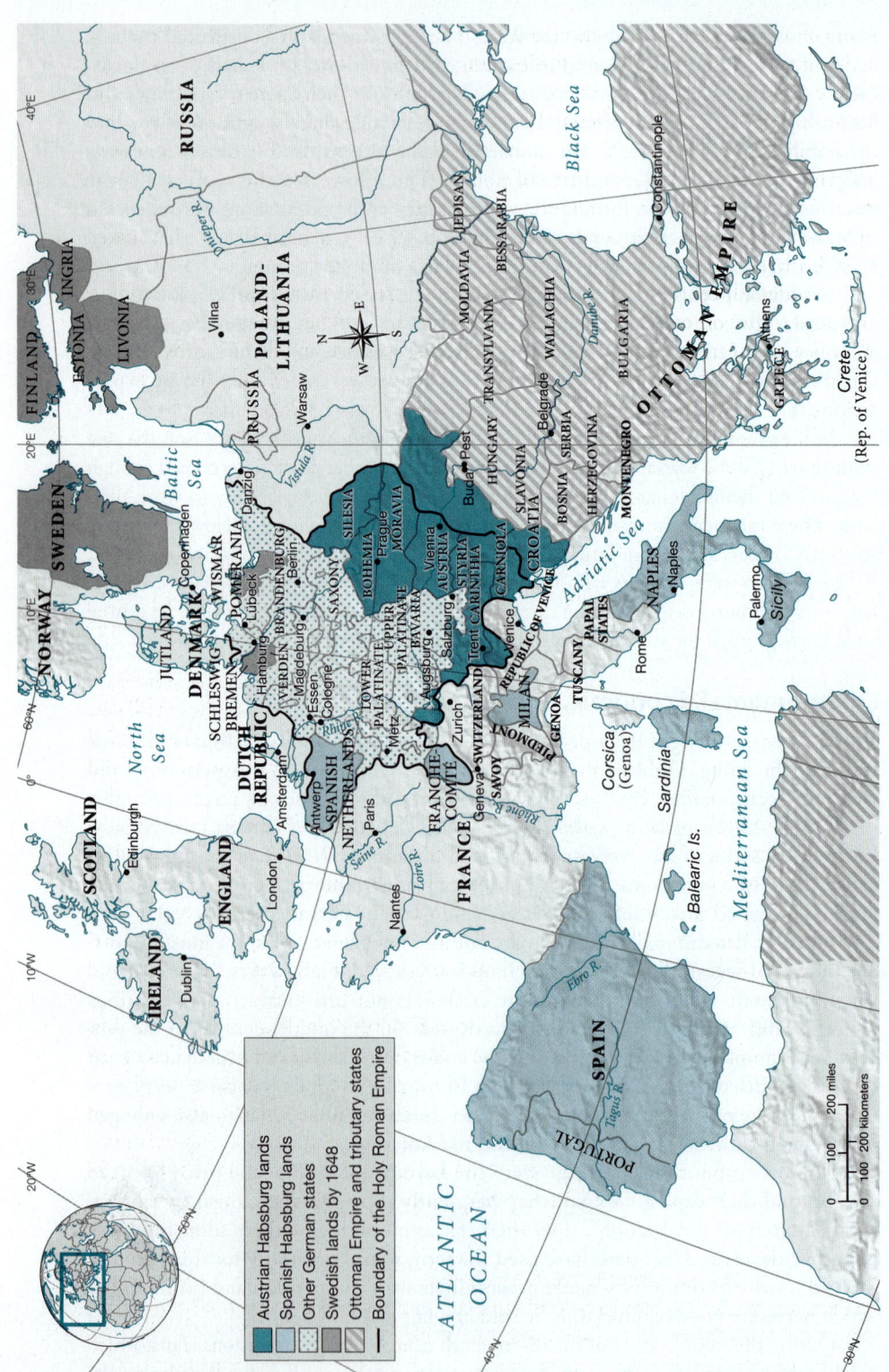

were common in England, France, and throughout the Spanish Empire, particularly during the 1640s. At the same time that he struggled to put down an uprising in Catalonia, the economic center of the realm, Spanish king Philip IV faced revolt in Portugal, the northern provinces of the Netherlands, and Spanish-occupied Sicily. France suffered an uprising in the same period that won enthusiastic support from both nobles and peasants, while the English monarch was tried and executed by his subjects and Russia experienced an explosive rebellion. In China a series of popular revolts culminated in the fall of the Ming empire in 1644, demonstrating the global reach of the seventeenth-century crisis.

Municipal and royal authorities struggled to overcome popular revolt in the mid-seventeenth century. They feared that stern repressive measures, such as sending in troops to fire on crowds, would create martyrs and further inflame the situation, while full-scale occupation of a city would be very expensive and detract from military efforts elsewhere. The limitations of royal authority gave some leverage to rebels. To quell riots, royal edicts were sometimes suspended, prisoners released, and discussions initiated. By the beginning of the eighteenth century rulers had gained much greater control over their populations.

## The Thirty Years' War

In addition to harsh economic conditions, popular unrest was greatly exacerbated by the impact of the decades-long conflict known as the **Thirty Years' War** (1618–1648), the first military conflict on a European scale. The background to the war was a shift in the balance between the population of Protestants and Catholics in the Holy Roman Empire that led to the deterioration of the Peace of Augsburg. Lutheran princes felt compelled to form the Protestant Union (1608), and Catholics retaliated with the Catholic League (1609). Dynastic interests were also involved; the Spanish Habsburgs strongly supported the goals of their Austrian relatives: the unity of the empire and the preservation of Catholicism within it.

The war began with a conflict in Bohemia between the Catholic League and the Protestant Union but soon spread through the Holy Roman Empire, drawing in combatants from across Europe. After a series of initial Catholic victories, the tide of the conflict turned due to the intervention of Sweden, under its brilliant young king Gustavus Adolphus (r. 1594–1632), and then France, whose chief minister, Cardinal Richelieu (REESH-uh-lyuh), intervened on the side of the Protestants to undermine Habsburg power.

The 1648 Peace of Westphalia that ended the Thirty Years' War marked a turning point in European history. The treaties that established the peace not only ended major conflicts fought over religious faith but also recognized the independent authority of almost three hundred German princes (Map 18.2), reconfirming the emperor's severely limited authority. The Augsburg agreement of 1555 became permanent, adding Calvinism to Catholicism and Lutheranism as legally permissible creeds. The United Provinces of the Netherlands, known as the Dutch Republic, won official freedom from Spain.

< **MAP 18.2    Europe After the Thirty Years' War**
Which country emerged from the Thirty Years' War as the strongest European power? What dynastic house was that country's major rival in the early modern period?

The Thirty Years' War was probably the most destructive event in central Europe prior to the world wars of the twentieth century. Perhaps one-third of urban residents and two-fifths of the rural population died, and agriculture and industry withered. Across Europe, states increased taxes to meet the cost of war, further increasing the suffering of a traumatized population.

## European Achievements in State-Building

In this context of warfare, economic crisis, popular revolt, and demographic decline, European rulers took urgent measures to restore order and rebuild their states. Despite differences in political systems, all these states sought to protect and expand their frontiers, raise taxes, consolidate central control, establish social welfare programs, and compete for colonies and trade in the New and Old Worlds. In so doing, they followed a broad pattern of state-building and consolidation of power found across Eurasia in this period.

Rulers who wished to increase their authority encountered formidable obstacles, including poor communications, entrenched local power structures, and ethnic and linguistic diversity. Nonetheless, over the course of the seventeenth century European governments achieved new levels of power and national unity. They did so by transforming emergency measures of wartime into permanent structures of government and by subduing privileged groups through the combined use of force and economic and social incentives. Increased state authority may be seen in four areas in particular: a tremendous growth in the size and professionalism of armies; much higher taxes; larger and more efficient bureaucracies; and territorial expansion both within Europe and overseas. A fifth important area of European state growth — government sponsorship of scientific inquiry — will be discussed in Chapter 19. Historians have used the term **fiscal-military state** to describe these increasingly centralized and bureaucratic states, which harnessed domestic resources to maintain a large army for internal order and to compete for territory within Europe and overseas.

# Absolutist States in Western and Central Europe

### What was absolutism, and how did it evolve in western and central Europe?

Rulers in absolutist states asserted that, because they were chosen by God, they were responsible to God alone. Under the rule of **absolutism**, monarchs claimed exclusive power to make and enforce laws, denying any other institution or group the authority to check their power. However, in practice absolutism was limited by the need to maintain legitimacy and compromise with elites. "Absolutist" monarchs thus felt constrained to uphold the laws of their predecessors and ruled in collaboration with institutions comprising representatives of privileged groups. Habsburg Spain and Austria as well as France provide key examples of the development of the absolutist state.

## Spain

The discovery of silver at Potosí in 1545 produced momentous wealth for Spain, allowing the Habsburg dynasty to dominate other European states and maintain its global empire. Yet Spain had inherent weaknesses that the wealth of empire had hidden. When Philip IV took the throne in 1621, he inherited a Spanish throne that encompassed different kingdoms with their own traditions and loyalties as well as a vast and overstretched overseas empire. Spanish silver had created great wealth but also dependency. While Creoles undertook new industries in the colonies and European nations targeted Spanish colonial trade, industry and finance in Spain itself remained undeveloped.

Spain's challenges mounted during the first half of the seventeenth century. Between 1610 and 1650 Spanish trade with the colonies in the New World fell 60 percent due to competition from colonial industries and from Dutch and English traders. To make matters worse, in 1609 the Crown expelled some three hundred thousand Moriscos, or former Muslims, significantly reducing the pool of skilled workers and merchants. At the same time, disease decimated the enslaved workers who toiled in South American silver mines. Moreover, the mines started to run dry; the quantity of metal produced steadily declined after 1620, and Dutch privateers seized the entire silver fleet in 1628.

Within Spain itself, the effects of the Little Ice Age greatly reduced the productivity of land. In order to stay afloat, Spanish aristocrats increased their land rents, but higher rents encouraged peasants to leave the land. In cities, the high price of food diminished demand for industrial goods, leading to low wages and unemployment for city dwellers.

For the central government, the expenses of war and imperial rule constantly exceeded income. Despite the efforts of Philip's able chief minister, Gaspar de

**Diego Rodríguez de Silva y Velázquez, *Las Meninas*, 1656** The royal princess Margaret Theresa is shown here surrounded by her ladies-in-waiting. The painter Velázquez has portrayed himself working on a canvas, while her parents, the king and queen of Spain, are reflected in the mirror behind the princess. (Alfredo Dagli Orti/Shutterstock)

Guzmán, Count-Duke of Olivares, it proved impossible to force the distinct kingdoms of the empire to shoulder the cost of its defense. To meet state debt, the Spanish Crown repeatedly devalued the coinage and declared bankruptcy, which resulted in the collapse of state credit and increased inflation.

Spain's situation worsened with internal rebellions and fresh military defeats during the Thirty Years' War and the remainder of the seventeenth century. The Treaty of Westphalia, which ended the Thirty Years' War, compelled Spain to recognize the independence of the Dutch Republic, and another treaty in 1659 granted extensive territories to France. Finally, in 1688 the Spanish Crown reluctantly recognized the independence of Portugal. With these losses, the era of Spanish dominance in Europe ended.

## The Foundations of French Absolutism

Although France was the largest and most populous state in western Europe, its position at the beginning of the seventeenth century appeared extremely weak. Struggling to recover from decades of religious civil war, France posed little threat to Spain's predominance in Europe. By the end of the century the countries' positions were reversed.

Henry IV (r. 1589–1610), who inaugurated the Bourbon dynasty, defused religious tensions and rebuilt France's economy. In 1598 he issued the Edict of Nantes, allowing Huguenots (French Protestants) the right to worship in 150 traditionally Protestant towns throughout France. He also invested in infrastructure and raised revenue by selling royal offices instead of charging high taxes. Despite his efforts at peace, Henry was murdered in 1610 by a Catholic zealot.

Cardinal Richelieu (1585–1642) became first minister of the French Crown on behalf of Henry's young son Louis XIII (r. 1610–1643). Richelieu designed his domestic policies to strengthen royal control. He extended the use of intendants, commissioners for each of France's thirty-two districts who were appointed by and were responsible to the monarch. By using the intendants to gather information and ensure royal edicts were enforced, Richelieu reduced the power of provincial nobles. Richelieu's main foreign policy goal was to destroy the Habsburgs' grip on territories that surrounded France. Consequently, Richelieu supported Habsburg enemies, including Protestants, during the Thirty Years' War.

Cardinal Jules Mazarin (1602–1661) succeeded Richelieu as chief minister for four-year-old Louis XIV, who inherited the throne in 1643. Mazarin's struggle to increase royal revenues to meet the costs of the Thirty Years' War led to the uprisings of 1648–1653 known as the Fronde. Much of the rebellion faded, however, when Louis XIV was declared king in his own right in 1651, ending the regency of his mother, Anne of Austria. The French people were desperate for peace and stability after the disorders of the Fronde and were willing to accept a strong monarch who could restore order.

## Louis XIV and Absolutism

During the long reign of Louis XIV (r. 1643–1715), known as the Sun King, the French monarchy overcame weakness and division to become the most powerful nation in western Europe. Louis based his authority on the **divine right of kings**:

God had established kings as his rulers on earth, and they were answerable ultimately to him alone. However, Louis also recognized that kings could not simply do as they pleased. They had to obey God's laws and rule for the good of the people.

Like rulers elsewhere in Eurasia, Louis XIV impressed his subjects with his discipline and hard work. He ruled his realm through several councils of state and insisted on taking a personal role in many of the councils' decisions. Despite increasing financial problems, Louis never called a meeting of the Estates General, the traditional French representative assembly composed of the three estates of clergy, nobility, and commoners. The nobility, therefore, had no means of united expression or action.

Louis also moved to impose religious unity on France, which he viewed as essential to the security of the state. In 1685 Louis revoked the Edict of Nantes. Around two hundred thousand Protestants, including some of the kingdom's most highly skilled artisans, fled France. Louis's insistence on "one king, one law, one religion" contrasts sharply with the religious tolerance exhibited by Muslim empires in the Middle East and South Asia (see "Non-Muslims Under Muslim Rule" in Chapter 17).

Despite his claims to absolute authority, there were multiple constraints on Louis's power. As a representative of divine power, he was obliged to rule in a way that seemed consistent with virtue and paternal care for his subjects. He had to uphold the laws issued by his royal predecessors. Moreover, he also relied on the collaboration of nobles. Without their cooperation, it would have been impossible for Louis to extend his power throughout France or wage his many foreign wars. In some regions of France, nobles, as well as leading clergymen and commoners, were organized into representative assemblies, known as provincial "estates." Among other prerogatives, these assemblies retained the right to allocate royal taxes, giving them an important role in regional governance.

## The Wars of Louis XIV

Louis XIV kept France at war for thirty-three of the fifty-four years of his personal rule. During his reign, the French army almost tripled in size and its professionalism greatly increased. Uniforms and weapons were standardized, and a system of training and promotion was devised. These developments were part of a European-wide phenomenon scholars have dubbed a "military revolution." Military competition among early modern European states was a key catalyst for the development of the fiscal-military state.

The results of Louis's military aggression were decidedly mixed. During the 1660s and 1670s, French armies won a number of important victories. The wars of the 1680s and 1690s, however, brought no additional territories and placed unbearable strains on French resources. Louis's last war, the War of the Spanish Succession (1701–1713), was endured by a French people suffering high taxes, crop failure, and widespread malnutrition and death. This war was the result of Louis's unwillingness to abide by a previous agreement to divide Spanish possessions between France and the Holy Roman emperor upon the death of the childless Spanish king Charles II (r. 1665–1700). In 1701 the English, Dutch, Austrians, and Prussians formed the Grand Alliance against Louis XIV. War dragged on until 1713, when it was ended by the Peace of Utrecht (Map 18.3).

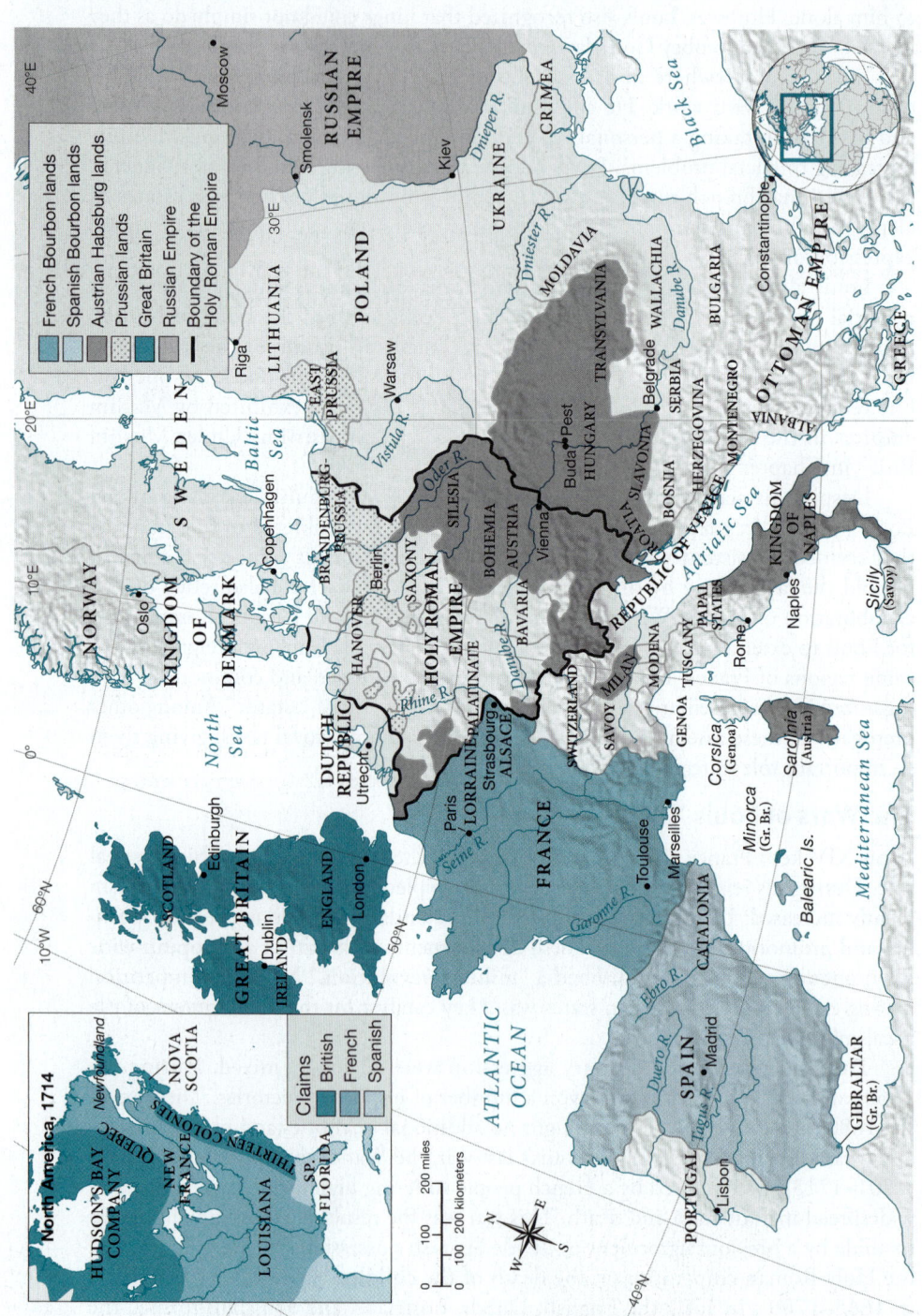

**Legend:**
- French Bourbon lands
- Spanish Bourbon lands
- Austrian Habsburg lands
- Prussian lands
- Great Britain
- Russian Empire
- Boundary of the Holy Roman Empire

RUSSIAN EMPIRE

Moscow
Smolensk
Kiev
UKRAINE
CRIMEA
Black Sea
*Dnieper R.*
*Dniester R.*
*Danube R.*
MOLDAVIA
WALLACHIA
TRANSYLVANIA
BULGARIA
Belgrade
SERBIA
BOSNIA
HERZEGOVINA
MONTENEGRO
ALBANIA
OTTOMAN EMPIRE
Constantinople
GREECE

POLAND
LITHUANIA
Riga
*Baltic Sea*
EAST PRUSSIA
Warsaw
*Vistula R.*
*Oder R.*
SILESIA
BRANDENBURG PRUSSIA
Berlin
SAXONY
BOHEMIA
Buda Pest
HUNGARY
SLAVONIA
CROATIA
AUSTRIA
Vienna
REPUBLIC OF VENICE
*Adriatic Sea*

S W E D E N
NORWAY
Oslo
KINGDOM OF DENMARK
Copenhagen
HANOVER
HOLY ROMAN EMPIRE
DUTCH REPUBLIC
Utrecht
*North Sea*
*Rhine R.*
BAVARIA
*Danube R.*
SWITZERLAND
SAVOY
MILAN
MODENA
GENOA
TUSCANY
PAPAL STATES
Rome
KINGDOM OF NAPLES
Naples
Sicily (Savoy)
Corsica (Genoa)
Sardinia (Austria)

LORRAINE
PALATINATE
Strasbourg
ALSACE
Paris
*Seine R.*
FRANCE
*Garonne R.*
Toulouse
Marseilles
Minorca (Gr. Br.)
Balearic Is.
*Mediterranean Sea*

SCOTLAND
Edinburgh
GREAT BRITAIN
ENGLAND
London
Dublin
IRELAND

ATLANTIC OCEAN

CATALONIA
*Ebro R.*
SPAIN
Madrid
*Duero R.*
*Tagus R.*
PORTUGAL
Lisbon
GIBRALTAR (Gr. Br.)

40°E
30°E
20°E
10°E
0°
10°W
60°N
50°N
40°N

**Inset map: North America, 1714**

Claims:
- British
- French
- Spanish

HUDSON'S BAY COMPANY
Newfoundland
NOVA SCOTIA
QUEBEC
NEW FRANCE
THIRTEEN COLONIES
LOUISIANA
SP. FLORIDA

N  E  W  S

0   100   200 miles
0   100   200 kilometers

## The Absolutist Palace

In 1682 Louis moved his court and government to the newly renovated palace at Versailles (vayr-SIGH), in the countryside southwest of Paris. The themes of the interior paintings and the sculptures in the gardens hailed Louis's power, with images of the Roman gods Apollo (the sun-god) and Neptune (the sea-god) making frequent appearances. The gardens' rational orderliness and symmetry showed that Louis's dominance extended even to nature, while their terraces and waterworks served as showcases for the latest techniques in military and civil engineering.

The palace was the center of French political, social, and cultural life, and all high-ranking nobles were required to spend at least part of the year living there. At court, nobles participated in an elaborate set of etiquette rituals focused on the king and the royal family. These rituals were far from meaningless or trivial. The king controlled immense resources and privileges; access to him meant favored treatment for government offices, military and religious posts, state pensions, honorary titles, and a host of other benefits.

A system of patronage — in which a higher-ranked individual protected a lower-ranked one in return for loyalty and services — flowed from the court to the provinces. Through this mechanism Louis gained cooperation from powerful nobles. Although they were denied public offices and posts, women played a central role in the patronage system. At court the king's wife, mistresses, and other female relatives recommended individuals for honors, advocated policy decisions, and brokered alliances between noble factions.

With Versailles as the center of European politics, French culture grew in international prestige. French became the language of polite society and international diplomacy, and France inspired a cosmopolitan European culture in the late seventeenth century that looked to Versailles as its center. Moreover, Louis's rival European monarchs built their own spectacular palaces, and palace building became a Europe-wide phenomenon.

## The Austrian Habsburgs

Absolutism was also the dominant form of monarchical rule among the more than one thousand states that composed the Holy Roman Empire. Prussia, a minor power with scattered holdings, emerged in the seventeenth and eighteenth centuries under the Hohenzollern dynasty as a major rival to the Austrian Habsburg dynasty (see "Enlightened Absolutism and Its Limits" in Chapter 19). Like all of central Europe, the Austrian Habsburgs emerged from the Thirty Years' War impoverished and

< **MAP 18.3**  **Europe After the Peace of Utrecht, 1715**
The series of treaties commonly called the Peace of Utrecht ended the War of the Spanish Succession and redrew the map of Europe. A French Bourbon king succeeded to the Spanish throne. France surrendered the Spanish Netherlands (later Belgium), then in French hands, to Austria and recognized the Hohenzollern rulers of Prussia. Spain ceded Gibraltar to Great Britain, for which it has been a strategic naval station ever since. Spain also granted Britain the asiento, the contract for supplying African slaves to America.

exhausted. Their efforts to destroy Protestantism in the German lands and to turn the weak Holy Roman Empire into a real state had failed. Henceforth, the Austrian Habsburgs turned away from a quest for imperial dominance and focused inward and eastward in an attempt to unify their diverse holdings.

Habsburg victory over Bohemia during the Thirty Years' War was an important step in this direction. Ferdinand II (r. 1619–1637) drastically reduced the power of the Bohemian Estates, the largely Protestant representative assembly. He also confiscated the landholdings of Protestant nobles and gave them to his supporters. After 1650 a large portion of the Bohemian nobility was of recent origin and owed its success to the Habsburgs.

With the support of this new nobility, the Habsburgs established direct rule over Bohemia. Under their rule, the condition of the serfs worsened substantially. The Habsburgs also successfully eliminated Protestantism in Bohemia. These changes were important steps in creating absolutist rule.

Ferdinand III (r. 1637–1657) continued to build state power. He centralized the government in the empire's German-speaking provinces, which formed the core Habsburg holdings, and established a permanent standing army. The Habsburg monarchy then turned east toward Hungary, which had been divided between the Ottomans and the Habsburgs in the early sixteenth century (see "The Expansion of the Ottoman Empire" in Chapter 17). Between 1683 and 1699 the Habsburgs pushed the Ottomans from most of Hungary and Transylvania. The recovery of all of the former kingdom of Hungary was completed in 1718.

Despite its reduced strength, the Hungarian nobility effectively thwarted the full development of Habsburg absolutism. Throughout the seventeenth century, Hungarian nobles periodically rose in revolt against the Habsburgs. In 1703, with the Habsburgs bogged down in the War of the Spanish Succession, the Hungarians rose in one last patriotic rebellion under Prince Francis Rákóczi (RAH-coht-see). Rákóczi and his forces were eventually defeated, but the Habsburgs agreed to restore many of the traditional privileges of the Hungarian aristocracy in return for the country's acceptance of Habsburg rule.

Elsewhere, the Habsburgs made significant achievements in state-building by forging consensus with the church and the nobility. A sense of common identity and loyalty to the monarchy grew among elites in Habsburg lands. Vienna became the political and cultural center of the empire.

# Alternatives to Absolutism

### What were alternatives to absolutism in early modern Europe?

While most European nations emerged from the crises of the seventeenth century with absolutist forms of government, other alternatives existed. **Constitutionalism** is the limitation of government by law, implying a balance between the authority and power of the government, on the one hand, and the rights and liberties of the subjects. It can take the form of **republicanism**, a form of government in which there is no monarch and power rests in the hands of the people as exercised through elected representatives. The Dutch Republic, one of the most important republican states in Europe, experienced a golden age in the seventeenth century. Some states, like the Polish-Lithuanian Commonwealth and England, evolved instead toward forms of constitutional monarchy, in which a monarchy (hereditary or elected) ruled but within legal limitations.

## The Polish-Lithuanian Commonwealth

After a marriage between their rulers in the Middle Ages, the kingdom of Poland and the Grand Duchy of Lithuania were governed as separate polities ruled by a common monarch. In 1569, the Union of Lublin formally joined the two territories in a confederation. The terms of the union submitted the monarch to oversight by a noble-dominated parliament, making the Polish-Lithuanian Commonwealth one of the earliest examples of a constitutional monarchy in Europe. Moreover, in contrast to almost all other European monarchies, the ruler was not hereditary but elected by a vote of all (male) members of the nobility. (The most important additional example of an elected ruler was the Holy Roman emperor, who was almost always the head of the Austrian Habsburg dynasty.)

The commonwealth was also noteworthy in being one of the most ethnically and religiously diverse European states, inhabited by Jews and Muslims as well as by Catholic, Protestant, and Orthodox Christians. In particular, it was the state with the largest Jewish population in the world at that time. Historians estimate that Jews constituted up to 10 percent of the population of Poland-Lithuania by the eighteenth century.

In the first half of the seventeenth century, the Polish-Lithuanian Commonwealth waged territorial war against Sweden and Russia, and it occupied Moscow from 1610 to 1612. It also benefited from remaining neutral during the Thirty Years' War. However, its political stability declined in the second half of the seventeenth century, and it fell under the influence of an increasingly powerful Russian Empire.

## The Failure of Absolutism in England

Rather than being achieved through a treaty of confederation, constitutional monarchy in England evolved through civil war against a would-be absolute monarch, a brief experiment with republicanism, and two efforts to restore monarchical rule. In 1603 beloved Queen Elizabeth was succeeded by her Scottish cousin James Stuart, who ruled England as James I (r. 1603–1625). Like Louis XIV, James believed in the absolute and divine rule of monarchs. James I and his son Charles I (r. 1625–1649) considered any legislative constraint a threat to their divine-right prerogative. Consequently, at every meeting of Parliament between 1603 and 1640, bitter squabbles erupted between the Crown and the House of Commons.

Religious issues also embittered relations between the king and the House of Commons. In the early seventeenth century many English people felt dissatisfied with the Church of England. Calvinist **Puritans** wanted to take the Reformation further by "purifying" the Anglican Church of Roman Catholic elements, including Crown-appointed bishops and elaborate ceremonies. James I responded to such ideas by declaring, "No bishop, no king." His son and successor, Charles I, further antagonized subjects by marrying a French Catholic princess and supporting the high-handed policies of Archbishop of Canterbury William Laud (1573–1645). Political and religious conflict in this period was exacerbated by economic distress caused by the severe weather conditions of the Little Ice Age and periodic outbreaks of plague.

Charles avoided direct confrontation with his subjects by refusing to call Parliament into session from 1629 to 1640, instead financing the realm through extraordinary levies. However, when Scottish Calvinists revolted against his religious policies, Charles was forced to summon Parliament to obtain funding for an army to put down the revolt. Angry with the king's behavior and sympathetic with the Scots' religious beliefs, the House of Commons passed the Triennial Act in 1641, which compelled the king to call Parliament every three years. The Commons also impeached Archbishop Laud and threatened to abolish bishops. King Charles, fearful of a Scottish invasion, reluctantly accepted these measures.

The next act in the conflict was precipitated by the outbreak of rebellion in Ireland. In 1641 the Catholic gentry of Ireland led an uprising in response to a feared invasion by British anti-Catholic forces. Without an army, Charles I could neither come to terms with the Scots nor respond to the Irish rebellion. After a failed attempt to arrest parliamentary leaders, Charles left London and began to raise an army. In response, Parliament formed its own army, the New Model Army.

The English Civil War (1642–1649) pitted the power of the king against that of Parliament. After three years of fighting, Parliament's army defeated the king's forces at the Battles of Naseby and Langport in the summer of 1645. Charles refused to concede defeat, and both sides waited for a decisive event. This arrived in the form of the army under the leadership of Oliver Cromwell, a member of the House of Commons and a devout Puritan. In 1647 Cromwell's troops captured the king and dismissed the members of Parliament who opposed Cromwell's actions. In 1649 the remaining representatives, known as the Rump Parliament, put Charles on trial for high treason. Charles was found guilty and beheaded on January 30, 1649.

## The Puritan Protectorate

With the execution of Charles, the monarchy was abolished and a commonwealth, or republican government, was proclaimed. Theoretically, legislative power rested in the surviving members of Parliament, and executive power was lodged in a council of state. In fact, the army that had defeated the king controlled the government, and Oliver Cromwell controlled the army. Though called the Protectorate, the rule of Cromwell (1653–1658) was a form of military dictatorship. Reflecting Puritan ideas of morality, Cromwell's state forbade sports, kept the theaters closed, and rigorously censored the press.

On the issue of religion, Cromwell favored some degree of tolerance, and all Christians except Roman Catholics had the right to practice their faiths. Cromwell had long associated Catholicism in Ireland with sedition and heresy, and he led an army there to reconquer the country in August 1649. Following Cromwell's reconquest, the English banned Catholicism in Ireland, executed priests, and confiscated land from Catholics for English and Scottish settlers.

The Protectorate collapsed when Cromwell died in 1658 and his ineffectual son succeeded him. By 1660 the English were ready to abandon their experiment with republicanism.

## Constitutional Monarchy

The Restoration of 1660 brought to the throne Charles II (r. 1660–1685), the eldest son of Charles I. Both houses of Parliament were also restored, as was the Anglican Church. However, Charles was succeeded by his Catholic brother James II, arousing fears of a return of Catholicism. A group of eminent persons in Parliament and the Church of England wrote to James's Protestant daughter Mary and her Dutch husband, Prince William of Orange, asking them to restore English liberties by taking the throne of England. In November 1688 William arrived on the English coast with five hundred ships and over twenty thousand soldiers, causing James II to flee for France. Early in 1689 William and Mary were jointly crowned as king and queen of England.

The English called the events of 1688 and 1689 a *revolution*, but they did not mean by this the radical overthrow of a political system. At the time, the word implied the return to an original state, a meaning derived from its origins as an astronomical term describing the circulation of celestial bodies. The men who brought about the revolution thus presented it as a return to the ancient rights and liberties of English subjects after the arbitrary rule of the Stuart kings.

The men who brought about the revolution framed this aspiration in the **Bill of Rights of 1689**, which was passed by Parliament and formally accepted by William and Mary. Law was to be made in Parliament; once made, it could not be suspended by the Crown. Parliament had to be called at least once every three years. The Bill of Rights also established the independence of the judiciary and mandated that there be no standing army in peacetime. Additional legislation granted freedom of worship to Protestant dissenters but not to Catholics. The Bill of Rights, along with other pieces of legislation, formed an informal constitution, one that persisted through the Act of Union creating Great Britain in 1707 and that remains in effect today.

The concept of a constitutional monarchy responsible to representatives of the people found its best defense in political philosopher John Locke's *Second Treatise of Civil Government* (1690). Locke (1632–1704) maintained that a government that oversteps its proper function — protecting the natural rights of life, liberty, and property — becomes a tyranny. Under a tyrannical government, he argued, the people have the natural right to rebellion. Constitutional monarchy did not equate with democracy. Sovereignty was placed in the king and Parliament, and Parliament represented the upper classes.

The events of 1688 and 1689 were referred to at the time as the "Glorious Revolution" because it supposedly restored English liberties with no bloodshed. In truth, William's arrival sparked riots and violence across the British Isles and in North American cities such as Boston and New York. Uprisings by supporters of James, known as Jacobites, occurred in 1689 in Scotland. In Ireland the two sides waged outright war from 1689 to 1691. William's victory at the Battle of the Boyne (1690) and the subsequent Treaty of Limerick (1691) sealed his accession to power.

## The Dutch Republic

In the late sixteenth century the seven northern provinces of the Netherlands fought for and won their independence from Spain. The independence of the Republic of the United Provinces of the Netherlands was recognized in 1648 in the treaty that ended the Thirty Years' War. Rejecting the rule of a monarch, the Dutch established a republic, a state in which power rested in the hands of the people and was exercised through elected representatives. Other examples of republics in early modern Europe included the Swiss Confederation and several autonomous city-states in Italy and in the Holy Roman Empire.

Among the Dutch, an oligarchy of wealthy businessmen called regents handled domestic affairs in each province's Estates, or assemblies. The provincial Estates held virtually all the power. A federal assembly, or States General, handled foreign affairs and war, but all issues had to be referred back to the local Estates for approval, and each of the seven provinces could veto any proposed legislation. Holland, the province with the largest navy and the most wealth, usually dominated the republic and the States General.

In each province, the Estates appointed an executive officer, known as the stadholder. Although in theory the stadholder was freely chosen by the Estates, in practice the reigning prince of Orange usually held the office of stadholder in several of the seven provinces of the republic. Tensions persisted between supporters of the House of Orange and those of the staunchly republican Estates, who suspected the princes of harboring monarchical ambitions. Global trade and commerce brought the Dutch the highest standard of living in Europe, perhaps in the world. Salaries were high, and all classes of society ate well. Consequently, the Netherlands experienced very few of the riots and popular revolts that characterized the rest of Europe.[2]

The moral and ethical bases of Dutch commercial wealth were thrift, frugality, and religious tolerance. Jews enjoyed a level of acceptance and assimilation in Dutch business and general culture unique in early modern Europe. In the Dutch Republic tolerance not only seemed the right way but also contributed to profits by attracting a great deal of foreign capital and investment.

# Colonial Expansion and Empire

### How did European nations compete for global trade and empire in the Americas and Asia?

For much of the sixteenth century the Spanish and Portuguese dominated European overseas trade and colonization (see "Conquest and Settlement" in Chapter 16). In the early seventeenth century, however, England, France, and the Netherlands challenged Spain's monopoly. They eventually succeeded in creating overseas empires, consisting of settler colonies in North America, slave plantations in the Caribbean, and scattered trading posts in West Africa and Asia. Competition among them was encouraged by mercantilist economic doctrine, which dictated that foreign trade was a zero-sum game in which one country's gains necessarily entailed another's loss.

## The Dutch Trading Empire

The so-called golden age of the Dutch Republic in the seventeenth century was built on its commercial prosperity and its highly original republican system of government. The Dutch came to dominate the European shipping business by putting profits from their original industry—herring fishing—into shipbuilding. They then took aim at Portugal's immensely lucrative Asian trade empire.

In 1599 a Dutch fleet returned to Amsterdam from a voyage to Southeast Asia carrying a huge cargo of spices. Those who had invested in the expedition received a 100 percent profit. The voyage led to the establishment in 1602 of the Dutch East India Company, founded with the stated intention of capturing the spice trade from the Portuguese.

In return for assisting Indonesian princes in local conflicts and disputes with the Portuguese, the Dutch won broad commercial concessions. Through agreements, seizures, and outright military aggression, they gained control of the western access to the Indonesian archipelago in the first half of the seventeenth century. Gradually, they acquired political domination over the archipelago itself. The Dutch were willing to use force more ruthlessly than the Portuguese were and had superior organizational efficiency. These factors allowed them to expel the Portuguese from Ceylon and other east Indian islands in the 1660s and henceforth dominate the production and trade of spices. The company also established the colony of Cape Town on the southern tip of Africa as a provisioning point for its Asian fleets.

The Dutch also aspired to a role in the Americas (Map 18.4). Founded in 1621, the Dutch West India Company aggressively sought to open trade with North and South America and capture Spanish territories there. The company captured or destroyed hundreds of Spanish ships, seized the Spanish silver fleet in 1628, and claimed portions of Brazil and the Caribbean. The Dutch also successfully interceded in the transatlantic slave trade, establishing a large number of trading stations on the west coast of Africa. Ironically, the nation that was known as a bastion of tolerance and freedom came to be one of the principal operators of the brutal slave trade starting in the 1640s.

## Colonial Empires of England and France

England and France followed the Dutch in challenging Iberian dominance overseas. Unlike the Iberian powers, whose royal governments financed exploration and directly ruled the colonies, England, France, and the Netherlands conducted the initial phase of colonization through chartered companies with monopolies over settlement and trade in a given area.

Just as the Spanish explorers had learned from the reconquista, English expansion drew on long experience at home conquering and colonizing Ireland. After an unsuccessful first colony at Roanoke (in what is now North Carolina), the English colony of Virginia, founded at Jamestown in 1607, gained a steady hold by producing tobacco for a growing European market. Indentured servants obtained free passage to the colony in exchange for several years of work and the promise of greater opportunity than could be found in England. In the 1670s English colonists from the Caribbean island of Barbados settled Carolina, where conditions were suitable for large rice plantations. During the late seventeenth century enslaved Africans replaced indentured servants as laborers on tobacco and rice plantations, and a harsh racial divide was imposed.

For the first settlers on the coast of New England, the reasons for seeking a new life in the colonies were more religious than economic. Many of these colonists were radical Protestants escaping Anglican repression. The small and struggling Puritan outpost of Plymouth Colony (1620) was followed by Massachusetts Bay Colony (1630), which grew into a prosperous settlement. Religious disputes in Massachusetts led to the dispersion of settlers into the new communities of Providence, Connecticut, Rhode Island, and New Haven. Because New England lacked the conditions for plantation agriculture, slavery was always a minor factor there.

Whereas the Spanish established wholesale dominance over Mexico and Peru and its indigenous inhabitants, English settlements hugged the Atlantic coastline and expelled indigenous people from their lands, leading to attacks by displaced groups and wars of reprisal and extermination. In place of the unified rule exerted by the Spanish Crown,

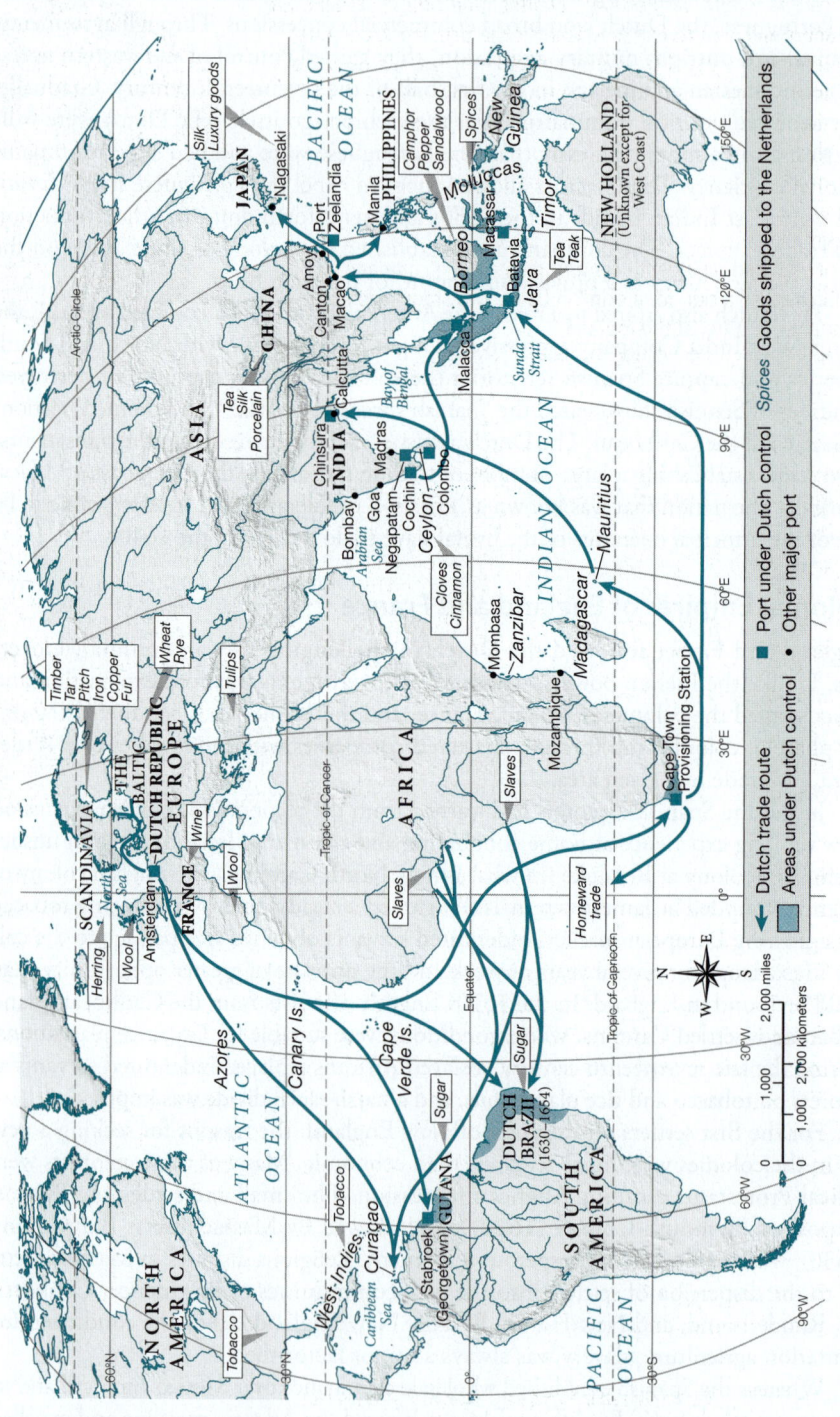

**The Fur Trade** In the early seventeenth century European fur traders relied on Native Americans' expertise and experience, leading to the equal relations depicted in this scene from the colony of New Sweden (in modern-day Pennsylvania). The action in the background of the engraving (below) shows violence among indigenous groups, rivalries exacerbated by contact with Europeans and their trade goods. Hudson's Bay Company, the English colonial trading company, issued its own tokens as currency in the fur trade. This token, dating from the mid-nineteenth century, displays the company's crest, which says "a skin for a skin" in Latin. Two stags face each other, with a fox at the top and four beavers on the shield. Traders received tokens for the pelts they sold and could use them to purchase goods from the company's store. European demand for beaver hats, made from the felted pelts of beavers, drove the tremendous expansion of the North American fur trade in the beginning of the seventeenth century. (engraving: From Geographia Americae with An Account of the Delaware Indians, Based on Surveys and Notes Made 1654–1656, by Peter Lindestrom, published by The Swedish Colonial Society/Visual Connection Archive; token: © National Maritime Museum, London, UK/The Image Works)

English colonization was haphazard and decentralized in nature, leading to greater colonial autonomy and diversity. As the English Crown grew more interested in colonial expansion, efforts were made to acquire the territory between New England in the north and Virginia in the south. The goal was to unify English holdings and minimize French and Dutch competition on the Atlantic seaboard. The results of these efforts were the mid-Atlantic colonies: the Catholic settlement of Maryland (1632); New York, captured from the Dutch in 1664; and the Quaker colony of Pennsylvania (1681).

The French represented yet another model of settlement and interaction, somewhat akin to the Portuguese in Asia and Africa. While the Spanish incorporated the large populations of pre-existing empires and the English expelled indigenous groups to provide agricultural land for their numerous colonists, the French focused on establishing trade and diplomatic relations with tribes that remained largely autonomous. In 1605 the French founded the settlement of Port-Royal on the Bay of Fundy in Acadia, as a base for fishing and the fur trade. In the following years, under the leadership of Samuel de Champlain, the French moved west into the

**< MAP 18.4   Seventeenth-Century Dutch Commerce**
Dutch wealth rested on commerce, and commerce depended on the huge Dutch merchant marine, manned by perhaps forty-eight thousand sailors. The fleet carried goods from all parts of the globe to the port of Amsterdam.

St. Lawrence River Valley, establishing the forts of Quebec (1608), Three Rivers (1634), and Montreal (1642). The French formed trade and military alliances with several indigenous nations, including the Montagnais, Hurons, and Algonquins, which allowed them to acquire valuable furs throughout the Great Lakes region. Contact with French traders, settlers, and missionaries resulted in devastating epidemics for their indigenous allies as well as increased political instability and violent conflict.

In the 1660s Louis XIV's government established direct royal control over New France (Canada) and tried to enlarge its population by sending colonists. Nevertheless, immigration to New Canada remained minuscule compared with the stream of settlers who came to British North America. The Jesuits, who were the most active missionary orders in New France, established a college in Quebec as early as 1635.

Following the waterways of the St. Lawrence River, the Great Lakes, and the Mississippi River, the French ventured into much of North America in the 1670s and 1680s. In 1673 the Jesuit Jacques Marquette and the merchant Louis Joliet sailed down the Mississippi as far as present-day Arkansas. In 1682 Robert de La Salle traveled the Mississippi to the Gulf of Mexico, opening the way for French occupation of Louisiana.

In the first decades of the seventeenth century, English and French captains also challenged Spain's hold over the Caribbean, seizing a number of islands. These islands acquired new importance after 1640, when the Portuguese brought sugar plantations to Brazil. Sugar and enslaved captives quickly followed in the West Indies (see "Sugar and Early Transatlantic Slavery" in Chapter 16), making the Caribbean plantations the most lucrative of all colonial possessions.

The northern European powers also expanded in Africa and Asia. During the seventeenth century, France and England—along with Denmark and other northern European powers—established fortified trading posts in West Africa as bases for purchasing slaves and in India and the Indian Ocean for spices and other luxury goods. Thus, by the end of the seventeenth century, a handful of European powers possessed overseas empires that truly spanned the globe.

## Mercantilism and Colonial Wars

**Mercantilism** was a collection of governmental policies for the regulation of economic activities by and for the state, with the aim of increasing state power. It derived from the idea that a state's international power was based on its wealth, specifically its supply of gold and silver. To accumulate wealth, a country always had to sell more goods abroad than it bought from foreign countries.

The economic policies of European states were driven by mercantilist theory. For example, Louis XIV's finance minister, Jean-Baptiste Colbert (1619–1683), followed mercantilist doctrine in enacting strict production regulations, increasing the number of guilds and encouraging foreign craftsmen to immigrate to France. He also abolished many domestic tariffs and raised tariffs on foreign products. These measures were intended to increase the quantity and quality of French exports and to discourage foreign imports.

Trade to and among European overseas possessions was also governed by mercantilist economic policy. The acquisition of colonies was intended to increase the wealth and power of the mother country, and to that end, European states imposed trading monopolies on their overseas colonies and trading posts. The mercantilist notion of a zero-sum game, in which any country's gain must come from another country's loss, led to hostile competition and outright warfare among European powers over their colonial possessions.

In England Oliver Cromwell established the first of a series of **Navigation Acts** in 1651, and the restored monarchy of Charles II extended them in 1660 and 1663. The acts required most goods imported into England and Scotland (Great Britain after 1707) to be carried on British-owned ships with British crews or on ships of the country producing the article. Moreover, these laws gave British merchants and shipowners a virtual monopoly on trade with British colonies. These economic regulations were intended to eliminate foreign competition and to encourage the development of a British shipping industry whose seamen could serve when necessary in the Royal Navy.

The Navigation Acts were a form of economic warfare against the Dutch, who were far ahead of the English in shipping and foreign trade in the mid-seventeenth century. In conjunction with three Anglo-Dutch wars between 1652 and 1674, the Navigation Acts seriously damaged Dutch shipping and commerce. By the late seventeenth century the Netherlands was falling behind England in shipping, trade, and settlement.

Thereafter France was England's most serious rival in the competition for overseas empire. France was continental Europe's leading military power. It was already building a powerful fleet and a worldwide system of rigidly monopolized colonial trade. In 1664 the French Crown founded the Company of the East Indies with hopes of competing with the Dutch for Asian trade. But the War of the Spanish Succession, the last of Louis XIV's many wars, tilted the balance in favor of England. The 1713 Peace of Utrecht forced France to cede its North American holdings in Newfoundland, Nova Scotia, and the Hudson Bay territory to Britain. Spain was compelled to give Britain control of its West African slave trade and to let Britain send one ship of merchandise into the Spanish colonies annually. These acquisitions primed Britain to take a leading role in the growing Atlantic trade of the eighteenth century, including the transatlantic slave trade (see Chapter 20). The treaty also banned the unification of France and Spain in order to protect the "balance of power" in Europe, the first time this phrase occurred in a peace treaty.

## People Beyond Borders

As they seized new territories, European nations produced maps proudly outlining their possessions. The situation on the ground, however, was often much more complicated than the lines on those maps would suggest. Many groups of people lived in the contested frontiers between empires, habitually crisscrossed their borders, or carved out niches within empires where they carried out their own lives in defiance of the official rules.

Restricted from owning land and holding many occupations in Europe, Jews were eager participants in colonial trade and established closely linked mercantile communities scattered across many different empires. Similarly, a community of Christian Armenians in Isfahan in the Safavid Empire (modern-day Iran) formed the center of a trade network extending from London to Manila and Acapulco (see "European Trade in Asia and the Islamic Powers' Response" in Chapter 17). Family ties and trust within these minority groups were a tremendous advantage in generating the financial credit and cooperation necessary for international commerce. Yet Jews and Armenians were minorities where they settled and vulnerable to persecution.

The nomadic Cossacks and Tartars who inhabited the steppes of the Don River basin that bordered the Russian and Ottoman Empires are yet another example of "in-between" peoples. The Cossacks and the Tartars maintained considerable political and cultural autonomy through the seventeenth century and enjoyed a degree of peaceful interaction. By the eighteenth century, however, both Ottoman and Russian rulers had expanded state control in their frontiers and had reined in the raiding and migration of nomadic steppe peoples. As their example suggests, the assertion of state authority in the seventeenth and eighteenth centuries made it progressively harder for all of these groups to retain autonomy from the grip of empire.

# The Russian Empire

**How did Russian rulers build a distinctive absolutist monarchy and expand into a vast Eurasian empire?**

Russia occupied a unique position among Eurasian states. With borders straddling eastern Europe and northwestern Asia, its development into a strong imperial state drew on elements from both continents. As in the Muslim empires in Central and South Asia and the Ming Dynasty in China, the expansion of Russia was a result of the weakening of the great Mongol and Timurid Empires. After declaring independence from the Mongols, the Russian tsars conquered a vast empire, extending through North Asia all the way to the Pacific Ocean. State-building and territorial expansion culminated during the reign of Peter the Great, who turned Russia toward the West by intervening in western European wars and politics and forcing his people to adopt elements of Western culture.

## Mongol Rule in Russia and the Rise of Moscow

In the thirteenth century the Mongols had conquered Kievan Rus, the medieval Slavic state that included most of present-day Ukraine, Belarus, and part of northwest Russia. For two hundred years the Mongols forced the Slavic princes to submit to their rule. The Mongols showed favor to the princes of the Grand Duchy of Moscow, a principality that emerged in the territory of the former Kievan Rus. The wealth and power they accrued from patronage by the Mongols allowed the princes of Moscow to surpass rival local rulers. Ivan III (r. 1462–1505), known as Ivan the Great, greatly expanded the principality of Moscow, westward toward the Baltic Sea and eastward to the Ural Mountains and the Siberian frontier.

By 1480 Ivan III was strong enough to declare the autonomy of Moscow. To legitimize his new position, Ivan and his successors borrowed elements of Mongol rule. They forced weaker Slavic principalities to render tribute and adopted Mongol institutions such as the tax system, postal routes, and census. Loyalty from the highest-ranking nobles, or boyars, helped the Muscovite princes consolidate their power.

Another source of legitimacy lay in Moscow's claim to the political and religious inheritance of the Byzantine Empire. After the empire's capital, Constantinople, fell to the Ottomans in 1453, the princes of Moscow saw themselves as heirs of the Byzantine caesars (emperors) and guardians of the Orthodox Christian Church. The marriage of Ivan III to the niece of the last Byzantine emperor further enhanced Moscow's assertion of imperial authority.

By the time of Ivan's death, a system of autocracy was already well developed in Muscovy. Derived from God, the ruler's power was limited only by religious precepts, not by laws or assemblies. The Russian tsar thus fulfilled claims to absolute power to a much greater extent than western European monarchs, who had to compromise and collaborate with elites in assemblies and other institutions.

## Building the Russian Empire

Developments in Russia took a chaotic turn with the reign of Ivan IV (r. 1533–1584), the famous Ivan the Terrible, who ascended to the throne at age three. His mother died when he was eight, leaving Ivan to suffer insults and neglect from the boyars at court. In 1547, at age sixteen, he pushed aside his advisers and had himself crowned "tsar of all Russia," the first Muscovite ruler to claim the title of *tsar*, the Russian term for the Roman and Byzantine caesars.

After the sudden death of his wife, Ivan began a campaign of persecution against those he suspected of opposing him. He executed members of leading boyar families, along with their families, friends, and servants. To replace them, Ivan created a new service nobility of several thousand men whom he rewarded with land to ensure their loyalty.

As landlords demanded more from the serfs who survived the persecutions, growing numbers of peasants fled toward recently conquered territories to the east and south. There they joined free groups and warrior bands, known as **Cossacks**, who had been living on the borders of Russian territory since the fourteenth century. Ivan responded by tying serfs ever more firmly to the land. Simultaneously, he ordered that urban dwellers be bound to their towns and jobs so that he could tax them more heavily. These restrictions checked the growth of the Russian middle classes and stood in sharp contrast to economic and social developments in western Europe.

Ivan's reign was successful in defeating the remnants of Mongol power, adding vast new territories to the realm, and laying the foundations for the huge multiethnic Russian Empire. In the 1550s, Ivan conquered the Muslim khanates of Kazan and Astrakhan and brought the fertile steppe region around the Volga River under Russian control. Ivan's efforts to expand to the west were less successful. His bid to secure control of Livonia, as a means of gaining access to the Baltic Sea, led to war with Sweden and the Grand Duchy of Lithuania. These conflicts encouraged Lithuania to formalize its ties to Poland with the Union of Lublin in 1569.

In the 1580s Cossacks fighting for the Russian state began the long conquest of Siberia. Because of the size and distance of the new territories, the Russian state did not initially seek to impose the Orthodox religion and maintained local elites in positions of honor and leadership, buying their loyalty with grants of land. In relying on cooperation from local elites and ruthlessly exploiting the common people, the Russians followed the pattern of the Spanish and other early modern European imperial states.

Following Ivan's death, Russia entered a chaotic period known as the Time of Troubles (1598–1613) that was triggered by a breakdown in dynastic succession and a severe famine in which up to one-third of the population perished. Political and social crisis led to civil war and an uprising of Cossacks and other groups supporting a contender for the throne. This breakdown in order allowed invading Polish-Lithuanian armies to occupy Moscow between 1610 and 1612. These threats brought the fractious Russian nobles together. An assembly of nobles elected the grandnephew of Ivan's wife, Michael Romanov (r. 1613–1645), the new hereditary tsar. They presented the election as an act of God, ensuring that the new tsar carried the same divine legitimacy as his predecessors.

With their legitimacy assured, the Romanov tsars, like their western European counterparts, made further achievements in territorial expansion and state-building. After a long war, Russia gained land to the west in Ukraine in 1667. By the end of the century it had completed the conquest of Siberia to the east. This vast territorial expansion brought Russian power to the Pacific Ocean and was only checked by the powerful Qing Dynasty. Like the French in Canada, the basis of Russian wealth in Siberia was furs, which the state collected by forced annual tribute payments from local peoples. Profits from furs and other natural resources, especially mining in the eighteenth century, funded expansion of the Russian bureaucracy and the army.

The growth of state power did nothing to improve the lot of the common people. In 1649 a new law code extended serfdom to all peasants in the realm, giving lords unrestricted rights over their serfs and establishing penalties for harboring runaways. Henceforth, Moscow maintained strict control of trade and administration throughout the empire.

The peace imposed by harsh Russian rule was disrupted in 1670 by a failed rebellion led by the Cossack Stenka Razin, who attracted a great army of urban poor and peasants. The ease with which Moscow crushed the rebellion by the end of 1671 testifies to the success of the Russian state in unifying and consolidating its empire.

## Peter the Great and Russia's Turn to the West

Heir to Romanov efforts at state-building, Peter the Great (r. 1682–1725) successfully created the Russian fiscal-military state. Peter built on the service obligations of Ivan the Terrible and his successors and continued their tradition of territorial expansion. His ambitions hinged on gaining access to the sea by extending Russia's borders to the Black Sea (controlled by the Ottomans) and to the Baltic Sea (dominated by Sweden).

Peter embarked on his first territorial goal by conquering the Ottoman fort of Azov in 1696 and quickly built Russia's first navy base nearby. In 1697 the tsar went on an eighteen-month tour of western European capitals. Peter was fascinated by foreign technology, and he hoped to forge an anti-Ottoman alliance to strengthen his hold on the Black Sea. Peter failed to secure a military alliance, but he

**Peter the Great** The compelling portrait above captures the strength and determination of the warrior-tsar in 1723, after more than three decades of personal rule. In his hand Peter holds the scepter, symbol of royal sovereignty, and across his breastplate is draped an ermine fur, a mark of honor. In the background are the battleships of Russia's new Baltic fleet and the famous St. Peter and St. Paul Fortress that Peter built in St. Petersburg. The image on the right portrays Peter dressed as a ship carpenter's apprentice during his incognito tour of western Europe. (tsar portrait: State Hermitage Museum, St. Petersburg, Russia/Bridgeman Images; carpenter's apprentice: Print Collector/Getty Images)

did learn his lessons from the growing power of the Dutch and the English. He also engaged more than a hundred foreign experts to return with him to Russia to help build the navy and improve Russian infrastructure.

To realize his second goal, Peter entered the Great Northern War (1700–1721) against Sweden. After a humiliating defeat at the Battle of Narva in 1700, Peter responded with measures designed to increase state power, strengthen his military, and gain victory. He required all nobles to serve in the army or in the civil administration—for life. Peter also created schools of navigation and mathematics, medicine, engineering, and finance to produce skilled technicians and experts. Furthermore, he established an interlocking military-civilian bureaucracy with fourteen ranks, and he decreed that everyone had to start at the bottom and work toward the top. He sought talented foreigners and placed them in his service. These measures gradually combined to make the army and government more powerful and efficient.

Peter also greatly increased the service requirements of commoners. He established a regular standing army of peasant-soldiers, drafted for life. In addition, he created special regiments of Cossacks and foreign mercenaries. To fund the army, taxes on peasants increased threefold during Peter's reign. Serfs were also arbitrarily assigned to work in the growing number of factories and mines that supplied the military.

In 1709 Peter's new war machine was able to crush Sweden's army in Ukraine at Poltava (Map 18.5). Russia's victory against Sweden was conclusive in 1721, and

**MAP 18.5   The Expansion of Russia, 1462–1689**
In little more than two centuries, Russia expanded from the small principality of Muscovy to an enormous multiethnic empire, stretching from the borders of western Europe through northern Asia to the Pacific.

Estonia and present-day Latvia came under Russian rule. The cost was high: warfare consumed 80 to 85 percent of all revenues. But Russia became the dominant power in the Baltic and very much a great European power.

After his victory at Poltava, Peter channeled enormous resources into building a new Western-style capital on the Baltic. The city of St. Petersburg was designed to reflect modern urban planning with wide, straight avenues; buildings set in a uniform line; and large parks. Each summer, twenty-five thousand to forty thousand peasants were sent to provide construction labor in St. Petersburg without pay.

There were other important consequences of Peter's reign. For Peter, modernization meant westernization, and both Westerners and Western ideas flowed into Russia for the first time. He required nobles to shave their heavy beards and wear Western clothing. He also required them to attend parties where young men and women would mix together and freely choose their own spouses. From these efforts a new elite class of Western-oriented Russians began to emerge.

Peter's reforms were unpopular with many Russians. For nobles, one of Peter's most detested reforms was the imposition of unigeniture — inheritance of land by one son alone. For peasants, the reign of the tsar saw a significant increase in the bonds of serfdom. Nonetheless, Peter's modernizing and westernizing of Russia paved the way for it to move somewhat closer to the European mainstream in its thought and institutions during the Enlightenment, especially under Catherine the Great (see "Enlightened Absolutism and Its Limits" in Chapter 19).

## Chapter Summary

Most parts of Europe experienced the first centuries of the early modern era as a time of crisis. Following the religious divides of the sixteenth-century Protestant and Catholic Reformations, Europeans in the seventeenth century suffered from economic stagnation, social upheaval, and renewed military conflict. Overcoming these obstacles, both absolutist and constitutional European states emerged from the seventeenth century with increased powers and more centralized control.

Monarchs in Spain, France, and Austria used divine right to claim they possessed absolute power and were not responsible to any representative institutions. Absolute monarchs overcame the resistance of the nobility both through military force and by confirming existing economic and social privileges. Poland-Lithuania, England, and the Netherlands defied the general trend toward absolute monarchy, adopting distinctive forms of constitutional rule.

As Spain's power weakened, other European nations bordering the Atlantic Ocean sought their own profits and glory from overseas empires, with England emerging in the early eighteenth century with a distinct advantage over its rivals. Henceforth, war among European powers would include conflicts over territories and trade in the colonies. European rulers' increased control over their own subjects thus went hand in glove with the expansion of European power in the world.

In Russia, Mongol conquest and rule set the stage for a harsh tsarist autocracy that was firmly in place by the time of the reign of Ivan the Terrible in the sixteenth century. The reign of Ivan and his successors saw a great expansion of Russian territory, laying the foundations for a huge multiethnic empire. Peter the Great forcibly turned Russia toward the West by adopting Western technology and culture.

## NOTES

1. Theodore K. Rabb, *The Struggle for Stability in Early Modern Europe* (Oxford: Oxford University Press, 1975), p. 10.
2. Simon Schama, *The Embarrassment of Riches: An Interpretation of Dutch Culture in the Golden Age* (New York: Alfred A. Knopf, 1987), pp. 165–170.

## MAKE CONNECTIONS LOOK AHEAD

The seventeenth century represented a difficult passage between two centuries of dynamism and growth in Europe. On one side lay the sixteenth century's religious enthusiasm and strife, overseas discoveries, rising populations, and vigorous commerce. On the other side stretched the eighteenth century's renewed population growth, economic development, and cultural flourishing. The first half of the seventeenth century was marked by harsh climate conditions and violent conflict across Europe and much of the world. Recurring crop failure, famine, and epidemic disease contributed to a stagnant economy and population loss. In the middle decades of the seventeenth century, the very survival of the European monarchies established in the Renaissance appeared in doubt.

With the re-establishment of order in the second half of the century, maintaining stability was of paramount importance to European rulers. While a few nations placed their trust in constitutionally limited governments, many more were ruled by monarchs proclaiming their absolute and God-given authority. Despite their political differences, most European states emerged from the period of crisis with shared achievements in state power, territorial expansion, and long-distance trade. In these achievements, they resembled the Qing in China, who also saw the consolidation of imperial authority in this period; by contrast, the Ottoman Empire recovered more slowly from the crises of the seventeenth century.

The eighteenth century was to see these power politics thrown into question by new Enlightenment aspirations for human society, which themselves derived from the inquisitive and self-confident spirit of the Scientific Revolution. These movements are explored in the next chapter. By the end of the eighteenth century demands for real popular sovereignty, colonial self-rule, and slave emancipation challenged the very bases of order so painfully achieved in the seventeenth century. Chapter 22 recounts the revolutionary movements that swept the late-eighteenth-century Atlantic world, while Chapters 25, 26, and 27 follow the story of European imperialism and the resistance of colonized peoples in Africa, Asia, and the Americas into the nineteenth century.

# Chapter 18 Review

## IDENTIFY KEY TERMS

Identify and explain the significance of each item below.

Protestant Reformation (p. 438)
Jesuits (p. 441)
moral economy (p. 443)
Thirty Years' War (p. 445)
fiscal-military state (p. 446)
absolutism (p. 446)
divine right of kings (p. 448)

constitutionalism (p. 452)
republicanism (p. 452)
Puritans (p. 453)
Bill of Rights of 1689 (p. 455)
mercantilism (p. 460)
Navigation Acts (p. 461)
Cossacks (p. 463)

## REVIEW THE MAIN IDEAS

Answer the focus questions from each section of the chapter.

1. How did the Protestant and Catholic Reformations change power structures in Europe and shape European colonial expansion? (p. 438)
2. What were the common crises and achievements of seventeenth-century European states? (p. 442)
3. What was absolutism, and how did it evolve in western and central Europe? (p. 446)
4. What were alternatives to absolutism in early modern Europe? (p. 452)
5. How did European nations compete for global trade and empire in the Americas and Asia? (p. 456)
6. How did Russian rulers build a distinctive absolutist monarchy and expand into a vast Eurasian empire? (p. 462)

## MAKE COMPARISONS AND CONNECTIONS

Analyze the larger developments and continuities within and across chapters.

1. This chapter has argued that, despite their political differences, rulers in absolutist and constitutionalist nations faced similar obstacles in the mid-seventeenth century and achieved many of the same goals. Based on the evidence presented here, do you agree with this argument? Why or why not?
2. Proponents of absolutism in western Europe believed that their form of monarchical rule was fundamentally different from and superior to what they saw as the "despotism" of Russia and the Ottoman Empire (Chapter 17). What was the basis of this belief, and how accurate do you think it was?
3. What common features did the Muslim empires of the Middle East and India (Chapter 17) share with European empires? How would you characterize interaction among these Eurasian empires?

## CHRONOLOGY

**ca. 1464–1591**   • Songhai Empire (Ch. 20)

**1501–1722**   • Safavid Empire in Persia (Ch. 17)

**1533–1584**   • Reign of Ivan the Terrible in Russia

**1556–1605**   • Akbar expands Mughal Empire (Ch. 17)

**1589–1610**   • Reign of Henry IV in France

**1598–1613**   • Time of Troubles in Russia

**1603–1867**   • Tokugawa Shogunate in Japan (Chs. 21, 26)

**1642–1649**   • English civil war, ending with the execution of Charles I

**1643–1715**   • Reign of Louis XIV in France

**1651**   • First of the Navigation Acts

**1652**   • East India Company settles Cape Town (Ch. 20)

**1653–1658**   • Oliver Cromwell's military rule in England (the Protectorate)

**1660**   • Restoration of English monarchy under Charles II

**1665–1683**   • Jean-Baptiste Colbert applies mercantilism to France

**1670–1671**   • Cossack revolt led by Stenka Razin

**1682–1725**   • Reign of Peter the Great in Russia

**1683–1718**   • Habsburgs push the Ottomans from Hungary

**1688–1689**   • Glorious Revolution in England

**1701–1713**   • War of the Spanish Succession

# 19

## New Worldviews and Ways of Life

### 1540–1790

**FROM THE MID-SIXTEENTH CENTURY ON, AGE-OLD PATTERNS OF** knowledge and daily life were disrupted by a series of transformative developments. In this period, scholars challenged, and eventually discarded, ancient frameworks for understanding the heavens. The resulting conception of the universe and its laws remained in force until Albert Einstein's discoveries in the first half of the twentieth century. Accompanied by new discoveries in botany, zoology, chemistry, and other domains, these developments constituted a fundamental shift in the basic framework for understanding the natural world and the methods for examining it known collectively as the "Scientific Revolution."

In the eighteenth century philosophers extended the use of reason from nature to human society. Self-proclaimed members of an "Enlightenment" movement, they wished to bring the same progress to human affairs that their predecessors had brought to the understanding of the natural world. The Enlightenment created concepts of human rights, equality, progress, and tolerance that still guide Western societies. At the same time, some Europeans used their new understanding of reason to proclaim their own superiority, thus rationalizing attitudes now regarded as racist and sexist. Despite these biases, European intellectual change drew on contact and exchange with non-European peoples, ideas, and natural organisms.

Changes in the material world encouraged the emergence of new ideas. With the growth of population, the revitalization of industry, and the creation of overseas empires and world trade networks, Europeans began to consume at a higher level. Feeding the growth of consumerism was the expansion of transatlantic trade and lower prices for colonial goods, often produced by enslaved people. During the eighteenth century ships crisscrossing the Atlantic circulated commodities, ideas, and people to all four continents bordering the ocean. As trade became more integrated and communication intensified, an Atlantic world of mixed identities and vivid debates emerged.

# The Scientific Revolution

**What revolutionary discoveries were made in the sixteenth and seventeenth centuries, and what was their global context?**

Building on developments in the Middle Ages and the Renaissance, tremendous advances in Europeans' knowledge of the natural world and techniques for establishing such knowledge took place between 1500 and 1700. Collectively known as the "Scientific Revolution," these developments emerged because many more people studied the natural world, using new methods to answer fundamental questions about the universe and how it operated. The authority of ancient Greek texts was replaced by a conviction that knowledge should be acquired by observation and experimentation and that mathematics could be used to understand and represent the workings of the physical world. By 1700 precise laws governing physics and astronomy were known, and a new emphasis on the practical uses of knowledge had emerged.

Hailed today as pioneers of a modern worldview, the major figures of the Scientific Revolution were for the most part devout Christians who saw their work as heralding the glory of creation and who combined older traditions of magic, astrology, and alchemy with their pathbreaking experimentation. Their discoveries took place in a broader context of international trade, imperial expansion, and cultural exchange. Alongside developments in modern science and natural philosophy, the growth of natural history in this period is now recognized by historians as a major achievement of the Scientific Revolution.

## The Muslim Contribution

Prior to the Scientific Revolution, learning flourished in many parts of the world. Between 750 and 950, Muslim scholars in the expanding Muslim world began translating the legacy of ancient Greek learning into Arabic, with the help of Christian and Jewish translators. The peaceful conditions and religious tolerance established by the Abbasid caliphate (750–1258) gave rise to a period of cultural flourishing known as the "Golden Age of Islam."

During this period, Muslim scholars thrived in cultural centers such as Baghdad, capital of the caliphate, and Córdoba, capital of Muslim Spain. They established the world's first institutions of higher learning, called *madrasas*, in Constantinople, Fez (Morocco), and Cairo, which were devoted to Islamic theology and law. In this fertile atmosphere, scholars surpassed the texts they had inherited in areas such as mathematics, physics, astronomy, and medicine. Arab and Persian mathematicians, for example, invented algebra, the concept of the algorithm, and decimal point notation, while Arab astronomers built observatories to collect celestial observations, and an Egyptian scholar, Ibn al-Haytham (d. 1042), revolutionized optics by demonstrating mathematically that light travels in straight lines.

Given the unsurpassed scientific and philosophical knowledge possessed by Arab and Muslim scholars in the tenth and eleventh centuries, one might have expected that modern science would have emerged in the Muslim world first. However, because the *madrasas* excluded study of the natural sciences, Muslim scholars did not benefit from institutions dedicated to the creation and dissemination of scientific knowledge. Thus, there was no cadre of students to carry on the work of the great scientific scholars patronized by Muslim rulers.

The re-establishment of stronger monarchies and the growth of trade in the High Middle Ages contributed to a renewal of learning in western Europe. As European scholars became aware of advances in knowledge made in Muslim territories, they traveled to Islamic lands in Iberia, Sicily, and the eastern Mediterranean to gain access to this knowledge. In the twelfth century these scholars translated many Greek texts into Latin, along with the commentaries of Arab scholars. With the patronage of kings and religious institutions, groups of scholars created universities in which these translated works, especially those of the ancient Greek philosopher Aristotle, dominated the curriculum.

As Europe recovered from the ravages of the Black Death in the late fourteenth and fifteenth centuries, the intellectual and cultural movement known as the Renaissance provided a crucial foundation for the Scientific Revolution. Scholars called humanists working in the wealthy city-states of Italy emphasized the value of classical education for creating a virtuous and civic-minded elite. The quest to restore the glories of the ancient past led to a new period of classical scholarship. The fall of Constantinople to the Ottomans in 1453 resulted in a great influx of little-known Greek works, as Christian scholars fled to Italy with their precious texts.

In this period, western European universities established new professorships of mathematics, astronomy, and natural philosophy. The prestige of the new fields was low, especially mathematics, which was reserved for practical problems but not used as a tool to understand the functioning of the physical world. Nevertheless, these professorships eventually enabled the union of mathematics with natural philosophy that was to be a hallmark of the Scientific Revolution.

## Scientific Thought to 1550

For medieval European scholars, philosophy was the path to true knowledge about the world, and its proofs derived from the authority of the ancients (as interpreted by Christian theologians) and their techniques of logical argumentation. Questions about the physical nature of the universe and how it functioned belonged to a minor branch of enquiry called natural philosophy, which was based primarily on the ideas of Aristotle, the great Greek philosopher of the fourth century B.C.E. According to the Christianized version of Aristotle, a motionless earth stood at the center of the universe and was encompassed by ten separate concentric crystal spheres in which were embedded the moon, sun, planets, and stars. Beyond the spheres was Heaven with the throne of God and the souls of the saved. Angels kept the spheres moving in perfect circles.

Aristotle's views also dominated thinking about physics and motion on earth. Aristotle had distinguished between the world of the celestial spheres and that of the earth—the sublunar world. The sublunar realm was made up of four imperfect, changeable elements: air, fire, water, and earth. Aristotle and his followers also believed that a uniform force moved an object at a constant speed and that the object would stop as soon as that force was removed. The great second-century Greek scholar Ptolemy amended Aristotle's physics by positing that the planets moved in small circles, called epicycles, each of which moved along a larger circle, or deferent. This theory accounted for the apparent backward motion of the planets (which in fact occurs as the earth passes the slower-moving outer planets or is passed by the faster-moving inner ones) and provided a surprisingly accurate model for predicting planetary motion.

Ptolemy's work also provided the basic foundation of knowledge about the earth. Rediscovered around 1410, his *Geography* presented crucial advances on medieval cartography by representing a round earth divided into 360 degrees with the major latitude marks. However, Ptolemy's map

**Model of Ptolemaic Astronomical System** This seventeenth-century brass model was used to demonstrate the Ptolemaic astronomical system, with the earth at the center and the sun, stars, and planets moving around it.
(Armillary sphere made by Adam Heroldt [fl. 1648]/Science Museum, London/ Bridgeman Images)

reflected the limits of ancient knowledge, showing only the continents of Europe, Africa, and Asia, with land covering three-quarters of the world.

## Astronomy and Physics

The first great departure from the medieval understanding of cosmology was the work of the German-Polish astronomer Nicolaus Copernicus (1473–1543). Copernicus studied astronomy, medicine, and church law at the famed universities of Kraków, Bologna, Padua, and Ferrara before taking up a church position in Prussia. Copernicus came to believe that Ptolemy's cumbersome rules detracted from the majesty of a perfect creator. He preferred an idea espoused by some ancient Greek scholars: that the sun, rather than the earth, was at the center of the universe. Without questioning the Aristotelian belief in crystal spheres, Copernicus theorized that the planets, including the earth, revolved around a fixed sun. In 1543, the year of his death, Copernicus published his findings in *On the Revolutions of the Heavenly Spheres*.

One astronomer who partially agreed with the **Copernican hypothesis** was Tycho Brahe (TEE-koh BRAH-hee) (1546–1601) in Denmark. Brahe established himself as Europe's leading astronomer with his detailed observations of a new star that appeared suddenly in 1572 and shone very brightly for almost two years. The new star, which was actually a distant exploding star, challenged the idea that the heavenly spheres were unchanging and therefore perfect. Impressed by his work, the king of Denmark provided funds for Brahe to build the most sophisticated observatory of his day.

Upon the king's death, Brahe acquired a new patron in the Holy Roman emperor Rudolph II, and he built a new observatory in Prague. For twenty years Brahe and his assistants observed the stars and planets with the naked eye in order to create new and improved tables of planetary motions, dubbed the *Rudolphine Tables* in honor of his patron.

Brahe's assistant, Johannes Kepler (1571–1630), carefully re-examined his predecessor's notations and came to believe that they could not be explained by Ptolemy's astronomy. Abandoning the notion of epicycles and deferents, Kepler used Brahe's data to develop three revolutionary laws of planetary motion. First, he demonstrated that the orbits of the planets around the sun are elliptical rather than circular. Second, he demonstrated that the planets do not move at a uniform speed in their orbits. A planet accelerates when it is close to the sun and slows as it moves farther away from the sun. Finally, Kepler's third law stated that the time a planet takes to make its complete orbit is precisely related to its distance from the sun.

Kepler's contribution was monumental. Whereas Copernicus had used mathematics to describe planetary movement, Kepler proved mathematically the precise relations of a sun-centered (solar) system. He thus united for the first time the theoretical cosmology of natural philosophy with mathematics. His work demolished the old system of Aristotle and Ptolemy, and with his third law he came close to formulating the idea of universal gravitation. In 1627 he also published the *Rudolphine Tables*. Based on his own and Tycho Brahe's observations, it listed more than one thousand stars and included tables detailing the positions of the sun, moon, and planets.

While Kepler was unraveling planetary motion, a young Florentine named Galileo Galilei (1564–1642) was challenging Aristotelian ideas about motion on earth. Galileo measured the movement of a rolling ball across a surface, repeating the action again and again to verify his results. In his famous acceleration experiment, he showed that a uniform force — in this case, gravity — produced a uniform acceleration. He also achieved new insight into the principle of inertia, hypothesizing that an object would continue in motion forever unless stopped by some external force.

On hearing details about the invention of the telescope in Holland, Galileo made one for himself in 1609. He quickly discovered that, far from being a perfect crystal sphere, the moon is cratered with mountains and valleys, just like the earth. He then discovered the first four moons of Jupiter, which clearly demonstrated that Jupiter could not possibly be embedded in an impenetrable crystal sphere as Aristotle and Ptolemy maintained. This discovery provided concrete evidence for the Copernican theory.

## Newton's Synthesis

By about 1640 the work of Brahe, Kepler, and Galileo had been largely accepted by the scientific community despite opposition from religious leaders. But the new findings failed to explain what forces controlled the movement of the planets and objects on earth. That challenge was taken up by English scientist Isaac Newton (1642–1727).

Newton arrived at some of his most basic ideas about physics in 1666 at age twenty-four but was unable to prove them mathematically. In 1684, after years of studying optics, Newton returned to mechanics for eighteen intensive months. The result was his towering accomplishment, a single explanatory system that integrated the astronomy of Copernicus, as corrected by Kepler's laws, with the physics of Galileo and his predecessors. Newton did this through a set of mathematical laws that explain motion and mechanics. These laws were published in 1687 in Newton's *Mathematical Principles of Natural Philosophy* (also known as the *Principia*).

The key feature of the Newtonian synthesis was the **law of universal gravitation**. According to this law, each body in the universe attracts every other body in a precise mathematical relationship, whereby the force of attraction is proportional to the quantity of matter of the objects and inversely proportional to the square of the distance between them. The whole universe was unified in one majestic system. Matter moved on earth and throughout the heavens according to the same laws, which could be understood and expressed in mathematical terms.

## Natural History and Empire

At the same time that they made advances in astronomy and physics, Europeans embarked on the pursuit of knowledge about unknown geographical regions. Because they were the first to acquire a large overseas territorial empire, the Spanish pioneered these efforts. The Spanish Crown sponsored many scientific expeditions to gather information and specimens, out of which emerged new discoveries that reshaped the fields of botany, zoology, cartography, and metallurgy, among others.

Plants were a particular source of interest because they offered tremendous profits in the form of spices, medicines, dyes, and cash crops. King Philip II of Spain sent his personal physician, Francisco Hernández, to New Spain for seven years in the 1560s. Hernández filled fifteen volumes with illustrations of three thousand plants previously unknown in Europe. He interviewed local healers about the plants' medicinal properties, thereby benefiting from centuries of Mesoamerican botanical knowledge.

Other countries followed the Spanish example as their global empires expanded, relying both on official expeditions and the private initiative of merchants, missionaries, and settlers. Over time, the stream of new information about plant and animal species overwhelmed existing intellectual frameworks. Carl Linnaeus (1707–1778) of Sweden sent his students on exploratory voyages around the world and, based on their observations and the specimens they collected, devised a system of naming and classifying living organisms still used today (with substantial revisions).

## Magic and Alchemy

Recent historical research on the Scientific Revolution has focused on the contribution of ideas and practices that we no longer recognize as science, such as astrology and alchemy. Many of the most celebrated astronomers were also astrologers. Used as a diagnostic tool in medicine, astrology formed a regular part of the curriculum of medical schools.

Centuries-old practices of magic and alchemy also remained important traditions for natural philosophers. Early modern practitioners of magic strove to understand and control hidden connections they perceived among different elements of the natural world, such as that between a magnet and iron. The idea that objects possessed hidden or "occult" qualities that allowed them to affect objects at a distance was a particularly important legacy of the magical tradition.

Johannes Kepler exemplifies the interaction among these different strands of interest in the natural world. His duties as court mathematician included casting horoscopes for the royal family, and he based his own life on astrological principles. He also wrote at length on cosmic harmonies and explained elliptical motion through ideas about the beautiful music created by the combined motion of the planets. Another example of the interweaving of ideas and beliefs is Sir Isaac Newton, who was both intensely religious and also fascinated by alchemy, whose practitioners believed (among other things) that base metals could be turned into gold.

# Important Changes in Scientific Thinking and Practice

### What intellectual and social changes occurred as a result of the Scientific Revolution?

The Scientific Revolution was not accomplished by a handful of brilliant individuals working alone. Advancements occurred in many fields as scholars developed new methods to seek answers to long-standing problems with the collaboration and assistance of skilled craftsmen who invented new instruments and helped conduct experiments. These results circulated in an international intellectual community from which women were usually excluded.

## The Methods of Science

One of the keys to the achievement of a new worldview in the seventeenth century was the development of better ways of obtaining knowledge. The English politician and writer Francis Bacon (1561–1626) was the greatest early propagandist for the experimental method. Rejecting the Aristotelian and medieval method of using speculative reasoning to build general theories, Bacon called for a new approach to scientific inquiry based on direct observation, free from past preconceptions and prejudices. The researcher who wants to learn more about leaves or rocks, for example, should not speculate about the subject but should rather collect a multitude of specimens and then compare and analyze them to derive general principles. Bacon's contribution was to formalize the empirical method, which had already been used by Brahe and Galileo, into the general theory of inductive reasoning known as **empiricism**.

On the continent more speculative methods retained support. In 1619 the French philosopher René Descartes (day-KAHRT) (1596–1650) experienced a life-changing intellectual vision. Descartes saw that there was a perfect correspondence between geometry and algebra and that geometrical spatial figures could be expressed as algebraic equations and vice versa. A major step forward in mathematics, Descartes's discovery of analytic geometry provided scientists with an important new tool.

Descartes used mathematics to elaborate a new vision of the workings of the cosmos. Drawing on ancient Greek atomist philosophies, Descartes developed the idea that matter was made up of identical "corpuscles" (tiny particles) that collided together in an endless series of motions, akin to the working of a machine. All occurrences in nature could be analyzed as matter in motion, and, according to Descartes, the total "quantity of motion" in the universe was constant. Descartes's mechanistic philosophy of the universe depended on the idea that space was identical to matter and that empty space—a vacuum—was therefore impossible.

Descartes's greatest achievement was to develop his initial vision into a whole philosophy of knowledge and science. When experiments proved that sensory impressions could be wrong, Descartes decided it was necessary to doubt them and everything that could reasonably be doubted, and then, as in geometry, to use deductive reasoning from self-evident truths, which he called "first principles," to ascertain scientific laws. For Descartes these innate ideas included the existence of God and mathematical principles. Descartes's reasoning ultimately reduced all substances to "matter" and "mind"—that is, to the physical and the spiritual. His view of the world as consisting of two fundamental entities is known as Cartesian dualism.

Both Bacon's inductive experimentalism and Descartes's deductive mathematical reasoning had flaws. Bacon's inability to appreciate the importance of mathematics and his obsession with practical results illustrated the limitations of antitheoretical empiricism. Likewise, some of Descartes's positions demonstrated the inadequacy of rigid, dogmatic rationalism. He believed, for example, that it was possible to deduce the whole science of medicine from first principles. Although insufficient on their own, Bacon's and Descartes's extreme approaches are combined in the modern scientific method, which began to crystallize in the late seventeenth century.

## Medicine, the Body, and Chemistry

The Scientific Revolution, which began with the study of the cosmos, soon transformed the understanding of the human body. For many centuries the ancient Greek physician Galen's explanation of the body carried the same authority as Aristotle's account of the universe. According to Galen, the body contained four humors: blood, phlegm, black bile, and yellow bile. Illness was believed to result from an imbalance of these humors.

Swiss physician and alchemist Paracelsus (1493–1541) was an early proponent of the experimental method in medicine and pioneered the use of chemicals to address what he saw as chemical, rather than humoral, imbalances. Another experimentalist, Flemish physician Andreas Vesalius (1514–1564), studied anatomy by dissecting human bodies, often those of executed criminals. In 1543, the same year Copernicus published *On the Revolutions of the Heavenly Spheres*, Vesalius issued *On the Structure of the Human Body*. Its two hundred precise drawings revolutionized the understanding of human anatomy, disproving Galen. In 1628 the experimental approach also led English royal physician William Harvey (1578–1657) to discover the circulation of blood through the veins and arteries.

Robert Boyle (1627–1691) was among the first scientists to perform controlled experiments and publish details of them; he also helped improve a number of scientific instruments. For example, he built and experimented with an air pump, which he used to investigate the properties of air and create a vacuum, thus disproving Descartes's belief that a vacuum could not exist in nature. Based on these experiments, he formulated a new law in 1662, now known as Boyle's law, which states that the pressure of a gas varies inversely with volume. Boyle also hypothesized that chemical substances were composed of tiny mechanical particles, out of which all other matter was formed.

## Science and Religion

It is sometimes assumed that the relationship between science and religion is fundamentally hostile and that the pursuit of knowledge based on reason and proof is incompatible with faith. Yet during the Scientific Revolution most scholars were devoutly religious and saw their work as contributing to the celebration of God's glory. However, the concept of heliocentrism, which displaced the earth from the center of the universe, threatened the understanding of the place of mankind in creation as stated in Genesis. All religions derived from the Old Testament thus faced difficulties accepting the Copernican system. The leaders of the Catholic Church were initially less hostile than Protestant and Jewish religious leaders, but in the first decades of the sixteenth century Catholic attitudes changed. In 1616 the Holy Office placed the works of Copernicus and his supporters, including Kepler, on a list of books Catholics were forbidden to read.

**Popularizing Science** The frontispiece illustration of Fontenelle's *Conversations on the Plurality of Worlds* (1686) invites the reader to share the pleasures of astronomy with an elegant lady and an entertaining teacher. The drawing shows the planets revolving around the sun. (Roger-Viollet/The Image Works)

Out of caution Galileo Galilei silenced his views on heliocentrism for several years, until 1623 saw the ascension of Pope Urban VIII, a man sympathetic to the new science. However, Galileo's 1632 *Dialogue on the Two Chief Systems of the World* went too far. Published in Italian and widely read, it openly lampooned the Aristotelian view and defended Copernicus. In 1633 Galileo was tried for heresy by the papal Inquisition. Imprisoned and threatened with torture, the aging Galileo recanted. Thereafter, the Catholic Church became more hostile to science, a change that helped account for the decline of science in Italy (but not in Catholic France) after 1640.

## Science and Society

The rise of modern science had many consequences. First, it created a new social group — the international scientific community. Members of this community were linked by common interests and values as well as by journals and scientific societies. The personal success of scientists and scholars depended on making new discoveries, and as a result science became competitive. Second, as governments intervened to support and sometimes direct research, the new scientific community became closely tied to the state and its agendas. National academies of science were created under state sponsorship in London in 1660, Paris in 1666, Berlin in 1700, and later across Europe.

It was long believed that the Scientific Revolution was the work of exceptional geniuses. More recently, historians have emphasized the importance of skilled craftsmen in the rise of science, particularly in the development of the experimental method. Many artisans developed a strong interest in emerging scientific ideas, and, in turn, the practice of science in the seventeenth century relied heavily on artisans' expertise in making instruments and conducting precise experiments.

Some things did not change in the Scientific Revolution. For example, scholars willing to challenge received ideas about the natural universe did not question traditional inequalities between the sexes. Instead the emergence of professional science may have worsened the inequality in some ways. When Renaissance courts served as centers of learning, talented noblewomen could find niches in study and research. The rise of a scientific community raised new barriers because the universities and academies that furnished professional credentials did not admit women.

There were, however, a number of noteworthy exceptions. In Italy universities and academies did accept women. Across Europe women worked as makers of wax anatomical models and as botanical and zoological illustrators. They were also very much involved in informal scientific communities, attending salons, conducting experiments, and writing learned treatises.

# The Rise and Spread of the Enlightenment

### How did the Enlightenment emerge, and what were major currents of Enlightenment thought?

The political, intellectual, and religious developments of the early modern period that gave rise to the Scientific Revolution further contributed to a series of debates about key issues in late-seventeenth- and eighteenth-century Europe and the wider world that came to be known as the **Enlightenment**. By shattering the unity of Western Christendom, the conflicts of the Reformation brought old religious certainties into question; the strong states that emerged to quell the disorder soon inspired questions about political sovereignty and its limits. Increased movement of peoples, goods, and ideas within and among the states of Asia, Africa, Europe, and its colonies offered examples of shockingly different ways of life and values. Finally, the tremendous achievements of the Scientific Revolution inspired intellectuals to believe that true answers to all the questions being asked could be found through the use of rational and critical thinking. In a characteristically optimistic spirit, Enlightenment thinkers embraced the belief that fundamental progress was possible in human society as well as science.

## The Early Enlightenment

Loosely united by certain key questions and ideas, the European Enlightenment (ca. 1690–1789) was a broad intellectual and cultural movement that gained strength gradually and did not reach its maturity until about 1750. Its origins in the late seventeenth century lie in a combination of developments, including political opposition to absolutist rule, religious conflicts between Protestants and Catholics and within Protestantism, and the attempt to apply principles and practices from the Scientific Revolution to improve living conditions in human society.

A key crucible for Enlightenment thought was the Dutch Republic, with its traditions of religious tolerance and republican rule. When Louis XIV demanded that all Protestants convert to Catholicism, many Huguenots fled the country and resettled in the Dutch Republic. From this haven of tolerance, French Huguenots and their supporters began to publish tracts denouncing religious intolerance and suggesting that only a despotic monarch would deny religious freedom. Their challenge to authority thus combined religious and political issues.

These dual concerns drove the career of one important early Enlightenment writer, Pierre Bayle (1647–1706), a Huguenot who took refuge from government persecution in the Dutch Republic. Bayle critically examined the religious beliefs and persecutions of the past in his *Historical and Critical Dictionary* (1697). Demonstrating that human beliefs had been extremely varied and very often mistaken, he concluded that nothing can ever be known beyond all doubt, a view known as skepticism.

The Dutch Jewish philosopher Baruch Spinoza (1632–1677) was a key figure in the transition from the Scientific Revolution to the Enlightenment. Deeply inspired by advances in the Scientific Revolution, Spinoza sought to apply natural philosophy to thinking about human society. He borrowed Descartes's emphasis on rationalism and his methods of deductive reasoning but rejected the French thinker's mind-body dualism. Instead Spinoza came to espouse monism, the idea that mind and body are united in one substance and that God and nature were merely two names for the same thing. He envisioned a deterministic universe in which good and evil were merely relative values and human actions were shaped by outside circumstances, not free will. Spinoza was excommunicated by the Jewish community of Amsterdam for his controversial religious ideas, but he was heralded by his Enlightenment successors as a model of personal virtue and courageous intellectual autonomy.

German philosopher and mathematician Gottfried Wilhelm von Leibniz (1646–1716) refuted both Cartesian dualism and Spinoza's monism. Instead he adopted the idea of an infinite number of substances, or "monads," from which all matter is composed according to a harmonious divine plan. His *Theodicy* (1710) declared that ours must be "the best of all possible worlds" because it was created by an omnipotent and benevolent God.

Out of this period of intellectual turmoil came John Locke's *Essay Concerning Human Understanding* (1690), perhaps the most important text of the early Enlightenment. In this work Locke (1632–1704) set forth a new theory about how human beings learn and form their ideas. Whereas Descartes based his deductive logic on the conviction that certain first principles, or innate ideas, are imbued in humans by God, Locke insisted that all ideas are derived from experience. According to Locke, the human mind at birth is like a blank tablet, or tabula rasa, on which understanding and beliefs are inscribed by experience. Human development is therefore determined by external forces, like education and social institutions, not innate characteristics. Locke's essay contributed to the theory of **sensationalism**, the idea that all human ideas and thoughts are produced as a result of sensory impressions.

## The Influence of the Philosophes

Divergences among the early thinkers of the Enlightenment show that, while they shared many of the same premises and questions, the answers they found differed widely. The spread of this spirit of inquiry and debate owed a great deal to the work of the **philosophes**, a group of French intellectuals who proclaimed that they were bringing the light of knowledge to their fellow humans.

To appeal to the public and get around the censors, the philosophes wrote novels and plays, histories and philosophies, and dictionaries and encyclopedias, all filled with satire and double meanings to evade censorship and spread their message. One of the greatest philosophes, the baron de Montesquieu (mahn-tuhs-KYOO) (1689–1755), pioneered this approach in *The Persian Letters* (1721). This work consists of letters supposedly written by two Persian travelers, who as outsiders see European customs in unique ways and thereby allow Montesquieu a vantage point for criticizing existing practices and beliefs.

Disturbed by the growth in royal power under Louis XIV and inspired by the example of the physical sciences, Montesquieu set out to apply the critical method to the problem of government in *The Spirit of Laws* (1748). Arguing that forms of government were shaped by history, geography, and customs, Montesquieu identified three main types: monarchies, republics, and despotisms. A great admirer of the English parliamentary system, Montesquieu argued for a separation of powers, with political power divided among different classes and legal estates holding unequal rights and privileges. Decades later, his theory of separation of powers had a great impact on the constitutions of the United States in 1789 and of France in 1791.

The most famous philosophe was François-Marie Arouet, known by the pen name Voltaire (1694–1778). In his long career, Voltaire wrote more than seventy witty volumes, hobnobbed with royalty, and died a millionaire through shrewd speculations. His early career, however, was turbulent, and he was twice arrested for insulting noblemen. To avoid a prison term, Voltaire moved to England for three years, and there he came to share Montesquieu's enthusiasm for English liberties and institutions.

Returning to France, Voltaire became the lover of Gabrielle-Emilie Le Tonnelier de Breteuil, marquise du Châtelet (1706–1749), a gifted noblewoman. Madame du Châtelet invited Voltaire to live in her country house at Cirey in Lorraine (a move accepted by her husband, a tolerant man with lovers of his own). Passionate about science, she studied physics and mathematics and published the first French translation of Newton's *Principia*. Excluded from the Royal Academy of Sciences because she was a woman, Madame du Châtelet had no doubt that women's limited role in science was due to their unequal education.

While living at Cirey, Voltaire wrote works praising England and popularizing English scientific progress. Yet, like almost all the philosophes, Voltaire was a reformer, not a revolutionary. He pessimistically concluded that the best form of government was a good monarch, since human beings "are very rarely worthy to govern themselves." Nor did Voltaire believe in social and economic equality. The only realizable equality, Voltaire thought, was that "by which the citizen only depends on the laws which protect the freedom of the feeble against the ambitions of the strong."[1]

Voltaire's philosophical and religious positions were much more radical. Voltaire believed in God, but, like many Enlightenment thinkers, he rejected the established church in favor of **deism**, belief in a distant, noninterventionist deity. Above all, Voltaire and most of the philosophes hated religious intolerance, which they believed led to fanaticism and cruelty.

The strength of the philosophes lay in their number, dedication, and organization. Their greatest achievement was a group effort — the seventeen-volume *Encyclopedia: The Rational Dictionary of the Sciences, the Arts, and the Crafts*, edited by Denis Diderot (1713–1784) and Jean le Rond d'Alembert (1717–1783). Completed in 1765 despite opposition from the French state and the Catholic Church, the *Encyclopedia* contained seventy-five thousand articles by leading scientists, writers, skilled workers, and progressive priests. Science and the industrial arts were exalted, religion and immortality questioned. Intolerance, legal injustice, and out-of-date social institutions were openly criticized.

After about 1770 a number of thinkers and writers began to attack the philosophes' faith in reason and progress. The most famous of these was the Swiss intellectual Jean-Jacques Rousseau (1712–1778). Like other Enlightenment thinkers, Rousseau was passionately committed to individual freedom. Unlike them, however, he attacked rationalism and civilization as destroying, rather than liberating, the individual. Warm, spontaneous feeling, Rousseau believed, had to complement and correct cold intellect. Rousseau's ideals greatly influenced the early Romantic movement, which rebelled against the culture of the Enlightenment in the late eighteenth century.

Rousseau's contribution to political theory in *The Social Contract* (1762) was based on two fundamental concepts: the general will and popular sovereignty. According to Rousseau, the **general will** is sacred and absolute, reflecting the common interests of all people, who have displaced the monarch as the holder of sovereign power. The general will is not necessarily the will of the majority, however. At times the general will may be the authentic, long-term needs of the people as correctly interpreted by a farseeing minority.

## Enlightenment Movements Across Europe

The Enlightenment was a movement of international dimensions, with thinkers traversing borders in a constant exchange of visits, letters, and printed materials. The Republic of Letters, as this international group of scholars and writers was called, was a truly cosmopolitan set of networks stretching from western Europe to its colonies in the Americas, to Russia and eastern Europe, and along the routes of trade and empire to Africa and Asia.

Within this broad international conversation, scholars have identified regional and national particularities. Outside France, many strains of Enlightenment thought sought to reconcile reason with faith, rather than emphasizing the errors of religious fanaticism and intolerance. Some scholars point to a distinctive "Catholic Enlightenment" that aimed to renew and reform the church from within, looking to divine grace rather than human will as the source of social progress.

The Scottish Enlightenment, centered in Edinburgh, was marked by an emphasis on common sense and scientific reasoning. A central figure in Edinburgh was David Hume (1711–1776). Building on Locke's writings on learning, Hume argued that the human mind is really nothing but a bundle of impressions. These impressions originate only in sensory experiences and our habits of joining these experiences together. Since our ideas ultimately reflect only our sensory experiences, our reason cannot tell us anything about questions that cannot be verified by sensory experience (in the form of controlled experiments or mathematics), such as the origin of the universe or the existence of God. Hume further argued, in opposition to Descartes, that reason alone could not supply moral principles and that they derived instead from emotions and desires, such as feelings of approval or shame. Hume's rationalistic inquiry thus ended up undermining the Enlightenment's faith in the power of reason by emphasizing the superiority of the passions over reason in driving human behavior.

Hume's ideas had a formative influence on another major figure of the Scottish Enlightenment, Adam Smith (1723–1790). In his *Theory of Moral Sentiments*

(1759), Smith argued that social interaction produced feelings of mutual sympathy that led people to behave in ethical ways, despite inherent tendencies toward self-interest. Smith believed that the thriving commercial life of the eighteenth century was likely to produce civic virtue through the values of competition, fair play, and individual autonomy. In *An Inquiry into the Nature and Causes of the Wealth of Nations* (1776), Smith attacked the laws and regulations created by mercantilist governments that, he argued, prevented commerce from reaching its full capacity (see "Mercantilism and Colonial Wars" in Chapter 18). For Smith, ordinary people were capable of forming correct judgments based on their own experience and should therefore not be hampered by government regulations. Instead, the pursuit of individual self-interest in a competitive market would lead to rising prosperity and greater social equality. Smith's **economic liberalism** became the dominant form of economic thought in the early nineteenth century.

Inspired by philosophers of moral sentiments, like Hume and Smith, as well as by physiological studies of the role of the nervous system in human perception, the celebration of sensibility became an important element of eighteenth-century culture. *Sensibility* referred to an acute sensitivity of the nerves and brain to outside stimuli that produced strong emotional and physical reactions. Novels, plays, and other literary genres depicted moral and aesthetic sensibility as a particular characteristic of women and the upper classes. The proper relationship between reason and the emotions became a key question.

After 1760 Enlightenment ideas were hotly debated in the German-speaking states, often in dialogue with Christian theology. Immanuel Kant (1724–1804) was the greatest German philosopher of his day. Kant posed the question of the age when he published a pamphlet in 1784 titled *What Is Enlightenment?* He answered, "*Sapere Aude* (dare to know)! 'Have the courage to use your own understanding' is therefore the motto of enlightenment." He argued that if intellectuals were granted the freedom to exercise their reason publicly in print, enlightenment would surely follow. Kant was no revolutionary; he also insisted that in their private lives, individuals must obey all laws, no matter how unreasonable. Like other Enlightenment figures in central and east-central Europe, Kant thus tried to reconcile absolutism and religious faith with a critical public sphere.

Along with other German intellectuals, such as Johann Gottlieb Fichte, Kant introduced a new strain of philosophy that became known as German idealism. Inspired by the work of David Hume, Kant argued that, since our senses provide access only to the appearance of things and not to "things in themselves," a gap existed between reality and perception. However, Kant was not willing to accept the religious skepticism and moral relativism these ideas produced in Hume. Instead, he came to believe that humans possessed a shared framework for understanding sensory impressions that did correspond to empirical reality. For Kant, these realities included the existence of God and universal moral law. Kant thus attempted to reconcile rationalism and empiricism, on the one hand, with faith and ethics on the other.

Fichte and other German philosophers after Kant took his idealism even further, arguing that there could be no independent existence for objects outside of our consciousness of them. By placing severe constraints on the capacity of human reason to generate knowledge, German idealism represented a sharp blow to the optimistic rationalism of earlier Enlightenment thinkers.

Important developments in Enlightenment thought also took place in the Italian peninsula. After achieving independence from Habsburg rule (1734), the kingdom of Naples entered a period of intellectual flourishing. In northern Italy a central figure was Cesare Beccaria (1738–1794). His *On Crimes and Punishments* (1764) was a passionate plea for reform of the penal system that decried the use of torture, arbitrary imprisonment, and capital punishment and advocated the prevention of crime over its punishment.

# Key Issues of Enlightenment Debate

### How did Enlightenment thinkers address issues of cultural and social difference and political power?

The Scientific Revolution and the political and religious conflicts of the late seventeenth century were not the only developments that influenced European thinkers. Europeans' increased interactions with non-European peoples and cultures also helped produce new ideas. Enlightenment thinkers struggled to assess differences between Western and non-Western cultures, often adopting Eurocentric views, but sometimes expressing admiration for other societies. These same thinkers focused a great deal of attention on other forms of cultural and social difference, developing new ideas about race, gender, and political power. Although new "scientific" ways of thinking often served to justify inequality, the Enlightenment did see a rise in religious tolerance, a particularly crucial issue for Europe's persecuted Jewish population.

## Global Contacts

In the wake of the great discoveries of the fifteenth and sixteenth centuries, the rapidly growing travel literature taught Europeans that the peoples of China, India, Africa, and the Americas had very different beliefs and customs. Educated Europeans began to look at truth and morality in relative, rather than absolute, terms.

The powerful and advanced nations of Asia were obvious sources of comparison with the West. Seventeenth-century Jesuit missionaries served as a conduit for transmission of knowledge to the West about Chinese history and culture. The philosopher and mathematician Leibniz corresponded with Jesuits stationed in China, coming to believe that Chinese ethics and political philosophy were superior but that Europeans had equaled China in science and technology; some scholars believe his concept of monads was influenced by Confucian teaching on the inherent harmony between the cosmic order and human society.[2]

During the eighteenth century Enlightenment opinion on China was divided. Voltaire and some other philosophes revered China — without ever visiting or seriously studying it — as an ancient culture replete with wisdom and learning, ruled by benevolent absolutist monarchs. They enthusiastically embraced Confucianism as a natural religion in which universal moral truths were uncovered by reason. By contrast, Montesquieu and Diderot criticized China as a despotic land ruled by fear.

Attitudes toward Islam and the Muslim world were similarly ambivalent. As the Ottoman military threat receded at the end of the seventeenth century, some Enlightenment thinkers assessed Islam favorably. Others, including Spinoza, saw Islamic culture as superstitious and favorable to despotism. In most cases, writing about Islam and

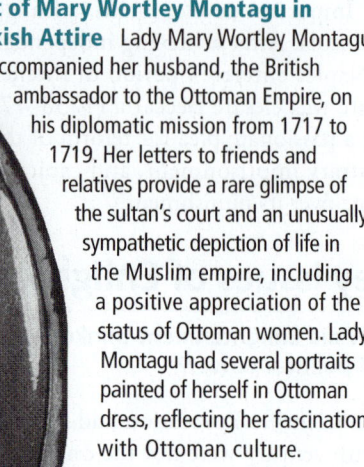

**Portrait of Mary Wortley Montagu in Turkish Attire** Lady Mary Wortley Montagu accompanied her husband, the British ambassador to the Ottoman Empire, on his diplomatic mission from 1717 to 1719. Her letters to friends and relatives provide a rare glimpse of the sultan's court and an unusually sympathetic depiction of life in the Muslim empire, including a positive appreciation of the status of Ottoman women. Lady Montagu had several portraits painted of herself in Ottoman dress, reflecting her fascination with Ottoman culture. (NYPL/Science Source/Getty Images)

Muslim cultures served primarily as a means to reflect on Western values and practices.

One writer with considerable personal experience in a Muslim country was Lady Mary Wortley Montagu, wife of the English ambassador to the Ottoman Empire. Her letters challenged prevailing ideas by depicting Turkish people as sympathetic and civilized. Montagu also disputed the notion that women were more oppressed in Ottoman society than at home in Europe.

Apart from debates about Asian and Muslim lands, the "discovery" of the New World and subsequent explorations in the Pacific Ocean also challenged existing norms and values in Europe. One popular idea, among Rousseau and others, was that indigenous peoples of the Americas were living examples of "natural man," who embodied the essential goodness of humanity uncorrupted by decadent society.

## New Definitions of Race

As scientists developed taxonomies of plant and animal species in response to discoveries in the Americas, they also began to classify humans into hierarchically ordered "races" and to speculate on the origins of perceived racial differences. The French naturalist Georges-Louis Leclerc, comte de Buffon (1707–1788), argued that humans originated with one species that then developed into distinct races due largely to climatic conditions.

Enlightenment thinkers such as David Hume and Immanuel Kant helped popularize these ideas. In *Of Natural Characters* (1748), Hume expressed his conviction that "negroes and in general all other species of men" were "naturally inferior to the whites."[3] In *On the Different Races of Man* (1775), Kant claimed that there were four human races, each of which derived from an original race. According to Kant, the closest descendants of the original race were the white inhabitants of northern Germany. (Scientists now know that humans originated in Africa.)

Using the word *race* to designate biologically distinct groups of humans was new in European thought. Previously, Europeans had grouped other peoples into "nations" based on their historical, political, and cultural affiliations, rather than on supposedly innate physical differences. While Europeans had long believed they were culturally superior to people from other nations, the new idea that racial difference was physical and innate rather than cultural taught them they were biologically superior as well. In turn, scientific racism helped legitimize and justify the tremendous growth of slavery that occurred during the eighteenth century.

Racist ideas did not go unchallenged. The abbé Raynal's *History of the Two Indies* (1770) fiercely attacked slavery and the abuses of European colonization. *Encyclopedia* editor Denis Diderot adopted Montesquieu's technique of criticizing European attitudes through the voice of outsiders in his dialogue between Tahitian villagers and their European visitors. Former slaves, like Olaudah Equiano and Ottobah Cugoano, published eloquent memoirs testifying to the horrors of slavery and the innate equality of all humans. These challenges to racism, however, were in the minority. More often, Enlightenment thinkers supported racial inequality.

## Women and the Enlightenment

The question of women's proper role in society and the nature of gender differences fascinated Enlightenment thinkers. Some philosophes championed greater rights and expanded education for women, claiming that the position and treatment of women were the best indicators of a society's level of civilization and decency. In the 1780s the marquis de Condorcet, a celebrated mathematician and contributor to the *Encyclopedia*, went so far as to urge that women should share equal rights with men. This was a rare position; most philosophes espoused modest reforms and did not challenge male superiority over women.

From the first years of the Enlightenment, women writers made crucial contributions both to debates about women's rights and to the broader Enlightenment discussion. In 1694 Mary Astell published *A Serious Proposal to the Ladies*, which encouraged women to aspire to the life of the mind and proposed the creation of a women's college. Astell also harshly criticized the institution of marriage. Echoing arguments made against the absolute authority of kings during the Glorious Revolution (see "Constitutional Monarchy" in Chapter 18), she argued that husbands should not exercise absolute control over their wives in marriage. Yet Astell, like most female authors of the period, was careful to acknowledge women's God-given duties to be good wives and mothers.

The explosion of printed literature during the eighteenth century brought significant numbers of women writers into print, but they remained a small proportion of published authors. In the second half of the eighteenth century, women produced some 15 percent of published novels, the genre in which they enjoyed the greatest success. They represented a much smaller percentage of nonfiction authors.[4]

If they remained marginal in the world of publishing, women played a much more active role in the informal dimensions of the Enlightenment: conversation, letter writing, travel, and patronage of artists and writers. A key element of their informal participation was as salon hostesses, or *salonnières* (sah-lahn-ee-EHRZ). **Salons**, which began in the early seventeenth century and reached their peak from 1740 to 1789, were weekly meetings held in wealthy households. They brought together writers, aristocrats, financiers, and noteworthy foreigners for meals and witty discussions of the latest trends in literature, science, and philosophy.

Women's prominent role as society hostesses and patrons of the arts and letters outraged some Enlightenment thinkers. According to Rousseau, women and men were radically different beings and should play diametrically opposed roles in life. Destined by nature to assume the active role in sexual relations, men were naturally suited for the rough-and-tumble worlds of politics and public life. Women's role was to attract male sexual desire in order to marry and have children. For Rousseau, French women's love for displaying themselves in public, attending salons, and pulling the strings of power was unnatural and had a corrupting effect on both politics and society. While many women enthusiastically espoused Rousseau's calls for a return to domesticity, a vocal minority emphatically disagreed.

Rousseau's emphasis on the natural laws governing women echoed a wider shift in ideas about gender during this period, as doctors, scientists, and philosophers increasingly agreed that women's essential characteristics were determined by their sexual organs and reproductive functions. This turn to nature, rather than tradition or scripture, as a means to understand human society had parallels in contemporary views on racial difference.

## Enlightened Absolutism and Its Limits

Enlightenment thinkers' insistence on questioning long-standing traditions and norms inevitably led to issues of power and politics. Most philosophes were political moderates, who distrusted the uneducated masses and hoped for reform, not revolution. As Enlightenment ideas reached from Parisian salons to the centers of government, some absolutist rulers, without renouncing their own absolute authority, took up the call to reform their governments in accordance with the rational and humane principles of the Enlightenment. The result was what historians have called the **enlightened absolutism** of the later eighteenth century. This concept was reflected in programs of reform in countries such as Prussia, Russia, and Austria.

Frederick II (r. 1740–1786) of Prussia, known as Frederick the Great, promoted religious tolerance and free speech and improved the educational system. Under his reign, Prussia's laws were simplified and torture of prisoners was abolished. In 1763, Prussia became the first country in the world to introduce compulsory public education at the elementary level. However, Frederick did not free the serfs of Prussia; instead he extended the privileges of the nobility over them.

Frederick's reputation as an enlightened prince was rivaled by that of Catherine the Great of Russia (r. 1762–1796). Catherine pursued three major goals. First, she worked hard to continue Peter the Great's efforts to bring the culture of western Europe to Russia. Catherine's second goal was domestic reform. Like Frederick, she restricted the practice of torture, allowed limited religious tolerance, and tried to improve education and local government. The philosophes applauded these measures and hoped more would follow.

These hopes were dashed by a massive uprising of serfs in 1733 under the leadership of a Cossack soldier named Emelian Pugachev. Although Pugachev was ultimately captured and executed, his rebellion shocked Russian rulers. After 1775 Catherine gave nobles absolute control of their serfs and extended serfdom into new areas. In 1785 she formally freed nobles from taxes and state service. Under Catherine the Russian nobility thus attained its most exalted position, and serfdom entered its most oppressive phase.

Catherine's third goal was territorial expansion. Her armies subjugated the last descendants of the Mongols and the Crimean Tartars and began the conquest of the Caucasus on the border between Europe and Asia. Her greatest coup was the partition of the Polish-Lithuanian Commonwealth, which took place in stages from 1772 to 1795 (Map 19.1). Poland did not regain its independence until the twentieth century.

Joseph II (r. 1780–1790), the Austrian Habsburg emperor, was perhaps the most sincere proponent of enlightened absolutism. Joseph abolished serfdom in 1781, and in 1789 he decreed that peasants could pay landlords in cash rather than through compulsory labor. When Joseph died at forty-nine, the Habsburg empire was in turmoil. His brother Leopold II (r. 1790–1792) canceled Joseph's radical edicts in order to re-establish order.

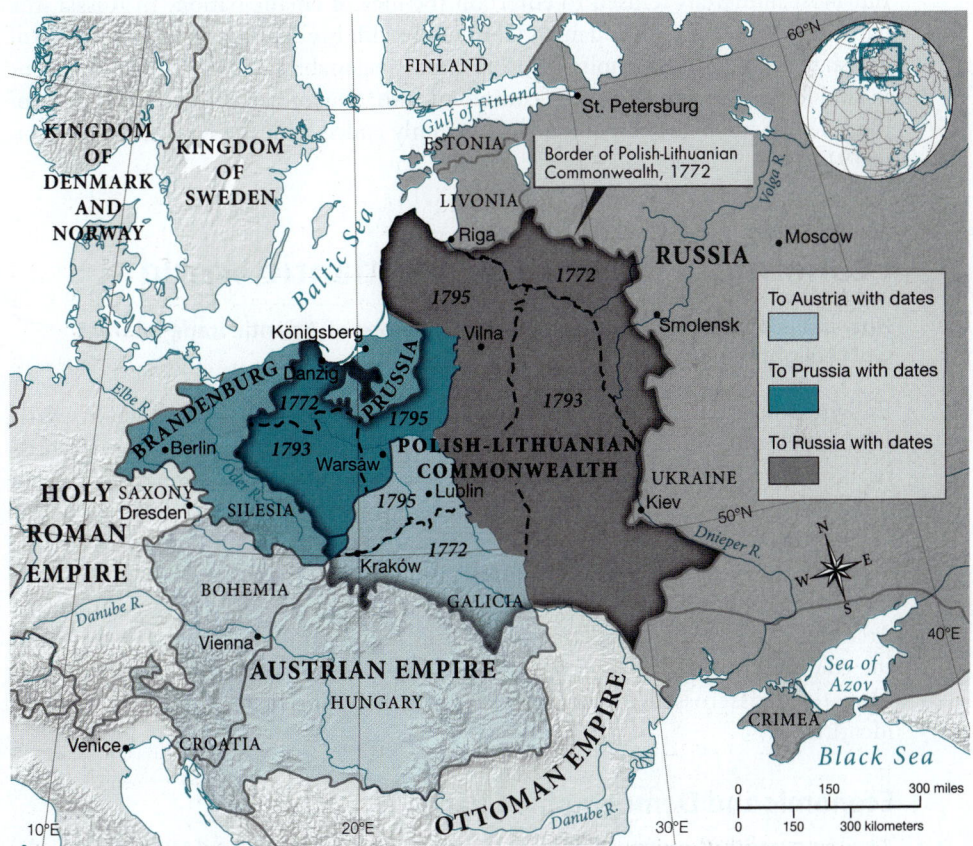

**MAP 19.1**   **The Partition of the Polish-Lithuanian Commonwealth, 1772–1795**
In 1772 the threat of war between Russia and Austria arose over Russian gains from the Ottoman Empire. To satisfy desires for expansion without fighting, Prussia's Frederick the Great proposed dividing parts of the Polish-Lithuanian Commonwealth among Austria, Prussia, and Russia. In 1793 and 1795 the three powers partitioned the remainder, and the commonwealth ceased to exist as an independent nation.

Perhaps the best example of the limitations of enlightened absolutism is the debates surrounding the possible emancipation of the Jews. For the most part, Jews in Europe were confined to tiny, overcrowded neighborhoods called *ghettoes*, a term that may have originated in the Jewish quarter of Venice with the Italian word *borghetto* meaning "little town." They were excluded by law from most occupations and could be ordered out of a kingdom at a moment's notice. For example, Catherine the Great expelled all Jews from Russia in 1727, an order she repeated in 1742.

In the eighteenth century an Enlightenment movement known as the **Haskalah** emerged from within the European Jewish community, led by the Prussian philosopher Moses Mendelssohn (1729–1786). Christian and Jewish Enlightenment philosophers, including Mendelssohn, began to advocate for freedom and civil rights for European Jews.

Arguments for tolerance won some ground, especially under Joseph II of Austria. But most monarchs refused to entertain the idea of emancipation. In Russia, the partition of the Polish-Lithuanian Commonwealth brought a very large number of Jewish subjects into the empire. In 1791 Catherine established the Pale of Settlement in land formerly belonging to the commonwealth. She forbade Jews to live outside of the Pale of Settlement, a requirement that only ended with the Russian Revolution of 1917.

# Economic Change and the Atlantic World

## How did economic and social change and the rise of Atlantic trade interact with Enlightenment ideas?

Enlightenment debates took place within a rapidly evolving material world. Agricultural reforms contributed to a rise in population that in turned fueled substantial economic growth in eighteenth-century Europe. A new public sphere emerged in the growing cities of Europe and its colonies in which people exchanged opinions in cafés, bookstores, and other spaces. A consumer revolution brought fashion and imported foods into the reach of common people for the first time.

These economic and social changes were fed by an increasingly integrated Atlantic economy that circulated finished European products, raw materials from the colonies, and enslaved people from Africa. Over time, the people, goods, and ideas that crisscrossed the ocean created distinctive Atlantic communities and identities.

## Economic and Demographic Change

The seventeenth century saw important gains in agricultural productivity in northwestern Europe that slowly spread throughout the continent. Using new scientific techniques of observation and experimentation, a group of scientists, government officials, and a few big landowners devised agricultural practices and tools that raised crop yields dramatically, especially in England and the Netherlands. These included new forms of crop rotation, better equipment, and selective breeding of livestock.

The controversial process of **enclosure**, fencing off common land to create privately owned fields, allowed a break with traditional methods but at the cost of reducing poor farmers' access to land.

Colonial plants also provided new sources of calories and nutrition. Introduced into Europe from the Americas—along with corn, squash, tomatoes, and many other useful plants—the potato provided an excellent new food source and offset the lack of fresh vegetables and fruits in common people's winter diet. The potato had become an important dietary supplement in much of Europe by the end of the eighteenth century.

Increases in agricultural productivity and better nutrition, combined with the disappearance of bubonic plague after 1720 and improvements in sewage and water supply, contributed to the tremendous growth of the European population in the eighteenth century. The explosion of population was a major phenomenon in all European countries, leading to a doubling of the number of Europeans between 1700 and 1835.

Population growth increased the number of rural workers with little or no land, and this in turn contributed to the development of industry in rural areas. The poor in the countryside increasingly needed to supplement their agricultural earnings with other types of work. **Cottage industry**, which consisted of manufacturing with hand tools in peasant cottages and work sheds, grew markedly in the eighteenth century, particularly in England and the Netherlands.

Despite the rise in rural industry, life in the countryside was insufficient to support the rapidly growing population. Many people thus left their small villages to join the tide of migration to the cities, especially after 1750. London and Paris swelled to over 500,000 people, while Naples and Amsterdam had populations of more than 100,000. It was in the bustling public life of these cities that the Enlightenment emerged and took root.

**Cottage Industry** Many steps went into making textiles. This 1791 illustration of the different tasks involved in spinning yarn is based on the artist's observations of linen manufacture in the north of Ireland. The yarn was spun on the wheel and then wound on the clock reel to measure it into "hanks" of set length. After being boiled in a pot over the fire and dried, the yarn was ready for weaving. (*Cottage Industry*, 1791/ British Library, London, UK/Bridgeman Images)

**MAP 19.2   The Atlantic Economy, 1701**

The growth of trade encouraged both economic development and military conflict in the Atlantic basin.
Four continents were linked together by the exchange of goods and slaves.

## The Atlantic Economy

European economic growth in the eighteenth century was spurred by the expansion of trade across the Atlantic Ocean. Commercial exchange in the Atlantic is often referred to as the triangle trade, designating a three-way transport of goods: European commodities to Africa; captured and enslaved Africans to the colonies; and colonial goods back to Europe. This model highlights some of the most important flows of trade but significantly over-simplifies the picture. For example, a brisk intercolonial trade existed, with the Caribbean slave colonies importing food from other American colonies in exchange for sugar and slaves (Map 19.2). Moreover, the Atlantic economy was inextricably linked to trade with the Indian and Pacific Oceans. The rising economic and political power of Europeans in the eighteenth century drew on connections established between the long-standing Asian and Atlantic trade worlds.

Over the course of the eighteenth century, the economies of European nations bordering the Atlantic Ocean relied more and more on colonial exports. In England sales to the mainland colonies of North America and the West Indian sugar islands soared from £500,000 to £4 million (Figure 19.1). Exports to England's colonies in Ireland and India also rose substantially from 1700 to 1800.

At the core of this Atlantic world was the misery and profit of the Atlantic slave trade (see "The African Slave Trade" in Chapter 20). The brutal practice intensified dramatically after 1700 and especially after 1750 with the growth of trade and the increase in demand for slave-produced goods. English dominance of the slave trade provided another source of large profits to the home country.

The French also profited enormously from colonial trade in the eighteenth century, even after losing their vast North American territories to England in 1763. The Caribbean colonies of Saint-Domingue (modern-day Haiti), Martinique, and Guadeloupe provided immense fortunes from slave-based plantation agriculture. The wealth generated from colonial trade fostered the confidence of the merchant classes in Nantes, Bordeaux, and other large cities, and merchants soon joined other elite groups clamoring for more political power.

The third major player in the Atlantic economy, Spain, also

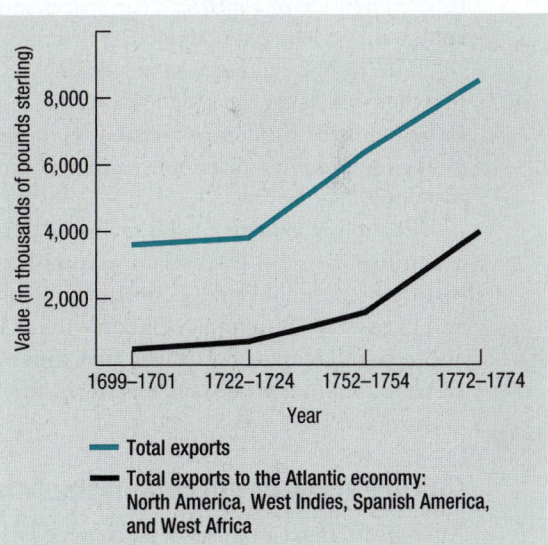

**FIGURE 19.1** **Exports of English Manufactured Goods, 1700–1774**
While trade between England and Europe stagnated after 1700, English exports to Africa and the Americas boomed and greatly stimulated English economic development.
(Source: Data from R. Davis, "English Foreign Trade, 1700–1774," *Economic History Review*, 2nd ser., 15 [1962]: 302–303.)

saw its colonial fortunes improve during the eighteenth century. Its mercantilist goals were boosted by a recovery in silver production. Spanish territory in North America expanded significantly in the second half of the eighteenth century. At the close of the Seven Years' War (1756–1763) (see "The Seven Years' War" in Chapter 22), Spain gained Louisiana from the French, and its influence extended westward all the way to northern California through the efforts of Spanish missionaries and ranchers.

Conflict among European powers in the late seventeenth century led to the rise of privateers in the Caribbean and elsewhere in the Atlantic world; these were ships sanctioned by their home government to attack and pillage those of enemy powers. Privateers operated with some semblance of legality, whereas the many pirates active in the Caribbean were outlaws subject to brutal punishment. The late seventeenth and early eighteenth centuries constituted the "golden age" of piracy, drawing poor European sailors and escaped slaves into the dangerous but lucrative activity.

## Urban Life and the Public Sphere

Urban life in the Atlantic world gave rise to new institutions and practices that encouraged the spread of Enlightenment thought. From about 1700 to 1789 the production and consumption of books grew significantly. Lending libraries, book-shops, cafés, salons, and Masonic lodges provided spaces in which urban people debated new ideas. Together these spaces and institutions helped create a new **public sphere** that celebrated open debate informed by critical reason.

The public sphere was an idealized space where members of society came together to discuss the social, economic, and political issues of the day. Although Enlightenment thinkers addressed their ideas to educated and prosperous readers, even poor and illiterate people learned about such issues as they were debated at the marketplace or tavern.

Economic growth in the second half of the eighteenth century also enabled a significant rise in the consumption of finished goods and new foodstuffs that historians have labeled a "consumer revolution." A boom in textile production and cheap reproductions of luxury items meant that the common people could afford to follow fashion for the first time. Colonial trade made previously expensive and rare foodstuffs, such as sugar, tea, coffee, chocolate, and tobacco, widely available.

## Culture and Community in the Atlantic World

As contacts among the Atlantic coasts of the Americas, Africa, and Europe became more frequent, and as European settlements grew into well-established colonies, new identities and communities emerged. The term **Creole** referred to people of Spanish or other European ancestry born in the Americas. Wealthy Creoles throughout the Atlantic colonies prided themselves on following European ways of life.

Over time, however, the colonial elite came to feel that their circumstances gave them different interests and characteristics from people of their home countries. Creoles adopted native foods, like chocolate, chili peppers, and squash, and sought relief from tropical disease in native remedies. Also, they began to turn against restrictions from their home countries: Creole traders and planters, along with their counterparts in English colonies, increasingly resented the regulations and taxes imposed by colonial bureaucrats, and such resentment would eventually lead to revolutions against colonial powers (see Chapter 22).

Not all Europeans in the colonies were wealthy or well educated. Numerous poor and lower-middle-class whites worked as clerks, shopkeepers, craftsmen, and laborers. With the exception of the English colonies of North America, white Europeans made up a minority of the population, outnumbered by indigenous peoples in Spanish America and, in the Caribbean, by the growing numbers of enslaved people of African descent. Since most European migrants were men, much of the colonial population of the Atlantic world descended from sexual exploitation of indigenous or African women by European men. Colonial attempts to identify and control racial categories profoundly influenced developing Enlightenment thought on racial differences.

In the Spanish and French Caribbean, as in Brazil, many slave masters acknowledged and freed their mixed-race children, leading to sizable populations of free people of color. In the second half of the eighteenth century, the prosperity of some free people of color brought a backlash from the white population of Saint-Domingue in the form of new race laws prohibiting nonwhites from marrying whites and forcing them to adopt distinctive attire. In the British colonies of the Caribbean and the southern mainland, by contrast, masters tended to leave their mixed-race progeny in slavery, maintaining a stark discrepancy between free whites and enslaved people of color.[5]

The identities inspired by the Atlantic world were equally complex. In some ways, the colonial encounter helped create new and more fixed forms of identity. Inhabitants of European nations whose loyalties had been to their towns and regions came to see themselves as "Spanish" or "English" when they crossed the Atlantic; similarly, colonial governments imposed the identity of "Indian" and "African" on peoples with vastly different linguistic, cultural, and political origins. The result was the creation of new Creole communities that melded cultural and social elements of various groups of origin with the new European cultures.

Mixed-race people represented complex mixtures of indigenous, African, and European ancestry, so their status was ambiguous. Spanish administrators applied purity of blood (*limpieza de sangre*) laws—originally used to exclude Jews and Muslims during the reconquista—to indigenous and African peoples. Some mixed-race people sought to enter Creole society and obtain its many official and unofficial privileges by passing as white. Over time, where they existed in any number, mestizos and free people of color established their own communities and social hierarchies based on wealth, family connections, occupation, and skin color.

Restricted from owning land and holding many occupations in Europe, Jews were eager participants in the new Atlantic economy and established a network of mercantile communities along its trade routes. As in the Old World, Jews in European colonies faced discrimination. They were considered to be white Europeans and thus ineligible for slavery, but they did not enjoy equal status with Christians. The status of Jews adds one more element to the complexity of Atlantic identities.

## The Atlantic Enlightenment

The colonies of British North America were deeply influenced by the Scottish Enlightenment, with its emphasis on pragmatic approaches to the problems of life. Following the Scottish model, leaders in the colonies adopted a moderate, "commonsense" version of the Enlightenment that emphasized self-improvement and ethical conduct. In most cases, this version of the Enlightenment was perfectly compatible with religion and was chiefly spread through the growing colleges and universities of the colonies.

Northern Enlightenment thinkers often depicted Spain and its American colonies as the epitome of the superstition and barbarity they contested. Nonetheless, the Bourbon dynasty that took power in Spain in the early eighteenth century followed its own course of enlightened absolutism, just like its counterparts in the rest of Europe. Under King Carlos III (r. 1759–1788) and his son Carlos IV (r. 1788–1808), Spanish administrators attempted to strengthen colonial rule and improve government efficiency. Enlightened administrators debated the status of indigenous peoples and whether it would be better for these peoples if they maintained their distinct legal status or were integrated into Spanish society.

Educated Creoles were well aware of the new currents of thought, and the universities, newspapers, and salons of Spanish America produced their own reform ideas. As in other European colonies, one effect of Enlightenment thought was to encourage Creoles to criticize the policies of the mother country and aspire toward greater autonomy.

# Chapter Summary

Decisive breakthroughs in astronomy and physics in the seventeenth century demolished the medieval synthesis of Aristotelian philosophy and Christian theology. The impact of these scientific breakthroughs on intellectual life was enormous, nurturing a new critical attitude in many disciplines. In addition, an international scientific community arose, and state-sponsored academies, which were typically closed to women, advanced scientific research.

Believing that all aspects of life were open to debate and skepticism, Enlightenment thinkers asked challenging questions about religious tolerance, political power, and racial and sexual difference. They drew inspiration from the new peoples and cultures encountered by Europeans and devised new ideas about race as a scientific and biological category. The ideas of the Enlightenment inspired absolutist rulers in central and eastern Europe, but real reforms were limited.

In the second half of the eighteenth century agricultural reforms helped produce tremendous population growth. Economic growth and urbanization favored the spread of Enlightenment thought by producing a public sphere in which ideas could be debated. The expansion of transatlantic trade made economic growth possible, as did the lowering of prices on colonial goods due to the growth of enslaved labor. Atlantic trade involved the exchange of commodities among Europe, Africa, and the Americas, but it was also linked with trade in the Indian and Pacific Oceans. The movement of people and ideas across the Atlantic helped shape the identities of colonial inhabitants.

## NOTES

1. Quoted in G. L. Mosse et al., eds., *Europe in Review* (Chicago: Rand McNally, 1964), p. 156.
2. D. E. Mungello, *The Great Encounter of China and the West, 1500–1800*, 2d ed. (Lanham, Md.: Rowman & Littlefield, 2005), p. 98.
3. Quoted in Emmanuel Chukwudi Eze, ed., *Race and the Enlightenment: A Reader* (Oxford: Blackwell, 1997), p. 33.
4. Aurora Wolfgang, *Gender and Voice in the French Novel, 1730–1782* (Aldershot, U.K.: Ashgate, 2004), p. 8.
5. Orlando Patterson, *Slavery and Social Death* (Cambridge, Mass.: Harvard University Press, 1982), p. 255.

## MAKE CONNECTIONS   LOOK AHEAD

Hailed as the origin of modern thought, the Scientific Revolution must also be seen as a product of its past. With curriculum drawn from Islamic cultural achievements, medieval universities gave rise to important new scholarship in mathematics and natural philosophy. Natural philosophers pioneered new methods of explaining and observing nature while drawing on centuries-old traditions of astrology, alchemy, and magic. A desire to control and profit from empire led the Spanish, followed by their European rivals, to explore and catalogue the flora and fauna of their American colonies. These efforts resulted in new frameworks in natural history.

Enlightenment ideas of the eighteenth century were a similar blend of past and present, progressive and traditional, inward-looking and cosmopolitan. Enlightenment thinkers advocated universal rights and liberties but also preached the biological inferiority of non-Europeans and women. Their principles often served as much to bolster absolutist regimes as to inspire revolutionaries to fight for human rights.

At the end of the eighteenth century, new notions of progress and social improvement would drive Europeans to embark on world-changing revolutions in politics and industry (see Chapters 22 and 23). These revolutions provided the basis for modern democracy and unprecedented scientific advancement. Yet some critics have seen a darker side. For them, the mastery over nature enabled by the Scientific Revolution now threatens to overwhelm the earth's fragile equilibrium, and the Enlightenment belief in the universal application of reason can lead to intolerance of other people's spiritual, cultural, and political values.

As the era of European exploration and conquest gave way to empire building, the eighteenth century witnessed increased consolidation of global markets and bitter competition among Europeans. The eighteenth-century Atlantic world thus tied the shores of Europe, the Americas, and Africa in a web of commercial and human exchange, including the horrors of slavery, discussed in Chapter 20. The Atlantic world also maintained strong ties with trade in the Pacific and the Indian Ocean.

# Chapter 19 Review

## IDENTIFY KEY TERMS

**Identify and explain the significance of each item below.**

Copernican hypothesis (p. 474)

law of universal gravitation (p. 475)

empiricism (p. 477)

Enlightenment (p. 480)

sensationalism (p. 481)

philosophes (p. 481)

deism (p. 482)

general will (p. 483)

economic liberalism (p. 484)

salons (p. 487)

enlightened absolutism (p. 488)

Haskalah (p. 490)

enclosure (p. 491)

cottage industry (p. 491)

public sphere (p. 494)

Creoles (p. 494)

## REVIEW THE MAIN IDEAS

**Answer the focus questions from each section of the chapter.**

1. What revolutionary discoveries were made in the sixteenth and seventeenth centuries, and what was their global context? (p. 471)

2. What intellectual and social changes occurred as a result of the Scientific Revolution? (p. 476)

3. How did the Enlightenment emerge, and what were major currents of Enlightenment thought? (p. 480)

4. How did Enlightenment thinkers address issues of cultural and social difference and political power? (p. 485)

5. How did economic and social change and the rise of Atlantic trade interact with Enlightenment ideas? (p. 490)

## MAKE COMPARISONS AND CONNECTIONS

**Analyze the larger developments and continuities within and across chapters.**

1. How did medieval and Renaissance developments contribute to the Scientific Revolution? Should the Scientific Revolution be seen as a sharp break with the past or as the culmination of long-term, gradual change?

2. The eighteenth century was the period of the European Enlightenment, which celebrated tolerance and human liberty. Paradoxically, it was also the era of a tremendous increase in slavery, which brought suffering and death to millions. How can you explain this paradox?

3. How did developments in population, global trade, and intellectual life affect each other in the eighteenth century? How and why did developments in one region affect other regions?

## CHRONOLOGY

| | |
|---|---|
| **1453** | • Ottoman conquest of Constantinople (Ch. 17) |
| **ca. 1500–1700** | • Scientific Revolution |
| **1501–1722** | • Safavid Empire in Persia (Ch. 17) |
| **1582–1610** | • Jesuit Matteo Ricci in China (Ch. 21) |
| **ca. 1600–1789** | • French salons led by elite women |
| **1644–1911** | • Manchus establish Qing Dynasty in China (Ch. 21) |
| **ca. 1690–1789** | • Enlightenment |
| **ca. 1700–1789** | • Growth of book publishing |
| **1738–1756** | • Major famine in West Africa (Ch. 20) |
| **1740–1786** | • Reign of Frederick the Great of Prussia |
| **1756–1763** | • Seven Years' War (Ch. 22) |
| **1762–1796** | • Reign of Catherine the Great of Russia |
| **1765** | • Philosophes publish *Encyclopedia: The Rational Dictionary of the Sciences, the Arts, and the Crafts* |
| **1770** | • Cook claims land in Australia for Britain (Ch. 26) |
| **1780–1790** | • Reign of Joseph II of Austria |
| **1780–1820** | • Peak of transatlantic slave trade (Ch. 20) |
| **1789–1807** | • Ottoman ruler Selim III introduces reforms (Ch. 25) |
| **1791** | • Establishment of the Pale of Settlement |

# 20

## Africa and the World

### 1400–1800

**AFRICAN STATES AND SOCIETIES OF THE EARLY MODERN PERIOD—** from the fifteenth through the eighteenth centuries—included a wide variety of languages, cultures, political systems, and levels of economic development. Kingdoms and stateless societies coexisted throughout Africa, from small Senegambian villages to the Songhai kingdom and its renowned city of Timbuktu in West Africa, and from the Christian state of Ethiopia to the independent Swahili city-states along the East African coast. By the fifteenth century Africans had developed a steady rhythm of contact and exchange. Across the vast Sahara, trade goods and knowledge passed back and forth from West Africa to North Africa, and beyond to Europe and the Middle East. The same was true in East Africa, where Indian Ocean traders touched up and down the African coast to deliver goods from Arabia, India, and Asia and to pick up the ivory, gold, spices, and other products representing Africa's rich natural wealth. In the interior as well, extensive trading networks linked African societies across the vast continent.

Modern European intrusion into Africa beginning in the fifteenth century profoundly affected these diverse societies and ancient trading networks. The intrusion led to the transatlantic slave trade, one of the greatest forced migrations in world history, through which Africa made a substantial, though involuntary, contribution to the building of the West's industrial civilization. In seventeenth-century Europe a growing, seemingly insatiable desire for sugar resulted in an increasing demand for slave labor in South America and the West Indies, where sugar was produced. In the eighteenth century Western technological changes created a demand for cotton and other crops that required extensive human labor, thus intensifying the West's "need" for African slaves.

# West Africa in the Fifteenth and Sixteenth Centuries

**What types of economic, social, and political structures were found in the kingdoms and states along the west coast and in the Sudan?**

In mid-fifteenth-century Africa, Benin (buh-NEEN) and a number of other kingdoms flourished along the two-thousand-mile west coast between Senegambia and the northeastern shore of the Gulf of Guinea. Further inland, in the region of the Sudan (soo-DAN), the kingdoms of Songhai (Song-GAH-ee), Kanem-Bornu (KAH-nuhm BOR-noo), and Hausaland benefited from the trans-Saharan caravan trade, which along with goods brought Islamic culture to the region. Stateless societies

**The Oba of Benin** The oba's palace walls were decorated with bronze plaques that date from about the sixteenth to eighteenth centuries. This plaque vividly conveys the oba's power, majesty, and authority. The two attendants holding his arms also imply that the oba needs the support of his people. The oba's legs are mudfish, which represent fertility, peace, well-being, and prosperity, but their elongation, suggesting electric eels, relates the oba's terrifying and awesome power to the eel's jolting shock. (National Museum, Lagos, Nigeria/ photo: André Held/akg-images)

such as those in the region of Senegambia (modern-day Senegal and the Gambia) existed alongside these more centralized states. Despite their political differences and whether they were agricultural, pastoral, or a mixture of both, West African cultures all faced the challenges presented by famine, disease, an often harsh environment and fickle climate, and the slave trade.

## The West Coast: Senegambia and Benin

The Senegambian states possessed a homogeneous culture and a common history. For centuries Senegambia—named for the Senegal and Gambia Rivers—served as an important entrepôt for desert caravan contact with North African and Middle Eastern Islamic civilizations (Map 20.1). Through the transatlantic slave trade, Senegambia came into contact with Europe and the Americas. Thus Senegambia felt the impact of Islamic culture to the north and of European influences from the maritime West.

The Senegambian peoples spoke Wolof, Serer, and Pulaar, all belonging to the West African language group. Both the Wolof-speakers and the Serer-speakers had clearly defined social classes: royalty, nobility, warriors, peasants, low-caste artisans

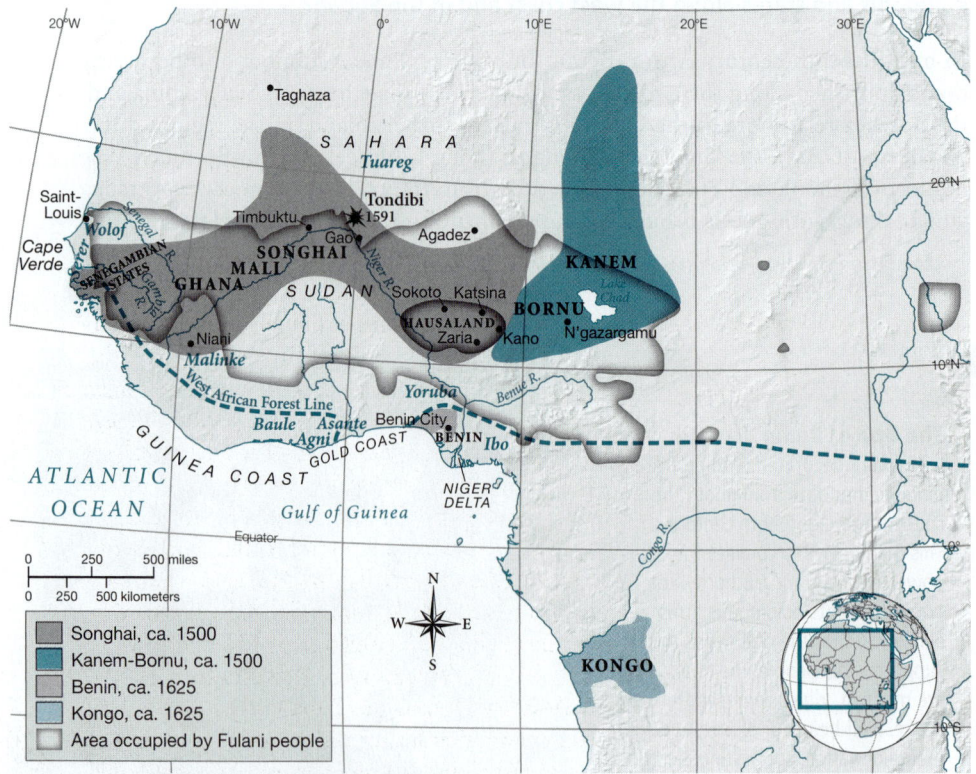

## MAP 20.1 West African Societies, ca. 1500–1800

The coastal region of West Africa witnessed the rise of a number of kingdoms in the sixteenth century.

such as blacksmiths and leatherworkers, and enslaved persons. The enslaved class consisted of individuals who were pawned for debt, house servants who could not be sold, and people who were acquired through war or purchase.

Senegambian slavery varied from society to society. In some places slaves were considered chattel property and were treated as harshly as they would be later in the Western Hemisphere. The word **chattel** originally comes from a Latin word meaning "head," as in "so many head of cattle." It reflects the notion that enslaved people are not human, but subhuman, like beasts of burden or other animals. Thus they can be treated like animals. But in Senegambia and elsewhere in Africa, many enslaved people were not considered chattel property and could not be bought and sold. Some even served as royal advisers and enjoyed great power and prestige.[1] Unlike in the Americas, where slave status passed forever from one generation to the next, in Africa the enslaved person's descendants were sometimes considered free.

Senegambia was composed of stateless societies, culturally homogeneous ethnic populations living in small groups of villages without a central capital. Among these stateless societies, **age-grade systems** evolved. Age-grades were groups of teenage males and females whom the society initiated into adulthood at the same time. Age-grades cut across family ties, created community-wide loyalties, and provided a means of local law enforcement, because each age-grade was responsible for the behavior of all its members.

The typical Senegambian community was a small, self-supporting agricultural village of closely related families. The average six- to eight-acre farm supported a moderate-size family. Millet and sorghum were the staple grains in northern Senegambia; farther south, forest dwellers cultivated yams as a staple. Social life centered on the family, and government played a limited role, interceding mostly to resolve family disputes and conflicts between families.

Alongside West African stateless societies like Senegambia were kingdoms and states ruled by kings who governed defined areas through bureaucratic hierarchies. The great forest kingdom of Benin emerged in the fifteenth and sixteenth centuries in what is now southern Nigeria (see Map 20.1). Over time, the position of its **oba**, or king, was exalted, bringing stability to the state. In the later fifteenth century the oba Ewuare strengthened his army and pushed Benin's borders as far as the Niger River in the east, westward into Yoruba country, and south to the Gulf of Guinea. During the late sixteenth and seventeenth centuries the office of the oba evolved from a warrior-kingship to a position of spiritual leadership.

At its height in the late sixteenth century, Benin controlled a vast territory, and European visitors described a sophisticated society. A Dutch visitor in the early 1600s, possibly Dierick Ruiters, described the capital, Benin City, as possessing a great, wide, and straight main avenue down the middle, with many side streets crisscrossing it. The visitor entered the city through a high, well-guarded gate framed on each side by a very tall earthen bulwark, or wall, with an accompanying moat. There was also an impressive royal palace, with at least four large courtyards surrounded by galleries leading up to it. William Bosman, another Dutch visitor writing a hundred years later, in 1702, described the prodigiously long and broad streets "in which continual Markets are kept, either of Kine [cattle], Cotton, Elephants Teeth, European Wares; or, in short, whatever is to be come at in this Country."[2] Visitors also noted that Benin City was kept scrupulously clean and had no beggars and that public security was so effective that theft was unknown. The period also witnessed remark-able artistic creativity in ironwork, carved ivory, and especially bronze portrait busts. Over nine hundred brass plaques survive, providing important information about Benin court life, military triumphs, and cosmological ideas.

In 1485 Portuguese and other Europeans began to appear in Benin in pursuit of trade, and over the next couple of centuries Benin grew rich from the profits made through the slave trade and the export of tropical products, particularly pepper and ivory. Its main European trading partners along this stretch of the so-called slave coast were the Dutch and Portuguese. In the early eighteenth century tributary states and stronger neighbors nibbled at Benin's frontiers, challenging its power. Benin, however, survived as an independent entity until the British conquered and burned Benin City in 1898 as part of the European imperialist seizure of Africa (see "The Scramble for Africa, 1880–1914" in Chapter 25).

## The Sudan: Songhai, Kanem-Bornu, and Hausaland

The Songhai kingdom, a successor state of the kingdoms of Ghana (ca. 900–1100) and Mali (ca. 1200–1450), dominated the whole semidesert Sahel region of the western and central Sudan (see Map 20.1). The imperial expansion of Songhai began during the reign of the Songhai king Sonni Ali (r. ca. 1464–1492) and continued under his eventual suc-cessor, Muhammad Toure (TOO-ray) (r. 1493–1528). From his capital at Gao, Toure extended his rule as far north as the salt-mining center at **Taghaza** (tah-GAHZ-ah) in the western Sahara and as far east as Agadez (AH-gah-dez) and Kano (KA-no). A convert to Islam, Toure returned from a pilgrimage to Mecca impressed by what he had seen there. He tried to bring about greater centralization in his own territories by building a strong army, improving taxation procedures, and replacing local Songhai officials with more effi-cient Arabs in an effort to substitute royal institutions for ancient kinship ties.

We know little about daily life in Songhai society because of the paucity of writ-ten records and surviving artifacts. Some information is provided by Leo Africanus (ca. 1493–1554), a Moroccan who published an account in 1526 of his many trav-els, which included a stay in the Songhai kingdom. As a scholar, Africanus was natu-rally impressed by Timbuktu, the second-largest city of the empire, which he visited in 1513. "Here [is] a great store of doctors, judges, priests, and other learned men, that are bountifully maintained at the King's court," he reported.[3] Many of these Islamic scholars had studied in Cairo and other Muslim learning centers. They gave Timbuktu a reputation for intellectual sophistication, religious piety, and moral justice.

Songhai under Muhammad Toure seems to have enjoyed economic prosperity. Leo Africanus noted the abundant food supply, which was produced in the southern savanna and carried on the Niger River to Timbuktu by a large fleet of canoes. The elite had immense wealth, and expensive North African and European luxuries — clothes, copperware, glass and stone beads, perfumes, and horses — were much in demand. The existence of many shops and markets implies the development of an urban culture. In Timbuktu merchants, scholars, judges, and artisans constituted a dis-tinctive bourgeoisie, or middle class. The presence of many foreign merchants, including Jews and Italians, gave the city a cosmopolitan atmosphere.

Slavery played an important role in Songhai's economy. On the royal farms scat-tered throughout the kingdom, enslaved people produced rice for the royal granaries.

Slaves could possess their own slaves, land, and cattle, but they could not bequeath any of this property; the king inherited all of it. Muhammad Toure greatly increased the number of royal slaves. He bestowed slaves on favorite Muslim scholars, who thus gained a steady source of income. Slaves were also sold at the large market at Gao, where traders from North Africa bought them to resell later in Cairo, Constantinople, Lisbon, Naples, Genoa, and Venice.

Despite its considerable economic and cultural strengths, Songhai had serious internal problems. Islam never took root in the countryside, and Muslim officials alienated the king from his people. Muhammad Toure's reforms were a failure. He governed diverse peoples—Tuareg, Mandinka, and Fulani as well as Songhai—who were often hostile to one another, and no cohesive element united them. Finally, the Songhai never developed an effective method of transferring power. Revolts, conspiracies, and palace intrigues followed the death of every king, and only three of the nine rulers in the dynasty begun by Muhammad Toure died natural deaths. Muhammad Toure himself was murdered by one of his sons. His death began a period of political instability that led to the kingdom's slow disintegration. The empire came to an end in 1591 when a Moroccan army of three thousand soldiers—many of whom were slaves of European origin equipped with European muskets—crossed the Sahara and inflicted a crushing defeat on the Songhai at Tondibi.

East of Songhai lay the kingdoms of Kanem-Bornu and Hausaland (see Map 20.1). Under the dynamic military leader Idris Alooma (IH-dris ah-LOW-mah) (r. 1571–1603), Kanem-Bornu subdued weaker peoples and gained jurisdiction over an extensive area. Well drilled and equipped with firearms, his standing army and camel-mounted cavalry decimated warriors fighting with spears and arrows. Idris Alooma perpetuated a form of feudalism by granting land to able fighters in return for loyalty and the promise of future military assistance. Kanem-Bornu also shared in the trans-Saharan trade, shipping eunuchs and young girls to North Africa in return for horses and firearms.

A devout Muslim, Idris Alooma elicited high praise from ibn-Fartura, who wrote a history of his reign called *The Kanem Wars*:

> Among the most surprising of his acts was the stand he took against obscenity and adultery, so that no such thing took place openly in his time. Formerly the people had been indifferent to such offences. . . . In fact he was a power among his people and from him came their strength.
>
> The Sultan was intent on the clear path laid down by the Qur'an . . . in all his affairs and actions.[4]

Idris Alooma built mosques at his capital city of N'gazargamu and substituted Muslim courts and Islamic law for African tribunals and ancient customary law. His eighteenth-century successors lacked his vitality and military skills, however, and the empire declined.

Between Songhai and Kanem-Bornu were the lands of the Hausa (HOUSE-uh). Hausa merchants carried on a sizable trade in slaves and kola nuts with North African communities across the Sahara. Obscure trading posts evolved into important Hausa city-states like Kano and Katsina (kat-SIN-ah), through which Islamic influences entered the region. Kano and Katsina became Muslim intellectual centers and in the fifteenth century attracted scholars from Timbuktu. The Muslim chronicler of the reign of King Muhammad Rimfa (RIMP-fah) (r. 1463–1499) of Kano records that the king introduced the Muslim practices of purdah (PUR-dah), or seclusion of women; Eid al-Fitr (eed al-FITR), the festival after the fast of Ramadan; and the assignment of eunuchs to high state offices.[5] As in Songhai and Kanem-Bornu, however, Islam made no strong imprint on the Hausa masses until the nineteenth century.

## Agriculture, Gender, and Marriage in West Africa

In West Africa, as elsewhere in Africa, agricultural production involved a sexual division of labor in which men did the heavy work of felling trees and clearing the land, while women then planted, weeded, and harvested. Between 1000 and 1400, cassava (manioc), bananas, and plantains came to West Africa from Asia. The Portuguese introduced maize (corn), sweet potatoes, and new varieties of yams from the Americas in the sixteenth century. Fish supplemented the diets of people living near bodies of water. According to former slave Olaudah Equiano, the Ibo people in the mid-eighteenth century ate plantains, yams, beans, and Indian corn, along with stewed poultry, goat, or bullock (castrated steer) seasoned with peppers.[6] However, such a protein-rich diet was probably exceptional.

Both nuclear and extended families were common in West Africa. Nuclear families averaged only five or six members, but the household of a Big Man (a local man of power) included his wives, married and unmarried sons, unmarried daughters, poor relations, dependents, and scores of children. Extended families were common among the Hausa and Mandinka peoples. On the Gold Coast in the seventeenth century, a well-to-do man's household might number 150 people; in the Kongo region in west-central Africa, several hundred.

Wives and children were highly desired in African societies because they could clear and cultivate the land and because they brought prestige, social support, and security in old age. The results were intense competition for women, inequality of access to them, an emphasis on male virility and female fertility, and serious tension between male generations. Polygyny was almost universal.

Men acquired wives in two ways. In some cases, couples simply eloped and began their union. More commonly, a man's family gave bride wealth to the bride's family as compensation for losing the fruits of her productive and reproductive abilities. She was expected to produce children, to produce food through her labor, and to pass on the culture in the raising of her children. Because it took time for a young man to acquire the bride wealth, all but the richest men delayed marriage until about age thirty. Women married at about the onset of puberty.

The easy availability of land in Africa reduced the kinds of generational conflict that occurred in western Europe, where land was scarce. Competition for wives between male generations, however, was fierce. On the one hand, myth and folklore stressed respect for the elderly, and the older men in a community imposed their authority over the younger ones. On the other hand, young men possessed the powerful asset of their labor, which could easily be turned into independence where so much land was available.

"Without children you are naked" goes a Yoruba (YORE-uh-bah) proverb, and children were the primary goal of marriage. Just as a man's virility determined his honor, so barrenness damaged a woman's status. A wife's infidelity was considered a less serious problem than her infertility. A woman might have six widely spaced pregnancies in her fertile years; the universal practice of breast-feeding infants for two, three, or even four years may have inhibited conception. Long intervals between births due to food shortages also may have limited pregnancies and checked population growth. Harsh climate, poor nutrition, and infectious diseases also contributed to a high infant mortality rate.

Disease posed perhaps the biggest obstacle to population growth. Even though West Africans had developed a relatively high degree of immunity to malaria and other parasitic diseases, malaria, spread by mosquitoes and rampant in West Africa, was the greatest killer, especially of infants. Acute strains of smallpox introduced by Europeans certainly did not help population growth, nor did venereal syphilis, which possibly originated in Latin America. As in Chinese and European communities in the early modern period, the sick depended on folk medicine, with African medical specialists administering a variety of treatments. Still, disease was common where the diet was poor and lacked adequate vitamins.

The devastating effects of famine represented another major check on population growth. Drought, poor soil, excessive rain, swarms of locusts, and rural wars that prevented land cultivation all meant later food shortages. In the 1680s famine extended from the Senegambian coast to the Upper Nile, and many people sold themselves into slavery for food. In the eighteenth century "slave exports" reached their peak in times of famine, and ships could fill their cargo holds simply by offering food. The worst disaster occurred from 1738 to 1756, when, according to one chronicler, the poor were reduced literally to cannibalism, also considered a metaphor for the complete collapse of civilization.[7]

Because the Americas had been isolated from the Eurasian-African landmass for thousands of years, parasitic diseases common in Europe, Africa, and Asia were unknown in the Americas before the Europeans' arrival. Enslaved Africans taken to the Americas brought with them the diseases common to tropical West Africa, such as yellow fever, dengue fever, malaria, and hookworm. Thus, the hot, humid disease environment in the American tropics, where the majority of enslaved Africans lived and worked, became more "African." On the other hand, cold-weather European diseases, such as chicken pox, mumps, measles, and influenza, prevailed in the northern temperate zone in North America and the southern temperate zone in South America. This difference in disease environment partially explains why Africans made up the majority of the unskilled labor force in the tropical areas of the Americas, and Europeans made up the majority of the unskilled labor force in the Western Hemisphere temperate zones, such as the northern United States and Canada.

## Trade and Industry

West African economies rested on agriculture, as did all premodern societies. There was some trade and industry, but population shortages encouraged local self-sufficiency, slowed transportation, and hindered exchange. There were very few large markets, and their relative isolation from the outside world and failure to attract large numbers of foreign merchants limited technological innovation.

For centuries black Africans had exchanged goods with North African merchants in centers such as Gao and Timbuktu. This long-distance trans-Saharan trade was conducted and controlled by Muslim-Berber merchants using camels. The two primary goods exchanged were salt, which came from salt mines in North Africa, and gold, which came mainly from gold mines in modern-day Mali, and later, modern Ghana.

As elsewhere around the world, water was the cheapest method of transportation, and many small dugout canoes and larger trading canoes plied the Niger and its delta region (see Map 20.1). On land West African peoples used pack animals (camels or donkeys) rather than wheeled vehicles; only a narrow belt of land in the Sudan was suitable for animal-drawn carts. When traders reached an area infested with tsetse flies, they transferred each animal's load to human porters. Such difficulties in transport severely restricted long-distance trade, so most people relied on the regional exchange of local specialties.

West African communities had a well-organized market system. At informal markets on riverbanks, fishermen bartered fish for local specialties. More formal markets existed within towns and villages or on neutral ground between them. Markets also rotated among neighboring villages on certain days. Local sellers were usually women; traders from afar were men.

Salt had long been one of Africa's most critical trade items, as it is essential to human health. The salt trade dominated the West African economies in the fifteenth, sixteenth, and seventeenth centuries. The main salt-mining center was at Taghaza (see Map 20.1) in the western Sahara. In the most wretched conditions, slaves dug the salt from desiccated lakes and loaded heavy blocks onto camels' backs. Nomadic **Tuareg** (Berber) peoples and later Moors (peoples of Berber and Arab descent) traded their salt south for gold, grain, slaves, and kola nuts. **Cowrie** (COW-ree) **shells**, imported from the Maldives in the Indian Ocean and North Africa, served as the medium of exchange. Gold continued to be mined and shipped from Mali until South American bullion flooded Europe in the sixteenth century. Thereafter, gold production in Mali steadily declined until the late twentieth and early twenty-first centuries, when it revived.

West African peoples engaged in many crafts, but the textile industry had the greatest level of specialization. The earliest fabric in West Africa was made of vegetable fiber. Muslim traders introduced cotton and its weaving in the ninth century. By the fifteenth century the Wolof and Mandinka regions had professional weavers producing beautiful cloth, but this cloth was too expensive to compete in the Atlantic and Indian Ocean markets after 1500. Although the relatively small quantities of cloth produced on very narrow looms (one to two inches wide) could not compete in a world market, they are the source of the famous multicolored African kente cloth made from threads of cotton, or cotton and silk, by the Akan people of Ghana and the Ivory Coast. The area around Kano, in northern Nigeria, is famous for the deeply dyed blue cloth produced on the narrowest looms in the world and favored by the Tuareg Berber peoples of North Africa.

# Cross-Cultural Encounters Along the East African Coast

**How did the arrival of Europeans and other foreign cultures affect the East African coast, and how did Ethiopia and the Swahili city-states respond to these incursions?**

East Africa in the early modern period faced repeated incursions from foreign powers. At the beginning of the sixteenth century Ethiopia faced challenges from the Muslim state of Adal, and then from Europeans. Jesuit attempts to substitute Roman Catholic liturgical forms for the Coptic Christian liturgies met with fierce resistance

## MAP 20.2  East Africa in the Sixteenth Century

In early modern times, the Christian kingdom of Ethiopia, first isolated and then subjected to Muslim and European pressures, played an insignificant role in world affairs. But the East African city-states, which stretched from Sofala in the south to Mogadishu in the north, had powerfully important commercial relations with Mughal India, China, the Ottoman world, and southern Europe.

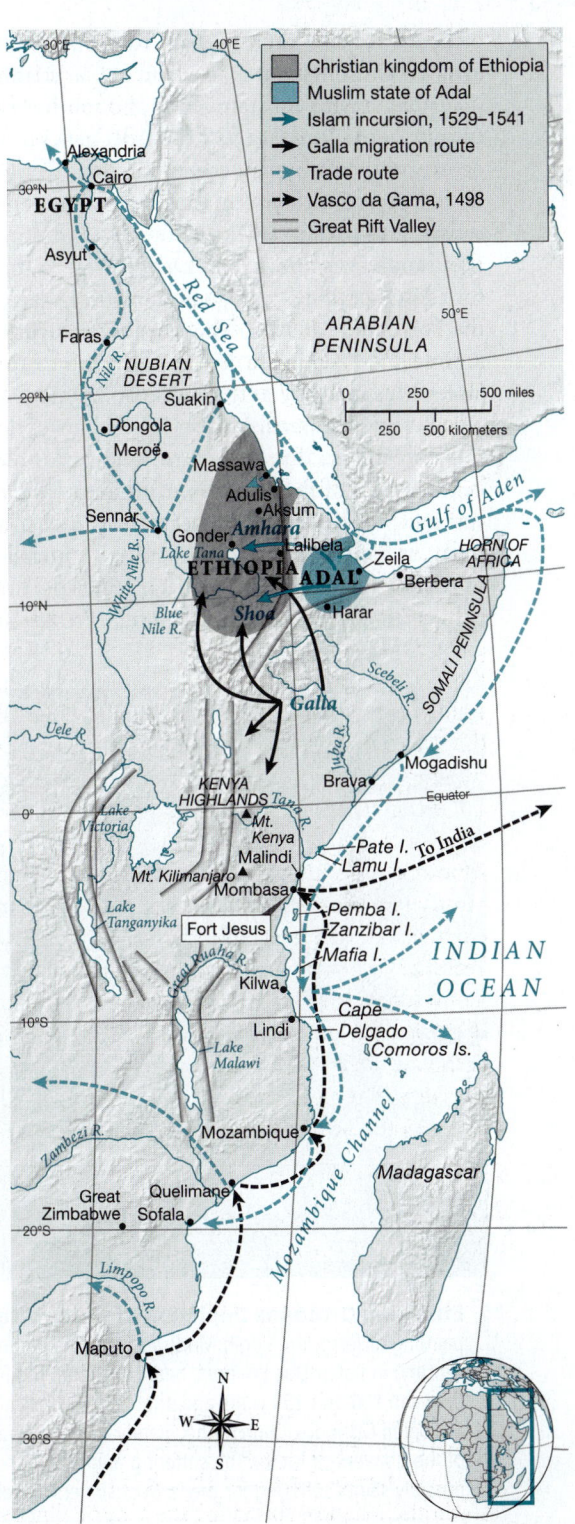

and ushered in a centuries-long period of hostility to foreigners. The wealthy Swahili city-states along the southeastern African coast also resisted European intrusions in the sixteenth century, with even more disastrous results. Cities such as Mogadishu, Kilwa, and Sofala used Arabic as the language of communication, and their commercial economies had long been tied to the Indian Ocean trade. The arrival of the Portuguese in 1498 proved catastrophic for those cities, and the Swahili coast suffered economic decline as a result.

## Muslim and European Incursions in Ethiopia, ca. 1500–1630

At the beginning of the sixteenth century the powerful East African kingdom of Ethiopia extended from Massawa in the north to several tributary states in the south (Map 20.2), but the ruling Solomonic dynasty in Ethiopia, in power since the thirteenth century, faced serious external threats. Alone among the states in northeast and eastern Africa, Ethiopia was a Christian kingdom that practiced **Coptic Christianity**, an orthodox form of the Christian faith that originated in Egypt in about 42–45. By the early 1500s Ethiopia was an island of Christianity surrounded by a sea of Muslim states.

Adal, a Muslim state along the southern base of the Red Sea, began incursions into Ethiopia, and in 1529 the Adal general Ahmad ibn-Ghazi inflicted a disastrous defeat on the Ethiopian emperor Lebna Dengel (r. 1508–1540). Ibn-Ghazi followed up his victory with systematic devastation of the land; destruction of many Ethiopian artistic and literary works, churches, and monasteries; and the forced conversion of thousands to Islam. Lebna Dengel fled to the mountains and appealed to Portugal for assistance. The Portuguese came to his aid, but Dengel was killed in battle before the Portuguese arrived. The Muslim occupation of Christian Ethiopia, which began around 1531, ended in 1543, after a joint Ethiopian and Portuguese force defeated a larger Muslim army at the Battle of Wayna Daga.

Portuguese participation in the battle, fighting alongside the Ethiopian Christian forces, was due in part to a centuries-old European myth. In the late twelfth century tales of Prester John, rumored to be a powerful Christian monarch ruling a vast and wealthy African empire, had reached western Europe. The search for Prester John, as well as for gold and spices, spurred the Portuguese to undertake a series of trans-African expeditions that reached Timbuktu and Mali in the 1480s and the Ethiopian court by 1508. Although Prester John was a mythical figure, Portuguese

**Ethiopian Orthodox Depiction of Jesus, Virgin, and Saints** This colorful fresco painting of Jesus, the Virgin Mary, and saints is in the Ura Kidane Mehret monastery (16th century) in Bahar Dar, Ethiopia, near Lake Tana. The fresco is one of several paintings, mostly done between 100 and 250 years ago, that portray biblical scenes and events and the history of the Ethiopian Orthodox Church. They nearly cover the walls of the church, which is part of a complex of the Convent of Mercy. The suffering figures in dark colors in the bottom right-hand corner are possibly saints suffering for the faith or sinners in Hell. (DEA/W. Buss/Getty Images)

emissaries triumphantly but mistakenly identified the Ethiopian emperor as Prester John.[8] It was their desire to convert Ethiopians from Coptic Christianity to Roman Catholicism that motivated the Portuguese to aid the Ethiopians in defeating Adal's Muslim forces in 1543.

No sooner had the Muslim threat ended than Ethiopia encountered three more dangers. The Galla, now known as the Oromo, moved northward in great numbers in the 1530s, occupying portions of Harar, Shoa, and Amhara. The Ethiopians could not defeat them militarily, and the Galla were not interested in assimilation. For the next two centuries the two peoples lived together in an uneasy truce. Simultaneously, the Ottoman Turks seized Massawa and other coastal cities. Then the Jesuits arrived and attempted to force Roman Catholicism on a proud people whose Coptic form of Christianity long antedated the European version. Since Ethiopian national sentiment was closely tied to Coptic Christianity, violent rebellion and anarchy ensued.

In 1633 the Jesuit missionaries were expelled. For the next two centuries hostility to foreigners, weak political leadership, and regionalism characterized Ethiopia. Civil conflicts between Galla and Ethiopians erupted continually. The Coptic Church, though lacking strong authority, survived as the cornerstone of Ethiopian national identity.

## The Swahili City-States and the Arrival of the Portuguese, ca. 1500–1600

The word **Swahili** means "People of the Coast" and refers to the people living along the East African coast and on the nearby islands. Although predominantly a Bantu-speaking people, the Swahili have incorporated significant aspects of Arab culture. The Arabic alphabet was used for the first written works in Swahili (although the Latin alphabet is now standard), and roughly 35 percent of Swahili words come from Arabic. Surviving texts in Swahili — from the earliest known Swahili documents dating from 1711 — provide historians with a glimpse of early Swahili history that is not possible when studying early nonliterate African societies. By the eleventh century the Swahili had accepted Islam, which provided a common identity and unifying factor for all the peoples along coastal East Africa. Living on the Indian Ocean coast, the Swahili also felt the influences of Indians, Indonesians, Persians, and even the Chinese.

Swahili civilization was overwhelmingly maritime. A fertile, well-watered, and intensely cultivated stretch of land extending down the coast yielded valuable crops. The region's considerable prosperity, however, rested on trade and commerce. The Swahili acted as middlemen in an Indian Ocean–East African economy that might be described as early capitalism. They exchanged cloves, ivory, rhinoceros horn, tortoise shells, inlaid ebony chairs, copra (dried coconut meat that yields coconut oil), and inland slaves for Arabian and Persian perfumes, toilet articles, ink, and paper; for Indian textiles, beads, and iron tools; and for Chinese porcelains and silks. In the fifteenth century the cosmopolitan city-states of Mogadishu, Pate, Lamu, Mombasa, and especially Kilwa enjoyed a worldwide reputation for commercial prosperity and high living standards.[9]

The arrival of the Portuguese explorer Vasco da Gama (VAS-ko dah GAH-ma) (see Map 16.2) in 1498 spelled the end of the Swahili cities' independence. Lured by the spice trade, Portugal wanted to build a maritime empire in the Indian Ocean.

Some Swahili rulers, such as the sultan of Malindi (ma-LIN-dee), quickly agreed to a trading alliance with the Portuguese. Others, such as the sultan of Mombasa (mahm-BAHS-uh), were tricked into commercial agreements. Swahili rulers who rejected Portuguese overtures saw their cities bombarded and attacked. To secure alliances made between 1502 and 1507, the Portuguese erected forts at the southern port cities of Kilwa, Zanzibar (ZAN-zuh-bahr), and Sofala. These fortified markets and trading posts served as the foundation of Portuguese commercial power on the Swahili coast. The better-fortified northern cities, such as Mogadishu, survived as important entrepôts for goods to India.

The Portuguese presence in the south did not yield the expected commercial fortunes. Rather than accept Portuguese commercial restrictions, the residents deserted the towns, and the local economies crumbled. Large numbers of Kilwa's people, for example, immigrated to northern cities. The gold flow from inland mines to Sofala (so-FALL-ah) slowed to a trickle. Swahili noncooperation successfully prevented the Portuguese from gaining control of the local coastal trade.

In the late seventeenth century pressures from the northern European maritime powers — the Dutch, French, and English, aided greatly by Omani Arabs — combined with local African rebellions to bring about the collapse of Portuguese influence in Africa. A Portuguese presence remained only at Mozambique in the far south and Angola (ahng-GO-luh) on the west coast.

# The African Slave Trade

**What role did slavery play in African societies before the transatlantic slave trade began, and what was the effect of European involvement?**

The exchange of peoples captured in local and ethnic wars within sub-Saharan Africa, the trans-Saharan slave trade with the Mediterranean Islamic world beginning in the seventh century, and the slave traffic across the Indian Ocean all testify to the long tradition and continental dimensions of the African slave trade before European intrusion. The enslavement of human beings was practiced in some form or another all over Africa — indeed, all over the world. Sanctioned by law and custom, enslaved people served critical and well-defined roles in the social, political, and economic organization of many African societies. Domestically these roles ranged from concubines and servants to royal guards and advisers. As was the case later in the Americas, some enslaved people were common laborers. In terms of economics, slaves were commodities for trade, no more or less important than other trade items, such as gold and ivory.

Over time, the trans-Saharan slave trade became less important than the transatlantic trade, which witnessed an explosive growth during the seventeenth and eighteenth centuries. The millions of enslaved Africans forcibly exported to the Americas had a lasting impact on African society and led ultimately to a wider use of slaves within Africa itself.

## The Institution of Slavery in Africa

Islamic practices strongly influenced African slavery. African rulers justified enslavement with the Muslim argument that prisoners of war could be sold and that captured people were considered chattel, or personal possessions, to be used any way the owner saw fit. Between 650 and 1600 Muslims transported perhaps as many as 4.82 million black slaves across the trans-Saharan trade route.[10] In the fourteenth and fifteenth centuries the rulers and elites of Mali and Benin imported thousands of white Slavic slave women, symbols of wealth and status, who had been seized in slave raids from the Balkans and Caucasus regions of the eastern Mediterranean by Turks, Mongols, and others.[11] In 1444, when Portuguese caravels landed 235 slaves at Algarve in southern Portugal, a contemporary observed that they seemed "a marvelous (extraordinary) sight, for, amongst them, were some white enough, fair enough, and well-proportioned; others were less white, like mulattoes; others again were black as Ethiops."[12]

Meanwhile, the flow of black people to Europe, begun during the Renaissance, continued. In the seventeenth and eighteenth centuries as many as two hundred thousand Africans entered European societies. Some arrived as slaves, others as servants; the legal distinction was not always clear. Eighteenth-century London, for example, had more than ten thousand blacks, most of whom arrived as sailors on Atlantic crossings or as personal servants brought from the West Indies. In England most were free, not slaves. Initially, a handsome black person was a fashionable accessory, a rare status symbol. Later, English aristocrats considered black servants too ordinary. The duchess of Devonshire offered her mother an eleven-year-old boy, explaining that the duke did not want a Negro servant because "it was more original to have a Chinese page than to have a black one; everybody had a black one."[13]

London's black population constituted a well-organized, self-conscious subculture, with black pubs, black churches, and black social groups assisting the black poor and unemployed. Some black people attained wealth and position, the most famous being Francis Barber, manservant of the sixteenth-century British literary giant Samuel Johnson and heir to Johnson's papers and to most of his sizable fortune.

In 1658 the Dutch East India Company began to allow the importation of slaves into the Cape Colony, which the company had founded on the southern tip of Africa at the Cape of Good Hope in 1652. Over the next century and a half about 75 percent of the slaves brought into the colony came from Dutch East India Company colonies in India and Southeast Asia or from Madagascar; the remaining 25 percent came from Africa. Most worked long and hard as field hands and at any other menial or manual forms of labor needed by their European masters. The Dutch East India Company was the single largest slave owner in the Cape Colony, employing its slaves on public works and company farms, but by 1780 half of all white men at the Cape had at least one slave. Slave ownership fostered a strong sense of racial and economic solidarity in the white master class.

Although in the seventeenth and eighteenth centuries Holland enjoyed a Europe-wide reputation for religious tolerance and intellectual freedom, in the Cape Colony the Dutch used a strict racial hierarchy and heavy-handed paternalism to maintain control over enslaved native and foreign-born peoples. In Muslim society the offspring of a free man and an enslaved woman were free, but in southern Africa such children remained enslaved. Because enslaved males greatly outnumbered enslaved females in the Cape Colony, marriage and family life were almost nonexistent for slaves. Because there were few occupations requiring special skills, those enslaved in the colony lacked opportunities to earn manumission, or freedom. And in contrast with North and South America and with Muslim societies, in the Cape

Colony only a very small number of those enslaved won manumission; most of these were women.[14]

The slave trade expanded greatly in East Africa's savanna and Horn regions in the late eighteenth century and the first half of the nineteenth century. Why this increased demand? Merchants and planters wanted slaves to work the sugar plantations on the Mascarene Islands, located east of Madagascar; the clove plantations on Zanzibar and Pemba; and the food plantations along the Kenyan coast. The eastern coast also exported enslaved people to the Americas, particularly to Brazil. In the late eighteenth and early nineteenth centuries, precisely when the slave trade to North America and the Caribbean declined, the Arabian and Asian markets expanded.

## The Transatlantic Slave Trade

Although the trade in African people was a worldwide phenomenon, the transatlantic slave trade involved the largest number of enslaved Africans. This forced migration of millions of human beings, extending from the early sixteenth to the late nineteenth centuries, represents one of the most inhumane, unjust, and shameful tragedies in human history. It also immediately provokes a troubling question: why, in the seventeenth and eighteenth centuries, did enslavement in the Americas become almost exclusively African?

European settlers first enslaved indigenous peoples, the Amerindians, to work on the sugar plantations in the New World (see "Sugar and Early Transatlantic Slavery" in Chapter 16). When they proved ill-suited to the harsh rigors of sugar production, the Spaniards brought in Africans.

One scholar has argued that a pan-European insider-outsider ideology prevailed across Europe. This cultural attitude permitted the enslavement of outsiders but made the enslavement of white Europeans taboo. Europeans could not bear the sight of other Europeans doing plantation slave labor. According to this theory, a similar pan-African ideology did not exist, as Africans had no problem with selling Africans to Europeans.[15] Several facts argue against the validity of this theory. English landlords exploited their Irish peasants with merciless severity, French aristocrats often looked on their peasantry with cold contempt, and Russian boyars treated their serfs with casual indifference and harsh brutality. These and other possible examples contradict the existence of a pan-European ideology or culture that opposed the enslavement of white Europeans. Moreover, the flow of white enslaved Slavic peoples from the Balkans into the eastern Mediterranean continued unabated during the same period.

Another theory holds that in the Muslim and Arab worlds by the tenth century, an association had developed between blackness and menial slavery. The Arab word *abd*, or "black," had become synonymous with *slave*. Although the great majority of enslaved persons in the Islamic world were white, a racial element existed in Muslim perceptions: not all slaves were black, but blacks were identified with slavery. In Europe, after the arrival of tens of thousands of sub-Saharan Africans in the Iberian Peninsula during the fifteenth century, Christian Europeans also began to make a strong association between slavery and black Africans. Therefore, Africans seemed the "logical" solution to the labor shortage in the Americas.[16]

Another important question relating to the African slave trade is this: why were African peoples enslaved in a period when serfdom was declining in western Europe, and when land was so widely available and much of the African continent had a labor shortage? The answer seems to lie in an environmental problem related to African agriculture. Partly because of the tsetse fly, which causes sleeping sickness and other diseases, and partly because of easily leached lateritic soils (containing high concentrations of oxides), farmers had great difficulty using draft animals, and tropical soils responded poorly to plowing. Thus, most field work in precolonial Africa was done with a hoe. Consequently, the individual African's agricultural productivity was low, and his or her economic value to society was less than the economic value of the more productive European peasant. Given the choice, it made no sense to transport the European peasant to the Americas, or to try and produce more with the African peasant in Africa. But in the Americas, enslaved Africans working with better tools and draft animals in a more fertile environment were more productive than they were in Africa. European slave dealers were therefore very willing to pay to have the Africans' higher productivity in the Americas.

The incidence of disease in the Americas also helps explain African enslavement. Smallpox took a terrible toll on Native Americans, and between 30 and 50 percent of Europeans exposed to malaria succumbed to that sickness. Africans had developed some immunity to both diseases, and in the Americas they experienced the lowest mortality rate of any people, making them, ironically, the most suitable workers for that environment.

Portuguese colonization of Brazil began in the early 1530s, and in 1551 the Portuguese founded a sugar colony at Bahia. Between 1551 and 1575, before the North American slave traffic began, the Portuguese delivered more African slaves to Brazil than ever reached British North America (Figure 20.1). Portugal essentially monopolized the slave trade until 1600 and continued to

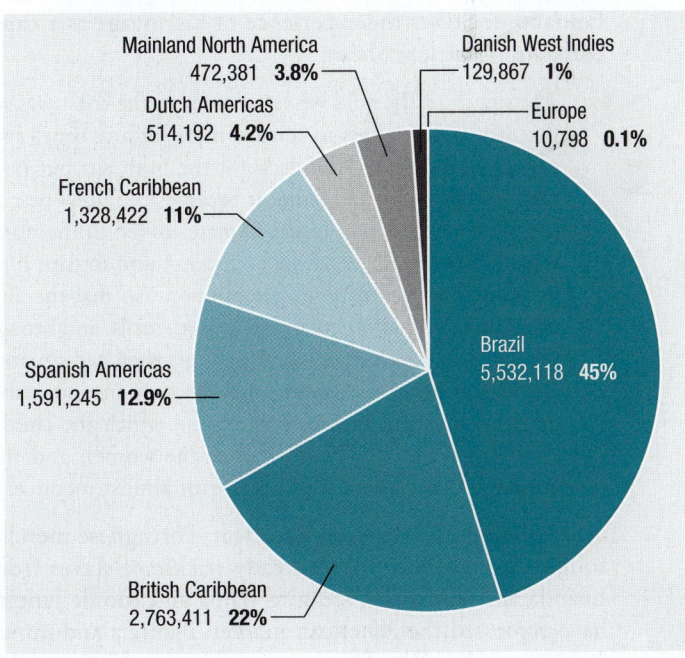

**FIGURE 20.1**
**Estimated Slave Imports by Destination, 1501–1866**
Brazil was the single largest importer of African slaves from 1501 to 1866. But when taken cumulatively, the British, French, Dutch, and Danish colonies of the Caribbean rivaled the much larger colony of Brazil for numbers of slaves imported from Africa.
(Source: Data from Emory University. "Assessing the Slave Trade: Estimates," in *Voyages: The Trans-Atlantic Slave Trade Database.* 2009. http://www.slavevoyages.org.)

Mainland North America 472,381 **3.8%**
Danish West Indies 129,867 **1%**
Dutch Americas 514,192 **4.2%**
Europe 10,798 **0.1%**
French Caribbean 1,328,422 **11%**
Spanish Americas 1,591,245 **12.9%**
Brazil 5,532,118 **45%**
British Caribbean 2,763,411 **22%**

play a significant role in the seventeenth century, though the trade was increasingly taken over by the Dutch, French, and English. From 1690 until the British House of Commons abolished the slave trade in 1807, England was the leading carrier of African slaves.

Population density and supply conditions along the West African coast and the sailing time to New World markets determined the sources of slaves. As the demand for slaves rose, slavers moved down the West African coast from Senegambia to the more densely populated hinterlands of the Bight of Benin and the Bight of Biafra. The abundant supply of Africans to enslave in Angola, the region south of the Congo River, and the quick passage from Angola to Brazil and the Caribbean established that region as the major coast for Portuguese slavers.

Transatlantic wind patterns partly determined exchange routes. Shippers naturally preferred the swiftest crossing — that is, from the African port nearest the latitude of the intended American destination. Thus Portuguese shippers carried their cargoes from Angola to Brazil, and British merchants sailed from the Bight of Benin to the Caribbean. The great majority of enslaved Africans were intended for the sugar and coffee plantations extending from the Caribbean islands to Brazil. Almost all Portuguese shipments went to satisfy the voracious Brazilian demand for slaves. Angola produced 26 percent of all African slaves and 70 percent of all Portuguese slaves. Trading networks extending deep into the interior culminated at two major ports on the Angolan coast, Luanda (loo-AHN-da) and Benguela. The Portuguese acquired a few slaves through warfare but secured the vast majority through trade with African dealers. Whites did not participate in the inland markets, which were run solely by Africans.

The so-called **Middle Passage** was the horrific voyage under appalling and often deadly conditions of enslaved Africans across the Atlantic to the Americas. Olaudah Equiano describes the experience of his voyage as a captured slave from Benin to Barbados in the Caribbean:

> The stench of the hold while we were on the coast was so intolerably loathsome that it was dangerous to remain there for any time, and some of us had been permitted to stay on the deck for the fresh air; but now that the whole ship's cargo were confined together it became absolutely pestilential. The closeness of the place and the heat of the climate, added to the number in the ship, which was so crowded that each had scarcely room to turn himself, almost suffocated us. This produced copious perspirations, so that the air soon became unfit for respiration from a variety of loathsome smells, and brought on a sickness among the slaves, of which many died. . . . This wretched situation was again aggravated by the galling of the chains, now become insupportable, and the filth of the necessary tubs [of human waste], into which the children often fell and were almost suffocated. The shrieks of the women and the groans of the dying rendered the whole a scene of horror almost inconceivable.[17]

Although the demand was great, Portuguese merchants in Angola and Brazil sought to maintain only a steady trickle of slaves from the African interior to Luanda and across the ocean to Bahia and Rio de Janeiro: a flood of slaves would have depressed the American market. Planters and mine operators from the provinces traveled to Rio to buy slaves. Between 1795 and 1808 approximately 10,000

Angolans per year stood in the Rio slave market. In 1810 the figure rose to 18,000; in 1828 it reached 32,000.[18]

The English ports of London, Bristol, and particularly Liverpool dominated the British slave trade. In the eighteenth century Liverpool was the world's greatest slave-trading port. In all three cities, small and cohesive merchant classes exercised great public influence. The cities also had huge stores of industrial products for export, growing shipping industries, and large amounts of ready cash for investment abroad.

Slaving ships from Bristol plied back and forth along the Gold Coast, the Bight of Benin, Bonny, and Calabar looking for African traders who were willing to supply them with slaves. Liverpool's ships drew enslaved people from Gambia, the Windward Coast, and the Gold Coast. British ships carried textiles, gunpowder and flint, beer and spirits, British and Irish linens, and woolen cloth to Africa. A collection of goods was grouped together into what was called the **sorting**. An English sorting might include bolts of cloth, firearms, alcohol, tobacco, and hardware; this batch of goods was traded for an enslaved individual or a quantity of gold, ivory, or dyewood.[19]

European traders had two systems for exchange. First, especially on the Gold Coast, they established factory-forts. These fortified trading posts were expensive to maintain but proved useful for fending off European rivals. Second, they used **shore trading**, in which European ships sent boats ashore or invited African dealers to bring traders and enslaved Africans out to the ships.

The shore method of buying slaves allowed the ship to move easily from market to market. The final prices of those enslaved depended on their ethnic origin, their availability when the shipper arrived, and their physical health when offered for sale in the West Indies or the North or South American colonies.

The supply of slaves for the foreign market was controlled by a small, wealthy African merchant class or by a state monopoly. By contemporary standards, slave raiding was a costly operation, and only black African entrepreneurs with sizable capital and labor could afford to finance and direct raiding drives.

The transatlantic slave trade was part of a much larger trading network that is known as the triangle trade. European merchants sailed to Africa on the first leg of the voyage to trade European manufactured goods for enslaved Africans. When they had filled their ships' holds with enslaved people, they headed across the Atlantic on the second leg of the voyage, the Middle Passage. When they reached the Americas, the merchants unloaded and sold their human cargoes and used the profits to purchase raw materials — such as cotton, sugar, and indigo — that they then transported back to Europe, completing the third leg of the commercial triangle.

Enslaved African people had an enormous impact on the economies and cultures of the Portuguese and Spanish colonies of South America and the Dutch, French, and British colonies of the Caribbean and North America. For example, on the sugar plantations of Mexico and the Caribbean; on the North American cotton, rice, and tobacco plantations; and in Peruvian and Mexican silver and gold mines, enslaved Africans not only worked in the mines and fields but also filled skilled, supervisory, and administrative positions and performed domestic service. In the United States enslaved Africans and their descendants influenced many facets of American culture,

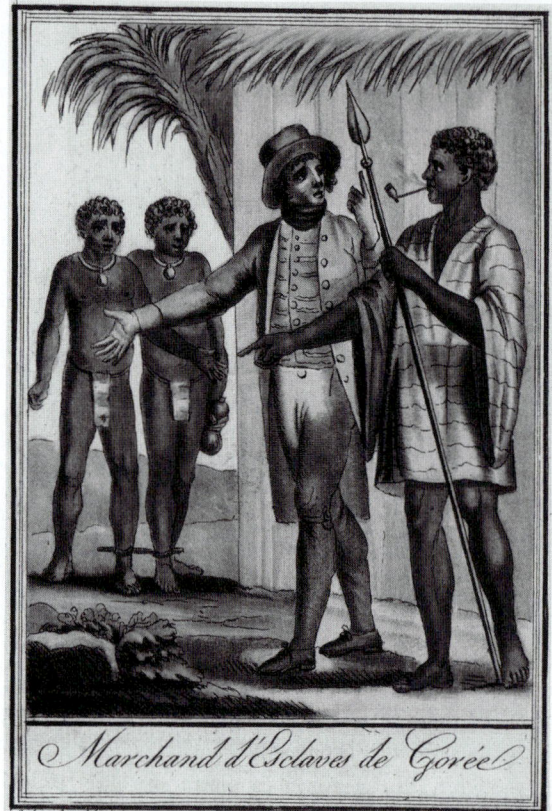

Marchand d'Esclaves de Gorée

**The African Slave Trade** A European slave trader discusses the exchange of goods for slaves brought to him by the African on the right at Gorée Island off the coast of Senegal. (DEA/M. Seemuller/ Getty Images)

such as language, music (ragtime and jazz), dance, and diet. Even the U.S. White House and Capitol building, where Congress meets, were built partly by slave labor.[20] The importance of the slave trade extended beyond the Atlantic world as well, as slave labor made possible the expansion of capitalism and the industrialization of Western societies.

## Impact on African Societies

What economic impact did European trade have on African societies? Africans possessed technology well suited to their environment. Over the centuries they had cultivated a wide variety of plant foods; developed plant and animal husbandry techniques; and mined, smelted, and otherwise worked a great variety of metals. Apart from a handful of items, most notably firearms, American tobacco and rum, and Portuguese brandy, European goods presented no novelty to Africans, but were desirable because of their low prices. Africans exchanged slaves, ivory, gold, pepper, and animal skins for those goods. African states eager to expand or to control commerce bought European firearms, although the difficulty of maintaining guns often gave gun owners only marginal superiority over skilled bowmen.[21]

The African merchants who controlled the production of exports gained the most from foreign trade. The king of Dahomey (duh-HO-mee) (modern-day Benin in West Africa), for example, had a gross income in 1750 of £250,000 (almost U.S. $33 million today) from the overseas export of his fellow Africans. A portion of his profit was spent on goods that improved his people's living standard. Slave-trading entrepôts, which provided opportunities for traders and for farmers who supplied foodstuffs to towns, caravans, and slave ships, prospered. But such economic returns did not spread very far.[22] International trade did not lead to Africa's economic development. Africa experienced neither technological growth nor the gradual spread of economic benefits in early modern times.

As in the Islamic world, women in sub-Saharan Africa also engaged in the slave trade. In Guinea these women slave merchants and traders were known as *nhara*.

**Sapi-Portuguese Saltcellar** Contact with the Sapi people of present-day Sierra Leone in West Africa led sixteenth-century Portuguese traders to commission this ivory saltcellar, for which they brought Portuguese designs. But the object's basic features—a spherical container and separate lid on a flat base, with men and/or women supporting, or serving as, beams below—are distinctly African. Here a Portuguese caravel sits on top with a man in the crow's nest. Four men stand below: two finely carved, regally dressed, and fully armed noblemen facing forward and two attendants in profile. (© akg-images/The Image Works)

They acquired considerable riches, often by marrying the Portuguese merchants and serving as go-betweens for these outsiders who were not familiar with the customs and languages of the African coast. One of them, Mae Aurélia Correia (1810?–1875?), led a life famous in the upper Guinea coastal region for its wealth and elegance. Between the 1820s and 1840s she operated her own trading vessels and is said to have owned several hundred slaves. Some of them she hired out as skilled artisans and sailors. She and her sister (or aunt) Julia amassed a fortune in gold, silver jewelry, and expensive cloth while living in European-style homes. Julia and her husband, a trader from the Cape Verde Islands, also owned their own slave estates where they produced peanuts.

The intermarriage of French traders and Wolof women in Senegambia created a métis, or mulatto, class. One such Afro-French family built the famous House of Slaves on the island of Gorée in the 1780s. In the emerging urban center of Saint-Louis, members of this small class adopted the French language, the Roman Catholic faith, and a French manner of life, and they exercised considerable political and economic power. However, European cultural influences did not penetrate West African society beyond the seacoast.

The political consequences of the slave trade varied from place to place. The trade enhanced the power and wealth of some kings and warlords in the short run but promoted conditions of instability and collapse over the long run. In the Kongo kingdom the perpetual Portuguese search for Africans to enslave undermined the monarchy, destroyed political unity, and led to constant disorder and warfare; as a result, power passed to the village chiefs. Likewise in Angola, the slave trade decimated and scattered the population and destroyed the local economy. By contrast, the military kingdom of Dahomey, which entered into the slave trade in the eighteenth century and made it a royal monopoly, prospered enormously. Dahomey's economic strength rested on the slave trade. The royal army raided deep into the interior, and in the late eighteenth century Dahomey became one of the major West African sources of slaves. When slaving expeditions failed to yield sizable catches and when European demand declined, the resulting depression in the Dahomean economy caused serious political unrest. Iboland, inland from the Niger Delta, from whose great port cities of Bonny and Brass the British drained tens of thousands of enslaved Africans, experienced minimal political effects. A high birthrate kept pace with the incursions of the slave trade, and Ibo societies remained demographically and economically strong.

What demographic impact did the slave trade have on Africa? Between approximately 1501 and 1866 more than 12 million Africans were forcibly exported to the Americas, 6 million were traded to Asia, and 8 million were retained as slaves within Africa. Figure 20.2 shows the estimated number of slaves shipped to the Americas in the transatlantic slave trade. Export figures do not include the approximately 10 to 15 percent who died during procurement or in transit.

The early modern slave trade involved a worldwide network of relationships among markets in the Middle East, Africa, Asia, Europe, and the Americas. But Africa was the crucible of the trade. There is no small irony in the fact that Africa, which of all the continents was most desperately in need of population because of its near total dependence on labor-intensive agriculture and pastoralism, lost so many millions to the trade. Although the British Parliament abolished the slave trade in 1807 and traffic in Africans to Brazil and Cuba gradually declined, within Africa the trade continued at the levels of the peak years of the transatlantic trade, 1780–1820. In the later nineteenth century developing African industries, using slave labor, produced a variety of products for domestic consumption and export. Again, there is irony in the fact that in the eighteenth century European demand for slaves expanded the trade (and wars) within Africa, yet in the nineteenth century European imperialists defended territorial aggrandizement by arguing that they were "civilizing" Africans by abolishing slavery.

Markets in the Americas generally wanted young male slaves. Asian and African markets preferred young females. Women were sought for their reproductive value, as sex objects, and because their economic productivity was not threatened by the possibility of physical rebellion, as might be the case with young men.

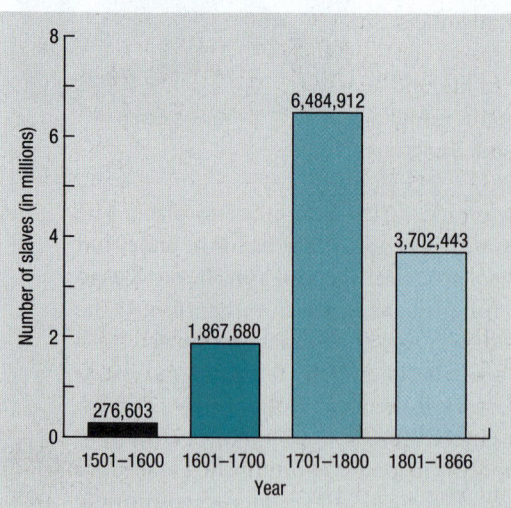

**FIGURE 20.2   The Transatlantic Slave Trade, 1501–1866**
The volume of slaves involved in the transatlantic slave trade peaked during the eighteenth century. These numbers show the slaves who embarked from Africa and do not reflect the 10 to 15 percent of enslaved Africans who died in transit.
(Source: Data from Emory University. "Assessing the Slave Trade: Estimates," in *Voyages: The Trans-Atlantic Slave Trade Database.* 2009. http://www.slavevoyages.org.)

Consequently, two-thirds of those exported to the Americas were male, one-third female. As a result, the population on Africa's western coast became predominantly female; the population in the East African savanna and Horn regions was predominantly male. The slave trade therefore had significant consequences for the institutions of marriage, the local trade in enslaved people (as these local populations became skewed with too many males or too many females), and the sexual division of labor. Although Africa's overall population may have shown modest growth from roughly 1650 to 1900, that growth was offset by declines in the Horn and on the eastern and western coasts. While Europe and Asia experienced considerable demographic and economic expansion in the eighteenth century, Africa suffered a decline.[23]

The political and economic consequences of the African slave trade are easier to measure than the human toll taken on individuals and societies. While we have personal accounts from many slaves, ships' captains and crews, slave masters, and others of the horrors of the slave-trading ports along Africa's coasts, the brutality of the Middle Passage, and the inhuman cruelty enslaved Africans endured once they reached the Americas, we know much less about the beginning of the slave's journey in Africa. Africans themselves carried out much of the "man stealing," the term used by Africans to describe the capturing of enslaved men, women, and children and marching them to the coast, where they were traded to Arabs, Europeans, or others. Therefore, we have few written firsthand accounts of the pain and suffering these violent raids inflicted, either on the person being enslaved or on the families and societies they left behind.

# Chapter Summary

In the early modern world, West African kingdoms and stateless societies existed side by side. Both had predominantly agricultural economies. Stateless societies revolved around a single village or group of villages without a central capital or ruler. Kings ruled over defined areas through bureaucratic hierarchies. The Sudanic empires in the Sahel controlled the north-south trans-Saharan trade in gold, salt, and other items. Led by predominantly Muslim rulers, these kingdoms belonged to a wider Islamic world and so had access to vast trade networks and some of the most advanced scholarship in the world. Still, Muslim culture affected primarily the royal and elite classes, seldom reaching the masses.

Europeans believed a wealthy (mythical) Christian monarch named Prester John ruled the Christian kingdom of Ethiopia. This fable attracted Europeans to Ethiopia and partly explains why the Portuguese helped the Ethiopians fight off Muslim incursions. Jesuit missionaries tried to convert Ethiopians to Roman Catholicism but were fiercely resisted and expelled in 1633.

Swahili city-states on Africa's southeastern coast possessed a Muslim and mercantile culture. The Swahili acted as middlemen in the East African–Indian Ocean trade network, which Portugal sought to conquer and control in the late fifteenth and early sixteenth centuries. Swahili rulers who refused to form trading alliances with the Portuguese were attacked. The Portuguese presence caused the economic decline and death of many Swahili cities.

Slavery existed across Africa before Europeans arrived. Enslaved people were treated relatively benignly in some societies but elsewhere as chattel possessions, suffering harsh and brutal treatment. European involvement in the slave trade began around 1550, when the Portuguese purchased Africans to work in Brazil. Africans proved more adaptive to the heat, humidity, and diseases of the tropics than Europeans or Amerindians. The Dutch East India Company used enslaved Africans and Southeast Asians in its Cape Colony. African entrepreneurs and merchants partnered in the trade, capturing people in the interior and exchanging them for firearms, liquor, and other goods with European slave ships. Some kingdoms experienced a temporary rise of wealth and power, but over time the slave trade was largely destabilizing. The individual suffering and social disruption in Africa caused by the enslavement of millions of Africans are impossible to estimate.

## NOTES

1. P. D. Curtin, *Economic Change in Precolonial Africa: Senegambia in the Era of the Slave Trade* (Madison: University of Wisconsin Press, 1975), pp. 34–35; J. A. Rawley, *The Transatlantic Slave Trade: A History* (Lincoln: University of Nebraska Press, 2005).

2. Pieter de Marees, *Description of the Gold Kingdom of Guinea*, trans. and ed. Albert van Dantzig and Adam Jones (1602; repr., Oxford: Oxford University Press, 1987), pp. 226–228; William Bosman, *A New Description of the Coast of Guinea*, ed. John Ralph Willis (London: Frank Cass, 1967), p. 461.

3. Quoted in R. Hallett, *Africa to 1875* (Ann Arbor: University of Michigan Press, 1970), p. 151.

4. A. ibn-Fartura, "The Kanem Wars," in *Nigerian Perspectives*, ed. T. Hodgkin (London: Oxford University Press, 1966), pp. 111–115.

5. "The Kano Chronicle," quoted in *Nigerian Perspectives*, ed. T. Hodgkin (London: Oxford University Press, 1966), pp. 89–90.

6. *Equiano's Travels: The Interesting Narrative of the Life of Olaudah Equiano*, ed. P. Edwards (Portsmouth, N.H.: Heinemann, 1996), p. 4.

7. J. Iliffe, *Africans: The History of a Continent* (Cambridge: Cambridge University Press, 2007), p. 68.

8. See A. J. R. Russell-Wood, *The Portuguese Empire: A World on the Move* (Baltimore: Johns Hopkins University Press, 1998), pp. 11–13.

9. Russell-Wood, *The Portuguese Empire*, pp. 35–38.

10. P. E. Lovejoy, *Transformations in Slavery: A History of Slavery in Africa* (Cambridge: Cambridge University Press, 1992), p. 25, Table 2.1, "Trans-Saharan Slave Trade, 650–1600."

11. Iliffe, *Africans*, p. 77.

12. Quoted in H. Thomas, *The Slave Trade* (New York: Simon and Schuster, 1997), p. 21.

13. G. Gerzina, *Black London: Life Before Emancipation* (New Brunswick, N.J.: Rutgers University Press, 1995), pp. 29–66 passim; quotation from p. 53.

14. R. Shell, *Children of Bondage: A Social History of the Slave Society at the Cape of Good Hope, 1652–1838* (Hanover, N.H.: University Press of New England, 1994), pp. 285–289.

15. See D. Eltis, *The Rise of African Slavery in the Americas* (Cambridge: Cambridge University Press, 2000), chap. 3; and the review/commentary by J. E. Inikori, *American Historical Review* 106.5 (December 2001): 1751–1753.

16. R. Blackburn, *The Making of New World Slavery: From the Baroque to the Modern, 1492–1800* (New York: Verso, 1998), pp. 79–80.

17. *Equiano's Travels*, pp. 23–26.

18. Rawley, *The Transatlantic Slave Trade*, pp. 45–47.

19. Robert W. July, *A History of the African People* (Prospect Heights, Ill.: Waveland Press, 1998), p. 171.

20. J. Thornton, *Africa and Africans in the Making of the Atlantic World* (New York: Cambridge University Press, 1992), pp. 138–142.

21. Robert W. July, *Precolonial Africa: An Economic and Social History* (New York: Scribner's, 1975), pp. 269–270.

22. A. G. Hopkins, *An Economic History of West Africa* (New York: Columbia University Press, 1973), p. 119.

23. P. Manning, *Slavery and African Life: Occidental, Oriental, and African Slave Trades* (New York: Cambridge University Press, 1990), pp. 22–23 and chap. 3, pp. 38–59.

## MAKE CONNECTIONS  LOOK AHEAD

During the period from 1400 to 1800 many parts of Africa experienced a profound transition with the arrival of Europeans all along Africa's coasts. Ancient trade routes, such as those across the Sahara or up and down the East African coast, were disrupted. In West Africa trade routes that had been purely internal now connected with global trade networks at European coastal trading posts. Along Africa's east coast the Portuguese attacked Swahili city-states in their effort to take control of the Indian Ocean trade nexus.

The most momentous consequence of the European presence along Africa's coast, however, was the introduction of the transatlantic slave trade. For more than three centuries Europeans, with the aid of African slave traders, enslaved millions of African men and women. Although many parts of Africa were untouched by the transatlantic slave trade, at least directly, areas where Africans were enslaved experienced serious declines in agricultural production, little progress in technological development, and significant increases in violence.

As we saw in Chapter 17 and will see in Chapter 21, early European commercial contacts with the empires of the Middle East and of South and East Asia were similar in many ways to those with Africa. Initially, the Portuguese, and then the English, Dutch, and French, did little more than establish trading posts at port cities and had to depend on the local people to bring them trade goods from the interior. Tropical diseases, particularly in India and Southeast Asia, took heavy death tolls on the Europeans, as they did in tropical Africa. What is more, while it was possible for the Portuguese to attack and conquer the individual Swahili city-states, Middle Eastern and Asian empires—such as the Ottomans in Turkey, the Safavids in Persia, the Mughals in India, and the Ming and Qing Dynasties in China—were, like the West African kingdoms, economically and militarily powerful enough to dictate terms of trade with the Europeans.

Resistance to enslavement took many forms on both sides of the Atlantic. In Haiti, as discussed in Chapter 22, resistance led to revolution and independence, marking the first successful uprising of non-Europeans against a colonial power. At the end of the nineteenth century, as described in Chapter 25, Europeans used the ongoing Arab-Swahili slave raids from Africa's eastern coast far into the interior as an excuse to invade and eventually colonize much of central and eastern Africa. The racial discrimination that accompanied colonial rule in Africa set the stage for a struggle for equality that led to eventual independence after World War II.

# Chapter 20 Review

## IDENTIFY KEY TERMS

**Identify and explain the significance of each item below.**

chattel (p. 503)

age-grade systems (p. 503)

oba (p. 503)

Taghaza (p. 504)

Tuareg (p. 508)

cowrie shells (p. 508)

Coptic Christianity (p. 509)

Swahili (p. 511)

Middle Passage (p. 516)

sorting (p. 517)

shore trading (p. 517)

## REVIEW THE MAIN IDEAS

**Answer the focus questions from each section of the chapter.**

1. What types of economic, social, and political structures were found in the kingdoms and states along the west coast and in the Sudan? (p. 501)

2. How did the arrival of Europeans and other foreign cultures affect the East African coast, and how did Ethiopia and the Swahili city-states respond to these incursions? (p. 508)

3. What role did slavery play in African societies before the transatlantic slave trade began, and what was the effect of European involvement? (p. 512)

## MAKE COMPARISONS AND CONNECTIONS

**Analyze the larger developments and continuities within and across chapters.**

1. In what ways did Islam enrich the Sudanic empires of West Africa?

2. Discuss the ways in which Africa came into greater contact with a larger world during the period discussed in this chapter.

3. How did the transatlantic slave trade affect West African society?

## CHRONOLOGY

| | |
|---|---|
| **1299–1922** | • Ottoman Empire (Chs. 17, 25, 28) |
| **1350–1520** | • European Renaissance (Ch. 15) |
| **1368–1644** | • Ming Dynasty in China (Ch. 21) |
| **1400–1600s** | • Salt trade dominates West African economy |
| **ca. 1464–1591** | • Songhai kingdom dominates the western Sudan |
| **1485** | • Portuguese and other Europeans first appear in Benin |
| **1493–1528** | • Muhammad Toure governs and expands kingdom of Songhai |
| **1498** | • Portuguese explorer Vasco da Gama sails around Africa |
| **1502–1507** | • Portuguese erect forts at Kilwa, Zanzibar, and Sofala on Swahili coast |
| **1521, 1533** | • Spanish conquest of Aztecs, then Incas (Ch. 16) |
| **1526–1761** | • Era of Mughal India (Ch. 17) |
| **1529** | • Adal defeats Ethiopian emperor; begins systematic devastation of Ethiopia |
| **1543** | • Joint Ethiopian and Portuguese force defeats Muslims in Ethiopia |
| **1571–1603** | • Idris Alooma governs kingdom of Kanem-Bornu |
| **1591** | • Moroccan army defeats Songhai |
| **1603–1867** | • Tokugawa Shogunate in Japan (Ch. 21) |
| **1644–1911** | • Qing Dynasty in China (Chs. 21, 26) |
| **1652** | • Dutch East India Company establishes colony at Cape of Good Hope |
| **1658** | • Dutch East India Company allows importation of slaves into Cape Colony |
| **1680s** | • Famine from Senegambian coast to Upper Nile |
| **1688–1689** | • English Glorious Revolution (Ch. 18) |
| **1738–1756** | • Major famine in West Africa |
| **1789** | • Olaudah Equiano publishes autobiography |

# 21

# Continuity and Change in East Asia

## 1400–1800

**THE FOUR CENTURIES FROM 1400 TO 1800 WERE A TIME OF GROWTH** and dynamic change throughout East Asia. Although both China and Japan suffered periods of war, each ended up with expanded territories. The age of exploration brought New World crops to the region, leading to increased agricultural output and population growth. It also brought new opportunities for foreign trade and new religions. Another link between these countries was the series of massive Japanese invasions of Korea in the late sixteenth century, which led to war between China and Japan.

In China the native Ming Dynasty (1368–1644) brought an end to Mongol rule. Under the Ming, China saw agricultural reconstruction, commercial expansion, and the rise of a vibrant urban culture. In the early seventeenth century, after the Ming Dynasty fell into disorder, the non-Chinese Manchus founded the Qing Dynasty (1644–1911) and added Taiwan, Mongolia, Tibet, and Xinjiang to their realm. By this period gunpowder was a major element in warfare. The Qing Empire thus was comparable to the other multiethnic empires of the early modern world, such as the Ottoman, Russian, and Habsburg Empires. In China itself the eighteenth century was a time of peace and prosperity.

In the Japanese islands the fifteenth century saw the start of civil war that lasted a century. At the end of the sixteenth century the world seemed to have turned upside down when a commoner, Hideyoshi, became the supreme ruler. He did not succeed in passing on his power to an heir, however. Power was seized by Tokugawa Ieyasu. Under the Tokugawa Shogunate (1603–1867), Japan restricted contact with the outside world and social mobility among its own people. Yet Japan thrived, as agricultural productivity increased and a lively urban culture developed.

# Ming China, 1368–1644

**What sort of state and society developed in China after the Mongols were ousted?**

The founding of the Ming Dynasty ushered in an era of peace and prosperity. By the beginning of the seventeenth century, however, the Ming government was beset by fiscal, military, and political problems.

## The Rise of Zhu Yuanzhang and the Founding of the Ming Dynasty

The founder of the **Ming Dynasty**, Zhu Yuanzhang (JOO yoowan-JAHNG) (1328–1398), began life in poverty during the last decades of Mongol rule. His home region was hit by drought and then plague in the 1340s, and when he was only sixteen years old, his father, oldest brother, and that brother's wife all died, leaving two penniless boys with three bodies to bury. With no relatives to turn to, Zhu Yuanzhang asked a monastery to accept him as a novice. The monastery itself was short of funds, and the monks soon sent Zhu out to beg for food. For three or four years he wandered through central China. Only after he returned to the monastery did he learn to read.

A few years later, in 1351, members of a religious sect known as the Red Turbans rose in rebellion against the government. Red Turban teachings drew on Manichaean ideas about the incompatibility of the forces of good and evil as well as on the cult of the Maitreya Buddha, who according to believers would in the future bring his paradise to earth to relieve human suffering. When the temple where Zhu Yuanzhang was living was burned down in the fighting, Zhu joined the rebels and rose rapidly.

Zhu and his followers developed into brilliant generals, and gradually they defeated one rival after another. In 1356 Zhu took the city of Nanjing and made it his base. In 1368 his armies took Beijing, which the Mongol emperor and his closest followers had vacated just days before. Then forty years old, Zhu Yuanzhang declared himself emperor of the Ming (Bright) Dynasty. As emperor, he is known as Taizu (TIGH-dzoo) or the Hongwu emperor.

Taizu started his reign wanting to help the poor. To lighten the weight of government taxes and compulsory labor, he ordered a full-scale registration of cultivated land and population so that these burdens could be assessed more fairly. He also tried persuasion. He issued instructions to be read aloud to villagers, telling them to be obedient to their parents, live in harmony with their neighbors, work contentedly at their occupations, and refrain from evil.

Although in many ways anti-Mongol, Taizu retained some Mongol practices, such as the hereditary service obligation for both artisan and military households. Garrisons were concentrated along the northern border and near the capital at Nanjing. Each garrison was allocated a tract of land that the soldiers took turns cultivating to supply their own food. Although in theory this system should have provided the Ming with a large but inexpensive army, in reality, men compelled to become soldiers did not necessarily make good fighting men. Consequently, like earlier dynasties, the Ming turned to non-Chinese northerners for much of its armed forces.

Taizu had deeply ambivalent feelings about men of education and sometimes brutally humiliated them in open court. When literary men began to avoid official life, Taizu made it illegal to turn down appointments or to resign from office. He began falling into rages that only the empress could stop, and after her death in 1382 no one could calm him. In 1376 Taizu had thousands of officials killed because they were found to have taken shortcuts in their handling of paperwork for the grain tax. In 1380 Taizu concluded that his chancellor was plotting to assassinate him, and thousands only remotely connected to the chancellor were executed. From then on, Taizu acted as his own chancellor, dealing directly with the heads of departments and ministries.

The next important emperor, called Chengzu or the Yongle emperor (r. 1403–1425), was also a military man. One of Taizu's younger sons, he took the throne by force from his nephew and often led troops into battle against the Mongols. Like his father, Chengzu was willing to use terror to keep government officials in line.

Early in his reign, Chengzu decided to move the capital from Nanjing to Beijing, which had been his own base as a prince and the capital during Mongol times. Constructed between 1407 and 1420, Beijing was a planned city. Like Chang'an in Sui and Tang times (581–907), it was arranged like a set of boxes within boxes and built on a north-south axis. The main outer walls were forty feet high and nearly fifteen miles around. Inside was the Imperial City, with government offices, and within that the palace itself, called the Forbidden City, with close to ten thousand rooms.

The areas surrounding Beijing were not nearly as agriculturally productive as those around Nanjing. To supply Beijing with grain, the Grand Canal connecting the city to the rice basket of the Yangzi River regions was broadened, deepened, and supplied with more locks and dams. The 15,000 boats and the 160,000 soldiers of the transport army who pulled loaded barges from the towpaths along the canal became the lifeline of the capital.

## Problems with the Imperial Institution

Taizu had decreed that succession should go to the eldest son of t...
the son's eldest son if the son predeceased his father, the system gen...
by earlier dynasties. In Ming times, the flaws in this system became app...
mediocre, obtuse, or erratic emperor followed another.

Because Taizu had abolished the position of chancellor, emperors turned ...
retaries and eunuchs to manage the paperwork. Eunuchs were essentially slaves ...
had been captured as boys and castrated. Society considered eunuchs the basest o...
servants, and Confucian scholars heaped scorn on them. Yet Ming emperors, like
rulers in earlier dynasties, often preferred the always-compliant eunuchs to high-
minded, moralizing civil service officials.

In Ming times, the eunuch establishment became huge. By the late fifteenth
century the eunuch bureaucracy had grown as large as the civil service, with each
having roughly twelve thousand positions. After 1500 the eunuch bureaucracy grew
even more rapidly, and by the mid-sixteenth century seventy thousand eunuchs were
in service throughout the country, with ten thousand in the capital. Tension between
the two bureaucracies was high. In 1420 Chengzu set up a eunuch-run secret service
to investigate cases of suspected corruption and sedition in the regular bureaucracy.

In hope of persuading emperors to make reforms, many Ming officials risked
their careers and lives by speaking out. To give an example, in 1519, when an emperor
announced plans to make a tour of the southern provinces, over a hundred officials
staged a protest by kneeling in front of the palace. The emperor ordered the officials
to remain kneeling for three days, then had them flogged; eleven died. Rarely did
such acts move an emperor to change his mind.

Although the educated public complained about the performance of emperors,
no one proposed or even imagined alternatives to imperial rule. High officials were
forced to find ways to work around uncooperative emperors, not always successfully.

## The Mongols and the Great Wall

The early Ming emperors held Mongol fighting men in awe and feared they might
form another great military machine of the sort Chinggis Khan (ca. 1162–1227) had
put together two centuries earlier. Although in Ming times the Mongols were never
united in a pan-Mongol federation, groups of Mongols could and did raid. Twice
they threatened the dynasty: in 1449 the khan of the western Mongols captured the
Chinese emperor, and in 1550 Beijing was surrounded by the forces of the khan of
the Mongols in Inner Mongolia. Fearful of anything that might strengthen the Mongols,
Ming officials were reluctant to grant any privileges to Mongol leaders, such as
trading posts along the borders. When trade was finally liberalized in 1570, friction
was reduced.

Two important developments shaped Ming-Mongol relations: the construction of the Great Wall and closer relations between Mongolia and Tibet. The Great
Wall, much of which survives today, was built as a compromise when Ming officials could agree on no other way to manage the Mongol threat. The wall extends
about 1,500 miles from northeast of Beijing into Gansu province. In the eastern
500 miles, the wall averages about 35 feet high and 20 feet across, with lookout
towers every half mile.

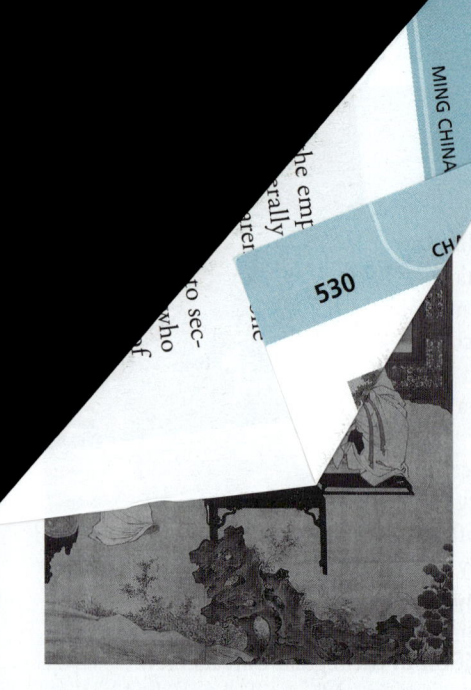

**holars as Collectors** The artist Du Jin (d. 1509) has icted two men of education and refinement in a garden, reciating a set of ancient objects. One can imagine that ne man seated on the chair has collected these objects, some probably discovered from ancient graves, and has invited his guest to examine them closely and offer his opinions of their age and significance. (Picturenow/ Getty Images)

Whether the wall did much to protect Ming China from the Mongols is still debated. Perhaps of more significance was the spread of Tibetan Buddhism among the Mongols. Tibet in this period was dominated by the major Buddhist monasteries, which would turn to competing Mongol leaders when they needed help. In 1577 the third Dalai Lama accepted the invitation of Altan Khan to visit Mongolia, and the khan declared that Tibetan Buddhism was the official religion of all the Mongols and that the Mongols would renounce blood sacrifice. When the third Dalai Lama's reincarnation was found to be the great-grandson of Altan Khan, the ties between Tibet and Mongolia, not surprisingly, became even stronger. From the perspective of Ming China, the growing influence of Buddhism among the Mongols seemed a positive development, as Buddhist emphasis on nonviolence was expected to counter the Mongols' love of war (though in fact the development of firearms was probably more crucial in the Mongols' loss of military advantage over their neighbors).

## The Examination Life

In sharp contrast to Europe in this era, Ming China had few social barriers. It had no hereditary aristocracy that could have limited the emperor's absolute power. Although China had no titled aristocracy, it did have an elite whose status was based above all on government office acquired through education. Unlike in many European countries of the era, China's merchants did not become a politically articulate class of the well-to-do. Instead the politically active class was educated men whose highest goals were government service.

Despite the harsh and arbitrary ways in which the Ming emperors treated their civil servants, demand for government jobs did not decline. The Ming government recruited almost all its officials through **civil service examinations**. Candidates had to study the Confucian classics and the interpretations of them by the twelfth-century Neo-Confucian scholar Zhu Xi (joo shee) (1130–1200), whose teachings were declared orthodox. To become officials, candidates had to pass examinations at the prefectural, the provincial, and the capital levels. To keep the wealthiest areas from dominating the exams, quotas were established for the number of candidates that each province could send to the capital.

Of course, boys from well-to-do families had a significant advantage because their families could start their education with tutors at age four or five, though less costly schools were becoming increasingly available as well. Families that for generations had pursued other careers—for example, as merchants or physicians—had more opportunities than ever for their sons to become officials through the exams. Clans sometimes operated schools for their members. Most of those who attended school stayed only a few years, but students who seemed most promising moved on to advanced schools where they practiced essay writing and studied the essays of men who had succeeded in the exams.

The examinations at the prefecture level lasted a day and drew hundreds if not thousands of candidates. The government compound would be taken over to give all candidates places to sit and write. The provincial and capital examinations were given in three sessions spread out over a week. In the first session, candidates wrote essays on passages from the classics. In the second and third sessions, candidates had to write essays on practical policy issues and on a passage from the *Classic of Filial Piety* (a brief text celebrating devotion to parents and other superiors). In addition, they had to show that they could draft state papers such as edicts, decrees, and judicial rulings.

The provincial examinations were major local events. From five thousand to ten thousand candidates descended on the city and filled up its hostels. To prevent cheating, no written material could be taken into the cells. Anyone caught wearing a cheat-sheet (an inner gown covered with the classics in minuscule script) was thrown out of the exam and banned from the next session as well. During the sessions candidates had time to write rough drafts of their essays, correct them, and then copy neat final versions. Throughout this time, tension was high.

After the papers were handed in, clerks recopied them and assigned them numbers to preserve anonymity. Proofreaders checked the copying before handing the papers to the assembled examiners, who divided them up to grade, which generally took about twenty days. Those 2 to 10 percent who passed could not spend long celebrating, however, because they had to begin preparing for the capital exams, less than a year away.

## Everyday Life in Ming China

For civil servants and almost everyone else, everyday life in Ming China followed patterns established in earlier periods. The family remained central to most people's lives, and almost everyone married. Beyond the family, people's lives were shaped by the type of work they did and where they lived.

Large towns and cities proliferated in Ming times and became islands of sophistication in the vast sea of rural villages. Printing reached the urban middle classes by the late Ming period, when publishing houses were putting out large numbers of books aimed at general audiences. To make their books attractive in the marketplace, entrepreneurial book publishers commissioned artists to illustrate them. By the sixteenth century more and more books were being published in the vernacular language (the language people spoke), especially short stories, novels, and plays. Ming vernacular short stories depicted a world much like that of their readers, full of shop clerks and merchants, monks and prostitutes, students and matchmakers.

The full-length novel made its first appearance during the Ming period. The plots of the early novels were heavily indebted to story cycles developed by oral storytellers over the course of several centuries. Plays were also very popular. Owners of troupes would purchase young children and train them to sing and perform. Jesuit missionary Matteo Ricci, who lived in China from 1582 to 1610, thought too many people were addicted to these performances:

> These groups of actors are employed at all imposing banquets, and when they are called they come prepared to enact any of the ordinary plays. The host at the banquet is usually presented with a volume of plays and he selects the one or several he may like. The guests, between eating and drinking, follow the plays with so much satisfaction that the banquet at times may last for ten hours.[1]

Farmers in this period continued to refashion the Chinese environment, intensifying their efforts to get as much food from their land as possible. The government strongly pushed the planting of useful trees, both fruit trees and mulberry trees needed to feed silkworms, and it has been estimated that 1 billion trees were planted during Taizu's reign. Farmers began to stock the rice paddies with fish, which continuously fertilized the rice fields, destroyed malaria-bearing mosquitoes, and enriched the diet. Farmers also grew cotton, sugarcane, and indigo as commercial crops. New World crops, especially sweet potatoes, allowed farmers to grow crops on hillsides or other areas previously left wild. Educated men, looking for ways to improve their lives, often encouraged farmers to cultivate these new crops.

Ethnic Chinese farmers also moved into territory that had previously been occupied mainly by other ethnic groups, especially in the southwest. The Ming rulers promoted the repopulation and colonization of war-devastated regions through reclamation of land and massive transfers of people. Immigrants to these areas received large plots and exemption from taxation for many years. In areas like the southwest that were rich in mineral ores, settlers took to mining.

Increased food production led to steady population growth and the multiplication of markets, towns, and small cities. Larger towns had permanent shops; smaller towns had periodic markets convening every five or ten days. The markets sold essential goods—such as pins, matches, oil for lamps, candles, paper, incense, and tobacco—to country people from the surrounding hamlets. They also offered the services of moneylenders, pawnbrokers, and craftsmen such as carpenters, barbers, joiners, and locksmiths.

## Ming Decline

Beginning in the 1590s the Ming government was beset by fiscal, military, and political problems. The government went nearly bankrupt helping defend Korea against a Japanese invasion. Then came a series of natural disasters: floods, droughts, locusts, and epidemics ravaged one region after another. At the same time, the Little Ice Age brought a drop in average temperatures that shortened the growing season and reduced harvests. In areas of serious food shortages, gangs of army deserters and laid-off soldiers began scouring the countryside in search of food. Once the gangs had stolen all their grain, hard-pressed farmers joined them just to survive. The Ming government had little choice but to try to increase taxes to deal with these threats, but the last thing people needed was heavier taxes.

Adding to the hardship was a sudden drop in the supply of silver. In place of the paper money that had circulated in Song and Mongol times, silver ingots came into general use as money in Ming times. Much of this silver originated in either Japan or the New World and entered China as payment for its silk and porcelain exports. When events in Japan and the Philippines led to disruption of trade, silver imports dropped. This led to deflation in China, which caused real rents to rise. Soon there were riots among urban workers and tenant farmers. In 1642 a group of rebels cut the dikes on the Yellow River, causing massive flooding. A smallpox epidemic soon added to the death toll. In 1644 the last Ming emperor, in despair, took his own life when rebels entered Beijing, opening the way for the start of a new dynasty.

# The Manchus and Qing China, to 1800

**Did the return of alien rule with the Manchus have any positive consequences for China?**

The next dynasty, the **Qing Dynasty** (1644–1911), was founded by the Manchus, a non-Chinese people who were descended from the Jurchens. In the late sixteenth century the Manchus began expanding their territories, and in 1644 they founded the Qing (CHING) Dynasty, which brought peace and in time prosperity. Successful Qing military campaigns extended the borders into Mongol, Tibetan, and Uighur regions, creating a multiethnic empire that was larger than any earlier Chinese dynasty.

## The Rise of the Manchus

In the Ming period, the Manchus lived in dispersed communities in what is loosely called Manchuria (the northeast of modern-day China). In the more densely populated southern part of Manchuria, the Manchus lived in close contact with Mongols, Koreans, and Chinese (Map 21.1). They were not nomads but rather hunters, fishers, and farmers. Like the Mongols, they also were excellent horsemen and archers and had a strongly hierarchical social structure, with elites and slaves. Slaves, often Korean or Chinese, were generally acquired through capture. Manchu villages were often at odds with each other over resources, and men did not leave their villages without arming themselves with bows and arrows or swords. Interspersed among these Manchu settlements were groups of nomadic Mongols who lived in tents.

The Manchus credited their own rise to Nurhaci (1559–1626). Over several decades, he united the Manchus and expanded their territories. Like Chinggis Khan, who had reorganized the Mongol armies to reduce the importance of tribal affiliations, Nurhaci created a new social basis for his armies in units called **banners**. Each banner was made up of a set of military companies and included the families and slaves of the soldiers. Each company had a hereditary captain, often from Nurhaci's own lineage. When new groups were defeated, their members were distributed among several banners to lessen their potential for subversion.

The Manchus entered China by invitation of the distinguished Ming general Wu Sangui, who was near the eastern end of the Great Wall when he heard that the rebels had captured Beijing. The Manchus proposed to Wu that they join forces and liberate Beijing. Wu opened the gates of the Great Wall to let the Manchus in, and within a couple of weeks they occupied Beijing. When the Manchus made clear that

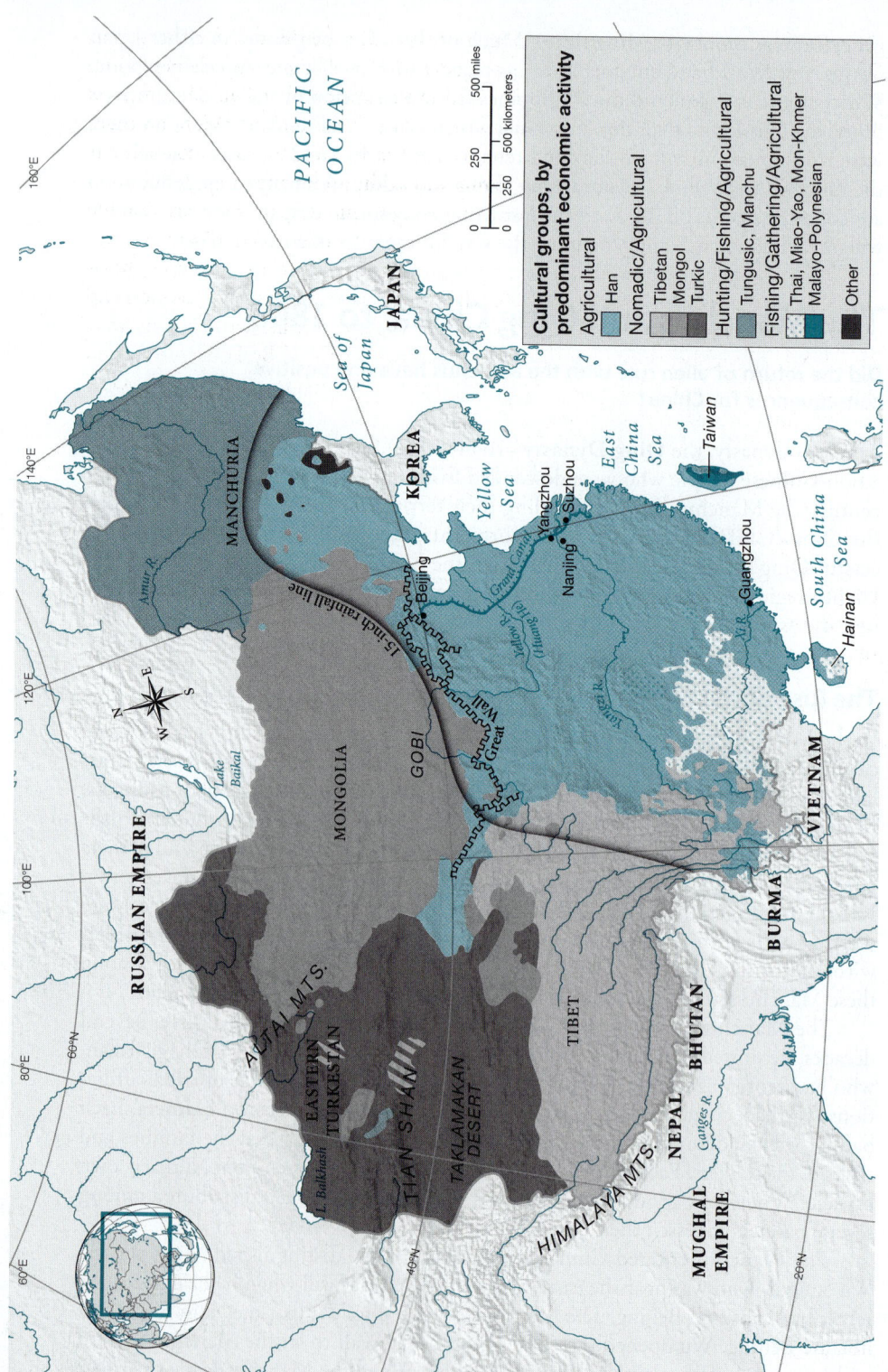

they intended to conquer the rest of the country and take the throne themselves, Wu and many other Chinese generals joined forces with them. With their Qing Dynasty established, in the summer of 1645 the Manchus ordered all Chinese men to shave the front of their heads and braid the rest in the Manchu fashion, an order many refused to comply with. Their resistance led Manchu commanders to order the slaughter of defiant cities. Before long, China was again under alien rule.

By this period, gunpowder weapons were a key element in warfare across much of Eurasia. China had invented gunpowder, and until the late 1400s it led the world in the development of gunpowder weapons and tactics. Centuries of peace, however, had slowed innovation. In the 1500s, the Ming adopted Portuguese cannon and muskets, and in the 1600s they added advanced Western artillery. In its early wars against the Manchus, the Ming court used cannon produced by Portuguese from Macao, which gave the Ming an advantage over the Manchus, until the Manchus also quickly adopted the technology.

Once the Qing were victorious, they put in place policies and institutions that gave China a respite from war and disorder. Most of the political institutions of the Ming Dynasty were taken over relatively unchanged, including the examination system. Population growth took off. Between 1700 and 1800 the Chinese population seems to have nearly doubled, from about 150 million to over 300 million. This growth has been attributed to many factors: global warming that extended the growing season, expanded use of New World crops, slowing of the spread of new diseases that had accompanied the sixteenth-century expansion of global traffic, and the efficiency of the Qing government in providing relief in times of famine.

Some scholars have recently argued that China's overall standard of living in the mid-eighteenth century was comparable to Europe's and that the standards of China's most developed regions, such as the lower Yangzi region, compared favorably to those of the most developed regions of Europe at the time, such as England and the Netherlands. Life expectancy, food consumption, and even facilities for transportation were at similar levels.

## Competent and Long-Lived Emperors

For more than a century, China was ruled by only three rulers, each of them hard-working, talented, and committed to making the Qing Dynasty a success. Two, the Kangxi and Qianlong emperors, had exceptionally long reigns.

Kangxi (KAHNG-shee) (r. 1661–1722) proved adept at meeting the expectations of both the Chinese and the Manchu elites. Kangxi could speak, read, and write Chinese and made efforts to persuade educated Chinese that the Manchus had a legitimate claim to rule, even trying to attract Ming loyalists who had been unwilling to serve the Qing. He undertook a series of tours of the south, where Ming loyalty had been strongest, and held a special exam to select men to compile the official history of the Ming Dynasty.

< **MAP 21.1  The Qing Empire, ca. 1800**
The sheer size of the Qing Empire in China almost inevitably led to its profound cultural influence on the rest of Asia.

Qianlong (chyan-luhng) (r. 1736–1796) understood that the Qing's capacity to hold the multiethnic empire together rested on their ability to appeal to all those they ruled. Besides speaking Manchu and Chinese, Qianlong learned to converse in Mongolian, Uighur, Tibetan, and Tangut, and he addressed envoys in their own languages. He became as much a patron of Tibetan Buddhism as of Chinese Confucianism. He initiated a massive project to translate the Tibetan Buddhist canon into Mongolian and Manchu and had huge multilingual dictionaries compiled.

To demonstrate to the Chinese scholar-official elite that he was a sage emperor, Qianlong worked on affairs of state from dawn until early afternoon and then turned to reading, painting, and calligraphy. He was ostentatious in his devotion to his mother, visiting her daily and tending to her comfort with all the devotion of the most filial Chinese son. He took several tours down the Grand Canal to the southeast, in part to emulate his grandfather, in part to entertain his mother, who accompanied him on these tours.

Despite these displays of Chinese virtues, the Qianlong emperor was alert to any signs of anti-Manchu thoughts or actions. He ordered full searches for books with disparaging references to the Manchus or to previous alien conquerors like the Jurchens and Mongols. Sometimes passages were deleted or rewritten, but when an entire book was offensive, it was destroyed.

Throughout Qianlong's reign, China remained an enormous producer of manufactured goods and led the way in assembly-line production. The government operated huge textile factories, but some private firms were even larger. Hangzhou had a textile firm that gave work to 4,000 weavers, 20,000 spinners, and 10,000 dyers and finishers. The porcelain kilns at Jingdezhen employed the division of labor on a large scale and were able to supply porcelain to much of the world. The growth of the economy benefited the Qing state, and the treasury became so full that the Qianlong emperor was able to cancel taxes on several occasions.

## Imperial Expansion

The Qing Dynasty put together a multiethnic empire that was larger than that of any earlier Chinese dynasty. Taiwan was acquired in 1683. In 1696 Kangxi led an army of eighty thousand men into Mongolia, and within a few years Manchu supremacy was accepted there. Cannon and muskets gave Qing forces military superiority over the Mongols, who were armed only with bows and arrows. Thus the Qing could dominate the steppe cheaply, effectively ending two thousand years of Inner Asian military advantage.

In the 1720s the Qing established a permanent garrison of banner soldiers in Tibet. By this time, the expanding Qing and Russian Empires were nearing each other. In 1689 the Manchu and the Russian rulers approved a treaty — written in Russian, Manchu, Chinese, and Latin — defining their borders in Manchuria and regulating trade. Another treaty in 1727 allowed a Russian ecclesiastical mission to reside in Beijing and a trade caravan to make a trip from Russia to Beijing once every three years.

The last region to be annexed was Chinese Turkestan (the modern province of Xinjiang). Both the Han and the Tang Dynasties had stationed troops in the region, exercising loose overlordship, but neither the Song nor the Ming had tried to control the area. The Qing won the region in the 1750s through a series of campaigns against Uighur and Dzungar Mongol forces.

# Japan's Middle Ages, ca. 1400–1600

## How did Japan change during this period of political instability?

In the twelfth century Japan entered an age dominated by military men, an age that can be compared to Europe's feudal age. The Kamakura Shogunate (1185–1333) had its capital in the east, at Kamakura. It was succeeded by the Ashikaga Shogunate (1338–1573), which returned the government to Kyoto (KYOH-toh) and helped launch, during the fifteenth century, the great age of Zen-influenced Muromachi culture. The sixteenth century brought civil war over succession to the shogunate, leading to the building of massive castles and the emergence of rulers of obscure origins who eventually unified the realm.

## Muromachi Culture

The headquarters of the Ashikaga shoguns were on Muromachi Street in Kyoto, and the refined and elegant style that they promoted is often called Muromachi culture. The shoguns patronized Zen Buddhism, the school of Buddhism associated with meditation and mind-to-mind transmission of truth.

Zen ideas of simplicity permeated the arts. The Silver Pavilion built by the shogun Yoshimasa (r. 1449–1473) epitomizes Zen austerity. Yoshimasa was also influential in the development of the tea ceremony, which celebrated the beauty of imperfect objects, such as plain or misshapen cups or pots. Spare monochrome paintings fit into this aesthetic, as did simple asymmetrical flower arrangements.

The shoguns were also patrons of the **Nō theater**. Nō drama originated in popular forms of entertainment, including comical skits and dances directed to the gods. It was transformed into high art by Zeami (1363–1443), an actor and playwright. Nō was performed on a bare stage with a pine tree painted across the backdrop. One or two actors wearing brilliant brocade robes performed, using stylized gestures and stances, one wearing a mask. The actors were accompanied by a chorus and a couple of musicians playing drums and flute. Many of the stories concerned ghosts consumed by jealous passions or the desire for revenge. The performers conveyed emotions and ideas as much through gestures, stances, and dress as through words. Zeami argued that the most meaningful moments came during silence, when the actor's spiritual presence allowed the audience to catch a glimpse of the mysterious and inexpressible.

## Civil War

Civil war began in Kyoto in 1467 as a struggle over succession to the shogunate. Rival claimants and their followers used arson as their chief weapon and burned down temples and mansions, destroying much of the city and its treasures. Once Kyoto was laid waste, war spread to outlying areas. When the shogun could no longer protect cities, merchants banded together to hire mercenaries. In the political vacuum, the Lotus League, a commoner-led religious sect united by faith in the saving power of the Lotus Sutra, set up a commoner-run government that collected taxes and settled disputes. In 1536, during eight days of fighting, the powerful Buddhist monastery Enryakuji attacked the League and its temples, burned much of the city, and killed men, women, and children who were thought to be believers.

In these confused and violent circumstances, power devolved to the local level, where warlords, from the **daimyo** (DIGH-myoh) class of regional lords, built their power bases. Many of the most successful daimyo were self-made men who rose from obscurity.

The violence of the period encouraged castle building. The castles were built not on mountaintops but on level plains, and they were surrounded by moats and walls made from huge stones. Inside a castle was an elegantly decorated many-storied keep. Though relatively safe from incendiary missiles, the keeps were vulnerable to Western-style cannon, introduced in the 1570s.

## The Victors: Nobunaga and Hideyoshi

The first daimyo to gain a predominance of power was Oda Nobunaga (1534–1582). A samurai of the lesser daimyo class, he recruited followers from masterless samurai who had been living by robbery and extortion. After he won control of his native province in 1559, he immediately set out to extend his power through central Japan. A key step was destroying the military power of the great monasteries. To increase revenues, he minted coins, the first government-issued money in Japan since 958. He also eliminated customs barriers and opened the little fishing village of Nagasaki to foreign commerce; it soon became Japan's largest port.

In 1582, in an attempted coup, Nobunaga was forced by one of his vassals to commit suicide. His general and staunchest adherent, Toyotomi Hideyoshi (1537–1598), avenged him and continued the drive toward unification of the daimyo-held lands, finally completed in 1590.

Like the Ming founder, Hideyoshi (HEE-deh-YOH-shee) was a peasant's son who rose to power through military talent. A series of campaigns brought all of Japan under Hideyoshi's control. Hideyoshi soothed the vanquished daimyo as Nobunaga had done—with lands and military positions—but he also required them to swear allegiance and to obey him down to the smallest particular. For the first time in over two centuries, Japan had a single ruler.

Hideyoshi did his best to ensure that future peasants' sons would not be able to rise as he had. His great sword hunt of 1588 collected weapons from farmers, who were no longer allowed to wear swords. Restrictions were also placed on samurai; they were prohibited from leaving their lord's service or switching occupations.

**Matsumoto Castle**
Hideyoshi built Matsumoto Castle between 1594 and 1597. Designed to be impregnable, it was surrounded by a moat and had a base constructed of huge stones. In the sixteenth and early seventeenth centuries Spanish and Portuguese missionaries compared Japanese castles favorably to European castles of the period. (Tanatat Pongpibool/Getty Images)

To improve tax collection, Hideyoshi ordered a survey of the entire country that tied each peasant household to the land. With the country pacified, Hideyoshi embarked on an ill-fated attempt to conquer Korea and China that ended only with his death, discussed later in this chapter.

# The Tokugawa Shogunate, to 1800

## What was life like in Japan during the Tokugawa peace?

On his deathbed, Hideyoshi set up a council of regents to govern during the minority of his infant son. The strongest regent was Hideyoshi's long-time supporter Tokugawa Ieyasu (toh-koo-GAH-wuh ee-eh-YAH-soo) (1543–1616). In 1600 at Sekigahara, Ieyasu smashed a coalition of daimyo defenders of the heir and began building his own government—thus ending the long period of civil war. In 1603 he took the title *shogun*. The **Tokugawa Shogunate** that Ieyasu fashioned lasted until 1867. This era is also called the Edo (AY-doh) period after the location of the shogunate in the city of Edo (now called Tokyo), starting Tokyo's history as Japan's most important city (Map 21.2).

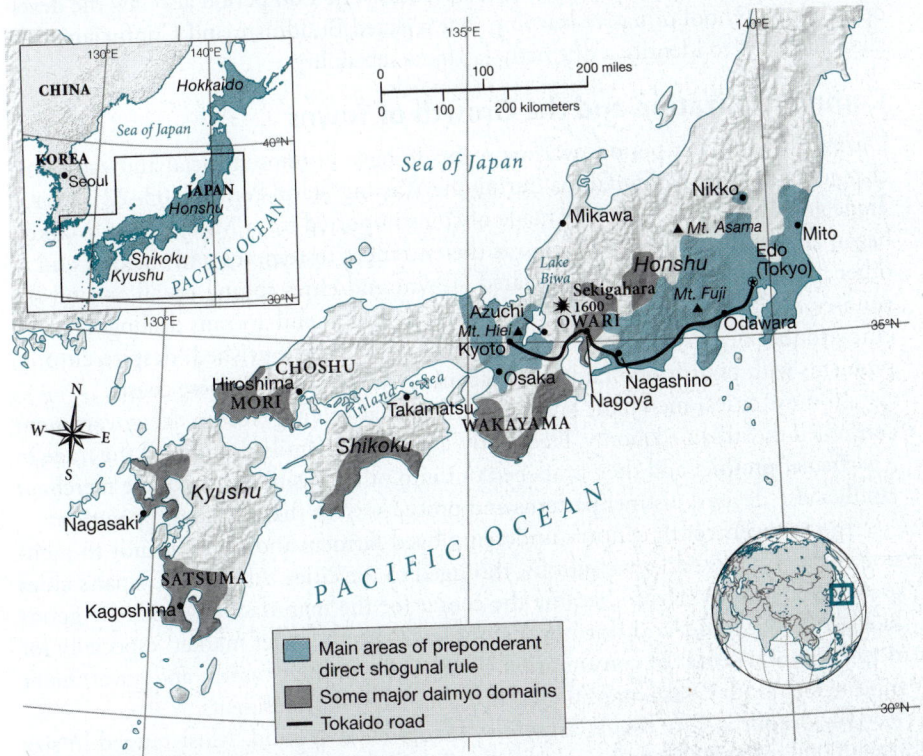

**MAP 21.2   Tokugawa Japan, 1603–1867**
The lands that the shogunate directly controlled were concentrated near its capital at Edo. The daimyo of distant places, such as the island of Kyushu, were required to make long journeys to and from Edo every year.

## Tokugawa Government

Over the course of the seventeenth century the Tokugawa shoguns worked to consolidate relations with the daimyo. In a scheme resembling the later residency requirements imposed by Louis XIV in France (see "The Absolutist Palace" in Chapter 18), Ieyasu set up the **alternate residence system**, which compelled the lords to live in Edo every other year and to leave their wives and sons there—essentially as hostages.

The peace imposed by the Tokugawa Shogunate brought a steady rise in population to about 30 million people by 1800. To maintain stability, the early Tokugawa shoguns froze social status. Daimyo were prohibited from moving troops outside their frontiers, making alliances, and coining money. Samurai and peasants were kept strictly apart. Samurai were defined as those permitted to carry swords. Prohibited from owning land, they had to live in castles (which evolved into castle-towns), and they depended on stipends from their lords, the daimyo. Likewise, merchants and artisans had to live in towns and could not own land.

After 1639 Japan limited its contacts with the outside world because of concerns both about the loyalty of subjects converted to Christianity by European missionaries and about the imperialist ambitions of European powers. However, China remained an important trading partner and source of ideas. The Edo period also saw the development of a school of native learning that rejected Buddhism and Confucianism as alien and tried to identify a distinctly Japanese sensibility.

## Commercialization and the Growth of Towns

During the civil war period, warfare seems to have promoted social and economic change, much as it had in China during the Warring States Period (403–221 B.C.E.). Trade grew, and greater use was made of coins imported from Ming China. Markets began appearing at river crossings, at the entrances to temples and shrines, and at other places where people congregated. Towns and cities sprang up all around the country, some of them around the new castles. Traders and artisans dealing in a specific product began forming guilds. Foreign trade also flourished, despite chronic problems with pirates who raided the Japanese, Korean, and Chinese coasts.

In most cities, merchant families with special privileges from the government controlled the urban economy. Frequently, a particular family dominated the trade in a particular product and then branched out into other businesses. Japanese merchant families also devised distinct patterns and procedures for their business operations.

In the seventeenth century underemployed farmers and samurai, not to mention the ambitious and adventurous, thronged to the cities. As a result, Japan's cities grew tremendously. Kyoto became the center for the manufacture of luxury goods like lacquer, brocade, and fine porcelain. Osaka was the chief market, especially for rice. Edo was a center of consumption by the daimyo, their vassals, and government bureaucrats. Both Osaka and Edo reached about a million residents.

Two hundred fifty towns came into being in this period. Most ranged in size from 3,000 to 20,000 people, but a few, such as Hiroshima, Kagoshima, and Nagoya, had populations of between 65,000 and 100,000. In addition, perhaps two hundred towns along the main road to Edo emerged to meet the needs of men traveling on the alternate residence system. In the eighteenth century perhaps 4 million people, 5 percent of the Japanese population, resided in cities or towns.

## The Life of the People in the Edo Period

The Tokugawa shoguns brought an end to civil war by controlling the military. Stripped of power and required to spend alternate years at Edo, many of the daimyo and samurai passed their lives in idle pursuit of pleasure. They spent extravagantly on paintings, concubines, boys, the theater, and the redecoration of their castles. These temptations, as well as more sophisticated pleasures and the heavy costs of maintaining alternate residences at Edo, gradually bankrupted the warrior class.

All major cities contained places of amusement for men — teahouses, theaters, restaurants, and houses of prostitution. Desperately poor parents sometimes sold their daughters to entertainment houses (as they did in China and medieval Europe), and the most attractive or talented girls, trained in singing, dancing, and conversational arts, became courtesans, later called geishas (GAY-shahz), "accomplished persons."

Cities were also the center for commercial publishing. The art of color woodblock printing was perfected during this period. As in contemporary China, the reading public eagerly purchased fiction and the scripts for plays. Ihara Saikaku (1642–1693) wrote stories of the foibles of townspeople in such books as *Five Women Who Loved Love* and *The Life of an Amorous Man*. One of the puppet plays of Chikamatsu Monzaemon (1653–1724) tells the story of the son of a business owner who, caught between duty to his family and love of a prostitute, decides to resolve the situation by double suicide. Similar stories were also performed in Kabuki theater, where plays could go on all day, actors wore elaborate makeup, and men trained to impersonate women performed female roles.

Almost as entertaining as attending the theater was watching the long processions of daimyo, their retainers, and their luggage as they passed back and forth to and from Edo every year. The shogunate prohibited most travel by commoners, but they could get passports to take pilgrimages, visit relatives, or seek the soothing waters of medicinal hot springs. Setting out on foot, groups of villagers would travel to such shrines as Ise, often taking large detours to visit Osaka or Edo to sightsee or attend the theater.

During the seventeenth and eighteenth centuries daimyo and upper-level samurai paid for their extravagant lifestyles by raising taxes on their subordinate peasants from 30 or 40 percent of the rice crop to 50 percent. Not surprisingly, this angered peasants, and peasant protests became chronic during the eighteenth century. Natural disasters also added to the peasants' misery. In 1783 Mount Asama erupted, spewing volcanic ash that darkened the skies all summer; the resulting crop failures led to famine. When famine recurred again in 1787, commoners rioted for five days in Edo, smashing merchants' stores and pouring sake and rice into the muddy streets. The shogunate responded by trying to control the floating population of day laborers without families in the city. At one point they were rounded up and transported to work the gold mines in an island off the north coast, where most of them died within two or three years.

This picture of peasant hardship tells only part of the story. Agricultural productivity increased substantially during the Tokugawa period. Peasants who improved their lands and increased their yields continued to pay the same assessed tax and could pocket the surplus as profit. They could also take on other work. At Hirano near Osaka, for example, 61.7 percent of all arable land was sown in cotton. The peasants ginned the cotton locally before transporting it to wholesalers in Osaka. In many rural places, as many peasants worked in the manufacture of silk, cotton, or vegetable oil as in the production of rice.

Coastal fishing also expanded during the Edo period. Fishermen learned to dry fish, making it easier to cope with uneven supplies. They also learned that dried fish could be pulverized and pressed into fishmeal cakes, which were in demand as fertilizer for commercial crops like cotton and tobacco. Fishermen began using larger boats with crews of up to fifty men who would spread huge nets to trap fish. They also began to hunt whales for their meat and blubber, which was used to make oil. Merchants organized whaling fleets with hundreds of men on numerous ships. The ships would steer migrating whales toward the shore, where they would be netted, killed with harpoons, and hauled onto the shore to be processed.

In comparison to farmers and fishermen, merchants had a much easier life, even if they had no political power. In 1705 the shogunate confiscated the property of a merchant in Osaka "for conduct unbecoming a member of the commercial class" (but more likely because too many samurai owed him money). The government seized 50 pairs of gold screens, 360 carpets, several mansions, 48 granaries and warehouses scattered around the country, and hundreds of thousands of gold pieces. Few merchants possessed such fabulous wealth, but many lived very comfortably.

Within a village, some families would be relatively well-off, others barely able to get by. The village headman generally came from the richest family, but he consulted a council of elders on important matters. Women in better-off families were much more likely to learn to read than women in poor families. Daughters of wealthy peasants studied penmanship, the Chinese classics, poetry, and the proper forms of correspondence, and they rounded out their education with travel. By contrast, girls from middle-level peasant families might have had from two to five years of formal schooling, focused on moral instruction.

By the fifteenth and sixteenth centuries Japan's family and marriage systems had evolved in the direction of a patrilocal, patriarchal system more like China's, and Japanese women had lost the prominent role in high society that they had occupied during the Heian period. It became standard for women to move into their husbands' homes, where they occupied positions subordinate to both their husbands and their mothers-in-law. In addition, elite families stopped dividing their property among all their children; instead they retained it for the sons alone or increasingly for a single son who would continue the family line. Wedding rituals involved both the

**Edo Craftsman at Work** Less than 3 inches tall, this ivory figure shows a parasol maker seated on the floor (the typical Japanese practice) eating his lunch, his tools by his side. (Private Collection/Photo © Boltin Picture Library/ Bridgeman Images)

exchange of betrothal gifts and the movement of the bride from her parents' home to her husband's home. She brought with her a trousseau that provided her with clothes and other items she would need for daily life, but not with land, which would have given her economic autonomy. On the other hand, her position within her new family was more secure, for it became more difficult for a husband to divorce his wife. If her husband fathered children with concubines, she was their legal mother.

A peasant wife shared responsibility for the family's economic well-being with her husband. If of poor or middling status, she worked alongside her husband in the fields, doing the routine work while he did the heavy work. If they were farm hands and worked for wages, the wife invariably earned a third or a half less than her husband. Wives of prosperous farmers never worked in the fields, but they reeled silk, wove cloth, helped in any family business, and supervised the maids. When cotton growing spread to Japan in the sixteenth century, women took on the jobs of spinning and weaving it.

Families were growing smaller in this period in response to the spread of single-heir inheritance. Japanese families restricted the number of children they had by practicing abortion and infanticide, turning to adoption when no heir survived.

Widows and divorcées of the samurai elite—where female chastity was the core of fidelity—were not expected to remarry. Among the peasant classes, by contrast, divorce seems to have been fairly common—the divorce rate was at least 15 percent in the villages near Osaka in the eighteenth century. A poor woman wanting a divorce could simply leave her husband's home. Sometimes Buddhist temple priests served as divorce brokers: they went to the village headman and had him force the husband to agree to a divorce. News of the coming of temple officials was usually enough to produce a letter of separation.

# Maritime Trade, Piracy, and the Entry of Europe into the Asian Maritime Sphere

**How did the sea link the countries of East Asia, and what happened when Europeans entered this maritime sphere?**

In the period 1400–1800 maritime trade and piracy connected China and Japan to each other and also to Korea, Southeast Asia, and Europe. Japan was a major base for pirates. Both Korea and Japan relied on Chinese coinage, and China relied on silver from Japan. During the fifteenth century China launched overseas expeditions. In the sixteenth century European traders appeared, eager for Chinese porcelains and silks, and Christian missionaries followed. Because of political developments in Europe, the international makeup of the European traders in East Asia changed, with the dominant groups being first the Portuguese, then the Dutch, and then the British.

## Zheng He's Voyages

Early in the Ming period, the Chinese government tried to revive the tribute system of the Han (206 B.C.E.–220 C.E.) and Tang (618–907) Dynasties, when China had dominated East Asia and envoys had arrived from dozens of distant lands. To invite more countries to send missions, the third Ming emperor (Chengzu, or Yongle) authorized an extraordinary series of voyages to the Indian Ocean under the command of the Muslim eunuch Zheng He (juhng huh) (1371–1433).

Zheng He's father had made the trip to Mecca, and the seven voyages that Zheng led between 1405 and 1433 followed old Arab trade routes. The first of the seven was made by a fleet of 317 ships, of which 62 were huge, 440 feet long. Each expedition involved from twenty thousand to thirty-two thousand men. Their itineraries included stops in Vietnam, Malaysia, Indonesia, Sri Lanka, India, and, in the later voyages, Hormuz (on the coast of Persia) and East Africa (see Map 16.1). At each stop Zheng He went ashore to visit rulers, transmit messages of China's peaceful intentions, and bestow lavish gifts. Rulers were invited to come to China or send envoys and were offered accommodation on the return voyages. Near the Straits of Malacca, Zheng's fleet battled Chinese pirates, bringing them under control. Zheng He made other shows of force as well, deposing rulers deemed unacceptable in Java, Sumatra, and Sri Lanka.

On the return of these expeditions, the Ming emperor was delighted by the exotic things the fleet brought back, such as giraffes and lions from Africa, fine cotton cloth from India, and gems and spices from Southeast Asia. Ma Huan, an interpreter who accompanied Zheng He, collected data on the plants, animals, peoples, and geography that they encountered and wrote a book titled *The Overall Survey of the Ocean's Shores*. Still, these expeditions were not voyages of discovery; they followed established routes and pursued diplomatic rather than commercial goals.

Why were these voyages abandoned? Officials complained about their cost and modest returns. As a consequence, after 1474 all the remaining ships with three or more masts were broken up and used for lumber. Chinese did not pull back from trade in the South China Sea and Indian Ocean, but the government no longer promoted trade, leaving the initiative to private merchants and migrants.

## Piracy and Japan's Overseas Adventures

One goal of Zheng He's expeditions was to suppress piracy, which had become a problem all along the China coast. Already in the thirteenth century social disorder and banditry in Japan had expanded into seaborne banditry, which occurred within the Japanese islands around the Inland Sea (Map 21.3), in the straits between Korea and Japan, and along the Korean and Chinese coasts. Pirates not only looted settlements but often captured people and held them for ransom. As maritime trade throughout East Asia grew more lively, sea bandits also took to attacking ships to steal their cargo. Although the pirates were called the "Japanese pirates" by both the Koreans and the Chinese, pirate gangs in fact recruited from all countries. The Ryūkyū (ryoo-kyoo) Islands and Taiwan became major bases.

Possibly encouraged by the exploits of these bandits, Hideyoshi, after his victories in unifying Japan, decided to extend his territory across the seas. In 1590, after receiving congratulations from Korea on his victories, Hideyoshi sent a letter asking the Koreans to allow his armies to pass through their country, declaring that his real target was China. He also sent demands for submission to countries of Southeast Asia and to the Spanish governor of the Philippines.

In 1592 Hideyoshi mobilized 158,000 soldiers and 9,200 sailors for his invasion and equipped them with muskets and cannon, which had recently been introduced into Japan. His forces overwhelmed Korean defenders and reached Seoul within three weeks and Pyongyang in two months. A few months later, in the middle of winter, Chinese armies arrived to help defend Korea, and Japanese forces were pushed back from Pyongyang. A stalemate remained in place until 1597, when Hideyoshi sent out new Japanese troops. This time the Ming army and the Korean navy were more

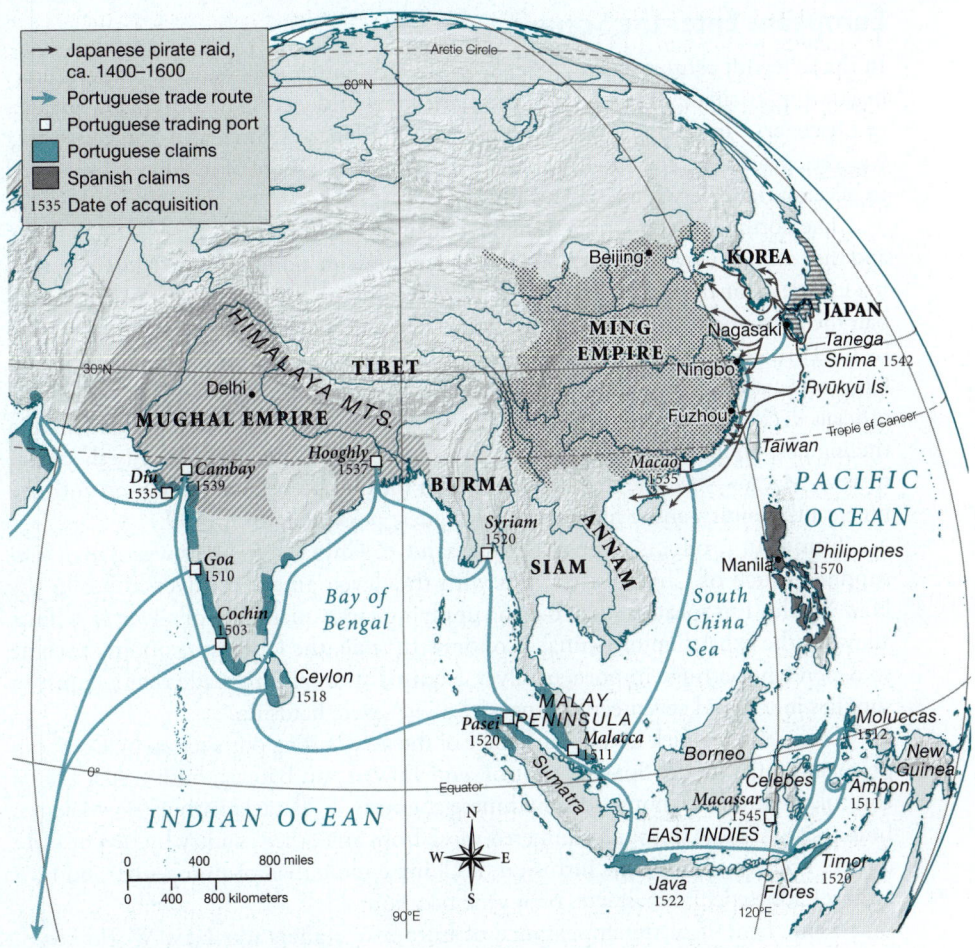

**MAP 21.3    East Asia, ca. 1600**
Pirates and traders often plied the same waters as seaborne trade grew in the sixteenth century.
The Portuguese were especially active in setting up trading ports.

successful in resisting the Japanese. In 1598, after Hideyoshi's death, the Japanese army withdrew from Korea, but Korea was left devastated.

After recovering from the setbacks of these invasions, Korea began to advance socially and economically. During the Joseon (joe-sun) Dynasty (1392–1910), the Korean elite (the yangban) turned away from Buddhism and toward strict Neo-Confucian orthodoxy. As agricultural productivity improved, the population grew from about 4.4 million in 1400 to about 8 million in 1600, 10 million in 1700, and 14 million in 1810 (or about half the size of Japan's population and one-twentieth of China's). With economic advances, slavery declined. When slaves ran away, landowners found that it was less expensive to replace them with sharecroppers than to recapture them. Between 1750 and 1790 the slave population dropped from 30 percent to 5 percent of the population. The hold of the yangban elite, however, remained strong. Through the eighteenth century about two dozen yangban families dominated the civil service examinations, leaving relatively few slots for commoners to rise to through study.

## Europeans Enter the Scene

In the sixteenth century Portuguese, Spanish, and Dutch merchants and adventurers began to participate in the East Asian maritime world (see "The European Voyages of Discovery" in Chapter 16). The trade among Japan, China, and Southeast Asia was very profitable, and the European traders wanted a share of it. They also wanted to develop trade between Asia and Europe.

The Portuguese and Dutch were not reluctant to use force to gain control of trade, and they seized many outposts along the trade routes, including Taiwan. Moreover, they made little distinction between trade, smuggling, and piracy. In 1521 the Ming tried to ban the Portuguese from China. Two years later an expeditionary force commissioned by the Portuguese king to negotiate a friendship treaty defeated its mission by firing on Chinese warships near Guangzhou. In 1557, without informing Beijing, local Chinese officials decided that the way to regulate trade was to allow the Portuguese to build a trading post on uninhabited land near the mouth of the Pearl River. The city they built there—Macao—became the first destination for Europeans going to China until the nineteenth century, and it remained a Portuguese possession until 1999.

European products were not in demand in China, but silver was. Japan had supplied much of China's silver, but with the development of silver mines in the New World, European traders began supplying large quantities of silver to China, allowing the expansion of China's economy. In time, the Chinese economy became so dependent on huge imports of silver acquired through this trade that a cutoff in supplies in the mid-seventeenth century caused severe hardship.

Chinese were quick to take advantage of the new trading ports set up by European powers. Manila, under Spanish control, and Taiwan and Batavia, both under Dutch control, all attracted thousands of Chinese colonists. In Batavia harbor (now Jakarta, Indonesia) Chinese ships outnumbered those from any other country by two or three to one. Local people felt the intrusion of Chinese more than of Europeans, and riots against Chinese led to massacres on several occasions.

A side benefit of the appearance of European traders was New World crops. Sweet potatoes, maize, peanuts, tomatoes, chili peppers, tobacco, and other crops were quickly adopted in East Asia. Sweet potatoes and maize in particular facilitated population growth because they could be grown on land previously thought too sandy or too steep to cultivate. Sweet potatoes became a common poor people's food.

## Christian Missionaries

The Spanish and Portuguese kings supported missionary activity, and merchant vessels soon brought Catholic missionaries to East Asia. The Jesuit priest Francis Xavier had worked in India and the Indies before China and Japan attracted his attention. In 1549 he was the first Christian missionary to arrive in Japan, landing on Kyushu, Japan's southernmost island (see Map 21.2). After he was expelled by the local lord, he traveled throughout western Japan as far as Kyoto, proselytizing wherever warlords allowed. He soon made many converts among the poor and even some among the daimyo. Xavier then set his sights on China but died on an uninhabited island off the China coast in 1552.

Other missionaries carried on his work, and by 1600 there were three hundred thousand baptized Christians in Japan. Most of them lived on Kyushu, where the

**Jesuit Astronomer** Johann Adam Schall von Bell (1592–1666) was a German Jesuit missionary, trained in astronomy, who entered China in 1622. After reaching Beijing in 1630, he joined other Jesuits who worked on calendar reform at the Chinese court, and he was able to stay on after the Manchus took over the government. This lithograph, later hand colored, was used as an illustration in a book published in Amsterdam two years after Bell's death. It draws attention especially to Bell's scientific instruments. (Pictures from History/Bridgeman Images)

shogun's power was weakest and the loyalty of the daimyo most doubtful. In 1615 bands of Christian samurai supported Tokugawa Ieyasu's enemies at the fierce Battle of Osaka. A couple of decades later, thirty thousand peasants in the heavily Catholic area of northern Kyushu revolted. The Tokugawa Shogunate thus came to associate Christianity with domestic disorder and insurrection and in 1639 stepped up its repression of Christianity. Foreign priests were expelled and thousands of Japanese Christians crucified.

Meanwhile, in China the Jesuits concentrated on gaining the linguistic and scholarly knowledge they would need to convert the educated class. The Jesuit Matteo Ricci studied for years in Macao before setting himself up in Nanjing and trying to win over members of the educated class. In 1601 he was given permission to reside in Beijing, where he made several high-placed conversions. He also interested educated Chinese men in Western geography, astronomy, and Euclidean mathematics.

Ricci and his Jesuit successors believed that Confucianism was compatible with Christianity. The Jesuits thought that both faiths shared similar concerns for morality and virtue, and they viewed the Confucian practice of making food offerings to ancestors as an expression of filial reverence rather than as a form of worship. The Franciscan and Dominican friars, who had taken a vow of poverty, disagreed with the Jesuit position. In 1715 religious and political quarrels in Europe led the pope to decide that the Jesuits' accommodating approach was heretical. Angry at this insult, the Kangxi emperor forbade all Christian missionary work in China.

## Learning from the West

Although both China and Japan ended up prohibiting Christian missionary work, other aspects of Western culture were seen as impressive and worth learning. The closed-country policy that Japan instituted in 1639 restricted Japanese from leaving the country and kept European merchants in small enclaves. Still, Japanese interest in Europe did not disappear. Through the Dutch enclave of Deshima on a tiny island in Nagasaki harbor, a stream of Western ideas, arts, and inventions trickled into Japan in the eighteenth century.

In China, too, both scholars and rulers showed an interest in Western learning. The Kangxi emperor frequently discussed scientific and philosophical questions with the Jesuits at court. When he got malaria, he accepted the Jesuits' offer of the medicine quinine. The court was impressed with the Jesuits' skill in astronomy and quickly appointed them to the Board of Astronomy. In 1674 the emperor asked them to re-equip the observatory with European instruments. In the visual arts the emperor and his successors employed Italian painters to make imperial portraits. Firearms and mechanical clocks were also widely admired. The court established its own clock and watch factory, and in 1673 the emperor insisted that the Jesuits manufacture cannon for him and supervise gunnery practice.

Admiration was not one-sided. In the early eighteenth century China enjoyed a positive reputation in Europe. The French philosopher Voltaire wrote of the rationalism of Confucianism and saw advantages to the Chinese political system because the rulers did not put up with parasitical aristocrats or hypocritical priests. Chinese medical practice also drew European interest. One Chinese practice that Europeans adopted was "variolation," an early form of smallpox inoculation.

## The Shifting International Environment in the Eighteenth Century

The East Asian maritime world underwent many changes from the sixteenth to the eighteenth centuries. As already noted, the Japanese pulled back their own traders and limited opportunities for Europeans to trade in Japan. In China the Qing government limited trading contacts with Europe to Guangzhou in the far south in an attempt to curb piracy. Portugal lost many of its bases to the Dutch, and by the eighteenth century the British had become as active as the Dutch. In the seventeenth century the British and Dutch sought primarily porcelains and silk, but in the eighteenth century tea became the commodity in most demand.

By the late eighteenth century Britain had become a great power and did not see why China should be able to dictate the terms of trade. Wanting to renegotiate relations, King George III sent Lord George Macartney to China in 1793 with six hundred cases of British goods, ranging from clocks and telescopes to Wedgwood pottery and landscape paintings. The Qianlong emperor, however, was not impressed. As he pointed out in his formal reply, the Qing Empire "possesses all things in prolific abundance and lacks no product within its own borders"; thus trading with Europe was a kindness, not a necessity.[2]

# Chapter Summary

After the fall of the Mongols, China was ruled by the native Ming Dynasty for nearly three centuries. The dynasty's founder ruled for thirty years, becoming more paranoid and despotic over time. Very few of his successors were particularly good rulers, yet China thrived in many ways. Population grew as food production increased. Educational levels were high as more and more men prepared for the civil service examinations. Urban culture was lively, and publishing houses put out novels, short stories, and plays in the vernacular language for large audiences.

In 1644 the Ming Dynasty fell to the non-Chinese Manchus. The Manchu rulers proved more competent than the Ming emperors and were able to both maintain peace and expand the empire to incorporate Mongolia, Tibet, and Central Asia. Population grew steadily under Manchu rule.

During the fifteenth and sixteenth centuries Japan was fragmented by civil war. As daimyo attacked and defeated each other, power was gradually consolidated, until Hideyoshi gained control of most of the country. Japan also saw many cultural developments during this period, including the increasing influence of Zen ideas on the arts and the rise of Nō theater.

After Hideyoshi's death, power was seized by Tokugawa Ieyasu, the founder of the Tokugawa Shogunate. During the seventeenth and eighteenth centuries Japan reaped the rewards of peace. The early rulers tried to create stability by freezing the social structure and limiting foreign contact to the city of Nagasaki. As the wealth of the business classes grew, the samurai, now dependent on fixed stipends, became progressively poorer. Samurai and others in search of work and pleasure streamed into the cities.

Between 1400 and 1800 maritime trade connected the countries of Asia, but piracy was a perpetual problem. Early in this period China sent out naval expeditions looking to promote diplomatic contacts, reaching as far as Africa. In the sixteenth century European traders arrived in China and Japan and soon developed profitable trading relationships. Trade with Europe brought silver, New World crops, new ideas, and more advanced weapons. The Catholic missionaries who began to arrive in Asia introduced Western science and learning as well as Christianity, until they were banned in both Japan and China. Although the shogunate severely restricted trade, some Western scientific ideas and technology entered Japan through the port of Nagasaki. Chinese, too, took an interest in Western painting, astronomy, and firearms. Because Europeans saw much to admire in East Asia in this period, ideas also flowed both ways.

## NOTES

1. L. J. Gallagher, trans., *China in the Sixteenth Century: The Journals of Matthew Ricci, 1583–1610* (New York: Random House, 1953), p. 23.
2. Pei-kai Cheng and M. Lestz, with J. Spence, eds., *The Search for Modern China: A Documentary History* (New York: W. W. Norton, 1999), p. 106.

## MAKE CONNECTIONS   LOOK AHEAD

During the four centuries from 1400 to 1800, the countries of East Asia became increasingly connected. On the oceans they were linked by trade and piracy, and for the first time a war involved China, Korea, and Japan. At the same time, their cultures and social structures were in no sense converging. The elites of China and Japan were very different: in Japan elite status was hereditary, while in China the key route to status and power involved doing well on a written examination. In Japan the samurai elite were expected to be skilled warriors, but in China the highest prestige went to men of letters. The Japanese woodblock prints that capture many features of the entertainment quarters in Japanese cities show a world distinct from anything in China.

By the end of this period, East Asian countries found themselves in a rapidly changing international environment, mostly because of revolutions occurring far from their shores. The next two chapters take up the story of these revolutions, first the political ones in America, France, and Haiti, and then the Industrial Revolution that began in Britain. In time, these revolutions would profoundly alter East Asia as well.

# Chapter 21 Review

## IDENTIFY KEY TERMS

**Identify and explain the significance of each item below.**

Ming Dynasty (p. 527)

civil service examinations (p. 530)

Qing Dynasty (p. 533)

banners (p. 533)

Nō theater (p. 537)

daimyo (p. 538)

Tokugawa Shogunate (p. 539)

alternate residence system (p. 540)

## REVIEW THE MAIN IDEAS

**Answer the focus questions from each section of the chapter.**

1. What sort of state and society developed in China after the Mongols were ousted? (p. 527)

2. Did the return of alien rule with the Manchus have any positive consequences for China? (p. 533)

3. How did Japan change during this period of political instability? (p. 537)

4. What was life like in Japan during the Tokugawa peace? (p. 539)

5. How did the sea link the countries of East Asia, and what happened when Europeans entered this maritime sphere? (p. 543)

## MAKE COMPARISONS AND CONNECTIONS

**Analyze the larger developments and continuities within and across chapters.**

1. How does the Qing Dynasty compare as an empire to other Eurasian empires of its day (Chapters 17 and 18)?

2. How were the attractions of city life in China and Japan of this period similar to those in other parts of Eurasia (Chapters 17 and 18)?

3. Can you think of any other cases in world history in which a farmer's son rose to the top of the power structure the way that Zhu Yuanzhang and Hideyoshi did? Why was this uncommon?

## CHRONOLOGY

**ca. 1350–1520**    • Italian Renaissance (Ch. 15)

**1368–1644**    • Ming Dynasty in China

**1405–1433**    • Zheng He's naval expeditions

**1407–1420**    • Construction of Beijing as Chinese capital

**1467–1600**    • Period of civil war in Japan

**1492**    • Columbus reaches America (Ch. 16)

**1517**    • Luther's Ninety-five Theses (Ch. 15)

**1549**    • First Jesuit missionaries land in Japan

**1557**    • Portuguese set up trading base at Macao

**1603–1867**    • Tokugawa Shogunate in Japan

**1631–1648**    • Construction of Taj Mahal under Shah Jahan in India (Ch. 17)

**1639**    • Japan restricts contact with the outside world and intensifies suppression of Christianity

**1644–1911**    • Manchus' Qing Dynasty in China

**ca. 1690–1789**    • The Enlightenment in Europe (Ch. 19)

**1763**    • Treaty of Paris recognizes British control over much of India (Ch. 17)

**1793**    • Lord Macartney's diplomatic visit to China

# 22

# Revolutions in the Atlantic World

## 1775–1825

**A GREAT WAVE OF REVOLUTION ROCKED THE ATLANTIC WORLD FROM 1775 to 1825.** As trade goods, individuals, and ideas circulated in ever-greater numbers across the Atlantic Ocean, debates and events in one locale soon influenced those in another. Changing social realities challenged the old order of life, and Enlightenment ideals of freedom and equality flourished, leading reformers in many places to demand fundamental changes in politics and government. At the same time, wars fought for dominance of the Atlantic economy burdened European governments with crushing debts, making them vulnerable to calls for reform.

The revolutionary era began in 1775 in North America, where the United States of America won freedom from Britain in 1783. Then in 1789 France became the leading revolutionary nation. It established first a constitutional monarchy, then a radical republic, and finally a new European empire under Napoleon that would last until 1815. Inspired both by the ideals of the revolution on the continent and by internal colonial conditions, enslaved people in the French colony of Saint-Domingue rose up in 1791, followed by colonial settlers and indigenous and enslaved people in Latin America. Their rebellion would eventually lead to the creation of independent nations in the Caribbean, Mexico, and South America. In Europe and its former colonies, the world of modern politics was born.

# Background to Revolution

## What were the factors behind the age of revolution in the Atlantic world?

The origins of revolutions in the Atlantic world were complex. No one cause lay behind them, nor was revolution inevitable or certain of success. However, a set of shared factors helped set the stage for reform. They included fundamental social and economic changes and political crises that eroded state authority; the impact of political ideas derived from the Enlightenment; and, perhaps most important, imperial competition and financial crises generated by the expenses of imperial warfare.

## Social Change

Eighteenth-century European society was legally divided into groups with special privileges, such as the nobility and the clergy, and groups with special burdens, such as the peasantry. Nobles were the largest landowners. They enjoyed exemption from many taxes and exclusive rights such as hunting and bearing swords. In most countries, various middle-class groups — professionals, merchants, and guild masters — enjoyed privileges that allowed them to monopolize all sorts of economic activity.

Traditional prerogatives persisted in societies undergoing dramatic change. Due to increased agricultural production, Europe's population rose rapidly after 1750, and its cities and towns swelled in size. Inflation kept pace with demography, making it increasingly difficult for urban people to find affordable food and living space. One way they kept up, and even managed to participate in the new consumer revolution, was by working harder and for longer hours. More positive developments were increased schooling and a rise in literacy rates, particularly among urban men.

Economic growth created new inequalities between rich and poor. While the poor struggled with rising prices, investors grew rich from the spread of rural

**The Awakening of the Third Estate**  French inhabitants were legally divided into three orders, or estates: the clergy, the nobility, and everyone else. This cartoon from July 1789 represents the third estate as a common man throwing off his chains and rising up against his oppression during the French Revolution, as the first estate (the clergy) and the second estate (the nobility) look on in fear.  (Musée de la Ville de Paris, Musée Carnavalet, Paris, France/Bridgeman Images)

manufacture and overseas trade. Old distinctions between the landed aristocracy and city merchants began to fade as enterprising nobles put money into trade and rising middle-class bureaucrats and merchants bought landed estates and noble titles. Marriages between nobles and wealthy, educated commoners (called the *bourgeoisie* [boorzh-wah-ZEE] in France) served both groups' interests, and a mixed-caste elite began to take shape.

Another social change involved the racial regimes established in European colonies. By the late eighteenth century European law accepted that only Africans and people of African descent were subject to slavery. Even free people of color—a term for nonslaves of African or mixed African-European descent—were subject to significant restrictions on their legal rights. European settlers in the colonies used extremely brutal methods to enforce their perceived racial superiority.

In Spanish America and Brazil, people of European and African descent intermingled with the very large indigenous population. Demographers estimate that indigenous people accounted for 60 to 75 percent of the population of Latin America at the end of the colonial period, in spite of tremendous population losses in the sixteenth and seventeenth centuries. The colonies that became Peru and Bolivia had indigenous majorities, while the regions that became Argentina and Chile had

European majorities. Until the reforms of Charles III, indigenous people and Spaniards were required by law to live in separate communities, although many of the former secretly fled to Spanish cities and haciendas to escape forced-labor obligations. Mestizos (meh-STEE-zohz), people of mixed European and indigenous descent, held a higher social status than other nonwhites, but a lower status than Europeans who could prove the "purity" of their blood.

## Demands for Liberty and Equality

In addition to destabilizing social changes, the ideals of liberty and equality helped fuel revolutions in the Atlantic world. The call for liberty was first of all a call for individual human rights. Supporters of the cause of individual liberty (who became known as "liberals" in the early nineteenth century) demanded freedom to worship according to the dictates of their consciences, an end to censorship, and freedom from arbitrary laws and from judges who simply obeyed orders from the government.

The call for liberty was also a call for a new kind of government. Reformers believed that the people had sovereignty — that is, that the people alone had the authority to make laws limiting an individual's freedom of action. In practice, this system of government meant choosing legislators who represented the people and were accountable to them. Monarchs might retain their thrones, but their rule should be constrained by the will of the people.

Equality was a more ambiguous idea. Eighteenth-century liberals argued that, in theory, all citizens should have identical rights and liberties. However, they accepted a number of distinctions. First, most male eighteenth-century liberals believed that equality between men and women was neither practical nor desirable. Women played an important informal role in the Atlantic revolutions, but in each case male legislators limited formal political rights — the right to vote, to run for office, to participate in government — to men. Second, few questioned the superiority of people of European descent over those of indigenous or African origin. Even those who believed that the slave trade was unjust and should be abolished, such as Thomas Jefferson, usually felt that emancipation was so socially and economically dangerous that it must be undertaken slowly and gradually, if at all.

Finally, liberals never believed that everyone should be equal economically. Great differences in wealth and income between rich and poor were perfectly acceptable, so long as every free white male had a legally equal chance at economic gain. However limited they appear to modern eyes, these demands for liberty and equality were revolutionary in the eighteenth-century context.

The two most important Enlightenment influences for late-eighteenth-century liberals were John Locke and the baron de Montesquieu. Locke maintained that England's long political tradition rested on "the rights of Englishmen" and on representative government through Parliament. He argued that if a government oversteps its proper function of protecting the natural rights of life, liberty, and private property, it becomes a tyranny. Montesquieu was also an admirer of England's Parliament. He believed that powerful "intermediary groups" — such as the judicial nobility of which he was a proud member — offered the best defense of liberty against despotism.

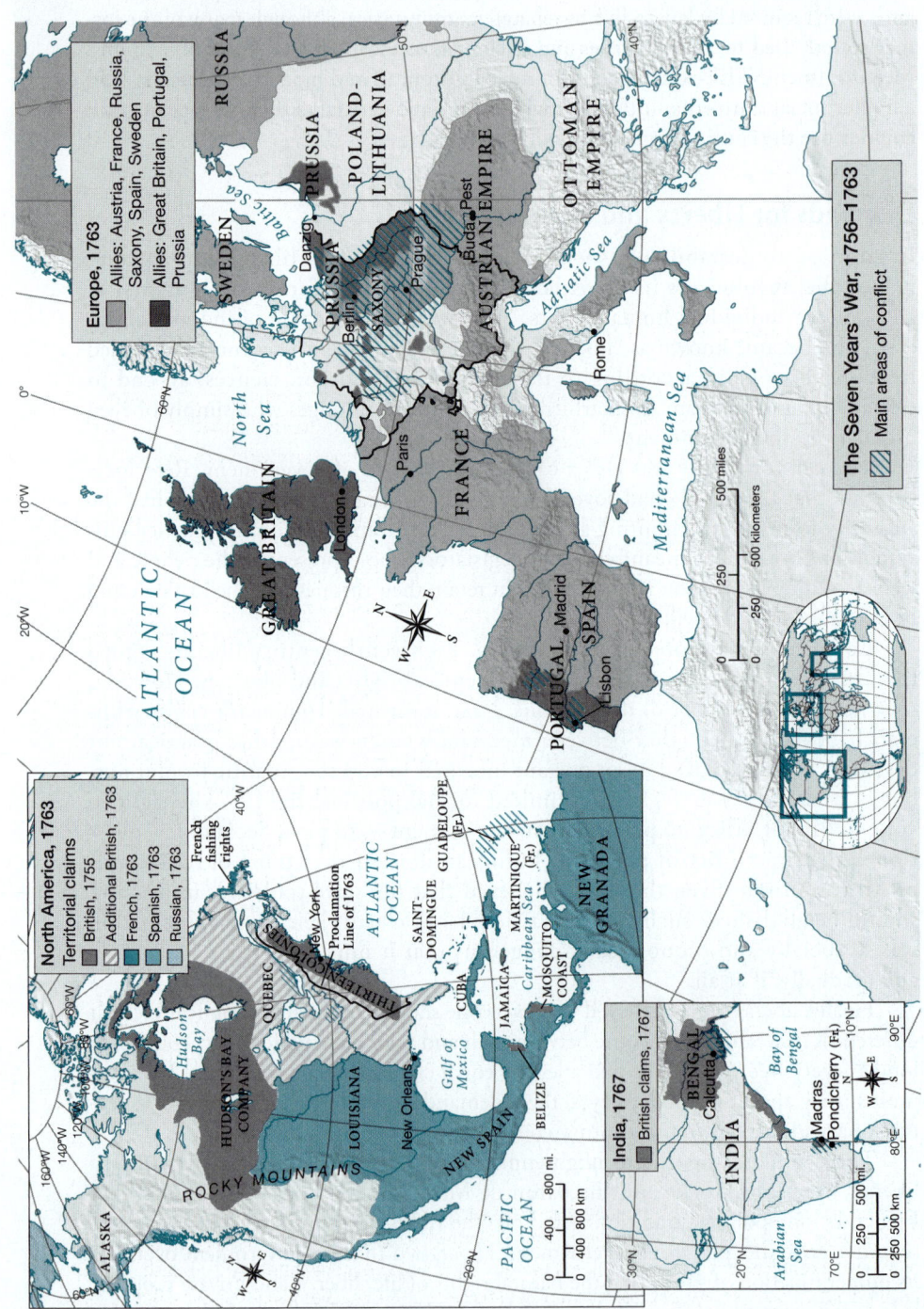

**Europe, 1763**

Allies: Austria, France, Russia, Saxony, Spain, Sweden

Allies: Great Britain, Portugal, Prussia

**The Seven Years' War, 1756–1763**

Main areas of conflict

**North America, 1763**

Territorial claims

British, 1755

Additional British, 1763

French, 1763

Spanish, 1763

Russian, 1763

**India, 1767**

British claims, 1767

The Atlantic revolutions began with aspirations for equality and liberty among the social elite. Soon, however, dissenting voices emerged as some revolutionaries became frustrated with the limitations of liberal notions of equality and liberty and clamored for a fuller realization of these concepts. Depending on location, their demands included political rights for women and free people of color, emancipation of the enslaved, better treatment of indigenous people, and government regulations to reduce economic inequality. The age of revolution was thus characterized by bitter conflicts over how far reform should go and to whom it should apply.

## The Seven Years' War

The roots of revolutionary ideology could be found in Enlightenment texts, but it was by no means inevitable that such ideas would result in revolution. Instead events — political, economic, and military — created crises that opened the door for radical action. One of the most important was the global conflict known as the Seven Years' War (1756–1763), known as the French and Indian War in North America.

The war's battlefields stretched from central Europe to India to North America, pitting a new alliance of England and Prussia against the French, Austrians, and, later, Spanish. Its origins were in conflicts left unresolved at the end of the War of the Austrian Succession in 1748, during which Prussia had seized the Austrian territory of Silesia. In central Europe, Austria's empress Maria Theresa vowed to win back Silesia and to crush Prussia. By the end of the Seven Years' War, Maria Theresa had almost succeeded, but Prussia survived with its boundaries intact.

In North America the encroachment of English settlers into territory claimed by the French in the Ohio Valley resulted in skirmishes that soon became war. Although the inhabitants of New France were greatly outnumbered by British colonists, their forces achieved major victories until 1758. Both sides relied on the assistance of Native American nations with whom they had long-standing trade contacts, and they actively sought new indigenous allies during the conflict. The tide of the war turned when the British diverted resources from Europe, using superior sea power to destroy the French fleet and choke French commerce around the world.

British victory on all colonial fronts was ratified in the 1763 **Treaty of Paris**. Canada and all French territory east of the Mississippi River passed to Britain, and France ceded Louisiana to Spain as compensation for Spain's loss of Florida to Britain. France also gave up most of its holdings in India, opening the way to British dominance on the subcontinent (Map 22.1).

< MAP 22.1  **The Seven Years' War in Europe, North America, and India, 1755–1763**
As a result of the war, France lost its vast territories in North America and India. In an effort to avoid costly conflicts with Native Americans living in the newly conquered territory, the British government in 1763 prohibited colonists from settling west of the Appalachian Mountains. One of the few remaining French colonies in the Americas, Saint-Domingue (on the island of Hispaniola) was the most profitable colony in the New World.

The war was ruinously expensive for all participants, and in its aftermath British, French, and Spanish governments had to increase taxes to repay loans, raising a storm of protest and demands for political reform. Since the Caribbean colony of Saint-Domingue (san-doh-MANGH) remained French, revolutionary turmoil in the mother country would directly affect its population. The seeds of revolutionary conflict in the Atlantic world were thus sown.

# The American Revolutionary Era, 1775–1789

### Why and how did American colonists forge a new, independent nation?

Increased taxes and government control sparked colonial protests in the New World, where the era of liberal political revolution began. After revolting against their home country, the thirteen mainland colonies of British North America succeeded in establishing a new unified government. Participants in the revolution believed they were demanding only the traditional rights of Englishmen. But those traditional rights were liberal rights, and in the American context they had strong democratic and popular overtones. Yet in challenging and recasting authority in the colonies, the revolution did not resolve the question of social and political equality, which continued to elude women and enslaved and indigenous people.

## The Origins of the Revolution

The high cost of the Seven Years' War doubled the British national debt. Anticipating further expenses to defend newly conquered territories, the British government broke with tradition and announced that it would maintain a large standing army in North America and tax the colonies directly. In 1765 Parliament passed the Stamp Act, which levied taxes on a long list of commercial and legal documents, diplomas, newspapers, almanacs, and playing cards. These measures seemed perfectly reasonable to the British, for a much heavier stamp tax already existed in Britain, and proceeds from the tax were to fund the defense of the colonies. Nonetheless, the colonists deeply resented the presence of British soldiers in their territories, which had always been policed and defended by their own militias. They also vigorously protested the Stamp Act by rioting and by boycotting British goods. Thus Parliament reluctantly repealed it.

This dispute raised an important political issue. The British government believed that Americans were represented in Parliament, albeit indirectly (like most British people), and that Parliament ruled throughout the empire. Many Americans felt otherwise, and came to see British colonial administration and parliamentary supremacy as grave threats to existing American liberties.

Americans' resistance to these threats was fed by the great degree of independence they had long enjoyed. In British North America, unlike in England and Europe, religious freedom was taken for granted. Colonial assemblies made the important laws, which were seldom overturned by the British government. Also, the right to vote was much more widespread than in England.

Moreover, greater political equality was matched by greater social and economic equality, at least for the free population. Almost all free male inhabitants served as part-time militia members and thus shared in the burden of military defense. There was no hereditary nobility, and independent farmers dominated colonial society. This was particularly true in the northern colonies, where the revolution originated.

In 1770 the so-called Boston Massacre, in which British troops occupying Boston fired on a rebellious crowd, inflamed anti-British feelings. In 1773 disputes over taxes and representation flared up again. Under the Tea Act of that year, the British East India Company secured a profitable monopoly on the tea trade, and colonial merchants were excluded. The price of tea was actually lowered for colonists, but the act generated a great deal of opposition because of its impact on local merchants.

In protest, Boston men disguised as Native Americans held a raucous Tea Party in which they boarded East India Company ships and threw tea from them into the harbor. The British responded with the Coercive Acts of 1774, which closed the port of Boston, curtailed local elections, and expanded the royal governor's power. County conventions in Massachusetts urged that the acts be "rejected as the attempts of a wicked administration to enslave America." Other colonial assemblies joined in the denunciations. In September 1774 the First Continental Congress met in Philadelphia. The more radical members of this assembly argued successfully against concessions to the English Crown. The British Parliament also rejected compromise, and in April 1775 fighting between the Massachusetts militia and British troops began at Lexington and Concord. On June 14, the newly convened Second Continental Congress approved the creation of a Continental Army, joining the independent colonial militias into a common army paid by Congress.

## Independence from Britain

As fighting spread, the colonists moved slowly toward open calls for independence. The uncompromising attitude of the British government and its use of German mercenaries did much to dissolve loyalties to the home country and to unite the separate colonies. *Common Sense* (1775), a brilliant attack by the recently arrived English radical Thomas Paine (1737–1809), also mobilized public opinion in favor of independence.

On July 4, 1776, the Second Continental Congress adopted the **Declaration of Independence**. Written by Thomas Jefferson and others, this document denounced the supposedly tyrannical acts committed by George III (r. 1760–1820) and proclaimed the natural rights of mankind and the sovereignty of the American states. The Declaration of Independence in effect universalized the traditional rights of English people and made them the individual rights of all men.

After the Declaration of Independence, the conflict often took the form of a civil war pitting patriots against Loyalists, those who maintained an allegiance to the Crown. The Loyalists, who numbered up to 20 percent of the total white population, tended to be wealthy and politically moderate. They were few in number in New England and Virginia, but more common in the Deep South and on the western frontier. British commanders also recruited Loyalists among enslaved people by promising freedom to any slave who left his master to fight for the mother country.

On the international scene, the French wanted revenge against the British for the humiliating defeats of the Seven Years' War. Thus they sympathized with the rebels and supplied guns and gunpowder. In 1778 the French government offered the Americans a formal alliance, and in 1779 and 1780 the Spanish and Dutch declared war on Britain. Catherine the Great of Russia helped organize the League of Armed Neutrality to protect neutral shipping rights and succeeded in hampering Britain's naval power.

Thus by 1780 Britain was engaged in an imperial war against most of Europe as well as the thirteen colonies. In these circumstances, and in the face of severe reverses in India, in the West Indies, and at Yorktown in Virginia, a new British government decided to cut its losses and end the war. Under the Treaty of Paris of 1783, Britain recognized the independence of the thirteen colonies and ceded all its territory between the Allegheny Mountains and the Mississippi River to the Americans.

## Framing the Constitution

The liberal program of the American Revolution was consolidated by the federal Constitution, the Bill of Rights, and the creation of a national republic. Assembling in Philadelphia in the summer of 1787, the delegates to the Constitutional Convention were determined to end the period of economic depression, social uncertainty, and weak central leadership that had followed independence. The delegates thus decided to grant the federal, or central, government important powers: regulation of domestic and foreign trade, the right to tax, and the means to enforce its laws.

The central government would operate in Montesquieu's framework of checks and balances, under which authority was distributed across three different branches — the executive, legislative, and judicial branches — which would prevent one interest from gaining too much power. The power of the federal government would in turn be checked by that of the individual states.

These proposals set off a great public debate. Opponents of the proposed Constitution — the **Antifederalists** — charged that the framers of the new document had taken too much power from the individual states and made the federal government too strong. Moreover, many Antifederalists feared for the individual freedoms for which they had fought. To overcome these objections, the Federalists promised to spell out these basic freedoms as soon as the new Constitution was adopted.

The result was the first ten amendments to the Constitution, which the first Congress passed shortly after it met in New York in March 1789. These amendments, ratified in 1791, formed an effective Bill of Rights to safeguard the individual. Most of them — trial by jury, due process of law, the right to assemble, freedom from unreasonable search — had their origins in English law and the English Bill of Rights of 1689. Other rights — freedom of speech, the press, and religion — reflected natural-law theory and the strong value colonists had placed on independence from the start. The second amendment reflected the colonists' belief that a citizen militia, in which all free male citizens were part-time soldiers, was the foundation of a free state.

## Limitations of Liberty and Equality

The American Constitution and the Bill of Rights exemplified the strengths and the limits of what came to be called classical liberalism. Liberty meant individual freedoms and political safeguards. Liberty also meant representative government, but it did not mean democracy, with its principle of one person, one vote. Equality meant equality before the law, not equality of political participation or wealth. It did not mean equal rights for the enslaved, Native Americans, or women.

A vigorous abolitionist movement during the 1780s led to the passage of emancipation laws in all northern states, but slavery remained prevalent in the South, and discord between pro- and antislavery delegates roiled the Constitutional Convention of 1787. The result was a compromise stipulating that an enslaved person would count as three-fifths of a person in tallying population numbers for taxation and proportional representation in the House of Representatives. This solution levied higher taxes on the South, but also guaranteed slaveholding states greater representation in Congress, which they used to oppose emancipation. Congress did ban slavery in federal territory in 1789, then the export of enslaved people from any state, and finally, in 1808, the import of slaves to any state.

The new republic also failed to protect the Native American groups whose lands fell within or alongside the territory ceded by Britain at the Treaty of Paris. The 1787 Constitution promised protection to Native Americans and guaranteed that their land would not be taken without consent. Nonetheless, the rights and interests of Native Americans were generally ignored as a growing colonial population pushed westward.

Women played a vital role in the American Revolution. They were essential participants in boycotts of British goods, which squeezed profits from British merchants and fostered the revolutionary spirit. After the outbreak of war, women raised funds for the Continental Army and took care of farms and workshops when their men went off to fight. Yet despite Abigail Adams's plea to her husband, John Adams, that the framers of the Declaration of Independence should "remember the ladies," women did not receive the right to vote in the new Constitution, an omission confirmed by a clause added in 1844.

# Revolution in France, 1789–1799

### Why and how did revolutionaries in France transform the nation?

Although inspired in part by events in North America, the French Revolution did not mirror the American example. It was more radical and more complex, more influential and more controversial. For Europeans and most of the rest of the world, it was the great revolution of the eighteenth century, the revolution that opened the modern era in politics.

## Breakdown of the Old Order

As did the American Revolution, the French Revolution had its immediate origins in state debt. The efforts of the ministers of King Louis XV (r. 1715–1774) to raise taxes to meet the expenses of the War of the Austrian Succession and the Seven Years' War were thwarted by the high courts, known as the parlements. The noble judges of the parlements resented this threat to their exemption from taxation and decried the government's actions as a form of royal despotism.

When renewed efforts to reform the tax system similarly failed in 1776, the government was forced to finance its enormous expenditures during the American war with borrowed money. As a result, the national debt soared. In 1786 the finance minister informed King Louis XVI (r. 1774–1792) that the nation was on the verge of bankruptcy.

Louis XVI's minister of finance convinced the king to call an assembly of notables in 1787 to gain support for major fiscal reforms. The assembled notables declared that sweeping tax changes required the approval of the **Estates General**, the representative body of all three estates, which had not met since 1614. Louis XVI's efforts to reject their demands failed, and in July 1788 he reluctantly called the Estates General into session.

## The National Assembly

The Estates General was composed of representatives from the three orders of society: the clergy, the nobility, and commoners. On May 5, 1789, the twelve hundred newly elected delegates of the three estates gathered in Versailles for the opening session of the Estates General. They met in an atmosphere of deepening economic crisis, triggered by a poor grain harvest in 1788.

The Estates General was almost immediately deadlocked by arguments about voting procedures. The government insisted that each estate should meet and vote separately, meaning that the two privileged estates could always outvote the third. Critics had demanded instead a single assembly dominated by the third estate. In his famous pamphlet *What Is the Third Estate?* the abbé Emmanuel Joseph Sieyès argued that the nobility was a tiny, overprivileged minority and that commoners constituted the true strength of the French nation.

The issue came to a crisis in June 1789 when delegates of the third estate refused to meet until the king ordered the clergy and nobility to sit with them in a single body. On June 17 the third estate voted to call itself the **National Assembly**. A few days later, the delegates, excluded from their hall because of "repairs," moved to an indoor tennis court where they swore the famous Tennis Court Oath, pledging not to disband until they had been recognized as a National Assembly.

The king's response was disastrously ambivalent. Although he made a conciliatory speech accepting the deputies' demands, he called a large army toward the capital to bring the Assembly under control, and on July 11 he dismissed his finance minister and other liberal ministers. On July 14, 1789, several hundred common people, fearing an attack by the king's army, stormed the Bastille (ba-STEEL), a royal prison, in search of weapons to defend the city. Ill-judged severity on the part of the Crown thus led to the first episodes of popular violence.

Uprisings also rocked the countryside. In July and August 1789 peasants throughout France began to rise in insurrection against their lords. Fear of marauders and vagabonds hired by vengeful landlords — called the Great Fear by contemporaries — seized the rural poor and fanned the flames of rebellion.

The National Assembly responded to the swell of popular anger with a surprise maneuver on the night of August 4, 1789. By a decree of the Assembly, all the old noble privileges — peasant serfdom where it still existed, exclusive hunting rights, the right to collect fees for having legal cases judged in the lord's court, the right to make peasants work on the roads, and a host of other entitlements—were abolished along with tithes paid to the church. On August 27, 1789, the Assembly further issued the Declaration of the Rights of Man and of the Citizen. This clarion call of the liberal revolution guaranteed equality before the law, representative government for a sovereign people, and individual freedom. It was quickly disseminated throughout France, the rest of Europe, and around the world.

The National Assembly's declaration had little practical effect for the poor and hungry people of Paris. The economic crisis worsened after the fall of the Bastille, as aristocrats fled the country and the luxury market collapsed. Foreign markets also shrank, and unemployment among the urban working class grew.

## Constitutional Monarchy

The next two years, until September 1791, saw the consolidation of the liberal revolution. In June 1790 the National Assembly abolished the nobility, and in July the king swore to uphold the as-yet-unwritten constitution. The king remained the head of state, but all lawmaking power now resided in the National Assembly, elected by the wealthiest half of French males. The constitution finally passed in September 1791 was the first in French history. It legalized divorce and broadened women's rights to inherit property and to obtain financial support for illegitimate children from fathers, but excluded women from political office and voting.

In addition to expanding women's legal rights, the National Assembly replaced the patchwork of historic provinces with eighty-three departments of approximately equal size. The deputies prohibited monopolies, guilds, and workers' associations and abolished barriers to trade within France. Thus the National Assembly applied the spirit of the Enlightenment in a thorough reform of France's laws and institutions.

The National Assembly also imposed a radical reorganization on religious life. It granted religious freedom to the small minority of French Jews and Protestants. Furthermore, in November 1789 it nationalized the property of the Catholic Church and abolished monasteries. In July 1790, the revolutionaries took further measures against the church. They established a national church with priests chosen by voters and required Catholic clergy to take an oath of loyalty to the new government. The pope formally condemned this measure, and only half the priests of France swore the oath. Many sincere Christians, especially those in the countryside, were appalled by these changes in the religious order. The attempt to remake the Catholic Church, like the abolition of guilds and workers' associations, sharpened the conflict between the educated classes and the common people that had been emerging in the eighteenth century.

## The National Convention

The outbreak and progress of revolution in France produced great excitement and a sharp division of opinion in Europe and the United States. Liberals and radicals saw a triumph of liberty over despotism, while conservative leaders were deeply troubled by the aroused spirit of reform. In 1790 Edmund Burke published *Reflections on the Revolution in France*, one of the great expressions of European conservatism. He derided abstract principles of "liberty" and "rights" and insisted on the importance of inherited traditions and privileges as a bastion of social stability.

The kings and nobles of continental Europe, who had at first welcomed the revolution in France as weakening a competing power, now feared its impact. In June 1791 the royal family was arrested and returned to Paris after a failed attempt to escape France. To the monarchs of Austria and Prussia, the arrest of a crowned monarch was unacceptable. Two months later they issued the Declaration of Pillnitz, proclaiming their willingness to intervene in France to restore Louis XVI's rule, if necessary.

The new French representative body, called the Legislative Assembly, was dominated by members of the **Jacobin club**, one of the many political clubs that had formed to debate the issues of the day. The Jacobins and other deputies reacted with patriotic fury to the Declaration of Pillnitz, and in April 1792 France declared war on Holy Roman Emperor Francis II of Austria.

France's crusade against tyranny went poorly at first. Prussian forces joined Austria against the French, who broke and fled at their first military encounter with this First Coalition of antirevolutionary foreign powers. The Legislative Assembly declared the country in danger, and volunteers rallied to the capital. In August the Assembly suspended the king from all his functions and imprisoned him.

The fall of the monarchy marked a rapid radicalization of the Revolution. In late September 1792 a new assembly, called the National Convention, was elected by universal manhood suffrage. The Convention proclaimed France a republic, a nation in which the people, instead of a monarch, held sovereign power. Under the leadership of the **Mountain**, the radical faction of the Jacobin club led by Maximilien Robespierre (ROHBZ-pyayr) and Georges Jacques Danton, the Convention tried and convicted the king for treason. On January 21, 1793, Louis was executed. His wife, Marie Antoinette, suffered the same fate later that year.

In February 1793 the National Convention declared war on Britain, the Dutch Republic, and Spain. Republican France was now at war with almost all of Europe, and it faced mounting internal opposition. Peasants in western France revolted against being drafted into the army, with the Vendée region of western France emerging as the epicenter of revolt. Devout Catholics, royalists, and foreign agents encouraged their rebellion.

By March 1793 the National Convention was locked in a struggle between two factions of the Jacobin club, the radical Mountain and the more moderate **Girondists** (juh-RON-dist). With the middle-class delegates so bitterly divided, the laboring poor of Paris emerged as the decisive political factor. The laboring poor and the petty traders were often known as the **sans-culottes** (san-koo-LAHT) ("without breeches") because their men wore trousers instead of the knee breeches of the wealthy. They demanded radical political action to guarantee them their daily bread. The Mountain, sensing an opportunity to outmaneuver the Girondists, joined with sans-culotte activists to engineer a popular uprising. On June 2, 1793, armed sans-culottes invaded the Convention and forced its deputies to arrest twenty-nine Girondist deputies for treason. All power passed to the Mountain.

This military and political crisis led to the most radical period of the Revolution, which lasted from spring 1793 until summer 1794. To deal with threats from within and outside France, the Convention formed the Committee of Public Safety in April 1793. Led by Robespierre, the Committee advanced on several fronts in 1793 and 1794. First, in September 1793 Robespierre and his colleagues established a planned economy. Rather than let supply and demand determine prices, the government set maximum allowable prices for key products. Though the state was too weak to enforce all its price regulations, it did fix the price of bread in Paris at levels the poor could afford.

The government also put the people to work producing arms, munitions, and uniforms for the war effort. The government told craftsmen what to produce, nationalized many small workshops, and requisitioned raw materials and grain. These economic reforms amounted to an emergency form of socialism, which thoroughly frightened Europe's propertied classes and greatly influenced the subsequent development of socialist ideology.

Second, the **Reign of Terror** (1793–1794) enforced compliance with republican beliefs and practices. Special revolutionary courts tried "enemies of the nation" for political crimes. As a result, some forty thousand French men and women were executed or died in prison. Presented as a necessary measure to save the republic, the Terror was a weapon directed against all suspected of opposing the revolutionary government.

In their efforts to impose unity, the Jacobins also took actions to suppress women's participation in political debate, which they perceived as disorderly and a distraction from women's proper place in the home. On October 30, 1793, the National Convention declared, "The clubs and popular societies of women, under whatever denomination are prohibited."

The third element of the Committee's program was to bring about a cultural revolution that would transform former royal subjects into republican citizens. The government sponsored revolutionary art and songs as well as secular holidays and open-air festivals to celebrate republican virtues. It also attempted to rationalize daily life by adopting the decimal system for weights and measures and a new calendar based on ten-day weeks. A campaign of de-Christianization aimed to eliminate Catholic symbols and beliefs. Fearful of the hostility aroused in rural France, however, Robespierre called for a halt to de-Christianization measures in mid-1794.

The final element in the program of the Committee of Public Safety was its appeal to a new sense of national identity and patriotism. With a common language and a common tradition reinforced by the revolutionary ideals of popular sovereignty and democracy, many French people developed an intense emotional attachment to the nation. This was the birth of modern nationalism, the strong identification with one's nation, which would have a profound effect on subsequent European history.

To defend the nation, a decree of August 1793 imposed a draft on all unmarried young men. By January 1794 French armed forces outnumbered those of their enemies almost four to one. To gain new recruits for colonial warfare, the Convention abolished slavery in all French colonies in February 1794. Soon, French armies were victorious on all fronts and domestic revolt was largely suppressed. The republic was saved.

## The Directory

The success of French armies led the Committee of Public Safety to relax emergency economic controls, but it extended the political Reign of Terror. The revolutionary tribunals sent many critics to the guillotine, including long-standing collaborators whom Robespierre believed had turned against him. A group of radicals and moderates in the Convention, knowing that they might be next, organized a conspiracy. They

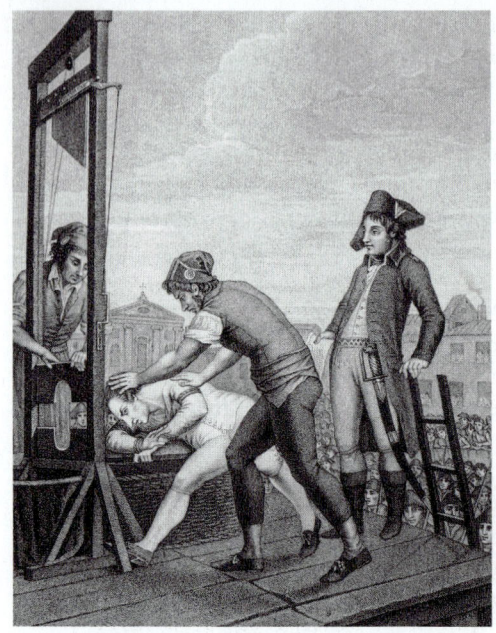

**The Execution of Robespierre** Completely wooden except for the heavy iron blade, the guillotine was devised by a French revolutionary doctor named Guillotin as a humane method of execution. The guillotine was painted red for Robespierre's execution. Large crowds witnessed the execution in a majestic public square in central Paris, then known as the Place de la Revolution and now called the Place de la Concorde (Harmony Square). (Musée de la Ville de Paris, Musée Carnavalet, Paris, France/Bridgeman Images)

howled down Robespierre when he tried to speak to the National Convention on July 27, 1794 — a date known as 9 Thermidor according to France's newly adopted republican calendar. The next day it was Robespierre's turn to be guillotined.

The respectable middle-class lawyers and professionals who had led the liberal Revolution of 1789 then reasserted their authority. This period of **Thermidorian reaction**, as it was called, harkened back to the moderate beginnings of the Revolution. In 1795 the National Convention abolished many economic controls and severely restricted local political organizations. In addition, the middle-class members of the National Convention wrote a new constitution restricting eligibility to serve as a deputy to men of substantial means. To prevent a new Robespierre from monopolizing power, the new Assembly granted executive power to a five-man body, called the Directory.

The Directory continued to support military expansion abroad, but war was no longer so much a crusade as a response to economic problems. Large, victorious armies reduced unemployment at home. However, the French people quickly grew weary of the corruption and ineffectiveness that characterized the Directory. This general dissatisfaction revealed itself clearly in the national elections of 1797, which returned a large number of conservative and even monarchist deputies. Fearing for its survival, the Directory used the army to nullify the elections and began to govern dictatorially. Two years later Napoleon Bonaparte ended the Directory in a coup d'état (koo day-TAH) and substituted a strong dictatorship for a weak one. While claiming to uphold revolutionary values, Napoleon would install authoritarian rule.

# Napoleon's Europe, 1799–1815

**How did Napoleon Bonaparte assume control of France and much of Europe, and what factors led to his downfall?**

For almost fifteen years, from 1799 to 1814, France was in the hands of a keen-minded military dictator of exceptional ability. Napoleon Bonaparte (1769–1821) realized the need to put an end to civil strife in France in order to create unity and consolidate his rule. And he did. But Napoleon saw himself as a man of destiny, and the glory of war and the dream of universal empire proved irresistible.

## Napoleon's Rule of France

Born on the Mediterranean island of Corsica into an impoverished noble family, Napoleon left home and became a lieutenant in the French artillery in 1785. Rising rapidly in the new army, Napoleon was placed in command of French forces in Italy and won brilliant victories there in 1796 and 1797. His next campaign, in Egypt, was a failure, but Napoleon returned to France before the fiasco was generally known. French aggression in Egypt and elsewhere provoked the British to organize a new alliance in 1798, the Second Coalition, which included Austria and Russia.

Napoleon soon learned that some prominent members of the legislature were plotting against the Directory. The dissatisfaction of these plotters stemmed not so much from the fact that the Directory was a dictatorship as from the fact that it was a weak dictatorship.

The young Napoleon, nationally revered for his military exploits, was an ideal figure of authority. On November 9, 1799, Napoleon and his conspirators ousted the Directors, and the following day soldiers disbanded the legislature. Napoleon was named first consul of the republic, and a new constitution consolidating his position was overwhelmingly approved in a plebiscite in December 1799. Republican appearances were maintained, but Napoleon became the real ruler of France.

Napoleon worked to maintain order and end civil strife by appeasing powerful groups in France, offering them favors in return for loyal service. Napoleon's bargain with the middle class was codified in the Civil Code of March 1804, also known as the **Napoleonic Code**, which reasserted two of the fundamental principles of the Revolution of 1789: equality of all male citizens before the law and absolute security of wealth and private property. Napoleon and the leading bankers of Paris established the privately owned Bank of France in 1800, which served the interests of both the state and the financial oligarchy. Napoleon won over peasants by defending the gains in land and status they had won during the Revolution.

At the same time, Napoleon consolidated his rule by recruiting disillusioned revolutionaries for the network of government officials. Nor were members of the old nobility slighted. In 1800 and again in 1802 Napoleon granted amnesty to noble émigrés on the condition that they return to France and take a loyalty oath. Members of this returning elite soon occupied high posts in the expanding centralized state. Napoleon also created a new imperial nobility to reward his most talented generals and officials.

Furthermore, Napoleon sought to restore the Catholic Church in France so that it could serve as a bulwark of social stability. Napoleon and Pope Pius VII (pontificate 1800–1823) signed the Concordat of 1801. Under this agreement the pope gained the right for French Catholics to practice their religion freely, but Napoleon's government now nominated bishops, paid the clergy, and exerted great influence over the church in France.

Order and unity had a price: authoritarian rule. In 1802, Napoleon re-established slavery in the colonies, hoping to profit from a revival of plantation agriculture. French women also lost many of the gains they had made in the 1790s. Under the Napoleonic

Code, women were dependents of either their fathers or their husbands, and they could not make contracts or have bank accounts in their own names. Napoleon also curtailed free speech and freedom of the press and manipulated voting in the occasional elections. After 1810 political suspects were held in state prisons, as they had been during the Terror.

## Napoleon's Expansion in Europe

After coming to power in 1799, Napoleon sent peace feelers to Austria and Britain, the dominant powers of the Second Coalition. When these overtures were rejected, French armies led by Napoleon decisively defeated the Austrians. Subsequent treaties with Austria in 1801 and Britain in 1802 consolidated France's hold on the territories its armies had won up to that point.

In 1802 Napoleon was secure but still driven to expand his power. Aggressively redrawing the map of German-speaking lands so as to weaken Austria and encourage the secondary states of southwestern Germany to side with France, Napoleon tried to restrict British trade with all of Europe. He then plotted to attack Britain, but his Mediterranean fleet was destroyed by Lord Nelson at the Battle of Trafalgar on October 21, 1805.

Austria, Russia, and Sweden joined with Britain to form the Third Coalition against France shortly before the Battle of Trafalgar. Yet the Austrians and the Russians were no match for Napoleon, who scored a brilliant victory over them at the Battle of Austerlitz in December 1805. Russia decided to pull back, and Austria accepted large territorial losses in return for peace as the Third Coalition collapsed.

Napoleon then reorganized the German states to his liking. In 1806 he abolished many tiny German states as well as the centuries-old Holy Roman Empire. In their place he established by decree the German Confederation of the Rhine, a union of fifteen German states minus Austria, Prussia, and Saxony.

Napoleon's intervention in German affairs alarmed the Prussians, who mobilized their armies. In October 1806 Napoleon attacked them and won two more victories at Jena and Auerstädt. The war with Prussia, now joined by Russia, continued into the following spring. After Napoleon won another victory, Alexander I of Russia was ready to negotiate for peace. In the treaties of Tilsit in 1807, Prussia lost half its population through land concessions. These included former Polish territories (acquired at the time of the partition of the Polish-Lithuanian Commonwealth), which Napoleon established as a French protectorate named the Grand Duchy of Warsaw. Russia accepted Napoleon's reorganization of western and central Europe and promised to enforce Napoleon's economic blockade against British goods.

## The Grand Empire and Its End

Napoleon's so-called **Grand Empire** encompassed virtually all of Europe except Great Britain. It consisted of three parts. The core, or first part, was an ever-expanding France (Map 22.2). The second part consisted of a number of dependent satellite kingdoms. The third part comprised the independent but allied states of Austria, Prussia, and Russia. After 1806 both satellites and allies were expected to support Napoleon's **Continental System**, a blockade in which no ship coming from Britain or her colonies was permitted to dock at any port that was controlled by the French.

**MAP 22.2  Napoleonic Europe in 1812**
At the height of the Grand Empire in 1810, Napoleon had conquered or allied with every major European power except Britain. But in 1812, angered by Russian repudiation of his ban on trade with Britain, Napoleon invaded Russia with disastrous results. Compare this map with Map 18.3, which shows the division of Europe in 1715.

The blockade was intended to destroy the British economy and, thereby, its ability to wage war.

In the areas incorporated into France and in the satellites, French rule sparked patriotic upheavals and encouraged the growth of reactive nationalism. The first great revolt occurred in Spain. In 1808 Napoleon deposed Spanish king Ferdinand

VII and placed his own brother Joseph on the throne. A coalition of Catholics, monarchists, and patriots rebelled against this attempt to turn Spain into a satellite of France. French armies occupied Madrid, but the foes of Napoleon fled to the hills and waged guerrilla warfare. Events in Spain sent a clear warning: resistance to French imperialism was growing.

Yet Napoleon pushed on. In 1810, when the Grand Empire was at its height, Britain still remained at war with France, helping the guerrillas in Spain and Portugal. The Continental System was a failure. Instead of harming Britain, the system provoked the British to set up a counter-blockade, which created hard times for French consumers. Perhaps looking for a scapegoat, Napoleon turned on Alexander I of Russia, who in 1811 openly repudiated Napoleon's prohibitions against British goods.

Napoleon's invasion of Russia began in June 1812 with a force that eventually numbered 600,000 (see Map 22.2). Napoleon believed he could win a rapid and decisive victory near the border that would force the Russians into negotiations. But, instead of fighting, the Russians retreated, drawing the French ever further into their territory. One hundred miles west of Moscow, the Russians finally faced the French army in the grueling Battle of Borodino, a clash that Napoleon himself described as the "most terrible" of the "fifty battles I have fought." Alexander ordered the evacuation of Moscow, which the Russians then burned in part, and he refused to negotiate. Finally, after five weeks in the scorched city, Napoleon ordered a disastrous retreat. When the frozen remnants of Napoleon's army staggered into Poland and Prussia in December, 370,000 men had died and another 200,000 had been taken prisoner.[1]

Leaving his troops to their fate, Napoleon raced to Paris to raise another army. Meanwhile, Austria and Prussia deserted Napoleon and joined Russia and Britain in the Treaty of Chaumont in March 1814, by which the four powers formed the Quadruple Alliance to defeat the French emperor. Less than a month later, on April 4, 1814, a defeated Napoleon abdicated his throne. The victorious allies then exiled Napoleon to the island of Elba off the coast of Italy.

In February 1815 Napoleon staged a daring escape from Elba. Landing in France, he issued appeals for support and marched on Paris. But Napoleon's gamble was a desperate long shot, for the allies were united against him. At the end of a frantic period known as the Hundred Days, they crushed his forces at Waterloo on June 18, 1815, and imprisoned him on the island of St. Helena, off the western coast of Africa. The restored Bourbon dynasty took power under Louis XVIII, a younger brother of Louis XVI.

# The Haitian Revolution, 1791–1804

**How did a slave revolt on colonial Saint-Domingue lead to the creation of the independent nation of Haiti in 1804?**

The events that led to the creation of the independent nation of Haiti constitute the third, and perhaps most extraordinary, chapter of the revolutionary era in the Atlantic world. The French colony that was to become Haiti reaped huge profits through a brutal system of slave-based plantation agriculture. News of revolution in France lit a powder keg of contradictory aspirations among white planters, free people of color, and the enslaved. Free people of color and, later, enslaved people rose up to claim their freedom, while planters struggled ruthlessly to retain their privilege and property. The uprising succeeded, despite invasion by the British and Spanish and Napoleon Bonaparte's bid to reimpose French control. In 1804 Haiti became the only nation in history to claim its freedom through slave revolt.

## Revolutionary Aspirations in Saint-Domingue

On the eve of the French Revolution, Saint-Domingue was inhabited by a variety of social groups who resented and mistrusted one another. The European population included French colonial officials, wealthy plantation owners and merchants, and poor artisans and clerks. Individuals of European descent born in the colonies were called Creoles, and over time they had developed their own interests, distinct from those of metropolitan France. Vastly outnumbering the white population were the colony's five hundred thousand enslaved people, along with a sizable population of some forty thousand free people of African and mixed African and European descent, known as "free people of color."

Most of the enslaved population performed grueling toil in the island's sugar plantations, with a smaller number working in coffee and indigo plantations or as urban artisans and servants. The planters used extremely harsh methods, such as beating, maiming, and executing slaves, to maintain their control. The 1685 Code Noir (Black Code) that legally regulated slavery was intended to provide minimal standards of humane treatment, but its tenets were rarely enforced. Masters calculated that they could earn more by working slaves ruthlessly and purchasing new ones when they died than by providing the food, rest, and medical care needed to allow the enslaved population to reproduce naturally. This meant that they sought a constant supply of newly enslaved people from Africa to work the plantations.

Despite their brutality, slaveholders on Saint-Domingue freed a certain number of their slaves, mostly their own mixed-race children, thereby producing one of the largest populations of free people of color in any slaveholding colony. The French Code Noir of 1685 granted free people of color the same legal status as whites, but from the 1760s on, white resentment over the prosperity and social standing that free people of color had acquired led colonial administrators to begin rescinding these rights. By the time of the French Revolution free people of color were subject to many discriminatory laws.

The political and intellectual turmoil of the 1780s, with its growing rhetoric of liberty, equality, and fraternity, raised new challenges and possibilities for each of Saint-Domingue's social groups. For enslaved people, news of abolitionist movements in France led to hopes that the mother country might grant them freedom. Free people of color looked to reforms in Paris as a means of gaining political enfranchisement and reasserting equal status with whites. The white Creole elite, however, was determined to protect its way of life, including slaveholding. They hoped to gain control of their own affairs, as had the North American colonists before them.

The National Assembly frustrated the hopes of all these groups. Cowed by colonial representatives who claimed that support for free people of color would result in slave insurrection, the Assembly refused to extend French constitutional safeguards to the colonies. At the same time, however, the Assembly also reaffirmed French monopolies over colonial trade, thereby angering planters as well.

In October 1790 Vincent Ogé (aw-ZHAY) (ca. 1750–1791), a free man of color, returned to Saint-Domingue from Paris determined to win rights for his people. He sent letters to the Provincial Assembly of Saint-Domingue demanding political rights for all free citizens. When Ogé's demands were refused and he faced threats of reprisals, he and his followers turned to armed insurrection. After initial victories, his army was defeated, and Ogé was executed. Revolutionary leaders in Paris were more sympathetic to Ogé's cause. In May 1791 the National Assembly granted political rights to free people of color born to two free parents who possessed sufficient property. When news of this legislation arrived in Saint-Domingue, the colonial governor refused to enact it. Violence then erupted between groups of Creoles and free people of color in parts of the colony.

## The Outbreak of Revolt

Just as the sans-culottes helped push forward more radical reforms in France, the second stage of revolution in Saint-Domingue also resulted from decisive action from below. In August 1791 the enslaved took events into their own hands. Groups of slaves held a series of nighttime meetings to plan a mass insurrection. In doing so, they drew on their own considerable military experience; the majority of them had been born in Africa, and many had served in the civil wars of the kingdom of Kongo and other conflicts before being taken into slavery.[2] They also drew on a long tradition of enslaved resistance prior to 1791, which had ranged from work slowdowns, to running away, to taking part in African-derived religious rituals and dances known as *vodou* (or voodoo). According to some sources, the August 1791 pact to take up arms was sealed by such a voodoo ritual.

Revolts began on a few plantations on the night of August 22. As the uprising spread, rebels joined together in an ever-growing army. During the next month enslaved combatants attacked and destroyed hundreds of sugar and coffee plantations. On April 4, 1792, as war loomed with the European states, the National Assembly issued a decree extending full citizenship rights to free men of African descent. The Assembly hoped this measure would win their political loyalty and their aid in defeating the slave rebellion.

Warfare in Europe soon spread to Saint-Domingue (Map 22.3). The Spanish colony of Santo Domingo, on the eastern side of the island of Hispaniola, had supported rebellion among the enslaved as a way to destabilize the French colony. In early 1793 the Spanish began to bring rebel leaders and soldiers into the Spanish army. Toussaint L'Ouverture (TOO-sahn LOO-vair-toor) (1743–1803), a former slave who had joined the revolt, was named a Spanish officer. In September the British navy blockaded the colony, and invading British troops captured French territory on the island. For the Spanish and British, revolutionary chaos provided a tempting opportunity to capture a profitable colony.

Desperate for forces to oppose France's enemies, commissioners sent by the newly elected National Convention promised freedom to enslaved men who fought for France. By October 1793 the commissioners had abolished slavery throughout the colony. On February 4, 1794, the Convention ratified the abolition of slavery and extended it to all French territories.

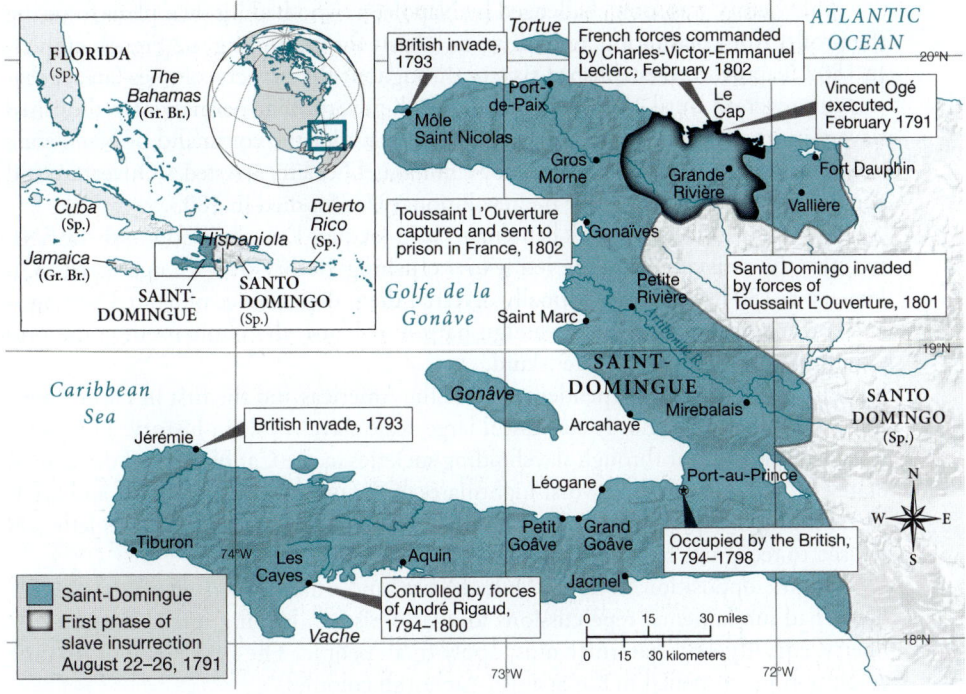

**MAP 22.3 The War of Haitian Independence, 1791–1804**
Neighbored by the Spanish colony of Santo Domingo, Saint-Domingue was the most profitable European colony in the Caribbean. In 1791 slave revolts erupted in the north near Le Cap, which had once been the capital. In 1770 the French had transferred the capital to Port-au-Prince, which in 1804 became the capital of the newly independent Haiti.

The tide of battle began to turn when Toussaint L'Ouverture switched sides and joined the French forces. By 1796 the French had regained control of the colony, and L'Ouverture had emerged as a key military leader. In March 1796, after he rescued the French colonial governor from hostile forces, L'Ouverture was named lieutenant governor of Saint-Domingue.

## The War of Haitian Independence

With Toussaint L'Ouverture acting increasingly as an independent ruler of the western province of Saint-Domingue, another general, André Rigaud (ree-GO) (1761–1811), set up his own government in the southern peninsula. Tensions mounted between L'Ouverture and Rigaud. While L'Ouverture was a freed slave of African descent, Rigaud belonged to the elite group of wealthy and educated free people of color. This elite resented the growing power of former slaves like L'Ouverture, who in turn accused the elite of adopting the prejudices of white settlers. Civil war broke out between the two sides in 1799, when L'Ouverture's forces, led by his lieutenant, Jean Jacques Dessalines (1758–1806), invaded the south. Victory over Rigaud in 1800 gave L'Ouverture control of the entire colony.

This victory was soon challenged by Napoleon, who had his own plans for using the profits from plantation agriculture as a basis for expanding the French empire. In 1802 Napoleon re-established slavery throughout the French colonies (an act that was not reversed until 1848, when the French government permanently abolished slavery in its remaining colonies). French forces under the command of Napoleon's brother-in-law, General Charles-Victor-Emmanuel Leclerc, arrested L'Ouverture and deported him to France, where the revolutionary leader died in 1803.

It was left to L'Ouverture's lieutenant, Jean Jacques Dessalines (duh-sah-LEEN), to unite the resistance, and he led it to a crushing victory over French forces. On January 1, 1804, Dessalines formally declared the independence of Saint-Domingue and the creation of the new sovereign nation of Haiti, the name used by the pre-Columbian inhabitants of the island.

Haiti, the second independent state in the Americas and the first in Latin America, was born from the only successful large-scale slave revolt in history. This event spread shock and fear through slaveholding societies in the Caribbean and the United States, bringing to life their worst nightmares of the utter reversal of power and privilege. Fearing the spread of rebellion to the United States, President Thomas Jefferson refused to recognize Haiti.

Despite opposition from the United States and other powers, Haitian independence had fundamental repercussions for world history, helping spread the idea that liberty, equality, and fraternity must apply to all people. The next phase of Atlantic revolution soon opened in the Spanish-American colonies.

# Revolutions in Latin America

**Why and how did the Spanish and Portuguese colonies of North and South America shake off European domination and develop into national states?**

In 1800 the Spanish Empire in the Americas stretched from the headwaters of the Mississippi River in present-day Minnesota to the tip of Cape Horn in the Antarctic (Map 22.4). Portugal controlled the vast territory of Brazil. Spain and Portugal believed that the great wealth of the Americas existed for the benefit of the Iberian powers, a stance that fostered bitterness and a thirst for independence in the colonies. Between 1806 and 1825 the colonies in Latin America were convulsed by upheavals that ultimately resulted in their independence. For Latin American republicans, their struggles were a continuation of the transatlantic wave of democratic revolution.

## The Origins of the Revolutions Against Colonial Powers

Spain's humiliating defeat in the War of the Spanish Succession (1701–1713) (see "The Wars of Louis XIV" in Chapter 18) prompted demands for a sweeping reform of all of Spain's institutions, including its colonial policies and practices. The new Bourbon dynasty initiated a decades-long effort known as the Bourbon reforms, which aimed to improve administrative efficiency and increase central control. Under Charles III (r. 1759–1788), Spanish administrators drew on Enlightenment ideals of rationalism and progress to strengthen colonial rule and thereby increase the fortunes and power of the Spanish state. They created a permanent standing army and enlarged colonial militias, sought to bring the church under tighter control, and dispatched intendants (government commissioners) with extensive new powers to oversee the colonies.

Additionally, Spain ended its policy of insisting that all colonial trade pass through its own ports and instead permitted free trade within the Spanish Empire. This was intended to favor Spain's competition with Great Britain and Holland by stimulating trade and thereby increasing the imperial government's tax revenues. In Latin America these actions stimulated the production and export of agricultural commodities that were in demand in Europe. Colonial manufacturing, however, which had been growing steadily, suffered a heavy blow under free trade. Colonial textiles and china, for example, could not compete with cheap Spanish products.

Madrid's tax reforms also aggravated discontent. Like Great Britain, Spain believed its colonies should bear some of the costs of their own defense. Accordingly, Madrid raised the prices of its monopoly products — tobacco and liquor — and increased sales taxes on many items. War with revolutionary France in the 1790s led to additional taxes and forced loans, all of which were widely resented. Moreover, high prices and heavier taxes imposed a great burden on indigenous communities, which bore the brunt of all forms of taxation and suffered from the corruption and brutality of tax collectors.

Political conflicts beyond the colonies also helped drive aspirations for independence. The French Revolution and the Napoleonic Wars, which involved France's occupation of Spain and Britain's domination of the seas, isolated Spain and weakened its control over its Latin American colonies.

Racial and ethnic divisions further fueled discontent. At this time, Creoles numbered approximately 3 million of a population of roughly 14 million. They resented the economic and political dominance of the roughly 200,000 **peninsulares** (puh-nihn-suh-LUHR-ayz), as the colonial officials and other natives of Spain or Portugal were called. The Creoles wanted to free themselves from Spain and Portugal and to rule the colonies themselves. They had little interest in improving the lot of indigenous people, who constituted by far the largest population group, or that of the mestizos of mixed Spanish and indigenous background and the mulattos of mixed Spanish and African heritage.

Slavery was practiced throughout Latin America, but unevenly. The Andes, Mexico, and Central America had relatively small enslaved populations. By contrast, regions dominated by plantation agriculture — especially the Caribbean islands and Brazil — relied on massive numbers of enslaved laborers. Sizable populations of free people of color existed throughout colonial Latin America, greatly outnumbering slaves in many cities. Despite prejudicial laws, they played an important role in urban public life, serving in large numbers in the militia units of cities such as Havana, Mexico City, Lima, and Buenos Aires. As in Saint-Domingue, white Creoles spurred a backlash against the rising social prominence of free people of color in the last decades of the eighteenth century.

A final factor contributing to rebellion was cultural and intellectual ideas. One set of such ideas was Enlightenment thought, which had been trickling into Latin America for decades (see "The Atlantic Enlightenment" in Chapter 19). By 1800 the Creole elite throughout Latin America was familiar with Enlightenment political thought and its role in inspiring colonial demands for independence. Another

**MAP 22.4  Latin America, ca. 1780 and 1830**

By 1830 almost all of Central America, South America, and the Caribbean islands had won independence. Note that the many nations that now make up Central America were unified when they first won independence from Mexico. Similarly, modern Venezuela, Colombia, and Ecuador were still joined in Gran Colombia.

**In 1830**

1811   Year independence gained

☐   Colony

OREGON COUNTRY (Joint U.S.-British occupation)

BRITISH NORTH AMERICA (CANADA) (Gr. Br.)

UNITED STATES 1783

San Antonio

MEXICO 1821

*Gulf of Mexico*

Mexico City

Veracruz

BAHAMA IS. (Gr. Br.)

Havana

CUBA (Spain)

HAITI 1804

PUERTO RICO (Spain)

BRITISH HONDURAS (Gr. Br.)

JAMAICA (Gr. Br.)

*Caribbean Sea*

Guatemala City   GUATEMALA

UNITED PROVINCES OF CENTRAL AMERICA 1823–1839

Panama

*ATLANTIC OCEAN*

TRINIDAD (Gr. Br.)

BR. GUIANA (Gr. Br.)

DUTCH GUIANA (Neth.)

FRENCH GUIANA (France)

Caracas

VENEZUELA

Socorro

Bogotá

GRAN COLOMBIA 1819–1830

Equator

Quito

*Galápagos Islands*

ECUADOR

PERU 1824

Lima

La Paz

BOLIVIA 1825

Sucre

EMPIRE OF BRAZIL 1822

Salvador

Rio de Janeiro

São Paulo

*PACIFIC OCEAN*

PARAGUAY

UNITED PROVINCES OF THE RIO DE LA PLATA 1816

Santiago

CHILE 1817

ARGENTINA

Buenos Aires

URUGUAY 1828

Montevideo

1811

N   W   E   S

PATAGONIA (Disputed between Argentina and Chile)

*Islas Malvinas (Falkland Islands)*

0   500   1,000 miles

0   500   1,000 kilometers

120°W    100°W    80°W    60°W    40°W    20°W

40°N   20°N   0°   20°S   40°S

important set of ideas consisted of indigenous traditions of justice and reciprocity, which often looked back to an idealized precolonial past. Local people perceived increased Spanish impositions as an assault on the traditional moral communities that bound them to each other and to the Crown. Creoles took advantage of indigenous symbols as a source of legitimacy, but this did not mean they were prepared to view indigenous people and mestizos as equals.

## Resistance, Rebellion, and Independence

The mid-eighteenth century witnessed frequent Andean Indian rebellions against increased taxation and the Bourbon Crown's other impositions. In 1780, under the leadership of a descendant of the Inca rulers who took the name Tupac Amaru II, a massive insurrection exploded in the Cuzco region (see Map 22.4). Indian chieftains from the region gathered a powerful force of indigenous people and people of mixed race. Rebellion swept across highland Peru, where many Spanish officials were executed. Shocked by the radical social and economic reforms promised by its leaders, Creoles joined forces with Spaniards and indigenous nobles to crush the rebellion. The government was obliged to concede to some of the rebels' demands by abolishing the repartimiento system, which required indigenous people to buy goods solely from tax collectors, and by establishing assemblies of local representatives in Cuzco.

As news of the rebellion of Tupac Amaru II trickled northward, it helped stimulate the 1781 Comuneros Revolt in the New Granada viceroyalty (see Map 22.4). In this uprising, an indigenous and mestizo peasant army commanded by Creole captains marched on Bogotá to protest high taxation, loss of communal lands, and state monopolies on liquor and tobacco. Dispersed by the ruling Spanish, who made promises they did not intend to keep, the revolt in the end did little to improve indigenous peoples' lives.

Authorities were shaken by these revolts and the many smaller uprisings that broke out through the eighteenth century, including slave rebellions in Venezuela in the 1790s. But the uprisings did not give rise directly to the independence movements that followed. Led from below, they did not question monarchical rule or the colonial relationship between Spain and Spanish America.

Two events outside of Spanish America did much to shape the ensuing struggle for independence. First, the revolution on Saint-Domingue and the subsequent independence of the nation of Haiti in 1804 convinced Creole elites, many of whom were slaveholders, of the potential for wide-scale rebellion among the enslaved (see Map 22.3). Their plans and strategies would henceforth be shaped by their determination to avoid a similar outcome in Spanish America.

Second, in 1808 Napoleon Bonaparte deposed Spanish king Ferdinand VII and placed his own brother on the Spanish throne. Spanish leaders meeting in exile defiantly began work on the nation's first constitution. Completed in 1812, the Constitution of Cadiz enshrined universal manhood suffrage, freedom of the press, limited monarchy, and other liberal principles. Colonial deputies obtained the right to representation in future assemblies, but not proportional to their population. Many future founding fathers of Latin American republics participated actively in the constitutional congress, which thus greatly influenced the spread of liberal ideas.

In the colonies, the political crisis engendered by Napoleon's coup encouraged movements for self-governance. In cities like Buenos Aires and Caracas, town councils, known as cabildos, took power into their own hands, ostensibly on behalf of deposed king Ferdinand. In July 1811 a regional congress in Caracas declared the independence of the United States of Venezuela and drafted a liberal constitution guaranteeing basic freedoms and abolishing the slave trade but restricting political participation to property owners. The republic failed after only one year, but patriots continued to fight royalist forces for the next eight years under the leadership of Simón Bolívar (1783–1830), who belonged to a wealthy land- and slave-owning family.

Bolívar and other Creole elites fighting for independence were forced to acknowledge that victory against Spain would require support from the nonwhites they had previously despised and who had often supported sympathetic royalist leaders against slave-owning Creoles. In return for promising to abolish slavery after independence, Bolívar received military and financial aid from the new Haitian nation. He granted immediate emancipation to enslaved men who joined the revolutionary struggle and named former slaves and free people of color to positions of authority in the army.

His victories over Spanish armies won Bolívar the presidency of the new republic of Gran Colombia (formerly the New Granada viceroyalty) in 1819. The republic passed laws for the gradual emancipation of slavery and issued a liberal constitution, similar to that of 1811. Bolívar and other military leaders continued attacks against the Spanish, eventually freeing or helping to liberate the future nations of Colombia, Ecuador, Peru, Chile, and Bolivia (named after the great liberator). Bolívar encouraged the new states to begin the process of manumission, a suggestion that met with great success in the Republic of Chile, which abolished slavery in 1823, but elsewhere encountered resistance from Creole slaveholders.

Dreaming of a continental political union, Bolívar summoned a conference of the new American republics in 1826 in Panama City. The meeting achieved little, however. The territories of Gran Colombia soon splintered (see Map 22.4), and a sadly disillusioned Bolívar went into exile.

The path to independence followed a different course in Mexico. Under Spain, Mexico had been united with Central America as the Viceroyalty of New Spain. In 1808, after Napoleon's coup, the Spanish viceroy assumed

**Triumph of Bolívar** Bolívar was treated as a hero everywhere he went in South America. (*Bolívar's Victory Parade in Caracas*, chalk lithograph by R. Weibezahl/Sammlung Archiv für Kunst und Geschichte, Berlin, Germany/akg-images)

control of the government of New Spain from its capital in Mexico City. Meanwhile, groups of rebels plotted to overthrow royalist power. Under the leadership of Miguel Hidalgo, a Jesuit priest who espoused social and racial equality, poor Creoles and indigenous and mestizo peasants rose up against the Spanish in 1810. After Hidalgo was caught and executed, another Catholic priest, José Maria Morelos y Pavón, emerged as a leader of anti-Spanish rebellion. In 1813 he convened a congress with the aim of establishing a new independent, national government. He was executed in 1815, but popular revolt continued to spread across Mexico.

By 1820 the desire for autonomy from Spain had spread among Creole elites. They joined forces with rebellious armies to make common cause against Spain and succeeded in winning over many royalist troops. In 1821 they issued a declaration of Mexican independence. Originally established as a constitutional monarchy, the new state became a republic in 1823. Gradual steps toward the abolition of slavery culminated in the freeing of all slaves by the end of the 1820s and the election of a president of African descent in 1829.

Portuguese Brazil followed a less turbulent path to independence than the Spanish-American republics. When Napoleon's troops entered Portugal, the royal family fled to Brazil and made Rio de Janeiro the capital of the Portuguese Empire. The king returned to Portugal in 1821 after the fall of Napoleon, leaving his son Pedro in Brazil as regent. Under popular pressure, Pedro proclaimed Brazil's independence in 1822, issued a constitution, and even led resistance against Portuguese troops. He accepted the title Emperor Pedro I (r. 1822–1831). Although Brazil remained a monarchy, Creole elites dominated society in Brazil, as they did elsewhere in Latin America. Because they had gained independence without military struggle, Brazil's Creole elites avoided making common cause with poor whites and people of color, and they refused to consider ending slavery once independence arrived.

## The Aftermath of Revolution in the Atlantic World

The Atlantic revolutions shared many common traits. They had common origins in imperial competition, war debt, social conflict, and Enlightenment ideals. Over the course of revolution, armed struggle often took the form of civil war, in which the participation of ordinary people—sans-culottes, enslaved people, free people of color, indigenous people and mestizos—played a decisive role. Perhaps their most important similarity was in the democratic limitations of the regimes these revolutions created and the frustrated aspirations they bequeathed to subsequent generations of marginalized citizens.

For the most part, the elite liberals who led the revolutions were not democrats and had no intention of creating regimes of full economic or social equality. The constitutions they wrote generally restricted political rights to landowners and middle-class men. Indigenous people may have gained formal equality as citizens, yet they found that the actual result was the removal of the privileged status they had negotiated with their original conquerors. Thus they suffered the loss of rights over their land and other resources. Moreover, none of the post-revolutionary constitutions gave women a role in political life.

The issue of slavery, by contrast, divided the revolutions. The American Revolution was led in part by slaveholding landowners, who were determined to retain slavery in its aftermath, while the more radical French republic abolished it through-out the French empire (a measure reversed by Napoleon). The independent nation of Haiti was built on the only successful slave revolt in history, but the need for revenue from plantation agriculture soon led to the return of coercive labor requirements, if not outright slavery. In Latin America independence speeded the abolition of slavery, bringing an immediate ban on the slave trade and gradual emancipation from the 1820s to the 1850s. Still, Cuba and Brazil, which had enormous slave populations, did not end slavery until 1886 and 1888, respectively.

The aftermath of the Atlantic revolutions brought extremely different fortunes to the new nations that emerged from them. France returned to royal rule with the restoration of the Bourbon monarchy in 1815. A series of revolutionary crises ensued in the nineteenth century as succeeding generations struggled over the legacies of monarchism, republicanism, and Bonapartism. It was not until 1871 that republi-canism finally prevailed. The transition to an independent republic was permanent and relatively smooth in the United States. Nevertheless, the unresolved conflict over slavery would lead to catastrophic civil war in 1860. Haiti faced crushing demands for financial reparations from France and the hostility of the United States and other powers.

The newly independent nations of Latin America had difficulty achieving eco-nomic and political stability when the wars of independence ended. In the 1830s regional separatism caused New Spain to break up into five separate countries. The failure of political union in New Spain and Gran Colombia isolated individual coun-tries, prevented collective action, and later paved the way for the political and eco-nomic intrusion of the United States and other powers. Spain's Caribbean colonies of Puerto Rico and Cuba remained loyal, in large part due to fears that slave revolt would spread from neighboring Haiti.

The Creole leaders of the revolutions had little experience in government, and the wars left a legacy of military, not civilian, leadership. Despite these disappoint-ments, liberal ideals of political and social equality born of the revolutionary era left a crucial legacy for future generations in Latin America (see Chapter 27).

# Chapter Summary

From 1775 to 1825 a wave of revolution swept through the Atlantic world. Its ori-gins included long-term social and economic changes, Enlightenment ideals of lib-erty and equality, and the costs of colonial warfare. British efforts to raise taxes after the Seven Years' War aroused violent protest in the American colonies. In 1776 the Second Continental Congress issued the Declaration of Independence, and by 1783 Britain was forced to recognize the independence of the thirteen colonies.

In 1789 delegates to the Estates General defied royal authority to declare them-selves a National Assembly, which promulgated France's first constitution in 1791. Led by the Jacobin club, the Assembly waged war on Austria and Prussia and pro-claimed France a republic. From the end of 1793, under the Reign of Terror, the Revolution pursued internal and external enemies ruthlessly and instituted economic controls to aid the poor. The weakness of the Directory government after the fall of Robespierre enabled Napoleon Bonaparte to claim control of France. Napoleon's relentless military ambitions allowed him to spread French power through much of Europe but ultimately led to his downfall.

After a failed uprising by free men of color, enslaved people rose in revolt in the French colony of Saint-Domingue in August 1791. Their revolt, combined with the outbreak of war and the radicalization of the French Revolution, led to a sequence of conflicts and rebellions that culminated in independence for the new Haitian nation in 1804.

Latin American independence movements drew strength from Spain's unpopular policies and the political crisis engendered by Napoleon's invasion of Portugal and Spain. Under the leadership of Simón Bolívar, the United States of Venezuela claimed independence in 1811. Led by Creole officers but reliant on nonwhite soldiers, rebel armies successfully fought Spanish forces over the next decade. Despite Bolívar's efforts to build a unified state, in the 1830s New Spain split into five separate countries. Mexico followed its own path to independence, becoming a republic in 1823. In Brazil the royal regent proclaimed independence in 1822 and reigned as emperor of the new state.

## NOTES

1. Donald Sutherland, *France, 1789–1815: Revolution and Counterrevolution* (New York: Oxford University Press, 1986), p. 420.
2. John K. Thornton, "'I Am the Subject of the King of Congo': African Political Ideology and the Haitian Revolution," *Journal of World History* 4.2 (Fall 1993): 181–214.

## MAKE CONNECTIONS  LOOK AHEAD

The Atlantic world was the essential context for a great revolutionary wave in the late eighteenth and early nineteenth centuries. The movement of peoples, commodities, and ideas across the Atlantic Ocean in the eighteenth century created a world of common debates, conflicts, and aspirations. Moreover, the high stakes of colonial empire heightened competition among European states, leading to a series of wars that generated crushing costs for overburdened treasuries. For the British and Spanish in their American colonies and the French at home, the desperate need for new taxes weakened government authority and opened the door to rebellion. In turn, the ideals of the French Revolution inspired enslaved and free people of African descent in Saint-Domingue and Latin America to rise up and claim the promise of liberty, equality, and fraternity for people of all races.

The chain reaction did not end with the liberation movements in Latin America that followed the Haitian Revolution. Throughout the nineteenth and early twentieth centuries, periodic convulsions occurred in Europe, the Americas, and elsewhere as successive generations struggled over the political rights first proclaimed by late-eighteenth-century revolutionaries (see Chapters 24 and 27). Meanwhile, as dramatic political events unfolded, a parallel economic revolution was gathering steam. This was the Industrial Revolution, the topic of the next chapter, which originated around 1780 and accelerated through the end of the eighteenth century. After 1815 the twin forces of industrialization and democratization would combine to transform Europe and the world.

# Chapter 22 Review

## IDENTIFY KEY TERMS

**Identify and explain the significance of each item below.**

Treaty of Paris (p. 557)

Declaration of Independence (p. 559)

Antifederalists (p. 560)

Estates General (p. 562)

National Assembly (p. 562)

Jacobin club (p. 564)

Mountain (p. 564)

Girondists (p. 564)

sans-culottes (p. 564)

Reign of Terror (p. 565)

Thermidorian reaction (p. 566)

Napoleonic Code (p. 567)

Grand Empire (p. 568)

Continental System (p. 568)

peninsulares (p. 575)

## REVIEW THE MAIN IDEAS

**Answer the focus questions from each section of the chapter.**

1. What were the factors behind the age of revolution in the Atlantic world? (p. 553)

2. Why and how did American colonists forge a new, independent nation? (p. 558)

3. Why and how did revolutionaries in France transform the nation? (p. 561)

4. How did Napoleon Bonaparte assume control of France and much of Europe, and what factors led to his downfall? (p. 566)

5. How did a slave revolt on colonial Saint-Domingue lead to the creation of the independent nation of Haiti in 1804? (p. 570)

6. Why and how did the Spanish and Portuguese colonies of North and South America shake off European domination and develop into national states? (p. 574)

## MAKE COMPARISONS AND CONNECTIONS

**Analyze the larger developments and continuities within and across chapters.**

1. What was revolutionary about the age of revolution? How did the states that emerged out of the eighteenth-century revolutions differ from the states that predominated in previous centuries?

2. To what extent would you characterize the revolutions discussed in this chapter as Enlightenment movements? (See "The Atlantic Enlightenment" in Chapter 19.) How did the increased circulation of goods, people, and ideas across the Atlantic in the eighteenth century contribute to the outbreak of revolution on both sides of the ocean?

3. Which do you think was more important, the achievements of these revolutions in terms of liberty and equality or the limitations imposed on these principles? How was it possible to declare the equality of all human beings, while denying equal rights to many categories of people?

## CHRONOLOGY

| | |
|---|---|
| **1715–1774** | • Reign of Louis XV |
| **1743–1803** | • Life of Toussaint L'Ouverture |
| **1756–1763** | • Seven Years' War |
| **1763** | • Treaty of Paris |
| **1774–1792** | • Reign of Louis XVI |
| **1775** | • Thomas Paine publishes *Common Sense* |
| **1775–1783** | • American Revolution |
| **1780–1820** | • Peak of transatlantic slave trade (Ch. 20) |
| **1784** | • British pass East India Company Act (Ch. 17) |
| **1789–1799** | • French Revolution |
| **1789–1807** | • Ottoman Ruler Selim III introduces reforms (Ch. 25) |
| **1790** | • Edmund Burke publishes *Reflections on the Revolution in France* |
| **1791–1804** | • Haitian Revolution |
| **1793** | • British diplomatic visit to China (Ch. 21) |
| **1799–1814** | • Reign of Napoleon Bonaparte |
| **1807** | • Slave trade declared illegal in British Empire (Ch. 25) |

# 23

# The Revolution in Energy and Industry

## 1760–1850

**WHILE THE REVOLUTIONS OF THE ATLANTIC WORLD WERE OPENING** a new political era, another revolution was beginning to transform economic and social life. The Industrial Revolution began in Great Britain around 1780 and soon began to influence continental Europe and the United States. Quite possibly only the development of agriculture during Neolithic times had a comparable impact and significance in world history. Non-Western nations began to industrialize after 1860.

Industrialization profoundly modified human experience. It changed patterns of work, transformed the social structure, altered the international balance of political power in favor of the most rapidly industrialized nations, and eventually contributed to global climate change. What was revolutionary about the Industrial Revolution was not its pace or that it represented a sharp break with the previous period. On the contrary, the Industrial Revolution built on earlier developments, and the rate of progress was slow. What was remarkable about the Industrial Revolution was that it inaugurated a period of sustained economic and demographic growth that has continued to the present. Although it took time, the Industrial Revolution eventually helped ordinary people in the West gain a higher standard of living, while also creating lasting environmental impacts.

# The Industrial Revolution in Britain

**Why did the Industrial Revolution begin in Britain, and how did it develop between 1780 and 1850?**

The Industrial Revolution began in Great Britain, the nation created by the formal union of Scotland, Wales, and England in 1707. The transformation in industry was something new in history, and it was unplanned. It originated from a unique combination of possibilities and constraints in late-eighteenth-century Britain. With no models to copy and no idea of what to expect, Britain pioneered not only in industrial technology but also in social relations and urban living.

## Why Britain?

Perhaps the most important debate in economic history focuses on how the Industrial Revolution originated and why it took place in western Europe, and Britain in particular, rather than in other economically vibrant parts of the world, such as Asia. Historians continue to debate this issue, but the best answer seems to be that Britain possessed a unique set of possibilities and constraints—abundant coal deposits, high wages, a relatively peaceful and centralized government, well-developed financial systems, innovative culture, highly skilled craftsmen, and a strong position in empire and global trade, including slavery—that spurred its people to adopt a capital-intensive, machine-powered system of production.

Thus a number of factors came together over the long term to give rise to the Industrial Revolution in Britain. The Scientific Revolution and the Enlightenment fostered a new worldview that embraced progress and the role of research and experimentation in understanding and mastering the natural world. Moreover, Britain's intellectual culture emphasized the public sharing of knowledge, including that of scientists and technicians from other countries.

In the economic realm, the seventeenth-century expansion of rural industry produced a surplus of English woolen cloth. Exported throughout Europe, English cloth brought commercial profits and high wages. By the eighteenth century the expanding Atlantic economy and trade with India and China were also serving Britain well. The mercantilist colonial empire Britain aggressively built, augmented by a strong position in Latin America and in the transatlantic slave trade, provided raw materials like cotton and a growing market for British manufactured goods. Strong demand for British manufacturing meant that British workers earned high wages compared to the rest of the world's laborers and that capital was available for investment in new industrial development.

Agriculture also played an important role in bringing about the Industrial Revolution. English farmers were second only to the Dutch in productivity in 1700, and they were continually adopting new methods of farming. Because of increasing efficiency, landowners were able to produce more food with a smaller workforce. The enclosure movement had deprived many small landowners of their land, leaving the landless poor to work as hired agricultural laborers or in rural industry. These groups created a pool of potential laborers for the new factories.

Abundant food and high wages in turn meant that the ordinary English family no longer had to spend almost everything they earned just to buy bread. Thus the family could spend more on manufactured goods and could pay to send their children to school. Britain's populace enjoyed high levels of education compared to that of the rest of Europe. Moreover, in the eighteenth century the members of the average British family—including women and girls—were redirecting their labor away from unpaid work for household consumption and toward work for wages that they could spend on goods.

Environmental factors also played an important role. In an age when it was much cheaper to ship goods by water than by land, no part of England was more than fifty miles from navigable water. Beginning in the 1770s a canal-building boom enhanced this advantage. Rivers and canals facilitated easy movement of England and Wales's enormous deposits of iron and coal. The abundance of coal combined with high wages in manufacturing placed Britain in a unique position among the nations of the world: its manufacturers had extremely strong incentives to develop technologies to draw on the power of coal to increase workmen's productivity. In regions with lower wages, such as India and China, the costs of mechanization outweighed potential gains in productivity.

A final factor favoring British industrialization was the heavy hand of the British state and its policies. Despite its rhetoric in favor of "liberty," Britain's parliamentary system taxed its population aggressively and spent the money on a navy to protect imperial commerce and on an army that could be used to quell uprisings by disgruntled workers. Starting with the Navigation Acts under Oliver Cromwell (see "Mercantilism and Colonial Wars" in Chapter 18), the British state also adopted aggressive tariffs, or duties, on imported goods to protect its industries.

All these factors combined to initiate the **Industrial Revolution**, a term first coined in 1799 to describe the burst of major inventions and technical changes underway. This technical revolution contributed to an impressive quickening in the annual rate of industrial growth in Britain. Whereas industry had grown at only 0.7 percent between 1700 and 1760 (before the Industrial Revolution), it grew at almost 3 percent between 1801 and 1831, when industrial transformation was in full swing.[1]

## Technological Innovations and Early Factories

The pressure to produce more goods for a growing market and to reduce the labor costs of manufacturing was directly related to the first decisive breakthrough of the Industrial Revolution: the creation of the world's first machine-powered factories in the British cotton textile industry. Technological innovations in the manufacture of cotton cloth led to a new system of production and social relationships.

The putting-out system that developed in the seventeenth-century textile industry involved a merchant who loaned, or "put out," raw materials to cottage workers who processed the raw materials in their own homes and returned the finished products to the merchant. There was always a serious imbalance in textile production based on cottage industry: the work of four or five spinners was needed to keep one weaver steadily employed. During the eighteenth century the putting-out system grew across Europe, but most extensively in Britain. The growth of demand only increased pressures on the supply of thread.

Many a tinkering worker knew that devising a better spinning wheel promised rich rewards. It proved hard to spin the traditional raw materials — wool and flax — with improved machines, but cotton was different. Cotton textiles had first been imported into Britain from India by the East India Company as a rare and delicate luxury for the upper classes. In the eighteenth century a lively market for cotton cloth emerged in West Africa, where the English and other Europeans traded it for enslaved people. By 1760 a tiny domestic cotton industry had emerged in northern England based on imported raw materials, but it could not compete with cloth produced by workers in India and other parts of Asia. International competition thus drove English entrepreneurs to invent new technologies to bring down labor costs.

After many experiments over a generation, a carpenter and jack-of-all-trades, James Hargreaves, invented his cotton-spinning jenny about 1765. At almost the same moment, a barber-turned-manufacturer named Richard Arkwright invented (or possibly pirated) another kind of spinning machine, the water frame. These breakthroughs produced an explosion in the infant cotton textile industry in the 1780s and made some inventors, like Richard Arkwright, extremely wealthy. In 1793, Eli Whitney's invention of the cotton gin, a machine for separating cotton fibers from seeds, vastly increased the productivity of cotton fields in the United States, leading to an expansion of slavery and an influx of raw materials for British manufacturers. The new machines were soon producing ten times as much cotton yarn as had been made in 1770.

Hargreaves's **spinning jenny** was simple, inexpensive, and powered by hand. In early models from six to twenty-four spindles were mounted on a sliding carriage, and each spindle spun a fine, slender thread. The machines were usually worked by women, who moved the carriage back and forth with one hand and turned a wheel to supply power with the other. Now it was the male weaver who could not keep up with the vastly more efficient female spinner.

Arkwright's **water frame** employed a different principle, using a series of rollers to stretch the yarn. It quickly acquired a capacity of several hundred spindles and demanded much more power than a single operator could provide. A solution was found in waterpower. The water frame required large specialized mills located beside rivers, factories that employed as many as one thousand workers. The major drawback of the water frame was that it could spin only a coarse, strong thread. Around 1780 a hybrid machine invented by Samuel Crompton proved capable of spinning very fine and strong thread in large quantities. Gradually, all cotton spinning was concentrated in large-scale factories.

These revolutionary developments in the textile industry allowed British manufacturers to compete successfully in international markets in both fine and coarse cotton thread. At first, the machines were too expensive to be adopted in continental Europe or elsewhere. Where wages were low and investment capital was scarce, there was little point in adopting mechanized production until the machines' productivity increased significantly and the cost of manufacturing the machines dropped, both of which occurred in the first decades of the nineteenth century.[2]

As a result of these developments, families using cotton in cottage industry were freed from their constant search for adequate yarn from scattered part-time spinners, because all the thread needed could be spun in the cottage on the jenny or obtained from a nearby factory. The income of weavers, now hard-pressed to keep up with the spinners, rose markedly until about 1792. In response, mechanics and capitalists sought to invent a power loom to save on labor costs. This Edmund Cartwright achieved in 1785.

The power looms of the factories worked poorly at first and did not fully replace handlooms until the 1820s. By 1831 the cotton textile industry accounted for fully 22 percent of the country's entire industrial production and British cotton textiles cost half as much as Indian ones.

## Steam Power and the Energy Revolution

Well into the eighteenth century, Europe, like other areas of the world, relied mainly on wood for energy, and human beings and animals performed most work. This dependence meant that Europe and the rest of the world remained poor in energy and power.

By the eighteenth century wood was in ever-shorter supply in Britain. Processed wood (charcoal) was mixed with iron ore in blast furnaces to produce pig iron that was further processed into steel, cast iron, or wrought iron. The iron industry's appetite for wood was enormous, and by 1740 the British iron industry was stagnating due to the depleted supply of fuel. As wood became ever more scarce, the British looked to coal as an alternative. They had first used coal in the late Middle Ages as a source of heat. By 1640 most homes in London were heated with coal, and it was also used in industry to provide heat for making beer, glass, soap, and other products. The breakthrough came when industrialists began to use coal to produce mechanical energy and to power machinery.

To produce more coal, mines had to be dug deeper and deeper and were constantly filling with water. Mechanical pumps, usually powered by animals walking in circles at the surface, had to be installed. Animal power was expensive and inconvenient. In an attempt to overcome these disadvantages, Thomas Savery in 1698 and Thomas Newcomen in 1705 invented the first primitive **steam engines**. Both engines burned coal to produce steam that drove the water pumps.

In 1763, James Watt (1736–1819), a skilled craftsman who made scientific instruments at the University of Glasgow, was called on to repair a Newcomen engine being used in a physics course. Watt discovered that the Newcomen engine could be significantly improved by adding a separate condenser. This invention, patented in 1769, greatly increased the efficiency of the steam engine.

The relatively advanced nature of the British economy provided Watt with the skilled workers, precision parts, and financial capital necessary to make his invention a practical success. In 1775, he partnered with Matthew Boulton, a wealthy English

**James Nasmyth's Mighty Steam Hammer** Nasmyth's invention was the forerunner of the modern pile driver, and its successful introduction in 1832 epitomized the rapid development of steam-power technology in Britain. In this painting by the inventor himself, workers manipulate a massive iron shaft being hammered into shape at Nasmyth's foundry near Manchester. (Ann Ronan Pictures/Print Collector/Getty Images)

industrialist, who had capital and exceptional skills in salesmanship. Among Britain's highly skilled locksmiths, tinsmiths, and millwrights, Watt found mechanics who could install, regulate, and repair his sophisticated engines. From ingenious manufacturers, Watt was gradually able to purchase precision parts. By the late 1780s the firm of Boulton and Watt had made the steam engine a practical and commercial success in Britain.

The coal-burning steam engine of Watt and his followers was the Industrial Revolution's most fundamental advance in technology. For the first time in history, humanity had, at least for a few generations, almost unlimited power at its disposal. Inventors and engineers could now devise and implement all kinds of power equipment to aid people in their work. Steam power began to replace waterpower in cotton-spinning mills during the 1780s, contributing greatly to that industry's phenomenal rise. Steam also took the place of waterpower in flour mills, in the malt mills used in breweries, in the flint mills supplying the pottery industry, and in the mills exported by Britain to the West Indies to crush sugarcane.

The British iron industry was also radically transformed. After 1770 the adoption of steam-driven bellows in blast furnaces allowed for great increases in the quantity of pig iron produced by British ironmakers. In the 1780s Henry Cort developed the puddling

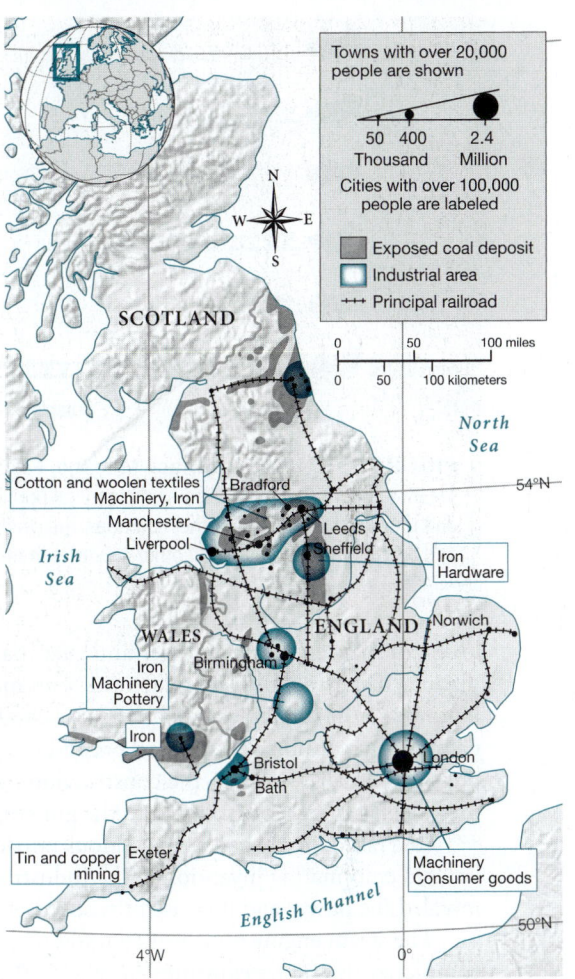

**MAP 23.1** **The Industrial Revolution in Great Britain, ca. 1850**

Industry concentrated in the rapidly growing cities of the north and the center of England, where rich coal and iron deposits were close to one another.

furnace, which allowed pig iron to be refined with coke, a smokeless and hot-burning fuel produced by heating coal to rid it of impurities.

Cort also developed steam-powered rolling mills, which quickly and efficiently pressed the molten iron into bars, further purifying them in the process. These technical innovations fostered a great boom in the British iron industry. In 1740 annual British iron production was only 17,000 tons. With the spread of coke smelting and the impact of Cort's inventions, production had reached 250,000 tons by 1806. In 1844 Britain produced 3 million tons of iron. Once expensive, iron became the cheap, basic, indispensable building block of the British economy.

## Steam-Powered Transportation

Steam power also revolutionized transportation. The first steam locomotive was built by Richard Trevithick after much experimentation. Then in 1829 George Stephenson's locomotive named *Rocket* sped down the track of the just-completed Liverpool and Manchester Railway at a maximum speed of 35 miles per hour. The line from Liverpool to Manchester was the first modern railroad, using steam-powered locomotives to carry customers to the new industrial cities. It was a financial as well as a technical success, and many private companies were organized to build more rail lines. Within twenty years they had completed the main trunk lines of Great Britain (Map 23.1). Other countries were quick to follow, with the first steam-powered trains operating in the United States in the 1830s and in Brazil, Chile, Argentina, and the British colonies of Canada, Australia, and India in the 1850s (Figure 23.1).

The arrival of the railroad had many significant consequences. It dramatically reduced the cost and uncertainty of shipping freight over land. Previously, markets had tended to be small and local; as the barrier of high transportation costs was

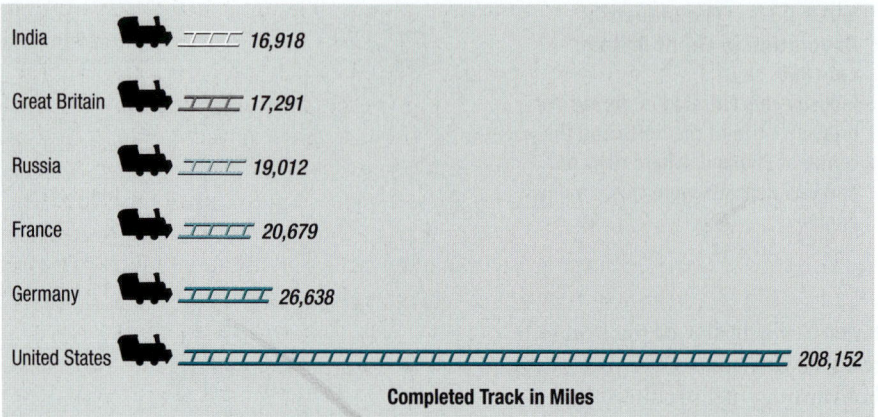

**FIGURE 23.1   Railroad Track Mileage, 1890**
Steam railroads were first used by the general public for shipping in England in the 1820s, and they quickly spread to other countries. The United States was an early adopter of railroads and by 1890 had surpassed all other countries in miles of track, as shown in this figure.

lowered, markets became larger and even nationwide. Larger markets encouraged manufacturers to build larger factories with more sophisticated machinery in a growing number of industries. Such factories could make goods more cheaply and gradually subjected most cottage workers and many urban artisans to severe competitive pressures. In all countries, the construction of railroads created a strong demand for unskilled labor and contributed to the growth of a class of urban workers.

The railroad also had a tremendous impact on cultural values and attitudes. The last and culminating invention of the Industrial Revolution, the railroad dramatically revealed the power and increased the speed of the new age.

The steam engine transformed water travel in a similar manner. French engineers completed the first steamships in the 1770s, and the first commercial steamships came into use in North America several decades later. The *Clermont*, designed by Robert Fulton, began to travel the Hudson River in New York State in 1807, shortly followed by ships belonging to brewer John Molson on the St. Lawrence River. The steamship brought the advantages of the railroad—speed, reliability, efficiency—to water travel.

## Industry and Population

In 1851 Great Britain celebrated the new era of industrial technology and its role as a world economic leader through an industrial fair called the Great Exhibition. Sponsored by the royal family and held in the newly built **Crystal Palace**, the fair drew more than 6 million visitors from all over Europe who marveled at the gigantic new exhibition hall. The building was made entirely of glass and iron, both of which were now cheap and abundant.

Britain's claim to be the "workshop of the world" was no idle boast, for it produced two-thirds of the world's coal and more than half of its iron and cotton cloth. More generally, in 1860 Britain produced a remarkable 20 percent of the entire world's output of industrial goods, whereas it had produced only about 2 percent of the world total in 1750.[3] As the British economy significantly increased its production of manufactured goods, the gross national product (GNP) rose roughly fourfold at constant prices between 1780 and 1851. At the same time, the population of Britain boomed, growing from about 9 million in 1780 to almost 21 million in 1851.

Rapid population growth in Great Britain was key to industrial development. More people meant a more mobile labor force, with a wealth of young workers in need of employment and ready to go where the jobs were. Sustaining the dramatic increase in population, in turn, was possible only through advances in agriculture and industry. But many contemporaries feared that the rapid growth in population would inevitably lead to disaster. In his *Essay on the Principle of Population* (1798), Thomas Malthus (1766–1834) argued that population would always tend to grow faster than the food supply. Malthus concluded that the only hope of warding off such "positive checks" to population growth as war, famine, and disease was "prudential restraint."[4] That is, young men and women had to limit the growth of population by marrying late in life. But Malthus was not optimistic about this possibility. The powerful attraction of the sexes would cause most people to marry early and have many children.

Economist David Ricardo (1772–1823) spelled out the pessimistic implications of Malthus's thought. Ricardo's depressing **iron law of wages** posited that, because of the pressure of population growth, wages would always sink to subsistence level. That is, wages would be just high enough to keep workers from starving.

Malthus, Ricardo, and their followers were proved wrong in the long run. However, until the 1820s, or even the 1840s, contemporary observers might reasonably have concluded that the economy and the total population were racing neck and neck, with the outcome very much in doubt. There was other problems as well. Perhaps workers, farmers, and ordinary people did not get their rightful share of the new wealth. Perhaps only the rich got richer, while the poor got poorer or made no progress. The spectacular growth of industry also had tremendous environmental consequences. We will turn to these issues after situating the process of industrialization in its European and global context.

# Industrialization in Europe and the World

**How did countries in Europe and around the world respond to the challenge of industrialization after 1815?**

As new technologies and a new organization of labor began to revolutionize production in Britain, other countries took notice and began to emulate its example. With the end of the Napoleonic Wars, European nations quickly adopted British inventions and achieved their own pattern of technological innovation and economic growth. By the last decades of the nineteenth century, western European countries as well as the United States and Japan had industrialized their economies to a considerable, albeit varying, degree.

Industrialization in other parts of the world proceeded more gradually, with uneven jerks and national and regional variations. Scholars are still struggling to explain these variations as well as the dramatic advantage in economic production that Western nations gained for the first time in history over non-Western ones. These questions are especially important because they may offer valuable lessons for poor countries that today are seeking to improve their material condition through industrialization and economic development. The latest findings on the nineteenth-century experience are encouraging. They suggest that there were alternative paths to the industrial world and that there was and is no need to follow a rigid, predetermined British model.

## National and International Variations

Comparative data on industrial production in different countries over time help give us an overview of what happened. One set of data, the work of a Swiss scholar, compares the level of industrialization on a per capita basis in several countries from 1750 to 1913. These data are far from perfect, but they reflect basic trends and are presented in Table 23.1 for closer study.

Table 23.1 presents a comparison of how much industrial product was produced, on average, for each person in a given country in a given year. All the numbers are expressed in terms of a single index number of 100, which equals the per capita level of industrial goods in Great Britain and Ireland in 1900. Every number in the table is thus a percentage of the 1900 level in Britain and is directly comparable with other numbers. The countries are listed in roughly the order that they began to use large-scale, power-driven technology.

What does this overview tell us? First, one sees in the first column that in 1750 all countries were fairly close together, including non-Western areas such as China

| TABLE 23.1 | PER CAPITA LEVELS OF INDUSTRIALIZATION, 1750–1913 | | | | | | |
|---|---|---|---|---|---|---|---|
| | 1750 | 1800 | 1830 | 1860 | 1880 | 1900 | 1913 |
| Great Britain | 10 | 16 | 25 | 64 | 87 | 100 | 115 |
| Belgium | 9 | 10 | 14 | 28 | 43 | 56 | 88 |
| United States | 4 | 9 | 14 | 21 | 38 | 69 | 126 |
| France | 9 | 9 | 12 | 20 | 28 | 39 | 59 |
| Germany | 8 | 8 | 9 | 15 | 25 | 52 | 85 |
| Austria-Hungary | 7 | 7 | 8 | 11 | 15 | 23 | 32 |
| Italy | 8 | 8 | 8 | 10 | 12 | 17 | 26 |
| Russia | 6 | 6 | 7 | 8 | 10 | 15 | 20 |
| China | 8 | 6 | 6 | 4 | 4 | 3 | 3 |
| India | 7 | 6 | 6 | 3 | 2 | 1 | 2 |

Note: All entries are based on an index value of 100, equal to the per capita level of industrialization in Great Britain in 1900. Data for Great Britain include Ireland, England, Wales, and Scotland.
Source: Data from P. Bairoch, "International Industrialization Levels from 1750 to 1980," *Journal of European Economic History* 11 (Spring 1982): 294, U.S. Journals at Cambridge University Press.

and India. Both China and India were technologically advanced and economically powerful up to 1800. However, the column headed 1800 shows that Britain had opened up a noticeable lead over all countries by 1800, and that gap progressively widened as the British Industrial Revolution accelerated through 1830 and reached full maturity by 1860.

Second, the table shows that Western countries began to emulate the British model successfully over the nineteenth century, with significant variations in the timing and in the extent of industrialization. Belgium led in adopting Britain's new technology, and it experienced a truly revolutionary surge between 1830 and 1860. France developed factory production more gradually and did not experience "revolutionary" growth in industrial output. Slow but steady economic growth in France was overshadowed by the spectacular rise of Germany and the United States after 1860 in what has been termed the "Second Industrial Revolution." In general, eastern and southern Europe began the process of industrialization later than northwestern and central Europe. Nevertheless, these regions made real progress in the late nineteenth century, as growth after 1880 in Austria-Hungary, Italy, and Russia suggests. This meant that all European states as well as the United States managed to raise per capita industrial levels in the nineteenth century.

These increases stood in stark contrast to the decreases that occurred at the same time in many non-Western countries, most notably in China and India, as Table 23.1 shows. European countries industrialized to a greater or lesser extent even as most of the non-Western world stagnated. Japan, which is not included in this table, stands out as an exceptional area of non-Western industrial growth in the second half of the nineteenth century. After the forced opening of the country to the West in the 1850s, Japanese entrepreneurs began to adopt Western technology and manufacturing methods, resulting in a production boom by the late nineteenth century (see "Industrialization" in Chapter 26). Differential rates of wealth- and power-creating industrial development, which heightened disparities within Europe, also greatly magnified existing inequalities between Europe and the rest of the world.

## Industrialization in Continental Europe

Throughout Europe the eighteenth century was an era of agricultural improvement, population increase, expanding foreign trade, and growing cottage industry. Thus, when the pace of British industry began to accelerate in the 1780s, continental businesses began to adopt the new methods as they proved their profitability. During the period of the revolutionary and Napoleonic Wars, from 1793 to 1815, however, western Europe experienced tremendous political and social upheaval that temporarily halted economic development. With the return of peace in 1815, western European countries again began to play catch-up.

They faced significant challenges. In the newly mechanized industries, British goods were being produced very efficiently, and these goods had come to dominate world markets. In addition, British technology had become so advanced that very few engineers or skilled technicians outside England understood it. Moreover, the technology of steam power involved large investments in the iron and coal industries

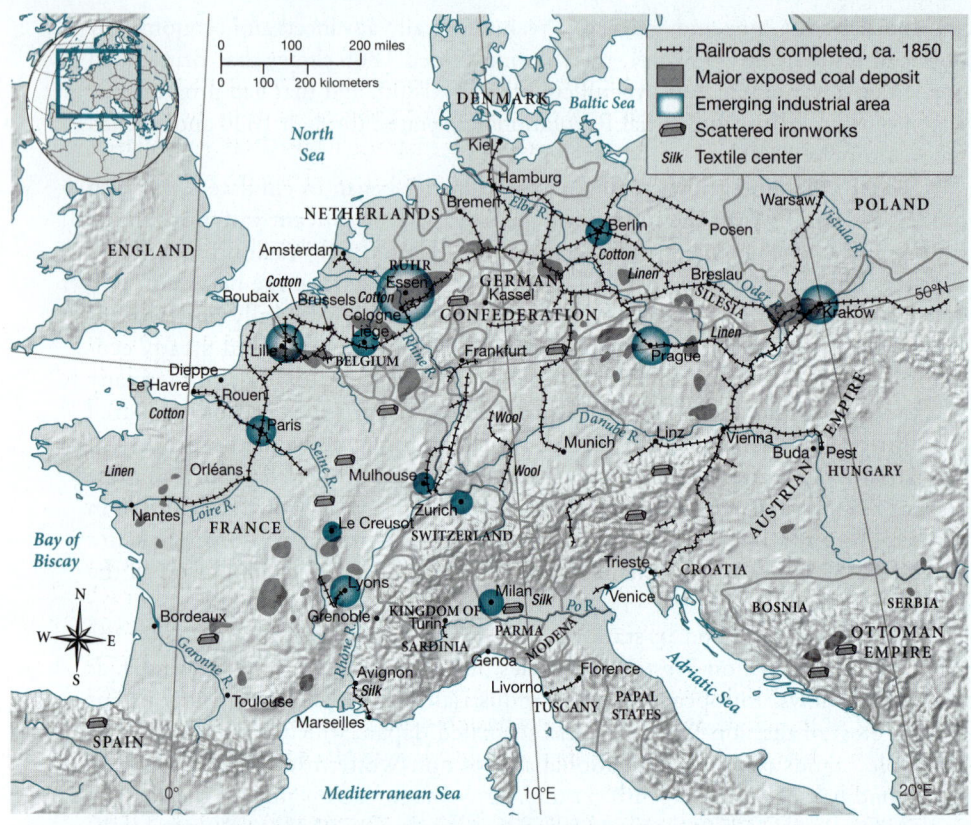

**MAP 23.2   Continental Industrialization, ca. 1850**

Although continental countries were beginning to make progress by 1850, they still lagged far behind Britain. For example, continental railroad building was still in an early stage, whereas the British rail system was essentially complete (see Map 23.1). Coal played a critical role in nineteenth-century industrialization, both as a power source for steam engines and as a raw material for making iron and steel.

and, after 1830, required the existence of railroads. Continental entrepreneurs had great difficulty amassing the large sums of money the new methods demanded, and laborers bitterly resisted the move to working in factories. All these factors slowed the spread of mechanization (Map 23.2).

Nevertheless, western European nations possessed a number of advantages that helped them respond to these challenges. First, most had rich traditions of putting-out enterprise, merchant capitalism, and skilled urban trades. These assets gave their firms the ability to adapt and survive in the face of new market conditions. Second, continental capitalists did not need to develop their own advanced technology. Instead they could "borrow" the new methods developed in Great Britain, as well as the engineers and some of the financial resources they lacked. Finally, European countries had strong, independent governments that were willing to use the power of the state to promote industry and catch up with Britain.

## Agents of Industrialization

Western European success in adopting British methods took place despite the best efforts of the British to prevent it. The British realized the great value of their technical discoveries and tried to keep their secrets to themselves. Until 1825 it was illegal for artisans and skilled mechanics to leave Britain; until 1843 the export of textile machinery and other equipment was forbidden. Many talented, ambitious workers, however, slipped out of the country illegally and became a powerful force in the spread of industrialization.

A second agent of industrialization consisted of talented European entrepreneurs such as Fritz Harkort (1793–1880). Serving in England as a Prussian army officer during the Napoleonic Wars, Harkort was impressed with what he saw. He then set up shop building steam engines in the Ruhr Valley, on the western border with France. In spite of problems obtaining skilled workers and machinery, Harkort succeeded in building and selling engines. However, his ambitious efforts failed to turn a profit. His career illustrates both the great efforts of a few important business leaders to duplicate the British achievement and the difficulty of the task.

National governments played an even more important role in supporting industrialization in continental Europe than in Britain. **Tariff protection** was one such support. The French, for example, responded to a flood of cheap British goods in 1815, after the Napoleonic Wars, by laying high taxes on imported goods. Customs agreements emerged among some German states starting in 1818, and in 1834 a number of states signed a treaty creating a customs union, or *Zollverein*. The treaty allowed goods to move between member states without tariffs, while erecting a single uniform tariff against other nations.

After 1815 continental governments also bore the cost of building roads, canals, and railroads to improve transportation. Belgium led the way in the 1830s and 1840s, building a state-owned railroad network that stimulated the development of heavy industry and made the country an early industrial leader. In France the state shouldered all the expense of acquiring and laying roadbed, including bridges and tunnels.

Finally, banks, like governments, also played a larger and more creative role on the continent than in Britain. Previously, almost all banks in Europe had been private. Because of the possibility of unlimited financial loss, the partners of private banks generally avoided industrial investment as being too risky.

In the 1830s, however, two important Belgian banks received permission from the growth-oriented government to establish themselves as corporations enjoying limited liability. That is, if the bank went bankrupt, stockholders would lose only their original investments in the bank's common stock, and they could not be forced to pay for additional losses out of other property they owned. Limited liability helped these banks attract investors. They mobilized impressive resources for investment in big companies, became industrial banks, and successfully promoted industrial development. Similar corporate banks became important in France and Germany in the 1850s and 1860s.

The combined efforts of skilled workers, entrepreneurs, governments, and industrial banks meshed successfully between 1850 and the financial crash of 1873. In Belgium, France, and the German states key indicators of modern industrial

***The Circle of the Rue Royale, Paris,* 1868**  The Circle of the Rue Royale was an exclusive club of aristocrats, bankers, railway owners, and other members of Parisian high society. This group exemplifies the consolidation of social and economic power that took place in the second half of the nineteenth century. (Heritage Images/Getty Images)

development increased at average annual rates of 5 to 10 percent. As a result, rail networks were completed in western Europe and much of central Europe, and the leading continental countries mastered the industrial technologies that had first been developed in Great Britain. In the early 1870s Britain was still Europe's most industrial nation, but a select handful of countries were closing the gap.

## The Global Picture

The Industrial Revolution did not have a transformative impact beyond Europe prior to the 1860s, with the exception of the United States and Japan. In many countries, national governments and pioneering entrepreneurs promoted industrialization but fell short of transitioning to an industrial economy. For example, in Russia the imperial government brought steamships to the Volga River and a railroad to the capital, St. Petersburg, in the first decades of the nineteenth century. By midcentury ambitious entrepreneurs had established steam-powered cotton factories using imported British machines. However, these advances did not lead to overall industrialization of the country. Instead Russia confirmed its role as provider of raw materials, especially timber and grain, to the hungry West.

Egypt, a territory of the Ottoman Empire, similarly began an ambitious program of modernization after a reform-minded viceroy took power in 1805. This program included the use of imported British technology and experts in textile manufacture and other industries. These industries, however, could not compete with lower-priced European imports. Like Russia, Egypt fell back on agricultural exports, such as sugar and cotton, to European markets.

Such examples of faltering efforts at industrialization could be found in many other places in the Middle East, Asia, and Latin America. Where European governments maintained direct or indirect control, they acted to maintain colonial markets as sources of raw materials and consumers for their own products, rather than encouraging the spread of industrialization. In India, which was a British colony, millions of poor textile workers lost their livelihood because they could not compete with industrially produced British cotton. The British charged stiff import duties on Indian cottons entering the kingdom, but prohibited the Indians from doing the same to British imports. The arrival of railroads in India in the mid-nineteenth century served the purpose of agricultural rather than industrial development.

Latin American economies were disrupted by the early-nineteenth-century wars of independence. As these countries' economies recovered in the mid-nineteenth century, they increasingly adopted steam power for sugar and coffee processing and for transportation. Like elsewhere, this technology first supported increased agricultural production for export and only later drove domestic industrial production.

The rise of industrialization in Britain, western Europe, and the United States thus caused other regions of the world to become increasingly economically dependent. Instead of industrializing, many territories underwent a process of deindustrialization or delayed industrialization. Their relative economic weakness made them vulnerable to the new wave of imperialism undertaken by industrialized nations in the second half of the nineteenth century (see "The New Imperialism, 1880–1914" in Chapter 25).

As for China, it did not adopt mechanized production until the end of the nineteenth century, but continued as a market-based, commercial society with a massive rural sector and industrial production based on traditional methods. In the 1860s and 1870s, when Japan was successfully adopting industrial methods, the Chinese government showed similar interest in Western technology and science. However, in the mid-nineteenth century China faced widespread uprisings, which drained attention and resources to the military; moreover, after the Boxer Uprising of 1900 (see "Republican Revolution" in Chapter 26), Western powers forced China to pay massive indemnities, further reducing its capacity to promote industrialization.

# New Patterns of Working and Living

### How did work evolve during the Industrial Revolution, and how did industrialization impact daily life and the environment?

Having first emerged in the British countryside in the late eighteenth century, factories and industrial labor began migrating to cities by the early nineteenth century. For some people, the Industrial Revolution brought improvements, but living and working conditions for the poor stagnated or even deteriorated until around 1850, especially in overcrowded industrial cities. Rapid and widespread industrialization increased atmospheric pollution and other environmental hazards, but coal smoke was not immediately recognized as a harmful pollutant.

## Work in Early Factories

The first factories of the Industrial Revolution were cotton mills, which began functioning in the 1770s along fast-running rivers and streams and were often located in sparsely populated areas. Cottage workers, accustomed to the putting-out system, were reluctant to work in the new factories even when they received relatively good wages. In a factory, workers had to keep up with the machine and follow its relentless tempo. Moreover, they had to show up every day, on time, and work long, monotonous hours under the constant supervision of demanding overseers.

Cottage workers were not used to that way of life. All members of the family worked hard and long, but in spurts, setting their own pace. Women and children could break up their long hours of spinning with other tasks. On Saturday afternoon the head of the family delivered the week's work to the merchant manufacturer and got paid. Saturday night was a time of relaxation and drinking, especially for men.

Also, early factories resembled English poorhouses, where totally destitute people went to live at public expense. The similarity between large brick factories and large stone poorhouses increased the cottage workers' fear of factories and their hatred of factory discipline. It was cottage workers' reluctance to work in factories that prompted early cotton mill owners to begin employing poor children instead. These so-called pauper apprentices, some as young as five or six years of age, worked long hours for little to no pay and meager food.

## Working Families and Children

By the 1790s the early labor pattern was rapidly changing. The use of pauper apprentices was in decline, and in 1802 it was forbidden by Parliament. Many more textile factories were being built, mainly in urban areas, where they could use steam power rather than waterpower and attract a workforce more easily than in the countryside. People came from near and far to work in the cities. Collectively, these wage laborers came to be known as the *working class*, a term first used in the late 1830s.

In some cases, workers accommodated to the system by carrying over familiar working traditions. Some came to the mills and the mines as family units, as they had worked on farms and in the putting-out system. The mill or mine owner bargained with the head of the family and paid him or her for the work of the whole family.

Ties of kinship were particularly important for newcomers, who often traveled great distances to find work. Many urban workers in Great Britain were from Ireland. They were forced out of rural Ireland by population growth and deteriorating economic conditions from 1817. Their numbers increased dramatically during the desperate years of the potato famine, from 1845 to 1851. Like many other immigrant groups held together by ethnic and religious ties, the Irish worked together, formed their own neighborhoods, and maintained their cultural traditions.

In the early decades of the nineteenth century, however, family labor gradually disappeared from the factories. As control and discipline passed into the hands of impersonal managers and overseers, adult workers began to protest against inhuman conditions on behalf of children. Some enlightened employers and social reformers in

**Workers at a U.S. Mill** Female workers at a U.S. cotton mill in 1890 take a break from operating belt-driven weaving machines to pose for this photograph, accompanied by their male supervisor. The first textile mills, established in the 1820s in Massachusetts, employed local farm girls. As competition intensified, conditions deteriorated and the mills increasingly relied on immigrant women who had few alternatives to the long hours, noise, and dangers of factory work. By 1900 more than 1 million women worked in factories in the United States. (Courtesy of George Eastman Museum)

Parliament agreed that more humane standards were necessary, and they used parliamentary reports to influence public opinion. For example, Robert Owen (1771–1858), a successful textile manufacturer, testified in 1816 before an investigating committee on the basis of his experience. He argued that employing children under ten years of age as factory workers was "injurious to the children, and not beneficial to the proprietors."[5] Workers also provided graphic testimony at such hearings as the reformers pressed Parliament to pass corrective laws.

These efforts resulted in a series of British Factory Acts from 1802 to 1833 that progressively limited the workday of child laborers and set minimum hygiene and safety requirements. The **Factory Act of 1833** stated that children between ages nine and thirteen could work a maximum of eight hours per day, not including two hours for education. Teenagers aged fourteen to eighteen could work up to twelve hours, while those under nine were banned from employment. The act also installed a system of full-time professional inspectors to enforce labor regulations. The Factory Acts constituted significant progress in preventing the exploitation of children. One unintended drawback of restrictions on child labor, however, was that they broke the pattern of whole families working together in the factory, because efficiency required standardized shifts for all workers. After 1833 the number of children employed in industry declined rapidly. The **Mines Act of 1842** prohibited underground work for all women and girls as well as for boys under ten.

## The Sexual Division of Labor

With the restriction of child labor and the collapse of the family work pattern in the 1830s came a new sexual division of labor. By 1850 the man was emerging as the family's primary wage earner, while the married woman found only limited job opportunities. Generally denied good jobs at high wages in the growing urban economy, wives were expected to concentrate on their duties at home. Evolving gradually, but largely in place by 1850, this new pattern of **separate spheres** in Britain constituted a major development in the history of women and of the family.

Several factors combined to create this new sexual division of labor. First, the new and unfamiliar discipline of the clock and the machine was especially hard on married women of the laboring classes. Factory discipline conflicted with child care in a way that labor on the farm or in the cottage had not.

Second, running a household in conditions of urban poverty was an extremely demanding job in its own right. There were no supermarkets, public transportation, or modern cooking and cleaning appliances. Taking on a brutal job outside the house had limited appeal for the average married woman from the working class. Thus many women might well have accepted the emerging division of labor as the best available strategy for family survival in the industrializing society.

Third, to a large degree the young, generally unmarried women who did work for wages outside the home were segregated from men and confined to certain "women's jobs" because the new sexual division of labor replicated long-standing patterns of gender segregation and inequality. In the preindustrial economy, a small sector of the labor market had always been defined as "women's work," especially tasks involving needlework, spinning, food preparation, child care, and nursing. This traditional sexual division of labor took on new overtones, however, in response to the factory system. The growth of factories and mines brought new opportunities for girls and boys to mix on the job, free of familial supervision. Such opportunities led to more unplanned pregnancies and fueled the illegitimacy explosion that had begun in the late eighteenth century and that gathered force until at least 1850. Thus, the segregation of jobs by gender was partly an effort by older people to control the sexuality of working-class youths.

A final factor encouraging working-class women to withdraw from paid labor was the domestic ideals emanating from middle-class women, who had largely embraced the "separate spheres" ideology. Middle-class reformers published tracts and formed societies to urge poor women to devote more care and attention to their homes and families.

## Living Standards for the Working Class

Although the evidence is complex and sometimes contradictory, most historians now agree that overall living standards for the working class did not rise substantially until 1850. Factory wages began to rise after 1815, but these gains were modest and were offset by a decline in married women's and children's participation in the labor force, meaning that many households had less total income than before. Moreover, many people still worked outside the factories as cottage workers or rural laborers, and in those sectors wages declined. Thus, the increased productivity of industry did not lead to an increase in the purchasing power of the British working classes. Only after 1830, and especially after 1840, did real wages rise substantially, so that the average worker earned roughly 30 percent more in real terms in 1850 than in 1770.[6]

Up to that point, the harshness of labor in the new industries probably outweighed their benefits for working people. With industrialization, workers toiled longer and harder at jobs that were often more grueling and more dangerous. In England nonagricultural workers labored about 250 days per year in 1760 as compared to 300 days per year in 1830, while the normal workday remained an exhausting eleven hours throughout the entire period.[7]

As the factories moved to urban areas, workers followed them in large numbers, leading to an explosion in the size of cities, especially in the north of England. By the end of the nineteenth century England had become by far the most urbanized country in Europe. Life in the new industrial cities, such as Manchester and Liverpool, was grim. Given extremely high rates of infant mortality, average life expectancy was around only twenty-five to twenty-seven years, some fifteen years less than the national average.[8] Migrants to the booming cities found expensive, hastily constructed, overcrowded apartments and inadequate sanitary systems. Another way to consider the workers' standard of living is to look at the goods they purchased, which also suggest stagnant or declining living standards until the middle of the nineteenth century. One important area of improvement was in the consumption of cotton goods, which became much cheaper and could be enjoyed by all classes. However, in other areas, food in particular, the modest growth in factory wages was not enough to compensate for rising prices.

From the 1850s onward, matters improved considerably as wages made substantial gains and the prices of many goods dropped. A greater variety of foods became available, including the first canned goods. Some of the most important advances were in medicine. Smallpox vaccination became routine, and surgeons began to use anesthesia in the late 1840s. By 1850 trains and steamships had revolutionized transportation for the masses, while the telegraph made instant communication possible for the first time in human history. Gaslights greatly expanded the possibilities of nighttime activity.

## Environmental Impacts of Industrialization

By the mid-seventeenth century, coal had replaced wood as the major fuel for domestic usage. The energy revolution brought about a massive rise in the use of coal to power steam engines in factories and trains as well as to heat blast furnaces, coke ovens, and pottery kilns. The consumption of coal in Britain rose from 10 million tons in 1800 to 60 million in 1856 and to 167 million by 1900.[9] Coal-fueled power transformed living conditions, conveying previously unimaginable levels of comfort, hygiene, and consumer choice on citizens of Western industrialized countries. It also allowed them to use their industrial might to build empires and dominate other countries.

**Environmental Impact of Industrialization** Flames from a coke-fired blast furnace light up the night sky in the village of Coalbrookdale, an early center of the English iron ore smelting industry. With smoke billowing from the furnace and broken machinery scattered in the foreground, this painting highlights the environmental degradation that accompanied industrialization. (Universal ImagesGroup/Getty Images)

However, coal burning had harsh environmental consequences. Soot and smoke from the chimneys of open coal fires pervaded London and other large cities. Burning coal produces toxic ash and emits smoke, soot, heavy metals like mercury and lead, and acidic gases, including sulfur dioxide and carbon dioxide (a greenhouse gas). Hydrochloric acid, a byproduct of the industrial production of goods such as soap, salt, and salt-glazed pottery, was also released into the atmosphere. Together, these gases created the phenomenon of *acid rain*, a term coined by a chemist in 1859.

In addition to atmospheric pollution, industrialization created many other environmental hazards. Running water and sewage systems were not widespread until the middle of the nineteenth century, meaning that rapidly expanding industrial cities lacked clean water and relied on outhouses and cesspools for handling human excrement. Garbage collection was haphazard, and rivers provided convenient dumping grounds for industrial and domestic waste, including sewage and dead animals. In the countryside, coal mines contaminated water and soil systems.

Contemporary writers and artists testified to the acrid and impenetrable smog that pervaded industrial cities. Describing London, one writer in the 1830s noted the "dense canopy of smoke that spread itself over her countless streets and squares, enveloping a million and a half beings in murky vapour."[10] Until the last decades of the nineteenth century, however, most British people viewed smoke belching from factory chimneys as a welcome symbol of economic prosperity. Rather than seeing it as harmful, they believed that acidic smoke purified the air of dangerous gases from decomposing organic waste (such as human sewage).

In the 1880s, middle-class reformers presented evidence that smoke had increased the incidence of respiratory diseases and rickets (caused by lack of exposure to the sun) and demanded antipollution laws. But they faced resistance from factory owners, workers fearful of unemployment, and a government committed to laissez-faire economic policies. Atmospheric pollution peaked in the late nineteenth century. Around 1900, electric power began to replace steam in industry, leading to substantial improvements in urban air quality over time. At the same time, the British government began to investigate atmospheric pollution, but regulation remained limited.

# Relations Between Capital and Labor

**How did the changes brought about by the Industrial Revolution lead to new social classes, and how did people respond?**

In Great Britain industrial development led to the creation of new social groups and intensified long-standing problems between capital and labor. A new class of factory owners and industrial capitalists arose. The demands of modern industry regularly brought the interests of the middle-class industrialists into conflict with those of the people who worked for them — the working class. As observers took note of these changes, they raised new questions about how industrialization affected social relationships. Meanwhile, the forced labor of enslaved people contributed to the industrialization process in multiple ways.

## The New Class of Factory Owners

Early industrialists operated in a highly competitive economic system. There were countless production problems, and success and large profits were by no means certain. Manufacturers therefore waged a constant battle to cut their production costs and stay afloat. Much of the profit had to go back into the business for new and better machinery.

Most early industrialists drew upon their families and friends for labor and capital, but they came from a variety of backgrounds. Many were from well-established merchant families with rich networks of contacts and support. Others were of modest means, especially in the early days. Artisans and skilled workers of exceptional ability had unparalleled opportunities. Members of ethnic and religious groups who had been discriminated against in traditional occupations jumped at the new chances and often helped each other.

As factories and firms grew larger, and opportunities declined, it became harder for a poor young mechanic to start a small enterprise and end up as a wealthy manufacturer. Expensive, formal education became more important for young men as a means of success and advancement. In Britain by 1830 and in France and Germany by 1860, leading industrialists were more likely to have inherited their well-established enterprises, and they were financially much more secure than their struggling parents had been.

Just like working-class women, the wives and daughters of successful businessmen also found fewer opportunities for active participation in Europe's business world. Rather than contributing as vital partners in a family-owned enterprise, as so many middle-class women had done before, these women were increasingly valued for their ladylike gentility.

## Responses to Industrialization

From the beginning, the British Industrial Revolution had its critics. Among the first were the Romantic poets. William Blake (1757–1827) called the early factories "satanic mills" and protested against the hard life of the London poor. William Wordsworth (1770–1850) lamented the destruction of the rural way of life. Some handicraft workers — notably the **Luddites**, who attacked factories in northern

England in 1811 and later—smashed the new machines, which they believed were putting them out of work. Middle-class reformers wrote of problems in the factories and new towns, while Malthus and Ricardo concluded that workers would earn only enough to stay alive.

This pessimistic view was accepted and reinforced by Friedrich Engels (1820–1895), the future revolutionary and colleague of Karl Marx (see "The Birth of Socialism" in Chapter 24). After studying conditions in northern England, this young son of a wealthy Prussian cotton manufacturer published in 1844 *The Condition of the Working Class in England*, a blistering indictment of the capitalist classes. Engels's influential account of capitalist exploitation and increasing worker poverty was embellished by Marx and later socialists.

Analysis of industrial capitalism, often combined with reflections on the French Revolution, led to the development of a new overarching interpretation—a new paradigm—regarding social relationships. Briefly, this paradigm argued that individuals were members of separate classes based on their relationship to the means of production, that is, the machines and factories that dominated the new economy. As owners of expensive industrial machinery and as dependent laborers in their factories, the two main groups of society had separate and conflicting interests. Accordingly, the comfortable, well-educated "public" of the eighteenth century came increasingly to be defined as the middle class ("middle" because they were beneath the small group of landowning aristocracy at the top of society who claimed to be above industrial activity), and the "people" gradually began to perceive themselves as composing a modern working class. This interpretation appealed to many because it seemed to explain what was happening. Therefore, conflicting classes existed, in part, because many individuals came to believe they existed and developed an awareness that they belonged to a particular social class—this awareness is what Karl Marx called **class-consciousness**.

## The Early Labor Movement in Britain

Not everyone worked in large factories and coal mines during the Industrial Revolution. In 1850 more British people still worked on farms than in any other single occupation. The second-largest occupation was domestic service, with more than 1 million household servants, 90 percent of whom were women.

Within industry itself, the pattern of artisans working with hand tools in small shops remained unchanged in many trades, even as others were revolutionized by technological change. For example, the British iron industry was completely dominated by large-scale capitalist firms by 1850. Yet the firms that fashioned iron into small metal goods employed on average fewer than ten wage workers who used handicraft skills.

Working-class solidarity and class-consciousness developed in small workshops as well as in large factories. In the northern factory districts, anticapitalist sentiments were frequent by the 1820s. Commenting in 1825 on a strike in the woolen center of Bradford and the support it had gathered from other regions, one newspaper claimed with pride that "it is all the workers of England against a few masters of Bradford."[11]

Such sentiments ran contrary to the liberal tenets of economic freedom. Liberal economic principles were embraced by statesmen and middle-class business owners in the late eighteenth century and continued to gather strength in the early nineteenth century. In 1799 Parliament passed the **Combination Acts**, which outlawed unions and strikes. In 1813 and 1814 Parliament repealed an old law regulating the wages of artisans and the conditions of apprenticeship. As a result of these and other measures, certain skilled artisan workers found aggressive capitalists ignoring traditional work rules and trying to flood their trades with unorganized women workers and children to beat down wages.

The capitalist attack on artisan guilds and work rules was bitterly resented by many craftworkers, who subsequently played an important part in Great Britain and in other countries in gradually building a modern labor movement. The Combination Acts were widely disregarded by workers. Craftsmen continued to take collective action, and societies of skilled factory workers also organized unions. Unions sought to control the number of skilled workers, to limit apprenticeship to members' own children, and to bargain with owners over wages. In the face of widespread union activity, Parliament repealed the Combination Acts in 1824, and unions were tolerated, though not fully accepted, after 1825.

The next stage in the development of the British trade-union movement was the attempt to create a single large national union. This effort was led not so much by working people as by social reformers such as Robert Owen. Owen, a self-made cotton manufacturer, had pioneered industrial relations by combining strict discipline with paternalistic concern for the health, safety, and work hours of his employees. After 1815 he experimented with cooperative and socialist communities. Then in 1834 Owen organized one of the largest and most visionary of the early national unions, the Grand National Consolidated Trades Union. When Owen's and other ambitious labor organizing schemes collapsed, the British labor movement moved once again after 1851 in the direction of craft unions. These unions won real benefits for members by fairly conservative means and thus became an accepted part of the industrial scene.

British workers also engaged in direct political activity in defense of their interests. After the collapse of Owen's national trade union, many working people went into the Chartist movement, which fought for universal manhood suffrage. Workers were also active in campaigns to limit the workday in factories to ten hours and to permit duty-free importation of wheat into Great Britain to secure cheap bread. Thus, working people developed a sense of their own identity and played an active role in shaping the new industrial system. They were neither helpless victims nor passive beneficiaries.

## The Impact of Slavery

Another mass labor force of the Industrial Revolution was composed of the millions of enslaved men, women, and children who toiled in European colonies in the Caribbean and in the nations of North and South America. Historians have long debated the extent to which revenue from slavery contributed to Britain's achievements in the Industrial Revolution.

Most now agree that profits from colonial plantations and slave trading were a small portion of British national income in the eighteenth century. Nevertheless, the impact of slavery on Britain's economy was much broader than direct profits alone.

In the mid-eighteenth century the need for items to exchange for colonial cotton, sugar, tobacco, and enslaved people stimulated demand for British manufactured goods in the Caribbean, North America, and West Africa. Britain's dominance in the slave trade also led to the development of finance and credit institutions that would help early industrialists obtain capital for their businesses.

The British Parliament abolished the slave trade in 1807 and freed all slaves in British territories in 1833, but by 1850 most of the cotton processed by British mills was supplied by the coerced labor of enslaved people in the southern United States. Thus, the Industrial Revolution was integrally connected to the Atlantic world and the misery of slavery.

## Chapter Summary

As markets for manufactured goods increased both domestically and overseas, Britain was able to respond with increased production, largely because of its stable government, abundant natural resources, and flexible labor force. The first factories arose as a result of innovations in the textile industry. The demand for improvements in energy led to innovations and improvements in the steam engine, which transformed the iron industry, among others. In the early nineteenth century transportation of goods was greatly enhanced with the adoption of steam-powered trains and ships.

After 1815 continental European countries gradually built on England's technical breakthroughs. Entrepreneurs set up their own factories and hired skilled local artisans along with English immigrants experienced in the new technologies. Newly established corporate banks worked in conjunction with government interventions in finance and tariff controls to promote railroads and other industries. Beginning around 1850 Japan and the United States also began to rapidly industrialize, but generally the Industrial Revolution spread more slowly outside Europe, as many countries were confined to producing agricultural goods and other raw materials to serve European markets.

The rise of modern industry had a profound impact on society, beginning in Britain in the late eighteenth century. Industrialization led to the growing size and wealth of the middle class and the rise of a modern industrial working class. Rigid rules, stern discipline, and long hours weighed heavily on factory workers, and improvements in the standard of living came slowly, but they were substantial by 1850. Married women withdrew increasingly from wage work and concentrated on child care and household responsibilities. The era of industrialization also fostered new attitudes toward child labor, encouraged protective factory legislation, and called forth a new sense of class feeling and an assertive labor movement. Enslaved labor in European colonies and the United States contributed to the rise of the Industrial Revolution by increasing markets for European goods, supplying raw materials, and encouraging the development of financial systems.

## NOTES

1. Nicholas Crafts, "Productivity Growth During the British Industrial Revolution: Revisionism Revisited," Working Paper, Department of Economics, University of Warwick, September 2014.

2. John Allen, *The British Industrial Revolution* (Cambridge: Cambridge University Press, 2009), pp. 1–2.

3. P. Bairoch, "International Industrialization Levels from 1750 to 1980," *Journal of European Economic History* 11 (Spring 1982): 269–333.

4. Quoted in J. Bowditch and C. Ramsland, eds., *Voices of the Industrial Revolution* (Ann Arbor: University of Michigan Press, 1961), p. 55, from Thomas Malthus, *Essay on the Principle of Population*, 4th ed. (1807).

5. Quoted in E. R. Pike, *"Hard Times": Human Documents of the Industrial Revolution* (New York: Praeger, 1966), p. 109.

6. Joel Mokyr, *The Enlightened Economy: An Economic History of Britain, 1700–1850* (New Haven, Conn.: Yale University Press, 2009), pp. 460–461.

7. H.-J. Voth, *Time and Work in England, 1750–1830* (Oxford: Oxford University Press, 2000), pp. 268–270; also pp. 118–133.

8. Mokyr, *The Enlightened Economy*, p. 455.

9. B. W. Clapp, *An Environmental History of Britain* (Abingdon: Routledge, 2013), p. 16.

10. Quoted in Peter Thorsheim, *Inventing Pollution: Coal, Smoke, and Culture in Britain Since 1800* (Athens: Ohio University Press, 2006), p. 5.

11. Quoted in D. Geary, ed., *Labour and Socialist Movements in Europe Before 1914* (Oxford: Berg, 1989), p. 29.

12. Kenneth Pomeranz, *The Great Divergence: China, Europe, and the Making of the Modern World Economy* (Princeton, N.J.: Princeton University Press, 2000).

## MAKE CONNECTIONS   LOOK AHEAD

For much of its history, Europe lagged behind older and more sophisticated civilizations in China and the Middle East. And yet by 1800 Europe had broken ahead of the other regions of the world in terms of wealth and power, a process that historians have termed "the Great Divergence."[12]

One prerequisite for the rise of Europe was its growing control over world trade, first in the Indian Ocean in the sixteenth and seventeenth centuries and then in the eighteenth-century Atlantic world. A second crucial factor behind the Great Divergence was the Industrial Revolution, which dramatically increased the pace of production and distribution while reducing their cost, thereby allowing Europeans to control other countries economically and politically. By the middle of the nineteenth century the gap between Western industrial production and standards of living and those of the non-West had grown dramatically, bringing with it the economic dependence of non-Western nations, meager wages for their largely impoverished populations, and increasingly aggressive Western imperial ambitions. In the late nineteenth century non-Western countries began to experience their own processes of industrialization. Today's world is witnessing a surge in productivity in China, India, and other non-Western nations, with uncertain consequences for the global balance of power. The world is also confronting the long-term environmental consequences of reliance on fossil fuels, with climate change posing a threat to global economic, political, and social stability.

# Chapter 23 Review

## IDENTIFY KEY TERMS

Identify and explain the significance of each item below.

Industrial Revolution (p. 587)  
spinning jenny (p. 588)  
water frame (p. 588)  
steam engines (p. 589)  
*Rocket* (p. 591)  
Crystal Palace (p. 592)  
iron law of wages (p. 593)  

tariff protection (p. 597)  
Factory Act of 1833 (p. 601)  
Mines Act of 1842 (p. 601)  
separate spheres (p. 602)  
Luddites (p. 605)  
class-consciousness (p. 606)  
Combination Acts (p. 607)

## REVIEW THE MAIN IDEAS

Answer the focus questions from each section of the chapter.

1. Why did the Industrial Revolution begin in Britain, and how did it develop between 1780 and 1850? (p. 586)
2. How did countries in Europe and around the world respond to the challenge of industrialization after 1815? (p. 593)
3. How did work evolve during the Industrial Revolution, and how did industrialization impact daily life and the environment? (p. 599)
4. How did the changes brought about by the Industrial Revolution lead to new social classes, and how did people respond? (p. 605)

## MAKE COMPARISONS AND CONNECTIONS

Analyze the larger developments and continuities within and across chapters.

1. Why did Great Britain take the lead in industrialization, and when did other countries begin to adopt the new techniques and organization of production?
2. How did historical developments between 1600 and 1800 contribute to the rise of Europe to world dominance in the nineteenth century? Argue for or against the following proposition: "Given contemporary trends, the dominance of the West in the nineteenth and twentieth centuries should be seen as a temporary aberration, rather than as a fundamental and permanent shift in the global balance of power."
3. How would you compare the legacy of the political revolutions of the late eighteenth century (Chapter 22) with that of the Industrial Revolution? Which seems to have created the most important changes, and why?

## CHRONOLOGY

| | |
|---|---|
| **ca. 1765** | • Hargreaves invents spinning jenny; Arkwright creates water frame |
| **1769** | • Watt patents modern steam engine |
| **ca. 1780–1850** | • Industrial Revolution and accompanying population boom in Great Britain |
| **1799** | • Combination Acts passed in England |
| **1802–1833** | • Factory Acts passed in England |
| **1805–1849** | • Muhammad Ali modernizes Egypt (Ch. 25) |
| **1810–1825** | • Latin American wars of independence (Ch. 22) |
| **1824** | • British Combination Acts repealed |
| **1829** | • Stephenson's *Rocket*; first modern railroad |
| **1830s** | • Industrial banks promote rapid industrialization of Belgium |
| **1830s–1850s** | • Steam-powered trains operating in the U.S. and South America (Ch. 27) |
| **1834** | • Creation of a *Zollverein* (customs union) among many German states |
| **1839–1842** | • Opium War in China (Ch. 26) |
| **1842** | • Mines Act passed in England |
| **1844** | • Engels, *The Condition of the Working Class in England* |
| **1850s** | • U.S. begins to industrialize rapidly |
| **1850s** | • Japan begins to adopt Western technologies (Ch. 26) |
| **1851** | • Great Exhibition held at Crystal Palace in London |
| **1857** | • Great Mutiny in India (Ch. 26) |
| **1860s** | • Rapid industrialization of Germany begins |

# 24

# Ideologies of Change in Europe

## 1815–1914

**THE MOMENTOUS TRANSFORMATIONS WROUGHT BY THE POLITICAL** and economic revolutions of the late eighteenth and early nineteenth centuries left a legacy of unfinished hopes and dreams for many Europeans: for democracy, liberty, and equality and for higher living standards for all. These aspirations clashed with unpredictable and tumultuous consequences over the course of the nineteenth century. After 1815 the powers that defeated Napoleon united under a revived conservatism to stamp out the spread of liberal and democratic reforms. But the political and social innovations made possible by the unfinished revolutions proved difficult to contain.

In politics, powerful ideologies—liberalism, nationalism, and socialism— emerged to oppose conservatism. All played critical roles in the political and social battles of the era and the great popular upheaval that eventually swept across Europe in the revolutions of 1848. These revolutions failed, however, and gave way to more sober—and more successful—nation building in the 1860s. European political leaders and middle-class nationalists also began to deal effectively with the challenges of the emerging urban society. One way they did so was through nationalism—mass identification with a nation-state that was increasingly responsive to the needs of its people. At the same time, the triumph of nationalism promoted bitter rivalries between states and peoples, spurred a second great wave of imperialism, and in the twentieth century brought an era of tragic global conflict.

# A Conservative Peace Gives Way to Radical Ideas

How did the allies fashion a peace settlement in 1815, and what radical ideas emerged between 1815 and 1848?

After finally defeating Napoleon, the conservative aristocratic monarchies of Russia, Prussia, Austria, and Great Britain—known as the Quadruple Alliance—reaffirmed their determination to hold France in line and to defeat the intertwined dangers of war and revolution. At the **Congress of Vienna** (1814–1815), they fashioned a lasting peace settlement that helped produce fifty years without major warfare in Europe. On the domestic front, they sought to restore order and limit the spread of revolutionary ideas.

Despite the congress's success on the diplomatic front, many observers at the time were frustrated by the high-handed dictates of the Great Powers and their refusal to adopt social reforms. After 1815 such critics sought to harness the radical ideas of the revolutionary age to new political movements. Many rejected **conservatism**, a political philosophy that stressed retaining traditional values and institutions, including hereditary monarchy and a strong landowning aristocracy. Radical thinkers developed alternative ideologies and tried to convince society to act on them.

## The Political and Social Situation After 1815

When the Quadruple Alliance, along with representatives of minor powers, met together at the Congress of Vienna, they combined leniency toward France with strong defensive measures. The Low Countries—Belgium and Holland—were united under an enlarged Dutch monarchy capable of opposing France more effectively. Prussia received considerably more territory along France's eastern border to stand as a "sentinel on the Rhine" against renewed French aggression. The congress recognized the neutrality of certain territories—for example, the cantons of Switzerland—as a means of creating buffer zones between potentially hostile states. One of the most hotly debated issues at the congress was the status of Poland, which had been dismantled in the 1790s and then re-created as a satellite state by Napoleon called the Duchy of Warsaw. The congress established a sovereign Kingdom of Poland ruled by the tsar of Russia and gave Poles living in Austrian, Prussian, and Russian territory the right to travel and communicate across national boundaries.

The congress returned France to the boundaries it possessed in 1792, which were larger than those of 1789. Even after Napoleon's brief return to power tested the allies' patience, France did not have to give up much additional territory and had to pay only modest reparations.

In their moderation toward France, the allies were motivated by self-interest and traditional ideas about the balance of power. To the peacemakers, especially to Klemens von Metternich (1773–1859), Austria's foreign minister, the balance of power meant an international equilibrium of political and military forces that would discourage aggression by any state or combination of states. This required, among other measures, ensuring the internal stability of France. The Quadruple Alliance members also agreed to meet periodically to discuss their common interests and to consider appropriate measures to maintain peace in Europe. This agreement represented a transformation of European diplomacy; the "congress system" it inaugurated lasted long into the nineteenth century.

The leaders of the congress reached their decisions with little recognition of the interests of smaller states and subject peoples within multiethnic states. They also left aside the question of the European territories of the Ottoman Empire, which Napoleon had schemed to divide between France and Russia. With the rise of nationalism, these neglected issues would pose serious threats to the post-1815 order. On a more positive note, the leading powers of the congress, led by Britain, issued a declaration condemning the slave trade and calling on European states to begin the process of abolition.

## Conservatism After 1815

In 1815, under Metternich's leadership, Austria, Prussia, and Russia formed the Holy Alliance, dedicated to crushing the ideas of the revolutionary era. Metternich's policies dominated the entire German Confederation of thirty-eight independent German states (Map 24.1). It was through the German Confederation that Metternich had the repressive Karlsbad Decrees issued in 1819. These decrees required member states to root out radical ideas in their universities and newspapers, and a permanent committee was established to investigate and punish any liberal or radical organizations.

Adhering to a conservative political philosophy, Metternich believed that strong governments were needed to protect society from its worst instincts. Like many European conservatives of his time, he believed that liberalism (see the next section), as embodied in revolutionary America and France, had been responsible for a generation of bloodshed and suffering. He blamed liberal revolutionaries for stirring up the lower classes, which he believed desired nothing more than peace and quiet.

Another belief that Metternich opposed, which was often allied with liberalism, was nationalism, the idea that each national group had a right to establish its own independent government. The Habsburg's Austrian Empire was a dynastic state

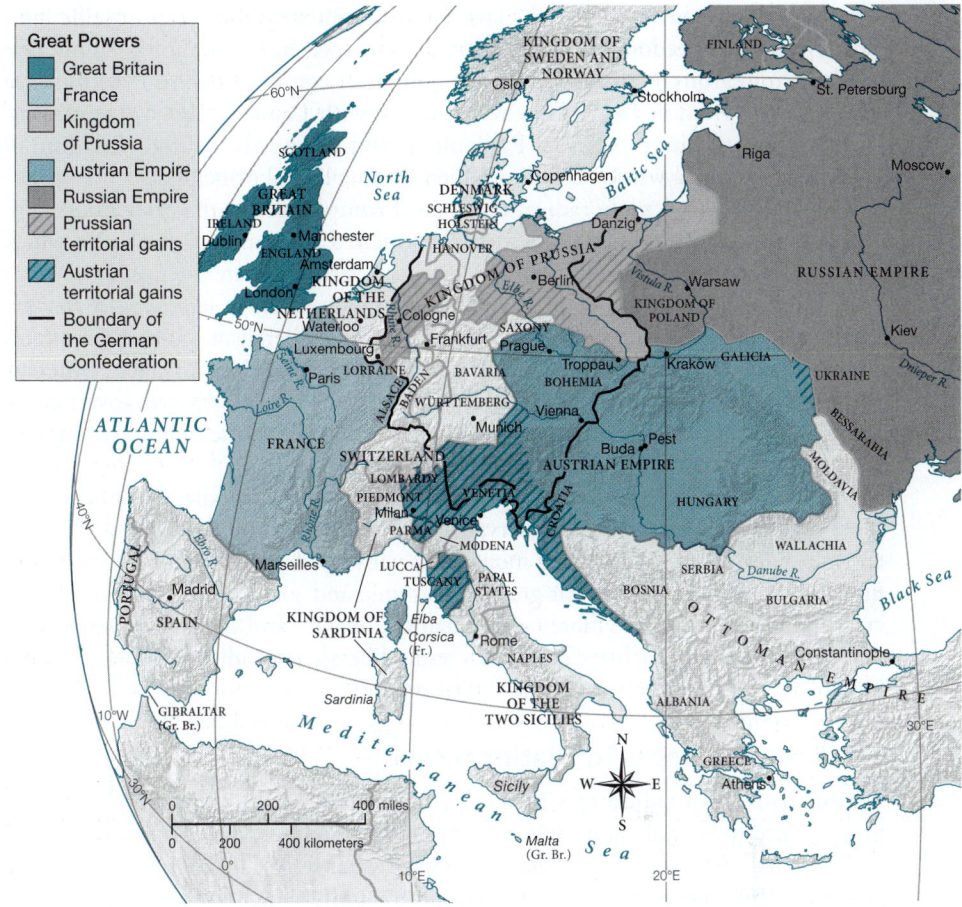

**MAP 24.1   Europe in 1815**

In 1815 Europe contained many different states, but after the defeat of Napoleon international politics was dominated by the five Great Powers: Russia, Prussia, Austria, Great Britain, and France. (The number rises to six if one includes the Ottoman Empire.)

dominated by Germans but containing many other national groups. This multinational state was both strong and weak. It was strong because of its large population and vast territories, but weak because of its many and potentially dissatisfied nationalities. In these circumstances, Metternich opposed both liberalism and nationalism, for Austria could not accommodate those ideologies and remain a powerful empire. Metternich's antinationalist efforts were supported by the two great multinational empires on Austria's borders, Russia and the Ottoman Empire.

## Liberalism and the Middle Class

The principal ideas of **liberalism** — liberty and equality — were by no means defeated in 1815. First realized in the American Revolution and then achieved in part in the French and Latin American Revolutions, liberalism demanded representative government and equality before the law. The idea of liberty also meant specific individual freedoms: freedom of the press, freedom of speech, freedom of assembly, and freedom from arbitrary arrest. In Europe only three countries had realized much of the liberal program in 1815. They were France, with Louis XVIII's Constitutional Charter; Great Britain, with its Parliament; and the newly created Kingdom of Poland, which had a written constitution enshrining liberal principles.

Liberalism faced more radical ideological competitors in the early nineteenth century. Opponents of liberalism especially criticized its economic principles, which called for unrestricted private enterprise and no government interference in the economy. This philosophy was popularly known as the doctrine of **laissez faire** (lay-say FEHR). In early-nineteenth-century Britain economic liberalism was embraced most enthusiastically by business groups and thus became a doctrine associated with corporate interests. Early-nineteenth-century liberals favored representative government, but they generally wanted property qualifications attached to the right to vote and to serve in Parliament.

As liberalism became increasingly identified with the middle class after 1815, some intellectuals and foes of conservatism felt that liberalism did not go nearly far enough. They called for replacing monarchies with republics, for democracy through universal male suffrage, and for greater economic and social equality. These democrats and republicans were more radical than the liberals, and they were more willing to endorse violence to achieve goals. As a result, liberals and radical republicans could join forces against conservatives only up to a point.

## The Growing Appeal of Nationalism

**Nationalism** was a radical new ideology that emerged in the years after 1815 — an idea destined to have an enormous influence in the modern world. Early advocates of the "national idea" argued that the members of what we would call today an ethnic group had their own spirit and their own cultural unity, which were manifested especially in a common language, history, and territory. In fact, such cultural unity was more a dream than a reality as local dialects abounded, historical memory divided the inhabitants of the different states as much as it unified them, and a variety of ethnic groups shared the territory of most states.

Nevertheless, many European nationalists sought to make the territory of each people coincide with well-defined boundaries in an independent nation-state. It was this political goal that made nationalism so explosive in central and eastern Europe after 1815, when there were either too few states (Austria, Russia, and the Ottoman Empire) or too many (the Italian peninsula and the German Confederation), and when different peoples overlapped and intermingled.

Between 1815 and 1850 most people who believed in nationalism also believed in either liberalism or radical democratic republicanism. A common faith in the creativity and nobility of the people was perhaps the single most important reason for the linking of these two concepts. Liberals and especially democrats saw the people as the ultimate source of all good government. They agreed that the benefits of self-government would be possible only if the people were united by common traditions that transcended class and local interests. Thus individual liberty and love of a free nation overlapped greatly.

Yet early nationalists also stressed the differences among peoples, and they developed a strong sense of "we" and "they." Thus, while European nationalism's main thrust was liberal and democratic, below the surface lurked ideas of national superiority and national mission.

## The Birth of Socialism

**Socialism**, a second radical doctrine after 1815, began in France. Early French socialists shared a sense of disappointment in the outcome of the French Revolution. They were also alarmed by the rise of laissez faire and the emergence of modern industry, which they saw as fostering inequality and selfish individualism. There was, they believed, an urgent need for a further reorganization of society to establish cooperation and a new sense of community.

Early French socialists felt an intense desire to help the poor, whose conditions had not been improved by industrial advances, and they preached greater economic equality between the rich and the poor. Inspired by the economic planning implemented in revolutionary France (see "The National Convention" in Chapter 22), they argued that the government should rationally organize the economy to control prices and prevent unemployment. Socialists also believed that government should regulate private property or that private property should be abolished and replaced by state or community ownership.

Up to the 1840s France was the center of socialism, as it had been the center of revolution in Europe, but in the following decades the German intellectual Karl Marx (1818–1883) would weave the diffuse strands of social thought into a distinctly modern ideology. Marx had studied philosophy at the University of Berlin before turning to journalism and economics. In 1848 the thirty-year-old Karl Marx and the twenty-eight-year-old Friedrich Engels published *The Communist Manifesto*, which became the guiding text of socialism.

Marx argued that middle-class interests and those of the industrial working class were inevitably opposed to each other. According to the *Manifesto*, the "history of all previously existing society is the history of class struggles." In Marx's view, one class had always exploited the other, and, with the advent of modern industry, society was split more clearly than ever before: between the well-educated and prosperous middle class — the **bourgeoisie** — and the modern working class — the **proletariat**.

Just as the bourgeoisie had triumphed over the feudal aristocracy in the French Revolution, Marx predicted that the proletariat would conquer the bourgeoisie in a new revolution. While a tiny majority owned the means of production and grew richer, the ever-poorer proletariat was constantly growing in size and in class-consciousness. Marx believed that the critical moment when class conflict would result in revolution was very near, as the last lines of *The Communist Manifesto* make clear:

> Germany . . . is on the eve of a bourgeois revolution, that is bound to be . . . the prelude to an immediately following proletarian revolution. . . .
>
> Let the ruling classes tremble at a Communist revolution. The proletarians have nothing to lose but their chains. They have a world to win. WORKING MEN OF ALL COUNTRIES, UNITE!

Marx drew on the arguments of Adam Smith and David Ricardo, who taught that labor was the source of all value. He went on to argue that profits rightfully belonged to the workers who had created them through their labor. Moreover, Marx incorporated Friedrich Engels's account of the terrible oppression of the new class of factory workers in England. Thus Marx pulled together powerful ideas and insights to create one of the great secular religions out of the intellectual ferment of the early nineteenth century.

# Reforms and Revolutions, 1815–1850

**Why did revolutions triumph briefly throughout most of Europe in 1848, and why did they fail?**

As liberal, nationalist, and socialist forces battered the conservatism of 1815, social and economic conditions continued to deteriorate for many Europeans, adding to the mounting pressures. In some countries, such as Great Britain, change occurred gradually and largely peacefully, but in 1848 radical political and social ideologies combined with economic crisis to produce revolutionary movements that demanded an end to repressive government. Between 1815 and 1848 many European countries, including France, Austria, and Prussia, experienced variations on this basic theme.

## Social and Economic Conflict

The slow and uneven spread of industrialization in Europe after 1815 meant that the benefits of higher productivity were not felt by many. In Great Britain, the earliest to industrialize, living standards only began to rise after 1850, and this trend took longer to spread to the continent. Indeed, for many people in the cities and countryside, the first half of the nineteenth century brought a decline in the conditions of daily life. In Europe's rapidly growing cities, migrants encountered shoddy housing, atmospheric pollution, and poor sanitation, ideal conditions for the spread of infectious disease.

Despite booming urbanization, much of the continent remained agricultural, and the traditional social hierarchy, dominated by a landowning aristocracy, persisted. Serfdom still existed in the Hungarian provinces of the Austrian Empire, Prussian Silesia, and Russia. In the early nineteenth century, however, the pressures of population growth, the adoption of new forms of agriculture, and the spread of exploitative rural industry destabilized these existing patterns. Many peasants lost access to collective land due to enclosure and the adoption of more efficient farming techniques. Meanwhile, the growing number of cottage workers resisted exploitation by merchant capitalists, and journeymen battled masters in urban industries.

Social malaise was exacerbated by the fact that the retracing of borders at the Congress of Vienna had placed many populations in new and unfamiliar states. Lack of loyalty to the central government only worsened popular anger over rising tax rates and other burdens. These simmering tensions broke to the surface in the 1840s, as widespread crop failure in 1845–1846 led to economic crisis.

In spring 1848 many people's grievances about enclosure and taxation resembled those of the eighteenth century. What transformed these conflicts was the political ideologies born from the struggles and unfulfilled hopes of the French Revolution — liberalism, nationalism, and socialism — as well as the newly invigorated conservatism that stood against them. These ideologies helped turn economic and social conflicts into the revolutions of 1848.

## Liberal Reform in Great Britain

The English parliamentary system guaranteed basic civil rights, but only about 8 percent of the population could vote. By the 1780s there was growing interest in reform, but the French Revolution threw the British aristocracy into a panic. After 1815, the British government put down popular protests over unemployment and the high cost of grain caused by the Napoleonic Wars with repressive legislation and military force.

By the early 1830s the social and economic disruption caused by industrialization began to be felt in politics. In 1832 pressure from the liberal middle classes and popular unrest convinced the king and the House of Lords that they must act. The Reform Bill of 1832 moved British politics in a more democratic direction by giving new industrial areas increased representation in the House of Commons and by increasing the number of voters by about 50 percent. Two years later, the New Poor Law called for unemployed and indigent families to be placed in workhouses rather than receiving aid from local parishes to remain in their own homes. With this act, Britain's rulers sought to relieve middle-class taxpayers of the burden of poor relief and to encourage unemployed rural workers to migrate to cities and take up industrial work.

Thus limited democratic reform was counterbalanced by harsh measures against the poor. Many working people protested their ongoing exclusion from voting and the terms of the New Poor Law. Between 1838 and 1848 they joined the Chartist movement (see "The Early Labor Movement in Britain" in Chapter 23), which demanded universal male suffrage. In 1847 the ruling conservative party, known as the Tories, sought to appease working people with the Ten Hours Act, which limited the workday for women and young people in factories to ten hours. Tory aristocrats championed such legislation in order to compete with the middle class for working-class support.

This competition meant that the parliamentary state relied on eliciting support from its people and thereby succeeded in managing unrest without the outbreak of revolution. Another factor favoring Great Britain's largely peaceful evolution in the nineteenth century was the fact that living standards had begun to rise by the late 1840s, as the benefits of industrialization finally began to be felt. Thus England avoided the violence and turmoil of the revolutions of 1848 that shook continental Europe.

The people of Ireland did not benefit from these circumstances. Ruled as a conquered people, the population was mostly composed of Irish Catholic peasants who rented land from a tiny minority of Protestant landowners, many of whom resided in England. Ruthlessly exploited and growing rapidly in numbers, the rural population around 1800 lived under terrible conditions.

Ireland's population doubled from 4 million to 8 million between 1780 and 1840, fueled in large part by the calories and nutritive qualities of the potato, which became the staple food crop in this period. However, the potato crop failed in 1845, 1846, 1848, and 1851 in Ireland and throughout much of Europe. Many suffered in Europe, but in Ireland, where dependency on the potato was much more widespread, the result was starvation and death. The British government, committed to laissez-faire economic policies, reacted slowly and utterly inadequately. One and a half million people died, while another million fled between 1845 and 1851, primarily to the United States and Great Britain. The Great Famine, as this tragedy came to be known, intensified anti-British feeling and promoted Irish nationalism.

## Revolutions in France

Louis XVIII's Constitutional Charter of 1814 was essentially a liberal constitution. It protected economic and social gains made by the middle class and the peasantry in the French Revolution, recognized intellectual and artistic freedom, and created a parliament with upper and lower houses. The charter was anything but democratic, however. Only a tiny minority of males had the right to vote for the representatives who, with the king and his ministers, made the nation's laws.

Louis's conservative successor, Charles X (r. 1824–1830), wanted to re-establish the old order in France. To rally French nationalism and gain popular support, he exploited a long-standing dispute with Algeria, a vassal state of the Ottoman Empire. In June 1830 a French force crossed the Mediterranean and took the capital of Algiers. The French continued to wage war against Algerian resistance until 1847, when they finally subdued the country. Bringing French and other European settlers to Algeria and expropriating large amounts of Muslim-owned land, the conquest of Algeria marked the rebirth of French colonial expansion after the defeats of the eighteenth century.

Buoyed by this success, Charles overplayed his hand and repudiated the Constitutional Charter. After three days of uprisings in Paris, which sparked a series of revolts by frustrated liberals and democrats across Europe, Charles fled. His cousin Louis Philippe (r. 1830–1848) accepted the Constitutional Charter of 1814 and assumed the title of the "king of the French people." Still, the situation in France remained fundamentally unchanged. Political and social reformers and the poor of Paris were bitterly disappointed.

During the 1840s this sense of disappointment was worsened by bad harvests and the slow development of industrialization, which meant that living conditions for the majority of the working classes were deteriorating rather than improving. Similar conditions prevailed across continental Europe, which was soon rocked by insurrections. In February full-scale revolution broke out in France, and its shock waves rippled across the continent.

Louis Philippe had refused to approve social legislation or consider electoral reform. Frustrated desires for change, high-level financial scandals, and crop failures in 1845 and 1846 united diverse groups of the king's opponents, including merchants, intellectuals, shopkeepers, and workers. In February 1848, as popular revolt broke out, barricades went up and Louis Philippe abdicated.

The revolutionaries quickly drafted a democratic constitution for France's Second Republic, granting the right to vote to every adult male. Colonial slavery and the death penalty were abolished, and national workshops were established for unemployed Parisian workers.

Yet there were profound differences within the revolutionary coalition in Paris. The socialism promoted by radical republicans frightened not only the liberal middle and upper classes but also the peasants, many of whom owned land. In elections for the new Constituent Assembly in April 1848, the monarchists won a clear majority. When the new government dissolved the national workshops in Paris, workers rose in a spontaneous insurrection. After three terrible "June Days" and the death or injury of more than ten thousand people, the republican army stood triumphant in a sea of working-class blood and hatred.

The revolution in France thus ended in failure. The middle and working classes had turned against each other. In place of a democratic republic, the Constituent Assembly completed a constitution featuring a strong executive. This allowed Louis Napoleon, nephew of Napoleon Bonaparte, to win a landslide victory in the December 1848 election based on promises to lead a strong government in favor of popular interests.

President Louis Napoleon at first shared power with a conservative National Assembly. But in 1851 he dismissed the Assembly and seized power. A year later he called on the French to make him hereditary emperor, and 97 percent voted to do so in a national plebiscite. Louis Napoleon then ruled France's Second Empire as Napoleon III, initiating policies favoring economic growth and urban development to appease the populace.

## The Revolutions of 1848 in Central Europe

Throughout central Europe, social conflicts were exacerbated by the economic crises of 1845 to 1846. News of the upheaval in France in 1848 provoked the outbreak of revolution. Liberals demanded written constitutions, representative government, and greater civil liberties from authoritarian regimes. When governments hesitated, popular revolts followed. Urban workers and students allied with middle-class liberals and peasants. In the face of these coalitions, monarchs made hasty concessions. Soon, however, popular revolutionary fronts broke down as they had in France.

Compared with the situation in France, where political participation by working people reached its peak, revolts in central Europe tended to be dominated by social elites. They were also more sharply divided between moderate constitutionalists and radical republicans. Unrest in the Austrian Empire began in 1846 in the Polish city of Kraków, which had been placed under the joint control of Russia, Prussia, and Austria at the Congress of Vienna. After a failed uprising by Polish nationalists, the city and its surrounding region were annexed by the Austrian Empire.

In early March 1848, news of the Parisian revolt inspired nationalists in the Hungarian parliament to demand autonomy from Austria, full civil liberties, and the abolition of feudal privileges. Ten days later, Viennese students and workers responded to the news from Paris by taking to the streets, and peasant disorders broke out. Faced with this disorder, the Habsburg emperor Ferdinand I (r. 1835–1848) capitulated and promised reforms and a liberal constitution. The coalition of revolutionaries was not stable, however. When the monarchy abolished serfdom, the newly free peasants lost interest in the political and social questions agitating the cities.

The revolutionary coalition was also weakened and ultimately destroyed by conflicting national aspirations. In April the Hungarian revolutionary leaders pushed through an extremely liberal constitution, but they also sought to create a unified Hungarian nation. The minority groups, including the Romanians, Serbs, Croats, and Slovaks that formed half the population, objected that such unification would hinder their own political autonomy and cultural independence. Likewise, Czech (CHEK) nationalists based in Bohemia and the city of Prague came into conflict with German nationalists. Thus nationalism within the Austrian Empire enabled the monarchy to play off one ethnic group against the other.

The monarchy's first breakthrough came in June when the army crushed a working-class revolt in Prague. In October the predominantly peasant troops of the regular Austrian army attacked the student and working-class radicals in Vienna and retook the city. When Ferdinand I abdicated in favor of his young nephew, Franz Joseph, only Hungary had yet to be brought under control. Fearing the spread of liberal ideas to his realm, Nicholas I of Russia (r. 1825–1855) obligingly lent his support. In June 1849, 130,000 Russian troops poured into Hungary and subdued the country. For a number of years the Habsburgs ruled Hungary as a conquered territory.

After Austria, Prussia was the largest and most influential kingdom in the German Confederation. Prior to 1848 middle-class Prussian liberals had sought to reshape Prussia into a liberal constitutional monarchy, which would lead the confederation's thirty-eight states into a unified nation. When artisans and factory workers in Berlin exploded in revolt in March 1848 and joined with middle-class liberals against the monarchy, Prussian king Frederick William IV (r. 1840–1861) caved in. On March 21 he promised to grant Prussia a liberal constitution and to merge Prussia into a new national German state.

Elections were held across the German Confederation for a national parliament, which convened to write a federal constitution for a unified German state. Members of the new parliament drafted a liberal constitution in March 1849 and elected King Frederick William of Prussia emperor of the new German state. But Frederick William contemptuously refused to accept this "crown from the gutter." When Frederick William tried to get the independent monarchs of the German-speaking lands to elect him emperor on his own terms, with authoritarian power, Austria balked. Supported by Russia, Austria forced Prussia to renounce all its unification schemes in late 1850.

Thus, across Europe, the uprisings of 1848, which had been inspired by the legacy of the late-eighteenth-century revolutionary era, were unsuccessful. Reform movements splintered into competing factions, while the forces of order proved better organized and more united, on both a domestic and international level.

# Nation Building in Italy, Germany, and Russia

**How did strong leaders and nation building transform Italy, Germany, and Russia?**

Louis Napoleon's triumph in 1848 and his authoritarian rule in the 1850s provided Europe's victorious forces of order with a new political model. To what extent might the expanding urban middle classes and even portions of the working classes rally to a strong and essentially conservative national state that also promised change? This was one of the great political questions in the 1850s and 1860s. In central Europe a resounding answer came with the national unification of Germany and Italy.

The Russian Empire also experienced profound political crises in this period, but they were unlike those in Germany or Italy because Russia was already a vast multinational state. It became clear to Russian leaders that they had to embrace the process of **modernization**, defined narrowly as the changes that enable a country to compete effectively with the leading countries at a given time.

## Cavour, Garibaldi, and the Unification of Italy

Italy had never been a united nation prior to 1850. A battleground for the Great Powers after 1494, Italy was reorganized in 1815 at the Congress of Vienna. Austria received the rich northern provinces of Lombardy and Venetia (vih-NEE-shuh). Sardinia and Piedmont fell under the rule of an Italian monarch, and Tuscany shared north-central Italy with several smaller independent states. The papacy ruled over central Italy and Rome, while a branch of the Bourbons ruled Naples and Sicily (Map 24.2).

**MAP 24.2  The Unification of Italy, 1859–1870**
The leadership of Sardinia-Piedmont, nationalist fervor, and Garibaldi's attack on the Kingdom of the Two Sicilies were decisive factors in the unification of Italy.

After 1815 the goal of a unified Italian nation captivated many Italians, but there was no agreement on how to achieve it. In 1848 the efforts of idealistic nationalist Giuseppe Mazzini (joo-ZEP-pay maht-SEE-nee) to form a democratic Italian republic were crushed by Austrian forces. Temporarily driven from Rome during the upheavals of 1848, a frightened Pope Pius IX (pontificate 1846–1878) turned against most modern trends, including national unification. At the same time, Victor Emmanuel, king of independent Sardinia, retained the moderate liberal constitution granted under duress in March 1848. To the Italian middle classes, Sardinia (see Map 24.2) appeared to be a liberal, progressive state ideally suited to drive Austria out of northern Italy and achieve the goal of national unification.

Sardinia had the good fortune of being led by Count Camillo Benso di Cavour. Cavour's national goals were limited and realistic. Cavour came from a noble family and embraced the economic doctrines and business activities associated with the prosperous middle class. Until 1859 he sought unity only for the states of northern and perhaps central Italy in a greatly expanded kingdom of Sardinia.

In the 1850s Cavour worked to consolidate Sardinia as a liberal constitutional state capable of leading northern Italy. He entered a secret alliance with Napoleon III, and in July 1858 he goaded Austria into attacking Sardinia. The combined Franco-Sardinian forces were victorious, but Napoleon III decided on a compromise peace with the Austrians in July 1859 to avoid offending French Catholics by supporting an enemy of the pope. Sardinia would receive only Lombardy, the area around Milan. Cavour resigned in protest.

Popular revolts and Italian nationalism salvaged Cavour's plans. While the war against Austria raged in the north, dedicated nationalists in central Italy had risen and driven out their rulers. Cavour returned to power in early 1860, and the people of central Italy voted overwhelmingly to join a greatly enlarged kingdom of Sardinia. Cavour had achieved his original goal of a north Italian state (see Map 24.2).

For superpatriots such as Giuseppe Garibaldi (1807–1882), the job of unification was still only half done. A poor sailor's son, Garibaldi personified the romantic revolutionary nationalism of 1848. Having led a unit of volunteers to several victories over Austrian troops in 1859, Garibaldi emerged in 1860 as an independent force in Italian politics.

Secretly supported by Cavour, Garibaldi landed on the shores of Sicily in May 1860, which spurred the peasantry to rebellion. Garibaldi captured Palermo and crossed to the mainland. When Garibaldi and Victor Emmanuel rode through Naples to cheering crowds, they symbolically sealed the union of north and south, of monarch and people.

The new kingdom of Italy, which did not include Venice until 1866 or Rome until 1870, was a parliamentary monarchy under Victor Emmanuel, neither radical nor democratic. Only a small minority of Italian males could vote. Despite political unity, the propertied classes and the common people were divided. A great social and cultural gap separated the industrializing north from the agrarian south.

## Bismarck and German Unification

In the aftermath of 1848 the German states, particularly Austria and Prussia, were locked in a political stalemate, each seeking to block the power of the other within the German Confederation. At the same time, powerful economic forces were undermining the political status quo. Modern industry was growing rapidly within the German customs union, or *Zollverein*. By 1853 all the German states except Austria had joined the customs union, and a new Germany excluding Austria was becoming an economic reality. Rising prosperity from the rapid growth of industrialization after 1850 gave new impetus to middle-class liberals.

By 1859 liberals had assumed control of the parliament that emerged from the upheavals of 1848 in Prussia. The national uprising in Italy in 1859, however, convinced Prussia's tough-minded Wilhelm I (r. 1861–1888) that political change and even war with Austria or France was possible. Wilhelm I pushed to raise taxes and increase the defense budget to double the army's size. The Prussian parliament, reflecting the middle class's desire for a less militaristic society, rejected the military budget in 1862, and the liberals triumphed in new elections. King Wilhelm then called on Count Otto von Bismarck (1815–1898) to head a new ministry and defy the parliament.

Born into the Prussian aristocracy, Bismarck (BIZ-mark) loved power, but he was also flexible and pragmatic in pursuing his goals. When Bismarck became chief minister in 1862, he declared that government would rule without parliamentary consent. Bismarck ordered the Prussian bureaucracy to collect taxes even though the parliament refused to approve the budget, and he reorganized the army. For their part, the voters of Prussia expressed their opposition to Bismarck's policies by sending large liberal majorities to the parliament from 1862 to 1866.

In 1866 Bismarck launched the Austro-Prussian War with the intent of expelling Austria from German politics. The war lasted only seven weeks, as the reorganized Prussian army defeated Austria decisively. Bismarck forced Austria to withdraw from German affairs and dissolved the existing German Confederation. The mainly Protestant states north of the Main River were grouped in the new North German Confederation, led by an expanded Prussia (Map 24.3). Each state retained its own local government, but the federal government—Wilhelm I and Bismarck—controlled the army and foreign affairs.

To make peace with the liberal middle class and the nationalist movement, Bismarck asked the Prussian parliament to approve after the fact all the government's "illegal" spending between 1862 and 1866. Overawed by Bismarck's achievements, middle-class liberals now jumped at the chance to cooperate, opting for national unity and military glory over the battle for truly liberal institutions. Bismarck also followed Napoleon III's example by creating a legislature with members of the lower house elected by universal male suffrage, allowing him to bypass the middle class and appeal directly to the people if necessary. The constitutional struggle in Prussia was over, and the German middle class was accepting the monarchical authority and aristocratic superiority that Bismarck represented.

The final act in the drama of German unification followed quickly with a patriotic war against France. The apparent issue—whether a distant relative of Prussia's Wilhelm I might become king of Spain—was only a diplomatic pretext. By 1870, alarmed by Prussia's growing power, French leaders had decided on a war to teach Prussia a lesson.

When war began in 1870, Bismarck had the wholehearted support of the south German states. The Germans quickly defeated Louis Napoleon's armies at Sedan on September 1, 1870. Three days later French patriots in Paris proclaimed a new French

**MAP 24.3　The Unification of Germany, 1866–1871**
This map shows how Prussia expanded and a new German Empire was created through two wars, the Austro-Prussian War of 1866 and the Franco-Prussian War of 1870–1871.

republic and vowed to continue fighting. But after five months, in January 1871, a starving Paris surrendered, and France accepted Bismarck's harsh peace terms. By this time the south German states had agreed to join a new German Empire.

The Franco-Prussian War released an enormous surge of patriotic feeling in Germany. The new German Empire had become Europe's most powerful state, and most Germans were enormously proud. Semi-authoritarian nationalism and a "new conservatism," which was based on an alliance of the propertied classes and sought the active support of the working classes, had triumphed in Germany.

## The Modernization of Russia

In the 1850s Russia was a poor agrarian society with a rapidly growing population. Almost 90 percent of the population lived off the land, and serfdom was still the basic social institution. Then the Crimean War of 1853 to 1856 arose from the breakdown of the balance of power established at the Congress of Vienna, European competition over influence in the Middle East, and Russian desires to expand into European territories held by the Ottoman Empire. France and Great Britain, aided by Sardinia and the Ottoman Empire, inflicted a humiliating defeat on Russia.

Russia's military defeat showed that it had fallen behind the industrializing nations of western Europe. Moreover, the war had caused hardship and raised the specter of massive peasant rebellion. Military disaster thus forced the new tsar, Alexander II (r. 1855–1881), and his ministers along the path of rapid social change and general modernization.

The first and greatest of the reforms was the freeing of the serfs. In 1861 the Emancipation Manifesto freed more than 23 million serfs on private land; this was followed in 1866 by the emancipation of some 30 million people on state-owned land. The emancipated peasants received, on average, about half of the land, which was to be collectively owned by peasant villages. The prices for the land were high, and collective ownership limited the possibilities of agricultural improvement and migration to urban areas. Thus the effects of the reform were limited. More successful was reform of the legal system, which established independent courts and equality before the law. The government also relaxed censorship and partially liberalized policies toward Russian Jews.

Russia's greatest strides toward modernization were economic rather than political. Rapid, government-subsidized railroad construction to 1880 enabled agricultural Russia to export grain and thus earn money for further industrialization. Industrial suburbs grew up around Moscow and St. Petersburg, and a class of modern factory workers emerged. Russia began seizing territory in far eastern Siberia, on the border with China; in Central Asia, north of Afghanistan; and in the Islamic lands of the Caucasus.

In 1881 an anarchist assassinated Alexander II, and the reform era came to an abrupt end. Political modernization remained frozen until 1905, but economic modernization sped forward in the massive industrial surge of the 1890s. The key leader was Sergei Witte (suhr-GAY VIH-tuh), the energetic minister of finance. Under Witte's leadership, the government doubled Russia's railroad network by the end of the century and promoted Russian industry with high protective tariffs.

By 1900 Russia was catching up with western Europe and expanding its empire in Asia. By 1903 Russia had established a sphere of influence in Chinese Manchuria and was eyeing northern Korea. When the protests of equally imperialistic Japan were ignored, the Japanese launched a surprise attack on Russian forces in Manchuria in February 1904. After Japan scored repeated victories, Russia was forced in September 1905 to accept a humiliating defeat.

Military disaster in East Asia brought political upheaval at home. On January 22, 1905, workers in St. Petersburg peacefully protesting for improved working conditions and higher wages were attacked by the tsar's troops outside the Winter Palace. This event, known as Bloody Sunday, set off a wave of strikes, peasant uprisings,

**Bloody Sunday, Russia, 1905** On January 22, 1905, Russian troops fired on striking workers who had peacefully assembled in front of the Winter Palace in St. Petersburg, hoping to present their grievances to the tsar. Over a hundred demonstrators died and many hundreds more were injured in the ensuing massacre. The event, known as Bloody Sunday, helped rouse resistance to the imperial government. (Laski Diffusion/Newsmakers/Getty Images)

and troop mutinies across Russia. The revolutionary surge culminated in October 1905 in a paralyzing general strike that forced the government to capitulate. The tsar, Nicholas II (r. 1894–1917), issued the **October Manifesto**, which granted full civil rights and promised a popularly elected Duma (DOO-muh) (parliament) with real legislative power.

Nonetheless, Nicholas II retained great powers and the Duma had only limited authority. Reform-minded deputies in the newly elected Duma were badly disappointed, and efforts to cooperate with the tsar's ministers broke down. In 1907 Nicholas II and his reactionary advisers rewrote the electoral law so as to greatly increase the weight of the propertied classes. On the eve of World War I, Russia was a partially modernized nation, a conservative constitutional monarchy with an agrarian but industrializing economy.

## Urban Life in the Age of Ideologies

**What was the impact of urban growth on cities, social classes, families, and ideas?**

By 1900 western Europe was urban and industrial as surely as it had been rural and agrarian in 1800. Rapid urban growth in the nineteenth century worsened long-standing overcrowding and unhealthy living conditions, lending support to voices calling for revolutionary change. In response, government leaders, city planners, reformers, and scientists urgently sought solutions to these challenges.

Over the long term, success in improving the urban environment and the introduction of social welfare measures encouraged people to put their faith in a responsive national state.

## Improving the Urban Environment

Since the Middle Ages, European cities had been centers of government, culture, and commerce. They had also been congested, dirty, and unhealthy. Industrialization greatly worsened these conditions. The steam engine freed industrialists from dependence on waterpower so that by 1800 they built new factories in cities, which had better shipping facilities and a large and ready workforce. Therefore, as industry grew, already overcrowded cities expanded rapidly.

In the 1820s and 1830s people in Britain and France began to worry about urban conditions. Parks and open areas were almost nonexistent, and narrow houses were built wall to wall in long rows. Highly concentrated urban populations lived in unsanitary conditions, with open drains and sewers flowing beside unpaved streets. Infected water contributed to a European cholera epidemic in 1831–1832, killing hundreds of thousands and contributing to social unrest.

The urban challenge—and the pressure of radical ideas, including those of the revolutions of 1848—eventually brought an energetic response. The most famous early reformer was Edwin Chadwick, a British official. Collecting detailed reports from local officials and publishing his findings in 1842, Chadwick concluded that the stinking excrement of communal outhouses could be carried off by water through sewers at less than one-twentieth the cost of removing it by hand. In 1848 Chadwick's report became the basis of Great Britain's first public health law, which created a national health board and gave cities broad authority to build modern sanitary systems. Such sanitary movements won dedicated supporters in the United States, France, and Germany from the 1840s on.

Early sanitary reformers were handicapped by the prevailing miasmatic theory of disease—the belief that people contract disease when they breathe foul odors from rotting waste. In the 1840s and 1850s keen observation by doctors and public health officials suggested that contagion spread through physical contact with filth and not by its odors, thus weakening the miasmatic idea. The breakthrough in understanding this process came with Louis Pasteur (1822–1895), who developed the **germ theory** of disease. By 1870 the work of Pasteur and others had demonstrated that specific living organisms caused specific diseases and that those organisms could be controlled. These discoveries led to the development of a number of effective vaccines. Surgeons also applied the germ theory in hospitals, sterilizing not only the wound but everything else in the operating room.

The achievements of the bacterial revolution coupled with the public health movement saved millions of lives, particularly after about 1890. In England, France, and Germany death rates declined dramatically, and diphtheria, typhoid, typhus, cholera, and yellow fever became vanishing diseases in the industrializing nations.

More effective urban planning after 1850 also improved the quality of city life. France took the lead during the rule of Napoleon III (r. 1848–1870), who believed that rebuilding Paris would provide employment, improve living conditions, and glorify his empire. Baron Georges Haussmann (HOWSS-mun) (1809–1884), whom

Napoleon III placed in charge of Paris, destroyed the old medieval core of Paris to create broad tree-lined boulevards, long open vistas, monumental buildings, middle-class housing, parks, and improved sewers and aqueducts. In addition to easing traffic and providing impressive views, the broad boulevards were intended to prevent a recurrence of the street barricades that had been built by revolutionary crowds in 1848. The rebuilding of Paris stimulated urban development throughout Europe, particularly after 1870.

Mass public transportation also greatly improved urban living conditions. In the 1890s countries in Europe and North America adopted a new innovation, the electric streetcar. Millions of riders hopped on board during the workweek. On weekends and holidays streetcars carried city people on outings to parks and the countryside, racetracks, and music halls.[1] Electric streetcars also gave people of modest means access to improved housing, as the still-crowded city was able to expand and become less congested.

Industrialization and the growth of global trade led to urbanization outside of Europe. The tremendous appetite of industrializing nations for raw materials, food, and other goods caused the rapid growth of port cities and mining centers across the world. These included Alexandria in Egypt, the major port for transporting Egyptian cotton, and mining cities like San Francisco in California and Johannesburg in South Africa. Many of these new cities consciously emulated European urban planning. For example, from 1880 to 1910 the Argentine capital of Buenos Aires modernized rapidly. The development of Buenos Aires was greatly stimulated by the arrival of many Italian and Spanish immigrants, part of a much larger wave of European migration in this period (see "Immigration" in Chapter 27).

## Social Inequality and Class

By 1850, the wages and living conditions of the working classes were finally showing real improvements. Greater economic rewards, however, did not significantly narrow the gap between rich and poor. In fact, economic inequality worsened in Europe over the course of the nineteenth century and reached its height on the eve of World War I. In every industrialized country around 1900, the richest 20 percent of households received anywhere from 50 to 60 percent of all national income, whereas the bottom 30 percent of households received 10 percent or less of all income. Despite the promises of the political and economic revolutions of the late eighteenth century, the gap between rich and poor in the early twentieth century was thus as great as or even wider than it had been in the eighteenth-century age of agriculture and aristocracy.

Despite extreme social inequality, society had not split into two sharply defined opposing classes, as Marx had predicted. Instead economic specialization created an almost unlimited range of jobs, skills, and earnings; one group or subclass blended into another in a complex, confusing hierarchy.

Between the tiny elite of the very rich and the sizable mass of the dreadfully poor existed a range of subclasses, each filled with individuals struggling to rise or at least to hold their own in the social order. A confederation of middle classes was loosely linked by occupations requiring mental, rather than physical, skill. As the upper middle class, composed mainly of successful industrialist families, gained in income and progressively lost all traces of radicalism after the trauma of 1848, they were drawn toward the aristocratic lifestyle.

One step below was a much larger group of moderately successful business owners and merchants, professionals in law and medicine, and midlevel managers of large public and private institutions. The expansion of industry and technology called for experts with specialized knowledge, and the most valuable of the specialties became solid middle-class professions. Next came independent shopkeepers, small traders, and tiny manufacturers—the lower middle class.

Food, housing, clothes, and behavior all expressed middle-class values. Employment of at least one full-time maid was the clearest sign that a family had crossed the divide from the working classes into the middle classes. Freed from domestic labor, the middle-class wife directed her servants, supervised her children's education, supported charitable associations, and used her own appearance and that of her home to display the family's status. The middle classes shared a code of expected behavior and morality that stressed hard work, self-discipline, and personal achievement.

At the beginning of the twentieth century about four out of five Europeans belonged to the working classes—that is, people whose livelihoods depended primarily on physical labor. Many of them were small landowning peasants and hired farm hands, especially in eastern Europe. The urban working classes were even less unified than the middle classes. Economic development and increased specialization during the nineteenth century expanded the traditional range of working-class skills, earnings, and experiences. Skilled, semiskilled, and unskilled workers accordingly developed widely divergent lifestyles and cultural values, and their differences contributed to a keen sense of social status and hierarchy within the working classes.

Highly skilled workers, who made up about 15 percent of the working classes, became known as the labor aristocracy. They were led by construction bosses and factory foremen. The labor aristocracy also included members of the traditional highly skilled handicraft trades that had not transitioned to mechanized production, as well as new kinds of skilled workers such as shipbuilders and railway locomotive engineers.

Below the labor aristocracy stood the complex world of semiskilled and unskilled urban workers. A large number of the semiskilled were factory workers who earned good wages and whose relative importance in the labor force was increasing. Below the semiskilled workers was a larger group of unskilled workers that included day laborers and domestic servants.

To make ends meet, many working-class wives had to join the ranks of working women in the "sweated industries." These industries resembled the old putting-out and cottage industries of earlier times, and they were similar to what we call sweatshops today. The women normally worked at home and were paid by the piece, often making clothing after the advent of the sewing machine in the 1850s.

Despite their harsh lives, the urban working classes found outlets for fun and recreation. Across Europe drinking remained a favorite working-class leisure-time activity along with sports and music halls. Religion continued to provide working people with solace and meaning, although church attendance among the urban working classes declined in the late nineteenth century, especially among men.

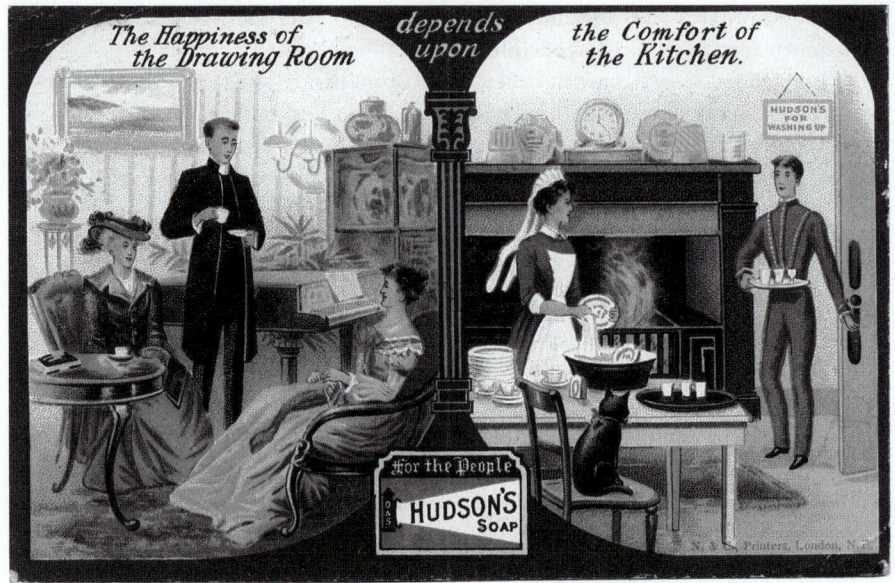

**Hudson's Soap Advertising Postcard, ca. 1903** Early-twentieth-century advertisements, such as this one for Hudson's Soap, reflected the strict class divisions of society. (Popperfoto/ Getty Images)

## The Changing Family

Industrialization and the growth of modern cities also brought great changes to the lives of women and families. As economic conditions improved, only women in poor families tended to work outside the home. The ideal became separate spheres, the strict division of labor by sex. This rigid division meant that married women faced great obstacles if they needed or wanted to move into the world of paid employment outside the home. Well-paying jobs were off-limits to women, and a woman's wage was almost always less than a man's, even for the same work.

Because they needed to be able to support their wives, middle-class men did not marry until they were well established in their careers. The system encouraged marriages between older men and younger women with little experience with adult life. Men were encouraged to see themselves as the protectors of their fragile and vulnerable wives.

As the ideology and practice of rigidly separate spheres narrowed women's horizons, their control and influence in the home became increasingly strong throughout Europe in the late nineteenth century. The comfortable home run by the middle-class wife was idealized as a warm shelter in a hard and impersonal urban world. By 1900 working-class families had adopted many middle-class values, but they did not have the means to fully realize the ideals of domestic comfort or separate spheres. Nevertheless, the working-class wife generally determined how the family's money was spent and took charge of all major domestic decisions. The woman's guidance of the household went hand in hand with the increased emotional importance of home and family for all social groups.

Ideas about sexuality within marriage varied. Many French marriage manuals of the late nineteenth century stressed that women had legitimate sexual needs. In the more puritanical United States, however, sex manuals recommended sexual abstinence for unmarried men and limited sexual activity for married men. Respectable women were thought to experience no sexual pleasure at all from sexual activity, and anything vaguely sexual was to be removed from their surroundings; even the legs of pianos were to be covered.

Medical doctors in both Europe and the United States began to study sexual desires and behavior more closely, and to determine what was considered "normal" and "abnormal." Same-sex attraction, labeled "homosexuality" for the first time, was identified as a "perversion." Governments increasingly regulated prostitution, the treatment of venereal disease, and access to birth control in ways that were shaped by class and gender hierarchies. Medical science also turned its attention to motherhood, and a wave of books instructed middle-class women on how to be better mothers.

Ideas about sexuality and motherhood were inextricably tied up with ideas about race. As European nations embarked on imperialist expansion in the second half of the nineteenth century, the belief in racial superiority that justified empire led to increased concerns about the possible dilution or weakening of the so-called European races. Maintaining healthy bodies, restricting sexuality, preventing interracial marriages, and ensuring that women properly raised their children were all components of racial strength, in the eyes of many European thinkers.

Women in industrializing countries also began to limit the number of children they bore. This revolutionary reduction in family size, in which the comfortable and well-educated classes took the lead, was founded on parents' desire to improve their economic and social position and that of their children. By having fewer youngsters, parents could give those they had advantages, from music lessons to expensive university educations.

The ideal of separate spheres and the gender division of labor meant that women lacked legal rights and faced discrimination in education and employment. Organizations founded by middle-class feminists campaigned for legal equality as well as for access to higher education and professional employment. In the late nineteenth century middle-class women scored some significant victories, such as the 1882 law giving British married women full property rights. Rather than contesting existing notions of women as morally superior guardians of the home, feminists drew on these ideas for legitimacy in speaking out about social issues.

Socialist women leaders usually took a different path. They argued that the liberation of working-class women would come only with the liberation of the entire working class. In the meantime, they championed the cause of working women and won some practical improvements. In a general way, these different approaches to women's issues reflected the diversity of classes and political views in urban society.

## Science for the Masses

Breakthroughs in industrial technology stimulated basic scientific inquiry as researchers sought to explain how such things as steam engines and blast furnaces actually worked. The result from the 1830s onward was an explosive growth of fundamental scientific discoveries that were increasingly transformed into material improvements for the general population.

A perfect example of the translation of better scientific knowledge into practical human benefits was the development of the branch of physics known as thermodynamics, the study of the relationship between heat and mechanical energy. By midcentury physicists had formulated the fundamental laws of thermodynamics, which were then applied to mechanical engineering, chemical processes, and many other fields. Electricity was transformed from a curiosity in 1800 to a commercial form of energy. By 1890 the internal combustion engine fueled by petroleum was an emerging competitor to steam and electricity.

Everyday experience and innumerable articles in newspapers and magazines impressed the importance of science on the popular mind. The methods of science acquired unrivaled prestige after 1850. Many educated people came to believe that the union of careful experiment and abstract theory was the only reliable route to truth and objective reality. The Enlightenment idea that natural processes were determined by rigid laws, leaving little room for either divine intervention or human will, won broad acceptance.

Living in an era of rapid change, nineteenth-century thinkers in Europe were fascinated with the ideas of evolution and dynamic development. The most influential of all nineteenth-century evolutionary thinkers was Charles Darwin (1809–1882). Darwin believed that all life had gradually evolved from a common ancestral origin in an unending "struggle for survival." Darwin's theory of **evolution** is summarized in the title of his work *On the Origin of Species by the Means of Natural Selection* (1859). He argued that small variations within individuals in one species enabled them to acquire more food and better living conditions and made them more successful in reproducing, thus allowing them to pass their genetic material to the next generation. When a number of individuals within a species became distinct enough that they could no longer interbreed successfully with others, they became a new species.

**Caricature of Darwin's Theory of Evolution**
Charles Darwin's advocacy of the theory of evolution aroused a storm of controversy. Many newspapers and magazines published satiric images mocking his idea that human beings had evolved from primates, such as this cartoon showing Darwin as a monkey with a human head. Darwin holds up a mirror to a monkey seated beside him, as if inviting the animal to reflect on the affinities between primate and human. (akg-images)

Darwin's theory of natural selection provoked resistance, particularly because he extended the theory to humans. His findings reinforced the teachings of secularists such as Marx, who scornfully dismissed religious belief in favor of agnostic or atheistic materialism. Many writers also applied the theory of biological evolution to human affairs. Herbert Spencer (1820–1903), an English philosopher, saw the human race as driven forward to ever-greater specialization and progress by a brutal economic struggle that determines the "survival of the fittest." The idea that human society also evolves, and that the stronger will become powerful and prosperous while the weaker will be conquered or remain poor, became known as **Social Darwinism**. Powerful nations used this ideology to justify nationalism and expansion, and colonizers to justify imperialism.

Not only did science shape society, but society also shaped science. As nations asserted their differences from one another, they sought "scientific" proof for those differences, which generally meant proof of their own superiority. European and American scientists, anthropologists, and physicians sought to prove that Europeans and those of European descent were more intelligent than other races, and that northern Europeans were more advanced than southern Europeans. Africans were described and depicted as "missing links" between chimpanzees and Europeans. This scientific racism extended to Jews, who were increasingly described as a separate and inferior race, not a religious group.

## Cultural Shifts

The French Revolution kindled the belief that radical reconstructions of politics and society were also possible in cultural and artistic life. The most significant expression of this belief in the early nineteenth century was the Romantic movement. In part a revolt against what was perceived as the cold rationality of the Enlightenment, **Romanticism** was characterized by a belief in emotional exuberance, unrestrained imagination, and spontaneity in both art and personal life. Preoccupied with emotional excess, Romantic works explored the awesome power of love and desire and of hatred, guilt, and despair. Where Enlightenment thinkers embraced secularization and civic life, Romantics delved into religious ecstasy and the hidden recesses of the self. The Romantics were passionately moved by nature and decried the growth of modern industry and industrial cities.

The French Romantic painter Eugène Delacroix (oo-ZHEHN deh-luh-KWAH) (1798–1863) depicted dramatic, colorful scenes that stirred the emotions. He frequently painted non-European places and people, whether lion hunts in Morocco or concubines in a sultan's harem. Like other Romantic works, Delacroix's art reveals the undercurrents of desire for and fascination with "exotic" and "savage" places in the nineteenth century.

It was in music that Romanticism realized most fully its goals of free expression and emotional intensity. Abandoning well-defined structures, the great Romantic composers used a wide range of forms to create musical landscapes and evoke powerful emotion. One of the greatest Romantic composers was Polish-born Frédéric Chopin (1810–1849), who wrote almost exclusively pieces for the solo piano. His music drew inspiration from Polish folk dances as well as from his tumultuous nine-year love affair with French novelist George Sand. Chopin's contemporary, the Hungarian-born Franz Liszt (1811–1886), was a prolific composer of many different types of music, including piano sonatas, operas, and religious music. Like Chopin, he drew on the music of his origins and wrote the famous "Hungarian Rhapsodies" from 1846 to 1853, which promoted Hungarian nationalism.

Romanticism also found a distinctive voice in literature. It had a precursor in the *Sturm und Drang* (storm and stress) movement in the German lands, which was epitomized by Johann Wolfgang von Goethe's novel *The Sorrows of Young Werther* (1774) about a sensitive student driven to suicide by a failed love affair. The novel became a European literary sensation and deeply influenced the period's youth, including Napoleon, who read the novel seven times.

In 1798 British Romantic poets William Wordsworth (1770–1850) and Samuel Taylor Coleridge (1772–1834) published their *Lyrical Ballads*, which abandoned flowery classical conventions for the language of ordinary speech. Wordsworth described his conception of poetry as the "spontaneous overflow of powerful feeling recollected in tranquility." Victor Hugo's (1802–1885) powerful novels exemplified the Romantic fascination with fantastic characters, strange settings, and strong emotions. The hero of Hugo's famous *Hunchback of Notre Dame* (1831) is the great cathedral's deformed bell-ringer, a "human gargoyle" overlooking the teeming life of fifteenth-century Paris.

In central and eastern Europe, in particular, literary Romanticism and early nationalism reinforced each other. Romantics turned their attention to peasant life and transcribed the folk songs, tales, and proverbs that the cosmopolitan Enlightenment had disdained. The brothers Jacob and Wilhelm Grimm were particularly successful at rescuing German fairy tales from oblivion.

Beginning in the 1840s Romanticism gave way to a new artistic genre, Realism. Influenced by the growing prestige of science in this period, Realist writers believed that literature should depict life exactly as it is. Forsaking poetry for prose and replacing the personal, emotional viewpoint of the Romantics with strict scientific objectivity, the Realists simply observed and recorded.

Realist writers focused on creating fiction based on contemporary everyday life. Beginning with a dissection of the middle classes, from which most of them sprang, many Realists eventually focused on the working classes, especially the urban working classes, which had been neglected in literature before this time. The Realists put a microscope to unexplored and taboo topics — sex, strikes, violence, alcoholism — shocking middle-class critics.

The Realists' claims of objectivity did not prevent the elaboration of a definite worldview. Realists such as the famous French novelist Émile Zola (1840–1902) and English novelist Thomas Hardy (1840–1928) were determinists. They believed that human beings, like atoms, are components of the physical world and that all human actions are caused by unalterable natural laws: heredity and environment determine human behavior; good and evil are merely social conventions. They were also critical of the failures of industrial society; by depicting the plight of poor workers, they hoped to bring about positive social change.

# Nationalism and Socialism, 1871–1914

**How did nationalism and socialism shape European politics in the decades before the Great War?**

After 1871 much of Europe's heartland was organized into strong national states. But in many places—in Ireland and Russia, Austria-Hungary and the Balkans—people continued to strive for national unity and independence. Nationalism served, for better or worse, as a new unifying political principle. At the same time, socialist parties grew rapidly. Governing elites manipulated national feeling to create a sense of unity to divert attention from underlying class conflicts, and increasingly channeled national sentiment in an antiliberal and militaristic direction, tolerating anti-Semitism and waging wars in non-Western lands. This policy helped manage domestic conflicts, but only at the expense of increasing the international tensions that erupted in World War I.

## Trends in Suffrage

There were good reasons why ordinary people felt increasing loyalty to their governments in central and western Europe by the turn of the twentieth century. Ordinary men felt they were becoming "part of the system," quite simply, because more of them could vote. By 1918 universal male suffrage had become the rule rather than the exception.

Women also began to demand the right to vote. The first important successes occurred in Scandinavia and Australia. In Sweden taxpaying single women and widows could vote in municipal elections after 1862. Australia and Finland gave women the right to vote in national elections and stand for parliament in 1902 and 1906, respectively (although restrictions on Aboriginal women's voting rights in Australia continued until the 1960s). In the western United States, women could vote in twelve states by 1913. One example among the thousands of courageous "suffragettes" was French socialist Hubertine Auclert (ew-ber-TEEN o-CLAIR), who in 1880–1881 led demonstrations, organized women in a property-tax boycott, and created the first suffragist newspaper in France.[2] Auclert and her counterparts elsewhere in Europe had little success before 1914, but they prepared the way for the female vote in many countries immediately after World War I.

As the right to vote spread, politicians and parties in national parliaments usually represented the people more responsively. The multiparty system prevailing in most countries meant that parliamentary majorities were built on shifting coalitions, which gave political parties leverage to obtain benefits for their supporters. Governments also passed laws to alleviate general problems, thereby acquiring greater legitimacy and appearing more worthy of support.

## The German Empire

The new German Empire was a federal union of Prussia and twenty-four smaller states. The separate states conducted much of the everyday business of government. Unifying the whole was a strong national government with a chancellor—Bismarck until 1890 — and a popularly elected parliament called the Reichstag (RIGHKS-tahg). Although Bismarck repeatedly ignored the wishes of the parliamentary majority, he nonetheless preferred to win the support of the Reichstag to lend legitimacy to his policy goals.

Bismarck was a fierce opponent of socialism. In 1878 he pushed through a law outlawing the German Social Democratic Party, but he was unable to force socialism out of existence. Bismarck then urged the Reichstag to enact new social welfare measures to gain the allegiance of the working classes. In 1883 the Reichstag created national health insurance, followed in 1884 by accident insurance and in 1889 by old-age pensions and retirement benefits. Together, these laws created a national social security system that was the first of its kind anywhere, funded by contributions from wage earners, employers, and the state.

Under Kaiser Wilhelm I (r. 1861–1888), Bismarck had managed the domestic and foreign policies of the state. In 1890 the new emperor, Wilhelm II (r. 1888–1918), eager to rule in his own right and to earn the workers' support, forced Bismarck to resign. Following Bismarck's departure, the Reichstag passed new laws to aid workers and to legalize socialist political activity.

Although Wilhelm II was no more successful than Bismarck in getting workers to renounce socialism, in the years before World War I the Social Democratic Party broadened its base and adopted a more patriotic tone. German socialists identified increasingly with the German state and concentrated on gradual social and political reform.

## Republican France

Although Napoleon III's reign made some progress in reducing antagonisms between classes, the Franco-Prussian War undid these efforts, and in 1871 France seemed hopelessly divided once again. The republicans who proclaimed the Third Republic in Paris refused to admit defeat by the Germans. They defended Paris with great heroism for weeks, until they were starved into submission by German armies in January 1871. When national elections then sent a large majority of conservatives and monarchists to the National Assembly, France's leaders decided they had no choice but to achieve peace by surrendering Alsace and Lorraine to Germany. Parisians exploded in patriotic frustration and proclaimed the Paris Commune in March 1871.

Commune leaders wanted to govern Paris without interference from the conservative French countryside. The National Assembly, led by conservative politician Adolphe Thiers, ordered the French army into Paris and brutally crushed the Commune. Twenty thousand people died in the fighting. As in June 1848, it was Paris against the provinces, French against French. Out of this tragedy France slowly formed a new national unity, achieving considerable stability before 1914.

The moderate republicans who governed France sought to preserve their creation by winning the loyalty of the next generation. Trade unions were fully legalized, and France ruthlessly acquired a colonial empire (see "The Scramble for Africa" in Chapter 25 and "Mainland Southeast Asia" in Chapter 26). A series of laws between 1879 and 1886 established free compulsory elementary education for both girls and boys, thereby greatly reducing the role of parochial Catholic schools, which had long been hostile to republicanism. In France and throughout the world, the general expansion of public education served as a critical nation- and nationalism-building tool in the late nineteenth century.

Although the educational reforms of the 1880s disturbed French Catholics, many of them rallied to the republic in the 1890s, and tensions between church and state eased. Unfortunately, the **Dreyfus affair** changed all that. In 1894 Alfred Dreyfus (DRY-fuss), a Jewish captain in the French army, was falsely accused and convicted of treason. In 1898 and 1899 the case split France apart once more. On one side was the army, which had manufactured evidence against Dreyfus, joined by anti-Semites and most of the Catholic establishment. On the other side stood the civil libertarians and most of the more radical republicans.

This battle, which eventually led to Dreyfus's being declared innocent, revived militant republican feeling against the church. Between 1901 and 1905 the government severed all ties between the state and the Catholic Church after centuries of close relations.

## Great Britain and the Austro-Hungarian Empire

The development of Great Britain and Austria-Hungary, two leading but quite different powers, throws a powerful light on the dynamics of nationalism in Europe before 1914. At home Britain made more of its citizens feel a part of the nation by passing consecutive voting rights bills that culminated with the establishment of universal male suffrage in 1884. Moreover, overdue social welfare measures were passed in a spectacular rush between 1906 and 1914. The ruling Liberal Party substantially raised taxes on the rich to pay for national health insurance, unemployment benefits, old-age pensions, and a host of other social measures. The state was integrating the urban masses socially as well as politically.

On the eve of World War I, however, the unanswered question of Ireland brought Great Britain to the brink of civil war. The terrible Irish famine of the 1840s and early 1850s had fueled an Irish revolutionary movement. The English slowly granted concessions, and in 1913 the British Parliament passed a bill granting Ireland self-government, or home rule.

The Irish Catholic majority in the southern counties ardently desired home rule. Irish Protestants in the northern counties of Ulster, however, vowed to resist home rule, fearing they would fall under the control of the majority Catholics. Unable to resolve the conflict as World War I started in August 1914, the British government postponed the question of Irish home rule indefinitely.

The Irish dilemma helps one appreciate how desperate the situation in the Austro-Hungarian Empire had become by the early twentieth century. Reacting to the upheaval of 1848, Austrian emperor Franz Joseph (r. 1848–1916) and his bureaucracy ruled Hungary as a conquered territory. This was part of broader efforts to centralize Austria and Germanize the language and culture of the different nationalities.

After its defeat by Prussia in 1866, however, a weakened Austria was forced to establish the so-called dual monarchy. The empire was divided in two, and the nationalistic Magyars gained virtual independence for Hungary. The two states were joined only by a shared monarch and common ministries for finance, defense, and foreign affairs. Still, the disintegrating force of competing nationalisms continued unabated, and the Austro-Hungarian Empire was progressively weakened and eventually destroyed by the conflicting national aspirations of its different ethnic groups. It was these ethnic conflicts in the Balkans that touched off the Great War in 1914 (see "The Outbreak of War" in Chapter 28).

## Jewish Emancipation and Modern Anti-Semitism

Revolutionary changes in political principles and the triumph of the nation-state brought equally revolutionary changes in Jewish life in western and central Europe. Beginning in France in 1791, Jews gradually gained civil rights. In the 1850s and 1860s liberals in Austria, Italy, and Prussia pressed successfully for legal equality for all regardless of religion. In 1871 the constitution of the new German Empire abolished restrictions on Jewish marriage, choice of occupation, place of residence, and property ownership.

By 1871 a majority of Jews in western and central Europe had improved their economic situations and entered the middle classes. Most Jews identified strongly with their respective nation-states and considered themselves patriotic citizens. Exclusion from government employment and discrimination in social relations continued, however, in central Europe.

Vicious anti-Semitism reappeared after the stock market crash of 1873, beginning in central Europe. Drawing on long traditions of religious intolerance, this hostility also drew on modern, supposedly scientific ideas about Jews as a separate race. Anti-Semitic beliefs were particularly popular among conservatives, extremist nationalists, and people who felt threatened by Jewish competition.

Anti-Semites also created modern political parties. In Austrian Vienna in the early 1890s, Karl Lueger (LOO-guhr), the popular mayor of Vienna from 1897 to 1910, combined fierce anti-Semitic rhetoric with his support of municipal ownership of basic services. In response to spreading anti-Semitism, a Jewish journalist named Theodor

**Jews Fleeing the Russian Army in 1914** Between 1880 and 1900, some 500,000 Russian Jews emigrated to the United States, and from 1900 to 1915, another 1.5 million followed them. An important factor behind the exodus was repression from the Russian government following the assassination of Tsar Alexander II in 1881. (Imagno/ Getty Images)

Herzl (1860–1904) turned from German nationalism to advocate Jewish political nationalism, or **Zionism**, and the creation of a Jewish state.

Before 1914 anti-Semitism was most oppressive in eastern Europe, where Jews also suffered from terrible poverty. In the Russian Empire, where there was no Jewish emancipation and 4 million of Europe's 7 million Jewish people lived in 1880, officials used anti-Semitism to channel popular discontent away from the government. The situation of Russian Jews dramatically worsened following the assassination of Tsar Alexander II in 1881. Believing his father's liberal policies, including the relaxation of laws against the Jews, were responsible for the assassination, his son and heir instituted a series of harsh new anti-Semitic laws.

Organized anti-Jewish violence, called pogroms, occurred in many places. The police and the army stood aside for days while peasants assaulted Jews and looted and destroyed their property. Official harassment continued in the following decades. Fleeing discrimination and violence and in search of economic and social betterment, approximately 2 million Russian Jews emigrated to the United States between 1880 and 1915.

## The Socialist Movement

Socialism appealed to large numbers of working men and women in the late nineteenth century, and the growth of socialist parties after 1871 was phenomenal. By 1912 the German Social Democratic Party, which espoused Marxist principles, had millions of followers and was the Reichstag's largest party. Socialist parties also grew in other countries, and Marxist socialist parties were linked together in an international organization.

As socialist parties grew and attracted large numbers of members, they looked more and more toward gradual change and steady improvement for the working class and less and less toward revolution. Workers themselves were progressively less inclined to follow radical programs for several reasons. As workers gained the right to vote and won real benefits, their attention focused more on elections than on revolutions. Workers were also not immune to nationalistic patriotism. Nor were workers a unified social group. Perhaps most important of all, workers' standard of living rose steadily after 1850, and the quality of life improved substantially in urban areas.

The growth of labor unions reinforced this trend toward moderation. In Great Britain new unions that formed for skilled workers after 1850 avoided radical politics and concentrated on winning better wages and hours for their members through collective bargaining and compromise. After 1890 unions for unskilled workers developed in Britain.

German unions were not granted important rights until 1869, and until the Anti-Socialist Laws were repealed in 1890 the government frequently harassed them as socialist fronts. But after most legal harassment was eliminated, union membership skyrocketed.

The German trade unions and their leaders were thoroughgoing revisionists. **Revisionism** was an effort by various socialists to update Marxist doctrines to reflect the realities of the time. The socialist Eduard Bernstein (1850–1932) argued in his

*Evolutionary Socialism* in 1899 that Marx's predictions of ever-greater poverty for workers had been proved false. Therefore, Bernstein suggested, socialists should reform their doctrines and win gradual evolutionary gains for workers through legislation, unions, and further economic development.

Socialist parties in other countries had clear-cut national characteristics. Socialists in Russia and the Austro-Hungarian Empire tended to be the most radical. In Great Britain the socialist but non-Marxist Labour Party formally committed to gradual reform. In Spain and Italy anarchism, seeking to smash the state rather than the bourgeoisie, dominated radical thought and action.

In short, socialist policies and doctrines varied from country to country. Socialism itself was to a large extent "nationalized." This helps explain why almost all socialist leaders supported their governments when war came in 1914.

# Chapter Summary

In 1814 the victorious allied powers sought to restore peace and stability in Europe. The conservative powers used intervention and repression as they sought to prevent the spread of radical political ideas. Despite their efforts, after 1815 ideologies of liberalism, nationalism, and socialism all developed to challenge the new order. The growth of these forces culminated in the liberal and nationalistic revolutions of 1848, revolutions that were crushed by resurgent conservative forces. In the second half of the nineteenth century Italy and Germany became unified nation-states, while Russia undertook a modernization program and struggled with popular discontent.

Living conditions in rapidly growing industrial cities declined until the mid-nineteenth century, when governments undertook major urban development, including new systems of sewerage, water supply, and public transportation. Major changes in the class structure and family life occurred, as the separate spheres ideology strengthened, and the class structure became more complex and diversified. The prestige of science grew tremendously, and scientific discoveries, such as Darwin's theory of natural selection, challenged traditional religious understandings of the world. In the realm of literature and the arts, the Romantic movement reinforced the spirit of change. Romanticism gave way to Realism in the 1840s.

Western societies became increasingly nationalistic as well as urban and industrial in the late nineteenth century. Nation-states became more responsive to the needs of their people, and they enlisted widespread popular support as political participation expanded, educational opportunities increased, and social security systems took shape. Even socialism became increasingly national in orientation, gathering strength as a champion of working-class interests in domestic politics. Yet even though nationalism served to unite peoples, it also drove them apart and contributed to the tragic conflicts of the twentieth century.

## NOTES

1. J. McKay, *Tramways and Trolleys: The Rise of Urban Mass Transport in Europe* (Princeton, N.J.: Princeton University Press, 1976), p. 81.
2. "*La Citoyenne* in the World: Hubertine Auclert and Feminist Imperialism," *French Historical Studies* 31.1 (Winter 2009): 63–84.

## MAKE CONNECTIONS   LOOK AHEAD

Much of world history in the past two and a half centuries can be seen as a struggle over the unfinished legacies of the late-eighteenth-century revolutions in politics and economics. Although defeated in 1848, the new political ideologies associated with the French Revolution re-emerged decisively after 1850. Nationalism, with its commitment to the nation-state, became the most dominant of the new ideologies. National movements brought about the creation of unified nation-states in two of the most fractured regions in Europe, Germany and Italy.

After 1870 nationalism and militarism, its frequent companion, touched off increased competition between the major European powers for raw materials and markets for manufactured goods. As discussed in the next two chapters, during the last decades of the nineteenth century Europe brutally colonized nearly all of Africa and large areas in Asia. In Europe itself nationalism promoted bitter competition between states, threatening the very progress and unity it had helped to build. In 1914 the power of unified nation-states turned on itself, unleashing an unprecedented conflict among Europe's Great Powers. Chapter 28 tells the story of this First World War.

Nationalism also sparked worldwide challenges to European dominance by African and Asian leaders who fought to liberate themselves from colonialism, and it became a rallying cry in nominally independent countries like China and Japan, whose leaders sought freedom from European and American influence and a rightful place among the world's leading nations. Chapters 25, 26, and 33 explore these developments. Likewise, Chapter 33 discusses how the problems of rapid urbanization and the huge gaps between rich and poor caused by economic transformations in America and Europe in the nineteenth century are now the concern of policy-makers in Africa, Asia, and Latin America.

Another important ideology of change, socialism, remains popular in Europe and elsewhere, with socialist parties democratically elected to office in many countries. Marxist revolutions that took absolute control of entire countries, as in Russia, China, and Cuba, occurred in the twentieth century.

## Chapter 24 Review

### IDENTIFY KEY TERMS

**Identify and explain the significance of each item below.**

Congress of Vienna (p. 613)
conservatism (p. 613)
liberalism (p. 615)
laissez faire (p. 616)
nationalism (p. 616)
socialism (p. 617)
bourgeoisie (p. 617)
proletariat (p. 617)
modernization (p. 623)

October Manifesto
(p. 628)
germ theory (p. 629)
evolution (p. 634)
Social Darwinism (p. 635)
Romanticism (p. 635)
Dreyfus affair (p. 639)
Zionism (p. 641)
revisionism (p. 641)

### REVIEW THE MAIN IDEAS

**Answer the focus questions from each section of the chapter.**

1. How did the allies fashion a peace settlement in 1815, and what radical ideas emerged between 1815 and 1848? (p. 613)

2. Why did revolutions triumph briefly throughout most of Europe in 1848, and why did they fail? (p. 618)

3. How did strong leaders and nation building transform Italy, Germany, and Russia? (p. 622)

4. What was the impact of urban growth on cities, social classes, families, and ideas? (p. 628)

5. How did nationalism and socialism shape European politics in the decades before the Great War? (p. 637)

### MAKE COMPARISONS AND CONNECTIONS

**Analyze the larger developments and continuities within and across chapters.**

1. How did the spread of radical ideas and the movements for reform and revolution explored in this chapter draw on the "unfinished" political and industrial revolutions of the late eighteenth century (Chapters 22, 23)?

2. How and why did the relationship between the state and its citizens change in the last decades of the nineteenth century?

3. How did the emergence of a society divided into working and middle classes affect the workplace, homemaking, family values, and gender roles?

## CHRONOLOGY

| | |
|---|---|
| **ca. 1790s–1840s** | • Romantic movement in literature and the arts |
| **1814–1815** | • Congress of Vienna |
| **1832** | • Reform Bill in Britain |
| **ca. 1840s–1890s** | • Realism dominates Western literature |
| **1845–1851** | • Great Famine in Ireland |
| **1846–1848** | • Mexican-American War (Ch. 27) |
| **1848** | • Revolutions in France, Austria, and Prussia |
| **1851–1864** | • Taiping Rebellion (Ch. 26) |
| **1853–1856** | • Crimean War |
| **1857** | • Great Mutiny / Great Revolt in India (Ch. 26) |
| **1859** | • Darwin, *On the Origin of Species by the Means of Natural Selection* |
| **1859–1870** | • Unification of Italy |
| **1861** | • Russian serfs freed |
| **1861–1865** | • U.S. Civil War (Ch. 27) |
| **1866–1871** | • Unification of Germany |
| **1880–1914** | • European "scramble for Africa" (Ch. 25) |
| **1898** | • Spanish-American War (Ch. 27) |
| **1904–1905** | • Russo-Japanese War |
| **1905** | • Revolution in Russia |
| **1906–1914** | • Social reform in Britain |

# 25

# Africa, the Ottoman Empire, and the New Imperialism

## 1800–1914

**WHILE INDUSTRIALIZATION AND NATIONALISM WERE TRANSFORMING** society in Europe and the neo-European countries (the United States, Canada, Australia, New Zealand, and, to an extent, South Africa), Western society itself was reshaping the world. European commercial interests went in search of new sources of raw materials and markets for their manufactured goods. At the same time, millions of Europeans and Asians emigrated abroad. What began as a relatively peaceful exchange of products with Africa and Asia in the early nineteenth century had transformed by century's end into a frenzy of imperialist occupation and domination that had a profound impact on both colonizer and colonized.

The political annexation of territory in the 1880s—the "New Imperialism," as it is often called by historians—was the capstone of Western society's underlying economic and technological transformation. More directly, Western imperialism rested on a formidable combination of superior military might and strong authoritarian rule, and it posed a brutal challenge to African and Asian peoples. Indigenous societies met this Western challenge in different ways and with changing tactics. By 1914 local elites in many lands were rallying their peoples and leading an anti-imperialist struggle for dignity and genuine independence that would triumph after 1945.

# Africa: From the Slave Trade to European Colonial Rule

**What were the most significant changes in Africa during the nineteenth century, and why did they occur?**

In the nineteenth and early twentieth centuries the different regions of Africa experienced gradual but monumental change. The transatlantic slave trade declined and practically disappeared by the late 1860s. In the early nineteenth century Islam expanded its influence south of the Sahara Desert, but Africa still generally remained free of European political control. After about 1880 further Islamic expansion to the south stopped, but the pace of change accelerated as France and Britain led European nations in the "scramble for Africa," dividing and largely conquering the continent. By 1900 the foreigners were consolidating their authoritarian empires.

## Trade and Social Change

The most important development in West Africa before the European conquest was the decline of the Atlantic slave trade and the simultaneous rise in exports of **palm oil** and other commodities. This shift in African foreign trade marked the beginning of modern economic development in sub-Saharan Africa. At the same time, and as a consequence, Africa suffered massive environmental and human degradation through deforestation, soil exhaustion and erosion, overgrazing, widespread substitution of subsistence crops for cash crops, large-scale mining operations that seriously harmed land and people, the denigration of local traditions and religions, and the disruption of families. Gender roles were reversed as well, as men now went off to work in the mines and cash-crop fields, while women tended small gardens and watched the children.

Although the trade in enslaved Africans was a global phenomenon, the transatlantic slave trade between Africa and the Americas became the most extensive and significant portion of it (see "The Transatlantic Slave Trade" in Chapter 20). Until 1700, and perhaps even 1750, most Europeans considered the African slave trade a legitimate business activity. After 1775 a broad campaign to abolish slavery developed in Britain and grew into one of the first peaceful mass political movements based on the mobilization of public opinion in British history. British women played a critical role in this movement, denouncing the immorality of human bondage and stressing the cruel treatment of female slaves and slave families. Abolitionists also argued for a transition to legitimate (nonslave) trade to end both the transatlantic slave trade and the internal African slave systems. In 1807 Parliament declared the slave trade illegal. Britain then began using its navy to seize slave runners' ships, liberate the captives, and settle them in the British port of Freetown in Sierra Leone, as well as in Liberia (see Map 25.1). Freed American slaves had established the colony of Liberia in 1821–1822.

British action had a limited impact at first. Britain's navy intercepted fewer than 10 percent of all slave ships, and the demand for slaves remained high on the sugar and coffee plantations of Cuba and Brazil until the 1850s and 1860s. The United States banned slave importation after January 1, 1808. From that time on, natural increase (slaves having children) mainly accounted for the subsequent growth of the African American slave population before the Civil War. Strong financial incentives remained, however, for Portuguese and other European slave traders and for those African rulers who relied on profits from the trade for power and influence.

As more nations joined Britain in outlawing the slave trade, shipments of human cargo slackened along the West African coast (see Map 25.1). At the same time the ancient but limited shipment of slaves across the Sahara and from the East African coast into the Indian Ocean and through the Red Sea expanded dramatically. Only in the 1860s did this trade begin to decline. As a result, total slave exports from all regions of sub-Saharan Africa declined only marginally, from 7.4 million in the eighteenth century to 6.1 million in the nineteenth century.[1] Abolitionists failed to achieve their vision that "legitimate trade" in tropical products would quickly replace illegal slave exports.

Nevertheless, beginning in West Africa, a legitimate trade did make steady progress for several reasons. First, with Britain encouraging palm tree cultivation as an alternative to the slave trade, palm oil sales from West Africa to Britain surged, from only one thousand tons in 1810 to more than forty thousand tons in 1855. Second, the sale of palm oil admirably served the self-interest of industrializing Europe. Manufacturers used palm oil to lubricate their giant machines and to make cheap soap and other cosmetics. Third, peanut production for export also grew rapidly, in part because both small, independent African family farmers and large-scale enterprises could produce peanuts for the substantial American and European markets.

Finally, powerful West African rulers and warlords who had benefited from the Atlantic slave trade redirected some of their slaves' labor into the production of legitimate goods for world markets. This was possible because local warfare and slave raiding continued to enslave large numbers of people in sub-Saharan Africa, so slavery and slave markets remained strong. Although some enslaved captives might still be sold abroad, now women were often kept as wives, concubines, or servants, while men were used to transport goods, mine gold, grow crops, and serve in slave armies. Thus the transatlantic slave trade's slow decline coincided with the most intensive use of slaves within Africa.

All the while, a new group of African merchants was emerging to handle legitimate trade, and some grew rich. Women were among the most successful of these merchants. There is a long tradition of West African women's active involvement in trade, but the arrival of Europeans provided new opportunities. The African wife of a European trader served as her husband's interpreter and learned all aspects of his business. When the husband died, as European men invariably did in the hot, humid, and mosquito-infested conditions of tropical West Africa, the African wife inherited his commercial interests, including his inventory and his European connections. Many such widows used their considerable business acumen to make small fortunes.

By the 1850s and 1860s legitimate African traders, flanked by Western-educated African lawyers, teachers, and journalists, had formed an emerging middle class in the West African coastal towns. Unfortunately for West Africans, in the 1880s and 1890s African business leadership gave way to imperial subordination.

## Islamic Revival and Expansion in Africa

The Sudanic savanna is that vast belt of flat grasslands stretching across Africa below the Sahara's southern fringe (the Sahel). By the early eighteenth century Islam had been practiced throughout this region for five hundred to one thousand years, depending on the area. City dwellers, political rulers, and merchants in many small states were Muslim. Yet the rural peasant farmers and migratory cattle raisers—the vast majority of the population—generally held on to traditional animist practices, worshipping ancestors, praying at local shrines, and invoking protective spirits. Since many Muslim rulers shared some of these beliefs, they did not try to convert their subjects in the countryside or enforce Islamic law.

A powerful Islamic revival began in the eighteenth century and gathered strength in the early nineteenth century. In essence, Muslim scholars and fervent religious leaders arose to wage successful **jihads** (JEE-hahds), or religious wars, against both animist rulers and Islamic states they deemed corrupt. The new reformist rulers believed African cults and religious practice could no longer be tolerated, and they often effected mass conversions of animists to Islam.

The most important of these revivalist states, the **Sokoto caliphate** (SOH-kuh-toh KAL-uh-fate), illustrates the pattern of Islamic revival in Africa. It was founded by Uthman dan Fodio (AHTH-mun dahn FOH-dee-oh) (1754–1817), a Muslim teacher who first won followers among both the Fulani herders and in the Muslim state of Gobir in the northern Sudan. After his religious community was attacked by Gobir's rulers, Uthman launched the jihad of 1804, one of the most important events in nineteenth-century West Africa. Uthman claimed the Hausa rulers of Muslim Gobir "worshipped many places of idols, and trees, and rocks, and sacrificed to them," killing and plundering their subjects without any regard for Islamic law.[2] He recruited young religious students and discontented Fulani cattle raisers to form the backbone of his jihadi fighters and succeeded in overthrowing the Hausa rulers and expanding Islam into the Sudan. In 1809 Uthman established the new Sokoto caliphate (see Map 20.1).

The triumph of the Sokoto caliphate had profound consequences for Africa and the Sudan. First, the caliphate was governed by a sophisticated written constitution based on Islamic history and law. This government of laws, rather than men, provided stability and made Sokoto one of the most prosperous regions in tropical

Africa. Second, because of Sokoto and other revivalist states, Islam became much more widely and deeply rooted in sub-Saharan Africa than ever before. Finally, as one historian explained, Islam had always approved of slavery for non-Muslims and Muslim heretics, and "the *jihads* created a new slaving frontier on the basis of rejuvenated Islam."[3] In 1900 the Sokoto caliphate had at least 1 million and perhaps as many as 2.5 million slaves.

Islam also expanded in East Africa. From the 1820s on, Arab merchants and adventurers pressed far into the interior in search of slaves and ivory, converting and intermarrying with local Nyamwezi (nyahm-WAY-zee) elites and establishing small Muslim states. The Arab immigrants brought literacy, administrative skills, and increased trade and international contact, as well as the intensification of slavery, to East Africa. In 1837 Sayyid Said (sa-EED sa-EED) (r. 1804–1856), the sultan of Oman, conquered Mombasa, the great port city in modern Kenya. After moving his capital from southern Arabia to the island of Zanzibar in 1840, Said gained control of most of the Swahili-speaking East African coast. He then routed all slave shipments from the coast to the Ottoman Empire and Arabia through Zanzibar. He also successfully encouraged Indian merchants to develop slave-based clove plantations in his territories. In the second half of the century, Tippu Tip (TI-pu TIP), an Arab-Zanzibari slave trader and entrepreneur, expanded these commercial ventures across the eastern interior and into Central Africa. In 1870, before Christian missionaries and Western armies began to arrive in force and halt Islam's spread, it appeared that most of the East and Central African populations would accept Islam within a generation.[4]

## The Scramble for Africa, 1880–1914

Between 1880 and 1914 Britain, France, Germany, Belgium, Spain, and Italy, worried that they would not get "a piece of that magnificent African cake" (in Belgian king Leopold II's graphic words), scrambled for African possessions. In 1880 Europeans controlled barely 20 percent of the African continent, mainly along the coast; by 1914 they controlled over 90 percent. Only Ethiopia in northeast Africa and Liberia on the West African coast remained independent (Map 25.1).

In explaining Europe's imperialist burst after 1880, certain events and individuals stand out. First, as the antislavery movement succeeded in shutting down the Atlantic slave trade by the late 1860s, slavery's persistence elsewhere attracted growing attention in western Europe and the Americas. Missionaries played a key role in publicizing the horrors of slave raids and the suffering of thousands of enslaved Africans. The public was led to believe that European conquest and colonization would end this human tragedy by bringing, in Scottish missionary David Livingstone's famous phrase, "Commerce, Christianity, and Civilization" to Africa.

Second, King Leopold II (r. 1865–1909) of Belgium also played a crucial role. His agents signed treaties with African chiefs and planted Leopold's flag along the Congo River. In addition, Leopold intentionally misled other European leaders to gain their support by promising to promote Christianity and civilization in his proposed Congo Free State. By 1883 Europe had caught "African fever," and the race for territory was on. Third, to lay down some rules for this imperialist competition,

French premier Jules Ferry and German chancellor Otto von Bismarck arranged a European conference on sub-Saharan Africa in Berlin in 1884–1885. The **Berlin Conference**, to which Africans were not invited, established the principle that European claims to African territory had to rest on "effective occupation" in order to be recognized by other states. A nation could establish a colony only if it had effectively taken

**MAP 25.1    The Partition of Africa**

The European powers carved up Africa after 1880 and built vast political empires.

possession of the territory through signed treaties with local leaders and had begun to develop it economically. Conference attendees recognized Leopold's rule over the Congo Free State.

In addition to developing rules for imperialist competition, participants at the Berlin Conference agreed to care for the native peoples' moral and material well-being, bring Christianity and civilization to Africa, and suppress slavery and the slave trade. These rules and agreements were contained in the General Act of the conference:

> All the Powers exercising sovereign rights or influence in the aforesaid territories bind themselves to watch over the preservation of the native tribes, and to care for the improvement of the conditions of their moral and material well-being, and to help in suppressing slavery, and especially the slave trade.
>
> They shall, without distinction of creed or nation, protect and favour all religious, scientific or charitable institutions and undertakings created and organized for the above ends, or which aim at instructing the natives and bringing home to them the blessings of civilization.[5]

In truth, however, these ideals ran a distant second to, and were not allowed to interfere with, the nations' primary goal of commerce—holding on to their old markets and exploiting new ones.

Fourth, the Berlin Conference coincided with Germany's emergence as an imperial power. In 1884 and 1885 Bismarck's Germany established **protectorates** (autonomous states or territories partly controlled and protected by a stronger outside power) over a number of small African kingdoms and societies (see Map 25.1). In acquiring colonies, Bismarck cooperated with France's Jules Ferry against the British. The French expanded into West Africa and also formed a protectorate on the Congo River. Meanwhile, the British began enlarging their West African enclaves and pushed northward from the Cape Colony and westward from the East African coast.

The British also moved southward from Egypt, which they had seized in 1882, but were blocked in the eastern Sudan by fiercely independent Muslims. In 1881 a pious Sudanese leader, Muhammad Ahmad (AH-mad) (1844–1885), proclaimed himself the "Mahdi" (MAH-dee) (a messianic redeemer of Islam) and led a revolt against foreign control of Egypt. In 1885 his army massacred a British force and took the city of Khartoum (khar-TOUM), forcing the British to retreat to Cairo. Ten years later a British force returned, building a railroad to supply arms and reinforcements as it went. In 1898 these troops, under the command of Field Marshal Horatio Hubert Kitchener, met their foe at Omdurman (AHM-dur-man), where Sudanese Muslims armed with spears were cut down by the recently invented machine gun. In the end eleven thousand Muslim fighters lay dead, while only twenty-eight Britons had been killed. Their commander received the title of "Lord Kitchener of Khartoum."

All European nations resorted to some violence in their colonies to retain control, subdue the population, appropriate land, and force African laborers to work long hours at physically demanding, and often dangerous, jobs. In no colony, however, was the violence and brutality worse than in Leopold II's Congo Free State. Rather than promoting Leopold's promised Christianity and civilization, the European companies operating in the Congo Free State introduced slavery,

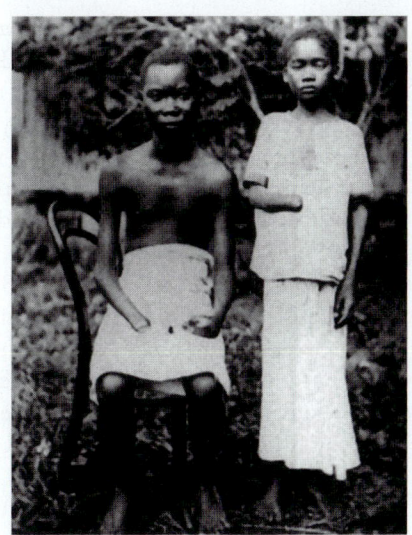

**Brutality in the Congo Free State** The brutality of King Leopold II's rule over the Congo Free State was unrivaled in any other European colony. Amputation of hands and feet was frequently used to punish workers, many of whom, as here, were children. Through cruel punishments like this, Europeans were able to intimidate and control the large African population. Another common practice was to send raiding parties deep into the interior to kill everyone in a village as a warning sign to surrounding villages that they must obey or face the same fate. The raiding parties would then return with baskets of severed hands to show how many people they had killed. (Universal Images Group/Bridgeman Images)

unimaginable savagery, and terror. Missionaries and others were not even allowed into the colony, to prevent them from reporting the horrors they would witness there.

Profits in the Congo Free State came initially from the ivory trade, but in the 1890s, after many of the Congo's elephant herds had been decimated, a new cash crop arose to take ivory's place. In the mid-1880s Scottish-born John Dunlop developed a process to make inflatable rubber tires. A worldwide boom in the demand for raw rubber soon followed, as new uses for rubber were found. By the mid-1890s rubber had surpassed ivory as the Congo Free State's major income producer, as more than half the colony possessed wild rubber vines growing thickly in the equatorial rain forest. The companies Leopold allowed to make profits in the Congo soon could not get enough rubber. Violence and brutality increased exponentially as Europeans and their well-armed mercenaries terrorized entire regions, cutting off hands, feet, and heads and wiping out whole villages to send the message that Africans must either work for the Europeans or die. The shed African blood is recalled in the colony's frightening nickname — the "red rubber colony." In the first years of the nineteenth century, human rights activists such as Edmund Morel (moh-REHL) exposed the truth about the horrific conditions in the Congo Free State. In 1908 Leopold was forced to turn over his private territory to Belgium as a colony, the Belgian Congo.

## Southern Africa in the Nineteenth Century

The development of southern Africa diverged from that of the rest of sub-Saharan Africa in important ways. Whites settled in large numbers, modern capitalist industry took off, and British imperialists had to wage all-out war.

When the British took possession of the Dutch Cape Colony during the Napoleonic Wars, there were about twenty thousand free Dutch citizens and twenty-five thousand African slaves, with substantial mixed-race communities on the northern frontier of white settlement. After 1815 powerful African chiefdoms; the Boers, or **Afrikaners** (descendants of the original Dutch settlers); and British colonial forces waged a complicated three-cornered battle to build strong states in southern Africa.

While the British consolidated their rule in the Cape Colony, the talented Zulu king Shaka (SHAHK-ah) (r. 1818–1828) was creating the largest and most powerful kingdom in southern Africa in the nineteenth century. Shaka's warriors, drafted by age groups and placed in highly disciplined regiments, perfected the use of a short stabbing spear in deadly hand-to-hand combat. The Zulu armies often destroyed their African enemies completely, sowing chaos and sending refugees fleeing in all directions. Shaka's wars led to the creation of Zulu, Tswana (TSWAH-nah), Swazi (SWAH-zee), Ndebele (n-deh-BELL-ee), and Sotho (SOO-too, not SOH-thoh) states in southern Africa. By 1890 these states were largely subdued by Dutch and British invaders, but only after many hard-fought frontier wars.

Between 1834 and 1838 the British abolished slavery in the Cape Colony and introduced racial equality before the law to protect African labor. In 1836 about ten thousand Afrikaner cattle ranchers and farmers, resentful of equal treatment of blacks by British colonial officials and missionaries after the abolition of slavery, began to make their so-called Great Trek northward into the interior. In 1845 another group of Afrikaners joined them north of the Orange River. Over the next thirty years Afrikaner and British settlers reached a mutually advantageous division of southern Africa. The British ruled the strategically valuable colonies of Cape Colony and Natal (nuh-TAHL) on the coast, and the Afrikaners controlled the ranch-land republics of Orange Free State and the Transvaal (TRANS-vahl) in the interior. The Zulu, Xhosa, Sotho, Ndebele, and other African peoples lost much of their land but remained the majority — albeit an exploited majority.

The discovery of incredibly rich deposits of diamonds in 1867 near Kimberley, and of gold in 1886 in the Afrikaners' Transvaal Republic around modern Johannesburg, revolutionized the southern African economy, making possible large-scale industrial capitalism and transforming the lives of all its peoples. The extraction of these minerals, particularly the deep-level gold deposits, required big foreign investment, European engineering expertise, and an enormous labor force. Thus small-scale miners soon gave way to powerful financiers, particularly Cecil Rhodes (1853–1902). Rhodes came from a large middle-class British family and at seventeen went to southern Africa to seek his fortune. By 1888 Rhodes's firm, the De Beers mining company, monopolized the world's diamond industry and earned him fabulous profits. The "color bar" system of the diamond fields gave whites the well-paid skilled positions and put black Africans in the dangerous, low-wage jobs far below the earth's surface. Southern Africa became one of the world's leading diamond and gold producers, pulling in black migratory workers from all over the region (as it does to this day).

The mining bonanza whetted the appetite of British imperialists led by the powerful Rhodes, who was considered the ultimate British imperialist. He once famously observed that the British "happen to be the best people in the world, with the highest ideals of decency and justice and liberty and peace, and the more of the world we inhabit, the better for humanity."[6] Between 1888 and 1893 Rhodes used missionaries and his British South Africa Company, chartered by the British government, to force African chiefs to accept British protectorates, and he managed to add Southern and Northern Rhodesia (modern-day Zimbabwe and Zambia) to the British Empire.

Southern Rhodesia is one of the most egregious examples of a region where Europeans misled African rulers to take their land. In 1888 the Ndebele (or Matabele) king, Lobengula (loh-ben-GUL-ah) (1845–1894), ruler over much of modern southwestern Zimbabwe, met with three of Rhodes's men, led by Charles Rudd, and signed the Rudd Concession. Lobengula believed he was simply allowing a handful of British fortune hunters a few years of gold prospecting in Matabeleland. Lobengula had been misled, however, by the resident London Missionary Society missionary (and Lobengula's supposed friend), the Reverend Charles Helm, as to the document's true meaning and Rhodes's hand behind it. Even though Lobengula soon repudiated the agreement, he opened the way for Rhodes's seizure of the territory.

In 1889 Rhodes's British South Africa Company received a royal charter from Queen Victoria to occupy Matabeleland on behalf of the British government. Though Lobengula died in early 1894, his warriors bravely fought Rhodes's private army in the First and Second Matabele Wars (1893–1894, 1896–1897), but were decimated by British Maxim guns. By 1897 Matabeleland had ceased to exist; it had been replaced by the British-ruled settler colony of Southern Rhodesia. Before his death, Lobengula asked Reverend Helm, "Did you ever see a chameleon catch a fly? The chameleon gets behind the fly and remains motionless for some time, then he advances very slowly and gently, first putting forward one leg and then the other. At last, when well within reach, he darts his tongue and the fly disappears. England is the chameleon and I am that fly."[7]

The Transvaal gold fields still remained in Afrikaner hands, however, so Rhodes and the imperialist clique initiated a series of events that sparked the South African War of 1899–1902 (also known as the Anglo-Boer War). The British needed 450,000 troops to crush the Afrikaners, who never had more than 30,000 men in the field. Often considered the first "total war," this conflict witnessed the British use of a scorched-earth strategy to destroy Afrikaner property, as well as concentration camps to detain Afrikaner families and their servants, thousands of whom died of illness. Africans were sometimes forced and sometimes volunteered to work for one side or the other; estimates of their number range from 15,000 to 40,000 for each side. They did everything from scouting and guard duty to heavy manual labor, driving wagons, and guarding the livestock.

The long and bitter war divided whites in South Africa, but South Africa's blacks were the biggest losers. The British had promised the Afrikaners representative government in return for surrender in 1902, and they made good on their pledge. In 1910 the Cape Colony, Natal, the Orange Free State, and the Transvaal formed a new self-governing Union of South Africa. After the peace settlement, because the white minority held almost all political power in the new union, and because Afrikaners outnumbered English-speakers, the Afrikaners began to regain what they had lost on the battlefield. South Africa, under a joint British-Afrikaner government within the British Empire, began the creation of a modern segregated society that culminated in an even harsher system of racial separation, or apartheid (uh-PAHRT-ayte), after World War II.

## Colonialism's Impact After 1900

By 1900 much of Africa had been conquered and a system of colonial administration was taking shape. In general, this system weakened or shattered the traditional social order.

The self-proclaimed political goal of the French and the British — the principal colonial powers — was to provide good government for their African subjects,
especially after World War I. "Good government" meant, above all, law and order.
It meant a strong, authoritarian government, which maintained a small army, built
up an African police force, and included a modern bureaucracy capable of taxing
and governing the population. Many African leaders and their peoples had chosen
not to resist the invaders' superior force, and others stopped fighting and turned to
other, less violent means of resisting colonial rule. Thus the goal of law and order was
widely achieved.

Colonial governments demonstrated much less interest in providing basic social
services. Education, public health, hospital, and other social service expenditures
increased after the Great War but still remained limited. Europeans feared the political implications of mass education and typically relied instead on the modest efforts
of state-subsidized mission schools. Moreover, they tried to make even their poorest
colonies pay for themselves through taxation.

Economically, the colonial goal was to draw the African interior into the world
economy on terms favorable to the dominant Europeans. Railroads linking coastal
trading centers to interior outposts facilitated easy shipment of raw materials out and
manufactured goods in. Railroads had two other important outcomes: they allowed
quick troop movements to put down local unrest, and they allowed many African
peasants to earn wages for the first time.

**Missionary School, South Africa, 1910** In this photo, African students are taught by a
Roman Catholic nun. In the early days of a mission station, before a school building had been
erected, nuns and priests held classes outside. Sometimes they also traveled to surrounding
African villages and held classes outside there. The students were generally given a mixture of
academic subject matter and religious instruction. (SZ Photo/Scherl/The Image Works)

The focus on economic development and low-cost rule explains why colonial governments were reluctant to move decisively against slavery within Africa. Officials feared that an abrupt abolition of slavery where it existed would disrupt production and lead to costly revolts by powerful slaveholding elites, especially in Muslim areas. Thus colonial regimes settled for halfway measures designed to satisfy humanitarian groups in Europe and also make all Africans, free or enslaved, participate in a market economy and work for wages. Even this cautious policy emboldened many slaves to run away, thereby facilitating a rapid decline of slavery within Africa.

Colonial governments also often imposed taxes. Payable only in labor or European currency, these taxes compelled Africans to work for their white overlords. Africans despised no aspect of colonialism more than forced labor, widespread until about 1920. In some regions, particularly in West Africa, African peasants continued to respond freely to the new economic opportunities by voluntarily shifting to export crops on their own farms. Overall, the result of these developments was an increase in wage work and production geared to the world market and a decline in nomadic herding and traditional self-sufficient farming of sustainable crops. In sum, the imposition of bureaucratic Western rule and the gradual growth of a world-oriented cash economy after 1900 had a revolutionary impact on large parts of Africa.

# The New Imperialism, 1880–1914

**What were the causes and consequences of European empire building after 1880?**

Western expansion into Africa and Asia reached its apex between about 1880 and 1914. In those years the leading European nations sent streams of money and manufactured goods to both continents and also rushed to create or enlarge vast overseas political empires. This frantic activity differed sharply from the limited economic penetration of non-Western territories between 1816 and 1880, which had left a China or a Japan "opened" but politically independent. By contrast, late-nineteenth-century empires recalled the old European colonial empires of the seventeenth and eighteenth centuries and led contemporaries to speak of the **New Imperialism**.

Characterized by a frenzied rush to plant the flag over as many people and as much territory as possible, the most spectacular manifestation of the New Imperialism was the seizure of nearly all of Africa. Less striking but equally important was Europe's extension of political control in Asia, the subject of Chapter 26.

## Causes of the New Imperialism

Many factors contributed to the West's late-nineteenth-century rush for territory in Africa and Asia, and controversies continue to rage over interpretation of the New Imperialism. Despite complexity and controversy, however, basic causes are clearly identifiable.

Economic motives played an important role in the extension of political empires, especially of the British Empire. By the 1870s France, Germany, and the United States were rapidly industrializing. For a century Great Britain had been the "workshop of the world," the dominant modern industrial power. Now it was losing its industrial leadership, as its share of global manufacturing output dropped from 33 percent to just 14 percent between 1870 and 1914, and facing increasingly tough competition in foreign markets. In this changing environment of widening economic internationalism, the world experienced one of the worst economic depressions in history, the Long Depression of 1873 to 1879 (originally called the Great Depression until the Great Depression of the 1930s supplanted it). To protect home industries, America and Europe (except for Britain and the Netherlands) raised tariff barriers, abandoning the century-long practice of free trade and laissez-faire capitalism. Unable to export their goods and faced with excess production, market saturation, and high unemployment, Britain, the other European powers, and the United States turned to imperial expansion, seeking African and Asian colonies to sell their products and acquire cheap raw materials. The Long Depression was arguably the single most important spark touching off the age of New Imperialism.

Economic gains from the New Imperialism proved limited, however, before 1914. The new colonies were too poor to buy much, and they offered few immediately profitable investments. Nonetheless, colonies became important for political and diplomatic reasons. Each leading European country considered them crucial to national security, military power, and international prestige.

Colonial rivalries reflected the increasing aggressiveness of Social Darwinian theories of brutal competition among races. As one prominent English economist argued in 1873, the "strongest nation has always been conquering the weaker . . . and the strongest tend to be best."[8] Thus European nations, considered as racially distinct parts of the dominant white race, had to seize colonies to prove their strength and virility. Moreover, since racial struggle was nature's inescapable law, the conquest of "inferior" peoples was just. Social Darwinism and harsh racial doctrines fostered imperialist expansion.

So, too, did the industrial world's unprecedented technological and military superiority. Three developments were crucial. First, the rapidly firing machine gun was an ultimate weapon in many unequal battles. Second, newly discovered **quinine** (KWIGH-nighn) effectively controlled malaria attacks, which had previously decimated Europeans in the tropics. Third, the introduction of steam power strengthened the Western powers in two ways. Militarily, they could swiftly transport their armies by sea or rail where they were most needed. Economically, steamships with ever-larger cargoes now made round-trip journeys to far-flung colonies much more quickly and economically. Small steamboats could travel back and forth along the coast and also carry goods up and down Africa's great rivers, as portrayed in the classic American film *The African Queen* (1951). Likewise, freight cars pulled by powerful steam engines—immune to disease, unlike animals and humans—replaced the thousands of African porters hitherto responsible for carrying raw materials from the interior to the coast.

Domestic political and class conflicts also contributed to overseas expansion. Conservative political leaders often manipulated colonial issues to divert popular attention from domestic problems and to create a false sense of national unity. Imperial propagandists relentlessly stressed that colonies benefited workers as well as capitalists, and they encouraged the masses to savor foreign triumphs and imperial glory.

Finally, special-interest groups in each country were powerful agents of expansion. Shipping companies wanted lucrative subsidies. White settlers wanted more land. Missionaries and humanitarians wanted to spread religion and stop the slave trade. Military men and colonial officials foresaw rapid advancement and high-paid positions in growing empires. The actions of such groups pushed the course of empire forward.

## A "Civilizing Mission"

To rationalize their aggressive and racist actions, Europeans and Americans argued that they could and should "civilize" supposedly primitive non-Western peoples. According to this view, Africans and Asians would benefit from Western education, modern economies, cities, advanced medicine, and higher living standards and eventually might be ready for self-government and Western democracy.

European imperialists also argued that imperial government protected colonized peoples from ethnic warfare, the slave trade within Africa, and other forms of exploitation by white settlers and business people. Thus the French spoke of their sacred "civilizing mission." In 1899 Rudyard Kipling (1865–1936), perhaps the most influential British writer of the 1890s, exhorted Westerners to unselfish service in distant lands (while warning of the high costs involved) in his poem "The White Man's Burden."

> Take up the White Man's Burden—
> Send forth the best ye breed—
> Go bind your sons to exile
> To serve your captives' need,
> To wait in heavy harness,
> On fluttered folk and wild—
> Your new-caught, sullen peoples
> Half-devil and half-child.[9]

Kipling's poem, written in response to America's seizure of the Philippines after the Spanish-American War, and his concept of a **white man's burden** won wide acceptance among American imperialists. This principle was an important factor in the decision to rule, rather than liberate, the Philippines after the Spanish-American War (see "The Philippines" in Chapter 26). Like their European counterparts, these Americans believed their civilization had reached unprecedented heights, enabling them to bestow unique benefits on all "less advanced" peoples.

Imperialists also claimed that peace and stability under European or American dominion permitted the spread of Christianity. In Africa Catholic and Protestant missionaries competed with Islam south of the Sahara, seeking converts and building schools. Many Africans' first real contact with Europeans and Americans was in mission schools. Some peoples, such as the Ibo in Nigeria, became highly Christianized. Such successes in black Africa contrasted with the general failure of missionary efforts in the Islamic world and in much of Asia.

## Critics of Imperialism

Imperial expansion aroused sharp, even bitter, critics. One forceful attack was delivered in 1902, after the unpopular South African War, by radical English economist J. A. Hobson (1858–1940) in his *Imperialism*. Hobson contended that the rush to acquire colonies resulted from the economic needs of unregulated (by governments) capitalism. Moreover, Hobson argued, the quest for empire diverted popular attention away from domestic reform and the need to reduce the great gap between rich and poor at home. These and similar arguments had limited appeal because most people fervently believed that imperialism was economically profitable for the homeland. Both Hobson and public opinion were wrong, however. Most British and European investors put the bulk of their money in the United States, Canada, Russia, and other industrializing countries. Sub-Saharan Africa accounted for less than 5 percent of British exports in 1890, and British investments in Africa flowed predominantly to the mines in southern Africa. Thus, while some sectors of the British economy did profit from imperial conquests, and trade with these conquests was greater just before the Great War than in 1870, overall profits from imperialism were marginal at best.

Hobson and many Western critics struck home, however, with their moral condemnation of whites' imperious rule over nonwhites. Kipling and his kind were lampooned as racist bullies whose rule rested on brutality, racial contempt, and the Maxim machine gun. Polish-born novelist Joseph Conrad (1857–1924), in *Heart of Darkness* (1902), castigated the "pure selfishness" of Europeans in "civilizing" Africa.

Critics charged Europeans with applying a degrading double standard and failing to live up to their own noble ideals. At home Europeans had won or were winning representative government, individual liberties, and a certain equality of opportunity. In their empires Europeans imposed military dictatorships on Africans and Asians, forced them to work involuntarily, and discriminated against them shamelessly.

## African and Asian Resistance

To African and Asian peoples, Western expansion represented a profoundly disruptive assault that threatened traditional ruling classes, economies, and ways of life. Christian missionaries and European secular ideologies challenged established beliefs and values. African and Asian societies experienced crises of identity, although the details of each people's story varied substantially.

Initially African and Asian rulers often responded to imperialist incursions by trying to drive the unwelcome foreigners away, as in China and Japan (see "The Opium War" and "The 'Opening' of Japan" in Chapter 26). Violent antiforeign reactions exploded elsewhere again and again, but the industrialized West's superior military technology almost invariably prevailed. In addition, Europeans sought to divide and conquer by giving special powers and privileges to some individuals and groups from among the local population, including traditional leaders such as chiefs, landowners, and religious figures; and Western-educated professionals and civil servants, including police officers and military officers. These local elites recognized the imperial power realities in which they were enmeshed and manipulated them to maintain or gain authority over the masses. Some concluded that the West was superior in certain ways and that they needed to reform and modernize their societies by copying some European achievements. By ruling indirectly through a local elite (backed by the implied threat of force), relatively small numbers of Europeans could maintain control over much larger populations without constant rebellion and protest. European empires were won by force, but they were maintained by cultural as well as military and political means.

Nevertheless, imperial rule was in many ways an imposing edifice built on sand. Acceptance of European rule was shallow and weak among the colonized masses, who were often quick to follow determined charismatic personalities who came to oppose the Europeans. Such leaders always arose, both when Europeans ruled directly, or indirectly through native governments, for at least two basic reasons.

First, the nonconformists—the eventual anti-imperialist leaders—developed a burning desire for human dignity. They felt such dignity was incompatible with, and impossible under, foreign rule. Second, potential leaders found in the Western world the necessary ideologies and justification for their protest, such as liberalism, with its credo of civil liberty and political self-determination. Above all, they found themselves attracted to the nineteenth-century Western ideology of nationalism, which asserted that every people had the right to control their own destiny. After 1917 anti-imperialist revolt found another weapon in Lenin's version of Marxist socialism.

# The Islamic Heartland Under Pressure

**How did the Ottoman Empire and Egypt try to modernize themselves, and what were the most important results?**

Stretching from West Africa into southeastern Europe and across Southwest Asia to the East Indies, Islamic civilization competed successfully with western Europe for centuries. Beginning in the late seventeenth century, however, the rising absolutist states of Austria and Russia began to challenge the Ottoman Empire and gradually to reverse Ottoman rule in southeastern Europe. In the nineteenth century European industrialization and nation building further altered the long-standing balance of power, and Western expansion eventually posed a serious challenge to Muslims everywhere.

## Decline and Reform in the Ottoman Empire

Although the Ottoman Empire began a slow decline after Suleiman (SOO-lay-man) the Magnificent in the sixteenth century, the relationship between the Ottomans and the Europeans in about 1750 was still one of roughly equal strength. This parity began to change quickly and radically, however, in the later eighteenth century, as the Ottomans fell behind western Europe in science, industrial skill, and military technology.

A transformation of the army was absolutely necessary to battle the Europeans more effectively and enhance the sultanate's authority within the empire. There were two primary obstacles to change, however. First, Ottoman military weakness reflected the decline of the sultan's "slave army," the janissary corps. With time, the janissaries—boys and other slaves raised in Turkey as Muslims, then trained to serve in the Ottoman infantry's elite corps—became a corrupt and privileged hereditary caste, absolutely opposed to any military innovations that might undermine their high status. Second, the empire was no longer a centralized military state. Instead local governors were becoming increasingly independent, pursuing their own interests and even seeking to establish their own governments and hereditary dynasties.

Sultan Selim III (r. 1789–1807) understood these realities, but when he tried to reorganize the army, the janissaries refused to use any "Christian" equipment. In 1807 they revolted and executed Selim in a palace revolution, one of many that plagued the Ottoman state. Selim's successor, the reform-minded Mahmud II (r. 1808–1839), proceeded cautiously, picking loyal officers and building his dependable artillery corps. In 1826 his council ordered the janissaries to drill in the European manner. As expected, the janissaries revolted and charged the palace, where they were mowed down by the waiting artillery.

The destruction and abolition of the janissaries cleared the way for building a new army, but it came too late to stop the rise of Muhammad Ali, the Ottoman governor in Egypt. In 1831 his French-trained forces occupied the Ottoman province of Syria and appeared ready to depose Mahmud II. The Ottoman sultan survived, but only with help from Britain, Russia, and Austria. The Ottomans were saved again in 1839, after their forces were routed trying to drive Muhammad Ali from Syria. In the last months of 1840 Russian diplomatic efforts, British and Austrian naval blockades, and threatened military action convinced Muhammad Ali to return Syria to the Ottomans. European powers preferred a weak and dependent Ottoman state to a strong and revitalized Muslim entity under a leader such as Muhammad Ali.

In 1839, realizing their precarious position, liberal Ottoman statesmen launched an era of radical reforms, which lasted until 1876 and culminated in a constitution

**Pasha Halim Receiving Archduke Maximilian of Austria**   As this painting suggests, Ottoman leaders became well versed in European languages and culture. They also mastered the game of power politics, playing one European state against another and to secure the Ottoman Empire's survival. The black servants on the right may be slaves from the Sudan.   (DEA/A. Dagli Orti/Getty Images)

and a short-lived parliament. Known as the **Tanzimat** (TAHN-zee-maht) (literally, "regulations" or "orders"), these reforms were designed to remake the empire on a western European model. The new decrees called for Muslim, Christian, and Jewish equality before the law and in business, security of life and property, and a modernized administration and military. New commercial laws allowed free importation of foreign goods, as British advisers demanded, and permitted foreign merchants to operate freely throughout an economically dependent empire. Under British pressure, slavery in the empire was drastically curtailed, though not abolished completely. Of great significance, growing numbers among the elite and the upwardly mobile embraced Western education, adopted Western manners and artistic styles, and accepted secular values to some extent.

Intended to bring revolutionary modernization such as that experienced by Russia under Peter the Great (see "Peter the Great and Russia's Turn to the West" in Chapter 18) and by Japan in the Meiji era (see "The Meiji Restoration" in Chapter 26), the Tanzimat achieved only partial success. The Ottoman state and society failed to regain its earlier power and authority for several reasons. First, implementation of the reforms required a new generation of well-trained and trustworthy officials, and that generation did not exist. Second, the liberal reforms failed to halt the growth of nationalism among Christian subjects in the Balkans (discussed below), which resulted in crises and defeats that undermined all reform efforts. Third, the Ottoman initiatives did not curtail the appetite of Western imperialism, and European bankers gained a stranglehold on Ottoman finances. In 1875 the Ottoman state had to declare partial bankruptcy and place its finances in the hands of European creditors.

Finally, the elaboration—at least on paper—of equal rights for citizens and religious communities failed to create greater unity within the state. Religious disputes increased, worsened by the Great Powers' relentless interference. This development embittered relations between religious communities, distracted the government from its reform mission, and split Muslims into secularists and religious conservatives. Islamic conservatives became the most dependable supporters of Sultan Abdülhamid II (ahb-DUHL-ah-mid) (r. 1876–1909), who abandoned the model of European liberalism in his long and repressive reign.

Meanwhile, the Ottoman Empire gradually lost control of its vast territories. Serbian nationalists rebelled and forced the Ottomans to grant Serbia local autonomy in 1816. The Greeks revolted against Ottoman rule in 1821 and won their national independence in 1830. As the Ottomans dealt with these uprisings by their Christian subjects in Europe, they failed to defend their Islamic provinces in North Africa. In 1830 French armies began their conquest of the Arabic-speaking province of Algeria.

Finally, during the Russo-Turkish War (1877–1878), absolutist Russia and a coalition of Balkan countries pushed southward into Ottoman lands and won a decisive victory. At the Congress of Berlin in 1878, the European Great Powers and the Ottoman Empire met to formally recognize Bulgarian, Romanian, Serbian, and Montenegrin independence. The Ottomans also lost territory to the Russians in the Caucasus, Austria-Hungary occupied the Ottoman provinces of Bosnia-Herzegovina (BAHZ-nee-uh HERT-suh-go-vee-nuh) and Novi Pazar (NOH-vi PAH-zar), and Great Britain took over Cyprus (SIGH-pruhs). The Ottoman Empire, now labeled the "sick man of Europe" in the European press, left the meeting significantly weakened and humiliated.

The combination of declining international power and conservative tyranny eventually led to a powerful resurgence of the modernizing impulse among idealistic Turkish exiles in Europe and young army officers in Istanbul. These fervent patriots, the so-called **Young Turks**, seized power in the 1908 revolution, overthrowing Sultan Abdülhamid II. They made his brother Mehmed V (r. 1909–1918) the figurehead sultan and forced him to implement reforms. The Young Turks helped prepare the way for the birth of modern secular Turkey after the defeat and collapse of the Ottoman Empire in World War I.

## Egypt: From Reform to British Occupation

The ancient land of the pharaohs had been ruled by a succession of foreigners from 525 B.C.E. to the Ottoman conquest in the early sixteenth century. In 1798, as France and Britain prepared for war in Europe, Napoleon Bonaparte invaded Egypt, thereby threatening British access to India, and occupied the territory for three years. Into the power vacuum left by the French withdrawal stepped an extraordinary Albanian-born Turkish general, Muhammad Ali (1769–1849).

Appointed Egypt's governor by Sultan Selim III in 1805, Muhammad Ali set out to build his own state on the strength of a large, powerful army organized along European lines. He also reformed the government and promoted modern industry. For a time Muhammad Ali's ambitious strategy seemed to work, but it eventually foundered when his armies occupied Syria and he threatened the Ottoman sultan, Mahmud II. In the face of European military might and diplomatic entreaties, Muhammad Ali agreed to peace with his Ottoman overlords and withdrew. In return he was given unprecedented hereditary rule over Egypt and Sudan. By his death in 1849, Muhammad Ali had established a strong and virtually independent Egyptian state within the Ottoman Empire.

To pay for a modern army and industrialization, Muhammad Ali encouraged the development of commercial agriculture geared to the European market, which had profound social implications. Egyptian peasants had been largely self-sufficient, growing food on state-owned land allotted to them by tradition. High-ranking officials and members of Muhammad Ali's family began carving private landholdings out of the state domain, and they forced the peasants to grow cash crops for European markets.

Muhammad Ali's modernization policies attracted growing numbers of Europeans to the banks of the Nile. Europeans served as army officers, engineers, doctors, government officials, and police officers. Others worked in trade, finance, and shipping. Above all, Europeans living in Egypt combined with landlords and officials to continue steering commercial agriculture toward exports. As throughout the Ottoman Empire, Europeans enjoyed important commercial and legal privileges and formed an economic elite.

In 1863 Muhammad Ali's grandson Ismail began his sixteen-year rule (r. 1863–1879) as Egypt's khedive (kuh-DEEV), or prince. He was a westernizing autocrat who received his education at France's leading military academy and dreamed of using European technology and capital to modernize Egypt and build a vast empire in northeastern Africa. He promoted cotton production, and exports to Europe soared. Ismail also borrowed large sums, and with his support the Suez Canal was completed by a French company in 1869, shortening the voyage from Europe to Asia by thousands of miles. Cairo acquired modern boulevards and Western hotels. As Ismail proudly declared, "My country is no longer in Africa, we now form part of Europe."[10]

Major cultural and intellectual changes accompanied the political and economic ones. The Arabic of the masses, rather than the conqueror's Turkish, became the official language, and young, European-educated Egyptians helped spread new skills and ideas in the bureaucracy. A host of writers, intellectuals, and religious thinkers responded to the novel conditions with innovative ideas that had a powerful impact in Egypt and other Muslim societies.

Three influential figures who represented broad families of thought were especially significant. The teacher and writer Jamal al-Din al-Afghani (jah-MAL al-DIN al-af-GHAN-ee) (1838/39–1897) argued for the purification of Islamic religious belief, Muslim unity, and a revolutionary overthrow of corrupt Muslim rulers and foreign exploiters. The more moderate Muhammad Abduh (AHB-duh) (1849–1905) launched the modern Islamic reform movement. Abduh concluded that Muslims should adopt a flexible, reasoned approach to change, modernity, science, social questions, and foreign ideas and not reject these out of hand.

Finally, the writer Qasim Amin (KAH-zim ah-MEEN) (1863–1908) represented those who found inspiration in the West in the late nineteenth century. In his influential book *The Liberation of Women* (1899), Amin argued forcefully that superior education for European women had contributed greatly to the Islamic world's falling far behind the West. In his view, the rejuvenation of Muslim societies required greater equality for women:

> History confirms and demonstrates that the status of women is inseparably tied to the status of a nation. Where the status of a nation is low, reflecting an uncivilized condition for that nation, the status of women is also low, and when the status of a nation is elevated, reflecting the progress and civilization of that nation, the status of women in that country is also elevated.[11]

Egypt changed rapidly during Ismail's rule, but his projects were reckless and enormously expensive. By 1876 the Egyptian government could not pay the interest on its colossal debt. Rather than let Egypt go bankrupt and repudiate its loans, France and Great Britain intervened, forcing Ismail to appoint French and British commissioners to oversee Egyptian finances. This meant that Europeans would determine the state budget and in effect rule Egypt.

Foreign financial control evoked a violent nationalistic reaction. Continuing diplomatic pressure, which forced Ismail to abdicate in favor of his weak son, Tewfiq (teh-FEEK) (r. 1879–1892), resulted in bloody anti-European riots in Alexandria in 1882. In response, the British fleet bombarded Alexandria, and a British expeditionary force occupied all of Egypt. British armies remained in Egypt until 1956.

Initially the British maintained the fiction that Egypt was an autonomous province of the Ottoman Empire, but in truth, the khedive was a mere puppet. In reality, the British consul, General Evelyn Baring, later Lord Cromer, ruled the country after 1883. Baring was a paternalistic reformer. He initiated tax reforms and made some improvements to conditions for peasants. Foreign bondholders received their interest payments, while Egyptian nationalists chafed under foreign rule.

# The Expanding World Economy

### What were the global consequences of European industrialization between 1800 and 1914?

Over the course of the nineteenth century the Industrial Revolution expanded and transformed economic relations across the face of the earth. As a result, the world's total income grew as never before, and international trade boomed. Western nations used their superior military power to force non-Western nations to open their doors to Western economic interests. Consequently, the largest share of the ever-increasing gains from trade flowed to the West, resulting in a stark division between rich and poor countries.

## The Rise of Global Inequality

From a global perspective, the ultimate significance of the Industrial Revolution was two-fold. First, it allowed those world regions that industrialized in the nineteenth century to increase their wealth and power enormously in comparison with those that did not. A gap between the industrializing regions (Europe, North America, and Japan) and the nonindustrializing regions (mainly Africa, Asia, and Latin America) opened and grew steadily throughout the nineteenth century (Figure 25.1). Moreover, this pattern of uneven global development became institutionalized, built into the structure of the world economy. Thus evolved a world of economic haves and have-nots, with the have-not peoples and nations far outnumbering the haves.

Second, in 1750 the average living standard was no higher in Europe as a whole than in the rest of the world. By 1914 the average person in the wealthiest countries had an income four or five times as great (and in Great Britain nine or ten times as great) as an average person's income in the poorest countries of Africa and Asia. The rise in average income and well-being reflected the rising level of industrialization in Great Britain and then in the other developed countries before World War I.

The reasons for these enormous income disparities have generated a great deal of debate. One school of interpretation stresses that the West used science, technology, capitalist organization, and even its critical worldview to create its wealth and greater physical well-being. An opposing school argues that the West used its

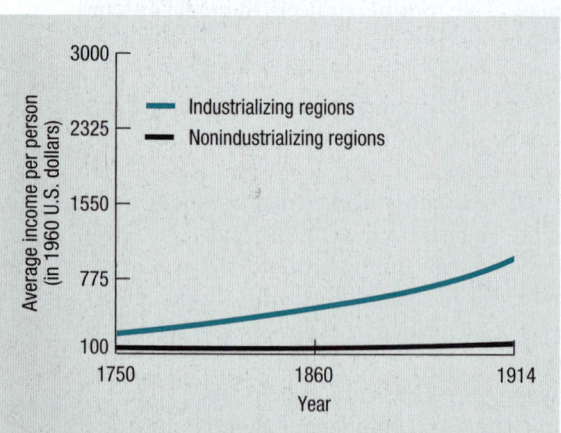

**Note:** Nonindustrializing regions include Africa, Asia, Latin America, and Oceania. Industrializing regions include all European countries, Canada, the United States, and Japan.

**FIGURE 25.1  The Growth of Average Income per Person Worldwide, 1750–1914**

Source of data: P. Bairoch and M. Lévy-Leboyer, eds., *Disparities in Economic Development Since the Industrial Revolution* (New York: Macmillan, 1980).

political, economic, and military power to steal much of its riches through its rapacious colonialism in the nineteenth and twentieth centuries.

These issues are complex, and there are few simple answers. As noted in Chapter 23, the wealth-creating potential of technological improvement and more intensive capitalist organization was great. At the same time, the initial breakthroughs in the late eighteenth century rested in part on Great Britain's having already used political force to dominate a substantial part of the world economy. In the nineteenth century other industrializing countries joined with Britain to extend Western dominion over the entire world economy. Unprecedented wealth was created, but the lion's share of that new wealth flowed to the West and its propertied classes and to a tiny indigenous elite of cooperative rulers, landowners, and merchants.

## The World Market

World trade was a powerful stimulus to economic development in the nineteenth century. In 1913 the value of world trade was about twenty-five times what it had been in 1800, even though prices of manufactured goods and raw materials were lower in 1913 than in 1800. In a general way, this enormous increase in international commerce summed up the growth of an interlocking world economy centered in Europe.

Great Britain played a key role in using trade to tie the world together economically. In 1815 Britain already possessed a colonial empire, including India, Canada, and Australia. The technological breakthroughs of the Industrial Revolution encouraged British manufacturers to seek export markets around the world. After Parliament repealed laws restricting grain importation in 1846, Britain also became the world's leading importer of foreign goods. Free access to Britain's market stimulated the development of mines and plantations in Africa and Asia.

The conquest of distance facilitated the growth of trade. Wherever railroads were built, they drastically reduced transportation costs, opened new economic opportunities, and called forth new skills and attitudes.

Much of the railroad construction undertaken in Africa, Asia, and Latin America connected seaports with inland cities and regions, as opposed to linking and developing cities and regions within a country. Thus railroads

**British East African Railway Poster**
Europeans constructed railroads in most of their African colonies to haul raw materials from the interior to coastal ports and to transport colonial officials, white settlers, and foreign tourists. Britain's East African railroad line from Kampala, Uganda, to the Kenyan port city of Mombasa was one of the most famous and most romanticized. Indians from British India did much of the construction and then remained in Kenya to form substantial Indian communities. President Theodore Roosevelt rode this train while on his 1909 African safari. (Pictorial Press Ltd./Alamy Stock Photo)

dovetailed with Western economic interests, facilitating the inflow and sale of Western manufactured goods and the export and development of local raw materials.

Steam power also revolutionized transportation by sea. Steam power was first used to supplant sails on the world's oceans in the late 1860s. Passenger and freight rates tumbled, and the shipment of low-priced raw materials from one continent to another became feasible.

The revolution in land and sea transportation helped European settlers seize vast, thinly populated territories and produce agricultural products and raw materials for sale in Europe. Improved transportation enabled Asia, Africa, and Latin America to export not only the traditional tropical products — spices, dyes, tea, sugar, coffee — but also new raw materials for industry, such as jute, rubber, cotton, and peanut and coconut oil. Intercontinental trade was enormously facilitated by the Suez Canal in Egypt and the Panama Canal in Central America. Of great importance, too, was large and continual investment in modern port facilities, which made loading and unloading cheaper, faster, and more dependable. Finally, transoceanic telegraph cables inaugurated rapid communications among the world's financial centers and linked world commodity prices in a global network.

The growth of trade and the conquest of distance encouraged Europeans to make massive foreign investments beginning about 1840, but not to European colonies or protectorates in Asia and Africa. About three-quarters of total European investment went to other European countries, the United States and Canada, Australia and New Zealand, and Latin America. Here booming, industrializing economies offered the most profitable investment opportunities. Much of this investment was peaceful and mutually beneficial for lenders and borrowers. The victims were Native Americans, Australian Aborigines (AB-or-ij-uh-nees), New Zealand Maoris (MAO-reez), and other native peoples who were displaced and decimated by the diseases, liquor, and weapons of an aggressively expanding Western society.

# The Great Global Migration

**What fueled migration, and what was the general pattern of this unprecedented movement of people?**

A poignant human drama was interwoven with this worldwide economic expansion: millions of people left their ancestral lands in one of history's greatest migrations, the so-called **great migration**. In the early eighteenth century the world's population entered a period of rapid growth that continued unabated through the nineteenth and twentieth centuries. Europe's population (including Asiatic Russia) more than doubled during the nineteenth century, from approximately 188 million in 1800 to roughly 432 million in 1900. Since African and Asian populations increased more slowly than those in Europe, Europeans and peoples of predominantly European origin jumped from about 22 percent of the world's total in 1850 to a high of about 38 percent in 1930.

Rapid population growth led to relative overpopulation in area after area in Europe and was a driving force behind emigration and Western expansion. Millions of country folk moved to nearby cities, and the more adventuresome went abroad, in search of work and economic opportunity. Some governments encouraged their excess populations to emigrate, even paying part of their expenses. Wars, famine, poverty, and, particularly in the case of Russian and eastern European Jews, bigotry and discrimination were also leading causes for emigrants to leave their ancestral homelands. More than 60 million people left Europe over the course of the nineteenth century, primarily for the rapidly growing "areas of European settlement"—North and South America, Australia, New Zealand, and Siberia. European emigration crested in the first decade of the twentieth century, when more than five times as many men and women departed as in the 1850s.

The European migrant was most often a small peasant landowner or a village craftsman whose traditional way of life was threatened by too little land, estate agriculture, and cheap factory-made goods. Determined to maintain or improve their precarious status, the vast majority of migrants were young and often unmarried. Many European migrants eventually returned home after some time abroad. Moreover, when the economic situation improved at home or when people began to win basic political and social reforms, migration slowed.

Ties of family and friendship played a crucial role in the movement of peoples. Over several years a given province or village might lose significant numbers of its inhabitants to migration. These people then settled together in rural enclaves or tightly knit urban neighborhoods in foreign lands thousands of miles away. Very often a strong individual—a businessman, a religious leader—blazed the way, and others followed, forming a **migration chain**.

A substantial number of Asians—especially Chinese, Japanese, Indians, and Filipinos—also responded to population pressure and rural hardship with temporary or permanent migration. At least 3 million Asians moved abroad before 1920. Most went as indentured laborers to work on the plantations or in the gold mines of Latin America, southern Asia, Africa, California, Hawaii, and Australia. White estate owners often used Asians to replace or supplement black Africans after the suppression of the Atlantic slave trade.

Asian migration would undoubtedly have been much greater if planters and mine owners desiring cheap labor had had their way. But usually they did not. Asians fled the plantations and gold mines as soon as possible, seeking greater opportunities in trade and towns. Here, however, they came into conflict with white settlers, who demanded a halt to Asian immigration. By the 1880s Americans and Australians were building **great white walls**—discriminatory laws designed to keep Asians out.

The general policy of "whites only" in the lands of large-scale European settlement meant that Europeans and people of European ancestry reaped the main benefits of the great migration. By 1913 people in Australia, Canada, and the United States all had higher average incomes than did people in Great Britain, still Europe's wealthiest nation. This, too, contributed to Western dominance in the increasingly lopsided world.

Within Asia and Africa the situation was different. Migrants from south China frequently settled in Dutch, British, and French colonies of Southeast Asia, where they established themselves as peddlers and small shopkeepers. These "overseas Chinese" gradually emerged as a new class of entrepreneurs and officeworkers. Traders from India and modern-day Lebanon performed the same function in much of sub-Saharan Africa after European colonization in the late nineteenth century. Thus in some parts of Asia and Africa the business class was both Asian and foreign, protected and tolerated by Western imperialists who found these business people useful.

## Chapter Summary

Following Europe's Industrial Revolution in the late eighteenth and early nineteenth centuries, European demands for raw materials and new markets reoriented Africa's economy. The transatlantic slave trade declined dramatically as Africans began producing commodities for export. This legitimate trade in African goods proved profitable and led to the emergence of a small black middle class. Islam revived and expanded until about 1870.

After 1880 a handful of Western nations seized most of Africa and parts of Asia and rushed to build authoritarian empires. The reasons for this empire building included trade rivalries, competitive nationalism in Europe, and self-justifying claims of a civilizing mission. European nations' unprecedented military superiority enabled them to crush resistance and impose their will.

The Ottoman Empire and Egypt prepared to become modern nation-states in the twentieth century by introducing reforms to improve the military, provide technical and secular education, and expand personal liberties. They failed, however, to defend themselves from Western imperialism. The Ottoman Empire lost territory but survived in a weakened condition. Egypt's Muhammad Ali reformed the government and promoted modern industry, but Egypt went bankrupt and was conquered and ruled by Britain. Western domination was particularly bitter for most Muslims because they saw it as profaning Islam and taking away their political independence.

Population pressures at home and economic opportunities abroad caused millions of European emigrants to resettle in the sparsely populated areas of European settlement in North and South America, Australia, and Asiatic Russia. Migration from Asia was much more limited, mainly because European settlers raised high barriers to prevent the settlement of Asian immigrants.

## NOTES

1. P. Lovejoy, *Transformations in Slavery: A History of Slavery in Africa*, 2d ed. (Cambridge: Cambridge University Press, 2000), p. 142.
2. Quoted in J. Iliffe, *Africans: The History of a Continent* (Cambridge: Cambridge University Press, 1995), p. 169.
3. Lovejoy, *Transformations in Slavery*, p. 15.
4. R. Oliver, *The African Experience* (New York: Icon Editions, 1991), pp. 164–166.
5. Quoted in H. Wheaton, *Elements of International Law* (London: Stevens & Sons, 1889), p. 804.
6. Quoted in Bernard Porter, *The Lion's Share: A Short History of British Imperialism, 1850–1970* (London: Longman, 1975), p. 134.
7. Quoted in Anthony Thomas, *Rhodes* (New York: St. Martin's Press, 1996), p. 194.
8. Walter Bagehot, *Physics and Politics, or Thoughts on the Application of the Principle of "Natural Selection" and "Inheritance" to Political Society* (New York: D. Appleton, 1873), pp. 43, 49.
9. Rudyard Kipling, *The Five Nations* (London, 1903).
10. Quoted in Earl of Cromer, *Modern Egypt* (London, 1911), p. 48.
11. Qasim Amin, *The Liberation of Women and the New Woman* (Cairo: The American University of Cairo Press, 2000), p. 6.

## MAKE CONNECTIONS   LOOK AHEAD

By the end of the nineteenth century broader industrialization across Europe increased the need for raw materials and markets, and with it came a rush to create or enlarge vast political empires abroad. The New Imperialism was aimed primarily at Africa and Asia, and in the years before 1914 the leading European nations not only created empires abroad, but also continued to send massive streams of migrants, money, and manufactured goods around the world. (The impact of this unprecedented migration is taken up in the next two chapters.) This political empire building contrasted sharply with the economic penetration of non-Western territories between 1816 and 1880, which had allowed Africa to develop a "legitimate trade" and end the transatlantic slave trade, and which left China and Japan "opened" but politically independent, as Chapter 26 will show.

European influence also grew in the Middle East. Threatened by European military might, modernization, and Christianity, Turks and Arabs tried to implement reforms that would ensure their survival and independence but also endeavored to retain key aspects of their cultures, particularly Islam. Although they made important advances in the modernization of their economies and societies, their efforts were not enough to overcome Western imperialism. With the end of World War I and the collapse of the Ottoman Empire, England and France divided much of the Middle East into colonies and established loyal surrogates as rulers in other, nominally independent, countries. Chapter 29 will take up the story of these developments.

Easy imperialist victories over weak states and poorly armed non-Western peoples encouraged excessive pride and led Europeans to underestimate the fragility of their accomplishments. Imperialism also made nationalism more aggressive and militaristic. As European imperialism was dividing the world after the 1880s, the leading European states were also dividing themselves into two opposing military alliances. As Chapter 28 will show, when the two armed camps stumbled into war in 1914, the results were disastrous. World War I set the stage for a new anti-imperialist struggle in Africa and Asia for equality and genuine independence, the topic of Chapters 31 and 32.

# Chapter 25 Review

## IDENTIFY KEY TERMS

**Identify and explain the significance of each item below.**

palm oil (p. 647)

jihad (p. 649)

Sokoto caliphate (p. 649)

Berlin Conference (p. 651)

protectorate (p. 652)

Afrikaners (p. 653)

New Imperialism (p. 657)

quinine (p. 658)

white man's burden (p. 659)

Tanzimat (p. 663)

Young Turks (p. 664)

great migration (p. 668)

migration chain (p. 669)

great white walls (p. 669)

## REVIEW THE MAIN IDEAS

**Answer the focus questions from each section of the chapter.**

1. What were the most significant changes in Africa during the nineteenth century, and why did they occur? (p. 647)

2. What were the causes and consequences of European empire building after 1880? (p. 657)

3. How did the Ottoman Empire and Egypt try to modernize themselves, and what were the most important results? (p. 661)

4. What were the global consequences of European industrialization between 1800 and 1914? (p. 666)

5. What fueled migration, and what was the general pattern of this unprecedented movement of people? (p. 668)

## MAKE COMPARISONS AND CONNECTIONS

**Analyze the larger developments and continuities within and across chapters.**

1. Explain the transitions in Africa from the slave trade to legitimate trade to colonialism in the late eighteenth and nineteenth centuries. How was Europe's Industrial Revolution (Chapter 23) related to these transitions?

2. Europeans had been visiting Africa's coasts for four hundred years before colonizing the entire continent in thirty years in the second half of the nineteenth century. Why hadn't they colonized Africa earlier, and what factors allowed them to do it then?

3. What were the causes of the great migration in the late nineteenth and early twentieth centuries?

## CHRONOLOGY

| | |
|---|---|
| **1805–1848** | • Muhammad Ali modernizes Egypt |
| **1806–1825** | • Latin American wars of independence (Ch. 22) |
| **1808–1839** | • Mahmud II rules Ottoman state and enacts reforms |
| **1809** | • Uthman dan Fodio founds Sokoto caliphate |
| **1830** | • France begins conquest of Algeria |
| **1839–1876** | • Western-style reforms (Tanzimat) in Ottoman Empire |
| **1858** | • Completion of British rule over India (Ch. 26) |
| **1859–1885** | • French conquest of Vietnam (Ch. 26) |
| **1861–1865** | • U.S. Civil War (Ch. 27) |
| **1867** | • Meiji Restoration in Japan (Ch. 26) |
| **1869** | • Completion of Suez Canal |
| **1870s–1914** | • Second Industrial Revolution (Ch. 23) |
| **1880–1914** | • Most of Africa falls under European rule; height of New Imperialism in Asia and Africa |
| **1884–1885** | • Berlin Conference |
| **1898** | • Spanish-American War (Ch. 27) |
| **1899** | • Kipling, "The White Man's Burden"; Amin, *The Liberation of Women* |
| **1899–1902** | • South African War |
| **1902** | • Conrad, *Heart of Darkness*; Hobson, *Imperialism* |
| **1908** | • Young Turks seize power in Ottoman Empire |
| **1911** | • Chinese revolution (Ch. 26) |

# 26

# Asia and the Pacific in the Era of Imperialism

## 1800–1914

**DURING THE NINETEENTH CENTURY THE SOCIETIES OF ASIA UNDERWENT** enormous changes as a result of population growth, social unrest, and the looming presence of Western imperialist powers. At the beginning of the century Spain, the Netherlands, and Britain had colonies in the Philippines, modern Indonesia, and India, respectively. By the end of the century much more land—most of the southern tier of Asia, from India to the Philippines—had been made colonies of Western powers. Most of these colonies became tied to the industrializing world as exporters of agricultural products or raw materials, including timber, rubber, tin, sugar, tea, cotton, and jute. The Western presence brought benefits, especially to educated residents of major cities, where the colonizers often introduced modern public health, communications, and educational systems. Still, cultural barriers between the colonizers and the colonized were huge, and the Western presence rankled.

Not all the countries in Asia were reduced to colonies. Although Western powers put enormous pressures on China and exacted many concessions from it, China remained politically independent. Much more impressively, Japan became the first non-Western nation to meet the many-sided challenge of Western expansion. Japan emerged from the nineteenth-century crisis stronger than any other Asian nation, becoming the first non-Western country to industrialize successfully. By the end of this period Japan had become an imperialist power itself.

# India and the British Empire in Asia

### In what ways did India change as a consequence of British rule?

Arriving in India on the heels of the Portuguese in the seventeenth century, the British East India Company outmaneuvered French and Dutch rivals and was there to pick up the pieces as the Mughal Empire decayed during the eighteenth century (see "From the British East India Company to the British Empire in India" in Chapter 17). By 1757 the company had gained control over much of India. During the nineteenth century the British government replaced the company, progressively unified the subcontinent, and harnessed its economy to British interests.

Travel and communication between Britain and India became much faster, safer, and more predictable in this period. The time it took to travel to India from Britain dropped from six months to three weeks, due both to the development of steamships and the 1869 opening of the Suez Canal. Whereas at the beginning of the nineteenth century someone in England had to wait a year or more to get an answer to a letter sent to India, by 1870 it took only a couple of months—or, if the matter was urgent, only a few hours by telegraph.

## The Evolution of British Rule

In India the British ruled with the cooperation of local princely allies. To assert their authority, the British disbanded and disarmed local armies, introduced simpler private property laws, and enhanced the powers of local princes and religious leaders, both Hindu and Muslim. The British administrators were on the whole competent and concerned about the welfare of the Indian peasants. Slavery was outlawed and banditry suppressed, and new laws designed to improve women's position in society were introduced. Sati (widow suicide) was outlawed in 1829, legal protection of widow remarriage was extended in 1856, and infanticide (disproportionately of female newborns) was banned in 1870.

**Breakfast at Home** In India the families of British civil servants could live more comfortably than they could back home. The artist Augustus Jules Bouvier captured their lifestyle in this 1842 engraving. (*The Breakfast*, plate 3 from "Anglo Indians," engraving by J. Bouvier, 1842/The Stapleton Collection/ Bridgeman Images)

The last armed resistance to British rule occurred in 1857. By that date the British military presence in India had grown to include 200,000 Indian sepoy troops and 38,000 British officers. In 1857 groups of sepoys, especially around Delhi, revolted in what the British called the **Great Mutiny** and the Indians called the **Great Revolt**. The sepoys' grievances were many, ranging from the use of fat from cows (sacred to Hindus) and pigs (regarded as filthy by Muslims) to grease rifle cartridges to high tax rates and the incorporation of low-caste soldiers into the army. The insurrection spread rapidly throughout northern and central India before it was finally crushed, primarily by native troops from other parts of India loyal to the British.

Although princely states were allowed to continue, after 1858 Britain ruled India much more tightly. India was governed by the British Parliament in London and administered by a civil service in India, the upper echelons of which were all white. In 1900 this elite consisted of fewer than 3,500 top officials for a population of 300 million.

## The Socioeconomic Effects of British Rule

The impact of British rule on the Indian economy was multifaceted. In the early stages, the British East India Company expanded agricultural production, creating large plantations. Early crops were opium to export to China (see "The Opium War") and tea to substitute for imports from China. India gradually replaced China as the leading exporter of tea to Europe. Clearing land for tea and coffee plantations, along with massive commercial logging operations, led to extensive deforestation.

To aid the transport of goods, people, and information, the colonial administration invested heavily in India's infrastructure. By 1855 India's major cities had all been linked by telegraph and railroads, and postal service was being extended to local villages. By 1900 the rail network extended 25,000 miles, serving 188 million passengers. By then over 370,000 Indians worked for the railroads. Irrigation also received attention, and by 1900 India had the world's most extensive irrigation system.

At the same time, Indian production of textiles suffered a huge blow. Britain imported India's raw cotton but exported machine-spun yarn and machine-woven cloth, displacing millions of Indian hand-spinners and hand-weavers. By 1900 India was buying 40 percent of Britain's cotton exports. Not until 1900 were small steps taken toward industrializing India. By 1914 about a million Indians worked in factories.

Although the economy expanded, the poor did not see much improvement in their standard of living. Tenant farming and landlessness increased with the growth in plantation agriculture, and increases in production were eaten up by increases in population. There was also a negative side to improved transportation. As Indians traveled more widely on the convenient trains, disease spread, especially cholera, which is transmitted by exposure to contaminated water. Pilgrims customarily bathed in and drank from sacred pools and rivers, worsening this problem. Despite improvements made to sanitation, in 1900 four out of every one thousand residents of British India still died of cholera each year.

## The British and the Indian Educated Elite

The Indian middle class probably gained more than the poor from British rule, because they were the ones to benefit from the English-language educational system Britain established in India. As a result of their education, high-caste Hindus came to form a new elite profoundly influenced by Western thought and culture. In addition, because Britain placed under the same general system of law and administration the various Hindu and Muslim peoples of the subcontinent who had resisted one another for centuries, university graduates tended to look on themselves as Indians more than as residents of separate states and kingdoms. This new perspective was a necessary step for the development of Indian nationalism.

Some Indian intellectuals sought to reconcile the values of the modern West and their own traditions. Rammohun Roy (1772–1833), who had risen to the top of the native ranks in the British East India Company, founded a college that offered instruction in Western languages and subjects. He also founded a society to reform traditional customs, especially child marriage, the caste system, and restrictions on widows. He espoused a modern Hinduism founded on the *Upanishads* (oo-PAH-nih-shadz), the ancient sacred texts of Hinduism.

The more that Western-style education was developed in India, the more the inequalities of the system became apparent to educated Indians. Indians were eligible to take the examinations for entry into the elite **Indian Civil Service**, the bureaucracy that administered the Indian government, but the exams were given in England. Since few Indians could travel such a long distance to take the test, in 1870 only 1 of the 916 members of the service was Indian. In other words, no matter how Anglicized educated Indians became, they could never become the white rulers' equals. The top jobs, the best clubs, the modern hotels, and even certain railroad compartments were sealed off to brown-skinned men and women. Most of the British elite considered the jumble of Indian peoples and castes to be racially inferior. The peasant masses might accept such inequality as the latest version of age-old class and caste hierarchies, but the well-educated, English-speaking elite eventually could not. They had studied not only Milton and Shakespeare but also English traditions of democracy, liberty, and national pride.

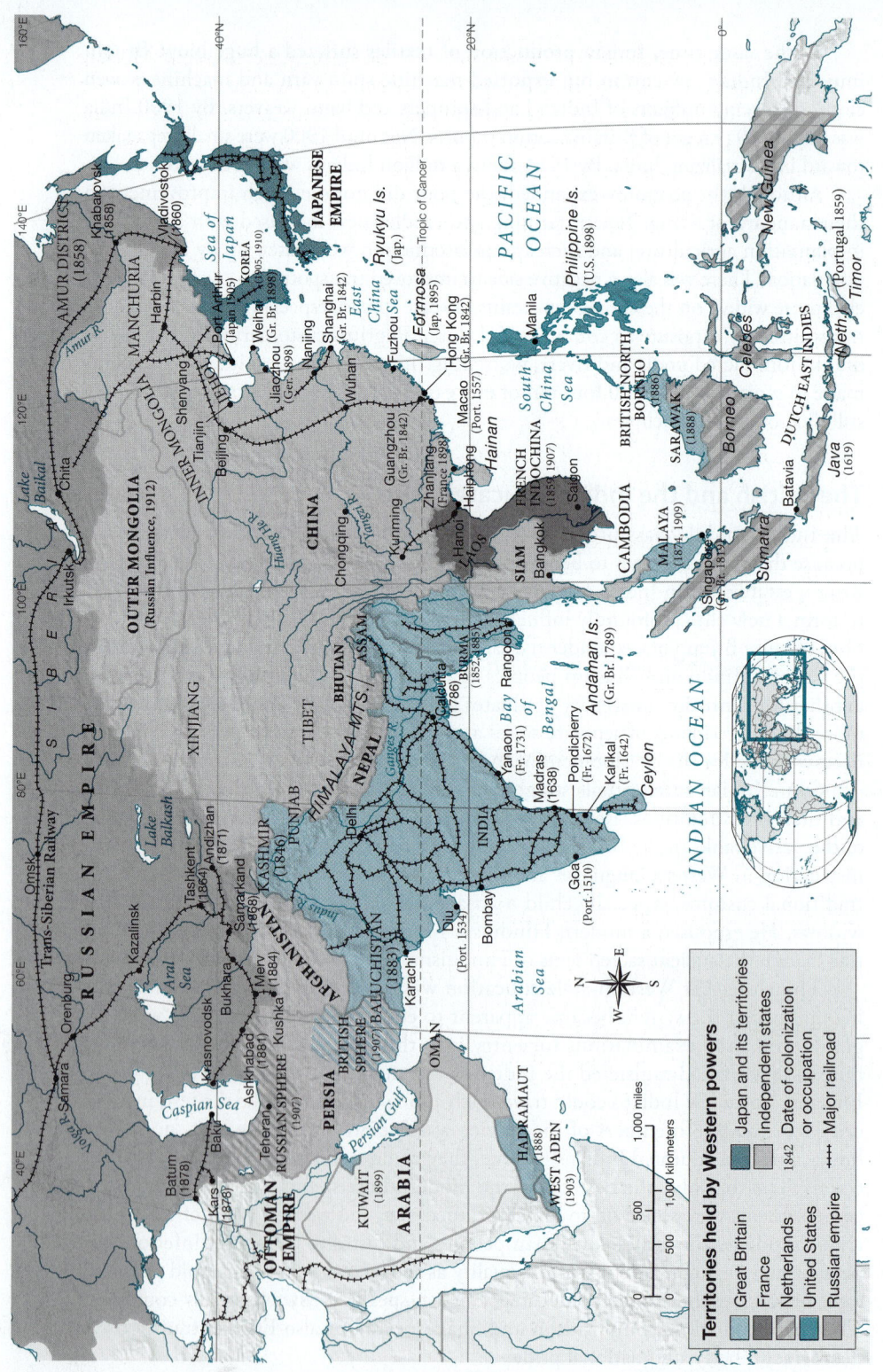

160°E
140°E
40°N
20°N
0°

AMUR DISTRICT (1858)
Khabarovsk (1858)
Vladivostok (1860)
Sea of Japan
JAPANESE EMPIRE
Ryukyu Is. (Jap.)
Tropic of Cancer

PACIFIC OCEAN

New Guinea
Timor (Portugal 1859) (Neth.)

MANCHURIA
Harbin
Port Arthur (Japan 1905)
Weiha (Gr. Br. 1898)
(1905,1910)
JEHOL
KOREA
East China Sea
Formosa (Jap. 1895)

Philippine Is. (U.S. 1898)

Amur R.
Shenyang
Jiaozhou (Ger. 1898)
Shanghai
Nanjing
Fuzhou Sea
Hong Kong (Gr. Br. 1842)
Manila

Chita
INNER MONGOLIA
Tianjin
Beijing
Wuhan
Macao (Port. 1557)
South China Sea

BRITISH NORTH BORNEO (1886)

SIBERIA
Irkutsk
OUTER MONGOLIA (Russian Influence, 1912)
CHINA
Guangzhou
Guangzhou (Gr. Br. 1842)
Zhanjiang (France 1898)
Hainan
SARAWAK (1888)
Borneo
Celebes

Lake Baikal
Chongqing
Kunming
Haiphong
Hanoi
FRENCH INDOCHINA (1859,1907)
Laos
DUTCH EAST INDIES

Huang He R.
Yangtze
XINJIANG
CAMBODIA
Saigon
Java (1619)
Batavia

RUSSIAN EMPIRE
Trans-Siberian Railway
Omsk
Lake Balkash
TIBET
BHUTAN
HIMALAYA MTS.
ASSAM
BURMA (1852,1885)
Rangoon (1786)
SIAM
Bangkok
MALAYA (1874,1909)
Sumatra
Singapore (Gr. Br. 1819)

Kazalinsk
Tashkent
Andizhan (1871)
NEPAL
Ganges R.
Calcutta
Bay of Bengal
Andaman Is. (Gr. Br. 1789)

Orenburg
Aral Sea
Samarkand (1868)
KASHMIR (1846)
PUNJAB
Delhi
INDIA
Yanaon (Fr. 1731)
Madras (1638)
Pondicherry (Fr. 1672)
Karikal (Fr. 1642)
Ceylon

Volga R.
Samara
Bukhara
Merv (1884)
Kushka (1881)
AFGHANISTAN
Indus R.
BALUCHISTAN (1883)
Diu (Port. 1534)
Goa (Port. 1510)
Bombay

Kazalinsk
Krasnovodsk
Ashkhabad (1881)
BRITISH SPHERE (1907)
Karachi

INDIAN OCEAN

Batum (1878)
Baku
Teheran
PERSIA
RUSSIAN SPHERE (1907)
Kars (1878)
Caspian Sea
OMAN
Arabian Sea

OTTOMAN EMPIRE
KUWAIT (1899)
ARABIA
HADRAMAUT (1888)
WEST ADEN (1903)
Persian Gulf

N
W   E
S

1,000 miles
1,000 kilometers
500
500
0
0

**Territories held by Western powers**

| | |
|---|---|
| Great Britain | Japan and its territories |
| France | Independent states |
| Netherlands | 1842 Date of colonization or occupation |
| United States | ╋╋╋ Major railroad |
| Russian empire | |

In the late nineteenth century the colonial ports of Calcutta, Bombay, and Madras, now all linked by railroads, became centers of intellectual ferment. In these and other cities, newspapers in English and in regional languages gained influence. By 1885, when a group of educated Indians came together to found the **Indian National Congress**, demands were increasing for the equality and self-government that Britain had already granted white-settler colonies such as Canada and Australia. The Congress Party called for more opportunities for Indians in the Indian Civil Service and reallocation of the government budget from military expenditures to the alleviation of poverty. The party advocated unity across religious and caste lines, but most members were upper-caste, Western-educated Hindus.

Defending British possessions in India became a key element of Britain's foreign policy during the nineteenth century and led to steady expansion of the territory Britain controlled in Asia. By 1852 the British had annexed Burma (now Myanmar), administering it as a province of India (Map 26.1). The establishment of a British base in Singapore was followed by expansion into Malaya (now Malaysia) in the 1870s and 1880s. In both Burma and Malaya, Britain tried to foster economic development, building railroads and promoting trade. Burma became a major exporter of timber and rice, Malaya of tin and rubber. So many laborers were brought into Malaya for the expanding mines and plantations that its population came to be approximately one-third Malay, one-third Chinese, and one-third Indian.

# Competition for Southeast Asia

### Why were most but not all Southeast Asian societies reduced to colonies?

At the beginning of the nineteenth century only a small part of Southeast Asia was under direct European control. By the end of the century most of the region would be in foreign hands.

## The Dutch East Indies

Although Dutch forts and trading posts in the East Indies dated back to the seventeenth century, in 1816 the Dutch ruled little more than the island of Java. Thereafter they gradually brought almost all of the 3,000-mile-long archipelago under their political authority. In extending their rule, the Dutch, like the British in India, brought diverse peoples with different languages and distinct cultural traditions into a single political entity (see Map 26.1).

Taking over the Dutch East India Company in 1799, the Dutch government modified the company's loose control of Java and gradually built a modern bureaucratic state. Javanese resistance to Dutch rule led to the bloody **Java War** (1825–1830). In 1830, after the war, the Dutch abolished the combination of tribute from rulers and forced labor from peasants that they had used to obtain spices, and they

< **MAP 26.1   Asia in 1914**
India remained under British rule, while China precariously preserved its political independence. The Dutch Empire in modern-day Indonesia was old, but French control of Indochina was a product of the New Imperialism.

established instead a particularly exploitive policy called the Culture System. Under this system, Indonesian peasants were forced to plant a fifth of their land in export crops, especially coffee and sugar, to turn over to the Dutch as tax.

At the end of the nineteenth century the Dutch began to encourage Western education in the East Indies. The children of local rulers and privileged elites, much like their counterparts in India, encountered new ideas in Dutch-language schools. They began to question the long-standing cooperation of local elites with Dutch colonialism, and they searched for a new national identity. Thus anticolonial nationalism began to take shape in the East Indies and would blossom after World War I.

## Mainland Southeast Asia

Unlike India and Java, mainland Southeast Asia had escaped European rule during the eighteenth century. In 1802 the **Nguyen Dynasty** (1802–1945) came to power in Vietnam, putting an end to thirty years of peasant rebellion and civil war. For the first time in the country's history, a single Vietnamese monarchy ruled the entire country. Working through a centralized bureaucracy fashioned on the Chinese model, the Nguyen (GWIHN) Dynasty energetically built irrigation canals, roads and bridges, and impressive palaces in Hue (HWAY), the new capital city. Construction placed a heavy burden on the peasants drafted to do the work, and this hardship contributed to a resurgence of peasant unrest.

Roman Catholic missionaries from France posed a second, more dangerous threat to Vietnam's Confucian ruling elite. Believing that Christianity would undermine Confucian moral values, in 1825 King Minh Mang (r. 1820–1841) outlawed the teaching of Christianity, and soon his government began executing Catholic missionaries and Vietnamese converts. Persecution continued under his successors, and as many as thirty thousand Vietnamese Christians were executed in the 1850s. In response, in 1859–1860 a French naval force seized Saigon and three surrounding provinces in southern Vietnam, making that part of Vietnam a French colony. In 1884–1885 France conquered the rest of the country, and Laos and Cambodia were added to form French Indochina in 1887. In all three countries the local rulers were left on their thrones, but France dominated and tried to promote French culture.

After Japan's victory over Russia in 1905, a new generation of Vietnamese saw Japan as a model for Vietnamese revitalization and independence. They went to Japan to study and planned for anticolonial revolution in Vietnam.

In all of Southeast Asia, only Siam (today Thailand) succeeded in preserving its independence. Siam was

**The French Governor General and the Vietnamese Emperor**  The twelfth emperor of the Nguyen Dynasty, Khai Dinh (1885–1925), had to find ways to get along with the French governor general (in this picture, Albert Sarraut) if he wished to preserve his dynasty. Seen here in 1917 or 1918, he had adopted Western leather shoes but otherwise tried to keep a distinct Vietnamese identity in his dress. (Maurice-Louis Branger/Roger-Viollet/Getty Images)

sandwiched between the British in Burma and the French in Indochina. Siam's very able king, Chulalongkorn (r. 1868–1910), took advantage of this situation to balance the two competitors against each other. Chulalongkorn had studied Greek and Latin and Western science and kept up with Western news by reading British newspapers from Hong Kong and Singapore. He outlawed slavery and implemented modernizing reforms that centralized the government so that it could more effectively control outlying provinces coveted by the imperialists. Independent Siam gradually developed a modern centralizing state similar to those constructed by Western imperialists in their Asian possessions.

## The Philippines

The United States became one of the imperialist powers in Asia when it took the Philippines from Spain in 1898. When the Spanish established rule in the Philippines in the sixteenth century, the islands had no central government or literate culture; order was maintained by village units dominated by local chiefs. Under the Spanish, Roman Catholic churches were established, and Spanish priests able to speak the local languages became the most common intermediaries between local populations and the new rulers. The government of Spain encouraged Spaniards to colonize the Philippines and granted them the exclusive right to control public affairs and collect taxes in a specific locality of the Philippines. A local Filipino elite also developed, aided by the Spanish introduction of private ownership of land. Manila developed into an important entrepôt in the galleon trade between Mexico and China, and this trade also attracted a large Chinese community, which handled much of the trade within the Philippines.

In the late nineteenth century wealthy Filipinos began to send their sons to study abroad, and a movement to press Spain for reforms emerged among those who had been abroad. When the Spanish cracked down on critics, a rebellion erupted in 1896.

In 1898 war between Spain and the United States broke out in Cuba (see "The Spanish-American War" in Chapter 27), and in May the American naval commodore George Dewey sailed into Manila Bay and sank the Spanish fleet anchored there. Dewey called on the Filipino rebels to help defeat the Spanish forces, but when the rebels declared independence, the U.S. government refused to recognize them. U.S. forces fought the Filipino rebels, and by the end of the insurrection in 1902 the war had cost the lives of five thousand Americans and about two hundred thousand Filipinos. In the following years the United States introduced a form of colonial rule that included public works and economic development projects, improved education and medicine, and, in 1907, an elected legislative assembly.

# China Under Pressure

**Was China's decline in the nineteenth century due more to internal problems or to Western imperialism?**

In 1800 most Chinese had no reason to question the concept of China as the central kingdom. A century later China's world standing had sunk precipitously. In 1900 foreign troops marched into China's capital to protect foreign nationals, and more and more Chinese had come to think that their government, society, and cultural values needed to be radically changed.

## The Opium War

Seeing little to gain from trade with European countries, the Qing (Manchu) emperors, who had been ruling China since 1644 (see "The Rise of the Manchus" in Chapter 21), permitted Europeans to trade only at the port of Guangzhou (Canton) and only through licensed Chinese merchants. Initially, the balance of trade was in China's favor. Great Britain and the other Western nations used silver to pay for tea, since they had not been able to find anything the Chinese wanted to buy. By the 1820s, however, the British had found something the Chinese would buy: opium. Grown legally in British-occupied India, opium was smuggled into China, where its use and sale were illegal. Huge profits and the cravings of addicts led to rapid increases in sales, from 4,500 chests a year in 1810 to 10,000 in 1830 and 40,000 in 1838. At this point it was China that suffered a drain of silver, since it was importing more than it was exporting.

To deal with this crisis, the Chinese government dispatched Lin Zexu to Guangzhou in 1839. He dealt harshly with Chinese who purchased opium and seized the opium stores of British merchants. Lin even wrote to Queen Victoria: "Suppose there were people from another country who carried opium for sale to England and seduced your people into buying and smoking it; certainly your honorable ruler would deeply hate it and be bitterly aroused."[1] But although for years the little community of foreign merchants had accepted Chinese rules, by 1839 the British, the dominant group, were ready to flex their muscles. British merchants wanted to create a market for their goods in China and get tea more cheaply by trading closer to its source in central China. They also wanted a European-style diplomatic relationship with China, with envoys and ambassadors, commercial treaties, and published tariffs. With the encouragement of their merchants in China, the British sent an expeditionary force from India with forty-two warships.

With its control of the seas, the British easily shut down key Chinese ports and forced the Chinese to negotiate. Dissatisfied with the resulting agreement, the British sent a second, larger force, which took even more coastal cities, including Shanghai. This **Opium War** was settled at gunpoint in 1842. The Treaty of Nanjing and subsequent agreements opened five ports to international trade, fixed the tariff on imported goods at 5 percent, imposed an indemnity of 21 million ounces of silver on China to cover Britain's war expenses, and ceded the island of Hong Kong to Britain. Through the clause on **extraterritoriality** (the legal principle that exempts individuals from local law), British subjects in China became answerable only to British law, even in disputes with Chinese. The treaties also had a "most-favored nation" clause, which meant that whenever one nation extracted a new privilege from China, it was extended automatically to Britain.

The treaties satisfied neither side. China continued to refuse to accept foreign diplomats at its capital in Beijing, and the expansion of trade fell far short of Western expectations. Between 1856 and 1860 Britain and France renewed hostilities with China. British and French troops occupied Beijing and set the emperor's summer palace on fire. Another round of harsh treaties gave European merchants and missionaries greater privileges and forced the Chinese to open several more cities to foreign trade.

## Internal Problems

China's problems in the nineteenth century were not all of foreign origin. By 1850 China, for centuries the world's most populous country, had more than 400 million people. As the population grew, farm size shrank, forests were put to the plow, surplus labor suppressed wages, and conflicts over rights to water and tenancy increased. Hard times also led to increased female infanticide, as families felt that they could not afford to raise more than two or three children and saw sons as necessities.

These economic and demographic circumstances led to some of the most destructive rebellions in China's history. The worst was the **Taiping Rebellion** (1851–1864), in which some 20 million people lost their lives, making it one of the bloodiest wars in world history. The Taiping (TIGH-ping) Rebellion was initiated by Hong Xiuquan (hong shoh-chwan) (1814–1864). After reading a Christian tract given to him by a missionary, Hong interpreted visions he had had to mean he was Jesus's younger brother and had a mission to wipe out evil in China. He soon gathered followers, whom he instructed to destroy idols and ancestral temples, give up opium and alcohol, and renounce foot binding and prostitution. In 1851 he declared himself king of the Heavenly Kingdom of Great Peace (Taiping), an act of open insurrection.

By 1853 the Taiping rebels had moved north and established their capital at the major city of Nanjing, which they held on to for a decade. From this base they set about creating a utopian society based on the equalization of landholdings and the equality of men and women. To suppress the Taipings, the Manchus had to turn to Chinese scholar-officials, who raised armies on their own, revealing the Manchus' military weakness.

## The Self-Strengthening Movement

After the various rebellions were suppressed, forward-looking reformers began addressing the Western threat. Under the slogan "self-strengthening," they set about modernizing the military along Western lines. Some of the most progressive reformers also initiated new industries, which in the 1870s and 1880s included railway lines, steam navigation companies, coal mines, telegraph lines, and cotton spinning and weaving factories.

These measures drew resistance from conservatives, who thought copying Western practices was compounding defeat. A highly placed Manchu official objected that "from ancient down to modern times" there had never been "anyone who could use mathematics to raise a nation from a state of decline or to strengthen it in times of weakness."[2] Yet knowledge of the West gradually improved with more translations and travel in both directions. Newspapers covering world affairs began publication in Shanghai and Hong Kong. By 1880 China had embassies in London, Paris, Berlin, Madrid, Washington, Tokyo, and St. Petersburg.

Despite the enormous effort put into trying to catch up, China was humiliated yet again at the end of the nineteenth century. First came the discovery that Japan had so successfully modernized that it easily defeated China in a contest over Korea. China's helplessness in the face of aggression led to a scramble among the European powers for concessions and protectorates in China. At the high point of this rush in 1898, it appeared that the European powers might actually divide China among themselves, the way they had recently divided Africa.

**Boxer Soldiers in Beijing** Although known in the foreign press for their cultivation of traditional martial arts, some Boxers were armed with modern rifles and became an intimidating presence in Tianjin and Beijing in 1899–1900. (Pictures from History/Bridgeman Images)

## Republican Revolution

In 1898 a group of educated young reformers gained access to the twenty-seven-year-old Qing emperor. They warned him of the fate of Poland (divided by the European powers in the eighteenth century; see "Enlightened Absolutism and Its Limits" in Chapter 19) and regaled him with the triumphs of the Meiji reformers in Japan. They proposed redesigning China as a constitutional monarchy with modern financial and educational systems. For three months the emperor issued a series of reform decrees. But the Manchu establishment and the empress dowager felt threatened and not only suppressed the reform movement but imprisoned the emperor as well. Hope for reform from the top was dashed.

A period of violent reaction swept the country, reaching its peak in 1900 with the uprising of a secret society that foreigners dubbed the **Boxers**. The Boxers blamed China's ills on foreigners, especially Christian missionaries. After the Boxers laid siege to the foreign legation quarter in Beijing, a dozen nations, including Japan, sent twenty thousand troops to lift the siege. In the negotiations that followed, China had to agree to cancel civil service examinations and pay a staggering indemnity.

After this defeat, gradual reform lost its appeal. More and more Chinese were studying abroad and learning about Western political ideas, including democracy and revolution. The most famous was Sun Yatsen (1866–1925). Sent by his peasant family to Hawaii, he learned English and then continued his education in Hong Kong. From 1894 on, he spent his time abroad organizing revolutionary societies. He joined forces with Chinese student revolutionaries studying in Japan, and together they sparked the **1911 Revolution**, which brought China's long history of monarchy to an end, to be replaced by a Western-style republic. China had escaped direct foreign rule but would never be the same.

# Japan's Rapid Transformation

**How was Japan able to quickly master the challenges posed by the West?**

During the eighteenth century Japan (much more effectively than China) kept foreign merchants and missionaries at bay. It limited trade to a single port (Nagasaki), where only the Dutch were allowed, and forbade Japanese to travel abroad. Because Japan's land and population were so much smaller than China's, the Western powers never expected much from Japan as a trading partner and did not press it as urgently. Still, the European threat was part of what propelled Japan to modernize.

## The "Opening" of Japan

Wanting to play a greater role in the Pacific, the United States decided to force the Japanese to open to trade. In 1853 Commodore Matthew Perry steamed into Edo (now Tokyo) Bay and demanded diplomatic negotiations with the emperor. Under threat of this **gunboat diplomacy**, and after consulting with the daimyo (major lords), the shogunate officials signed a treaty with the United States that opened two ports and permitted trade.

Japan at this time was a complex society. The emperor in Kyoto had no effective powers. For more than two hundred years real power had been in the hands of the Tokugawa shogun in Edo (AY-doh) (see "Tokugawa Government" in Chapter 21). The country was divided into numerous domains, each under a daimyo (DIGH-myoh). Each daimyo had under him samurai, warriors who had hereditary stipends and privileges, such as the right to wear a sword. Peasants and merchants were also legally distinct classes, and in theory social mobility from peasant to merchant or merchant to samurai was impossible. After two centuries of peace, there were many more samurai than were needed to administer or defend the country, and many lived very modestly. They were proud, however, and felt humiliated by the sudden American intrusion and the unequal treaties that the Western countries imposed. Some began agitating against the shogunate under the slogan "Revere the emperor and expel the barbarians."

When foreign diplomats and merchants began to settle in Yokohama after 1858, radical samurai reacted with a wave of antiforeign terrorism and antigovernment assassinations. The response from Western powers was swift and unambiguous. An allied fleet of American, British, Dutch, and French warships was sent to demolish key Japanese forts, further weakening the power and prestige of the shogun's government.

## The Meiji Restoration

In 1867 a coalition of reform-minded daimyo led a coup that overthrew the Tokugawa Shogunate. The samurai who led this coup declared a return to direct rule by the emperor, which had not been practiced in Japan for more than six hundred years. This emperor was called the Meiji (MAY-jee) emperor and this event the **Meiji Restoration**. The domain leaders who organized the coup, called the Meiji Oligarchs, moved the boy emperor to Tokyo castle but kept real power in their own hands.

The battle cry of the Meiji reformers had been "strong army, rich nation." Convinced that they could not beat the West until they had mastered the secrets of its military and industrial might, the oligarchs initiated a series of measures to reform Japan along modern Western lines. Within four years a delegation was traveling the world to learn what made the Western powers strong. Its members examined everything from the U.S. Constitution to the factories, shipyards, and railroads that made the European landscape so different from Japan's.

Japan under the shoguns had been decentralized, with most of the power over the population in the hands of the many daimyo. By elevating the emperor, the oligarchs were able to centralize the government. In 1871 they abolished the domains and merged the domain armies, dismantling the four-class legal system. This amounted to stripping the samurai (7 to 8 percent of the population) of their privileges. Even their monopoly on the use of force was eliminated: the new army recruited commoners along with samurai. Not surprisingly, some samurai rose up against their loss of privileges. None of these uncoordinated uprisings made any difference.

Several leaders of the Meiji Restoration, in France on a fact-finding mission during the Franco-Prussian War of 1870–1871, were impressed by the active participation of French citizens in the defense of Paris. For Japan to survive in the hostile international environment, they concluded, ordinary people had to be trained to fight. Consequently, a conscription law, modeled on the French law, was issued in 1872. To improve the training of soldiers, the new War College was organized along German lines, and German instructors were recruited to teach there. Young samurai were trained to form the new professional officer corps.

Many of the new institutions established in the Meiji period reached down to the local level. Schools open to all were rapidly introduced beginning in 1872. Teachers were trained in newly established teachers' colleges, where they learned to inculcate discipline, patriotism, and morality. Another modern institution that reached the local level was a national police force, and soon one- or two-man police stations were set up throughout the country. These policemen came to act as local agents of the central government, enforcing public health rules, conscription laws, and codes of behavior.

In 1889 Japan became the first non-Western country to adopt the constitutional form of government. A commission sent abroad to study European constitutional governments had come to the conclusion that the German constitutional monarchy would provide the best model for Japan, rather than the more democratic governments of the British, French, and Americans. Japan's new government set up a two-house parliament. The upper house of lords was drawn largely from former daimyo and nobles, and the lower house was elected by a limited electorate (about 5 percent of the adult male population in 1890). The emperor was declared "sacred and inviolable." He had the right to appoint the prime minister and cabinet.

Cultural change during the Meiji period was as profound as political change. For more than a thousand years China had been the major source of ideas and technologies introduced into Japan. But in the late nineteenth century China, beset by Western pressure, had become an object lesson on the dangers of stagnation. The influential author Fukuzawa Yukichi began urging Japan to pursue "civilization and enlightenment," by which he meant Western civilization. Soon Japanese were being told to conform to Western taste, eat meat, wear Western-style clothes, and drop customs that Westerners found odd, such as married women's blackening their teeth.

## Industrialization

The leaders of the Meiji Restoration, wanting to strengthen Japan's military capacity, promoted industrialization. The government recruited foreign experts and sent Japanese abroad to study science and engineering.

The government also played an active role in getting railroads, mines, and factories started. Early on, the Japanese government decided to compete with China in the export of tea and silk to the West. Introducing the mechanical reeling of silk gave Japan a strong price advantage in the sale of silk, and Japan's total foreign trade increased tenfold from 1877 to 1900. The next stage was to develop heavy industry.

A huge indemnity exacted from China in 1895, as part of the peace agreement, was used to establish the Yawata Iron and Steel Works. The third stage of Japan's industrialization would today be called import substitution. Factories such as cotton mills were set up to help cut the importation of Western consumer goods.

Most of the great Japanese industrial conglomerates known as *zaibatsu* (zigh-BAHT-dzoo), such as Mitsubishi, got their start in this period, often founded by men with government connections. Sometimes the government set up plants that it then sold to private investors at bargain prices. Successful entrepreneurs were treated as patriotic heroes.

As in Europe, the early stages of industrialization brought hardship to the countryside. Farmers often rioted as their incomes failed to keep up with prices or as their tax burdens grew. Workers in modern industries were no happier, and in 1898 railroad workers went on strike for better working conditions and overtime pay. Still, rice production increased, death rates dropped as public health was improved, and the population grew from about 33 million in 1868 to about 45 million in 1900.

## Japan as an Imperial Power

During the course of the Meiji period, Japan became an imperial power, making Taiwan and Korea into its colonies. The conflicts that led to Japanese acquisition of both of them revolved around Korea.

In the second half of the nineteenth century, Korea found itself caught between China, Japan, and Russia, each trying to protect or extend its sphere of influence. Westerners also began demanding that Korea be "opened." Korea's first response was to insist that its foreign relations be handled through Beijing. Matters were complicated by the rise in the 1860s of a religious cult with strong xenophobic elements.

In 1871 the U.S. minister to China took five warships to try to open Korea, but left after exchanges of fire resulted in 250 Koreans dead without any progress in getting the Korean government to make concessions. Japan tried next and in 1876 forced the Korean government to sign an unequal treaty and open three ports to Japanese trade. On China's urging, Korea also signed treaties with the European powers in an effort to counterbalance Japan.

Over the next couple of decades reformers in China and Japan tried to encourage Korea to adopt its own self-strengthening movement, but Korean conservatives did their best to undo reform efforts. In 1894, when a religious cult rose in a massive revolt, both China and Japan sent military forces, claiming to come to the Korean government's aid. They ended up fighting each other instead in what is known as the Sino-Japanese War. With its decisive victory, Japan gained Taiwan from China and was able to make Korea a protectorate. In 1910 Korea was formally annexed as a province of Japan.

Japan also competed aggressively with the leading European powers for influence and territory in China, particularly in the northeast (Manchuria). There Japanese and Russian imperialism met and collided. In 1904 Japan attacked Russian forces and, after its 1905 victory in the bloody **Russo-Japanese War**, emerged with a valuable foothold in China—Russia's former protectorate over Port Arthur (see Map 26.1).

Japan's victories over China and Russia changed the way European nations looked at Japan. Through negotiations Japan was able to eliminate extraterritoriality in 1899 and gain control of its own tariffs in 1911. Within Japan, the success of the military in raising Japan's international reputation added greatly to its political influence.

# The Pacific Region and the Movement of People

**What were the causes and consequences of the vast movement of people in the Pacific region?**

The nineteenth century was marked by extensive movement of people into, across, and out of Asia and the broad Pacific region. Many of these migrants moved from one Asian country to another, but there was also a growing presence of Europeans in Asia, a consequence of the increasing integration of the world economy.

## Settler Colonies in the Pacific: Australia and New Zealand

The largest share of the Europeans who moved to the Pacific region in the nineteenth century went to the settler colonies in Australia and New Zealand (Map 26.2). In 1770 the English explorer James Cook visited New Zealand, Australia, and Hawaii. All three of these places in time became destinations for migrants.

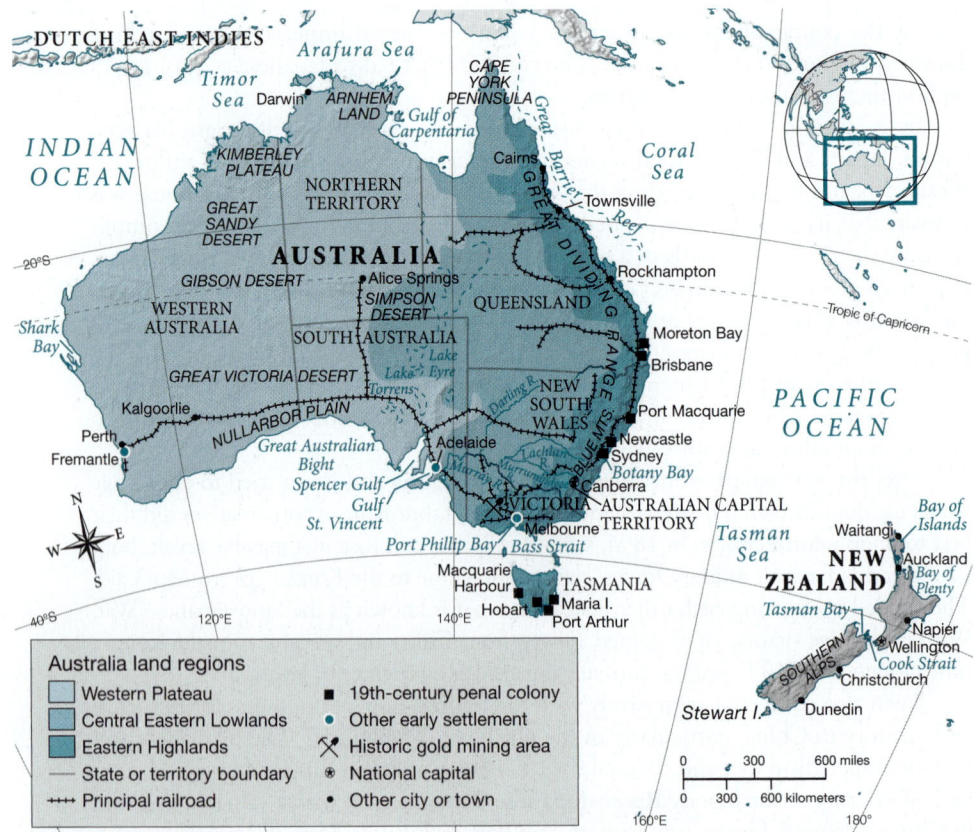

**MAP 26.2  Australia**

Because of the vast deserts in western Australia, cities and industries developed mainly in the east. Australia's early geographical and cultural isolation bred a sense of inferiority. Air travel, the communications revolution, and the massive importation of Japanese products and American popular culture have changed that.

Between 200 and 1300 C.E. Polynesians settled numerous islands of the Pacific, from New Zealand in the south to Hawaii in the north and Easter Island in the east. Thus most of the lands that explorers like Cook encountered were occupied by societies with chiefs, crop agriculture, domestic animals such as chickens and pigs, excellent sailing technology, and often considerable experience in warfare. Australia had been settled millennia earlier by a different population. When Cook arrived in Australia, it was occupied by about three hundred thousand Aborigines who lived entirely by food gathering, fishing, and hunting. Like the Indians of Central and South America, the people in all these lands fell victim to Eurasian diseases and died in large numbers.

Australia was first developed by Britain as a penal colony. Between 1787 and 1869, when the penal colony system was abolished, a total of 161,000 convicts were transported to Australia. After the end of the Napoleonic Wars in 1815, a steady stream of nonconvicts chose to relocate to Australia. Australia is warm, and much of it is desert. Raising sheep proved suitable to Australia's climate, and wool exports steadily increased, from 75,400 pounds in 1821 to 24 million pounds in 1845.

To encourage migration, the Australian government offered free passage and free land to immigrants. By 1850 Australia had five hundred thousand inhabitants. The discovery of gold in Victoria in 1851 quadrupled that number in a few years. The gold rush also provided the financial means for cultural development. Public libraries, museums, art galleries, and universities opened in the thirty years after 1851. These institutions dispensed a distinctly British culture.

Not everyone in Australia was of British origin, however. Chinese and Japanese built the railroads and ran the shops in the towns and the market gardens nearby. Filipinos and Pacific Islanders did the hard work in the sugarcane fields. Afghans and their camels controlled the carrying trade in some areas. But fear that Asian labor would lower living standards and undermine Australia's distinctly British culture led to efforts to keep Australia white.

An unintended consequence of introducing European plants and animals was their escape from farms and harm to native plants and animals. The best-known case is rabbits, purposely imported and released to please hunters in the late 1850s. Within a decade rabbits had become so prevalent that 2 million could be killed each year without having any noticeable effect on the population. Before the end of the century, fences were being widely built to try to keep out rabbits. Today there are an estimated 200 million rabbits in Australia, viewed as a major environmental threat.

Australia gained independence in stages. In 1850 the British Parliament passed the Australian Colonies Government Act, which allowed the four most populous colonies to establish colonial legislatures, determine the franchise, and frame their own constitutions. In 1902 Australia became one of the first countries in the world to give women the vote.

By 1900 New Zealand's population had reached 750,000, only a fifth of Australia's. One major reason more people had not settled these fertile islands was the resistance of the native Maori people. They quickly mastered the use of muskets and tried for decades to keep the British from taking their lands.

Foreign settlement in Hawaii began gradually. Initially, whalers stopped there for supplies, as they did at other Pacific Islands. Missionaries and businessmen came next, and soon other settlers followed, both whites and Asians. A plantation economy developed

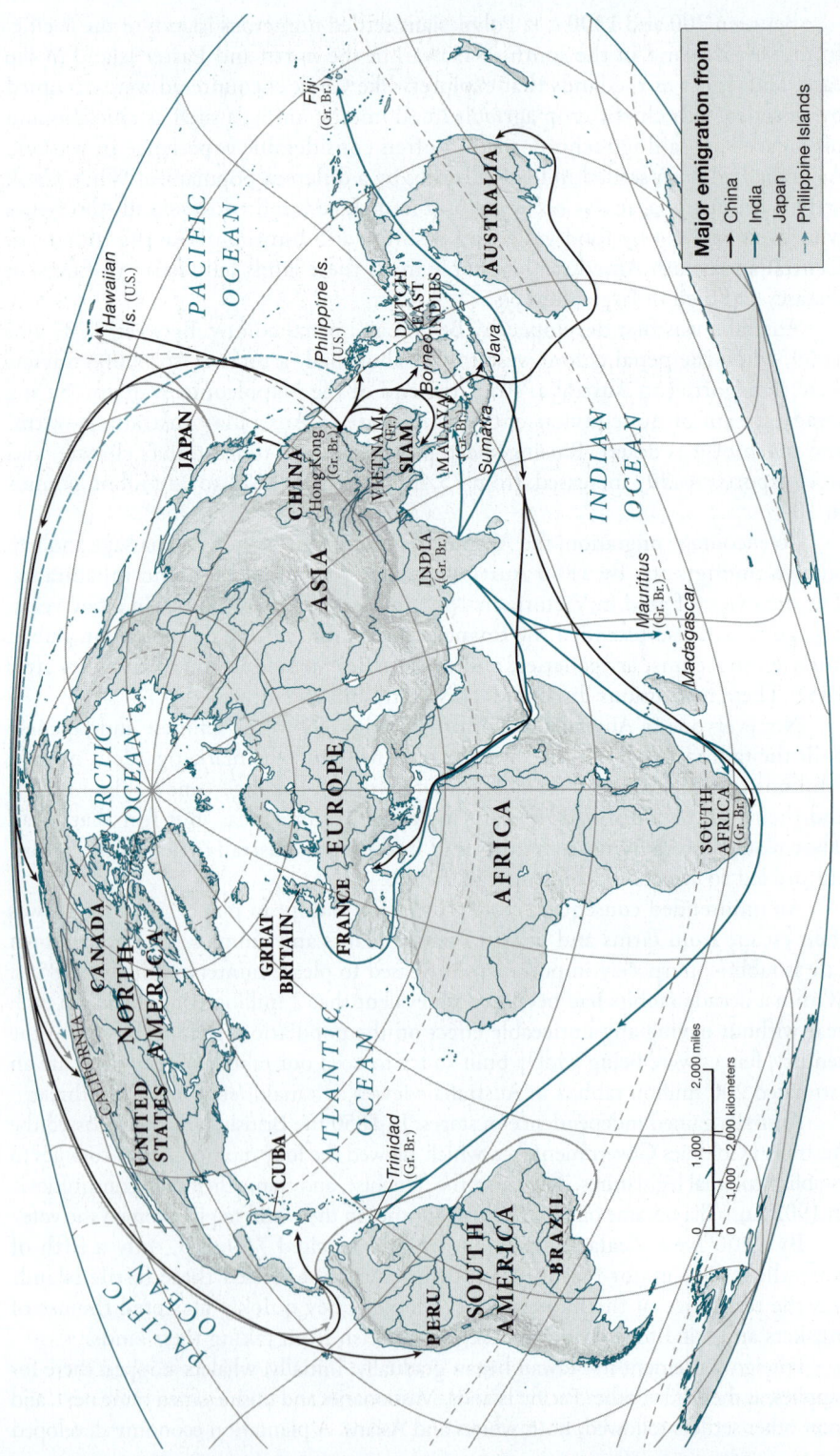

Major emigration from

- China
- India
- Japan
- Philippine Islands

**Maori Chief, 1885**
This photograph depicts Chief Wahanui of the Ngati Maniapoto tribe with his family and friends. The chief had fought in the Maori wars against the British in 1864–1865. Twenty years later, he and his family had adopted many elements of Western material culture.
(Albumen print by Alfred Burton [1834–1914]/Private Collection/ © Michael Graham-Stewart/ Bridgeman Images)

centered on sugarcane. In the 1890s leading settler families overthrew the native monarchy, set up a republic, and urged the United States to annex Hawaii, which it did in 1898.

## Asian Emigration

Like Europeans, Asians left their native countries in unprecedented numbers in the nineteenth century (Map 26.3). As in Europe, both push and pull factors prompted people to leave home. Between 1750 and 1900 world population grew rapidly, in many places tripling. China and India were extremely densely populated countries—China with more than 400 million people in the mid-nineteenth century, India with more than 200 million. Not surprisingly, these two giants were the leading exporters of people in search of work or land. On the pull side were the new opportunities created by the flow of development capital into previously underdeveloped areas. In many of the European colonies in Asia the business class came to consist of both Asian and European migrants. Asian diasporas formed in many parts of the world, with the majority in Asia itself, especially Southeast Asia.

By the nineteenth century Chinese formed key components of mercantile communities throughout Southeast Asia. Chinese often assimilated in Siam and Vietnam, but they rarely did so in Muslim areas such as Indonesia, Catholic areas such as the Philippines, and primitive tribal areas such as northern Borneo. In these places distinct Chinese communities emerged, usually dominated by speakers of a single Chinese dialect.

## < MAP 26.3  Emigration Out of Asia, 1820–1914

As steamships made crossing oceans quicker and more reliable, many people in Asia left their home countries to find new opportunities elsewhere. European imperialism contributed to this flow, especially by recruiting workers for newly established plantations or mines. Many emigrants simply wanted to work a few years to build their savings and planned to return home. Often, however, they ended up staying in their new countries and forming families there.

After Singapore was founded by the British in 1819, Chinese rapidly poured in, soon becoming the dominant ethnic group. In British-controlled Malaya, some Chinese built great fortunes in the tin business, while others worked in the mines. Chinese also settled in the Spanish-controlled Philippines and in Dutch-controlled Indonesia.

Discovery of gold in California in 1848, Australia in 1851, and Canada in 1858 encouraged Chinese to book passage to those places. In California few arrived soon enough to strike gold, but they quickly found work building railroads, and others took up mining in Wyoming and Idaho.

Indian entrepreneurs were similarly attracted by the burgeoning commerce of the growing British Empire. The bulk of Indian emigrants were **indentured laborers**, recruited under contract. The rise of indentured labor from Asia was a direct result of the outlawing of the African slave trade in the early nineteenth century by Britain and the United States. Sugar plantations in the Caribbean and elsewhere needed new sources of workers, and planters in the British colonies discovered that they could recruit Indian laborers to replace blacks. Later in the century many Indians emigrated to British colonies in Africa, the largest numbers to South Africa.

In areas outside the British Empire, China offered the largest supply of ready labor. Starting in the 1840s contractors arrived at Chinese ports to recruit labor for plantations and mines in Cuba, Peru, Hawaii, Sumatra, South Africa, and elsewhere. Chinese laborers did not have the British government to protect them and seem to have suffered even more than Indian workers.

India and China sent more people abroad than any other Asian countries during this period, but they were not alone. As Japan started to industrialize, its cities could not absorb all those forced off the farms, and people began emigrating in significant numbers, many to Hawaii and later to South America. Emigration from the Philippines also was substantial, especially after it became a U.S. territory in 1898.

Asian migration to the United States, Canada, and Australia—the primary destinations of European emigrants—would undoubtedly have been greater if it had not been so vigorously resisted by the white settlers in those regions. In 1882 Chinese were barred from becoming American citizens, and the immigration of Chinese laborers was suspended. Australia also put a stop to Asian immigration with the Commonwealth Immigration Restriction Act of 1901, which established the "white Australia policy" that remained on the books until the 1970s.

Most of the Asian migrants discussed so far were illiterate peasants or business people, not members of traditional educated elites. By the beginning of the twentieth century, however, another group of Asians was going abroad in significant numbers: students. On their return they contributed enormously to the intellectual life of their societies, increasing understanding of the modern Western world and also becoming the most vocal advocates of overthrowing the old order and driving out the colonial masters.

Among the most notable of these foreign-educated radicals were Mohandas Gandhi (1869–1948) (see "Gandhi's Resistance Campaign in India" in Chapter 29) and Sun Yatsen. Sun developed his ideas about the republican form of government while studying in Hawaii and Hong Kong. Gandhi, after studying law in Britain, took a job in South Africa, where he became involved in trying to defend the interests of the Indians who lived and worked there. It was there that he gradually elaborated his idea of passive resistance.

# The Countries of Asia in Comparative Perspective

**What explains the similarities and differences in the experiences of Asian countries in this era?**

At the start of the nineteenth century the societies of Asia varied much more than those of any other part of the world. In the temperate zones of East Asia, the old established monarchies of China, Japan, and Korea were all densely populated and boasted long literary traditions and traditions of unified governments. They had ties to each other that dated back many centuries and shared many elements of their cultures. South of them, in the tropical and subtropical regions, cultures were more diverse. India was just as densely populated as China, Japan, and Korea, but politically and culturally less unified, with several major languages and dozens of independent rulers reigning in kingdoms large and small, not to mention the growing British presence. In both India and Southeast Asia, Islam was much more important than it was in East Asia. All the countries with long written histories and literate elites were at a great remove from the thinly populated and relatively primitive areas without literate cultures and sometimes even without agriculture, such as Australia and some of the islands of the Philippines and Indonesia.

## The Impact of Foreign Domination

The nineteenth century gave the societies of Asia more in common in that all of them in one way or another had come into contact with the expanding West. Still, the Western powers did not treat all the countries the same way. Western powers initially wanted manufactured goods from the more developed Asian societies, especially Indian cotton textiles and Chinese porcelains. At the beginning of the nineteenth century Britain had already gained political control over large parts of India and was intent on forcing China to trade on terms more to its benefit. It paid virtually no attention to Korea and Japan, not seeing in them the same potential for profit. The less developed parts of Asia also attracted increasing Western interest, not because they could provide manufactured goods, but because they offered opportunities for Western development, much as the Americas had earlier.

The West that the societies of Asia faced during the nineteenth century was itself rapidly changing, and the steps taken by Western nations to gain power in Asia naturally also changed over time. Western science and technology were making rapid advances, which gave European armies progressively greater advantages in weaponry. The Industrial Revolution made it possible for countries that industrialized early, such as Britain, to produce huge surpluses of goods for which they had to find markets; this development shifted their interest in Asia from a place to buy goods to a place to sell goods. Britain had been able to profit from its colonization of India, and this profit both encouraged it to consolidate its rule and invited its European rivals to look for their own colonies. For instance, rivalry with Britain led France to seek colonies in Southeast Asia not only for their own sake but also as a way to keep Britain from extending its sphere of influence any farther.

There were some commonalities in the ways Asian countries responded to pressure from outside. In the countries with long literary traditions, often the initial response of the established elite was to try to drive the unwelcome foreigners away. This was the case in China, Japan, and Korea in particular. Violent antiforeign reactions exploded again and again, but the superior military technology of the industrialized West almost invariably prevailed. Some Asian leaders insisted on the need to preserve their cultural traditions at all costs. Others came to the opposite conclusion that the West was indeed superior in some ways and that they would have to adopt European ideas or techniques for their own purposes. This can be seen both among Indians who acquired education in English and in many of the Meiji reformers in Japan. The struggles between the traditionalists and the westernizers were often intense. As nationalism took hold in the West, it found a receptive audience among the educated elites in Asia. How could the assertion that every people had the right to control its own destiny not appeal to the colonized?

## Environmental and Economic Forces

The countries of Asia in the nineteenth century also shared the consequences of rapid economic and environmental change. Some changes were largely positive. Whether they were colonized or not, most countries in Asia witnessed the spread of new technologies. Railroads, telegraphs, modern sanitation, and a wider supply of inexpensive manufactured goods brought fundamental changes in everyday life not only to lands under colonial rule, such as India and Vietnam, but also, if less rapidly, to places that managed to remain independent, such as China and Japan. In fact, the transformation of Japan between 1860 and 1900 was extraordinary. By 1914 Japan had urban conveniences and educational levels comparable to those in Europe.

But negative effects of change were not trivial. Deforestation was pervasive. In areas like China that had experienced deforestation for millennia, the process reached more extreme forms as farmers stripped away all vegetation in their search for fuels for their stoves. In mainland Southeast Asia, where there still were great tropical forests, some were cleared to convert to paddy fields to grow rice for export. In Island Southeast Asia, the extraction of resources by imperial powers led to the harvesting of teak and other highly valued trees at unsustainable levels and the creation of plantations for growing sugar, tobacco, and coffee, employing wage labor. In India, the British colonial government approved clearing large tracts of land for plantations, especially for tea and opium cultivation. It also introduced what it saw as modern scientific forestry that tried to maximize the revenue from forests by controlling the harvesting of trees.

Climate anomalies also had a broad negative impact on Asia in the nineteenth century. In 1815 the eruption of Mount Tambora in eastern Indonesia was one of the most powerful volcanic eruptions in history, resulting in tens of thousands of deaths in the Indonesian islands and hardship around the world because of "the year without a summer" as ash blown into the atmosphere reduced the amount of sunlight reaching the earth.

Equally catastrophic was the effect on monsoon rains of the El Niño Southern Oscillation (ENSO) of 1876–1878, which caused major droughts in India and north China, among other places. The resulting great famines were widely witnessed and written about by the foreign press in both countries, and efforts were made to provide relief, but otherwise the experience in the two countries was quite different because of their different political systems. In India, the recent expansion of the rail lines should have made it easier to move grain, but imperial government officials, reluctant to interfere too much with market forces and wanting to continue commodity exports, provided only skimpy food to those willing to do heavy labor. The total death toll there has been estimated at 5.5 million people. In China, the Qing government had devoted its reduced revenues to modernizing its military and otherwise dealing with the foreign threat and so was unable to perform its traditional role of providing relief from granaries filled in more prosperous times. Foreign missionaries in China saw the famine as an opportunity to show the power of Christian charity and raised large funds for famine relief, which in turn stimulated the wealthy Chinese elite in the southeast, far from the famine lands, to raise funds for relief themselves to show that China's traditional Confucian values were just as generous to the poor. Still, the death toll was on the order of 10 to 12 million people.

# Chapter Summary

In the nineteenth century the countries of Asia faced new challenges. In India Britain extended its rule to the whole subcontinent, though often the British ruled indirectly through local princes. Britain brought many modern advances to India, such as railroads and schools. Slavery was outlawed, as was widow suicide and infanticide. Resistance to British rule took several forms. In 1857 Indian soldiers in the employ of the British rose in a huge revolt, and after Britain put down this rebellion it ruled India much more tightly. Indians who received English education turned English ideas of liberty and representative rule against the British and founded the Indian National Congress, which called for Indian independence.

By the end of the nineteenth century, most countries in Southeast Asia, from Burma to the Philippines, had been made colonies of Western powers, which developed them as exporters of agricultural products or raw materials, including rubber, tin, sugar, tea, cotton, and jute. The principal exception was Siam (Thailand), whose king was able to play the English and French off against each other and institute centralizing reforms. In the Philippines more than three centuries of Spanish rule ended in 1898, but Spain was replaced by another colonial power: the United States.

In the nineteenth century China's world standing declined as a result of both foreign intervention and internal unrest. The government's efforts to suppress opium imports from Britain led to military confrontation with the British and to numerous concessions that opened China to trade on Britain's terms. Within its borders, China faced unprecedented population pressure and worsening economic conditions that resulted in uprisings in several parts of the country. Further humiliations by the Western powers led to concerted efforts to modernize, but China never quite caught up. Inspired by Western ideas of republican government, revolutionaries tried to topple the dynasty, finally succeeding in 1911–1912.

Japan was the one Asian country to quickly transform itself when confronted by the military strength of the West. It did this by overhauling its power structure. The Meiji oligarchs centralized and strengthened Japan's power by depriving the samurai of their privileges, writing a constitution, instituting universal education, and creating a modern army. At the same time they guided Japan toward rapid industrialization. By the early twentieth century Japan had become an imperialist power with colonies in Korea and Taiwan.

The nineteenth century was also a great age of migration. Citizens of Great Britain came east in large numbers, many to join the Indian civil service or army, others to settle in Australia or New Zealand. Subjects of Asian countries also went abroad, often leaving one Asian country for another. Asian students traveled to Europe, Japan, or the United States to continue their educations. Millions more left in search of work. With the end of the African slave trade, recruiters from the Americas and elsewhere went to India and China to secure indentured laborers. Asian diasporas formed in many parts of the world.

By the turn of the twentieth century the countries in the Asia and Pacific region varied greatly in wealth and power, for several reasons. The countries did not start with equivalent circumstances. Some had long traditions of unified rule; others did not. Some had manufactured goods that Western powers wanted; others offered raw materials or cheap labor. The timing of the arrival of Western powers also made a difference, especially because Western military superiority increased over time. European Great Power rivalry had a major impact, especially after 1860. Similarities in the experiences of Asian countries were also notable and included many of the benefits (and costs) of industrialization seen elsewhere in the world, such as modernizations in communication and transportation, extension of schooling, and the emergence of radical ideologies. Particularly important was the shared experience of environmental stress, which could aggravate droughts and other natural disasters.

## NOTES

1. Ssu-yu Teng and J. K. Fairbank, *China's Response to the West: A Documentary Survey* (New York: Atheneum, 1971), p. 26.
2. Teng and Fairbank, *China's Response to the West*, p. 76, modified.

## MAKE CONNECTIONS    LOOK AHEAD

The nineteenth century brought Asia change on a much greater scale than did any earlier century. Much of the change was political—old political orders were ousted or reduced to tokens by new masters, often European colonial powers. Old elites found themselves at a loss when confronted by the European powers with their modern weaponry and modern armies. Cultural change was no less dramatic as the old elites pondered the differences between their traditional values and the ideas that seemed to underlie the power of the European states. In several places ordinary people rose in rebellion, probably in part because they felt threatened by the speed of cultural change. Material culture underwent major changes as elites experimented with Western dress and architecture and ordinary people had opportunities to travel on newly built railroads. Steamships, too, made long-distance travel easier, facilitating the out-migration of people seeking economic opportunities far from their countries of birth.

In the Americas, too, the nineteenth century was an era of unprecedented change and movement of people. Colonial empires were being overturned there, not imposed as they were in Asia in the same period. The Americas were on the receiving end of the huge migrations taking place, while Asia, like Europe, was much more an exporter of people. The Industrial Revolution brought change to all these areas, both by making available inexpensive machine-made products and by destroying some old ways of making a living. Intellectually, in both Asia and the Americas the ideas of nationalism and nation building shaped how people, especially the more educated, thought about the changes they were experiencing.

# Chapter 26 Review

## IDENTIFY KEY TERMS

**Identify and explain the significance of each item below.**

Great Mutiny / Great Revolt (p. 676)      Taiping Rebellion (p. 683)

Indian Civil Service (p. 677)             Boxers (p. 684)

Indian National Congress (p. 679)         1911 Revolution (p. 684)

Java War (p. 679)                         gunboat diplomacy (p. 685)

Nguyen Dynasty (p. 680)                   Meiji Restoration (p. 685)

Opium War (p. 682)                        Russo-Japanese War (p. 687)

extraterritoriality (p. 682)              indentured laborers (p. 692)

## REVIEW THE MAIN IDEAS

**Answer the focus questions from each section of the chapter.**

1. In what ways did India change as a consequence of British rule? (p. 675)

2. Why were most but not all Southeast Asian societies reduced to colonies? (p. 679)

3. Was China's decline in the nineteenth century due more to internal problems or to Western imperialism? (p. 681)

4. How was Japan able to quickly master the challenges posed by the West? (p. 684)

5. What were the causes and consequences of the vast movement of people in the Pacific region? (p. 688)

6. What explains the similarities and differences in the experiences of Asian countries in this era? (p. 693)

## MAKE COMPARISONS AND CONNECTIONS

**Analyze the larger developments and continuities within and across chapters.**

1. How quickly was Asia affected by the Industrial Revolution in Europe (Chapter 23)? Explain your answer.

2. How do the experiences of European colonies in Asia compare to those in Africa (Chapter 25)?

3. How does China's response to the challenge of European pressure compare to that of the Ottoman Empire (Chapter 25) during the same period?

## CHRONOLOGY

| | |
|---|---|
| **1806–1825** | • Latin American wars of independence (Ch. 22) |
| **1807** | • Slave trade abolished in British Empire (Ch. 25) |
| **1839–1842** | • Opium War |
| **1848** | • Revolutions in France, Austria, and Prussia (Ch. 24) |
| **1851** | • Gold found in Australia, leads to increased immigration |
| **1853** | • Commodore Perry opens Japanese ports to foreign trade |
| **1857** | • Great Mutiny / Great Revolt by Indian sepoys against British rule |
| **1859–1885** | • Vietnam becomes a colony of France |
| **1861** | • Serfs freed in Russia (Ch. 24) |
| **1861–1865** | • U.S. Civil War (Ch. 27) |
| **1867** | • Meiji Restoration in Japan |
| **1872** | • Universal public schools established in Japan |
| **1885** | • Indian National Congress founded |
| **1895** | • Japan defeats China, gains Taiwan |
| **1898** | • U.S. takes control of Philippines from Spain |
| **1904–1905** | • Japan attacks and defeats Russia |
| **1910** | • Korea becomes a province of Japan |
| **1912** | • China's monarchy replaced by a republic |

# 27

# The Americas in the Age of Liberalism

## 1810–1917

**INDEPENDENCE BROUGHT STRIKING CHANGE AND STUBBORN** continuities to the Americas. With the exception of Haiti's revolution, American nations gained independence with their colonial social orders mostly intact. Slavery endured in the United States, Cuba, and Brazil until the second half of the nineteenth century. In Spanish America land remained concentrated in the hands of colonial elites. Territorial expansion displaced most of the indigenous communities that had withstood colonialism. By 1900 millions of immigrants from Europe, the Middle East, and Asia had settled in the Americas.

Though new political systems and governing institutions emerged, political rivals struggled to share power. Liberal republicanism became the most common form of government. But there were exceptions, such as the monarchy that ruled Brazil until 1889 and the parliamentary system tied to Britain that developed in Canada, which retained a symbolic role for the British monarch. Economically, the United States nurtured expanding internal markets and assumed an influential place in Atlantic and Pacific trade. Across Latin America, new nations with weak internal markets and often poorly consolidated political systems struggled to accumulate capital or industrialize.

# New Nations

**How and why did nation-state consolidation vary across the Americas?**

After American nations gained their independence between 1783 and 1825, each began a long and often-violent process of state-building and consolidating its eventual national territory. In countries such as Mexico and Argentina new governments failed to establish the legitimacy and authority needed to bring political stability. In the United States long-standing tensions culminated in the Civil War, while in Cuba nationalists fought a long struggle for independence from Spain.

## Liberalism and Caudillos in Spanish America

To establish political and economic frameworks, American nations reached for ideologies that circulated in the Atlantic world in the age of revolutions. The dominant ideology of the era was liberalism. Liberals sought to create representative republics with strong central governments framed by constitutions that defined and protected individual rights, in particular the right to freely own and buy and sell private property. Beginning with the United States, colonies that became independent nations in the Americas all adopted liberal constitutions.

The U.S. Constitution was an example of liberalism: it defined individual rights, but those individual rights were subordinated to property rights. Slaves were considered property rather than individuals with constitutional rights. Only property owners could vote, women in marriage could not control property, and the new government did not recognize the property of Indians. In the Americas, liberalism mainly served **oligarchs** — the small number of individuals and families who had monopolized political power and economic resources since the colonial era. Liberalism preserved slavery, created tools that allowed the wealthy and powerful to continue to concentrate landownership in the countryside, gave industrialists a free hand over their workers, and concentrated political power in the hands of those who held economic power.

By the end of the nineteenth century liberalism commingled with other ideologies such as Social Darwinism and scientific racism (see "Science for the Masses" in Chapter 24). This combination also inspired the imperial ambitions of the United States toward Mexico and the **Circum-Caribbean**, the region that includes the Antilles as well as the lands that bound the Caribbean Sea in Central America and northern South America.

The implementation of liberalism took different shapes. The United States deferred questions about the continuation of slavery as well as federal authority until its Civil War (1861–1865). After the North prevailed, liberal economic growth gave rise to business and industrial empires and stimulated the immigration of millions of people to provide cheap labor for the booming economy. In Spanish America wars of independence left behind a weak consensus about government that led to long cycles of civil war across many countries.

The lack of a shared political culture among powerful groups in Spanish America created a crisis of confidence. Large landowners held great local power that they refused to yield to politicians in a distant capital. Political factions feared that if a rival faction won power, it would not abide by the rules and limits framed by the constitution, or that a rival would use its governing authority to crush its opponents. The power vacuum that resulted was often filled by caudillos, leaders who ruled by force of personality and through the strength of the faction supporting them rather than through laws and institutions. This form of leadership is known as **caudillismo** (COW-deeh-is-moh). The rule of a caudillo often provided temporary stability amid the struggles between liberals and conservatives, but caudillos cultivated their own prestige at the expense of building stable political institutions.

## Mexico and the United States

The rumblings of independence first stirred Mexico in 1810. A century later the country was engulfed in the first great social upheaval of the twentieth century, the Mexican Revolution. In the century between these events, Mexico declined politically and economically from its status as the most prosperous and important colony of the Spanish Empire. It lost most of its national territory as Central American provinces broke away to become independent republics and as the United States expanded westward and captured or purchased Mexico's northern lands.

Mexicans experienced political stabilization and economic growth again in the second half of the nineteenth century when liberal leaders, especially the dictator Porfirio Díaz (r. 1876–1911), imposed order and attracted foreign investment. But as Díaz himself is said to have remarked, "Poor Mexico, so far from God, so close to the United States."[1] Under the doctrine of **manifest destiny**, the United States claimed and resettled all the territory spanning from its original Atlantic states to the Pacific Ocean. In this process of expansion, it seized lands from Indian nations and Mexico (Map 27.1).

As it pursued westward expansion, the United States remained economically integrated into the expanding and industrializing British Empire, and U.S. merchants retained access to Atlantic markets and credit. But regional differences increased. In the first half of the nineteenth century the North grew rapidly, becoming the center of immigration, banking, and industrialization. In the South, by contrast, slavery and tenant farming kept much of the population at the economic margins and weakened internal markets. Slavery also inhibited immigration, since immigrants avoided settling in areas where they had to compete with unfree labor.

The dichotomy between the economies of the U.S. North and South repeated itself in the difference between the economies of the United States and Latin America. Latin American economies were organized around the export of agricultural and mineral commodities like sugar and silver, not around internal markets as in the United States, and these export economies were disrupted by the independence process.

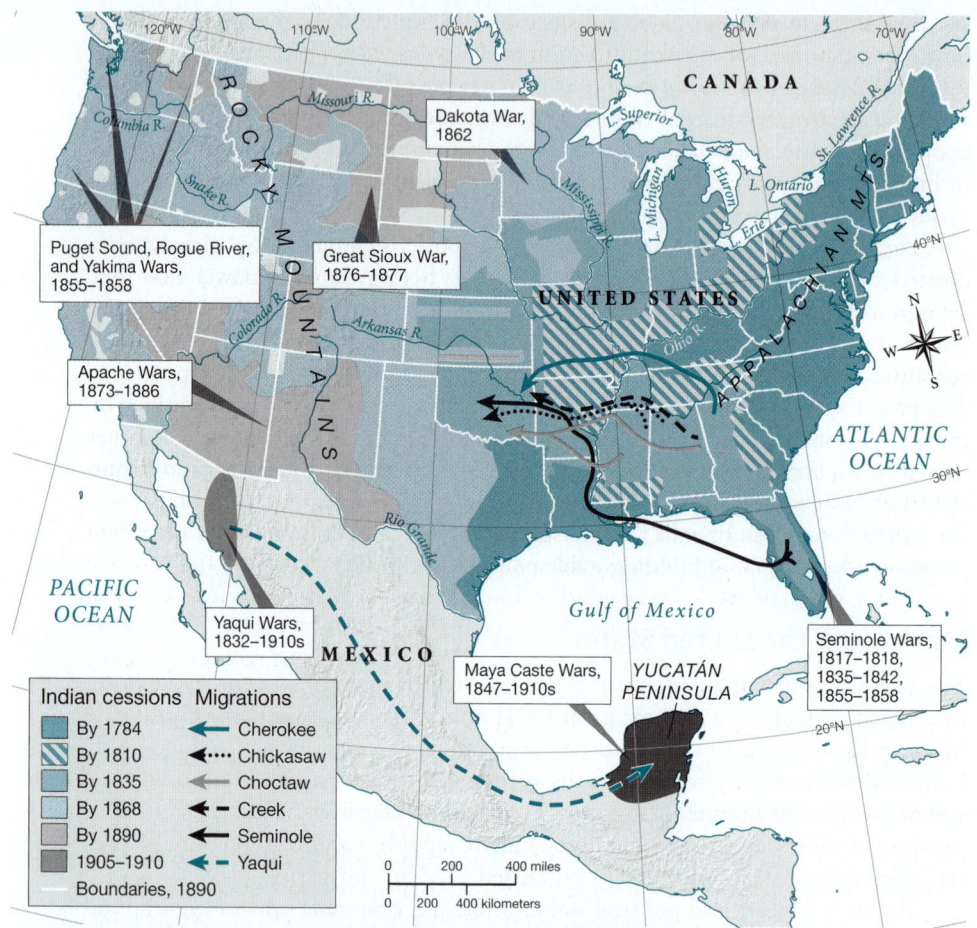

**MAP 27.1   Displacement of Indigenous Peoples, 1780s–1910s**
The United States and Mexico waged repeated wars to claim the lands of Native American nations. This was the last stage of the process of conquest and dispossession that began with the arrival of Europeans in the Americas three centuries earlier. As national armies seized native lands, displaced native peoples were forcibly removed, leading to the deaths of thousands and the destruction of cultures.

Mexico's challenges after independence resulted mainly from the inability of its political leaders to establish a consensus about how to govern the new nation. The general who led the war against Spain, Agustín de Iturbide, proclaimed himself emperor in 1822. When he was deposed a year later, the country's southern provinces broke away, becoming Guatemala, Honduras, Nicaragua, El Salvador, and Costa Rica. Power in Mexico rested in the hands of regional caudillos, and the presidency changed hands frequently as rival factions competed against each other. Antonio López de Santa Anna, the most powerful of Mexico's caudillos, held the presidency ten times between 1833 and 1854—three separate times in 1833 alone.

The fate of the major silver mine in Mexico illustrates the challenges presented by independence. La Valenciana in central Mexico was the most productive silver mine in the world. It was one of the first places where the newly invented steam engine was used to pump water out of shafts, allowing miners to work below the water table. The machinery was destroyed during Mexico's war of independence (1810–1821), and the flooded mine ceased operation. Neither private investors nor the new government had the capital necessary to reactivate the mine after independence.

Mexico entered a vicious cycle: with diminished capital and economic activity, tax revenues evaporated, public administration disintegrated, and the national government became unmanageable. The lack of political stability, in turn, drove investors away. The consequences are striking: in 1800 Mexico produced half the goods and services that the United States did; by 1845 production had dropped to only 8 percent. Per capita income fell by half.[2]

Politically and economically weakened, Mexico was vulnerable to expansionist pressure from the United States. Its northern territories attracted the ambitions of U.S. politicians, land speculators, and settlers. In the 1820s settlers from the U.S. South petitioned the Mexican government for land grants in the province of Texas, in return for which they would adopt Mexican citizenship. The U.S. government encouraged these settlers to declare the independence of Texas in 1836.

After Texas and Florida became U.S. states in 1845, President James Polk expanded the nation's border westward, precipitating the Mexican-American War (1846–1848). In defeat, Mexico ceded half its national territory to the United States through the **Treaty of Guadalupe Hidalgo** (1848). With the U.S. acquisition of Florida from Spain in 1819 and the conquest of Mexican territory, many Latinos — U.S. citizens or residents of Latin American origin or descent — became U.S. citizens not because they moved to the United States but because the United States moved to them.

## Liberal Reform in Mexico

In 1853 Mexican president Santa Anna unintentionally ushered in a new era of liberal consolidation and economic reform by triggering a backlash against his sale of Mexican territory along the northern border to the United States in a deal known as the Gadsden Purchase. Many Mexicans thought Santa Anna betrayed the nation and threw their support behind a new generation of liberal leaders. Beginning with the presidency of Ignacio Comonfort (pres. 1855–1858), these liberals carried out sweeping legal and economic changes called *La Reforma*, or "the reform."

Liberal reformers sought to make all individuals equal under the law and established property ownership as a basic right and national goal. The first major step in La Reforma was the Juárez Law (1855), which abolished old legal privileges for military officers and members of the clergy. The law was written by Minister of Justice Benito Juárez (hoo-AH-rehs), an Indian from Oaxaca (whah-HAH-kah) whose first language was Zapotec. Juárez began life as a farmer but earned a law degree and became the most important force in consolidating Mexico's political system in the decades after independence. An even more consequential measure, the **Lerdo Law** (1856), banished another legacy of colonialism: "corporate lands," meaning lands owned by groups or institutions, such as the Catholic Church, a major landowner, rather than by individual property owners. Liberals saw those landholdings as backward and inefficient and wanted to replace them with individual farm owners.

These reforms triggered a backlash from conservative landowners and the church. When liberals ratified a new constitution in 1857, the Catholic Church threatened to excommunicate anyone who swore allegiance to it. Conservatives revolted, triggering a civil war called the Wars of Reform (1857–1861). Liberal forces led by Benito Juárez defeated the conservatives, who then conspired with French emperor Napoleon III to invite a French invasion of Mexico. Napoleon III saw an opportunity to re-establish France's American empire. His propaganda gave currency to the term *Latin America*, used to assert that France had a natural role to play in Mexico because of a common "Latin" origin.

The French army invaded Mexico in 1862. The main resistance French forces faced was the defense mounted by a young officer named Porfirio Díaz, who slowed the invaders' advance through the city of Puebla on their way to Mexico City. The day of the Battle of Puebla, May 5, became a national holiday (known in the United States as "Cinco de Mayo"). Mexican conservatives and Napoleon III installed his Austrian cousin Maximilian of Habsburg as emperor of Mexico.

The deposed Juárez led a guerrilla war against the French troops backing Maximilian. When the U.S. Civil War ended in 1865, the U.S. government sought to root out France's influence on its border and threw its support behind Juárez, pressuring France to remove its troops. Bolstered by surplus Civil War armaments that flooded across the border into Mexico, Juárez's nationalists prevailed and executed Maximilian. Conservatives had been completely discredited: they had conspired with another country to install a foreign leader through a military invasion.

We can compare Benito Juárez, who governed the restored republic until 1876, with Abraham Lincoln. Both rose from humble rural origins to become able liberal lawyers. They became agile political and military leaders who prevailed in civil wars. The decade between the Wars of Reform and Juárez's restoration of the republic in 1867 can also be compared to the U.S. Civil War: both were watersheds in which questions that had lingered since independence were violently resolved and liberalism emerged as the dominant political philosophy.

## Brazil: A New World Monarchy

Brazil gained independence in 1822 as a monarchy ruled by Emperor Pedro I, the son and heir of the Portuguese emperor. The creation of a Brazilian monarchy marked the culmination of a process that began in 1808, when Napoleon's armies crossed the Pyrenees from France to invade the Iberian Peninsula. Napoleon toppled the Spanish Crown, but the Portuguese royal family, many of the government's bureaucrats, and most of the aristocracy fled aboard British warships to Portugal's colony of Brazil. This would be the first and only time a European empire would be ruled from one of its colonies.

Before the Portuguese court relocated to Brazil, colonial policies had restricted many activities in Brazil in order to keep the colony dependent and subordinate to Portugal. It was only with the arrival of the imperial court that Brazil gained its first printing press, library, and schools for engineering, medicine, law, and the arts.

With the flight of the emperor to Brazil in 1808 and the declaration of independence by his son in 1822, Brazil achieved something that had eluded many Latin American nations: it retained territorial unity under relative political stability. A liberal constitution adopted in 1824 lasted until a republican military coup in 1889. It established a two-chamber parliament and a role for the emperor as a political intermediary. Pedro I was not adept in this role and abdicated in 1831, leaving behind a regency governing in the name of his young son, Pedro II. In 1840, at the age of fourteen, Pedro II declared himself an adult and assumed the throne, ruling Brazil for the next forty-nine years.

Independent Brazil had many continuities with its colonial past. It remained the society with the largest number of African slaves in the Americas. It also continued to be economically and militarily dependent on Britain, just as its mother country, Portugal, had been in the eighteenth century. Britain negotiated with Brazil a "Friendship Treaty" that allowed British industrial goods to enter the country with very low tariffs. The flood of cheap British imports inhibited Brazilian industrialization. British economic and political influence, as well as special privileges enjoyed by British citizens in Brazil, were examples of **neocolonialism**, the influence that European powers and the United States exerted over politically and economically weaker countries after independence.

# Slavery and Abolition

**Why did slavery last longer in the United States, Brazil, and Cuba than elsewhere in the Americas, and how did resistance by enslaved people shape abolition?**

In former Spanish-American colonies, the abolition of slavery quickly followed independence. In British colonies, slavery ended in 1834, and the British navy suppressed the Atlantic slave trade. But in the United States, Cuba, and Brazil, slavery endured well into the nineteenth century. In each of these countries the question of abolition became entwined with the disputes over the nature of government, federal authority in the United States, independence for Cuba, and monarchy versus republicanism in Brazil.

## Slave Societies in the Americas

Africans and their descendants were enslaved in every country of the Americas. The experiences in slavery and freedom of Africans and African Americans, defined here as the descendants of enslaved Africans anywhere in the New World, varied considerably. Several factors shaped their experiences: the nature of slave regimes in different economic regions, patterns of manumission (individual slaves' gaining

**A Government Functionary Leaving Home with His Family and Servants, 1839**
This lithograph is a depiction of Brazilian patriarchal and slave society social hierarchies that are shown through differences of gender, race, and age. The male patriarch is followed by members of the household ordered by their diminishing rank. (Bibliothèque Nationale, Paris, France/© Archives Charmet/Bridgeman Images)

their freedom), the nature of abolition (the ending of the institution of slavery), and the proportion of the local population they represented.

The settlement of Africans as slaves was the most intense in areas that relied on plantation agriculture. Plantations cultivated a single crop — especially sugar, coffee, tobacco, and cotton — on a vast scale that supplied distant global markets. Cotton from Alabama was spun by looms in New England or Britain; sugar and coffee from Brazil were consumed in European salons. Enslaved Africans played many other roles as well. From Buenos Aires to Boston, slavery was widespread in port cities, where it was fed by easy access to the slave trade and the demand for street laborers such as porters. And across the Americas, enslaved women were forced into domestic service, a role that conferred social prestige on their masters, but which also added sexual abuse to the miseries that enslaved people endured.

## Independence and Abolition

Slavery and abolition became intertwined with the process of political independence, with the different experiences of the United States and Haiti shaping views across the rest of the Americas. In Haiti independence was achieved in a revolution in which slaves turned against their oppressors. By contrast, the United States gained its independence in a war that did not result in widespread slave revolt, and its liberal government preserved slavery. When merchants and landowners in other colonies contemplated independence, they weighed whether the U.S. or the Haitian experience awaited them. As a result, independence movements proceeded the slowest in colonies with large subjected populations.

British efforts to keep their North American colonies, as well as a combination of moral and economic appeals for the abolition of slavery in British territories, hastened the end of the slave trade to the Americas. When British forces fought to prevent the independence of the United States, they offered freedom to slaves who joined them. Many did so, and after the British defeat and withdrawal, they migrated to Spanish Florida, the Caribbean, and West Africa.

In 1807 British abolitionists pressured Parliament to end the slave trade, and Parliament abolished slavery in Canada and Britain's Caribbean colonies in 1834. To reduce economic competition, the British government pressured other nations to follow suit. A British naval squadron patrolled the Atlantic to suppress the slave trade, capturing slave ships, freeing their captives, and resettling them in a colony established in Sierra Leone in 1787 to settle former slaves who had sided with Britain in the American Revolution.

In Spanish America, after independence movements enlisted the participation of slaves and offered freedom in return, new national governments enacted gradual abolition. The first step toward abolition was often through **free womb laws** that freed children born to enslaved women. These laws, passed across independent Spanish America between 1811 and 1825, created gradual abolition but did not impose an immediate financial loss on slaveholders: to the contrary, the free children of slaves remained apprenticed to their masters until they reached adulthood. Similar laws hastened the abolition of slavery in the Northern states of the United States.

The combination of free womb laws and manumission as a reward for military service meant that unlike in the United States, by the time slavery was abolished in Latin American countries, most peoples of African descent had already gained their freedom (Map 27.2).

## MAP 27.2   Abolition in the Americas

The process of abolition in the Americas was gradual and varied across regions. In some areas, such as Mexico and parts of New England, slavery was abolished soon after independence, while in the U.S. South it lasted until the end of the Civil War. In Texas slavery was abolished by the Mexican government, but when Texas became part of the United States, slavery was legally reinstated. In British territories slavery was abolished in 1834. Across Latin America the abolition of slavery was hastened by civil wars that mobilized slaves as combatants. The last country to abolish slavery, Brazil, did so only in 1888.

In the United States the questions of nation-building and slavery remained connected. The Constitution gave individual states autonomy in matters such as slavery. As slavery expanded in the South and was gradually abolished in the North, tensions over westward expansion culminated in the Civil War. When Abraham Lincoln, opposed to the spread of slavery, was elected president in 1860, Southern political leaders seceded and formed the Confederate States of America. Lincoln declared the secession illegal and waged war to preserve the territorial integrity of the United States. The ensuing civil war resulted in the deaths of over 750,000 combatants and civilians.

In 1862 Lincoln put pressure on Confederate states to rejoin the Union by issuing the Emancipation Proclamation. The proclamation abolished slavery in all states that remained opposed to the Union on January 1, 1863. It was intended as leverage to bring the rebel states back, not to abolish slavery altogether; consequently, it freed slaves only in states that had seceded. Nevertheless, the proclamation hastened the demise of slavery. After the Confederacy surrendered in 1865, the Thirteenth Amendment to the Constitution fully abolished slavery. Subsequent amendments recognized the citizenship and rights of people formerly enslaved.

Two aspects made slavery and abolition different in the United States than in Latin America: gradual abolition in the North, which made slavery regional; and the often violent Southern white backlash against military defeat and Reconstruction, which codified racial segregation. But the absence of segregation did not mean the North was antiracist: segregation is a form of racism but hardly the only one. Instead race relations in the northern and western states of the United States resembled those of Latin America, where racial prejudice and discrimination persisted through informal practices in employment, housing, and lending. Meanwhile, the U.S. South erected a distinct edifice of laws and extralegal violence to preserve white supremacy.

## Abolition in Cuba and Brazil

Cuba and Brazil followed long paths to abolition. In Cuba nationalist rebels fought for independence from Spain in the Ten Years' War (1868–1878). Many enslaved and free blacks joined the anticolonial struggle, and rebel leaders supported abolition. Spanish authorities who sought to defuse the armed conflict granted freedom to those who fought on the Spanish side in the war, to the children of slaves born since 1868, and to slaves over age sixty. By 1878 Spanish forces had defeated the nationalists, but the conflict had set in motion an irreversible process of abolition.

In Brazil an 1871 law granted freedom to children born to slaves, and an 1885 law granted freedom to slaves over age sixty. At best, these laws were half measures, aimed at placating abolitionists without disrupting the economic reliance on slave labor. At worst, they mocked the meaning of abolition by preserving slave owners' control over the labor of the children of slaves, while freeing masters from their obligations to care for elderly slaves.

Slave resistance accelerated abolition in Cuba and Brazil. As in the United States, where the mass flight of enslaved people during the Civil War helped cripple the Confederacy economically, the rising numbers of people fleeing plantations made slavery unsustainable. In Brazil, the vast interior presented those escaping with opportunities to resettle out of the reach of slave society. Slavery was finally abolished in Cuba in 1886 and in Brazil in 1888, making them the last regions of the Americas to end slavery.

# Export-Led Growth and Social Unrest

**As Latin America became more integrated into the world economy, how did patterns of economic growth shape political culture and social reactions?**

Beginning in the 1850s, the consolidation of liberalism in the Americas created conditions for a return of foreign investment that brought economic growth. But as liberal reforms created new economic pressures, rural workers and indigenous communities led reform and resistance movements such as those unleashed by the Mexican Revolution.

## Latin America Re-enters the World Economy

By the second half of the nineteenth century, Latin American elites found ways to balance liberal political ideas about the way national governments should be structured with liberal economic policies that favored large landowners. Political stability and economic growth returned. Foreign investment intensified. By the turn of the twentieth century Latin American countries were firmly tied to the world economy. Indigenous and rural communities paid a high price for this return to economic growth: as the value of agricultural exports increased, so did the value of land. Governments, foreign investors, and large landowners seized indigenous lands through war, legal action, or coercion at a dizzying rate.

For example, in the late 1880s the Argentine government sold off lands it took from indigenous communities. The land was inexpensive, but because it was sold in such large parcels, the few who could purchase it did so by mortgaging existing landholdings. Though reformers had imagined the creation of a class of small farmers, the result was the opposite: more than 20 million acres were sold to just 381 landowners who created vast estates known as **latifundios**.[3]

Liberal economic policies and the intensification of foreign trade concentrated land in the hands of wealthy exporters. Governments represented the interests of large landowners by promoting commodity exports and industrial imports, following the liberal economic principle of comparative advantage (that countries should export what they could produce the most efficiently and import what other countries could produce more cheaply and efficiently). Brazil became the world's largest exporter of coffee and experienced a brief but intense boom in rubber production. Argentina became one of the most efficient and profitable exporters of grains and beef. Chile and Peru served the international market for fertilizers by exporting nitrates and bat guano.

These export booms depended on imported capital and technology. In the Circum-Caribbean this came mostly from investors in the United States, while in South America it often came from Britain.

British capital and technology built Argentina's network of railroads and refrigerated meatpacking plants. Chile's nitrate-mining industry was expanded through the War of the Pacific (1879–1883), a conflict in which Chile seized territory in bordering Peru and Bolivia. As a result, Bolivia lost its access to the Pacific and became a landlocked nation. The war and its outcomes revealed British influence as well: to finance the war, the Chilean government issued bonds bought by British investors. The bonds were repaid through the sale of concessions for mining the nitrate-rich

**MAP 27.3  The War of the Triple Alliance, 1865–1870**
The War of the Triple Alliance, also known as the Paraguay War, was the bloodiest war in South American history. Fought between Paraguay and the allied countries of Argentina, Brazil, and Uruguay, the war resulted in Paraguay losing a large part of its population and nearly 60,000 square miles of territory.

lands that Chile conquered from Bolivia. In 1878 British companies controlled 13 percent of nitrate mining. By 1890 they controlled 90 percent.

The War of the Triple Alliance, or Paraguay War (1865–1870), also brought liberal change to Brazil (Map 27.3). In 1865 Paraguayan leader Francisco Solano López declared war against Argentina, Brazil, and Uruguay after they threatened landlocked Paraguay's use of Uruguay's port of Montevideo, the international shipping point for Paraguay's imports and exports. The war was devastating for Paraguay, which lost more than half its population. But the war also brought repercussions for the victors.

In Brazil, where Emperor Pedro II's calls for volunteers to enlist in the army fell on deaf ears, the army enlisted enslaved people, who, if they served honorably and survived, would be granted freedom. What did it mean that the free citizens of a nation would not mobilize to defend it, and that the nation prevailed only through the sacrifices borne by its enslaved? For many, especially officers who were veterans of the conflict, the lesson was that being a monarchy that relied on slavery made Brazil a weak and backward nation. Veteran officers and liberal opponents of the war formed republican and abolitionist movements. These officers overthrew the monarchy in 1889 and established a liberal republican government.

## The Porfiriato and Liberal Stability in Mexico

When Porfirio Díaz became president of Mexico in 1876, the hero of the Battle of Puebla inherited a country in which much had been achieved. President Juárez had established national unity against the French invasion. His generation of liberal leaders had also created a legal and political framework based on the 1857 constitution. But Mexico was a country that faced enormous challenges. Per capita income was less than it had been at independence in 1821. The country had barely four hundred miles of railroads, compared to more than seventy thousand miles in the United States. Díaz's first challenge was to attract foreign investment.

Porfirio Díaz built a regime—the **Porfiriato**—with unprecedented stability and ruled, with a single term out of power, from 1876 to 1911. He ruled by the mantra "*pan o palo*," bread or the stick, rewarding supporters and ruthlessly punishing opponents. The political stability he created made Mexico a haven for foreign investment, particularly from the United States. Foreign trade increased tenfold, and the country became the third-largest oil producer in the world. Railroads rapidly expanded, reaching fifteen thousand miles of track by 1910, much of it connecting Mexico to the United States. Railroads also connected regions long isolated from each other and sustained national markets for the first time since the colonial era.

The Porfiriato was a modernizing regime. The government swelled with technocrats called *científicos* (see-en-TEE-fee-kohs), on whom Díaz lavished great rewards. By contrast, the Porfiriato considered indigenous peoples racially inferior and suppressed them. This was the case of the Yaqui Indians of Sonora, at the border with Arizona (see Map 27.1). Díaz's army vanquished Yaqui communities, seized their land, and dispatched survivors to the Yucatán, where they worked as slaves on plantations cultivating *henequén* (hen-eh-KEN), a plant whose fibers were used in the hay-baling machines increasingly used by U.S. farmers.

As foreign investment made land valuable, small landholders became vulnerable. Large landowners and speculators used the Lerdo Law to usurp peasant lands. In addition, the 1883 Law of Barren Lands allowed real estate companies to identify land that was not being cultivated (often land that communities allowed to lie fallow as they rotated crops) so it could be surveyed and auctioned off. The abuse of these laws had devastating consequences: by 1910, even though most of Mexico's population of 12 million remained rural, 80 percent of peasants did not own any land. The expansion of railroads made land valuable, and liberal reforms created the tools to transfer that value from peasants to investors. Given Mexico's proximity to the United States, that process was swifter and more intense than it was elsewhere in Latin America, and it led to the first great social upheaval of the twentieth century.

## The Mexican Revolution

Porfirio Díaz declared himself the unanimous winner of Mexico's 1910 elections. His defeated challenger, wealthy landowner and liberal lawyer Francisco Madero, issued a manifesto calling the election illegitimate and pronouncing himself the provisional president of Mexico. Madero's call to arms was the spark that ignited a powder keg of grievances from peasants whose lands had been taken or threatened, as well as from exploited urban workers.

Peasants and workers across the country rose up, drove out Díaz, and anointed Madero provisional president. Madero proved to be a weak reformer, and armed peasant groups rose up again, this time against him. The U.S. ambassador, who considered Madero to be inadequate in his defense of U.S. business interests, conspired with the commander of Madero's army to assassinate him in 1912. Mexico's revolution now deepened, as factions around the country joined the fighting.

The ideological leadership of the Mexican Revolution came from Emiliano Zapata and his supporters, who hailed from rural communities south of Mexico City whose lands were threatened. The Zapatistas made their demands in a document called the **Plan de Ayala** (ai-YAH-lah) that called for the return of all land, forests,

**Emiliano Zapata and Pancho Villa in Mexico's Presidential Palace, 1914** Villa sits in the presidential chair topped with the golden eagle, and Zapata appears next to him on the right, holding a sombrero. Two small children peer over their shoulders as each leader insists he will not claim the presidency since his goal was reform and not power. (George Rinhart/Getty Images)

and waters taken from rural communities. Their pledge to fight until these demands were met was taken up by many armed groups across Mexico, particularly the army commanded by the charismatic Pancho Villa (pahn-choh VEE-yah). They found allies as well in the Red Brigades of anarchist and socialist workers who controlled the capital, Mexico City, during much of the war.

Though they controlled most of Mexico at the height of the revolution, supporters of the Plan de Ayala were gradually beaten back by the faction that would eventually prevail, a group called the Constitutionalists, led by politician Venustiano Carranza and Álvaro Obregón, a skilled general who emulated tactics and strategies employed in Europe in the First World War. But to consolidate political control and to convince rebels like those supporting Zapata and Villa to put down their arms, their constitution included key demands from the Plan de Ayala and from urban workers.

In meeting some demands of peasants and workers, Mexico's 1917 constitution imposed the most significant limits to liberalism yet attempted in the Americas. It broke the fundamental liberal embrace of private property by asserting that all land, water, and subsoil resources belong to the nation, which allows their use for the public good. This clause allowed the government to expropriate lands from large estates to make grants of collective land called *ejidos* (eh-HEE-dohz) to rural communities. Over 80 million acres of farmland and forests would be redistributed as ejidos. The constitution included the most advanced labor code in the world at the time, guaranteeing workers the right to unionize and strike, an eight-hour workday, a minimum wage, and protections for women workers, including maternity leave.

By agreeing to these reforms, the Constitutionalist faction was able to consolidate control over a new political order that would enjoy remarkable stability: the political party that emerged from the Constitutionalists would hold presidential power for almost all of the next one hundred years.

# Immigration

**What factors influenced immigration to the Americas? How did immigrants shape—and how were they shaped by—their new settings?**

During the late nineteenth and early twentieth centuries, unprecedented numbers of people from Europe, Asia, and the Middle East settled across North and South America. The largest wave of immigrants—some 28 million between 1860 and 1914—settled in the United States. Another 8 million had settled in Argentina and Brazil by 1930. This cycle of immigration was a product of liberal political and economic reforms that abolished slavery, established stable political systems, and created a framework for integrating immigrants as factory and farm laborers.

## Immigration to Latin America

In 1852 the Argentine political philosopher Juan Bautista Alberdi published *Bases and Points of Departure for Argentine Political Organization*, in which he argued that the development of his country depended on immigration. Believing that whites were racially superior, he urged massive immigration from northern Europe and the United States:

> Each European who comes to our shores brings more civilization in his habits, which will later be passed on to our inhabitants, than many books of philosophy. . . . Do we want to sow and cultivate in America English liberty, French culture, and the diligence of men from Europe and from the United States? Let us bring living pieces of these qualities.[4]

Alberdi's ideas, guided by the aphorism "to govern is to populate," won immediate acceptance and were even incorporated into the Argentine constitution, which declared, "The Federal government will encourage European immigration." Other countries of the Americas, also influenced by Social Darwinism, adopted similar immigration policies.

Coffee barons in Brazil, *latifundiarios* (owners of vast estates) in Argentina, and investors in nitrate and copper mining in Chile made enormous profits that they reinvested in new factories. From the outset, Latin America had been tied to the Industrial Revolution in Britain and northern Europe as a provider of raw materials and as a consumer of industrial goods. In the major exporting countries of Argentina, Brazil, and Mexico, domestic industrialization now began to take hold in the form of textile mills, food-processing plants, and mechanized transportation such as modern ports and railroads.

**The 1907 Rio Blanco Strike**  Mexico industrialized under the Porfiriato in ways that were highly exploitative of workers. At the Rio Blanco Mill, workers waged a strike against the requirement that they spend their wages at company stores, which typically inflated prices. Police killed between fifty and seventy workers to suppress the strike. (The Stapleton Collection/Bridgeman Images)

By the turn of the twentieth century an industrial working class had begun to emerge. In Brazil and Argentina these workers, who were mainly European immigrants, proved unexpectedly contentious: they brought with them radical ideologies that challenged liberalism, particularly anarchism and **anarcho-syndicalism**, a version of anarchism that advocated placing power in the hands of workers' unions. The workers clashed with bosses and political leaders who rejected the idea that workers had rights. The authorities suppressed worker organizations such as unions, and they resisted implementing labor laws such as a minimum wage, restrictions on child labor, the right to strike, or factory safety regulations.

Radicalized workers mounted labor actions that at times grew into general strikes with over one hundred thousand workers picketing. But outside of Mexico, the movements of urban workers did not merge with rural unrest in the formula that produced revolution.

Although Europe was a significant source of immigrants to Latin America, so were Asia and the Middle East. In the late nineteenth and early twentieth centuries, large numbers of Japanese arrived in Brazil, most settling in São Paulo state, creating the largest ethnic Japanese community outside of Japan. From the Middle East, Lebanese, Turks, and Syrians also entered Brazil. South Asian laborers went to Trinidad, Jamaica, Guyana, and other British territories in the Caribbean, mostly as indentured servants under five-year contracts. Perhaps one-third returned to India, but the rest stayed, saved money, and bought small businesses or land. After slavery was abolished in Cuba in 1886, some work in the cane fields was done by Chinese indentured laborers. Likewise, the abolition of slavery in Mexico led to the arrival of thousands of Chinese bonded servants.

Thanks to the influx of new arrivals, Buenos Aires, São Paulo, Mexico City, Montevideo, Santiago, and Havana experienced spectacular growth. By 1914 Buenos Aires had emerged as one of the most cosmopolitan cities in the world, with a population of 3.6 million. As Argentina's political capital, the city housed its government bureaucracies and agencies. The meatpacking, food-processing, flour-milling, and wool industries were concentrated there as well. Elegant shops near the Plaza de Mayo catered to the expensive tastes of the elite upper classes that constituted about 5 percent of the population. By contrast, the thousands of immigrants who toiled twelve hours a day, six days a week, on docks and construction sites and in meatpacking plants were crowded into the city's one-room tenements.

Immigrants brought wide-ranging skills that helped develop industry and commerce. In Argentina, Italian and Spanish settlers stimulated the expansion of cattle ranching, meat processing, wheat farming, and the shoe industry. In Brazil, Italians gained a leading role in the coffee industry, and Japanese farmers made the country self-sufficient in rice production. Chinese laborers built Peruvian railroads, and in sections of large cities such as Lima, the Chinese dominated the ownership of shops and restaurants.

## Immigration to the United States

After the Civil War ended in 1865, the United States underwent an industrial boom powered by exploitation of the country's natural resources. The federal government turned over vast amounts of land and mineral resources to private industrialists for development. In particular, railroad companies — the foundation of industrial expansion — received 130 million acres. By 1900 the U.S. railroad system was 193,000 miles long, connected every part of the nation, and represented 40 percent of the railroad mileage in the world, and it was all built by immigrant labor.

Between 1860 and 1914, 28 million immigrants came to the United States. Though many became settlers, industrial America developed through the labor of immigrants. Chinese, Scandinavian, and Irish immigrants laid railroad tracks. At the Carnegie Steel Corporation, Slavs and Italians produced one-third of the world's total steel supply in 1900. As in South America, immigration fed the growth of cities. In 1790 only 5.1 percent of Americans were living in centers of twenty-five hundred or more people. By 1860 this figure had risen to 19.9 percent, and by 1900 almost 40 percent of the population lived in cities. Also by 1900, three of the largest cities in the world were in the United States — New York City with 3.4 million people, Chicago with 1.7 million, and Philadelphia with 1.4 million.

Working conditions for new immigrants were often deplorable. Industrialization had created a vast class of workers who depended entirely on wage labor. Employers paid women and children much less than men. Some women textile workers earned as little as $1.56 for seventy hours of work, while men received from $7 to $9 for the same work. Because business owners resisted government efforts to install costly safety devices, working conditions in mines and mills were frightful. In 1913 alone, even after some safety measures had been instituted, twenty-five thousand people died in industrial accidents. Between 1900 and 1917 seventy-two thousand railroad workers died on the job. Workers responded to these conditions with strikes, violence, and, gradually, unionization.

Immigrants faced more than economic exploitation: they were also subjected to harsh ethnic stereotypes and faced pressure to culturally assimilate. An economic depression in the 1890s increased resentment toward immigrants. Powerful owners of mines, mills, and factories fought the organization of labor unions, fired thousands of workers, slashed wages, and ruthlessly exploited their workers. Workers in turn feared that immigrant labor would drive salaries lower. Some of this antagonism sprang from racism, some from old Protestant prejudice against Catholicism, the faith of many of the new arrivals. Anti-Semitism against Jewish immigrants from eastern Europe intensified.

East Asian immigrants in the U.S. West faced increasingly violent acts by white mobs, often called race riots, as well as legal restrictions culminating in the Chinese Exclusion Act of 1882. The Exclusion Act denied Chinese laborers entrance to the

**"The Chinese Must "Go!"** Anti-immigrant sentiment intensified as immigration to the United States accelerated in the late nineteenth and early twentieth centuries. This 1880 campaign advertisement presented Chinese immigrants as a threat to native-born workers. (Sarin Images/Granger)

country and barred Chinese workers in the United States from becoming citizens. Chung Sen, an immigrant returning to China after the Exclusion Act, reflected on his American experience: "The ill treatment of . . . [my] countrymen may perhaps be excused on the grounds of race, color, language and religion, but such prejudice can only prevail among the ignorant. In civility . . . [Americans] are very properly styled barbarians."[5] This hostility extended to immigration from Japan as well, which the United States restricted in 1907; later Japanese immigrants settled in South America.

In Latin America, oligarchs encouraged immigration from Europe, the Middle East, and Japan because they believed these "whiter" workers were superior to black or indigenous workers. By contrast, in the United States the descendants of northern European Protestants developed prejudices and built social barriers out of their belief that Catholic Irish, southern and eastern European, or Jewish immigrants were not white enough.

## Immigration to Canada

Beginning in the 1840s, Canada gradually gained autonomy from Britain, and in 1867 it achieved independence as the Dominion of Canada (Map 27.4). British authorities agreed to grant the provinces political independence to avoid the disruption and loss of influence that followed U.S. independence, and in return the Dominion retained a symbolic role for the British monarchy. By 1900 Canada still had only a little over 5 million people (as compared to 13.6 million in Mexico and 76 million in the United States). As in the United States and Latin America, the expansion of Canada came at

**< MAP 27.4   The Dominion of Canada, 1871**
Shortly after the Dominion of Canada came into being as a self-governing nation within the British Empire in 1867, new provinces were added. Vast areas of Canada were too sparsely populated to achieve provincial status. Alberta and Saskatchewan did not become part of the Dominion until 1905; Newfoundland was added only in 1949.

the expense of native peoples, whose population dropped by half or more during the century, many succumbing to the newcomers' diseases. By 1900 there were only about 127,000 indigenous people left in Canada. French Canadians were the largest minority in the population, and they remained distinct in language, law, and religion.

Immigration to Canada increased in the 1890s. Between 1897 and 1912, 961,000 people entered Canada from the British Isles, 594,000 from Europe, and 784,000 from the United States. Some immigrants went to work in the urban factories of Hamilton, Toronto, and Montreal. However, immigrants from continental Europe—mainly from Poland, Germany, Scandinavia, Russia, and Ukraine—flooded the midwestern plains and soon transformed the prairies into one of the world's major grain-growing regions. Between 1891 and 1914 wheat production soared from 2 million bushels per year to 150 million bushels. Mining expanded, and British Columbia, Ontario, and Quebec produced large quantities of wood pulp, much of it sold to the United States. Canada's great rivers were harnessed to supply hydroelectric power for industrial and domestic use. But Canada remained a predominantly agricultural country, with less than 10 percent of its population engaged in manufacturing.

## Settler Colonialism and Its Impacts

In western Canada and the United States, as well as in Argentina and Chile, state policies and railroad companies selling land encouraged migrants and immigrants to move into areas that had been predominantly indigenous. This pattern of migration was **settler colonialism**, the practice of displacing indigenous or pre-existing populations and creating culturally, economically, and demographically distinct societies in their place. Settler colonialism took place in other parts of the world as well, including South Africa, Australia, and New Zealand (see "Settler Colonies in the Pacific: Australia and New Zealand" in Chapter 26).

As in other regions, settler colonialism in western North America and southern South America was sharply racial: it took lands from indigenous peoples and favored settlers of European descent. Seneca Indian Eli S. Parker, an officer in the Union army who was an aide to Ulysses Grant during the Civil War, spoke sarcastically of "the mercy of the American people [which] granted them the right to occupy and cultivate certain lands until someone stronger wanted them." Canadian Mohawk writer E. Pauline Johnson called this colonialism "might and doubtful right."[6]

The displacement of Native Americans was echoed in policies restricting other minority groups, such as the Chinese Exclusion Act. Though some African Americans settled in the West, Oregon's constitution prohibited African Americans from entering state territory, while other areas imposed less formal exclusion. Even as Canadian authorities encouraged western settlement by European immigrants, they pressed African Americans fleeing slavery in the United States to migrate to British colonies in the Caribbean.

Settler colonialism was remarkable for its ambition: settlers renamed and reimagined the landscape, often demarcating it with a new industrial product, barbed wire fencing; they redistributed land and resources in new ways; and they invented new traditions configured as frontier culture. They developed new legal systems and institutions as well as new forms of production that were often connected to distant markets by the railroads that had brought them. The settlers' reconfiguration of vast regions of the Americas was so thorough that it seemed a preordained and divine right.

The ways in which settlers transformed pampas, plains, and prairies had deep environmental repercussions. Cattle introduced by ranchers carried parasites that were lethal to bison, and new crops such as wheat and hay, as well as invasive species, displaced native grasses, affecting animal and plant life as much as people. Farming consumed nutrients that had taken centuries to accumulate in the soil and disrupted ecosystems, resulting in erosion and heightened flooding.

In North America, settlers were encouraged to believe that "rain follows the plough": that turning grassland into farmland would increase rainfall and support intensified farming. Above-average rainfall in the 1870s and the 1880s seemed to prove this. As rainfall returned to its mean, however, hardship ensued for many settlers, as was captured in a folk song:

> Nebraska land, Nebraska land,
> As on thy desert soil I stand
> And look away across the plains,
> I wonder why it never rains.[7]

Grazing and farming practices caused an environmental disaster. As settlers disrupted the western plains' ecosystem of flora, fauna, and microbes, they unleashed erosion and desertification that resulted in the Dust Bowl, a wave of dust storms in the 1930s that blew western soils into the atmosphere, sometimes reaching hundreds of miles into the Atlantic Ocean.

Areas of settler colonialism were often at the forefront of women's suffrage. Canada's western provinces were the first to grant women the right to vote in 1916. In the United States, all of the states west of the Mississippi granted women the right to vote before the Nineteenth Amendment made it a national right in 1919. Women were first elected to statewide or federal office in Montana, New Mexico, North Dakota, Texas, and Wyoming.

Among the factors contributing to this acceleration of suffrage in the West was the process of establishing new legal and governing frameworks; because this process coincided with the rise of the suffrage movement, new legislatures were more receptive to political demands. In addition, the racial character of settler colonialism was expressed in suffrage racism, by which white communities came together to actively exclude minorities. In California, for instance, suffragists formed alliances with advocates for Chinese exclusion.

In Argentina and Chile, military campaigns produced a similar pattern of displacement by targeting the Mapuche Indians on both sides of the Andes. Between 1861 and 1883, Chile's "Pacification of Araucania" campaign made lands available to immigrants from Germany, Italy, Switzerland, and Britain. In the 1870s, the Argentine government launched the "Conquest of the Desert," a military campaign whose name evoked the idea that indigenous lands were an uncivilized wilderness; under this campaign the military seized the southern region of Patagonia. It was followed by the "Conquest of the Chaco," which seized regions in northwestern Argentina. These wars were accompanied by ambitious railroad construction that linked inland areas to the coast, the introduction of barbed wire fencing, and the development of new strains of cattle and grain that made Argentina a leading exporter of beef and wheat, mostly produced by immigrant tenant farmers from Italy, Germany, and Britain.

# A New American Empire

## How did U.S. policies in the Caribbean and Central America resemble European imperialism, and how did they differ?

By 1890 the United States had claimed the contiguous territories it acquired through purchase, war, and displacement. Its frontier was closed. It then redirected its expansionist pressures outward, beginning with the remnants of the Spanish Empire: Cuba and Puerto Rico in the Caribbean, and the Philippine Islands and Guam in the Pacific. Emulating the imperialism of European nations like Britain and France, the United States claimed control of land and people that served its economic interests and justified its domination through theories of white supremacy and by arguing that it was advancing civilization.

## U.S. Intervention in Latin America

Between 1898 and 1932 the U.S. government intervened militarily thirty-four times in ten nations in the Caribbean and Central America to extend and protect its economic interests. U.S. influence in the Circum-Caribbean was not new, however, and stretched back to the early nineteenth century. In 1823 President James Monroe proclaimed in the **Monroe Doctrine** that the United States would keep European influence out of Latin America. This doctrine asserted that Latin America was part of the U.S. sphere of influence. U.S. intervention in Latin America was also a byproduct of the manifest destiny ideal of consolidating national territory from the Atlantic to the Pacific. Often the easiest way to connect the two sides of the continent was through Latin America.

The California gold rush of the 1840s created incentives to move people and goods quickly and inexpensively between the eastern and western parts of the United States decades before its transcontinental railroad was completed in 1869. It was cheaper, faster, and safer to travel to the east or west coast of Mexico and Central America, traverse the continent where it was narrower, and continue the voyage by sea. The Panama Railway, the first railroad constructed in Central America, served exactly this purpose and was built with U.S. investment in 1855.

Facing pressure from abolitionists against expanding the slave regime westward, planters and politicians in the U.S. South responded by seeking opportunities to annex new lands in Latin America and the Caribbean. They eyed Cuba, the Dominican Republic, El Salvador, and Nicaragua. In Nicaragua, Tennessean William Walker employed a mercenary army to depose the government and install himself as president (1856–1857). One of his first acts was to reinstate slavery. He was overthrown by armies sent from Costa Rica, El Salvador, and Honduras.

By the end of the nineteenth century U.S. involvement in Latin America had intensified, first through private investment and then through military force. In 1893 a group of U.S. investors formed the Santo Domingo Improvement Company, which bought the foreign debt of the Dominican Republic and took control of its customs houses in order to repay investors and creditors. After the government propped up by the U.S. company fell, President Theodore Roosevelt introduced what would be known as the **Roosevelt Corollary** to the Monroe Doctrine, which stated that the

United States, as a civilized nation, would correct the "chronic wrongdoing" of its neighbors, such as failure to protect U.S. investments.

In 1903 and 1904 Roosevelt deployed Marines to the Dominican Republic to protect the investments of U.S. firms. Marines occupied the Dominican Republic again from 1916 to 1924. The violent and corrupt dictator Rafael Trujillo (troo-HEE-yo) ruled from 1930 to 1961 with the support of the United States. When he eventually defied the United States, he was assassinated by rivals acting with the encouragement of the U.S. government.

Versions of the Dominican Republic's experience played out across the Circum-Caribbean. U.S. Marines occupied Haiti from 1915 to 1934 and Nicaragua from 1912 to 1934. These occupations followed a similar pattern of using military force to protect private U.S. investments in banana and sugar plantations, railroads, mining, ports, and utilities. And as U.S. forces departed, they left power in the hands of dictators who served U.S. interests. These dictators governed not through popular consent but through force, corruption, and the support of the United States.

## The Spanish-American War

In Cuba a second war of independence erupted in 1895 after it had failed to gain freedom from Spain in the Ten Years' War (1868–1878). A brutal war of attrition ensued, and by 1898 the countryside was in ruins and Spanish colonial control was restricted to a handful of cities. Cuban nationalists were on the verge of defeating the Spanish forces and gaining independence. But before they could realize this goal, the United States intervened, resulting in the Spanish-American War (1898).

The U.S. intervention began with a provocative act: sailing the battleship *Maine* into Havana harbor. This was an aggressive act because the battleship was capable of bombarding the entire city. But soon after it laid anchor, the *Maine* exploded and sank, killing hundreds of sailors. The U.S. government accused Spain of sinking the warship, a charge Spain denied, and demanded that the Spanish government provide restitution. Later investigations determined that a kitchen fire spread to the main munitions storage and blew up the ship. The sinking of the *Maine* led to war. After the U.S. Navy and Marines defeated Spanish forces in the Pacific and the Caribbean, the United States acquired Guam and Puerto Rico and launched a military occupation of Cuba and the Philippines.

Puerto Rico and Guam became colonies directly ruled by U.S. administrators, and residents of both island territories did not gain the right to elect their own leaders until after the Second World War. They remained commonwealths (territories that are not states, and, for many, a euphemism for colonies) of the United States. The U.S. government also established direct rule in the Philippines, brushing aside the government established by Filipino nationalists who had fought for freedom from Spain. Nationalists then fought against the United States in the Philippine-American War (1899–1902) in an unsuccessful effort to establish an independent government.

Cuba alone gained independence, but U.S. pressure limited that independence. The Platt Amendment, which the United States imposed as a condition of Cuban independence, gave the U.S. Senate the power to annul Cuban laws, withheld Cuba's right to establish foreign treaties, and granted the United States control over Guantanamo Bay, where it established a permanent naval base. In addition to imposing legal limits on Cuban independence, the United States repeatedly occupied the island. Between 1917 and 1922 U.S. administrator Enoch Crowder governed Cuba from his staterooms on the battleship *Minnesota*.

The constraints that the U.S. government imposed on Cuban politics, along with its willingness to deploy troops and periodically establish military rule, created a safe and fertile environment for U.S. investment. As the first U.S. commander of Cuba, General Leonard Wood equated good government with investor confidence: "When people ask me what I mean by stable government, I tell them 'money at six percent.'"[8] During the war of independence that had raged since 1895, Cuban farmers had been bankrupted, with 100,000 farms and 3,000 ranches destroyed. U.S. investors flooded in, and by 1919 half of the island's sugar mills were owned by U.S. businesses. Small farms were consolidated into estates as twenty-two companies took hold of 20 percent of Cuba's national territory. U.S. companies like Coca-Cola and Hershey were among the new landowners, producing their most important ingredient: sugar.

The United States exported its prevailing racial prejudices to its new Caribbean territories. In Cuba, U.S. authorities encouraged political parties to exclude black Cubans. Black war veterans established the Independent Party of Color in 1908 to press for political inclusion. Party leaders Evaristo Estenoz and Pedro Ivonet sought to use the party's potential electoral weight to incorporate black Cubans into government and education. The party was banned in 1910, and in 1912 its leaders organized a revolt that led to a violent backlash by the army and police, supported by U.S. Marines. The campaign against members of the party was followed by a wave of lynchings of black Cubans across the island.

In Puerto Rico the influence of U.S. racism was more direct. In 1913, as the U.S. Congress debated granting Puerto Ricans U.S. citizenship, the federal judge for Puerto Rico appointed by President Woodrow Wilson objected and wrote to the president that Puerto Ricans "have the Latin American excitability and I think Americans should go slowly in granting them anything like autonomy. Their civilization is not at all like ours yet." Later the judge declared, "The mixture of black and white in Porto Rico threatens to create a race of mongrels of no use to anyone, a race of Spanish American talkers. A governor of the South, or with knowledge of southern remedies for that trouble could, if a wise man, do much."[9]

The United States instituted the "remedies" to which the judge alluded, such as the sterilization of many thousands of Puerto Rican women as part of a policy aimed at addressing what the government saw as overpopulation on the island. In addition, Puerto Rican men drafted into U.S. military service were organized into segregated units, as African Americans were.

## The Panama Canal

U.S. imperialism in the Caribbean extended beyond Cuba and Puerto Rico to the prize the United States had pursued for decades: a canal to connect the Atlantic and Pacific Oceans. The canal would transport cargo between the east and west of the United States much less expensively than rail. In the mid-nineteenth century the U.S. railroad tycoon Cornelius Vanderbilt tried but failed to build a canal through Nicaragua. Later, a consortium of French investors pursued the construction of a canal in the Colombian province of Panama, encouraged by the success of the Suez Canal. Engineers and laborers completed some excavation before the French company went bankrupt.

After the Spanish-American War gave the United States more control of the Caribbean, U.S. authorities negotiated with the Colombian government for the right to continue the project started by the French company. When the Colombian congress balked at the U.S. demand that it should have territorial control of the canal, the U.S. government encouraged an insurrection in Panama City and recognized the rebels as leaders of the new country of Panama. The new Panamanian government gave the United States permanent rights to the canal and the land upon which it was built, which became known as the Canal Zone. The Canal Zone became an unincorporated U.S. territory, similar in status to Puerto Rico and Guam. It housed canal workers as well as U.S. military installations.

Tens of thousands of migrant workers from around the Caribbean provided labor for construction of the canal, which opened in 1914. U.S. authorities instituted the same segregationist policies applied in their other Caribbean territories. Workers were divided into a "gold roll" of highly paid white U.S. workers and a "silver roll" of mostly black workers, who came from Barbados, Panama, Nicaragua, Colombia, and other parts of the Caribbean. They were paid lower wages, faced much higher rates of death and injury, and lived in less healthy conditions. The Canal Zone itself functioned as a segregated enclave: U.S. residents could move freely between it and Panamanian territory, but it was closed to Panamanians except those who entered through labor contracts.

# Chapter Summary

In the century after independence, political consolidation and economic integration varied across the Americas. The North of the United States became the continent's main engine of capital accumulation, immigration, and industrialization. In the U.S. South and Brazil, reliance on slavery weakened internal markets, inhibited immigration, and slowed industrialization. In Spanish America the lack of a governing consensus until the second half of the nineteenth century resulted in "lost decades" after independence, in which new countries fell behind not only relative to other regions of the world, but even relative to their past colonial experiences.

The cycle of war that began in the 1850s and continued for the next two decades reshaped the Americas politically and economically, consolidating a liberal order that placed great wealth in few hands while dealing misery and dislocation to many others. Liberalism had a modernizing influence on trade and industry, but it further concentrated wealth. Just as the United States waged wars against the Indians and pushed its frontier westward, other countries including Mexico, Chile, and Argentina had their own "Indian wars" and frontier expansion. Likewise, Mexico, Chile, and Argentina had their own "Indian wars" and frontier expansion. Racial prejudice kept most African Americans at the social and economic margins.

By the beginning of the twentieth century, the economies of American nations were tightly integrated into the world economy, and powerful currents of immigration further deepened ties between continents. The industrialization that began in the northeast of the United States developed elsewhere in the continent, but the lead in industrialization held by the United States allowed it to increasingly impose its will over other nations. The economic and social dislocations produced by the liberal model of export-oriented economic growth also awoke growing social demands by the rural and urban poor. These boiled over the most dramatically in Mexico's 1910 revolution; in other locations as well, workers' demands for the right to organize for better wages and for political representation became too insistent to ignore.

## NOTES

1. Jürgen Buchenau, *Mexican Mosaic: A Brief History of Mexico* (Wheeling, Ill.: Harlan-Davidson, 2008), p. 2.

2. Jaime E. Rodriguez O., *Down from Colonialism: Mexico's Nineteenth Century Crisis* (Los Angeles: Chicano Studies Center Research Publications, UCLA, 1983), p. 15.

3. David Rock, *Argentina, 1516–1987: From Spanish Colonization to Alfonsín* (Berkeley: University of California Press, 1987), p. 154.

4. Quoted in Nicolas Shumway, *The Invention of Argentina* (Berkeley: University of California Press, 1991), p. 147.

5. Quoted in Ken Burns, *The West*, Episode 7, "Barbarians" (1996), https://www.pbs.org/weta/thewest/program/episodes/seven/barbarians.htm.

6. Eli S. Parker, *Transactions of the Buffalo Historical Society: Red Jacket*, vol. 3 (Buffalo, N.Y.: Buffalo Historical Society, 1885), p. 42; second quotation from Joan Magee, *Loyalist Mosaic: A Multi-ethnic Heritage* (Toronto: Dundrum, 1984), p. 216.

7. Roger L. Welsch, *A Treasury of Nebraska Pioneer Folklore* (Lincoln: University of Nebraska Press, 1984), pp. 48–49.

8. Quoted in Luis A. Pérez, *The War of 1898: The United States and Cuba in History and Historiography* (Chapel Hill: University of North Carolina Press, 1998), p. 32.

9. Quoted in Arturo Morales Carrión, *Puerto Rico: A Political and Cultural History* (New York: W. W. Norton, 1983), pp. 187–188.

## MAKE CONNECTIONS   LOOK AHEAD

In the Americas the century or so between independence and World War I was a time of nation building. Colonial governments were overthrown, new constitutions were written, settlement was extended, slavery was ended, and immigrants from around the world settled. Although wealth was unevenly distributed, in most of these countries it was not hard to find signs of progress: growing cities, expanding opportunities for education, and modern conveniences. This progress came with harsh costs for indigenous communities, rural peasants, and the growing ranks of urban industrial workers. The great upheaval of the Mexican Revolution was a reaction against these costs, and it resulted in a society that curbed some of the excesses facilitated by liberalism.

World War I, the topic of the next chapter, affected these countries in a variety of ways. Canada followed Britain into the war in 1914 and sent six hundred thousand men to fight, losing many in some of the bloodiest battles of the war. The United States did not join the war until 1917, but quickly mobilized several million men and in 1918 began sending soldiers and materials in huge numbers. Even countries that maintained neutrality, as all the Latin American countries other than Brazil did, felt the economic impact of the war deeply, especially the increased demand for food and manufactured goods. For the working class the global demand for exported foods drove up the cost of living, but the profits that oligarchs accumulated fueled the process of industrialization.

# Chapter 27 Review

## IDENTIFY KEY TERMS

**Identify and explain the significance of each item below.**

oligarchs (p. 700)

Circum-Caribbean (p. 700)

caudillismo (p. 701)

manifest destiny (p. 701)

Treaty of Guadalupe Hidalgo (p. 703)

Lerdo Law (p. 703)

neocolonialism (p. 705)

free womb laws (p. 706)

latifundios (p. 709)

Porfiriato (p. 711)

Plan de Ayala (p. 711)

anarcho-syndicalism
(p. 714)

settler colonialism (p. 718)

Monroe Doctrine (p. 720)

Roosevelt Corollary (p. 720)

## REVIEW THE MAIN IDEAS

**Answer the focus questions from each section of the chapter.**

1. How and why did nation-state consolidation vary across the Americas? (p. 700)

2. Why did slavery last longer in the United States, Brazil, and Cuba than elsewhere in the Americas, and how did resistance by enslaved people shape abolition? (p. 705)

3. As Latin America became more integrated into the world economy, how did patterns of economic growth shape political culture and social reactions? (p. 709)

4. What factors influenced immigration to the Americas? How did immigrants shape—and how were they shaped by—their new settings? (p. 713)

5. How did U.S. policies in the Caribbean and Central America resemble European imperialism, and how did they differ? (p. 720)

## MAKE COMPARISONS AND CONNECTIONS

**Analyze the larger developments and continuities within and across chapters.**

1. How did the embrace of liberalism in Latin America resemble or differ from its expression in other parts of the world?

2. How did factors that influenced the Mexican Revolution express themselves in other parts of the Americas?

3. In what ways did the United States come to resemble European powers in building overseas empires (Chapters 25, 26)? How did U.S. expansionism and the colonialism practiced by Britain and France differ?

4. How did neocolonialism make Latin America after independence resemble regions of Asia and Africa (Chapters 25, 26) that were subjected to direct colonial rule?

## CHRONOLOGY

**1780–1850**   • Industrial Revolution in Britain (Ch. 23)

**1810–1825**   • Wars of independence in Latin America

**1846–1848**   • Mexican-American War

**1848**   • Marx and Engels publish *The Communist Manifesto* (Ch. 24)

**1857–1861**   • Mexican Wars of Reform

**1858**   • British Parliament begins to rule India (Ch. 26)

**1861–1865**   • U.S. Civil War

**1865–1870**   • Paraguay War (War of the Triple Alliance)

**1867**   • Japan's Meiji Restoration promotes reforms and industrialization (Ch. 26)

**1867**   • Dominion of Canada formed

**1868–1878**   • Cuban Ten Years' War

**1879–1883**   • War of the Pacific

**1884–1885**   • Berlin Conference formalizes European colonization in Africa (Ch. 25)

**1886**   • Abolition of slavery in Cuba

**1888**   • Abolition of slavery in Brazil

**1889**   • Brazilian monarchy overthrown and republic established

**1898**   • Spanish-American War

**1904**   • U.S. secures the rights to build and control the Panama Canal

**1910**   • Mexican Revolution erupts

# 28

# World War and Revolution

## 1914–1929

**IN SUMMER 1914 THE NATIONS OF EUROPE WENT WILLINGLY TO WAR.** They believed they had no other choice, but everyone confidently expected a short war leading to a decisive victory. Such a war, they believed, would "clear the air." Then European society could continue as before. They were wrong. The First World War was long, global, indecisive, and tremendously destructive. It quickly degenerated into a senseless military stalemate lasting four years. To the shell-shocked generation of survivors, it became simply the Great War.

In March 1917, as Russia suffered horrendous losses on the eastern front, its war-weary people rebelled against their tsar, Nicholas II, forcing him to abdicate. Moderate reformists established a provisional government but made the fatal decision to continue the war against Germany. In November Vladimir Lenin and his Communist Bolshevik Party staged a second revolution, this time promising an end to the war. The Germans forced a harsh peace on the Russians, but Lenin believed this a small price to pay for the establishment of history's first Communist state. Few then could have realized how profoundly this event would shape the course of the twentieth century.

When the Great War's victorious Allies, led by Great Britain, France, and the United States, gathered in Paris in 1919 to write the peace, they were well aware of the importance of their decisions. Some came to Paris seeking revenge, some came looking for the spoils of war, and some promoted nationalist causes, while a few sought an idealistic end to war. The process was massive and complex, but in the end few left Paris satisfied with the results. The peace and prosperity the delegates had so earnestly sought lasted barely a decade.

# The First World War, 1914–1918

**What were the long-term and immediate causes of World War I, and how did the conflict become a global war?**

The First World War clearly marked a major break in the course of world history. The maps of Europe and southwest Asia were redrawn, nationalist movements took root and spread across Asia (the subject of the next chapter), America consolidated its position as a global power, and the world experienced, for the first time, industrialized, total war. Europe's Great Powers started the war and suffered the most — in casualties, in costs, in destruction, and in societal and political upheaval. Imperialism also brought the conflict to the Middle East, Africa, and Asia, making this a global war of unprecedented scope. The young soldiers who went to war believed in the pre-1914 world of order, progress, and patriotism. Then, in the words of German soldier and writer Erich Remarque (rih-MAHRK), the "first bombardment showed us our mistake, and under it the world as they had taught it to us broke in pieces."[1]

## Origins and Causes of the Great War

Scholars began arguing over the Great War's origins soon after it began, and the debate continues a century after its end. The victorious Allied powers expressed their opinion — that Germany caused the war — in the Versailles treaty. But history seldom offers such simple answers, particularly to questions so complex. The war's origins lie in the nineteenth century, and its immediate causes lie in the few years and months before the war, especially one particular morning in June 1914.

Any study of the Great War's origins must begin with nationalism, one of the major ideologies of the nineteenth century, and its armed companion, **militarism**, the glorification of the military as the supreme ideal of the state with all other interests subordinate to it. European concerns over national security, economies, welfare, identities, and overseas empires set nation against nation, alliance against alliance, and army against army until they all went to war at once.

Competition between nations intensified greatly when Germany became a unified nation-state and the most powerful country in Europe in 1871. A new era in international relations began, as Chancellor Bismarck declared Germany a "satisfied" power, having no territorial ambitions within Europe and desiring only peace.

But how to preserve the peace? Bismarck's first concern was to keep rival France diplomatically isolated and without military allies. His second concern was to prevent Germany from being dragged into a war between the two rival empires, Austria-Hungary and Russia, as they sought to fill the power vacuum created in the Balkans by the Ottoman Empire's decline. To these ends, Bismarck brokered a series of treaties and alliances, all meant to ensure the balance of power in Europe and to prevent the outbreak of war.

In 1890 Germany's new emperor, Wilhelm II, forced Bismarck to resign and then abandoned many of Bismarck's efforts to ensure German security through promoting European peace and stability. Wilhelm refused to renew a nonaggression pact Bismarck had signed with Russia in 1887, for example, which prompted France to court the tsar, offering loans and arms, and sign a Franco-Russian Alliance in 1892. With France and Russia now allied against Germany, Austria, and Italy, Great Britain's foreign policy became increasingly crucial. Many Germans and some Britons felt that the ethnically related Germanic and Anglo-Saxon peoples were natural allies. However, the good relations that had prevailed between Prussia and Great Britain since the mid-eighteenth century gave way after 1890 to a bitter Anglo-German rivalry.

There were several reasons for this development. Germany and Great Britain's commercial rivalry in world markets and Kaiser Wilhelm's publicly expressed intention to create a global German empire unsettled the British. German nationalist militarists saw a large navy as the legitimate mark of a great world power, and their decision in 1900 to add a fleet of big-gun battleships to their already expanding navy heightened tensions. British leaders considered this expansion a military challenge to their long-standing naval supremacy.

Thus British leaders set about shoring up their exposed position with their own alliances and agreements. Britain improved its relations with the United States, concluded an alliance with Japan in 1902, and in the Anglo-French Entente (ahn-TAHNT) of 1904 settled all outstanding colonial disputes with France. Frustrated by Britain's closer relationship with France, Germany's leaders decided to test the entente's strength by demanding an international conference to challenge French control over Morocco. At the Algeciras (al-jih-SIR-uhs) (Spain) Conference in 1906, Germany's crude bullying only forced France and Britain closer together, and Germany left the meeting empty-handed.

The Moroccan crisis was something of a diplomatic revelation. Britain, France, Russia, and even the United States began to view Germany as a potential threat. At the same time, German leaders began to suspect sinister plots to encircle Germany and block its development as a world power. In 1907 Russia and Britain settled

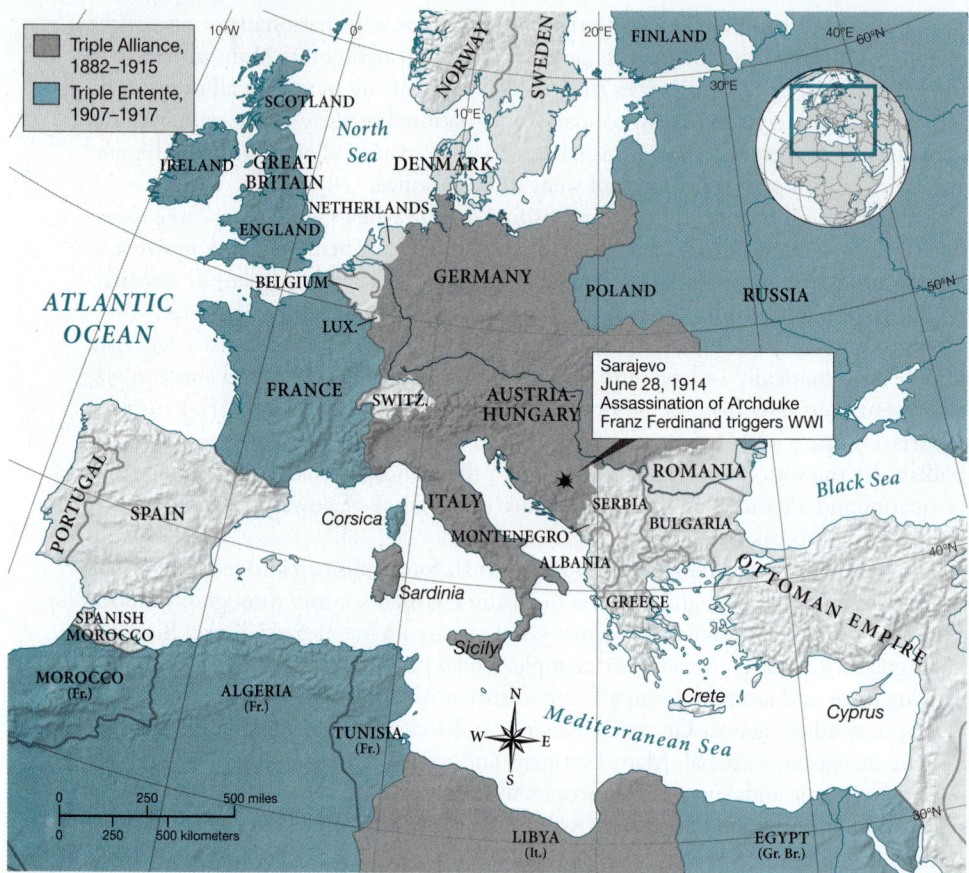

**MAP 28.1** **European Alliances at the Outbreak of World War I, 1914**
By the time war broke out, Europe was divided into two opposing alliances: the Triple Entente of Britain, France, and Russia and the Triple Alliance of Germany, Austria-Hungary, and Italy. Italy switched sides and joined the Entente in 1915.

their outstanding differences and signed the Anglo-Russian Agreement. This treaty, together with the earlier Franco-Russian Alliance of 1892 and Anglo-French Entente of 1904, served as a catalyst for the **Triple Entente**, the alliance of Great Britain, France, and Russia in the First World War (Map 28.1).

By 1909 Europe's leading nations were divided into two hostile blocs, both ill-prepared to deal with upheaval in the Balkans.

## The Outbreak of War

In 1897, the year before he died, the prescient Bismarck is reported to have remarked, "One day the great European War will come out of some damned foolish thing in the Balkans."[2] By the early twentieth century a Balkans war seemed inevitable. The reason was simple: nationalism was destroying the Ottoman Empire in Europe and threatening to break up the Austro-Hungarian Empire.

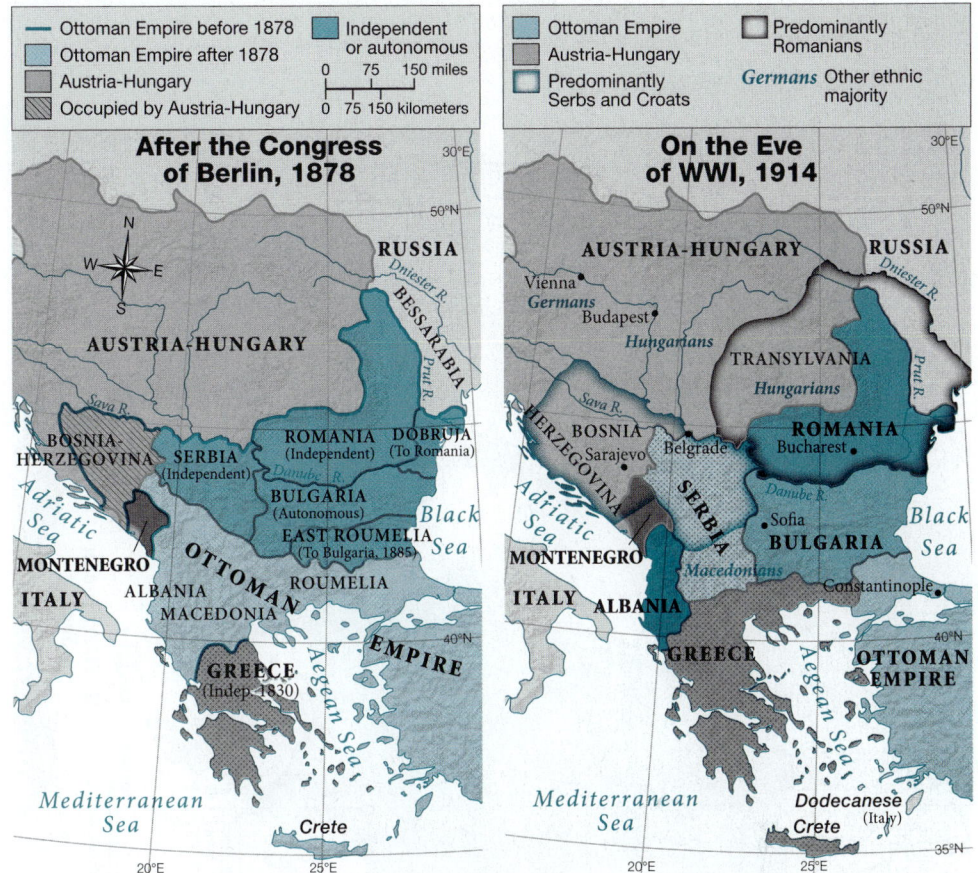

**MAP 28.2  The Balkans, 1878–1914**
The Ottoman Empire suffered large territorial losses after the Congress of Berlin in 1878 but remained a power in the Balkans. By 1914 ethnic boundaries that did not follow political boundaries had formed, and Serbian national aspirations threatened Austria-Hungary.

Serbia led the way, becoming openly hostile to both Austria-Hungary and the Ottoman Empire. The Slavic Serbs looked to Slavic Russia for support of their national aspirations. In 1908, to block Serbian expansion, Austria formally annexed Bosnia and Herzegovina, with their large Serbian, Croatian (kroh-AY-shuhn), and Muslim populations. Serbia erupted in rage but could do nothing without Russia's support.

Then two nationalist wars, the first and second Balkan wars in 1912 and 1913, finally destroyed the centuries-long Ottoman presence in Europe (Map 28.2). This sudden but long-expected event elated Balkan nationalists but dismayed Austria-Hungary's leaders, who feared that Austria-Hungary might next be broken apart.

Within this tense context, Serbian nationalist Gavrilo Princip (gah-VRIH-loh prin-SIP) assassinated Archduke Franz Ferdinand, heir to the Austro-Hungarian throne, and his wife, Sophie, on June 28, 1914, during a state visit to the Bosnian capital of Sarajevo (sar-uh-YAY-voh). Austria-Hungary's leaders held Serbia responsible and

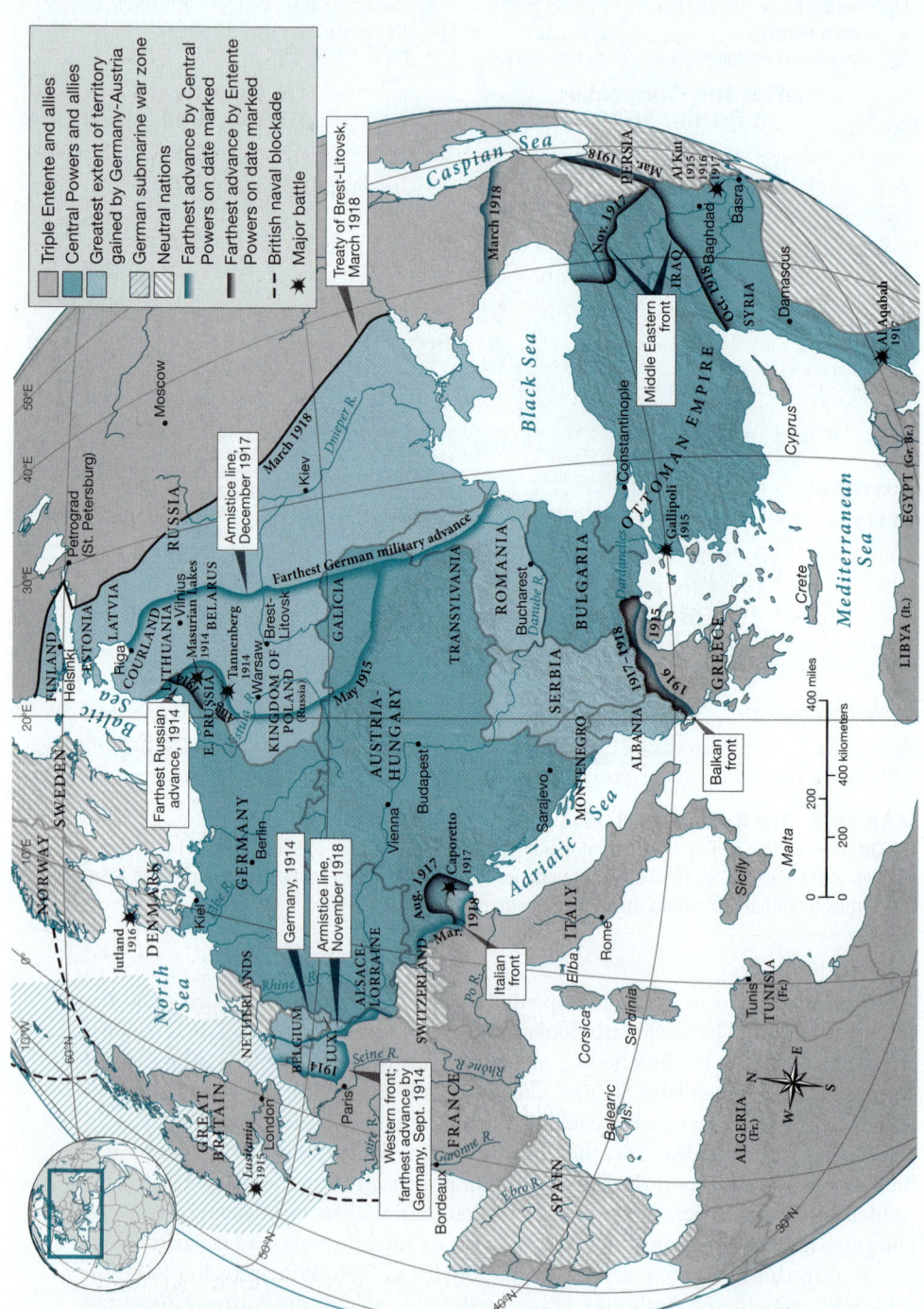

**Legend:**
- Triple Entente and allies
- Central Powers and allies
- Greatest extent of territory gained by Germany-Austria
- German submarine war zone
- Neutral nations
- Farthest advance by Central Powers on date marked
- Farthest advance by Entente Powers on date marked
- British naval blockade
- ★ Major battle

Treaty of Brest-Litovsk, March 1918

*Caspian Sea*

March 1918

Moscow

Petrograd (St. Petersburg)

50°E

40°E

30°E

RUSSIA

March 1918

Kiev

*Dnieper R.*

Armistice line, December 1917

Farthest German military advance

FINLAND

Helsinki

*Baltic Sea*

ESTONIA

Riga

LATVIA

COURLAND

Vilnius

LITHUANIA

BELARUS

1914

Masurian Lakes

Tannenberg 1914

Warsaw

KINGDOM OF POLAND (Russia)

Brest-Litovsk

GALICIA

May 1915

Farthest Russian advance, 1914

E. PRUSSIA

*Vistula R.*

20°E

SWEDEN

NORWAY

10°E

0°

60°N

*North Sea*

Jutland 1916

DENMARK

Kiel

*Elbe R.*

GERMANY

Berlin

Germany, 1914

Armistice line, November 1918

Lusitania 1915

GREAT BRITAIN

London

NETHERLANDS

BELGIUM

LUX.

1914

Paris

*Seine R.*

ALSACE-LORRAINE

*Rhine R.*

SWITZERLAND

Western front; farthest advance by Germany, Sept. 1914

FRANCE

*Loire R.*

*Rhône R.*

*Garonne R.*

Bordeaux

SPAIN

*Ebro R.*

TRANSYLVANIA

AUSTRIA-HUNGARY

Vienna

Budapest

Caporetto 1917

Aug. 1917

Mar. 1918

Italian front

Po R.

ITALY

Rome

Elba

Corsica (Fr.)

Sardinia

ROMANIA

Bucharest

*Danube R.*

SERBIA

MONTENEGRO

Sarajevo

ALBANIA

BULGARIA

1917 1918

1915

1916

Balkan front

GREECE

Crete

*Adriatic Sea*

Malta

Sicily

Tunis

TUNISIA (Fr.)

ALGERIA (Fr.)

Balearic Isls.

*Black Sea*

Constantinople

Gallipoli 1915

*Dardanelles*

OTTOMAN EMPIRE

Nov. 1917

Middle Eastern front

Mar. 1918

PERSIA

IRAQ

Oct. 1918

Baghdad

Al Kut 1915 1916 1917

Basra

SYRIA

Damascus

Al 'Aqabah 1917

Cyprus

*Mediterranean Sea*

EGYPT (Gr. Br.)

LIBYA (It.)

400 miles

400 kilometers

200

200

0

0

N E S W

on July 23 presented Serbia with an unconditional ultimatum that included demands amounting to Austrian control of the Serbian state. When Serbia replied moderately but evasively, Austria declared war on Serbia on July 28 (Map 28.3).

Of prime importance in Austria-Hungary's fateful decision was Germany's unconditional support. Kaiser Wilhelm II and his chancellor, Theobald von Bethmann-Hollweg (THEE-uh-bawld von BAYT-mahn-hawl-vayk), realized that war between Austria and Russia was likely, for Russia could not stand by and watch the Serbs be crushed. Yet Bethmann-Hollweg hoped that while Russia (and its ally France) might go to war, Great Britain would remain neutral.

Anticipating a possible conflict, Europe's military leaders had been drawing up war plans and timetables for years, and now these, rather than diplomacy, began to dictate policy. On July 28, as Austrian armies bombarded Belgrade, Tsar Nicholas II ordered a partial mobilization against Austria-Hungary but almost immediately found this was impossible. Russia had assumed a war with both Austria and Germany, and it could not mobilize against one without mobilizing against the other. Therefore, on July 29 Russia ordered full mobilization and in effect declared general war. The German general staff had also prepared for a two-front war. Its Schlieffen (SHLEE-fuhn) plan, first drafted in 1905, called for first knocking out France with a lightning attack through neutral Belgium to capture Paris before turning on a slower-to-mobilize Russia. On August 3 German armies invaded Belgium. Great Britain declared war on Germany the following day. In each country the great majority of the population rallied to defend its nation and enthusiastically embraced war in August 1914.

## Stalemate and Slaughter

When the Germans invaded Belgium in August 1914, the Belgian army defended its homeland and then fell back to join a rapidly landed British army corps near the Franco-Belgian border. Instead of quickly capturing Paris in a vast encircling movement, German soldiers were advancing slowly along an enormous front. On September 6 the French attacked the German line at the Battle of the Marne (MAHRN). For three days France threw everything into the attack, forcing the Germans to fall back (see Map 28.3).

The two stalled armies then dug in behind rows of trenches, mines, and barbed wire. A "no-man's land" of one hundred to three hundred yards lay between the two combatants. Eventually an unbroken line of parallel zigzag trenches stretched over four hundred miles from the Belgian coast to the Swiss frontier. By November 1914 the slaughter on the western front had begun in earnest. For four years battles followed the same plan: after ceaseless heavy artillery shelling to "soften up" the enemy, young soldiers went "over the top" of the trenches in frontal attacks on the enemy's line.

< **MAP 28.3**   **The First World War in Europe**
The trench war on the western front was concentrated in Belgium and northern France, while the war in the east encompassed an enormous territory.

**John Nash, *Over the Top*** John Nash was an English artist who served as a soldier with the First Battalion Artists' Rifles from 1916 to 1918 and then served as an official war artist in 1918. This painting depicts the Artists' Rifles leaving their trench to attack at Welsh Ridge in France on December 30, 1917. In a unit of eighty men, Nash was one of only twelve soldiers not wounded or killed by German shelling and gunfire; many of the casualties occurred during the first few minutes of the advance. (Imperial War Museum, London, UK/IWM/Getty Images)

German writer Erich Remarque described a typical attack in his celebrated novel *All Quiet on the Western Front* (1929):

> We see men living with their skulls blown open; we see soldiers run with their two feet cut off. . . . Still the little piece of convulsed earth in which we lie is held. We have yielded no more than a few hundred yards of it as a prize to the enemy. But on every yard there lies a dead man.[3]

The human cost of **trench warfare** was staggering, while territorial gains were minuscule. In the Battle of the Somme (SAWM) in summer 1916, the British and French gained an insignificant 125 square miles at a cost of 600,000 dead or wounded. The Germans lost 500,000 men. That same year the unsuccessful German attack on Verdun (vehr-DUHN) cost 700,000 lives on both sides. The slaughter was made even greater by new weapons of war—including chemical gases, tanks, airplanes, flamethrowers, and the machine gun. British poet Siegfried Sassoon (1886–1967) wrote of the Somme offensive, "I am staring at a sunlit picture of Hell."[4] The year 1917 was equally terrible.

On the eastern front, the Russians moved into eastern Germany but suffered appalling losses against the Germans at the Battles of Tannenberg and the Masurian Lakes in August and September 1914 (see Map 28.3). German and Austrian forces then reversed the Russian advances of 1914 and forced the Russians to retreat deep into their own territory in the 1915 eastern campaign. A staggering 2.5 million Russians were killed, wounded, or taken prisoner.

These changing tides of victory and hopes of territorial gains brought neutral countries into the war. Italy, a member of the Triple Alliance since 1882, declared its neutrality in 1914. Then, in May 1915, Italy joined the Triple Entente of Great Britain, France, and Russia in return for promises of Austrian territory. In September Bulgaria joined the Triple Alliance in order to settle old scores with Serbia.

## The War Becomes Global

In October 1914 the Ottoman Empire joined with Austria and Germany, by then known as the Central Powers. A German alliance permitted the Turks to renounce the limitations on Ottoman sovereignty imposed by Europeans in the nineteenth century and also to settle old grievances with Russia, the Turks' historic enemy.

The entry of the Ottoman Turks pulled the entire Middle East into the war and made it truly a global conflict. While Russia attacked the Ottomans in the Caucasus, the British protected their rule in Egypt. In 1915, at the Battle of Gallipoli (guh-LIP-uh-lee), British forces tried to take the Dardanelles (dahr-duh-NELZ) and Constantinople from the Ottoman Turks but were badly defeated. Casualties were high on both sides and included thousands of Australians and New Zealanders. Deeply loyal to the mother country, Australia sent 329,000 men and vast economic aid to Britain during the war. Over 100,000 New Zealanders also served in the war, almost a tenth of New Zealand's entire population, and they suffered a 58 percent casualty rate — one of the highest of any country. Nearly 4,000 native New Zealand Maori soldiers also fought at Gallipoli and on the western front. Ormond Burton, a New Zealand infantryman, later observed that "somewhere between the landing at Anzac [a cove on the Gallipolian peninsula] and the end of the battle of the Somme, New Zealand very definitely became a nation."[5]

The British had more success inciting Arabs to revolt against their Turkish over-lords. The foremost Arab leader was Hussein ibn-Ali (1856–1931), who governed much of the Ottoman Empire's territory along the Red Sea (see Map 29.1). In 1915 Hussein won vague British commitments for an independent Arab kingdom, with himself as king of the Arabs. In return, he joined forces with the British under T. E. Lawrence, who in 1917 led Arab tribesmen and Indian soldiers in a successful guerrilla war against the Turks on the Arabian peninsula. In the Ottoman province of Iraq, Britain occupied Basra (BAHS-rah) in 1914 and captured Baghdad in 1917. In 1918 British armies, aided by imperial forces from Egypt, India, Australia, and New Zealand, smashed the old Ottoman state. Thus war brought revolutionary change to the Middle East.

Japan, allied with the British since 1902, joined the Triple Entente on August 23, 1914, and began attacking German-controlled colonies and territories in the Pacific. Later that year Japan seized Germany's holdings on the Shandong (shan-dawng) Peninsula in China.

War also spread to colonies in Africa and East Asia. Colonized peoples provided critical supplies and fought in Europe, Africa, and the Ottoman Empire. More than a million Africans and Asians served in the various armies of the warring powers, with more than double that number serving as porters to carry equipment. Drawn primarily from Senegal, French West Africa, and British South Africa, over 140,000 Africans fought on the western front, and 31,000 of them died there.

Many of these men joined up to get clothes (uniforms), food, and money for enlisting. Others did so because colonial recruiters promised them better lives when they returned home. Most were illiterate and had no idea of why they were going or what they would experience. One West African infantryman, Kande Kamara, later wrote:

> We black African soldiers were very sorrowful about the white man's war. . . .
> I didn't really care who was right — whether it was the French or the Germans —
> I went to fight with the French army and that was all I knew. The reason for war
> was never disclosed to any soldier. . . . We just fought and fought until we got
> exhausted and died.[6]

The war had a profound impact on these colonial troops. Fighting against and killing Europeans destroyed the impression that the Europeans were superhuman.

New concepts like nationalism and individual freedoms—ideals for which the Europeans were supposedly fighting—were carried home to become rallying cries for future liberation struggles.

A crucial turning point in the expanding conflict came in April 1917 when the United States declared war on Germany. American intervention grew out of the war at sea and sympathy for the Triple Entente. At the beginning of the war Britain and France had established a naval blockade to strangle the Central Powers. In early 1915 Germany launched a counter-blockade using the new and deadly effective submarine. Then in May a German submarine sank the British passenger liner *Lusitania* (loo-sih-TAY-nee-uh) (which, besides regular passengers, was secretly and illegally carrying war materials to Britain). More than 1,000 people died, including 139 U.S. citizens. When President Woodrow Wilson protested vigorously, Germany was forced to restrict its submarine warfare for almost two years or face almost certain war with the United States.

Early in 1917 the German military command—confident that improved submarines could starve Britain into submission before the United States could come to its rescue—resumed unrestricted submarine warfare. This was a reckless gamble. The United States declared war on Germany and eventually tipped the balance in favor of the Triple Entente.

# The Home Front

### How did total war affect the home fronts of the major combatants?

The war's impact on civilians was no less massive than on the men crouched in trenches. Total war mobilized entire populations, led to increased state power, and promoted social equality. It also led to dissent and a growing antiwar movement.

## Mobilizing for Total War

Within months of the outbreak of the Great War, national unity governments began to plan and control economic and social life in order to wage **total war**. Governments imposed rationing, price and wage controls, and even restrictions on workers' freedom of movement. These total-war economies blurred the old distinction between soldiers on battlefields and civilians at home. As the ability of central governments to manage and control highly complicated economies increased, their powers were strengthened, often along socialist lines.

Germany went furthest in developing a planned economy to wage total war. Soon after war began, the Jewish industrialist Walter Rathenau (RAHT-uh-now) convinced the German government to set up the War Raw Materials Board to ration and distribute raw materials. Food was also rationed, and the board successfully produced substitutes, such as synthetic rubber and synthetic nitrates, for scarce war supplies. Following the terrible Battles of Verdun and the Somme in 1916, military leaders forced the Reichstag (RIGHKS-tahg) to accept the Auxiliary Service Law, which required all males between seventeen and sixty to work only at jobs considered critical to the war effort. Women also worked in war factories, mines, and steel mills.

As mature liberal democracies, France and Great Britain mobilized economically for total war less rapidly and less completely than autocratic Germany, aided by the fact that they could import materials from their colonies and from the United States. When it became apparent that the war was not going to end quickly, however, the Western Allies all passed laws giving their governments sweeping powers over all areas of the nation's daily life—including industrial and agricultural production, censorship, education, health and welfare, the curtailment of civil liberties, labor, and foreign aliens.

## The Social Impact of War

The social impact of total war was no less profound than the economic impact, though again there were important national variations. The military's insatiable needs—nearly every belligerent power resorted to conscription to put soldiers in the field—created a tremendous demand for workers at home. This situation brought about momentous changes.

One such change was increased power and prestige for labor unions. Unions cooperated with war governments in return for real participation in important decisions. This entry of labor leaders into policymaking councils paralleled the entry of socialist leaders into the war governments.

Women's roles also changed dramatically. In every belligerent country, large numbers of women went to work in industry, transportation, and offices. A former parlor maid reportedly told her boyfriend as he prepared to leave for France:

> While you are at the front firing shells, I am going into a munitions factory to make shells. The job will not be as well paid as domestic service, it will not be as comfortable as domestic service; it will be much harder work, but it will be my bit, and every time you fire your gun you can remember I am helping to make the shells.[7]

Moreover, women became highly visible—not only as munitions workers but also as bank tellers, mail carriers, and even police officers. Women also served as nurses and doctors at the front. In general, the war greatly expanded the range of women's activities and changed attitudes toward women. Although at war's end most women were quickly let go and their jobs were given back to the returning soldiers,

**Women Working at a Munitions Factory** These women, working at the Woolwich munitions factory in southeast London, are shoveling thousands of cartridge shells into wooden boxes to be shipped to the front in France. Women worked in munitions factories in all the warring nations, handling highly explosive materials and toxic chemicals and operating dangerous machines. Women's war efforts were rewarded in some countries after the war when they received the right to vote. (© TopFoto/The Image Works)

their many-sided war effort caused Britain, Germany, the United States, and Austria to grant them the right to vote after the war.

Recent scholarship has shown, however, that traditional views of gender—of male roles and female roles—remained remarkably resilient and that there was a significant conservative backlash in the postwar years. Even as the war progressed, many men, particularly soldiers, grew increasingly hostile toward women. Some were angry at mothers, wives, and girlfriends for urging them to enlist and fight in the horrible war. Soldiers with wives and girlfriends back home grew increasingly convinced that they were cheating on them. Others worried that factory or farm jobs had been taken by women and there would be no work when they returned home. Men were also concerned that if women received the vote at war's end, they would vote themselves into power. These concerns, as well as the fear that women would lose their femininity, are reflected in a letter from Private G. F. Wilby, serving in East Africa, to his fiancée in London, Ethel Baxter, in August 1918:

> Whatever you do, don't go in Munitions or anything in that line—just fill a Woman's position and remain a woman. . . . I want to return and find the same loveable little woman that I left behind—not a coarse thing more of a man than a woman.[8]

War also promoted social equality, blurring class distinctions and lessening the gap between rich and poor. Greater equality was reflected in full employment, rationing according to physical needs, and a sharing of hardships. Society became more uniform and more egalitarian.

## Growing Political Tensions

During the war's first two years, belief in a just cause and patriotic nationalism united soldiers and civilians behind their various national leaders. Each government employed censorship and propaganda to maintain popular support.

By spring 1916, however, cracks were appearing under the strain of total war. In April Irish nationalists in Dublin unsuccessfully rose up against British rule in the Easter Rebellion. Strikes and protest marches over inadequate food flared up on every home front. In April 1917 nearly half the French infantry divisions mutinied for two months after suffering enormous losses in the Second Battle of the Aisne (EN). Later that year there was a massive mutiny of Russian soldiers supporting the revolution.

The Central Powers experienced the most strain. In October 1916 a young socialist assassinated Austria's chief minister. By 1917 German political unity was also collapsing, and prewar social conflicts were re-emerging. A coalition of Socialists and Catholics in the Reichstag called for a compromise "peace without annexations or reparations." Thus Germany, like its ally Austria-Hungary and its enemy France, began to crack in 1917. But it was Russia that collapsed first and saved the Central Powers—for a time.

# The Russian Revolution

### What factors led to the Russian Revolution, and what was its outcome?

The 1917 Russian Revolution, directly related to the Great War, opened a new era with a radically new prototype of state and society that changed the course of the twentieth century.

## The Fall of Imperial Russia

Imperial Russia in 1914 was still predominantly a rural and nonurbanized society. Industrialization came late to Russia and, although rapidly expanding, was still in its early stages. Peasants still made up perhaps 80 percent of the population. Besides the royal family and the nobility, the rest of Russian society consisted of the bourgeoisie (the elite, educated upper and middle classes, such as liberal politicians, propertied and professional classes, military officers, and landowners) and the proletariat (the urban working class, which remained small, and rank-and-file soldiers and sailors). These two factions contended for power when the tsar abdicated in 1917.

Like their allies and their enemies, Russians embraced war with patriotic enthusiasm in 1914. For a moment Russia was united, but soon the war began to take its toll. Russia quickly exhausted its supplies of shells and ammunition, and better-equipped German armies inflicted terrible losses—1.5 million casualties and nearly 1 million captured in 1915 alone. Russian soldiers were sent to the front without rifles; they were told to find their arms among the dead. The Duma (DOO-muh), Russia's lower house of parliament, and *zemstvos* (ZEMST-vohs), local governments, led the effort toward full mobilization on the home front. These efforts improved the military situation, but overall Russia mobilized less effectively for total war than did the other warring nations.

Although limited industrial capacity was a serious handicap in a war against highly industrialized Germany, Russia's real problem was leadership. A kindly, slightly dull-witted man, Tsar Nicholas II (r. 1894–1917) distrusted the moderate Duma and rejected any democratic sharing of power. As a result, the Duma, whose members came from the elite classes, and the popular masses became increasingly critical of the tsar's leadership and the appalling direction of the war. In response, Nicholas (who had no military background) traveled to the front in September 1915 to lead Russia's armies—and thereafter received all the blame for Russian losses.

His departure was a fatal turning point. His German-born wife, Tsarina Alexandra, took control of the government and the home front. She tried to rule absolutely in her husband's absence with an uneducated Siberian preacher, Rasputin (ra-SPOO-tin), as her most trusted adviser. In a desperate attempt to right the situation, three members of the high aristocracy murdered Rasputin in December 1916. In this convulsive atmosphere, the government slid steadily toward revolution.

Large-scale strikes, demonstrations, and protest marches were now commonplace, as were bread shortages. On March 8, 1917, a women's bread march in Petrograd (formerly St. Petersburg) started riots, which spread throughout the city. While his ministers fled the city, the tsar ordered that peace be restored, but discipline broke down, and the soldiers and police joined the revolutionary crowd. The Duma declared a provisional government on March 12, 1917. Three days later, Nicholas abdicated, and he and his family were placed under house arrest by the provisional government. When the Bolsheviks seized power in November 1917 they moved the royal family to Yekaterinburg, and there they were all executed in July 1918.

## The Provisional Government

The **March Revolution** was joyfully accepted throughout the country. A new government formed in May 1917, with the understanding that an elected democratic government, ruling under a new constitution drafted by a future Constituent

Assembly, would replace it when circumstances permitted. The provisional government established equality before the law; freedom of religion, speech, and assembly;
the right of unions to organize and strike; and other classic liberal measures.

The provisional government soon made two fatal decisions, however, that turned
the people against it. First, it refused to confiscate large landholdings and give them to
peasants, fearing that such drastic action in the countryside would only complete
the disintegration of Russia's peasant army. Second, the government decided that the
continuation of war was still the all-important national duty and that international
alliances had to be honored. Neither decision was popular. The peasants believed that
when the tsar's autocratic rule ended, so too did the nobles' title to the land, which
was now theirs for the taking. The army believed that the March Revolution meant
the end of the war.

From its first day, the provisional government had to share power (dual power)
with a formidable rival that represented the popular masses — the **Petrograd Soviet**
(or council) of Workers' and Soldiers' Deputies, a huge, fluctuating mass organization composed of two to three thousand workers, soldiers, and socialist intellectuals.
This counter-government, or half government, issued its own radical orders, further
weakening the provisional government. Most famous of these was Army Order No. 1,
issued in March 1917, which stripped officers of their authority and gave power to
elected committees of common soldiers.

Order No. 1 led to a total collapse of army discipline. Peasant soldiers began
"voting with their feet," to use Lenin's graphic phrase, returning to their villages to
get a share of the land that peasants were seizing from landowners, either through
peasant soviets (councils) or by force, in a great agrarian upheaval. Through the summer of 1917, the provisional government, led from July by the socialist Alexander
Kerensky, became increasingly more conservative and authoritarian as it tried to
maintain law and order and protect property (such as nobles' land and factories). The
government was being threatened from one side by an advancing German army and
from the other by proletarian forces, urban and rural alike, shouting "All power to
the soviets!" and calling for an even more radical revolution.

## Lenin and the Bolshevik Revolution

According to most traditional twentieth-century accounts of the two Russian
revolutions in 1917, written by both anti-Soviet Russian and Western scholars, in
March Russia successfully overthrew the tsar's autocratic rule and replaced it with
a liberal, Western-style democracy. Then in November a small group of hard-core
radicals, led by Vladimir Lenin, somehow staged a second revolution and installed
an atheistic Communist government. More recently, however, and especially since
the Soviet archives were opened in the 1990s following the dissolution of the Soviet
Union, a different picture has emerged. Scholars are recognizing that the second revolution had widespread popular support and that Lenin was often following events as
much as leading them.

Born into the middle class, Vladimir Ilyich Lenin (1870–1924) became an
enemy of imperial Russia when his older brother was executed for plotting to kill the
tsar in 1887. As a law student Lenin studied Marxist doctrines with religious ferocity.
Exiled to Siberia for three years because of socialist agitation, after his release Lenin

lived in western Europe for seventeen years and developed his own revolutionary interpretations of Marxist thought (see "The Birth of Socialism" in Chapter 24).

Three interrelated ideas were central for Lenin. First, he stressed that only violent revolution could destroy capitalism. Second, Lenin believed that a socialist revolution was possible even in an agrarian country like Russia. According to classical Marxist theory, a society must reach the capitalist, industrial stage of development before its urban workers, the proletariat, can rise up and create a Communist society. Lenin thought that although Russia's industrial working class was small, the peasants, who made up the bulk of the army and navy, were also potential revolutionaries. Third, Lenin believed that at a given moment revolution was determined more by human leadership than by vast historical laws. He called for a highly disciplined workers' party, strictly controlled by a dedicated elite of intellectuals and full-time revolutionaries like him. This "vanguard of the proletariat" would not stop until revolution brought it to power.

Lenin's ideas did not go unchallenged by other Russian Marxists. At a Social Democratic Labor Party congress in London in 1903, Lenin demanded a small, disciplined, elitist party; his opponents wanted a more democratic party with mass membership. The Russian Marxists split into two rival factions. Because his side won one crucial vote at the congress, Lenin's camp became known as **Bolsheviks**, or "majority group"; his opponents were Mensheviks, or "minority group."

In March 1917 Lenin and nearly all the other leading Bolsheviks were living in exile abroad or in Russia's remotest corners. After the March Revolution, the German government provided safe passage for Lenin from his exile in Switzerland across Germany and back into Russia, hoping he would undermine Russia's sagging war effort. They were not disappointed. Arriving in Petrograd on April 16, Lenin attacked at once, issuing his famous April Theses. To the Petrograd Bolsheviks' great astonishment, he rejected all cooperation with what he called the "bourgeois" provisional government and instead called for exactly what the popular masses themselves were demanding: "All power to the soviets!" and "Peace, Land, Bread!" Bolshevik support increased through the summer, culminating in mass demonstrations in Petrograd on July 16–20 by soldiers, sailors, and workers. Lenin and the Bolshevik Central Committee had not planned these demonstrations and were completely unprepared to support them. Nonetheless, the provisional government labeled Lenin and other leading Bolsheviks traitors and ordered them arrested. Lenin had to flee to Finland.

Meanwhile, however, the provisional government itself was collapsing. The coalition between liberals and socialists was breaking apart as their respective power bases — bourgeoisie and proletariat — demanded they move further to the right or left. Prime Minister Kerensky's unwavering support for the war lost him all credit with the army, the only force that might have saved him and democratic government in Russia. In early September an attempted right-wing military coup failed as Petrograd workers organized themselves as Red Guards to defend the city and then convinced the coup's soldiers to join them. Lenin, from his exile in Finland, now called for an armed Bolshevik insurrection before the Second All-Russian Congress of Soviets met in early November.

In October the Bolsheviks gained a fragile majority in the Petrograd Soviet. Lenin did not return to Russia until mid-October and even then remained in hiding. It was Lenin's supporter Leon Trotsky (1879–1940) who brilliantly executed

**Lenin and Stalin at Lenin's Country House at Gorki** This controversial photo, supposedly taken by Lenin's sister in 1922, two years before Lenin's death, has stirred much scholarly debate. Some argue that Stalin had himself airbrushed into the photo later to support his claim as Lenin's legitimate successor. Even if the photo is authentic, it appears to have been retouched later, on Stalin's orders, to clear his severely pockmarked face; to make his shorter and stiffer left arm, injured in a childhood accident, appear normal; and to make him taller (he was only 5 feet 4 inches tall) and larger than the smaller and more passive-looking Lenin. (Haynes Archive/Popperfoto/Getty Images)

the Bolshevik seizure of power. On November 6 militant Trotsky followers joined with trusted Bolshevik soldiers to seize government buildings and arrest provisional government members. That evening Lenin came out of hiding and took control of the revolution. The following day revolutionary forces seized the Winter Palace, and Kerensky capitulated. At the Congress of Soviets, a Bolshevik majority declared that all power had passed to the soviets and named Lenin head of the new government.

The Bolsheviks came to power for three key reasons. First, by late 1917 democracy had given way to anarchy as the popular masses no longer supported the provisional government. Second, in Lenin and Trotsky the Bolsheviks had truly superior leaders who were utterly determined to provoke a Marxist revolution. Third, the Bolsheviks appealed to soldiers, urban workers, and peasants who were exhausted by war and eager for socialism.

## Dictatorship and Civil War

The Bolsheviks' true accomplishment was not taking power but keeping it and conquering the chaos they had helped create. Once again, Lenin was able to profit from developments over which he and the Bolsheviks had no control. Since summer 1917 an unstoppable peasant revolution had swept across Russia, as peasants divided among themselves the estates of the landlords and the church. Thus Lenin's first law, which supposedly gave land to the peasants, actually merely approved what peasants were already doing. Lenin then met urban workers' greatest demand with a decree giving local workers' committees direct control of individual factories.

The Bolsheviks proclaimed their regime a "provisional workers' and peasants' government," promising that a freely elected Constituent Assembly would draw up a new constitution. However, when Bolshevik delegates won fewer than one-fourth of the seats in free elections in November, the Constituent Assembly was permanently disbanded by Bolshevik soldiers acting under Lenin's orders.

Lenin then moved to make peace with Germany, at any price. That price was very high. Germany demanded the Soviet government surrender all its western territories in the Treaty of Brest-Litovsk (BREHST lih-TAWFSK) in March 1918. With Germany's defeat eight months later, the treaty was nullified, but it allowed Lenin time to escape the disaster of continued war and pursue his goal of absolute political power for the Bolsheviks — now renamed Communists — within Russia.

The war's end and the demise of the democratically elected Constituent Assembly revealed Bolshevik rule as a dictatorship. "Long live the [democratic] soviets; down with the Bolsheviks" became a popular slogan. Officers of the old army organized so-called White opposition to the Bolsheviks in southern Russia, Ukraine, Siberia, and west of Petrograd and plunged the country into civil war from November 1917 to October 1922. The Whites came from many political factions and were united only by their hatred of the Bolsheviks — the Reds. In almost five years of fighting, 125,000 Reds and 175,000 Whites and Poles were killed before the Red Army, formed in March 1918 under Trotsky's command, claimed final victory.

The Bolsheviks' Red Army won for several reasons. Strategically, they controlled the center, while the disunited Whites attacked from the fringes. Moreover, the Whites' poorly defined political program failed to unite all of the Bolsheviks' foes under a progressive democratic banner. Most important, the Communists developed a better army, against which the divided Whites were no match.

The Bolsheviks also mobilized the home front. Establishing **War Communism** — the application of the total-war concept to a civil conflict — they seized grain from peasants, introduced rationing, nationalized all banks and industry, and required everyone to work. Although these measures contributed to a breakdown of normal economic activity, they also served to maintain labor discipline and to keep the Red Army supplied.

Revolutionary terror also contributed to the Communist victory. The old tsarist secret police was re-established as the Cheka (CHEHK-kah), which hunted down and executed thousands of real or supposed foes, including the tsar and his family. During the so-called Red Terror of 1918–1920, the Cheka sowed fear, silenced opposition, and executed an estimated 250,000 "class enemies."

Finally, foreign military intervention in the civil war ended up helping the Communists. The Allies sent troops to prevent war materiel that they had sent to the provisional government from being captured by the Germans. After the Soviet government nationalized all foreign-owned factories without compensation and refused to pay foreign debts, Western governments began to support White armies. While these efforts did little to help the Whites' cause, they did permit the Communists to appeal to the ethnic Russians' patriotic nationalism.

# The War's Consequences

### What were the global consequences of the First World War?

In spring 1918 the Germans launched their last major attack against France and failed. A defeated Germany finally agreed to an armistice on November 11, following ones already signed by the Austrian-Hungarian (November 3) and Ottoman (October 30) leaders. All three monarchies fell and their empires broke apart.

In January 1919 the victorious Western Allies came together in Paris hoping to establish a lasting peace.

Laboring intensively, the Allies soon worked out peace terms with Germany, created the peacekeeping League of Nations, and reorganized eastern Europe and southwest Asia. The 1919 peace settlement, however, failed to establish a lasting peace or to resolve the issues that had brought the world to war. World War I and the treaties that ended it shaped the course of the twentieth century, often in horrible ways. Surely this was the ultimate tragedy of the Great War that cost $332 billion and left 10 million people dead and another 20 million wounded.

## The End of the War

Peace and an end to the war did not come easily. Victory over revolutionary Russia had temporarily boosted sagging German morale, and in spring 1918 the German army attacked France once more. The German offensive was turned back in July at the Second Battle of the Marne, where 140,000 fresh American soldiers saw action. Adding 2 million men in arms to the war effort by August, the late but massive American intervention decisively tipped the scales in favor of Allied victory.

By September British, French, and American armies were advancing steadily on all fronts. On October 4 the German emperor formed a new, more liberal German government to sue for peace. As negotiations over an armistice dragged on, the frustrated German people rose up. On November 3 sailors in Kiel (KEEL) mutinied, and throughout northern Germany soldiers and workers established revolutionary councils on the Russian soviet model. With army discipline collapsing, Kaiser Wilhelm abdicated and fled to Holland. Socialist leaders in Berlin proclaimed a German republic on November 9 and agreed to tough Allied terms of surrender. The armistice went into effect at 11 o'clock on November 11, 1918.

## The Paris Peace Treaties

Seventy delegates from twenty-seven nations attended the opening of the Paris Peace Conference at the Versailles (vayr-SIGH) Palace on January 18, 1919. By August 1920 five major treaties with the defeated powers had been agreed upon. The most well-known, the Treaty of Versailles, laid out peace terms with Germany and also included the Covenant of the League of Nations and an article establishing the International Labour Organization. The conference also yielded a number of minor treaties, unilateral declarations, bilateral treaties, and League of Nations mandates (Map 28.4). The delegates had met with great expectations. A young British diplomat later wrote that the victors "were journeying to Paris . . . to found a new order in Europe. We were preparing not Peace only, but Eternal Peace."[9]

This idealism was strengthened by President Wilson's January 1918 peace proposal, his Fourteen Points. Wilson stressed national self-determination and the rights of small countries and called for the creation of a **League of Nations**, a permanent international organization designed to protect member states from aggression and avert future wars.

The real powers at the conference were the "Big Three": the United States, Great Britain, and France. Germany and Russia were excluded, and Italy's role was limited. President Wilson wanted to immediately deal with the establishment of a League of Nations, while Prime Ministers Lloyd George of Great Britain and, especially,

**MAP 28.4   Territorial Changes in Europe After World War I**
The Great War brought tremendous changes to eastern Europe. Empires were shattered, new nations were established, and a dangerous power vacuum was created by the relatively weak states established between Germany and Soviet Russia.

Georges Clemenceau (klem-uhn-soh) of France were primarily concerned with punishing Germany.

Although personally inclined to make a somewhat moderate peace with Germany, Lloyd George felt pressured for a victory worthy of the sacrifices of total war. As Rudyard Kipling summed up the general British feeling at war's end, the Germans were "a people with the heart of beasts."[10] For his part, Clemenceau wanted revenge and lasting security for France, which, he believed, required the creation of a buffer state between France and Germany, Germany's permanent demilitarization, and vast German reparations. Wilson, supported by Lloyd George, would hear none of this.

In the end, Clemenceau agreed to a compromise, abandoning the French demand for a Rhineland buffer state in return for a formal defensive alliance with the United States and Great Britain.

On June 28, 1919, in the great Hall of Mirrors at Versailles (where Germany had forced France to sign the armistice ending the Franco-Prussian War), German representatives of the ruling moderate Social Democrats and the Catholic Party reluctantly signed the treaty.

Germany's African colonies were mandated to Great Britain, France, South Africa, and Belgium. Germany's hold over the Shandong Peninsula in China passed to Japan, provoking an eruption of outrage among Chinese nationalists (see "The Rise of Nationalist China" in Chapter 29). Germany's territorial losses within Europe were minor: Alsace-Lorraine was returned to France, and parts of Germany were ceded to the new Polish state (see Map 28.4). The treaty limited Germany's army to one hundred thousand men and allowed no new military fortifications in the Rhineland.

More harshly, the Allies demanded that Germany (with Austria) accept responsibility for the war and pay reparations equal to all civilian damages caused by the war, although the Allies left the actual reparations figure to be set at a later date when tempers had cooled. These much-criticized "war-guilt" and "reparations" clauses reflected British and French popular demands for revenge, but were bitterly resented by the German people.

The **Treaty of Versailles** and the other agreements reached in Paris were seen as the first steps toward re-establishing international order, albeit ones that favored the victorious Allies, and they would have far-reaching consequences for the remainder of the twentieth century and beyond.

In eastern Europe, Poland regained its independence (see Map 19.1), and the independent states of Austria, Hungary, Czechoslovakia, and a larger Romania were created out of the Austro-Hungarian Empire (see Map 28.4). A greatly expanded Serbian monarchy united Slavs in the western Balkans and took the name Yugoslavia.

Promises of independence made to Arab leaders were largely brushed aside, and Britain and France extended their power in the Middle East, taking advantage of the breakup of the Ottoman Empire. Article 22 of the Covenant of the League of Nations established a **mandate system**, whereby territories previously controlled by the defeated states, principally the Ottoman Empire and imperial Germany, were given to individual states among the allied powers as "advanced nations," to administer "as a sacred trust for the benefit of its native people." Accordingly, France received Lebanon and Syria, and Britain took Iraq and Palestine. Palestine was to include a Jewish national homeland first promised by Britain in 1917 in the Balfour Declaration (see "Nationalist Movements in the Middle East" in Chapter 29). Only Hussein's Arab kingdom of Hejaz (hee-JAZ) received independence. These Allied acquisitions, although officially League of Nations mandates, were simply colonialism under another name. They left colonized peoples in the Middle East, Asia (see Chapter 29), and Africa bitterly disappointed and demonstrated that the age of Western and Eastern imperialism lived on.

## American Rejection of the Versailles Treaty

The 1919 peace settlement was not perfect, but for war-shattered Europe it was an acceptable beginning. Moreover, Allied leaders wanted a quick settlement for another reason: they detested Lenin and feared his Bolshevik Revolution might spread. The remaining problems could be worked out in the future.

Such hopes were dashed, however, when the United States quickly reverted to its prewar preferences for isolationism and the U.S. Senate, led by Republican Henry Cabot Lodge, rejected the Versailles treaty on November 19, 1919. Wilson obstinately rejected all attempts at compromise on the treaty, ensuring that it would never be ratified in any form and that the United States would never join the League of Nations. Moreover, the Senate refused to ratify Wilson's defensive alliance with France and Great Britain. Using U.S. action as an excuse, Great Britain also refused to ratify its defensive alliance with France. Betrayed by its allies, France stood alone, and the great hopes of early 1919 had turned to ashes by year's end.

# The Search for Peace and Political Stability, 1919–1929

**How did leaders deal with the political dimensions of uncertainty and try to re-establish peace and prosperity in the interwar years?**

The pursuit of real and lasting peace in the first half of the interwar years proved difficult for many reasons. Germany hated the Treaty of Versailles. France was fearful and isolated. Britain was undependable, and the United States had turned its back on Europe's problems. Eastern Europe was in ferment, and no one could predict Communist Russia's future. Moreover, the international economic situation was poor and was greatly complicated by war debts and disrupted patterns of trade. Yet for a time, from 1925 to late 1929, it appeared that peace and stability were within reach.

## Germany and the Western Powers

Nearly all Germans and many other observers immediately and for decades after believed the Versailles treaty represented a harsh dictated peace and should be revised or repudiated as soon as possible. Many right-wing Germans, including Adolf Hitler, believed there had been no defeat; instead they believed German soldiers had been betrayed (*Dolchstoss*—"stabbed in the back") by liberals, Marxists, Jews, and other "November criminals" who had surrendered in order to seize power.

Historians have recently begun to reassess the treaty's terms, however, and many scholars currently view them as relatively reasonable. They argue that much of the German anger toward the Allies was based more on perception than reality. With the collapse of Austria-Hungary, the dissolution of the Ottoman Empire, and the revolution in Russia, Germany emerged from the war an even stronger power in eastern Europe than before, and an economically stronger and more populated nation than France or Great Britain. Moreover, when contrasted with the extremely harsh Treaty of Brest-Litovsk that Germany had forced on Lenin's Russia, and the peace terms Germany had intended to impose on the Allies if it won the war, the Versailles treaty was far from being a vindictive and crippling peace. Had it been, Germany could hardly have become the economic and military juggernaut that it was only twenty years later.

This is not to say, however, that France did not seek some degree of revenge on Germany for both the Franco-Prussian War (see "Bismarck and German Unification" and Map 24.3 in Chapter 24) and the Great War. Most of the war on the western front had been fought on French soil. The expected reconstruction costs and the amount of war debts France owed to the United States were staggering. Thus the French believed that heavy German reparations were an economic necessity that could hold Germany down indefinitely and would enable France to realize its goal of security.

The British felt differently. Prewar Germany had been Great Britain's second-best market, and after the war a healthy, prosperous Germany appeared to be essential to the British economy. In addition, the British were suspicious of France's army — the largest in Europe — and the British and French were at odds over their League of Nations mandates in the Middle East.

While France and Britain drifted in different directions, the Allied reparations commission completed its work and announced in April 1921 that Germany had to pay the enormous sum of 132 billion gold marks ($33 billion) in annual installments of 2.5 billion gold marks. The young German republic — known as the Weimar Republic — made its first reparations payment in that year. Then in 1922, wracked by rapid inflation and political assassinations, and motivated by hostility and arrogance as well, the Weimar Republic announced its inability to pay more and proposed a reparations moratorium for three years.

The British were willing to accept a moratorium, but the French were not. Led by their prime minister, Raymond Poincaré (pwan-kah-RAY) (1860–1934), the French decided they had to either call Germany's bluff or see the entire peace settlement dissolve to their great disadvantage. In January 1923 French and Belgian armies occupied the Ruhr (ROO-uhr) district, industrial Germany's heartland, creating the most serious international crisis of the 1920s.

Strengthened by a wave of patriotism, the German government ordered the people of the Ruhr to stop working and to resist French occupation nonviolently. The French responded by sealing off not only the Ruhr but also the entire Rhineland from the rest of Germany, letting in only enough food to prevent starvation.

By summer 1923 France and Germany were engaged in a great test of wills. French armies could not collect reparations from striking workers at gunpoint. But French occupation was paralyzing Germany and its economy, and the German government was soon forced to print money to pay its bills. Prices soared, and German money rapidly lost all value. In 1919 one American dollar equaled nine German marks; by November 1923 it took over 4.2 trillion German marks to purchase one American dollar. As retired and middle-class people saw their savings wiped out, many Germans felt betrayed. They hated and blamed for their misfortune the Western governments, their own government, big business, the Jews, the workers, and the Communists. The crisis left them psychologically prepared to follow radical right-wing leaders.

In August 1923, as the mark's value fell and political unrest grew throughout Germany, Gustav Stresemann (GOOS-tahf SHTRAY-zuh-mahn) (1878–1929) became German chancellor. Stresemann adopted a compromising attitude. He called off the peaceful resistance campaign in the Ruhr and in October agreed in principle to pay reparations but asked first for a re-examination of Germany's ability to pay. Poincaré accepted. Thus, after five years of hostility and tension, Germany and France, with British and American help, decided to try compromise and cooperation.

## Hope in Foreign Affairs

In 1924 an international committee of financial experts headed by American banker Charles G. Dawes met to re-examine reparations. Under the terms of the resulting **Dawes Plan** (1924), Germany's yearly reparations were reduced and linked to the level of German economic prosperity. Germany would also receive large loans from the United States to promote German recovery, as well as to pay reparations to France and Britain, thus enabling those countries to repay the large sums they owed the United States. This circular flow of international payments was complicated and risky, but it worked for a while, facilitating a worldwide economic recovery in the late 1920s.

The economic settlement was matched by a political settlement. In 1925 European leaders met in Locarno, Switzerland. Germany and France solemnly pledged to accept their common border, and both Britain and Italy agreed to fight either France or Germany if one invaded the other. Stresemann also agreed to settle boundary disputes with Poland and Czechoslovakia by peaceful means, and France promised those countries military aid if Germany attacked them. Other developments also strengthened hopes for international peace. In 1926 Germany joined the League of Nations, and in 1928 fifteen countries signed the Kellogg-Briand Pact. The signing nations "condemned and renounced war as an instrument of national policy."

The pact fostered the cautious optimism of the late 1920s and also encouraged the hope that the United States would accept its international responsibilities.

## Hope in Democratic Government

European domestic politics also offered reason for hope. During the Ruhr occupation and the great inflation, Germany's republican government appeared ready to collapse. But the moderate businessmen who tended to dominate the various German coalition governments believed that economic prosperity demanded good relations with the Western powers, and they supported parliamentary government at home. Elections were held regularly, and as the economy boomed in the aftermath of the Dawes Plan, republican democracy appeared to have growing support among a majority of Germans.

There were, however, sharp political divisions in the country. Many unrepentant nationalists and monarchists populated the right and the army. In November 1923 an obscure politician named Adolf Hitler, who had become leader of an obscure workers party, the National Socialist German Workers Party, in July 1921, proclaimed a "national socialist revolution" in a Munich beer hall. Hitler's plot to seize government control was poorly organized and easily crushed. Hitler was sentenced to prison, where he outlined his theories and program in his book *Mein Kampf* (*My Struggle*, 1925). Members of Germany's Communist Party received directions from Moscow, and they accused the Social Democrats of betraying the revolution. The working classes were divided politically, but a majority supported the socialist, but nonrevolutionary, Social Democrats.

France's situation was similar to Germany's. Communists and socialists battled for the workers' support. After 1924 the democratically elected government rested mainly in the hands of moderate coalitions, and business interests were well represented. France's great accomplishment was the rapid rebuilding of its war-torn northern region, and good times prevailed until 1930.

Britain, too, faced challenges after 1920. The great problem was unemployment, which hovered around 12 percent throughout the 1920s. The state provided unemployment benefits and a range of additional social services. These and other measures kept living standards from seriously declining, defused class tensions, and pointed the way to the welfare state Britain established after World War II.

The wartime trend toward greater social equality also continued in Britain, helping to maintain social harmony. Relative social harmony was accompanied by the rise of the Labour Party, which, under Prime Minister Ramsay MacDonald (1866–1937), governed the country in 1924 and 1929–1935. The Labour Party sought a gradual and democratic move toward socialism, so that the middle classes were not overly frightened as the working classes won new benefits.

The British Conservatives under Stanley Baldwin (1867–1947) showed the same compromising spirit on social issues, and Britain experienced only limited social unrest in the 1920s and 1930s. In 1922 Britain granted southern, Catholic Ireland full autonomy after a bitter guerrilla war, thereby removing another source of prewar friction. Thus developments in both international relations and domestic politics gave the leading democracies cause for cautious optimism in the late 1920s.

# The Age of Anxiety

**In what ways were the anxieties of the postwar world expressed or heightened by revolutionary ideas in modern thought, art, and science and in new forms of communication?**

Many people hoped that happier times would return after the war, along with the familiar prewar ideals of peace, prosperity, and progress. The war had caused such social, economic, and psychological upheaval, however, that great numbers of men and women felt themselves increasingly adrift in an age of anxiety and continual crisis.

## Uncertainty in Philosophy and Religion

Before 1914 most people in the West still believed in Enlightenment philosophies of progress, reason, and individual rights. As the century began, progress was a daily reality, apparent in the rising living standard, the taming of the city, the spread of political rights to women and workers, and the growth of state-supported social programs. Just as there were laws of science, many thinkers felt, there were laws of society that rational human beings could discover and wisely act on. Even before the war, however, some philosophers, such as the German Friedrich Nietzsche (NEE-chuh) (1844–1900), called such faith in reason into question. The First World War accelerated the revolt against established philosophical certainties. Logical positivism, often associated with Austrian philosopher Ludwig Wittgenstein (VIHT-guhn-shtighn) (1889–1951), rejected most concerns of traditional philosophy—from God's existence to the meaning of happiness—as nonsense and argued that life must be based on facts and observation. Others looked to **existentialism** for answers. Highly diverse and even contradictory, existential thinkers were loosely united in a search for moral values in a terrifying and uncertain world. They did not believe that a supreme being had established humanity's fundamental nature and given life its meaning. In the words of the French existentialist Jean-Paul Sartre (1905–1980), "Man's existence precedes his essence. . . . To begin with he is nothing. He will not be anything until later, and then he will be what he makes of himself."[11]

In contrast, the loss of faith in human reason and in continual progress led to a renewed interest in Christianity. After World War I several thinkers and theologians began to revitalize Christian fundamentals, and intellectuals increasingly turned to religion between about 1920 and 1950. Sometimes described as Christian existentialists because they shared the loneliness and despair of atheistic existentialists, these believers felt that religion was one meaningful answer to terror and anxiety. In the words of a famous Roman Catholic convert, English novelist Graham Greene, "One began to believe in heaven because one believed in hell."[12]

## The New Physics

For people no longer committed to traditional religious beliefs, a belief in unchanging natural laws offered some comfort. These laws seemed to determine physical processes and permit useful solutions to more and more problems. A series of discoveries beginning around the turn of the century, however, challenged the established certainties of Newtonian physics (see "Newton's Synthesis" in Chapter 19).

An important first step toward the new physics was the British physicist J. J. Thomson's 1897 discovery of subatomic particles, which proved that atoms were not stable and unbreakable. The following year Polish-born physicist Marie Curie (1867–1934) and her French husband, Pierre (1859–1906), discovered radium and demonstrated that it constantly emits subatomic particles and thus does not have a constant atomic weight. Building on this, German physicist Max Planck (1858–1947) showed in 1900 that subatomic energy is emitted in uneven little spurts, which he called "quanta," and not in a steady stream, as previously believed.

In 1905 the German-Jewish genius Albert Einstein (1879–1955) further undermined Newtonian physics. His theory of special relativity postulated that time and space are relative to the observer's viewpoint and that only the speed of light is constant for all frames of reference in the universe. In addition, Einstein's theory that matter and energy are interchangeable and that even a particle of matter contains enormous levels of potential energy would later become the scientific basis for the atomic bomb.

The 1920s opened the "heroic age of physics," in the apt words of one of its leading pioneers, Ernest Rutherford (1871–1937). In 1919 Rutherford first split the atom. Breakthrough followed breakthrough, but some discoveries raised new doubts about reality. In 1927 German physicist Werner Heisenberg (VEHR-nuhr HIGH-zuhn-burg) theorized his "uncertainty principle," whereby any act of measurement in quantum physics is affected by, and blurred by, the experimenter. Thus, if experiments in an exact science like physics can be distorted by human observation, what other areas of human knowledge are similarly affected? Is ultimate truth unknowable?

The implications of the new theories and discoveries were disturbing to millions of people in the 1920s and 1930s. The new universe was strange and troubling, and, moreover, science appeared distant from human experience and human problems.

## Freudian Psychology

With physics presenting an uncertain universe so unrelated to ordinary human experience, questions about the power and potential of the human mind assumed special significance. The findings and speculations of psychologist Sigmund Freud (1856–1939) were particularly disturbing.

Before Freud, most psychologists assumed that human behavior resulted from rational thinking by the conscious mind. By analyzing dreams and hysteria, Freud developed a very different view of the human psyche. Freud concluded that human behavior was governed by three parts of the self: **id, ego, superego**. The primitive, irrational unconscious, which he called the id, was driven by sexual, aggressive, and pleasure-seeking desires and was locked in constant battle with the mind's two other parts: the rationalizing conscious — the ego — which mediates what a person can do, and ingrained moral values — the superego — which specify what a person should do. Thus, for Freud, human behavior was a product of a fragile compromise between instinctual drives and the controls of rational thinking and moral values.

## Twentieth-Century Literature

Western literature was also influenced by the general intellectual climate of pessimism, relativism, and alienation. In the twentieth century many writers adopted the limited, often confused viewpoint of a single individual. Like Freud, these novelists focused on the complexity and irrationality of the human mind.

Some novelists used the stream-of-consciousness technique with its reliance on internal monologues to explore the psyche. The most famous stream-of-consciousness novel is *Ulysses*, published by Irish novelist James Joyce (1882–1941) in 1922. Abandoning conventional grammar and blending foreign words, puns, bits of knowledge, and scraps of memory together in bewildering confusion, the language of *Ulysses* was intended to mirror modern life itself.

Creative writers rejected the idea of progress; some even described "anti-utopias," nightmare visions of things to come. In 1918 Oswald Spengler (1880–1936) published *The Decline of the West*, in which he argued that Western civilization was in its old age and would soon be conquered by East Asia. Likewise, T. S. Eliot (1888–1965) depicted a world of growing desolation in his famous poem *The Waste Land* (1922). Franz Kafka's (1883–1924) novels *The Trial* (1925) and *The Castle* (1926) portrayed helpless individuals crushed by inexplicably hostile forces.

## Modern Architecture, Art, and Music

Like scientists and intellectuals, creative artists rebelled against traditional forms and conventions at the end of the nineteenth century and beginning of the twentieth. This **modernism** in architecture, art, and music, which grew more influential after the war, meant constant experimentation and a search for new kinds of expression.

The United States pioneered in the new architecture. In the 1890s the Chicago School of architects, led by Louis H. Sullivan (1856–1924), used cheap steel, reinforced concrete, and electric elevators to build skyscrapers and office build-ings lacking almost any exterior ornamentation. The buildings of Frank Lloyd Wright (1867–1959) were renowned for their sometimes-radical design, their creative use of wide varieties of materials, and their appearance of being part of the landscape.

In Europe architectural leadership centered in German-speaking countries. In 1919 Walter Gropius (1883–1969) merged the schools of fine and applied arts at Weimar into a single interdisciplinary school, the Bauhaus. Throughout the 1920s the Bauhaus movement stressed good design for everyday life and **functionalism**— that is, a building should serve the purpose for which it is designed. The movement attracted enthusiastic students from all over the world.

Art increasingly took on a nonrepresentational, abstract character. In 1907 in Paris the famous Spanish painter Pablo Picasso (1881–1973), along with Georges Braque (BRAHK), Marcel Duchamp, and other artists, established Cubism — an artistic approach concentrated on a complex geometry of zigzagging lines and sharply angled overlapping planes. Since the Renaissance, artists had represented objects from a single viewpoint and had created unified human forms. In his first great Cubist work, *Les Demoiselles d'Avignon* (lay dehm-wuh-ZEHL da-vee-NYAWN) (1907), Picasso's figures present a radical new view of reality with a strikingly non-Western depiction of the human form. Their faces resemble carved African masks, reflecting the growing importance of non-Western artistic traditions in Europe in the early twentieth century.

The ultimate stage in the development of abstract, nonrepresentational art occurred around 1910. Artists such as the Russian-born Wassily Kandinsky (1866–1944) turned away from nature completely. "The observer," said Kandinsky, "must learn to look at [my] pictures . . . as form and color combinations . . . as a represen-tation of mood and not as a representation of *objects*."[13]

Radicalization accelerated after World War I. The most notable new develop-ments were New Objectivity (*Sachlichkeit* [SAHK-leech-kight] in German), Dadaism (DAH-dah-ihz-uhm), and Surrealism. New Objectivity emerged from German art-ists' experiences in the Great War and the Weimar Republic. Paintings by artists like George Grosz (GRAWSH) and Otto Dix were provocative, emotionally disturbing, and harshly satirical. Dadaism attacked all accepted standards of art and behavior, delighting in outrageous conduct. After 1924 many Dadaists were attracted to Surreal-ism. Surrealists, such as Salvador Dalí (1904–1989), painted fantastic worlds of wild dreams and complex symbols.

Developments in modern music were strikingly parallel to those in painting. Attracted by the emotional intensity of expressionism, composers depicted unseen inner worlds of emotion and imagination. Just as abstract painters arranged lines and color but did not draw identifiable objects, so modern composers arranged sounds atonally without creating recognizable harmonies. Led by composers such as the Austrian Arnold Schönberg (SHUHN-buhrg) (1874–1951) and the Russian Igor Stravinsky (1882–1971), modern composers turned their backs on long-established musical conventions. The pulsating, dissonant rhythms and the dancers' earthy rep-resentation of lovemaking in Stravinsky's ballet *The Rite of Spring* nearly caused a riot when first performed in Paris in 1913.

## Movies and Radio

In the decades following the First World War, motion pictures became the main entertainment of the masses worldwide. During the First World War the United States became the dominant force in the rapidly expanding silent-film industry, and Charlie Chaplin (1889–1978), an Englishman working in Hollywood, demonstrated that in the hands of a genius the new medium could combine mass entertainment and artistic accomplishment.

Motion pictures also became powerful tools of indoctrination, especially in countries with dictatorial regimes. Lenin encouraged the development of Soviet film making, and Sergei Eisenstein (1898–1948), the most famous of his film makers, and others dramatized the Communist view of Russian history. In Germany Hitler, who rose to power in 1933, turned to a talented film maker, Leni Riefenstahl (REE-fuhn-shtahl) (1902–2003), for a masterpiece of documentary propaganda, *Triumph of the Will*, based on the 1934 Nazi Party rally at Nuremberg. Her film was a brilliant and all-too-powerful depiction of Germany's rebirth as a great power under Nazi leadership.

Motion pictures offered ordinary people a temporary escape from the hard realities of international tensions, uncertainty, unemployment, and personal frustrations. They remained the most popular form of mass entertainment until the advent of television after World War II.

Radio also dominated popular culture after the Great War. In 1920 the first public broadcasts were made in Great Britain and the United States. Every major country quickly established national broadcasting networks. LOR, Radio Argentina, became the first formal radio station in the world when it made its first broadcast in August 1920. Radios were revolutionary in that they were capable of reaching all of a nation's citizens at once, offering them a single perspective on current events and teaching them a single national language and pronunciation.

**The Universal Appeal of Radio** Russian emigre Madame Asta Souvrina sits with her dog, named Bernhardt of Russia, as they listen with earphones to the radio in January 1922. Madame Souvrina was driven out of Russia by the Bolsheviks. The radio appears to have been put together by hand from a crystal radio kit. (Library of Congress/Corbis Historical/Getty Images)

# Chapter Summary

Nationalism, militarism, imperialism, and the alliance system increased political tensions across Europe at the end of the nineteenth century. Franz Ferdinand's assassination in 1914 sparked a regional war that soon became global. Four years of stalemate and slaughter followed. Entire societies mobilized for total war, and government powers greatly increased. Women earned greater social equality, and labor unions grew. Many European countries adopted socialism as a realistic economic blueprint.

Horrible losses on the eastern front led to Russian tsar Nicholas II's abdication in March 1917. A provisional government controlled by moderate social democrats replaced him but refused to withdraw Russia from the war. A second Russian revolution followed in November 1917, led by Lenin and his Bolshevik Party. The Bolsheviks established a radical Communist regime, smashed existing capitalist institutions, and posed an ongoing challenge to Europe and its colonial empires.

The "war to end all wars" brought only a fragile truce. The Versailles treaty took away Germany's colonies, limited its military, and demanded admittance of war guilt and exorbitant war reparations. Separate treaties redrew the maps of Europe and the Middle East. Allied wartime solidarity faded, and Germany remained unrepentant, setting the stage for World War II. Globally, the European powers refused to extend self-determination to their colonies, instead creating a mandate system that sowed further discontent among colonized peoples.

In the 1920s moderate political leaders sought to create an enduring peace and rebuild prewar prosperity through compromise. By decade's end they seemed to have succeeded: Germany experienced an economic recovery, France rebuilt its war-torn regions, and Britain's Labour Party expanded social services. Ultimately, however, these measures were short-lived.

The war's horrors, particularly the industrialization of war that slaughtered millions, shattered Enlightenment ideals and caused widespread anxiety. In the interwar years philosophers, artists, and writers portrayed these anxieties in their work. Movies and the radio initially offered escape but soon became powerful tools of indoctrination and propaganda.

## NOTES

1. Erich Maria Remarque, *All Quiet on the Western Front*, trans. A. W. Wheen (New York: Fawcett, 1996), p. 13.
2. Quoted in Winston Churchill, *The World Crisis, 1911–1918* (New York: Free Press, 2005), p. 96.
3. Remarque, *All Quiet*, pp. 134–135.
4. Siegfried Sassoon, *The Memoirs of George Sherston: Memoirs of an Infantry Officer* (New York: Literary Guild of America, 1937), p. 74.
5. Quoted in Keith Sinclair, *The Growth of New Zealand Identity, 1890–1980* (Auckland, N.Z.: Longman Paul, 1987), p. 24.
6. Quoted in Svetlana Palmer and Sarah Wallis, eds., *Intimate Voices from the First World War* (New York: William Morrow, 2003), p. 221.
7. Ethel Alec-Tweedie, *Women and Soldiers*, 2d ed. (London: John Lane, 1918), p. 29.

8. Quoted in Janet S. K. Watson, "Khaki Girls, VADS, and Tommy's Sisters: Gender and Class in First World War Britain," *The International History Review* 19 (1997): 49.

9. Quoted in H. Nicolson, *Peacemaking 1919* (New York: Grosset & Dunlap Universal Library, 1965), pp. 8, 31–32.

10. Quoted in Nicolson, *Peacemaking 1919*, p. 24.

11. Quoted in John Macquarrie, *Existentialism* (New York: Penguin Books, 1972), p. 15.

12. G. Greene, *Another Mexico* (New York: Viking Press, 1939), p. 3.

13. Quoted in A. H. Barr, Jr., *What Is Modern Painting?* 9th ed. (New York: Museum of Modern Art, 1966), p. 25.

## MAKE CONNECTIONS  LOOK AHEAD

The Great War continues to influence global politics and societies, more than a century after the guns went silent in November 1918. To understand the origins of many modern world conflicts, one must study first the intrigues and treaties and the revolutions and upheavals that were associated with this first truly world war.

In Chapter 30 we will see how the conflict contributed to a worldwide depression, the rise of totalitarian dictatorships, and a Second World War more global and destructive than the first. In the Middle East the Ottoman Empire came to an end, allowing France and England to carve out mandated territories—including modern Iraq, Palestine/Israel, and Lebanon—that remain flash points for violence and political instability in the twenty-first century. Nationalism, the nineteenth-century European ideology of change, took root in Asia, partly driven by Wilson's promise of self-determination. In Chapter 29 the efforts of various nationalist leaders—Atatürk in Turkey, Gandhi in India, Mao Zedong in China, Ho Chi Minh in Vietnam, and others—to throw off colonial domination will be examined, as well as the rise of ultranationalism in Japan, which led it into World War II and to ultimate defeat.

America's entry into the Great War placed it on the world stage, a place it has not relinquished as a superpower in the twentieth and twenty-first centuries. Russia, too, eventually became a superpower, but this outcome was not so clear in 1919 as its leaders fought for survival in a vicious civil war. By the outbreak of World War II Joseph Stalin had solidified Communist power, and the Soviet Union and the United States would play leading roles in defeating totalitarianism in Germany and Japan. But at war's end, as explained in Chapter 31, the two superpowers found themselves opponents in a Cold War that lasted for much of the rest of the twentieth century.

# Chapter 28 Review

## IDENTIFY KEY TERMS

**Identify and explain the significance of each item below.**

militarism (p. 729)
Triple Entente (p. 730)
trench warfare (p. 734)
total war (p. 736)
March Revolution (p. 739)
Petrograd Soviet (p. 740)
Bolsheviks (p. 741)
War Communism (p. 743)
League of Nations (p. 744)

Treaty of Versailles
　(p. 746)
mandate system (p. 746)
Dawes Plan (p. 749)
*Mein Kampf* (p. 749)
existentialism (p. 750)
id, ego, superego (p. 752)
modernism (p. 752)
functionalism (p. 753)

## REVIEW THE MAIN IDEAS

**Answer the focus questions from each section of the chapter.**

1. What were the long-term and immediate causes of World War I, and how did the conflict become a global war? (p. 728)

2. How did total war affect the home fronts of the major combatants? (p. 736)

3. What factors led to the Russian Revolution, and what was its outcome? (p. 738)

4. What were the global consequences of the First World War? (p. 743)

5. How did leaders deal with the political dimensions of uncertainty and try to re-establish peace and prosperity in the interwar years? (p. 747)

6. In what ways were the anxieties of the postwar world expressed or heightened by revolutionary ideas in modern thought, art, and science and in new forms of communication? (p. 750)

## MAKE COMPARISONS AND CONNECTIONS

**Analyze the larger developments and continuities within and across chapters.**

1. The war between Austria and Serbia should have been a small regional conflict in one corner of Europe. How did nationalism, militarism, and the New Imperialism contribute to its expansion into a global conflict?

2. In what ways would someone transported in time from 1900 to 1925 have been shocked and surprised at the changes that had occurred in that short time?

3. How did the mandate system established by the League of Nations reflect the Social Darwinian ideas of the late nineteenth century (Chapter 24)?

## CHRONOLOGY

| | |
|---|---|
| **1910** | • Mexican Revolution (Ch. 27) |
| **1914** | • Panama Canal opens (Ch. 27) |
| **1914–1918** | • World War I |
| **June 28, 1914** | • Assassination of Archduke Franz Ferdinand of Austria-Hungary |
| **August 1914** | • Japan joins the Triple Entente |
| **October 1914** | • Ottoman Empire joins Central Powers |
| **1915** | • Armenian genocide in the Ottoman Empire begins (Ch. 29) |
| **May 1915** | • Italy joins the Triple Entente; Germans sink the *Lusitania* |
| **1916** | • Arab revolt against Ottoman rule begins (Ch. 29) |
| **1917** | • March Revolution; tsar abdicates; Bolsheviks seize power; Lenin heads new government |
| **1917–1922** | • Russian civil war |
| **April 1917** | • U.S. declares war on Germany |
| **March 1918** | • Treaty of Brest-Litovsk |
| **November 1918** | • Armistice ends the war; revolution in Germany |
| **1919** | • Treaty of Versailles |
| **1920** | • Gandhi launches nonviolent campaign against British rule in India (Ch. 29) |
| **July 29, 1921** | • Adolf Hitler becomes Führer (leader) of the Nazi Party |
| **October 1923** | • Mustafa Kemal elected first president of the Republic of Turkey (Ch. 29) |
| **1924** | • Dawes Plan |
| **1927** | • Chinese civil war begins with Nationalists' attack on Communists (Ch. 29) |
| **1928** | • Kellogg-Briand Pact |
| **1929** | • Great Depression begins (Ch. 30) |

# 29

# Nationalism in Asia

## 1914–1939

CHAPTER PREVIEW

**The First World War's Impact on Nationalist Trends**
- Why did modern nationalism develop in Asia between the First and Second World Wars, and what was its appeal?

**Nationalist Movements in the Middle East**
- How did the Ottoman Empire's collapse in World War I shape nationalist movements in the Middle East?

**Toward Self-Rule in India**
- What role did Gandhi and his campaign of militant nonviolence play in leading India to independence from the British?

**Nationalist Struggles in East and Southeast Asia**
- How did nationalism shape political developments in East and Southeast Asia?

**FROM ASIA'S PERSPECTIVE, THE FIRST WORLD WAR WAS LARGELY A** European civil war that shattered Western imperialism's united front, underscored the West's moral bankruptcy, and convulsed prewar relationships throughout Asia. Most crucially, the war sped the development of modern Asian nationalism. Before 1914 the nationalist gospel of anti-imperialist political freedom and racial equality had already won converts among Asia's westernized, educated elites. In the 1920s and 1930s it increasingly won the allegiance of the masses. Nationalism in Asia between 1914 and 1939 became a mass movement with potentially awesome power.

The modern nationalism movement was never monolithic. In Asia especially, where the new and often narrow ideology of nationalism was grafted onto old, rich, and complex civilizations, the shape and eventual outcome of nationalist movements varied enormously. Between the outbreaks of the First and Second World Wars, each Asian country developed a distinctive national movement rooted in its own unique culture and history. Each nation's people created their own national reawakening, which reinvigorated thought and culture as well as politics and economics. Nationalist movements gave rise in Asia to conflict both within large, multiethnic states and between independent states.

The Asian nationalist movement witnessed the emergence of two of the true giants of the twentieth century. Mohandas Gandhi in India and Mao Zedong in China both drew their support from the peasant masses in the world's two most populous countries. Gandhi successfully used campaigns of peaceful nonviolent resistance to British colonial rule to gain Indian independence. Mao, on the other hand, used weapons of war and socialist promises of equality to defeat his westernized nationalist opponents and establish a modern Communist state.

# The First World War's Impact on Nationalist Trends

**Why did modern nationalism develop in Asia between the First and Second World Wars, and what was its appeal?**

In the late nineteenth and early twentieth centuries the peoples of Asia adapted the European ideology of nationalism to their own situations. The Great War profoundly affected Asian nationalist aspirations by altering relations between Asia and Europe. For four years Asians watched Kipling's haughty bearers of "the white man's burden" (see "A 'Civilizing Mission'" in Chapter 25) vilify and destroy each other. Japan's defeat of imperial Russia in 1905 (see "Japan as an Imperial Power" in Chapter 26) had shown that an Asian power could beat a European Great Power; Asians now viewed the entire West as divided and vulnerable.

## Asian Reaction to the War in Europe

The Great War was a global conflict, but some peoples were affected more significantly than others. The Japanese and Ottoman Turks were directly involved, fighting with the Allies and Central Powers, respectively. The Chinese, who overthrew their emperor in 1911, were more concerned with internal events and the threat from Japan than with the war in Europe. In British India and French Indochina the war's impact was unavoidably greater. Total war required the British and the French to draft their colonial subjects into the conflict. An Indian or Vietnamese soldier who fought in France and came in contact there with democratic and republican ideas, however, was less likely to accept foreign rule when he returned home. The British and the French therefore had to make rash promises to gain the support of these colonial peoples and other allies during the war. After the war the nationalist genie the colonial powers had called on refused to slip meekly back into the bottle.

U.S. president Wilson's war aims also raised the hopes of peoples under imperial rule. In January 1918 Wilson proposed his Fourteen Points (see "The Paris Peace

Treaties" in Chapter 28), whose key idea was national self-determination for the peoples of Europe and the Ottoman Empire. Wilson recommended in Point 5 that in all colonial questions "the interests of native populations be given equal weight with the desires of European governments," and he seemed to call for national self-rule. This message had enormous appeal for educated Asians, fueling their hopes of freedom.

## The Mandates System

After winning the war, the Allies tried to re-establish or increase their political and economic domination of their Asian and African colonies. Although fatally weakened, Western imperialism remained very much alive in 1918, partly because President Wilson was no revolutionary. At the Paris Peace Conference Wilson compromised on colonial questions in order to achieve some of his European goals and create the League of Nations.

The compromise at the Paris Peace Conference between Wilson's vague, moralistic idealism and the European determination to maintain control over colonial empires was a system of League of Nations mandates over Germany's former colonies and the old Ottoman Empire. Article 22 of the League of Nations Covenant, which was part of the Treaty of Versailles, assigned territories "inhabited by peoples incapable of governing themselves" to various "developed nations." "The well-being and development of such peoples" were declared "a sacred trust of civilization." The **Permanent Mandates Commission**, whose members came from European countries with colonies, was created to oversee the developed nations' fulfillment of their international responsibility. Thus the League elaborated a new principle—development toward the eventual goal of self-government—but left its implementation to the colonial powers themselves. Industrialized Japan was the only Asian state to obtain mandates.

The mandates system demonstrated that Europe was determined to maintain its imperial power and influence. Bitterly disappointed patriots throughout Asia saw the system as an expansion of the imperial order. Yet they did not give up. They preached national self-determination and struggled to build mass movements capable of achieving freedom and independence.

In this struggle Asian nationalists were encouraged by Soviet communism. After seizing power in 1917, Lenin declared that the Asian inhabitants of the new Soviet Union were complete equals of the Russians with a right to their own development. The Communists also denounced European and American imperialism and pledged to support revolutionary movements in colonial countries. The example, ideology, and support of Soviet communism exerted a powerful influence in the 1920s and 1930s, particularly in China and French Indochina.

## Nationalism's Appeal

There were at least three reasons for the upsurge of nationalism in Asia. First and foremost, nationalism provided the most effective means of organizing anti-imperialist resistance both to direct foreign rule and to indirect Western domination. Second, nationalism called for fundamental changes and challenged old political and social practices and beliefs. As in Russia after the Crimean War, in Turkey after the Ottoman Empire's collapse, and in Japan after the Meiji Restoration, the nationalist creed after World War I went hand in hand with acceptance of modernization by the educated elites, who used modernization to contest the influence and power of conservative traditionalists. Third, nationalism offered a vision of a free and prosperous future and provided an ideology to ennoble the sacrifices the struggle would require.

Nationalism also had a dark side. As in Europe (see "The Growing Appeal of Nationalism" in Chapter 24), Asian nationalists developed a strong sense of "we" and "they." "They" were often the enemy. European imperialists were just such a "they," and nationalist feelings generated the will to challenge European domination. But, as in Europe, Asian nationalism also stimulated bitter conflicts and wars between peoples, in three different ways.

First, as when the ideology of nationalism first developed in Europe in the early 1800s, Asian (and African) elites were often forced to create a national identity in colonies that Europeans had artificially created, or in multiethnic countries held together by authoritarian leaders but without national identities based on shared ethnicities or histories. Second, nationalism stimulated conflicts between relatively homogeneous peoples in large states, rallying, for example, Chinese against Japanese and vice versa. Third, nationalism often heightened tensions between ethnic or religious groups within states. In nearly all countries there were ancient ethnic and religious differences and rivalries. Imperial rulers of colonial powers (like the British and French) and local authoritarian rulers (like the Chinese emperor) exploited these ethnic and religious differences to "divide and conquer" the peoples in their empires. When the rigid imperial rule ended, the different national, religious, or even ideological (communists versus capitalists) factions turned against each other, each seeking to either seize control of or divide the existing state and to dominate the enemy "they" within its borders. This habit of thinking in terms of "we" versus "they" was, and still is, a difficult frame of mind to abandon, and these divisions made it difficult for nationalist leaders to unite people under a common national identity.

Nationalism's appeal in Asia was not confined to territories under direct European rule. Europe and the United States had forced even the most solid Asian states, China and Japan, to accept humiliating limitations on their sovereignty. Thus the nationalist promise of genuine economic independence and true political equality with the West appealed as powerfully in old but weak states like China as in colonial territories like British India.

# Nationalist Movements in the Middle East

## How did the Ottoman Empire's collapse in World War I shape nationalist movements in the Middle East?

The most flagrant attempt to expand Western imperialism occurred in southwest Asia (Map 29.1). There the British and the French successfully encouraged an Arab revolt in 1916 and destroyed the Ottoman Empire. Europeans then sought to replace Turks as principal rulers throughout the region. Turkish, Arab, and Persian nationalists, as well as Jewish nationalists arriving from Europe, reacted violently. They struggled to win nationhood, and as the Europeans were forced to make concessions, they sometimes came into sharp conflict with each other, most notably in Palestine.

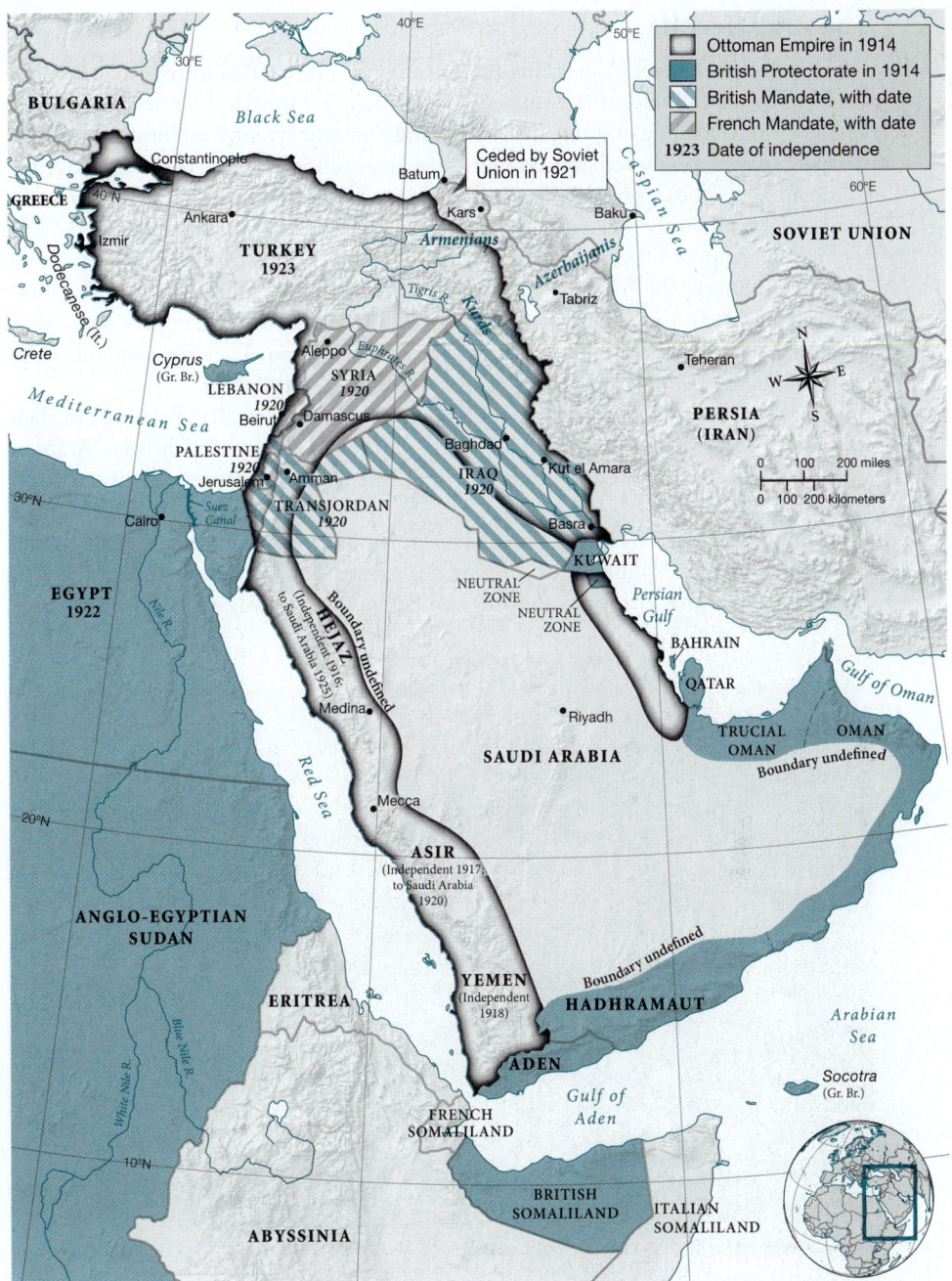

**MAP 29.1   The Partition of the Ottoman Empire, 1914–1923**
By 1914 the Ottoman Turks had been pushed out of the Balkans, and their Arab provinces were on the edge of revolt. That revolt erupted in the First World War and contributed greatly to the Ottomans' defeat. When the Allies then attempted to implement their plans, including independence for the Armenian people, Mustafa Kemal arose to forge in battle the modern Turkish state.

## The Arab Revolt

Long subject to European pressure, the Ottoman Empire failed to reform and modernize in the late nineteenth century (see "The Islamic Heartland Under Pressure" in Chapter 25). Declining international stature and domestic tyranny led idealistic exiles to engage in revolutionary activity and motivated army officers to seize power and save the Ottoman state. These patriots, the so-called Young Turks, succeeded in the 1908 revolution, and subsequently they were determined to hold together the remnants of the vast multiethnic empire. Defeated in the Balkan war of 1912 and stripped of practically all territory in Europe, the Young Turks redoubled their efforts in southwest Asia. The most important of their possessions were Syria—consisting of modern-day Lebanon, Syria, Israel, the West Bank, the Gaza Strip, and Jordan—and Iraq. The Ottoman Turks also claimed the Arabian peninsula but exercised only loose control there.

For centuries the largely Arab populations of Syria and Iraq had been tied to their Ottoman rulers by their common faith in Islam (though there were Christian Arabs as well). Yet beneath the surface, ethnic and linguistic tensions simmered between Turks and Arabs.

Young Turk actions after 1908 made the embryonic "Arab movement" a reality. The majority of Young Turks promoted a narrow Turkish nationalism. They further centralized the Ottoman Empire and extended the sway of Turkish language

**Refugees from the Armenian Genocide** An estimated 1.5 million Armenians were killed, or died from hunger and exhaustion, during forced deportation marches carried out by the Ottoman Turks in 1915–1917. This photo shows some of the 100,000 to 200,000 Armenians who survived. They had been driven into the Syrian Desert and were later discovered at As-Salt in northern Jordan. The refugees were later taken by the British to Jerusalem, and some of their descendants still live in the Armenian Quarter there. (Pictures from History/Bridgeman Images)

and culture. In 1909 the Turkish government brutally slaughtered thousands of Armenian Christians, a prelude to the wholesale massacre of more than a million Armenians during the First World War. Meanwhile, Arab discontent grew.

During World War I the Turks aligned themselves with Germany and Austria-Hungary (see "The War Becomes Global" in Chapter 28). As a result, the Young Turks drew all of the Middle East into what had been up to that point a European war. Arabs opposed to Ottoman rule found themselves allied with the British, who encouraged the alliance with vague promises of an independent Arab kingdom. After British victories on the Arabian peninsula in 1917 and 1918, many Arab patriots expected a large, unified Arab state to rise from the dust of the Ottoman collapse. Within two years, however, Arab nationalists felt bitterly betrayed by Great Britain and its allies.

Arab bitterness was partly directed at secret wartime treaties between Britain and France to divide and rule the old Ottoman Empire. In the 1916 **Sykes-Picot Agreement**, Britain and France secretly agreed that France would receive modern-day Lebanon, Syria, and much of southern Turkey, and Britain would receive Palestine, Jordan, and Iraq. The Sykes-Picot Agreement contradicted British promises concerning Arab independence after the war and left Arab nationalists feeling cheated and betrayed.

A related source of Arab frustration was Britain's wartime commitment to a Jewish homeland in Palestine. The **Balfour Declaration** of November 1917, made by the British foreign secretary Arthur Balfour, declared:

> His Majesty's Government views with favour the establishment in Palestine of a national home for the Jewish People, and will use their best endeavors to facilitate the achievement of this object, it being clearly understood that nothing shall be done which may prejudice the civil and religious rights of existing non-Jewish communities in Palestine.[1]

As a careful reading reveals, the Balfour Declaration made contradictory promises to European Jews and Middle Eastern Arabs.

Some British Cabinet members believed the Balfour Declaration would appeal to German, Austrian, and American Jews and thus help the British war effort. Others sincerely supported the Zionist vision of a Jewish homeland, but also believed that Jews living in this homeland would be grateful to Britain and thus help maintain British control of the Suez Canal.

In 1914 Jews made up about 11 percent of the predominantly Arab population in the Ottoman territory that became, under British control, Palestine. The "national home for the Jewish People" mentioned in the Balfour Declaration implied to the Arabs — and to the Zionist Jews as well — some kind of Jewish state that would be incompatible with majority rule.

After Faisal bin Hussein's failed efforts at the Paris Peace Conference to secure Arab independence, Arab nationalists met in Damascus at the General Syrian Congress in 1919 and unsuccessfully called again for political independence. Ignoring Arab opposition, the British mandate in Palestine formally incorporated the Balfour Declaration and its commitment to a Jewish national home. In March 1920 the Syrian National Congress proclaimed Syria independent, with Faisal bin Hussein as king. A similar congress declared Iraq an independent kingdom.

Western reaction to events in Syria and Iraq was swift and decisive. A French army stationed in Lebanon attacked Syria, taking Damascus in July 1920. Faisal fled, and the French took over. Meanwhile, the British put down an uprising in Iraq and established effective control there. Western imperialism appeared to have replaced Turkish rule in the Middle East (see Map 29.1).

## The Turkish Revolution

Days after the end of the First World War, French and then British troops entered Constantinople to begin a five-year occupation of the Ottoman capital. A young English official wrote that he found the Ottoman Empire "utterly smashed." The Turks were "worn out" from the war, and without bitterness they awaited the construction of a "new system."[2] The Allies' new system was blatant imperialism, which proved harsher for the defeated Turks than for the Arabs now free from Turkish rule. A treaty forced on the helpless sultan dismembered Turkey and reduced it to a puppet state. Great Britain and France occupied parts of Turkey, and Italy and Greece claimed shares as well. There was a sizable Greek minority in western Turkey, and Greek nationalists cherished the "Great Idea" of a modern Greek empire modeled on long-dead Christian Byzantium. In 1919 Greek armies carried by British ships landed on the Turkish coast at Smyrna and advanced into the interior. Turkey seemed finished.

But Turkey produced a great leader and revived to become an inspiration to the entire Middle East. Mustafa Kemal (moo-STAH-fah kuh-MAHL) (1881–1938), considered the father of modern Turkey, was a military man sympathetic to the Young Turk movement. After the armistice, he watched with anguish the Allies' aggression and the sultan's cowardice. In early 1919 he began working to unify Turkish resistance.

The sultan, bowing to Allied pressure, initially denounced Kemal, but the cause of national liberation proved more powerful. The catalyst was the Greek invasion and attempted annexation of much of western Turkey. A young Turkish woman described feelings she shared with countless others:

> After I learned about the details of the Smyrna occupation by Greek armies, I hardly opened my mouth on any subject except when it concerned the sacred struggle. . . . I suddenly ceased to exist as an individual. I worked, wrote and lived as a unit of that magnificent national madness.[3]

Refusing to acknowledge the Allied dismemberment of their country, the Turks battled on through 1920 despite staggering defeats. The next year the Greeks advanced almost to Ankara, the nationalist stronghold in central Turkey. There Mustafa Kemal's forces took the offensive and won a great victory. The Greeks and their British allies sued for peace. The resulting **Treaty of Lausanne** (1923) recognized a truly independent Turkey, and Turkey lost only its former Arab provinces (see Map 29.1).

Mustafa Kemal believed Turkey should modernize and secularize along Western lines. His first moves, beginning in 1923, were political. Kemal called on the National Assembly to depose the sultan and establish a republic, and he had himself elected president. Kemal savagely crushed the demands for independence of ethnic minorities within Turkey like the Armenians and the Kurds, but he realistically abandoned all thought of winning back lost Arab territories. He then created a one-party system in order to work his will.

Kemal's most radical changes pertained to religion and culture. For centuries most believers' intellectual and social activities had been regulated by Islamic religious authorities. Profoundly influenced by the example of western Europe, Mustafa Kemal set out, like the philosophes of the Enlightenment, to limit religious influence in daily affairs, but, like Russia's Peter the Great, he employed dictatorial measures rather than reason and democracy to reach his goal. Kemal decreed a revolutionary separation of church and state. Secular law codes inspired by European models replaced religious courts. State schools replaced religious schools and taught such secular subjects as science, mathematics, and social sciences.

Mustafa Kemal also struck down many entrenched patterns of behavior. Women, traditionally secluded and inferior to males in Islamic society, received the right to vote. Civil law on a European model, rather than the Islamic code, now governed marriage. Women could seek divorces, and no man could have more than one wife at a time. Men were forbidden to wear the tall red fez of the Ottoman era as headgear; government employees were ordered to wear business suits and felt hats, erasing the visible differences between Muslims and "infidel" Europeans. The old Arabic script was replaced with a new Turkish alphabet based on Roman letters, which facilitated massive government efforts to spread literacy after 1928. Finally, in 1935, surnames on the European model were introduced. The National Assembly granted Mustafa Kemal the surname Atatürk, which means "father of the Turks."

By his death in 1938, Atatürk and his supporters had consolidated their revolution. Government-sponsored industrialization was fostering urban growth and new attitudes, encouraging Turks to embrace business and science. Poverty persisted in rural areas, as did some religious discontent among devout Muslims. But

**Atatürk and His Wife, Latifah Uşaklıgil** Though they were only married for two years (1923–1925), Latifah Uşaklıgil came to symbolize the ideal modern Turkish woman. She came from a well-educated and wealthy family, and she studied law in Paris at the Sorbonne. She was studying English in London when she returned to Turkey toward the end of the war of Turkish independence (1919–1923). Latifah Uşaklıgil dressed in the latest modern Western fashions, and, as First Lady of Turkey, appeared frequently in public, which was quite uncommon at the time. Here they are pictured making an official appearance together during a trip to Bursa in 1923. (Bettmann/Getty Images)

like the Japanese after the Meiji Restoration, the Turkish people had rallied around the nationalist banner to repulse European imperialism and were building a modern secular nation-state.

## Modernization Efforts in Persia and Afghanistan

In Persia (renamed Iran in 1935) strong-arm efforts to build a unified modern nation ultimately proved less successful than in Turkey. In the late nineteenth century Persia had also been subject to extreme foreign pressure, which stimulated efforts to reform the government as a means of reviving Islamic civilization. In 1906 a nationalistic coalition of merchants, religious leaders, and intellectuals revolted. The despotic shah was forced to grant a constitution and establish a national assembly, the **Majlis** (MAHJ-lis).

Yet the 1906 Persian revolution was doomed to failure, largely because of European imperialism. Without consulting Iran, in 1907 Britain and Russia divided the country into spheres of influence. Britain's sphere ran along the Persian Gulf; the Russian sphere encompassed the whole northern half of Persia (see Map 29.1). Thereafter Russia intervened constantly. It blocked reforms, occupied cities, and completely dominated the country by 1912. When Russian power collapsed in the Bolshevik Revolution, British armies rushed into the power vacuum. By bribing corrupt Persians, Great Britain in 1919 negotiated a treaty allowing the installation of British "advisers" in every government department.

The Majlis refused to ratify the treaty, and the blatant attempt to make Persia a British satellite aroused the national spirit. In 1921 reaction against the British brought to power a military dictator, Reza Shah Pahlavi (PAH-luh-vee) (1877–1944), who proclaimed himself shah in 1925 and ruled until 1941.

Inspired by Turkey's Mustafa Kemal, Reza Shah had three basic goals: to build a modern nation, to free Persia from foreign domination, and to rule with an iron fist. The challenge was enormous. Persia was a vast, undeveloped country. The rural population was mostly poor and illiterate, and among the Persian majority were sizable ethnic minorities with their own aspirations. Furthermore, Iran's powerful religious leaders hated Western (Christian) domination but were equally opposed to a more secular, less Islamic society.

To realize his vision of a strong Persia, the shah created a modern army, built railroads, and encouraged commerce. He won control over ethnic minorities such as the Kurds in the north and Arab tribesmen on the Iraqi border. He reduced the privileges granted to foreigners and raised taxes on the powerful Anglo-Persian Oil Company, which had been founded in 1909 to exploit the first great oil strike in the Middle East. Yet Reza Shah was less successful than Atatürk.

Because the European-educated elite in Persia was smaller than the comparable group in Turkey, the idea of re-creating Persian greatness on the basis of a secularized society attracted relatively few determined supporters. Many powerful religious leaders turned against Reza Shah, and he became increasingly brutal, greedy, and tyrannical.

Afghanistan, meanwhile, was nominally independent in the nineteenth century, but the British imposed political restrictions and constantly meddled in the country's affairs. In 1919 emir Amanullah Khan (1892–1960) declared war on the British government in India and won complete independence for the first time. Amanullah (ah-man-UL-lah) then decreed revolutionary modernizing reforms designed to hurl his primitive country into the twentieth century. He established modern, secular schools for both boys and girls, and adult education classes for the predominantly illiterate population. He did away with seclusion and centuries-old dress codes for women, abolished slavery, created the country's first constitution in 1923, restructured and reorganized the economy, and established a legislative assembly and secular (rather than Islamic) court system. The result was tribal and religious revolt, civil war, and retreat from reform. Islam remained both religion and law. A powerful but primitive patriotism enabled Afghanistan to win political independence from the West, but not to build a modern society.

## Gradual Independence in the Arab States

French and British mandates forced Arab nationalists to seek independence by gradual means after 1920. Arab nationalists were indirectly aided by Western taxpayers who wanted cheap — that is, peaceful — empires. As a result, Arabs won considerable control over local affairs in the mandated states, except Palestine, though the mandates remained European satellites in international and economic affairs.

In Iraq the British chose Faisal bin Hussein, whom the French had deposed in Syria, as king. Faisal obligingly gave British advisers broad behind-the-scenes control. The king also accepted British ownership of Iraq's oil fields, consequently giving the West a stranglehold on the Iraqi economy. Given the severe limitations imposed on him, Faisal (r. 1921–1933) proved to be an able ruler, gaining his peoples' support and encouraging moderate reforms. In 1932 he secured Iraqi independence at the price of a restrictive long-term military alliance with Great Britain.

Egypt had been occupied by Great Britain since 1882 and had been a British protectorate since 1914. Following intense nationalist agitation after the Great War, Great Britain in 1922 proclaimed Egypt formally independent but continued to occupy the country militarily and control its politics. In 1936 the British agreed to restrict their troops to their bases in the Suez Canal Zone.

The French compromised less in their handling of their mandated Middle East territories. Following the Ottoman Empire's collapse after World War I, the French designated Lebanon as one of several ethnic enclaves within a larger area that became part of the French mandate of Syria. They practiced a policy of divide and rule and generally played off ethnic and religious minorities against each other. In 1926 Lebanon became a separate republic but remained under the control of the French mandate. Arab nationalists in Syria finally won promises of Syrian independence in 1936 in return for a friendship treaty with France.

In short, the Arab states gradually freed themselves from Western political mandates but not from Western military threats or from pervasive Western influence. Since large Arab landowners and urban merchants increased their wealth and political power after 1918, they often supported the Western hegemony. Radical nationalists, on the other hand, recognized that Western control of the newly discovered Arab oil fields was proof that economic independence and genuine freedom had not yet been achieved.

## Arab-Jewish Tensions in Palestine

Relations between the Arabs and the West were complicated by the tense situation in the British mandate of Palestine, and that situation deteriorated in the interwar years. Both Arabs and Jews denounced the British, who tried unsuccessfully to compromise with both sides. Arab nationalist anger, however, was aimed primarily at Jewish settlers. The key issue was Jewish migration from Europe to Palestine.

Jewish nationalism, known as Zionism, took shape in Europe in the late nineteenth century under Theodor Herzl's leadership (see "Jewish Emancipation and Modern Anti-Semitism" in Chapter 24). Herzl believed that only a Jewish state could guarantee Jews dignity and security. The Zionist movement encouraged some of the world's Jews to settle in Palestine, but until 1921 the great majority of Jewish emigrants preferred the United States.

After 1921 the situation changed radically. An isolationist United States drastically limited immigration from eastern Europe, where war and revolution had kindled anti-Semitism. Moreover, the British began honoring the Balfour Declaration despite Arab protests. Thus Jewish immigration to Palestine from turbulent Europe in the interwar years grew rapidly, particularly after Adolf Hitler became German chancellor in 1933. By 1939 Palestine's Jewish population had increased almost fivefold since 1914 and accounted for about 30 percent of all inhabitants.

Jewish settlers in Palestine faced formidable difficulties. Although much of the land purchased by the Jewish National Fund was productive, the sellers of such land were often wealthy absentee Arab landowners who cared little for their Arab tenants' welfare. When the Jewish settlers replaced those long-time Arab tenants, Arab farmers and intellectuals burned with a sense of injustice. Moreover, most Jewish immigrants came from urban backgrounds and preferred to establish new cities like Tel Aviv or to live in existing towns, where they competed with the Arabs. The land issue combined with economic and cultural friction to harden Arab protest into hatred. The British gradually responded to Arab pressure and tried to slow Jewish immigration. This effort satisfied neither Jews nor Arabs, and between 1936 and 1939 the three communities (Arab, Jewish, and British) were engaged in an undeclared civil war. On the eve of the Second World War, the frustrated British proposed an independent Palestine with the number of Jews permanently limited to only about one-third of the total population. Zionists felt themselves in grave danger of losing their dream of an independent Jewish state.

Nevertheless, in the face of adversity Jewish settlers gradually succeeded in forging a cohesive community in Palestine. Hebrew, for centuries used only in religious worship, was revived as a living language in the 1920s–1930s to bind the Jews in Palestine together. Despite its slow beginnings, rural development achieved often remarkable results. The key unit of agricultural organization was the **kibbutz**, a collective farm on which each member shared equally in the work, rewards, and defense. An egalitarian socialist ideology also characterized industry, which grew rapidly. By 1939 a new but old nation was emerging in the Middle East.

# Toward Self-Rule in India

**What role did Gandhi and his campaign of militant nonviolence play in leading India to independence from the British?**

The nationalist movement in British India grew out of two interconnected cultures, Hindu and Muslim. While the two joined together to challenge British rule, they also came to see themselves as fundamentally different. Nowhere has modern nationalism's power both to unify and to divide been more strikingly demonstrated than in India.

## British Promises and Repression

Indian nationalism had emerged in the late nineteenth century, and when the First World War began, the British feared an Indian revolt. Instead Indians supported the war effort. About 1.2 million Indian soldiers and laborers voluntarily served in Europe, Africa, and the Middle East. The British government in India and the native Indian princes sent large supplies of food, money, and ammunition. In return, the British opened more good government jobs to Indians and made other minor concessions.

As the war in distant Europe ground on, however, inflation, high taxes, food shortages, and a terrible influenza epidemic created widespread suffering and discontent. The prewar nationalist movement revived, becoming stronger than ever, and moderates and radicals in the Indian National Congress Party joined forces. Moreover, in 1916 Hindu leaders in the Congress Party hammered out an alliance—the **Lucknow Pact**—with India's Muslim League. The Lucknow (LUHK-noh) Pact forged a powerful united front of Hindus and Muslims and called for putting India on an equal footing with self-governing British dominions like Canada, Australia, and New Zealand.

The British response to the Lucknow Pact was mixed. In August 1917 the British called for the "gradual development of self-governing institutions with a view to the progressive realization of responsible government in India."[4] But the proposed self-government was much more limited than that granted the British dominions. In late 1919 the British established a dual administration: part Indian and elected, part British and authoritarian. Such uncontroversial activities as agriculture and health were transferred from British to Indian officials, but sensitive matters like taxes, police, and the courts remained solely in British hands.

Old-fashioned authoritarian rule also seriously undermined whatever positive impact this reform might have had. The 1919 Rowlatt Acts indefinitely extended wartime "emergency measures" designed to curb unrest and root out "conspiracy." The result was a wave of rioting across India.

Under these tense conditions a crowd of some ten thousand gathered to celebrate a Sikh religious festival in an enclosed square in the Sikh (SEEK) holy city of Amritsar (ahm-RIHT-suhr) in the northern Punjab province. Unknown to the crowd, the local English commander, General Reginald Dyer, had banned all public meetings that very day. Dyer marched his troops into the square and, without warning, ordered them to fire into the crowd until the ammunition ran out. Official British records of the Amritsar Massacre list 379 killed and 1,137 wounded, but these figures remain hotly contested as being too low. Tensions flared, and India stood on the verge of more violence and repression. That India took a different path to national liberation was due largely to Mohandas K. Gandhi (1869–1948), the most influential Indian leader of modern times.

## The Roots of Militant Nonviolence

Gandhi grew up in a well-to-do family, and after his father's death he went to study law in England, where he passed the English bar. Upon returning to India, he decided in 1893 to try a case for some wealthy Indian merchants in the British colony of Natal (part of modern South Africa). It was a momentous decision.

In Natal Gandhi took up the plight of the expatriate Indian community. White plantation owners had been importing thousands of poor Indians as indentured laborers since the 1860s. Some of these Indians, after completing their period of indenture, remained in Natal as free persons and economic competitors. In response, the Afrikaner (of Dutch descent) and British settlers passed brutally discriminatory laws. Poor Indians had to work on plantations or return to India. Rich Indians, who had previously had the vote in Natal, lost that right in 1896. Gandhi undertook his countrymen's legal defense.

Meanwhile, Gandhi was searching for a spiritual theory of social action. He studied Hindu and Christian teachings and gradually developed a weapon for the poor and oppressed that he called **satyagraha** (suh-TYAH-gruh-huh). Gandhi conceived of satyagraha, loosely translated as "soul force," as a means of striving for truth and social justice through love and a willingness to suffer the oppressor's blows, while trying to convert him or her to one's views of what is true and just. Its tactic was active nonviolent resistance.

When South Africa's white government severely restricted Asian immigration and internal freedom of movement, Gandhi put his philosophy into action and organized a nonviolent mass resistance campaign. Thousands of Indian men and women marched in peaceful protest and withstood beatings, arrest, and imprisonment.

In 1914 South Africa's exasperated whites agreed to many of the Indians' demands. They passed a law abolishing discriminatory taxes on Indian traders, recognized the legality of non-Christian marriages, and permitted the continued immigration of free Indians.

## Gandhi's Resistance Campaign in India

In 1915 Gandhi returned to India a hero. The masses hailed him as a mahatma, or "great soul"—a Hindu title of veneration for a man of great knowledge and humanity. In 1920 Gandhi launched a national campaign of nonviolent resistance to British rule. He urged his countrymen to boycott British goods, jobs, and honors and told peasants not to pay taxes.

The nationalist movement had previously touched only the tiny, prosperous, Western-educated elite. Now both the illiterate masses of village India and the educated classes heard Gandhi's call for militant nonviolent resistance. It particularly appealed to the masses of Hindus who were not members of the warrior caste or the so-called military races and who were traditionally passive and nonviolent. The British had regarded ordinary Hindus as cowards. Gandhi told them that they could be courageous and even morally superior:

> What do you think? Wherein is courage required—in blowing others to pieces from behind a cannon, or with a smiling face to approach a cannon and be blown to pieces? Who is the true warrior—he who keeps death always as a bosom-friend, or he who controls the death of others? Believe me that a man devoid of courage and manhood can never be a passive resister.[5]

Gandhi made the Indian National Congress into a mass political party, welcoming members from every ethnic group and cooperating closely with the Muslim minority.

In 1922 some Indian resisters turned to violence, murdering twenty-two policemen. Savage riots broke out, and Gandhi abruptly called off his campaign, observing that he had "committed a Himalayan blunder in placing civil disobedience before those who had never learnt the art of civil disobedience."[6] Arrested for fomenting rebellion, Gandhi served two years in prison. Upon his release Gandhi set up a commune, established a national newspaper, and set out to reform Indian society and improve the lot of the poor. For Gandhi moral improvement, social progress, and the national movement went hand in hand. Above all, Gandhi nurtured national identity and self-respect. He also tried to instill in India's people the courage to overcome their fear of their colonial rulers and to fight these rulers with nonviolence.

During Gandhi's time in prison (1922–1924) the Indian National Congress had splintered into various factions, and Gandhi spent the years after his release quietly trying to reunite the organization. In 1929 the radical nationalists, led by Jawaharlal Nehru (juh-WAH-hur-lahl NAY-roo) (1889–1964), pushed through the National Congress a resolution calling for virtual independence within a year. The British stiffened in their resolve against Indian independence, and Indian radicals talked of a bloody showdown.

Into this tense situation Gandhi masterfully reasserted his leadership, taking a hard line toward the British but insisting on nonviolent methods. He organized a massive resistance campaign against the tax on salt, which gave the British a veritable monopoly on the salt that was absolutely necessary for survival in India's heat and humidity and affected every Indian family. From March 12 to April 6, 1930, Gandhi led tens of thousands of people in a spectacular march to the sea, where he made salt in defiance of the law. A later demonstration at the British-run Dharasana

**Gandhi on the Salt March, March 1930** A small, frail man, Gandhi possessed enormous courage and determination. His campaign of nonviolent resistance to British rule inspired the Indian masses and mobilized a nation. Here he is shown walking on his famous march to the sea to protest the English-Indian government's monopoly on salt production. (© SZ Photo/Scherl/Bridgeman Images)

(dahr-AH-sahn-nah) salt works resulted in many of the 2,500 nonviolent marchers being beaten senseless by policemen in a brutal and well-publicized encounter. Over the next months the British arrested Gandhi and sixty thousand other protesters for making and distributing salt. But the protests continued, and in 1931 the frustrated and unnerved British released Gandhi from jail and sat down to negotiate with him over Indian self-rule. Negotiations resulted in a new constitution, the Government of India Act, in 1935, which greatly strengthened India's parliamentary representative institutions and gave Indians some voice in the administration of British India.

Despite his best efforts, Gandhi failed to heal a widening split between Hindu and Muslims. Indian nationalism, based largely on Hindu symbols and customs, increasingly disturbed the Muslim minority, represented by the Muslim League led by the Western-educated Bombay lawyer Muhammad Ali Jinnah (jee-NAH) (1876–1948). Tempers mounted, and both sides committed atrocities. By the late 1930s Muslim League leaders were calling for the creation of a Muslim nation in British India, a "Pakistan," or "land of the pure." As in Palestine, the rise of conflicting nationalisms in India based on religion would lead to tragedy (see "Independence in India, Pakistan, and Bangladesh" in Chapter 31).

# Nationalist Struggles in East and Southeast Asia

**How did nationalism shape political developments in East and Southeast Asia?**

Because of the efforts of the Meiji reformers, nationalism and modernization were well developed in Japan by 1914. Japan competed politically and economically with the world's leading nations, building its own empire and proclaiming its special mission in Asia. Initially China lagged behind, but after 1912 the pace of nationalist development began to quicken.

By promoting extensive modernization in the 1920s, the Chinese nationalist movement managed to reduce the power and influence both of the warlords who controlled large territories in the interior and of the imperialist West. This achievement was soon undermined, however, by an internal civil war followed by war with an expanding Japan. Nationalism also flourished elsewhere in Asia, scoring a major victory in the Philippines.

## The Rise of Nationalist China

The 1911 Revolution led by Sun Yatsen (1866–1925) overthrew the Qing (CHING) Dynasty, and after four thousand years of monarchy the last Chinese emperor, Puyi (1906–1967), abdicated in February 1912. Sun Yatsen (soon yaht-SEHN) proclaimed China a republic and thereby opened an era of unprecedented change for Chinese society. In 1912 he turned over leadership of the republican government to the other central figure in the revolution, Yuan Shigai (yoo-AHN shee-KIGH). Originally called out of retirement to save the Qing Dynasty, Yuan (1859–1916) betrayed its Manchu leaders and convinced the revolutionaries that he could unite the country peacefully and prevent foreign intervention. Once elected president of the republic, however, Yuan concentrated on building his own power. In 1913 he used military force to dissolve China's parliament and ruled as a dictator. China's first modern revolution had failed.

The extent of the failure became apparent only after Yuan's death in 1916, when the central government in Beijing almost disintegrated. For more than a decade thereafter, power resided in a multitude of local military leaders, the so-called warlords. Their wars, taxes, and corruption created terrible suffering.

Foreign imperialism intensified the agony of warlordism. Japan's expansion into Shandong and southern Manchuria during World War I angered China's growing middle class and enraged China's young patriots (see Map 29.2). On May 4, 1919, five thousand students in Beijing exploded in anger against the decision of the Paris Peace Conference to leave the Shandong Peninsula in Japanese hands. This famous incident launched the **May Fourth Movement**, which opposed both foreign domination and warlord government.

The May Fourth Movement, which was both strongly pro-Marxist and passionately anti-imperialist, looked to the October 1917 Bolshevik Revolution in Russia as a model for its own nationalist revolution. In 1923 Sun Yatsen decided to ally his Nationalist Party, or Guomindang (gwoh-mihn-dang), with Lenin's Communist Third International and the newly formed Chinese Communist Party. The result was the first of many so-called national liberation fronts.

Sun, however, was no Communist. In his *Three Principles of the People*, elaborating on the official Nationalist Party ideology—nationalism, democracy, and people's livelihood—nationalism remained of prime importance:

> Compared to the other peoples of the world we have the greatest population and our civilization is four thousand years old; we should be advancing in the front rank with the nations of Europe and America. But the Chinese people . . . do not have national spirit. . . . If we do not earnestly espouse nationalism and weld together our four hundred million people into a strong nation, there is a danger of China's being lost and our people being destroyed. If we wish to avert this catastrophe, we must . . . bring this national spirit to the salvation of the country.[7]

Democracy, in contrast, had a less exalted meaning. Sun equated it with firm rule by the Nationalists, who would improve people's lives through land reform and welfare measures.

Sun planned to use the Nationalist Party's revolutionary army to crush the warlords and reunite China under a strong central government. When Sun unexpectedly died in 1925, Jiang Jieshi (known in the West as Chiang Kai-shek) (1887–1975) took his place. In 1926 and 1927 Jiang Jieshi (jee-ang jee-shee) led Nationalist armies in a successful attack on warlord governments in central and northern China. In 1928 the Nationalists established a new capital at Nanjing. Foreign states recognized the Nanjing government, and superficial observers believed China to be truly reunified.

In fact, national unification was only skin-deep. China remained a vast agricultural country plagued by foreign concessions, regional differences, and a lack of modern communications. Moreover, the uneasy alliance between the Nationalist Party and the Chinese Communist Party had turned into a bitter, deadly rivalry. Fearful of Communist subversion of the Nationalist government, Jiang decided in April 1927 to liquidate his left-wing "allies" in a bloody purge. Chinese Communists went into hiding and vowed revenge.

## China's Intellectual Revolution

Nationalism was the most powerful idea in China between 1911 and 1929, but it was only one aspect of a complex intellectual revolution, generally known as the **New Culture Movement**, that hammered at traditional Chinese thought and custom, advocated cultural renaissance, and pushed China into the modern world. The New Culture Movement was founded around 1916 by young Western-oriented intellectuals in Beijing. These intellectuals attacked Confucian ethics, which subordinated subjects to rulers, sons to fathers, and wives to husbands. As modernists, they advocated new and anti-Confucian virtues: individualism, democratic equality, and the critical scientific method. They also promoted the use of simple, understandable written language as a means to clear thinking and mass education. China, they said, needed a whole new culture, a radically different worldview.

Many intellectuals thought the radical worldview China needed was Marxist socialism. It, too, was Western in origin, "scientific" in approach, and materialist in its denial of religious belief and Confucian family ethics. But while liberalism and individualism reflected the bewildering range of Western thought since the Enlightenment, Marxist socialism offered the certainty of a single all-encompassing creed. As one young Communist intellectual exclaimed, "I am now able to impose order on all the ideas which I could not reconcile; I have found the key to all the problems which appeared to me self-contradictory and insoluble."[8]

Marxism provided a means of criticizing Western dominance, thereby salving Chinese pride. Chinese Communists could blame China's pitiful weakness on rapacious foreign capitalistic imperialism. Thus Marxism, as modified by Lenin and applied by the Bolsheviks in the Soviet Union, appeared as a means of catching up with the hated but envied West. For Chinese believers, it promised salvation soon.

Chinese Communists could and did interpret Marxism-Leninism to appeal to the masses—the peasants. Mao Zedong (sometimes spelled Mao Tse-tung) in particular quickly recognized the impoverished Chinese peasantry's enormous revolutionary potential. A member of a prosperous, hard-working peasant family, Mao Zedong (maow-dzuh-dahng) (1893–1976) converted to Marxist socialism in 1918. He began his revolutionary career as an urban labor organizer. In 1925 protest strikes by Chinese textile workers against their Japanese employers unexpectedly spread from the big coastal cities to rural China, prompting Mao (like Lenin in Russia) to reconsider the peasants. Investigating the rapid growth of radical peasant associations in Hunan province, Mao argued passionately in a 1927 report:

> The force of the peasantry is like that of the raging winds and driving rain. It is rapidly increasing in violence. No force can stand in its way. The peasantry will tear apart all nets which bind it and hasten along the road to liberation. They will bury beneath them all forces of imperialism, militarism, corrupt officialdom, village bosses and evil gentry.[9]

Mao's first experiment in peasant revolt—the Autumn Harvest Uprising of September 1927—was not successful, but Mao learned quickly. He advocated equal distribution of land and broke up his forces into small guerrilla groups. After 1928 he and his supporters built up a self-governing Communist soviet, centered at Jiangxi (jee-AHNG-shee) in southeastern China, and dug in against Nationalist attacks.

China's intellectual revolution also stimulated profound changes in popular culture and family life. After the 1911 Revolution Chinese women enjoyed increasingly greater freedom and equality, and gradually gained unprecedented educational and economic opportunities. Thus rising nationalism and the intellectual revolution interacted with monumental changes in Chinese family life.

## From Liberalism to Ultranationalism in Japan

The nearly total homogeneity of the Japanese population (98.5 percent ethnic Japanese) was a major factor in the Meiji reformers' efforts to build a powerful, nationalistic, modern state and resist Western imperialism. Their spectacular success deeply impressed Japan's fellow Asians. The Japanese, alone among Asia's peoples, had mastered modern industrial technology by 1910 and had fought victorious wars against both China and Russia. The First World War brought more triumphs. In 1915 Japan seized Germany's Asian holdings and retained most of them as League of Nations mandates. The Japanese economy expanded enormously. Profits soared as Japan won new markets that wartime Europe could no longer supply.

In the early 1920s Japan made further progress on all fronts. In 1922 Japan signed a naval arms limitation treaty with the Western powers and returned some of its control over the Shandong Peninsula to China. These conciliatory moves reduced tensions in East Asia. At home Japan seemed headed toward genuine democracy. The electorate expanded twelvefold between 1918 and 1925 as all males over twenty-five won the vote. Two-party competition was intense. Japanese living standards were the highest in Asia. Literacy was universal.

Japan's remarkable rise was accompanied by serious problems. Japan had a rapidly growing population but scarce natural resources. As early as the 1920s Japan was exporting manufactured goods in order to pay for imports of food and essential raw materials. Deeply enmeshed in world trade, Japan was vulnerable to every boom and bust. These economic realities broadened support for Japan's colonial empire. Before World War I Japanese leaders saw colonial expansion primarily in terms of international prestige and national defense. They believed that control of Taiwan, Korea, and Manchuria provided an essential "outer ring of defense" to protect the home islands from Russian attack and Anglo-American imperialism. Now, in the 1920s, Japan's colonies also seemed essential for markets, raw materials, and economic growth.

Japan's rapid industrial development also created an imbalanced "dualistic" economy. The modern sector consisted of a handful of giant conglomerate firms, the **zaibatsu** (zigh-BAHT-dzoo), or "financial combines." Zaibatsu firms wielded enormous economic power and dominated the other sector of the economy, an unorganized multitude of peasant farmers and craftsmen. The result was financial oligarchy, corruption of government officials, and a weak middle class.

Behind the façade of party politics, Japanese elites — the emperor, high government officials, big business and military leaders — jockeyed savagely for power. Cohesive leadership, which had played such an important role in Japan's modernization by the Meiji reformers, had ceased to exist. By far the most serious challenge to peaceful progress was fanatical nationalism. As in Europe, ultranationalism first emerged in Japan in the late nineteenth century but did not flower fully until the First World War and the 1930s.

Though their views were often vague, Japan's ultranationalists shared several fundamental beliefs. They were violently anti-Western, rejecting democracy, big business, and Marxist socialism. Reviving old myths, they stressed the emperor's godlike qualities and the samurai warrior's code of honor, obedience, and responsibility. Despising party politics, they assassinated moderate leaders and plotted armed uprisings to achieve their goals. Above all else, the ultranationalists preached foreign expansion. Like Western imperialists shouldering "the white man's burden," Japanese ultranationalists thought their mission was a noble one. "Asia for the Asians" was their anti-Western rallying cry. As the famous ultranationalist Kita Ikki wrote in 1923, "Our seven hundred million brothers in China and India have no other path to independence than that offered by our guidance and protection."[10]

The ultranationalists were noisy and violent in the 1920s, but it took the Great Depression of the 1930s to tip the scales decisively in their favor. The worldwide depression hit Japan like a tidal wave in 1930. Exports and wages collapsed; unemployment and raw suffering soared. The ultranationalists blamed the system, and people listened.

## Japan Against China

Among those who listened with particular care were young Japanese army officers in Manchuria, the underpopulated, resource-rich province of northeastern China controlled by the Japanese army since its victory over Russia in 1905. The rise of Chinese nationalism embodied in the Guomindang unification of China challenged Japanese control over Manchuria. In response, junior Japanese officers in Manchuria, in cooperation with top generals in Tokyo, secretly manufactured an excuse for aggression in late 1931. They blew up some Japanese-owned railroad tracks near the city of Shenyang (Mukden) and then, with reinforcements rushed in from Korea, quickly occupied all of Manchuria in "self-defense."

In 1932 Japan proclaimed Manchuria an independent state, renaming it Manchukuo, and in 1934 installed Puyi, the last Qing emperor, as puppet emperor over the puppet state. When the League of Nations condemned Japanese aggression in Manchuria, Japan resigned in protest. Japanese aggression in Manchuria proved that the army, though reporting directly to the Japanese emperor, was an independent force subject to no outside control.

For China the Japanese conquest of Manchuria was disastrous. Japanese aggression in Manchuria drew attention away from modernizing efforts. The Nationalist government promoted a massive boycott of Japanese goods but lost interest in social reform. Above all, the Nationalist government after 1931 completely neglected land reform and the Chinese peasants' grinding poverty. A contemporaneous Chinese economist spelled out the revolutionary implications: "It seems clear that the land problem in China today is as acute as that of eighteenth-century France or nineteenth-century Russia."[11] Mao Zedong agreed.

Having abandoned land reform, partly because they themselves were often landowners, the Nationalists under Jiang Jieshi devoted their energies between 1930 and 1934 to great campaigns of encirclement and extermination of the Communists' rural power base in southeastern China. In 1934 they closed in for the kill, but,

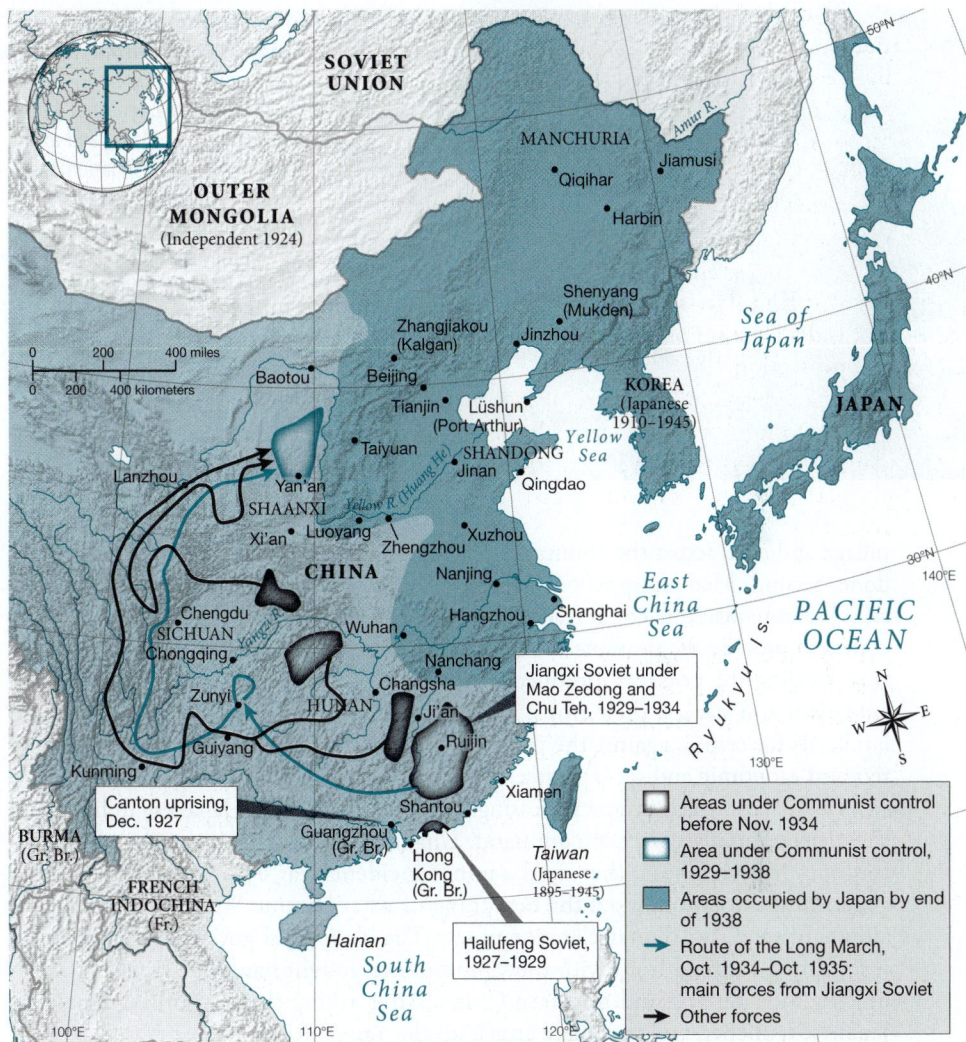

**MAP 29.2**   **The Chinese Communist Movement and the War with Japan, 1927–1938**
After urban uprisings ordered by Stalin failed in 1927, Mao Zedong succeeded in forming a self-governing Communist soviet in mountainous southern China. Relentless Nationalist attacks between 1930 and 1934 finally forced the Long March to Yan'an, where the Communists were well positioned for guerrilla war against the Japanese.

in one of the most incredible sagas of modern times, the main Communist army broke out, beat off attacks, and retreated 6,000 miles in twelve months to a remote region on the northwestern border (Map 29.2). Of the estimated 100,000 men and women who began the **Long March**, only 8,000 to 10,000 reached the final destination in Yan'an (YEH-nahn).

There Mao built up his forces once again, established a new territorial base, and won local peasant support in five unprecedented ways. First, Mao's forces did not

**Mao Zedong and the Chinese Long March** Mao's Communist forces were welcomed by the peasants during the Long March and at the army's final destination at Yan'an because the soldiers treated them with respect. In Yan'an they set up schools and health clinics, helped the farmers with their crops, and tried and punished the warlords and landlords. Here Mao talks with some peasants while on the Long March. (akg-images)

pillage and rape across the countryside as imperialist and warlord armies had always done. Second, Mao set up schools, albeit for Marxist education, so the nearly universally illiterate peasants could learn to read and write. Third, Mao established health clinics to provide the peasants with basic medical care. Fourth, Mao's armies, rather than stealing the peasants' produce, put down their weapons and helped the peasants plant and harvest their crops. Fifth, Communist courts tried the warlords and landlords for crimes against the peasants, who for the first time in Chinese history received economic and social justice.

In Japan politics became increasingly chaotic. In 1937 the Japanese military and the ultranationalists were in command. Unable to force China to cede more territory in northern China, they used a minor incident near Beijing as a pretext for a general attack. This marked the beginning of what became World War II in Asia, although Japan issued no declaration of war. The Nationalist government, which had just formed a united front with the Communists, fought hard, but Japanese troops quickly took Beijing and northern China. After taking the port of Shanghai, the Japanese launched an immediate attack up the Yangzi River.

Foretelling the horrors of World War II, the Japanese air force bombed Chinese cities and civilian populations with unrelenting fury. Nanjing, the capital, fell in December 1937. Entering the city, Japanese soldiers went berserk and committed dreadful atrocities over seven weeks. They brutally murdered an estimated 200,000 to 300,000 Chinese civilians and unarmed soldiers, and raped 20,000 to 80,000 Chinese women. The "Rape of Nanjing" combined with other Japanese atrocities to outrage world opinion. The Western powers denounced Japanese aggression but, with tensions rising in Europe, took no action.

By late 1938 Japanese armies occupied sizable portions of coastal China (see Map 29.2). But the Nationalists and the Communists had retreated to the interior, and both refused to accept defeat. In 1939, as Europe edged toward another great war, China and Japan were bogged down in a savage stalemate. This undeclared war—called by historians the Second Sino-Japanese War (1937–1945)—provided a spectacular example of conflicting nationalisms.

## Striving for Independence in Southeast Asia

The tide of nationalism was also rising in Southeast Asia. Nationalists in French Indochina and the Philippines urgently wanted genuine political independence and freedom from foreign rule. In French Indochina they ran up against an imperialist stone wall. The obstacle to Filipino independence came from America and Japan.

The French in Indochina, as in all their colonies, refused to export the liberal policies contained in the stirring words of their own Declaration of the Rights of Man and of the Citizen: liberty, equality, and fraternity. This uncompromising attitude stimulated the growth of an equally stubborn Communist opposition under Ho Chi Minh (hoh chee mihn) (1890–1969), which despite ruthless repression emerged as the dominant anti-French force in Indochina.

In the Philippines, however, a well-established nationalist movement achieved greater success. As in colonial Latin America, the Spanish in the Philippines had been indefatigable missionaries. By the late nineteenth century the Filipino population was 80 percent Catholic. Filipinos shared a common cultural heritage and a common racial origin. Education, especially for girls, was advanced for Southeast Asia, and already in 1843 a higher percentage of people could read in the Philippines than in Spain itself. Economic development helped to create a westernized elite, which turned first to reform and then to revolution in the 1890s.

Filipino nationalists were bitterly disillusioned when the United States, having taken the Philippines from Spain in the Spanish-American War of 1898, ruthlessly beat down a patriotic revolt and denied the universal Filipino desire for independence. The Americans claimed the Philippines was not ready for self-rule and might be seized by Germany or Britain if it could not establish a stable, secure government. As the imperialist power in the Philippines, the United States encouraged education and promoted capitalistic economic development. And as in British India, an elected legislature was given some real powers.

As in India and French Indochina, demands for independence grew. One important contributing factor was American racial attitudes. Americans treated Filipinos as inferiors and introduced segregationist practices borrowed from the American South. American racism made passionate nationalists of many Filipinos. However, it was the Great Depression that had the most radical impact on the Philippines.

As the United States collapsed economically in the 1930s, the Philippines suddenly appeared to be a liability rather than an asset. American farm groups lobbied for protection from cheap Filipino sugar. To protect American jobs, labor unions demanded an end to Filipino immigration. Responding to public pressure, in 1934 Congress made the Philippines a self-governing commonwealth and scheduled independence for 1944. Sugar imports were reduced, and immigration was limited to only fifty Filipinos per year.

Some Filipino nationalists denounced the continued U.S. presence, but others were less certain that it was the immediate problem. Japan was fighting in China and expanding economically into the Philippines and throughout Southeast Asia. By 1939 a new threat to Filipino independence would come from Japan itself.

# Chapter Summary

The Ottoman Empire's collapse in World War I left a power vacuum that both Western imperialists and Asian nationalists sought to fill. Strong leaders, such as Turkey's Mustafa Kemal, led successful nationalist movements in Turkey, Persia, and Afghanistan. British and French influence over the League of Nations–mandated Arab states declined in the 1920s and 1930s as Arab nationalists pushed for complete independence. The situation in Palestine, where the British had promised both Palestinians and Jewish Zionists independent homelands, deteriorated in the interwar years as increasingly larger numbers of European Jews migrated there.

Britain's centuries-long colonial rule over the Indian subcontinent met increasing resistance from Indian nationalists, particularly from Indian National Congress leaders, in the first decades of the twentieth century. Gandhi's active, nonviolent resistance campaign, which he called satyagraha, was principally responsible for convincing the British that their colonial hegemony in India was doomed. China's 1911 Revolution successfully ended the ancient dynastic system before the Great War, while the 1919 May Fourth Movement renewed nationalist hopes after it. Jiang Jieshi's Nationalist Party and Mao Zedong's Communists, however, would violently contest who would rule over a unified China. Japan, unlike China, industrialized early and by the 1920s seemed headed toward genuine democracy, but militarists and ultranationalists then launched an aggressive campaign of foreign expansion based on "Asia for Asians," which contributed to the buildup to World War II. As the Great Depression took hold, Filipino nationalists achieved independence from the United States. The diversity of these nationalist movements, arising out of separate historical experiences and distinct cultures, helps explain why Asian nationalists, like European nationalists, developed a strong sense of "we" and "they." In Asia "they" included other Asians as well as Europeans.

## NOTES

1.  Howard M. Sachar, *A History of Israel: From the Rise of Zionism to Our Time* (New York: Alfred A. Knopf, 1985), p. 109.
2.  H. Armstrong, *Turkey in Travail: The Birth of a New Nation* (London: John Lane, 1925), p. 75.
3.  Quoted in Lord Kinross, *Atatürk: A Biography of Mustafa Kemal, Father of Modern Turkey* (New York: Morrow, 1965), p. 181.
4.  Lawrence James, *Raj: The Making and Unmaking of British India* (New York: St. Martin's Press, 1998), p. 458.
5.  Quoted in E. Erikson, *Gandhi's Truth: On the Origins of Militant Nonviolence* (New York: W. W. Norton, 1969), p. 225.
6.  M. K. Gandhi, *Non-Violent Resistance (Satyagraha)* (New York: Schocken Books, 1961), p. 365.
7.  Quoted in W. T. de Bary, W. Chan, and B. Watson, *Sources of Chinese Tradition* (New York: Columbia University Press, 1964), pp. 768–769.
8.  Quoted in J. F. Fairbank, E. O. Reischauer, and A. M. Craig, *East Asia: Tradition and Transformation* (Boston: Houghton Mifflin, 1973), p. 774.
9.  Quoted in B. I. Schwartz, *Chinese Communism and the Rise of Mao* (Cambridge, Mass.: Harvard University Press, 1951), p. 74.
10. Quoted in W. T. de Bary, R. Tsunoda, and D. Keene, *Sources of Japanese Tradition*, vol. 2 (New York: Columbia University Press, 1958), p. 269.
11. Institute of Pacific Relations, *Agrarian China: Selected Source Material from Chinese Authors* (Chicago: University of Chicago Press, 1938), p. 1.

## MAKE CONNECTIONS  LOOK AHEAD

Just as nationalism drove politics and state-building in Europe in the nineteenth century, so it took root across Asia in the late nineteenth and early twentieth centuries. While nationalism in Europe developed out of a desire to turn cultural unity into political reality and create imagined communities out of millions of strangers, in Asia nationalist sentiments drew their greatest energy from opposition to European imperialism and domination. Asian modernizers, aware of momentous advances in science and technology and of politics and social practices in the West, also pressed the nationalist cause by demanding an end to outdated conservative traditions that they argued only held back the development of modern, independent nations capable of throwing off Western domination and existing as equals with the West.

The nationalist cause in Asia took many forms and produced some of the twentieth century's most remarkable leaders. In Chapter 32 we will discuss how nationalist leaders across Asia shaped the freedom struggle and the resulting independence according to their own ideological and personal visions. China's Mao Zedong is the giant among the nationalist leaders who emerged in Asia, but he replaced imperialist rule with one-party Communist rule. Gandhi's dream of a unified India collapsed with the partition of British India into Hindu India and Muslim Pakistan and Bangladesh. India and Pakistan remain bitter, and nuclear-armed, enemies today, as we will see in Chapter 33. Egypt assumed a prominent position in the Arab world after World War II under Gamal Nasser's leadership and, after a series of wars with Israel, began to play a significant role in efforts to find a peaceful resolution to the Israeli-Palestinian conflict. That conflict, however, continues unabated as nationalist and religious sentiments inflame feelings on both sides. Ho Chi Minh eventually forced the French colonizers out of Vietnam, only to face another Western power, the United States, in a long and deadly war. As described in Chapter 31, a unified Vietnam finally gained its independence in 1975, but, like China, the country was under one-party Communist control.

Japan remained an exception to much of what happened in the rest of Asia. After a long period of isolation, the Japanese implemented an unprecedented program of modernization and westernization in the late nineteenth century. Japan continued to model itself after the West when it took control of former German colonies as mandated territories after the Great War and occupied territory in China, Korea, Vietnam, Taiwan, and elsewhere. In the next chapter we will see how ultranationalism drove national policy in the 1930s, ultimately leading to Japan's defeat in World War II.

# Chapter 29 Review

## IDENTIFY KEY TERMS

**Identify and explain the significance of each item below.**

Permanent Mandates Commission (p. 761)

Sykes-Picot Agreement (p. 765)

Balfour Declaration (p. 765)

Treaty of Lausanne (p. 766)

Majlis (p. 768)

kibbutz (p. 770)

Lucknow Pact (p. 771)

satyagraha (p. 772)

May Fourth Movement (p. 775)

New Culture Movement (p. 776)

zaibatsu (p. 777)

Long March (p. 779)

## REVIEW THE MAIN IDEAS

**Answer the focus questions from each section of the chapter.**

1. Why did modern nationalism develop in Asia between the First and Second World Wars, and what was its appeal? (p. 760)

2. How did the Ottoman Empire's collapse in World War I shape nationalist movements in the Middle East? (p. 762)

3. What role did Gandhi and his campaign of militant nonviolence play in leading India to independence from the British? (p. 770)

4. How did nationalism shape political developments in East and Southeast Asia? (p. 774)

## MAKE COMPARISONS AND CONNECTIONS

**Analyze the larger developments and continuities within and across chapters.**

1. Asian leaders adopted several of the ideologies of change that evolved in nineteenth-century Europe (Chapter 24) to unite their peoples against European imperialism in the twentieth century. Give examples of some of these ideologies and where they were adopted.

2. How were Indian, Chinese, and Turkish responses to European imperialism in the twentieth century affected by the different individual histories of these nations (Chapters 25, 26)?

3. Compare and contrast Japan's actions as a modern, imperial power in the late nineteenth century and the first three decades of the twentieth century with those of the European imperial powers at the same time (Chapters 25, 26).

## CHRONOLOGY

| | |
|---|---|
| **1898** | • Spanish-American War (Ch. 27) |
| **1910** | • Mexican Revolution (Ch. 27) |
| **1914–1918** | • World War I (Ch. 28) |
| **1916** | • Sykes-Picot Agreement divides Ottoman Empire between France and Britain |
| **1916** | • Lucknow Pact forms alliance between Hindus and Muslims in India |
| **1916** | • New Culture Movement in China begins |
| **1917** | • Balfour Declaration expresses British support for Jewish homeland in Palestine |
| **1917–1922** | • Russian Revolution and civil war (Ch. 28) |
| **1919** | • Afghanistan achieves independence |
| **1919–1920** | • Paris Peace Conference and treaties (Ch. 28) |
| **1923** | • Treaty of Lausanne ends war in Turkey |
| **1927** | • Jiang Jieshi, leader of Chinese Nationalist Party, purges Communist allies |
| **1929–1939** | • Great Depression (Ch. 30) |
| **1930** | • Gandhi's march to the sea to protest the British salt tax |
| **1931** | • Japan occupies Manchuria |
| **1932** | • Iraq gains independence in return for military alliance with Great Britain |
| **1933** | • Hitler and Nazi Party take power in Germany (Ch. 30) |
| **1934** | • Mao Zedong leads Chinese Communists on Long March |
| **1934** | • Philippines gains self-governing commonwealth status from U.S. |
| **1937** | • Japanese militarists launch attack on China |

# 30

# The Great Depression and World War II

## 1929–1945

**THE YEARS OF ANXIETY AND POLITICAL MANEUVERING IN EUROPE** after World War I were made much worse when a massive economic depression spread around the world following the American stock market crash of October 1929. An increasingly interconnected global economy now collapsed. Free-market capitalism appeared to have run its course. People everywhere looked for relief to new leaders, some democratically elected,

786

many not. In Europe, on the eve of the Second World War, few liberal democratic governments survived. Worldwide, in countries such as Brazil, Japan, the Soviet Union, and others, as well as in Europe, dictatorships seemed the wave of the future.

The mid-twentieth-century era of dictatorship is a deeply disturbing chapter in the history of civilization. The key development was not only the resurgence of authoritarian rule, but also the rise of a particularly ruthless brand of totalitarianism that reached its fullest realization in the Soviet Union, Nazi Germany, and Japan in the 1930s. Stalin, Hitler, and Japan's military leaders intervened radically in society and ruled with unprecedented severity. Hitler's sudden attack on Poland in 1939 started World War II in Europe. His successes encouraged the Japanese to expand their stalemated Chinese campaign into a vast Pacific war. By war's end, millions had died on the battlefields and in the bombed-out cities. Millions more died in the Holocaust, in Stalin's Soviet Union from purges and forced imposition of communism, and during Japan's quest to create an "Asia for Asians."

# The Great Depression, 1929–1939

**What caused the Great Depression, and what were its consequences?**

Like the Great War, the Great Depression must be spelled with capital letters. Beginning in 1929 an exceptionally long and severe economic depression struck the entire world with ever-greater intensity, and recovery was uneven and slow. Only the Second World War brought it to an end.

## The Economic Crisis

Though economic activity was already declining moderately in many countries by early 1929, the U.S. stock market crash in October of that year really started the Great Depression. The American stock market boom was built on borrowed money. Two factors explain why. First, the wealth gap (or income inequality) between America's rich and poor reached its greatest extent in the twentieth century in 1928–1929. One percent of Americans then held 70 percent of all America's wealth. Eventually, with not enough money to go around, the remaining 99 percent of Americans had to borrow to make even basic purchases—as a result, the cost of farm credit, install- ment loans, and home mortgages skyrocketed. Then a point was reached where the 99 percent could borrow no more, so they stopped buying.

Second, wealthy investors and speculators took increasingly greater investment risks. One such popular risk was to buy stocks by paying only a small fraction of the total purchase price and borrowing the remainder from their stockbrokers or from banks. Such buying "on margin" was extremely dangerous. When prices started fall- ing, the hard-pressed margin buyers started selling to pay their debts. The result was a financial panic. Countless investors and speculators were wiped out in a matter of days or weeks, and the New York stock market's crash started a domino effect that hit most of the world's major stock exchanges.

The financial panic in the United States triggered a worldwide financial crisis. Throughout the 1920s American bankers and investors had lent large sums to many countries, and as panic spread, New York bankers began recalling their short-term loans. Frightened citizens around the world began to withdraw their bank savings, leading to general financial chaos. The recall of American loans also accelerated the collapse in world prices, as business people dumped goods in a frantic attempt to get cash to pay what they owed.

The financial chaos led to a drastic decline in production in country after country. Between 1929 and 1933 world output of goods fell by an estimated 38 percent. Countries now turned inward and tried to go it alone. Many followed the American example, in which protective tariffs were raised in 1930 to their highest levels ever to seal off shrinking national markets for American producers only.

Although historians' opinions differ, two factors probably best explain the relentless slide to the bottom from 1929 to early 1933. First, the international economy lacked leadership able to maintain stability when the crisis came. Neither the seriously weakened Britain nor the United States—the world's economic leaders—stabilized the international economic system in 1929. Instead Britain and the United States cut back international lending and erected high tariffs.

Second, in almost every country, governments cut their budgets and reduced spending instead of running large deficits to try to stimulate their economies. That is, governments needed to put large sums of money into the economy to stimulate job growth and spending. After World War II such a "counter-cyclical policy," advocated by the British economist John Maynard Keynes (1883–1946), became a well-established weapon against depression. But in the 1930s orthodox economists generally regarded Keynes's prescription with horror.

## Mass Unemployment

The need for large-scale government spending was tied to mass unemployment. The 99 percent's halt in buying contributed to the financial crisis, which led to production cuts, which in turn caused workers to lose their jobs and have even less money to buy goods. This led to still more production cuts, and unemployment soared. In Britain unemployment had averaged 12 percent in the 1920s; between 1930 and 1935 it averaged more than 18 percent. Germany and Austria had some of the highest unemployment rates, 30–32 percent in 1932. The worst unemployment was in the United States. In the 1920s unemployment there had averaged only 5 percent; in 1933 it soared to about 33 percent of the entire labor force: 14 million people were out of work. This was the only time in American history when more people left America than immigrated in—including thousands of Mexican Americans who suffered increasing hostility, accused of stealing jobs from those who considered themselves to be "real Americans." Perhaps a hundred thousand Americans migrated to the Soviet Union, attracted by communism's promises of jobs and a new life.

Mass unemployment created great social problems. Poverty increased dramatically, although in most industrialized countries unemployed workers generally received some meager unemployment benefits or public aid that prevented starvation. Millions of unemployed people lost their spirit, and homes and ways of life were disrupted in countless personal tragedies. In 1932 workers in Manchester,

England, appealed to their city officials—a typical appeal echoed throughout the Western world:

> We tell you that thousands of people . . . are in desperate straits. We tell you that men, women, and children are going hungry. . . . We tell you that great numbers are being rendered distraught through the stress and worry of trying to exist without work. . . .
>
> If you do not provide useful work for the unemployed—what, we ask, is your alternative? Do not imagine that this colossal tragedy of unemployment is going on endlessly without some fateful catastrophe. Hungry men are angry men.[1]

## The New Deal in the United States

The Great Depression and the response to it marked a major turning point in American history. Herbert Hoover (U.S. pres. 1929–1933) and his administration initially reacted with limited action. When the financial crisis struck Europe with full force in summer 1931 and boomeranged back to the United States, banks failed and unemployment soared. In 1932 industrial production fell to about 50 percent of its 1929 level.

In these desperate circumstances Franklin Delano Roosevelt (U.S. pres. 1933–1945) won a landslide presidential victory in 1932 with promises of a "**New Deal** for the forgotten man." Roosevelt's basic goal was to preserve capitalism by reforming it. Rejecting socialism and government ownership of industry, Roosevelt advocated forceful federal government intervention in the economy. His commitment to national relief programs marked a profound shift from the traditional stress on family support and local community responsibility.

Roosevelt attacked mass unemployment by creating new federal agencies that launched a vast range of public works projects so the federal government could directly employ as many people as financially possible. The Works Progress Administration (WPA), set up in 1935, employed one-fifth of the entire U.S. labor force at some point in the 1930s, and these workers constructed public buildings, bridges, and highways.

In 1935 the U.S. government established a national social security system with old-age pensions and unemployment benefits. The 1935 National Labor Relations Act declared collective bargaining to be U.S. policy, and union membership more than doubled. In general, between 1935 and 1938 government rulings and social reforms chipped away at the privileges of the wealthy and tried to help ordinary people.

Despite undeniable accomplishments in social reform, the New Deal was only partly successful as a response to the Great Depression. Unemployment was still a staggering 10 million when war broke out in Europe in 1939. The New Deal brought fundamental reform, but it never did pull the United States out of the depression; only the Second World War did that.

## The European Response to the Depression

The American stock market's collapse in October 1929 set off a chain of economic downturns that hit Europe, particularly Germany and Great Britain, the hardest. Postwar Europe had emerged from the Great War deeply in debt and in desperate need of investment capital to rebuild. The United States became the primary creditor and financier. Germany borrowed, for example, to pay Britain war reparations, and then Britain took that money and repaid its war debts and investment loans to America. When the American economy crashed, the whole circular system crashed with it.

Of all the Western democracies, the Scandinavian countries under socialist leadership responded most successfully to the challenge of the Great Depression. When the economic crisis struck in 1929, Sweden's socialist government pioneered the use of large-scale deficits to finance public works projects and thereby maintain production and employment. Scandinavian governments also increased social welfare benefits. All this spending required a large bureaucracy and high taxes. Yet both private and cooperative enterprise thrived, as did democracy. Some observers considered Scandinavia's welfare socialism an appealing middle way between what they considered to be sick capitalism and cruel communism or fascism.

In Britain, Ramsay MacDonald's Labour government (1929–1931) and, after 1931, the Conservative-dominated coalition government followed orthodox economic theory. The budget was balanced, but unemployed workers received barely enough welfare support to live. Nevertheless, the economy recovered considerably after 1932, reflecting the gradual reorientation of the British economy. Britain concentrated increasingly on the national, rather than the international, market. Old export industries, such as textiles and coal, continued to decline, but new industries, such as automobiles and electrical appliances, grew. These developments encouraged British isolationism and often had devastating economic consequences for Britain's far-flung colonies and dominions, which depended heavily upon reciprocal trade with Great Britain and the United States.

The Great Depression came late to France because it was relatively less industrialized and more isolated from the world economy. But once the depression hit, it stayed. Economic stagnation both reflected and heightened an ongoing political crisis, as liberals, democratic socialists, and Communists fought for control of the French government with conservatives and the far right. The latter groups agitated against parliamentary democracy and turned to Mussolini's Italy and Hitler's Germany for inspiration. At the same time, the Communist Party and many workers looked to Stalin's Russia for guidance.

Frightened by the growing popularity of Hitler- and Mussolini-style right-wing dictatorships at home and abroad, the Communist, Socialist, and Radical Parties in France formed an alliance—the **Popular Front**—for the May 1936 national elections. Following its clear victory, the Popular Front government launched a far-reaching New Deal–inspired program of social and economic reform. Popular with workers (because it supported unions) and the lower middle class, these measures were quickly sabotaged by rapid inflation, rising wages, a decline in overseas exports, and cries of socialist revolution from frightened conservatives. Politically, the Popular Front lost many left-wing supporters when it failed to back the republican cause in the Spanish Civil War while Hitler and Mussolini openly armed and supported Franco's nationalists. In June 1937, with the country hopelessly divided, the Popular Front collapsed.

## Worldwide Effects

The Great Depression's magnitude was unprecedented, and its effect rippled well beyond Europe and the United States. Because many countries and colonies in Africa, Asia, and Latin America were nearly totally dependent on one or two export commodities—such as coffee beans or cocoa—for income, the implementation of protectionist trade policies by the leading industrial nations had devastating effects.

The Great Depression hit the vulnerable commodity economies of Latin America especially hard. With foreign sales plummeting, Latin American countries could not buy the industrial goods they needed from abroad. The global depression provoked a profound shift toward economic nationalism after 1930, as popularly based governments worked to reduce foreign influence and gain control of their own economies and natural resources. These efforts were fairly successful. By the late 1940s factories in Argentina, Brazil, and Chile could generally satisfy domestic consumer demand for the products of light industry. But as in Hitler's Germany, the deteriorating economic conditions in Latin America also gave rise to dictatorships, some of them modeled along European Fascist lines.

The Great Depression marked a decisive turning point in the development of African nationalism. For the first time, educated Africans faced widespread unemployment. African peasants and small business people who had been drawn into world trade, and who sometimes profited from booms, also felt the economic pain, as did urban workers. In some areas the result was unprecedented mass protest.

While Asians were somewhat affected by the Great Depression, the consequences varied greatly by country or colony and were not as serious generally as they were elsewhere. That being said, where the depression did hit, it was often severe. The price of rice fell by two-thirds between 1929 and 1932. Also crippling to the region's economies was Asia's heavy dependence on raw material exports. With debts to local moneylenders fixed in value and taxes to colonial governments hardly ever reduced, many Asian peasants in the 1930s struggled under crushing debt and suffered terribly.

When the Great Depression reached China in the early 1930s, it hit the rural economy the hardest. China's economy depended heavily on cash-crop exports and these declined dramatically, while cheap foreign agricultural goods—such as rice and wheat—were dumped in China. While Chinese industrial production dropped off after 1931, it quickly recovered. Much of this growth was in the military sector, as China tried to catch up with the West and also prepare for war with Japan.

In Japan the terrible suffering caused by the Great Depression caused ultranationalists and militarists to call for less dependence on global markets and the expansion of a self-sufficient empire. Such expansion began in 1931 when Japan invaded Chinese Manchuria, which became a major source of the raw materials needed to feed Japanese industrial growth. Japan recovered more quickly from the Great Depression than did any other major industrial power because of prompt action by the civilian democratic government, but the government and large corporations continued to be blamed for the economic downturn. By the mid-1930s this lack of confidence, combined with the collapsing international economic order, Europe's and America's increasingly isolationist and protectionist policies, and a growing admiration for Nazi Germany and its authoritarian, militaristic model of government, had led the Japanese military to topple the civilian authorities and dictate Japan's future.

# Authoritarian States

**What was the nature of the new totalitarian dictatorships, and how did they differ from conservative authoritarian states and from each other?**

Both conservative and radical totalitarian dictatorships arose in Europe in the 1920s and the 1930s. Although they sometimes overlapped in character and practice, they were profoundly different in essence.

## Conservative Authoritarianism

The traditional form of antidemocratic government in world history was conservative authoritarianism. Like Russia's tsars and China's emperors, the leaders of such governments relied on obedient bureaucracies, vigilant police departments, and trustworthy armies to control society. They forbade or limited popular participation in government and often jailed or exiled political opponents. Yet they had neither the ability nor the desire to control many aspects of their subjects' lives. As long as the people did not try to change the system, they often enjoyed considerable personal independence.

After the First World War, conservative authoritarianism revived, especially in Latin America. Conservative dictators also seized power in Spain and Portugal, and in the less developed eastern part of Europe. There were several reasons for this development. These lands lacked strong traditions of self-government, and many new states, such as Yugoslavia, were torn by ethnic conflicts. Dictatorship appealed to nationalists and military leaders as a way to repress such tensions and preserve national unity. Large landowners and the church were still powerful forces in these predominantly agrarian areas and often looked to dictators to protect them from progressive land reform or Communist agrarian upheaval. Conservative dictatorships were concerned more with maintaining the status quo than with mobilizing the masses or forcing society into rapid change or war.

## Radical Totalitarian Dictatorships

By the mid-1930s a new kind of radical dictatorship—termed totalitarian—had emerged in the Soviet Union, Germany, and, to a lesser extent, Italy. Scholars disagree over the definition of totalitarianism, its origins, and to what countries and leaders the term should apply. Moreover, when the Cold War began in the late 1940s, conservatives, particularly in the United States, commandeered the term as shorthand for the "evil" Communist regimes in the Soviet Union and its satellites. Liberals, especially in the 1960s, used the term more loosely to refer to every system they felt inhibited freedom—from local police to the U.S. Pentagon. Thus by the 1980s many scholars questioned the term's usefulness. More recently, with these caveats, scholars have returned to the term to explain and understand fascism, Nazism, and communism in the 1920s, 1930s, and 1940s.

It can be argued that **totalitarianism** began with the total war effort of 1914–1918 (see "Mobilizing for Total War" in Chapter 28), as governments acquired total control over all areas of society in order to achieve one supreme objective: victory. This provided a model for future totalitarian states. As the French thinker Élie Halévy (AY-lee ah-LAY-vee) observed in 1936, the varieties of modern totalitarian tyranny — fascism, Nazism, and communism — could be thought of as "feuding brothers" with a common father: the nature of modern war.[2]

The consequences of the Versailles treaty (1919) and the severe economic and political problems that Germany and Italy faced in the 1920s left both those countries ripe for new leadership, but not necessarily totalitarian dictators. It was the Great Depression that must be viewed as the immediate cause of the modern totalitarian state.

In 1956 American historians Carl Friedrich and Zbigniew Brzezinski (z-BIG-nyef bzheh-ZIN-skee) identified at least six key features of modern totalitarian states: (1) an official ideology; (2) a single ruling party; (3) complete control of "all weapons of armed combat"; (4) complete monopoly of all means of mass communication; (5) a system of terror, physical and psychic, enforced by the party and the secret police; and (6) central control and direction of the entire economy.[3]

While all these features were present in Stalin's Communist Soviet Union and Hitler's Nazi Germany, there were some major differences. Most notably, Soviet communism seized private property for the state and sought to level society by crushing the middle classes. Nazi Germany also criticized big landowners and industrialists but, unlike the Communists, did not try to nationalize private property, so the middle classes survived. This difference in property and class relations led some scholars to speak of "totalitarianism of the left" — Stalinist Russia — and "totalitarianism of the right" — Nazi Germany.

Moreover, Soviet Communists ultimately had international aims: they sought to unite the workers of the world. Mussolini and Hitler claimed they were interested in changing state and society on a national level only, although Hitler envisioned a greatly expanded "living space," or *lebensraum* (LAY-buhns-rowm), for Germans in eastern Europe and Russia. Both Mussolini and Hitler used the term **fascism** (FASH-iz-uhm) to describe their movements' supposedly "total" and revolutionary character. Orthodox Marxist Communists argued that the Fascists were powerful capitalists seeking to destroy the revolutionary working class and thus protect their enormous profits. So while Communists and Fascists both sought the overthrow of existing society, their ideologies clashed, and they were enemies.

European Fascist movements shared many characteristics, including extreme, often expansionist, nationalism; anti-socialism aimed at destroying working-class movements; a dynamic and violent leader; a crushing of human individualism; alliances with powerful capitalists and landowners; and glorification of war and the military. Fascists, especially in Germany, also embraced racial homogeneity. Indeed, while class was the driving force in communist ideology, race and racial purity were profoundly important to Nazi ideology.

Although 1930s Japan has sometimes been called a Fascist society, most recent scholars disagree with this label. Japanese political philosophers were attracted by some European Fascist ideas, such as Hitler's desire for eastward expansion, which would be duplicated by Japan's expansion to the Asian mainland. Other appealing concepts included nationalism, militarism, the corporatist economic model,

**The Spread of Fascism in Spain, 1937**  In the 1920s and 1930s most European countries had Fascist sympathizers. Between 1936 and 1939 Fascist nationalist forces led by General Francisco Franco, pictured here, fought a brutal war against the government of Spain's left-leaning, democratic Second Spanish Republic. Socialist and liberal volunteers from around the world came to Spain to fight against Franco's army, as recounted in Ernest Hemingway's novel *For Whom the Bell Tolls*. Pablo Picasso portrayed the destruction to one town caused by German Nazi and Italian Fascist warplanes, supporting Franco, in his famous painting *Guernica*. Following the nationalist victory, Franco ruled Spain as a dictator for thirty-six years.  (© Imagno/Austrian Archives/The Image Works)

and a single, all-powerful political party. The idea of a Japanese dictator, however, clashed with the emperor's divine status. There were also various ideologically unique forces at work in Japan, including ultranationalism, militarism (building on the historic role of samurai warriors in Japanese society), reverence for traditional ways, emperor worship, and the profound changes to Japanese society beginning with the Meiji Restoration in 1867 (see "The Meiji Restoration" in Chapter 26). These also contributed to the rise of a totalitarian, but not Fascist, state before the Second World War.

In summary, the concept of totalitarianism remains a valuable tool for historical understanding. It correctly highlights that in the 1930s Germany, the Soviet Union, and Japan made an unprecedented "total claim" on the beliefs and behaviors of their respective citizens.[4] However, none of these nations were successful in completely dominating their citizens. Thus totalitarianism is an idea never fully achieved.

# Stalin's Soviet Union

## How did Stalin and the Communist Party build a totalitarian order in the Soviet Union?

Joseph Stalin (1879–1953) consolidated his power following Lenin's death in 1924 and by 1927 was the de facto leader of the Soviet Union. In 1928 he launched the first **five-year plan** — a "revolution from above,"[5] as he so aptly termed it, to transform Soviet society along socialist lines, and to generate a Communist society with new attitudes, new loyalties, and a new socialist humanity. Stalin and the Communist Party used constant propaganda, enormous sacrifice, and unlimited violence and state control to establish a dynamic, modern totalitarian state in the 1930s.

## From Lenin to Stalin

By spring 1921 Lenin and the Bolsheviks had won the civil war, but they ruled a shattered and devastated land. Facing economic disintegration, the worst famine in generations, riots by peasants and workers, and an open rebellion by previously pro-Bolshevik sailors at Kronstadt (kruhn-SHTAHT), Lenin changed course. In March 1921 he announced the **New Economic Policy (NEP)**, which re-established limited economic freedom in an attempt to rebuild agriculture and industry. Peasant producers could sell their surpluses in free markets, as could private traders and small handicraft manufacturers. Heavy industry, railroads, and banks, however, remained wholly nationalized.

The NEP was successful both politically and economically. Politically, it was a necessary but temporary compromise with the Soviet Union's overwhelming peasant majority. Economically, the NEP brought rapid recovery. In 1926 industrial output surpassed prewar levels, and peasants were producing almost as much grain as before the war.

As the economy recovered, an intense power struggle began in the Communist Party's inner circles, for Lenin left no chosen successor when he died in 1924. The principal contenders were Stalin and Leon Trotsky. While Trotsky appeared to be the stronger of the two, in the end Stalin won because he gained the support of the party, the only genuine source of power in the one-party state.

Stalin gradually achieved absolute power between 1922 and 1927. He used the moderates to crush Trotsky and then turned against the moderates and destroyed them as well. Stalin's final triumph came at the party congress of December 1927, which condemned all deviation from the general party line as formulated by Stalin.

## The Five-Year Plans

The 1927 party congress marked the end of the NEP and the beginning of socialist five-year plans. The first five-year plan had staggering economic objectives. In just five years, total industrial output was to increase by 250 percent and agricultural production by 150 percent. By 1930 economic and social change was sweeping the country in a frenzied effort to modernize and industrialize, much like in Britain in the nineteenth century, and dramatically changing the lives of ordinary people, sometimes at great personal cost. One worker complained, "The workers . . . made every effort to fulfill the industrial and financial plan and fulfilled it by more than 100 percent, but how are they supplied? The ration is received only by the worker, except for rye flour, his wife and small children receive nothing. Workers and their families wear worn-out clothes, the kids are in rags, their naked bellies sticking out."[6]

Stalin unleashed his "second revolution" because, like Lenin, he was deeply committed to socialism. Stalin was also driven to catch up with the advanced and presumably hostile Western capitalist nations. In February 1931 Stalin famously declared:

> It is sometimes asked whether it is not possible to slow down the tempo a bit. . . .
> No, comrades, it is not possible! The tempo must not be reduced! . . . To slacken
> the tempo would mean falling behind. And those who fall behind get beaten.
> No, we refuse to be beaten! . . . We are fifty or a hundred years behind the
> advanced countries. We must make good this distance in ten years. Either we do
> it, or we shall be crushed.[7]

Domestically, there was the peasant problem. For centuries peasants had wanted to own the land, and finally they had it. Sooner or later, the Communists reasoned, the peasants would become conservative capitalists and threaten the regime. Stalin therefore launched a preventive war against the peasantry to bring it under the state's absolute control.

That war was **collectivization** — the forcible consolidation of individual peasant farms into large, state-controlled enterprises. Beginning in 1929 peasants were ordered to give up their land and animals and become members of collective farms. As for the kulaks, the better-off peasants, Stalin instructed party workers to "break their resistance, to eliminate them as a class."[8] Stripped of land and livestock, many starved or were deported to forced-labor camps for "re-education."

Because almost all peasants were poor, the term *kulak* soon meant any peasant who opposed the new system. Whole villages were often attacked. One conscience-stricken colonel in the secret police confessed to a foreign journalist:

> I am an old Bolshevik. I worked in the underground against the Tsar and then
> I fought in the Civil War. Did I do all that in order that I should now surround
> villages with machine guns and order my men to fire indiscriminately into
> crowds of peasants? Oh, no, no![9]

Forced collectivization led to disaster. Many peasants slaughtered their animals and burned their crops in protest. Nor were the state-controlled collective farms more productive. Grain output barely increased, and collectivized agriculture made no substantial financial contribution to Soviet industrial development during the first five-year plan.

In Ukraine Stalin instituted a policy of all-out collectivization with two goals: to destroy all expressions of Ukrainian nationalism, and to break the Ukrainian peasants' will so they would accept collectivization and Soviet rule. Stalin began by purging Ukraine of its intellectuals and political elite. He then set impossibly high grain quotas for the collectivized farms. This grain quota had to be turned over to the government before any peasant could receive a share. Many scholars and dozens of governments and international organizations have declared Stalin's and the Soviet government's policies a deliberate act of genocide. As one historian observed:

> Grain supplies were sufficient to sustain everyone if properly distributed. People died mostly of terror-starvation (excess grain exports, seizure of edibles from the starving, state refusal to provide emergency relief, bans on outmigration, and forced deportation to food-deficit locales), not poor harvests and routine administrative bungling.[10]

The result was a terrible man-made famine, called in Ukrainian the *Holodomor* (HAU-lau-dau-mohr) (Hunger extermination), in Ukraine in 1932 and 1933, which probably claimed 3 to 5 million lives.

Collectivization was a cruel but real victory for Communist ideologues who were looking to institute their brand of communism and to crush opposition as much as improve production. By 1938, 93 percent of peasant families had been herded onto collective farms at a horrendous cost in both human lives and resources. Regimented as state employees and dependent on the state-owned tractor stations, the collectivized peasants were no longer a political threat.

The industrial side of the five-year plans was more successful. Soviet industry produced about four times as much in 1937 as in 1928. No other major country had ever achieved such rapid industrial growth. Heavy industry led the way, and urban development accelerated: more than 25 million people migrated to cities to become industrial workers during the 1930s.

The sudden creation of dozens of new factories demanded tremendous resources. Funds for industrial expansion were collected from the people through heavy hidden sales taxes. Firm labor discipline also contributed to rapid industrialization. Trade unions lost most of their power, and individuals could not move without police permission. When factory managers needed more hands, they were sent "unneeded" peasants from collective farms.

Foreign engineers were hired to plan and construct many of the new factories. Highly skilled American engineers, hungry for work in the depression years, were particularly important until newly trained Soviet experts began to replace them after 1932. Thus Stalin's planners harnessed the skill and technology of capitalist countries to promote the surge of socialist industry.

## Life and Culture in Soviet Society

Daily life was hard in Stalin's Soviet Union. Despite these hardships, many Communists saw themselves as heroically building the world's first socialist society while capitalism crumbled and fascism rose in the West.

Offsetting the hardships were the important social benefits Soviet workers received, such as old-age pensions, free medical services and education, and day-care centers for children. Unemployment was almost unknown. Moreover, there was the possibility of personal advancement. Rapid industrialization required massive numbers of trained experts. Thus the Stalinist state broke with the egalitarian policies of the 1920s and provided tremendous incentives to those who acquired specialized skills. A growing technical and managerial elite joined the political and artistic elites in a new upper class, whose members were rich and powerful.

Soviet society's radical transformation profoundly affected women's lives. The Russian Bolshevik Revolution immediately proclaimed complete equality of rights for women. In the 1920s divorce and abortion were made easily available, and women were urged to work outside the home. After Stalin came to power, however, he encouraged a return to traditional family values.

The most lasting changes for women involved work and education. Peasant women continued to work on farms, and millions of women now toiled in factories and heavy construction. The more determined women entered the ranks of the better-paid specialists in industry and science. By 1950, 75 percent of all doctors in the Soviet Union were women.

Culture was thoroughly politicized through constant propaganda and indoctrination. Party activists lectured workers in factories and peasants on collective farms, while newspapers, films, and radio broadcasts recounted socialist achievements and warned of capitalist plots.

## Stalinist Terror and the Great Purges

In the mid-1930s the push to build socialism and a new society culminated in ruthless police terror and a massive purging of the Communist Party. In August 1936 sixteen prominent "Old Bolsheviks" — party members before the 1917 revolution — confessed to all manner of plots against Stalin in spectacular public show trials in Moscow. Then in 1937 the secret police arrested a mass of lesser party officials and newer members, torturing them and extracting confessions for more show trials. In addition to the party faithful, union officials, managers, intellectuals, army officers, and countless ordinary citizens were struck down. One Stalin functionary admitted, "Innocent people were arrested: naturally — otherwise no one would be frightened. If people were arrested only for specific misdemeanors, all the others would feel safe and so become ripe for treason."[11] In all, at least 8 million people were arrested, and millions of these were executed. Those not immediately executed were sent to gulags (GOO-lagz) — labor camps from which few escaped. Many were simply worked to death as they provided convict labor for Stalin's industrialization drive in areas of low population.

Stalin recruited 1.5 million new members to replace those purged. Thus more than half of all Communist Party members in 1941 had joined since the purges. This new generation of Stalin-formed Communists served the leader effectively until his death in 1953 and then governed the Soviet Union until the early 1980s. Stalin's mass purges remain baffling, for most historians believe those purged posed no threat and confessed to crimes they had not committed. Some historians have challenged the long-standing interpretation that blames the great purges on Stalin's cruelty or madness. They argue that Stalin's fears were exaggerated but genuine and were shared by many in the party and in the general population. Investigations and trials snowballed into a mass hysteria, a new witch-hunt.[12] Historians who have accessed recently opened Soviet archives, however, continue to hold that Stalin was intimately involved with the purges and personally directed them, abetted by amenable informers, judges, and executioners. Oleg Khlevniuk, a Ukrainian historian familiar with these archives, writes, "Theories about the elemental, spontaneous nature of the terror, about a loss of central control over the course of mass repression, and about the role of regional leaders in initiating the terror are simply not supported by the historical record."[13] In short, a ruthless and paranoid Stalin found large numbers of willing collaborators for crime as well as for achievement.

# Mussolini and Fascism in Italy

### How did Italian fascism develop?

Benito Mussolini's Fascist movement and his seizure of power in 1922 were important steps in the rise of dictatorships between the two world wars. Mussolini and his supporters were the first to call themselves "Fascists." His dictatorship was brutal and theatrical, and it contained elements of both conservative authoritarianism and modern totalitarianism.

## The Seizure of Power

In the early twentieth century Italy was a liberal state with civil rights and a constitutional monarchy. On the eve of the First World War, the parliamentary regime granted universal male suffrage. But there were serious problems. Poverty was widespread, and many peasants were more attached to their villages and local interests than to the national state. Church-state relations were often tense. Class differences were also extreme, and by 1912 the Socialist Party's radical wing led the powerful revolutionary socialist movement.[14]

World War I worsened the political situation. Having fought on the Allied side almost exclusively for purposes of territorial expansion, Italian nationalists were disappointed with Italy's modest gains at the Paris Peace Conference. Workers and peasants also felt cheated: to win their support during the war, the government had promised social and land reform, which it failed to deliver after the war.

The Russian Revolution inspired and energized Italy's revolutionary socialist movement, and radical workers and peasants began occupying factories and seizing land in 1920. These actions scared and mobilized the property-owning classes. Thus by 1921 revolutionary socialists, antiliberal conservatives, and frightened property owners were all opposed — though for different reasons — to the liberal parliamentary government.

Into these crosscurrents of unrest and fear stepped Benito Mussolini (1883– 1945). Mussolini began his political career as a Socialist Party leader and radical newspaper editor before World War I. Expelled from the Italian Socialist Party for supporting the war, and wounded on the Italian front in 1917, Mussolini returned home and began organizing bitter war veterans into a band of Fascists — Italian for "a union of forces."

At first Mussolini's program was a radical combination of nationalist and socialist demands. As such, it competed directly with the well-organized Socialist Party and failed to attract followers. When Mussolini realized his violent verbal assaults on rival Socialists won him growing support from conservatives and the frightened middle classes, he began to shift gears and to exalt nation over class. By 1921 he was ridiculing and dismissing the Marxist interpretation of history:

> We deny the existence of two classes, because there are many more than two classes. We deny that human history can be explained in terms of economics. We deny your internationalism. That is a luxury article, which only the elevated can practice, because peoples are passionately bound to their native soil.[15]

Mussolini and his private army of **Black Shirts** also turned to physical violence. Few people were killed, but Socialist newspapers, union halls, and local Socialist Party headquarters were destroyed, eventually pushing Socialists out of the city governments of northern Italy. A skillful politician, Mussolini convinced his followers they were opposing the "Reds," while also promoting a real revolution of the little people against the established interests.

With the government breaking down in 1922, Mussolini stepped forward as the savior of order and property. In October 1922 thirty thousand Fascists marched on Rome, threatening the king and demanding he appoint Mussolini prime minister. Victor Emmanuel III (r. 1900–1946), forced to choose between Fascists or Socialists, asked Mussolini to form a new cabinet. Thus, after widespread violence and a threat of armed uprising, Mussolini seized power "legally."

## The Regime in Action

In 1924 Mussolini declared his desire to "make the nation Fascist"[16] and imposed a series of repressive measures. Press freedom was abolished, elections were fixed, and the government ruled by decree. Mussolini arrested his political opponents, disbanded all independent labor unions, and put dedicated Fascists in control of Italy's schools. He created a Fascist youth movement, Fascist labor unions, and many other Fascist organizations. He trumpeted his goal in a famous slogan of 1926: "Everything in the state, nothing outside the state, nothing against the state."[17] By year's end Italy was a one-party dictatorship under Mussolini's unquestioned leadership.

Mussolini was only primarily interested, however, in personal power. Rather than destroy the old power structure, he remained content to compromise with the conservative classes that controlled the army, the economy, and the state. He controlled labor but left big business to regulate itself, profitably and securely. There was no land reform.

Mussolini also drew increasing support from the Catholic Church. In the **Lateran Agreement** of 1929, he recognized the Vatican as a tiny independent state and agreed to give the church heavy financial support. The pope in return urged Italians to support Mussolini's government.

Like Stalin and Hitler, Mussolini favored a return of traditional roles for women. He abolished divorce and told women to stay at home and produce children. In 1938 women were limited by law to a maximum of 10 percent of the better-paying jobs in industry and government.

Mussolini's government passed no racial laws until 1938 and did not persecute Jews savagely until late in the Second World War, when Italy was under Nazi control. Nor did Mussolini establish a truly ruthless police state. Only twenty-three political prisoners were condemned to death between 1926 and 1944. Mussolini's Fascist Italy, though repressive and undemocratic, was never really totalitarian.

# Hitler and Nazism in Germany

**Why were Hitler and his Nazi regime initially so popular, and how did their actions lead to World War II?**

The most frightening dictatorship developed in Nazi Germany. Here Nazism asserted an unlimited claim over German society and proclaimed the ultimate power of its leader, Adolf Hitler. Nazism's aspirations were truly totalitarian.

## The Roots of Nazism

**Nazism** grew out of many complex concepts, of which the most influential were extreme nationalism and racism. These ideas captured the mind of the young Adolf Hitler (1889–1945) and evolved into Nazism.

The son of an Austrian customs official, Hitler did poorly in high school and dropped out at age sixteen. He then headed to Vienna, where he was exposed to extreme Austro-German nationalists who believed Germans to be a superior people and central Europe's natural rulers. They advocated union with Germany and violent expulsion of "inferior" peoples from the Austro-Hungarian Empire.

From these extremists Hitler eagerly absorbed virulent anti-Semitism, racism, and hatred of Slavs. He developed an unshakable belief in the crudest distortions of Social Darwinism (see "Science for the Masses" in Chapter 24), the superiority of Germanic races, and the inevitability of racial conflict. The Jews, he claimed, directed an international conspiracy of finance capitalism and Marxist socialism against German culture, German unity, and the German race. Anti-Semitism and racism became Hitler's most passionate convictions.

Hitler greeted the Great War's outbreak as a salvation. The struggle and discipline of serving as a soldier in the war gave his life meaning, and when Germany suddenly surrendered in 1918, Hitler's world was shattered. Convinced that Jews and Marxists had "stabbed Germany in the back," he vowed to fight on.

In late 1919 Hitler joined a tiny extremist group in Munich called the German Workers' Party. By 1921 Hitler had gained absolute control of this small but growing party, now renamed the National Socialist German Worker's Party, or Nazi Party. A master of mass propaganda and political showmanship, Hitler worked his audiences into a frenzy with wild attacks on the Versailles treaty, the Jews, war profiteers, and Germany's Weimar Republic.

In late 1923 Germany under the Weimar Republic was experiencing unparalleled hyperinflation and seemed on the verge of collapse (see "Germany and the Western Powers" in Chapter 28). Hitler, inspired by Mussolini's recent victory, attempted an armed uprising in Munich. Despite the failure of the poorly organized plot and Hitler's arrest, Nazism had been born.

## Hitler's Road to Power

At his trial Hitler violently denounced the Weimar Republic and attracted enormous publicity. During his brief prison term in 1924 he dictated *Mein Kampf* (*My Struggle*), in which he expounded on his basic ideas on race and anti-Semitism, the notion of territorial expansion based on "living space" for Germans, and the role of the leader-dictator, called the *Führer* (FYOOR-uhr).[18]

The Nazis remained a small splinter group until the 1929 Great Depression shattered the economic prosperity and stability of the late 1920s. By the end of 1932, 32 percent or more of Germany's labor force was unemployed. Industrial production fell by one-half between 1929 and 1932. No factor contributed more to Hitler's success than this economic crisis.

Hitler rejected free-market capitalism and advocated government programs to promote recovery. He pitched his speeches to middle- and lower-middle-class groups and to skilled workers. As the economy collapsed, great numbers of these people "voted their pocketbooks"[18] and deserted the conservative and moderate parties for the Nazis. In the July 1932 election the Nazis won 14.5 million votes—38 percent of the total—and became the largest party in the Reichstag.

Hitler and the Nazis appealed strongly to German youth; Hitler himself was only forty in 1929. In 1931 almost 40 percent of Nazi Party members were under thirty, compared with 20 percent of Social Democrats. "National Socialism is the organized will of the youth,"[19] proclaimed the official Nazi slogan. National recovery, exciting and rapid change, and personal advancement made Nazism appealing to millions of German youths.

Hitler also came to power because of the breakdown of democratic government. Germany's economic collapse in the Great Depression convinced many voters that the country's republican leaders were incompetent and corrupt. Disunity on the left was another nail in the republic's coffin. The Communists refused to cooperate with the Social Democrats, even though the two parties together outnumbered the Nazis in the Reichstag.

Finally, Hitler excelled in backroom politics. In 1932 he succeeded in gaining support from key people in the army, big business, and politics, who thought they could manipulate and use him to their own advantage. Thus in January 1933 President Paul von Hindenburg (1847–1934) legally appointed Hitler, leader of Germany's largest party, as German chancellor.

## The Nazi State and Society

Hitler quickly established an unshakable dictatorship. When the Reichstag building was partly destroyed by fire in February 1933, Hitler blamed the Communist

**Young People in Hitler's Germany** This photo from 1930 shows Hitler admiring a young boy dressed in the uniform of Hitler's storm troopers, a paramilitary organization of the Nazi Party that supported Hitler's rise to power in the 1920s and early 1930s. Only a year after the founding of the storm troopers in 1921, Hitler began to organize Germany's young people into similar paramilitary groups in an effort to militarize all of German society. The young paramilitaries became the Hitler Youth, who eventually numbered in the millions. (Popperfoto/Getty Images)

Party. He convinced President von Hindenburg to sign dictatorial emergency acts that abolished freedom of speech and assembly and most personal liberties. He also called for new elections in an effort to solidify his political power.

When the Nazis won only 44 percent of the votes, Hitler outlawed the Communist Party and arrested its parliamentary representatives. Then on March 23, 1933, the Nazis forced through the Reichstag the so-called **Enabling Act**, which gave Hitler absolute dictatorial power for four years.

Hitler and the Nazis took over the government bureaucracy, installing many Nazis in top positions. Hitler next outlawed strikes and abolished independent labor unions, which were replaced by the Nazi Labor Front. Professional people—doctors and lawyers, teachers and engineers—also saw their independent organizations swallowed up in Nazi associations. Publishing houses and universities were put under Nazi control, and students and professors publicly burned forbidden books. Modern art and architecture were ruthlessly prohibited. Life became violently anti-intellectual. As the cynical Joseph Goebbels, later Nazi minister of propaganda, put it, "When I hear the word 'culture' I reach for my gun."[20] By 1934 a brutal dictatorship characterized by frightening dynamism and total obedience to Hitler was already largely in place.

In 1934 Hitler also ordered that all civil servants and members of the German armed forces swear a binding oath of "unquestioning obedience" to Adolf Hitler. The SS—Hitler's elite personal guard—grew rapidly. Under Heinrich Himmler (1900–1945), the SS took over the political police (the Gestapo) and expanded its network of concentration camps.

From the beginning, German Jews were a special object of Nazi persecution. By late 1934 most Jewish lawyers, doctors, professors, civil servants, and musicians had been banned from their professions. In 1935 the infamous Nuremberg Laws classified as Jewish anyone having three or more Jewish grandparents and deprived Jews of all rights of citizenship. By 1938 roughly one-quarter of Germany's half million Jews had emigrated, sacrificing almost all their property in order to leave Germany.

In late 1938 the attack on the Jews accelerated and grew more violent. On November 9 and 10, 1938, the Nazis initiated a series of well-organized attacks against Jews throughout Nazi Germany and some parts of Austria. This infamous event is known as Kristallnacht (krees-TAHL-nahkht), or Night of Broken Glass, after the broken glass that littered the streets following the frenzied destruction of Jewish homes, shops, synagogues, and neighborhoods by German civilians and uniformed storm troopers. U.S. consul David Buffum reported of the Nazis in Leipzig:

> The most hideous phase of the so-called "spontaneous" action, has been the wholesale arrest and transportation to concentration camps of male German Jews between the ages of sixteen and sixty. . . . Having demolished dwellings and hurled most of the effects to the streets, the insatiably sadistic perpetrators threw many of the trembling inmates into a small stream that flows through the Zoological Park, commanding horrified spectators to spit at them, defile them with mud and jeer at their plight.[21]

Many historians consider this night the beginning of Hitler's Final Solution against the Jews, and after this event it became very difficult for Jews to leave Germany.

Some Germans privately opposed these outrages, but most went along or looked the other way. Although this lack of response reflected the individual's helplessness in a totalitarian state, it also reflected the strong popular support Hitler's government enjoyed.

## Hitler's Popularity

Hitler had promised the masses economic recovery—"work and bread"—and he delivered. The Nazi Party launched a large public works program to pull Germany out of the depression. In 1935 Germany turned decisively toward rearmament. Unemployment dropped steadily, and by 1938 the Nazis boasted of nearly full employment. For millions of Germans economic recovery was tangible evidence that Nazi promises were more than show and propaganda.

For ordinary German citizens, in contrast to those deemed "undesirable" (Jews, Slavs, Gypsies, Jehovah's Witnesses, Communists, and homosexuals), Hitler's government offered greater equality and more opportunities. In 1933 class barriers in Germany were generally high. Hitler's rule introduced changes that lowered these barriers. The new Nazi elite included many young and poorly educated dropouts, rootless lower-middle-class people like Hitler who rose to the top with breathtaking speed. More generally, however, the Nazis tolerated privilege and wealth only as long as they served party needs.

Yet Hitler and the Nazis failed to bring about a real social revolution. The well-educated classes held on to most of their advantages, and only a modest social leveling occurred in the Nazi years. Significantly, the Nazis shared with the Italian Fascists the stereotypical view of women as housewives and mothers. Only when facing labor shortages during the war did they reluctantly mobilize large numbers of German women for office and factory work.[22]

Not all Germans supported Hitler, and a number of German groups actively resisted him after 1933. Tens of thousands of political enemies were imprisoned, and thousands were executed. In the first years of Hitler's rule, the principal resisters were trade-union Communists and Socialists. Catholic and Protestant churches produced a second group of opponents. Their efforts were directed primarily at preserving genuine religious life, however, not at overthrowing Hitler. Finally, in 1938 and again during the war, some high-ranking army officers, who feared the consequences of Hitler's reckless aggression, plotted, unsuccessfully, against him.

## Aggression and Appeasement, 1933–1939

After Germany's economic recovery and Hitler's success in establishing Nazi control of society, Hitler turned to the next item on his agenda: aggressive territorial expansion. Germany's withdrawal from the League of Nations in October 1933 indicated its determination to rearm. When in March 1935 Hitler established a general military draft and declared the "unequal" Versailles treaty disarmament clauses null and void, leaders in Britain, France, and Italy issued a rather tepid joint protest and warned him against future aggressive actions.

But the emerging united front against Hitler quickly collapsed. Britain adopted a policy of appeasement, granting Hitler everything he could reasonably want (and more) in order to avoid war. British appeasement, which practically dictated

French policy, had the support of many powerful British conservatives who, as in Germany, underestimated Hitler. The British people, still horrified by the memory, the costs, and the losses of the First World War, generally supported pacifism rather than war.

Some British leaders at the time, however, such as Winston Churchill, bitterly condemned appeasement as peace at any price. After the war, British appeasement came to be viewed as "the granting from fear or cowardice of unwarranted concessions in order to buy temporary peace at someone else's expense."[23] Beginning in the 1990s some historians have argued that British leaders had no real choice but to appease Hitler in the 1930s, because neither Great Britain nor France was prepared psychologically or militarily to fight another war.[24]

In March 1936 Hitler marched his armies without notice into the demilitarized Rhineland, violating the Treaties of Versailles and Locarno. France would not move without British support, and Britain refused to act. As Britain and France opted for appeasement, Hitler found powerful allies, particularly Mussolini, who in October 1935 had attacked the independent African kingdom of Ethiopia. Western powers had condemned the Italian aggression, but Hitler supported Italy energetically. In October 1936 Italy and Germany established the so-called Rome-Berlin Axis. Japan, which wanted support for its occupation of Manchuria, joined the Axis alliance in 1940.

At the same time, Germany and Italy intervened in the Spanish Civil War (1936–1939), where their support helped General Francisco Franco's Fascist movement defeat republican Spain. Republican Spain's only official aid in the fight against Franco came from the Soviet Union.

In late 1937 Hitler moved forward with his plans to crush Austria and Czechoslovakia as the first step in his long-contemplated drive to the east for living space. On March 12, 1938, German armies moved into Austria unopposed, and Austria became two provinces of Greater Germany (Map 30.1).

Simultaneously, Hitler demanded that the pro-Nazi, German-speaking territory of western Czechoslovakia — the Sudetenland — be turned over to Germany. Democratic Czechoslovakia was prepared to defend itself, but appeasement triumphed again. In September 1938 British prime minister Arthur Neville Chamberlain (1869–1940) and French negotiators met with Hitler in Munich and agreed with him that the Sudetenland should be ceded to Germany immediately. Returning to London from the Munich Conference, Chamberlain told cheering crowds that he had secured "peace with honour . . . peace for our time."[25] Sold out by the Western powers, Czechoslovakia gave in.

Hitler's armies occupied the remainder of Czechoslovakia, however, in March 1939. This time, there was no possible rationale of self-determination for Nazi aggression. When Hitler used the question of German minorities in Danzig as a pretext to confront Poland, Chamberlain declared that Britain and France would fight if Hitler attacked his eastern neighbor. Hitler did not take these warnings seriously and pressed on.

Through the 1930s Hitler had constantly referred to ethnic Slavs in the Soviet Union and other countries as *Untermenschen* (OON-ter-men-schen) (inferior people), and relations between the two countries had grown increasingly tense. War between Germany and the Soviet Union seemed inevitable,

**MAP 30.1   The Growth of Nazi Germany, 1933–1939**
Until March 1939 Hitler brought ethnic Germans into the Nazi state; then he turned on the Slavic peoples, whom he had always hated. He stripped Czechoslovakia of its independence and prepared for an attack on Poland in September 1939.

and, indeed, Stalin believed that Great Britain and France secretly hoped the Nazis and Bolsheviks would destroy each other. Then, in an about-face that stunned the world, sworn enemies Hitler and Stalin signed a nonaggression pact in August 1939. Each dictator promised to remain neutral if the other became involved in war. An attached secret protocol divided eastern Europe into German and Soviet zones "in the event of a political and territorial reorganization."[26] Stalin agreed to the pact for three reasons: he distrusted Western intentions, he needed more time to build up Soviet industry and military reserves, and Hitler offered territorial gain.

For Hitler, everything was now set. He told his generals on the day of the nonaggression pact, "My only fear is that at the last moment some dirty dog will come up with a mediation plan."[27] On September 1, 1939, the Germans attacked Poland from three sides. Two days later, Britain and France, finally true to their word, declared war on Germany. The Second World War in Europe had begun.

# The Second World War, 1939–1945

How did Germany and Japan build empires in Europe and Asia, and how did the Allies defeat them?

World war broke out because Hitler's and Japan's ambitions were essentially unlimited. Nazi soldiers scored enormous successes in Europe until late 1942, establishing a vast empire of death and destruction. Japan attacked the United States in December 1941 and then moved to expand its empire throughout Asia and the Pacific Ocean. Eventually, the mighty Grand Alliance of Britain, the United States, and the Soviet Union overwhelmed the aggressors in manpower and military strength. Thus the Nazi and Japanese empires proved short-lived.

## Hitler's Empire in Europe, 1939–1942

Using planes, tanks, and trucks in the first example of a **blitzkrieg** (BLITZ-kreeg), or "lightning war," Hitler's armies crushed Poland in four weeks. The Soviet Union quickly took its share agreed to in the secret protocol—the eastern half of Poland and the Baltic states of Lithuania, Estonia, and Latvia. In spring 1940 the Nazi lightning war struck again. After occupying Denmark, Norway, and Holland, German motorized columns broke through southern Belgium and into France.

As Hitler's armies poured into France, aging marshal Henri-Philippe Pétain, a national hero of the Great War, formed a new French government—the so-called Vichy (VIH-shee) government—and accepted defeat. By July 1940 Hitler ruled practically all of western continental Europe; Italy was an ally, the Soviet Union a friendly neutral (Map 30.2). Only Britain, led by Winston Churchill (1874–1965), remained unconquered.

To prepare for an invasion of Britain, Germany first needed to gain control of the air. In the Battle of Britain, which began in July 1940, German planes attacked British airfields and key factories, dueling with British defenders high in the skies. In September Hitler began indiscriminately bombing British cities to break British morale. British aircraft factories increased production, and Londoners defiantly dug in. By September Britain was winning the air war, and Hitler abandoned his plans for an immediate German invasion of Britain.

Hitler now allowed his lifetime obsession of creating a vast eastern European empire for the "master race" to dictate policy. In June 1941 Germany broke the Nazi-Soviet nonaggression pact and attacked the Soviet Union. By October Leningrad was practically surrounded, Moscow was besieged, and most of Ukraine had been conquered. But the Soviets did not collapse, and when a severe winter struck German armies outfitted in summer uniforms, the invaders were stopped.

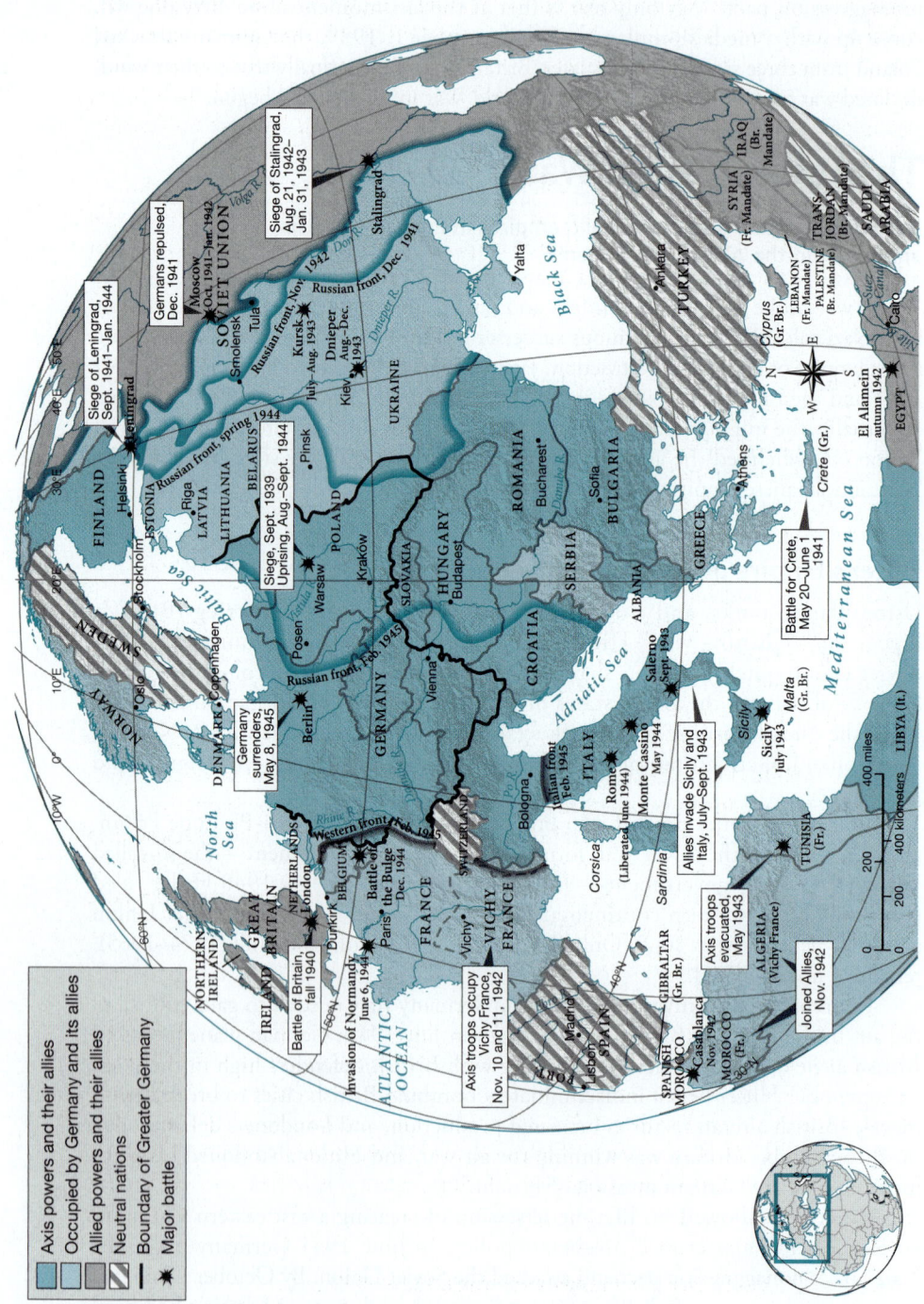

Axis powers and their allies

Occupied by Germany and its allies

Allied powers and their allies

Neutral nations

Boundary of Greater Germany

Major battle

Although stalled in Russia, Hitler ruled an enormous European empire. He now began building a **New Order** based on the guiding principle of Nazi totalitarianism: racial imperialism. Within the New Order, the Dutch, Norwegians, Swedes, and Danes received preferential treatment, for the Germans believed they were racially related to the German "Aryan" master race. The French, an "inferior" Latin people, occupied the middle position. At the bottom of the New Order were the harshly treated "subhumans," Jews and Slavs.

Hitler envisioned a vast eastern colonial empire where enslaved Poles, Ukrainians, and Russians would die or be killed off while Germanic peasants would resettle the abandoned lands. Himmler and the elite SS corps implemented a program of destruction in the occupied territories to create a "mass settlement space" for Germans.

## The Holocaust

Finally, the Nazi state condemned all European Jews to extermination in the **Holocaust**. After Warsaw fell in 1939, the Nazis forced Jews in the occupied territories to move to urban ghettos, while German Jews were sent to occupied Poland. After Germany attacked Russia in June 1941, forced expulsion spiraled into extermination. In late 1941 Hitler and the Nazi leadership ordered the SS to speed up planning for "the final solution of the Jewish question."[28] Throughout the Nazi empire Jews were systematically arrested, packed like cattle onto freight trains, and dispatched to extermination camps.

Arriving at their destination, small numbers of Jews were sent to nearby slave labor camps, where they were starved and systematically worked to death. Most victims were taken to "shower rooms," which were actually gas chambers. By 1945 about 6 million Jews had been murdered.

Who was responsible for this terrible crime? After the war, historians laid the guilt on Hitler and the Nazi leadership, arguing that ordinary Germans had little knowledge of the extermination camps, or that those who cooperated had no alternative given the brutality of Nazi terror and totalitarian control. Beginning in the 1990s studies appeared revealing a much broader participation of German people in the Holocaust and popular indifference (or worse) to the Jews' fate.[29] In most occupied countries local non-German officials also cooperated in the arrest and deportation of Jews.

## Japan's Asian Empire

By late 1938, 1.5 million Japanese troops were bogged down in China, holding a great swath of territory but unable to defeat the Nationalists and the Communists (see "Japan Against China" in Chapter 29). In 1939, as war broke out in Europe, the Japanese redoubled their ruthless efforts in China. Implementing a savage policy of "kill all, burn all, destroy all," Japanese troops committed shocking atrocities, including the so-called Rape of Nanjing. During Japan's war in China—the second

< **MAP 30.2   World War II in Europe and Africa, 1939–1945**
The map shows the extent of Hitler's empire at its height, before the Battle of Stalingrad in late 1942 and the subsequent advances of the Allies until Germany surrendered on May 7, 1945.

**Liberated Nazi Concentration Camp Prisoners** The Nazis operated over 1,200 camps and subcamps in all the countries occupied by Germany. These included forced-labor, POW, re-education, transit, and the more infamous "death" or "extermination" camps. Although the Jews made up the single largest number of victims, the Nazis also arrested and executed homosexuals, Communists, Roma (or gypsies), Jehovah's Witnesses, Soviet prisoners of war, Christian clergymen, intellectuals, and those accused of being "asocial" or "deviant." The Nazis murdered around 6 million Jews and 11 million others during the Holocaust. The prisoners in this photo are survivors of the Ebensee subcamp of the Mauthausen concentration camp, liberated by the Allies on May 5, 1945. (National Archives/Getty Images)

Sino-Japanese War (1937–1945)—the Japanese are estimated to have killed 4 million Chinese people.

In August 1940 the Japanese announced the formation of a self-sufficient Asian economic zone. Although they spoke of liberating Asia from Western imperialism and of "Asia for the Asians," their true intentions were to eventually rule over a vast Japanese empire. Ultranationalists moved to convince Japan's youth that Japan had a sacred liberating mission in Asia.

For the moment, however, Japan needed allies. In September 1940 Japan signed a formal alliance (the Axis alliance) with Germany and Italy, and Vichy France granted the Japanese dominion over northern French Indochina. The United States, upset with Japan's occupation of Indochina and fearing embattled Britain would collapse if it lost its Asian colonies, froze scrap iron sales to Japan and applied further economic sanctions in October.

As 1941 opened, Japan's leaders faced a critical decision. At the time, the United States was the world's largest oil producer and supplied over 90 percent of Japan's oil needs. Japan had only a year and a half's worth of military and economic oil reserves, which the war in China and the Japanese military and merchant navies were quickly drawing down. The Netherlands' colonial possessions in Indonesia (Netherlands East Indies) could supply all of Japan's oil, rubber, and tin needs, but the Japanese feared an attack there would bring American reprisal. On July 26, 1941, President Roosevelt embargoed all oil exports to Japan and froze its assets in the United States. Japan now had to either recall its forces from China or go to war before running out of oil. It chose war.

On December 7, 1941, Japan launched a surprise attack on the U.S. fleet in Pearl Harbor in the Hawaiian Islands. Japan hoped to cripple its Pacific rival, gain time to build a defensible Asian empire, and eventually win an ill-defined compromise peace.

The Japanese attack was a limited success. The Japanese sank or crippled every American battleship, but by chance all the American aircraft carriers were at sea and escaped unharmed. Hours later the Japanese destroyed half of the American Far East Air Force stationed at Clark Air Base in the Philippines. Americans were humiliated by these unexpected defeats, which soon overwhelmed American isolationism and brought the United States into the war.

Hitler immediately declared war on the United States. Simultaneously, Japanese armies successfully attacked European and American colonies in Southeast Asia. Small but well-trained Japanese armies defeated larger Dutch and British armies to seize the Netherlands East Indies and the British colonies of Hong Kong, Malaya, and Singapore. After American forces surrendered the Philippines in May 1942, Japan held a vast empire in Southeast Asia and the western Pacific (Map 30.3).

The Japanese claimed they were freeing Asians from Western imperialism, and they called their empire the Greater East Asian Co-Prosperity Sphere. Most local populations were glad to see the Western powers go, but Asian faith in "co-prosperity" and support for Japan steadily declined as the war progressed. Although the Japanese set up anticolonial governments and promised genuine independence, real power always rested with Japanese military commanders and their superiors in Tokyo. Moreover, the Japanese never treated local populations as equals, and the occupiers exploited local peoples for Japan's wartime needs.

The Japanese often exhibited great cruelty toward prisoners of war and civilians. Dutch, Indonesian, and perhaps as many as two hundred thousand Korean women were forced to provide sex for Japanese soldiers as "comfort women." Recurring cruel behavior aroused local populations against the invaders.

## The Grand Alliance

While the Nazis and the Japanese built their empires, Great Britain (the greatest colonial power), the United States (the greatest capitalist power), and the Soviet Union (the greatest Communist power) joined together in an unlikely military pact called the Grand Alliance. The vagaries of war, rather than choice, brought them together. Stalin had been cooperating with Hitler before Germany attacked Russia in June 1941, and the United States entered the war only after the Japanese attack on Pearl Harbor in December.

Grand Alliance leaders agreed to a **Europe first policy** set forth by Churchill and adopted by Roosevelt. Only after defeating Hitler would the Allies mount an all-out attack on Japan. To encourage mutual trust, the Allies adopted the principle of the unconditional surrender of Germany and Japan, and no unilateral treaties

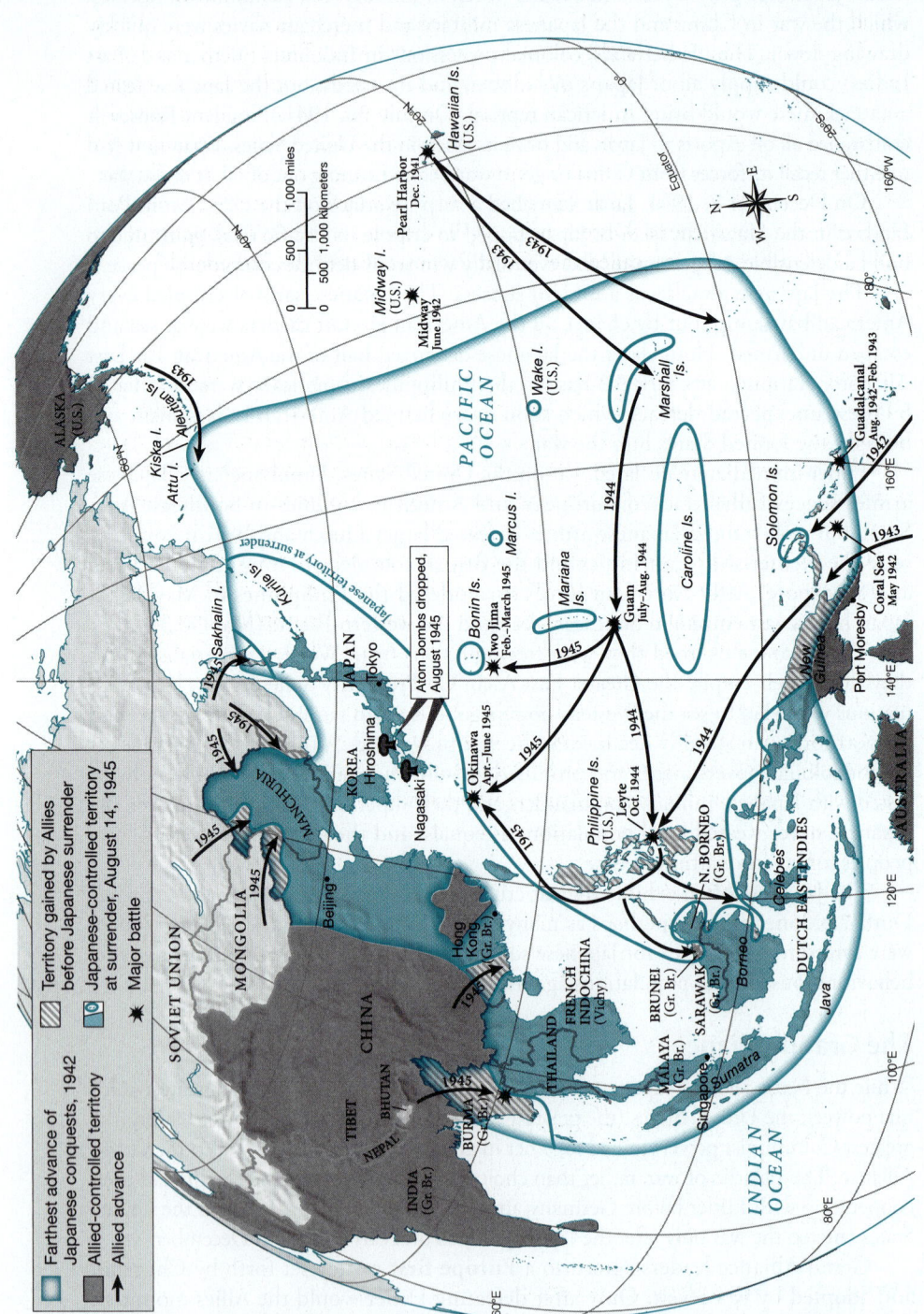

(as Russia had signed with Germany in World War I). This policy cemented the Grand Alliance because it denied Germany and Japan any hope of dividing their foes.

The Grand Alliance's military resources were awesome. The United States possessed a unique capacity to wage global war with its large population and mighty industry, which it harnessed in 1943 to outproduce not only the Axis powers but also the rest of the world combined.[30] The British economy was totally and effectively mobilized, and the country became an important staging area for the war in Europe. As for the Soviet Union, so great was its economic strength that it might well have defeated Germany without Western help. Stalin drew on the massive support of the people for what the Soviets called the "Great Patriotic War of the Fatherland."

## The War in Europe, 1942–1945

Halted at the gates of Moscow and Leningrad in 1941, the Germans renewed their offensive against the Soviet Union in 1942 and attacked Stalingrad in July. The Soviet armies counterattacked, quickly surrounding the entire German Sixth Army of 300,000 men. By late January 1943 only 123,000 soldiers were left to surrender. In summer 1943 the larger, better-equipped Soviet armies took the offensive and began to push the Germans back (see Map 30.2).

Not yet prepared to attack Germany directly through France, the Western Allies engaged in heavy fighting in North Africa (see Map 30.2). In autumn 1942 British forces defeated German and Italian armies at the Battle of El Alamein (el a-luh-MAYN) in Egypt. Shortly thereafter an Anglo-American force took control of the Vichy French colonies of Morocco and Algeria.

Having driven the Axis powers from North Africa by spring 1943, Allied forces invaded Italy. War-weary Italians deposed Mussolini, and the new Italian government accepted unconditional surrender in September 1943. Italy, it seemed, was liberated. But German commandos rescued Mussolini and made him head of a puppet government. German armies seized Rome and all of northern Italy. They finally surrendered only on April 29, 1945. Two days earlier Mussolini had been captured by partisan forces, and he was executed the next day.

On June 6, 1944, American and British forces under General Dwight Eisenhower landed on the beaches of Normandy, France, in history's greatest naval invasion. More than 2 million men and almost 0.5 million vehicles pushed inland and broke through the German lines.

In early February 1945 a sick and feeble Franklin Roosevelt met with Stalin and Churchill at Yalta in the Russian Crimea to negotiate plans for the remainder of the war in Europe, Russia's participation in the war in Asia, and the postwar world. Roosevelt was later severely criticized by some for supposedly "handing over" eastern Europe and northeast Asia (North Korea in particular) to the Soviet Union. Other scholars have noted, however, that Stalin made substantial concessions as well.

**< MAP 30.3** **World War II in the Pacific**
In 1942 Japanese forces overran an enormous amount of territory, which the Allies slowly recaptured in a long, bitter struggle.

**Roosevelt, Churchill, and Stalin at Yalta**  In February 1945, three months before his death, President Roosevelt met with the other two leaders of the Grand Alliance, Churchill and Stalin, at the Crimean resort town of Yalta. With victory against Germany clearly in sight, they met to discuss the reconstruction of war-torn Europe, the treatment and occupation of Germany and eastern Europe after the war, and the Soviet Union's entry into the war in the Pacific. Although Stalin made some important concessions, many historians argue that Roosevelt was already too ill to join Churchill in demanding stronger guarantees from Stalin regarding self-determination for eastern Europe. (Franklin D. Roosevelt Presidential Library and Museum of the National Archives and Records Administration/U.S. National Archives/photo CT53-70:5)

In March 1945 American troops crossed the Rhine and entered Germany. The Soviets had been advancing steadily since July 1943, and on April 26, 1945, the Red Army met American forces on the Elbe River in Germany. As Soviet forces fought their way into Berlin, Hitler committed suicide in his bunker on April 30. On May 7 the remaining German commanders capitulated.

## The War in the Pacific, 1942–1945

While gigantic armies clashed on land in Europe, the greatest naval battles in history decided the fate of the war in Asia. In April 1942 the Japanese devised a plan to take Port Moresby in New Guinea and also destroy U.S. aircraft carriers in an attack on Midway Island (see Map 30.3). Having broken the secret Japanese code, the Americans skillfully won a series of decisive naval victories. First, in the Battle of the Coral Sea in May 1942, an American carrier force halted the Japanese advance on Port Moresby. Then, in the Battle of Midway in June 1942, American pilots sank all four of the attacking Japanese aircraft carriers and established overall naval equality with Japan in the Pacific.

The United States gradually won control of the sea and air as it geared up its war industry. By 1943 the United States was producing one hundred thousand aircraft a year, almost twice as many as Japan produced in the entire war. In July 1943 the Americans and their Australian allies opened an "island-hopping" campaign toward Japan. By 1944 hundreds of American submarines were hunting in "wolf packs," decimating shipping and destroying economic links in Japan's far-flung, overextended empire.

The Pacific war was brutal—a "war without mercy"—and atrocities were committed on both sides.[31] Aware of Japanese atrocities in China and the Philippines, the U.S. forces seldom took Japanese prisoners after the Battle of Guadalcanal in August 1942, killing even those rare Japanese soldiers who offered to surrender. American forces moving across the central and western Pacific in 1943 and 1944 faced unyielding resistance, and this resistance hardened soldiers as American casualties kept rising. A product of spiraling violence, mutual hatred, and dehumanizing racial stereotypes, the war without mercy intensified as it moved toward Japan.

In June 1944 U.S. bombers began a relentless bombing campaign of the Japanese home islands. In October 1944 American forces under General Douglas MacArthur landed on Leyte Island in the Philippines. In the ensuing Battle of Leyte Gulf, the Japanese lost 13 large warships, including 4 aircraft carriers, while the Americans lost only 3 small ships. The Japanese navy was practically finished.

In spite of massive defeats, Japanese troops continued to fight on. Indeed, the bloodiest battles of the Pacific war took place on Iwo Jima in February 1945 and on Okinawa in June 1945. American commanders believed that an invasion of Japan might cost 1 million American casualties and possibly 10 to 20 million Japanese lives. In fact, Japan was almost helpless, its industry and cities largely destroyed by intense American bombing. As the war in Europe ended in April 1945, Japanese leaders were divided. Hardliners argued that surrender was unthinkable; Japan had never been invaded or lost a war. A peace faction sought a negotiated end to the war.

On July 26 Truman, Churchill, and Stalin issued the Potsdam Declaration, which demanded unconditional surrender. The declaration left unclear whether the Japanese emperor would be treated as a war criminal. The Japanese, who considered Emperor Hirohito a god, sought clarification and amnesty for him. The Allies remained adamant that the surrender be unconditional. The Japanese felt compelled to fight on.

On August 6 and 9, 1945, the United States dropped atomic bombs on Hiroshima and Nagasaki in Japan. Also on August 9, Soviet troops launched an invasion of the Japanese puppet state of Manchukuo (Manchuria, China). To avoid a Soviet invasion and further atomic bombing, the Japanese announced their surrender on August 14, 1945. The Second World War, which had claimed the lives of more than 50 million soldiers and civilians, was over.

## Chapter Summary

The 1929 American stock market crash triggered a global Great Depression. Western democracies expanded their powers and responded with relief programs. Authoritarian and Fascist regimes arose to replace some capitalist democracies. Only World War II ended the depression.

The radical totalitarian dictatorships of the 1920s and 1930s were repressive, profoundly antiliberal, and exceedingly violent. Mussolini set up the first Fascist government, a one-party dictatorship, but it was never truly a totalitarian state on the order of Hitler's Germany or Stalin's Soviet Union. In the Soviet Union Stalin launched a socialist "revolution from above" to modernize and industrialize the U.S.S.R. Mass purges of the Communist Party in the 1930s led to the imprisonment and deaths of millions.

Hitler and the Nazi elite rallied support by recalling the humiliation of World War I and the terms of the Versailles treaty, condemning Germany's leaders, building on racist prejudices against "inferior" peoples, and warning of a vast Jewish conspiracy to harm Germany and the German race. The Great Depression caused German voters to turn to Hitler for relief. After he declared the Versailles treaty disarmament clause null and void, British and French leaders tried appeasement. On September 1, 1939, his unprovoked attack on Poland forced the Allies to declare war, starting World War II.

Nazi armies first seized Poland and Germany's western neighbors and then turned east. Here Hitler planned to build a New Order based on racial imperialism. In the Holocaust that followed, millions of Jews and other "undesirables" were systematically exterminated. In Asia the Japanese created the Greater East Asian Co-Prosperity Sphere. This was a sham, as "Asia for the Asians" meant nothing but Japanese domination and control. After Japan attacked Pearl Harbor, the United States entered the war. In 1945 the Grand Alliance of the United States, Britain, and the Soviet Union defeated, outproduced, and outmanned Germany and Japan.

## NOTES

1. Quoted in S. B. Clough et al., eds., *Economic History of Europe: Twentieth Century* (New York: Harper & Row, 1968), pp. 243–245.
2. E. Halévy, *The Era of Tyrannies* (Garden City, N.Y.: Doubleday, 1965), pp. 265–316, esp. p. 300.
3. Carl J. Friedrich and Zbigniew K. Brzezinski, *Totalitarian Dictatorship and Autocracy*, 2d ed. (Cambridge, Mass.: Harvard University Press, 1965), pp. 21–23.
4. I. Kershaw, *The Nazi Dictatorship: Problems and Perspectives of Interpretation*, 2d ed. (London: Edward Arnold, 1989), p. 34.
5. See Robert C. Tucker, *Stalin in Power: The Revolution from Above, 1928–1941* (New York: W. W. Norton, 1992).
6. Lewis Siegelbaum and Andrei Sokolov, *Stalinism as a Way of Life: A Narrative in Documents* (New Haven, Conn.: Yale University Press, 2000), pp. 38–39.
7. Joseph Stalin, "Speech to First All-Congress Conference of Managers of Socialist Industry, February 4, 1931," in Joseph Stalin, *Leninism* (London: George Allen & Unwin, 1940), pp. 365–366.
8. Robert Service, *Stalin: A Biography* (Cambridge, Mass.: Harvard University Press, 2005), p. 266.
9. Quoted in I. Deutscher, *Stalin: A Political Biography*, 2d ed. (New York: Oxford University Press, 1967), p. 325, fn. 1.
10. Steven Rosefielde, *Red Holocaust* (New York: Routledge, 2010), p. 259, fn. 12.
11. Malcolm Muggeridge, *Chronicles of Wasted Time. Chronicle 1: The Green Stick* (New York: William Morrow, 1973), pp. 234–235.
12. M. Malia, *The Soviet Tragedy: A History of Socialism in Russia, 1917–1991* (New York: Free Press, 1995), pp. 227–270; see also the controversial work by historian John Archibald Getty, *Origins of the Great Purges: The Soviet Communist Party Reconsidered, 1933–1938* (New York: Cambridge University Press, 1985).
13. Oleg V. Khlevniuk, *Master of the House: Stalin and His Inner Circle* (New Haven, Conn.: Yale University Press, 2009), p. xix.

14. R. Vivarelli, "Interpretations on the Origins of Fascism," *Journal of Modern History* 63 (March 1991): 41.
15. Ion Smeaton Munro, *Through Fascism to World Power: A History of the Revolution in Italy* (London: Alexander MacLehose, 1933), p. 120.
16. Christopher Seton-Watson, *Italy from Liberalism to Fascism, 1870–1925* (London: Methuen, 1967), p. 661.
17. Seton-Watson, *Italy from Liberalism to Fascism*, p. 661.
18. W. Brustein, *The Logic of Evil: The Social Origins of the Nazi Party, 1925–1933* (New Haven, Conn.: Yale University Press, 1996), pp. 52, 182.
19. Karl Dietrich Bracher, *The German Dictatorship: The Origins, Structure, and Effects of National Socialism*, trans. Jean Steinberg (New York: Praeger, 1970), p. 146.
20. Quoted in R. Stromberg, *An Intellectual History of Modern Europe* (New York: Appleton-Century-Crofts, 1966), p. 393.
21. Quoted in R. Moeller, *The Nazi State and German Society: A Brief History with Documents* (Boston: Bedford/St. Martin's, 2010), p. 108.
22. See Claudia Koonz, *Mothers in the Fatherland: Women, the Family, and Nazi Politics* (New York: St. Martin's Press, 1987).
23. D. N. Dilks, "Appeasement Revisited," *University of Leeds Review* 15 (1972): 28–56.
24. See Frank McDonough, *Neville Chamberlain, Appeasement, and the British Road to War* (Manchester: Manchester University Press, 1998).
25. Winston Churchill, *The Second World War: The Gathering Storm* (Boston: Houghton Mifflin, 1948), p. 318.
26. Izidors Vizulis, *The Molotov-Ribbentrop Pact of 1939: The Baltic Case* (New York: Praeger, 1990), p. 16.
27. Anthony Read, *The Devil's Disciples: Hitler's Inner Circle* (New York: W. W. Norton, 2004), pp. 571–572.
28. Jeremy Noakes and Geoffrey Pridham, eds., "Message from Hermann Göring to Reinhard Heydrich, 31 July, 1941," in *Documents on Nazism, 1919–1945* (New York: Viking Press, 1974), p. 486.
29. See, for example, Christopher Browning, *Ordinary Men: Reserve Police Battalion 101 and the Final Solution in Poland* (New York: HarperCollins, 1992); Robert Gellately, *Backing Hitler: Consent and Coercion in Nazi Germany* (Oxford: Oxford University Press, 2001); Ian Kershaw, *Hitler, the Germans, and the Final Solution* (New Haven, Conn.: Yale University Press, 2008).
30. H. Willmott, *The Great Crusade: A New Complete History of the Second World War* (New York: Free Press, 1989), p. 255.
31. J. Dower, *War Without Mercy: Race and Power in the Pacific War* (New York: Pantheon, 1986).

## MAKE CONNECTIONS  LOOK AHEAD

If anyone still doubted the interconnectedness of all the world's inhabitants following the Great War, those doubts faded as events on a truly global scale touched everyone as never before. First a Great Depression shook the financial foundations of the wealthiest capitalist economies and the poorest producers of raw materials and minerals. Another world war followed, bringing global death and destruction. At war's end, as we shall see in Chapter 31, the world's leaders revived Woodrow Wilson's idea of a League of Nations and formed the United Nations in 1946 to prevent such tragedies from ever reoccurring.

Although the United Nations was an attempt to bring nations together, the postwar world became more divided than ever. Chapter 31 will describe how two new superpowers — the United States and the Soviet Union — emerged from World War II to engage one another in the Cold War for nearly the rest of the century. Then in Chapters 32 and 33 we will see how less developed nations in Asia, Africa, and Latin America emerged after the war. Many of them did so by turning the nineteenth-century European ideology of nationalism against its creators, breaking the bonds of colonialism.

# Chapter 30 Review

## IDENTIFY KEY TERMS

**Identify and explain the significance of each item below.**

New Deal (p. 789)
Popular Front (p. 790)
totalitarianism (p. 792)
fascism (p. 793)
five-year plan (p. 795)
New Economic Policy (NEP) (p. 795)
collectivization (p. 796)
Black Shirts (p. 800)

Lateran Agreement
  (p. 800)
Nazism (p. 801)
Enabling Act (p. 803)
blitzkrieg (p. 807)
New Order (p. 809)
Holocaust (p. 809)
Europe first policy (p. 811)

## REVIEW THE MAIN IDEAS

**Answer the focus questions from each section of the chapter.**

1. What caused the Great Depression, and what were its consequences? (p. 787)

2. What was the nature of the new totalitarian dictatorships, and how did they differ from conservative authoritarian states and from each other? (p. 792)

3. How did Stalin and the Communist Party build a totalitarian order in the Soviet Union? (p. 795)

4. How did Italian fascism develop? (p. 799)

5. Why were Hitler and his Nazi regime initially so popular, and how did their actions lead to World War II? (p. 801)

6. How did Germany and Japan build empires in Europe and Asia, and how did the Allies defeat them? (p. 807)

## MAKE COMPARISONS AND CONNECTIONS

**Analyze the larger developments and continuities within and across chapters.**

1. Compare the effects of the Great Depression on the peoples and economies of Europe, Latin America, and East Asia. How did governments in these regions and their citizens respond to this economic cataclysm?

2. Which ideologies of change from nineteenth-century Europe (Chapter 24) contributed to the outbreak of World War II? What new ideologies arose at this time that led the world to war?

3. Is it possible to compare the death and destruction of the Great War with that of World War II? Why or why not? Did the horrors of total war in World War I somehow make the greater scale of mass killing and devastation more acceptable in World War II? Explain.

## CHRONOLOGY

| | |
|---|---|
| **1922** | • Mussolini seizes power in Italy |
| **1924–1929** | • Buildup of Nazi Party in Germany |
| **1927** | • Stalin is de facto ruler of the Soviet Union |
| **1929** | • Start of collectivization in Soviet Union |
| **1929–1939** | • Great Depression |
| **1931** | • Japan invades Manchuria |
| **1932–1933** | • Famine in Ukraine |
| **1933** | • Hitler appointed German chancellor |
| **1933** | • Franklin Roosevelt launches New Deal in U.S. |
| **1935** | • Mussolini invades Ethiopia |
| **1936–1939** | • Spanish Civil War |
| **1936–1939** | • Civil war in Palestine (Ch. 29) |
| **1939–1945** | • World War II |
| **1940** | • Japan signs formal alliance with Germany and Italy |
| **1940** | • Germany defeats France; Battle of Britain |
| **1941–1945** | • The Holocaust |
| **1941** | • Japan attacks Pearl Harbor; U.S. enters war |
| **1944** | • Allied invasion at Normandy, France |
| **August 1945** | • Atomic bombs dropped on Japan |
| **August 1945** | • World War II ends |

# 31

# Decolonization, Revolution, and the Cold War

## 1945–1968

---

**CHAPTER PREVIEW**

**The World Remade**
- How did the Cold War and decolonization shape the postwar world?

**Nation Building in South Asia and the Middle East**
- How did religion and the legacies of colonialism affect the formation of new nations in South Asia and the Middle East after World War II?

**Revolution and Resurgence in East and Southeast Asia**
- How did the Cold War shape reconstruction, revolution, and decolonization in East and Southeast Asia?

**Decolonization in Africa**
- What factors influenced decolonization in Africa after World War II?

**Populist and Revolutionary Pathways in Latin America**
- Why did populism emerge as such a powerful political force in Latin America?

**The Limits of Postwar Prosperity**
- Why did the world face growing social unrest in the 1960s?

---

**AFTER THE SECOND WORLD WAR, THE WORLD FACED DEEP AND SWIFT** currents of change that swept from the decolonization of Asia and Africa to social revolutions such as those in China and Cuba. These transformations were the outcome of movements that began well before the Second World War and were accelerated by the war's upheaval. The transformations took place in the context of the Cold War, a rivalry between the United States and the Soviet Union.

820

As people around the world pushed back against centuries of Western expansion and demanded national self-determination and racial equality, new nations emerged and most colonial territories gained independence between 1945 and the early 1960s. A revolution in China consolidated Communist rule and initially followed the Soviet model, but then veered in new directions. Rather than form an allied Communist front, China and the Soviet Union became economic and political rivals.

The Cold War that emerged between the United States and U.S.S.R. did not involve direct armed conflict between the two nations, but instead became a global experience in which each country backed rival factions in struggles around the world. The Cold War also imposed a division between western European countries allied to the United States and eastern European nations that the Soviet Union brought into its zone of influence.

# The World Remade

## How did the Cold War and decolonization shape the postwar world?

After the end of World War II, rivalry between the United States and the Soviet Union divided postwar Europe and became a long, tense standoff that came to be called the **Cold War**. As this war took shape, three events separated by barely two years foreshadowed the changes that would take place in the world: the independence of India and Pakistan in 1947; the establishment of the state of Israel in 1948; and the Communist revolution in China in 1949. All had their roots in the decades preceding the Second World War — and even predating the First World War. Yet each was shaped by the war and its outcomes.

## The Cold War

In Europe the victorious Allies agreed initially on a path for moving Germany away from Nazism, but they failed to agree on the political order that would follow the war. In Germany, the Allies conducted a process of **denazification** that removed Nazi officials from positions of power, banned Nazi organizations, and dismantled institutions connected to Nazism. In Nuremberg, the city where Nazi leaders had met in 1935 to turn their anti-Semitism into laws, many leading Nazis were convicted for crimes committed during the Holocaust and for other atrocities.

For Soviet leaders, however, Germany remained a menace to the Soviet Union, and Joseph Stalin insisted that his country needed control of eastern Europe to guarantee its postwar military security. While U.S. president Roosevelt had been inclined to accommodate these demands, his successor, Harry Truman, demanded free elections throughout eastern Europe. Stalin refused, and the conflict over this question grew into the Cold War.

Truman's unwavering stance was bolstered by the United States' status as the only country that possessed atomic weapons at the end of the war. Just as the U.S. sense of security came from having a monopoly on the atomic bomb, Stalin pursued security by militarily occupying eastern Europe and imposing compliant governments that would provide a buffer against the threat of western European aggression. These countries were considered Soviet satellites — nations whose politics and economics were modeled on and dictated by the Soviet Union.

President Truman misread these occupations as a campaign for world domination, and such fears were fed by Communist movements in Greece and China, beyond Stalin's occupation zone. In October 1945 Truman issued the **Truman Doctrine**, which promised military and economic support to governments threatened by Communist control. The doctrine aimed at "containing" communism to areas already occupied by the Soviet army.

Following up his announcement, Truman asked Congress for military aid for Greece and Turkey. Soon after, Secretary of State George C. Marshall proposed a broader package of economic and food aid — the **Marshall Plan** — to help Europe rebuild. Stalin refused Marshall Plan assistance for eastern Europe. The Soviet Union's support for the overthrow of the democratically elected Czechoslovakian government in 1948 and its replacement by a Communist government shocked the U.S. Congress into approving the Marshall Plan in April 1948.

These actions set in motion a lasting pattern of escalating reactions to real and perceived provocations between the United States and the Soviet Union. Stalin retaliated against the Marshall Plan and other moves by the Allies by blocking road traffic through the Soviet zone of Germany to Berlin, prompting the United States and its allies to airlift millions of tons of provisions to the West Berliners. After 324 days the Soviet government backed down: containment seemed to work. In 1949 the United States formed an anti-Soviet military alliance of Western governments: the North Atlantic Treaty Organization (**NATO**). Stalin countered by tightening his hold on his satellites, which were united in 1955 under the Warsaw Pact. Thus Europe became divided into two hostile blocs. British prime minister Winston Churchill warned that an "iron curtain has descended across the Continent."

The Soviet Union, with its massive army arrayed across eastern Europe, and the United States, with its industrial strength and atomic weapons, emerged as superpowers whose might dwarfed that of other countries. Superpower status reached an awkward balance after the Soviet Union developed its own atomic weapons in 1949. Both nations pitched themselves into a military and geopolitical confrontation that stopped short of outright war (Map 31.1).

**Berlin Airlift** Children standing on the rubble of a destroyed building watch a U.S. Air Force cargo plane arrive with supplies to support West Berliners during the Soviet blockade (1948–1949). (Bettmann/Getty Images)

An ideological divide defined the rivalry between the United States and the Soviet Union. The United States saw itself as the defender of a "free world" governed by liberal principles such as free markets, private property, and individual rights protected by democratic constitutions. The Soviet Union defined itself as the defender of the rights of workers and peasants against their exploiters, the rights of colonial peoples against their colonizers, and economic development based on planning and equitable distribution. The Cold War sharpened the distinctions between these models, creating opposing paths that the superpowers pressured other countries to follow.

## MAP 31.1   Cold War Europe in the 1950s

Europe was divided by an "iron curtain" during the Cold War. None of the Communist countries of eastern Europe were participants in the Marshall Plan.

## The United Nations

In 1945 representatives of fifty nations met in San Francisco to draft a charter for a new intergovernmental organization called the United Nations. Like that of its predecessor, the League of Nations (see "The Paris Peace Treaties" in Chapter 28), the immediate goal of the United Nations was to mediate international conflicts in order to preserve peace. But in 1945 the founders of the United Nations foresaw a more ambitious role than the League of Nations had played: the UN would also support decolonization; promote economic development; and expand access to health care, worker protections, environmental conservation, and gender equity.

The United Nations was divided into two bodies: a General Assembly that met annually and included all nations that signed the UN Charter; and a Security Council made up of five regional powers, each of which held veto power over the council's decisions, making it a body that in effect functioned only through unanimous consent. Roosevelt intended the Security Council to include the United States, the Soviet Union, Great Britain, China, and Brazil. Because of U.S. influence over Latin America, British and Soviet leaders feared the Brazilian seat would simply be a second vote for the United States, so they insisted that France instead be the fifth member of the Security Council. After the Chinese Revolution in 1949, the government of Taiwan held China's seat until the United Nations transferred it to the People's Republic of China in 1971.

The UN gave critical support to decolonization efforts. Its charter defended the right of self-determination, and it served as a forum for liberation movements to make claims or negotiate the terms of independence. The UN also provided a platform for opponents of colonialism to condemn those colonial powers that resisted calls for independence. In addition, UN member nations volunteered military forces to serve around the world as peacekeepers, who provided a buffer to ease violent disputes and served as observers to ensure that agreements were being met or that abuses were not being committed in conflict areas.

In its early years, the United Nations mediated Indonesia's demand for independence from the Netherlands, which fought a four-year war to reoccupy the former colony that killed 150,000 Indonesian combatants and civilian Indonesians. The UN also deployed peacekeepers in the newly created border between India and Pakistan, and it helped determine the terms under which Britain relinquished control of Palestine and Jordan and under which Israel was established in 1948. The agenda of the United Nations evolved as new member states joined. In 1960 alone, eighteen African nations were seated at the UN, forming part of an "Afro-Asian bloc" committed to rapidly completing the decolonization process and advancing postcolonial economic development.

## The Politics of Liberation

The term *Third World* emerged in the 1950s among observers who viewed Africa, Asia, and Latin America as a single entity, different from both the capitalist, industrialized "First World" and the Communist, industrialized "Second World." The idea of a Third World had particular appeal amid the Cold War rivalry because it suggested an autonomous space outside of Cold War pressures. Despite deep differences between them, most so-called Third World countries in Africa, Asia, and Latin

America were poor and economically underdeveloped—meaning less industrialized—and were thus also referred to as "nonindustrial" or "industrializing" nations.

Many parts of the world were still under colonial rule by European countries at the end of the Second World War, though this status was challenged by nationalist liberation movements. The roots of many liberation movements often reached back to the nineteenth century, and they endured ongoing repression by colonial powers. But after colonial powers were weakened by the Second World War, nationalist movements grew more insistent. The quest for liberation took many forms. Economically, nations emerging from colonialism sought industrialization and development to end dependence on former colonizers. Politically, they sought alliances with other industrializing nations to avoid the neocolonial influences of more powerful nations. Intellectually, they reacted against Western assumptions of white supremacy.

The former colonies faced intense pressure to align themselves ideologically and economically with either the United States or the Soviet Union, and few could resist the pressure or the incentives those powers brought to bear. Nonetheless, to varying degrees, they tried to operate independently from the two superpowers in a number of ways. In 1955 leaders of twenty-nine recently independent nations in Asia and Africa met in Bandung, Indonesia, to create a framework for political and economic cooperation so they could emerge from colonialism without having to resubordinate their nations either to their former colonizers or to pressures from the Cold War superpowers. The participants outlined principles for rejecting pressure from the superpowers and supporting decolonization. In 1961 nations participating in the Bandung conference met in Yugoslavia, where Marxists who had come to power in the struggle against Nazi Germany zealously guarded their independence from the Soviet Union, to form the Non-Aligned Nations Movement.

## Dependency and Development Theories

In 1948 the United Nations established the Economic Commission for Latin America (ECLA) in Santiago, Chile, to study economic development. Under the direction of Argentine economist Raúl Prebisch, ECLA produced one of Latin America's main intellectual contributions to the twentieth century: a diagnosis of reasons why less industrialized regions of the world lagged economically and technologically behind Europe and the United States. These ideas were known as **dependency theory**.

According to dependency theory, the first regions to industrialize in the nineteenth century—western Europe and the United States—locked in a lasting economic advantage magnified by colonialism and neocolonialism. This advantage trapped countries in Latin America, Africa, and Asia in roles as exporters of agricultural and mineral commodities and importers of capital and technology. According to this analysis, the prosperity of Europe and the United States was built on the impoverishment of other regions, an inequality that increased over time as the value of commodities decreased relative to the value of manufactured and technological goods.

How could this pattern be broken? Could a country that grew coffee become a country that manufactured cars? This question would be asked many times around the world in the second half of the twentieth century, and it would be answered in many ways.

One approach was **modernization theory**, which suggested that societies passed through phases of development from primitive to modern, and that adopting the political, economic, or cultural practices of places like the United States was the best remedy for poverty. This theory shaped U.S. foreign aid programs, which deployed armies of experts offering advice in areas ranging from revising legal codes to digging wells. These experts often did not understand local conditions, believing that the American way was always best. Regardless of their intentions, these projects were often riddled with unintended negative consequences, which led to mistrust of U.S. aid.

For peoples emerging from colonialism, dependency theory was more appealing. Newly independent nations faced enormous pressures: rural poverty pushed millions into cities where good jobs were scarce. Cities and the countryside alike had insufficient schools and health care. Dependency theorists favored state planning to both induce industrialization and distribute resources more equitably. A common tool to do this was **import substitution industrialization (ISI).** ISI practices included trade barriers to keep some foreign goods out and subsidies to incentivize domestic industry to substitute them. Dependency theorists believed that even ISI was not enough and that deep social reforms were needed, such as the redistribution of large farming estates to rural workers, as well as state control of major industries and banks.

The governments that attempted land redistribution or the nationalization of foreign firms faced a backlash by landowners, foreign corporations, and political conservatives. In many cases, reformist governments were deposed in military coups supported by the United States. One example was Guatemala, where a democratically elected government pursued the redistribution of land held by large U.S. companies. The government was overthrown in 1954 in a coup organized by the U.S. Central Intelligence Agency.

The experience in Guatemala hardened Cold War views. The United States expanded its containment doctrine to Latin America, where it stepped in to block governments whose reforms it interpreted as Communist. For Latin American reformers, the events in Guatemala suggested that peaceful, gradual change would be blocked by the United States and that more radical paths were needed. One person drawing this lesson was an Argentine medical student volunteering in Guatemala at the time of the coup. Ernesto "Che" Guevara (CHAY goo-eh-vahrah) (1928–1967) developed an approach to revolution using tactics he outlined in a manual called *Guerilla Warfare*. Guevara believed that private property and wage labor were forms of exploitation that could be overthrown by free workers volunteering their labor to help liberate others.

Within Catholicism, an aspiration for social change crystallized into a movement called **liberation theology**. The movement emerged in Latin America amid reforms of the Catholic Church by Pope John XXIII (pontificate 1958–1963), who called on clergy to engage with the contemporary world—a world characterized by poverty and exclusion. In 1968 the Latin American Council of Bishops gathered in Medellín, Colombia, and invoked dependency theory as it called on clergy to exercise a "preferential option for the poor" by working toward "social justice," including land redistribution, the recognition of peasants' and labor unions, and condemnation of economic dependency and neocolonialism.

Priests who embraced liberation theology challenged governments, fought against landowners and business owners they saw as oppressors, and formed community organizations, or ecclesiastical base communities, where the residents of poor neighborhoods could gather to discuss their problems and devise solutions. After the 1970s Popes John Paul II (pontificate 1978–2005) and Benedict XVI (pontificate 2005–2013) suppressed liberation theology and silenced its most outspoken thinkers. Advocates of liberation theology greeted the 2013 naming of a pope from Latin America, Francis, as a return to the focus on fighting poverty and social exclusion within the Catholic Church.

## Interpreting the Postcolonial Experience

Many intellectuals who came of age during and after the struggle for political emancipation embraced a vision of solidarity among peoples oppressed by colonialism and racism. Some argued that genuine freedom required a total rejection of Western values in addition to an economic and political break with the former colonial powers. Frantz Fanon (1925–1961) expressed these views in his *Black Skin, White Masks* (1952), which reflects on the dehumanizing effects of racism, and *The Wretched of the Earth* (1961), which explores the psychology of being colonized.

Fanon, an Afro-Caribbean psychologist from Martinique, saw decolonization as a necessarily violent process whereby colonizers and their vision of the world are replaced by those of the colonized, whom he called "the wretched of the earth." Fanon believed that throughout Africa and Asia the former imperialists and their local collaborators — the "white men with black faces" — remained the enemy:

> During the colonial period the people are called upon to fight against oppression; after national liberation, they are called upon to fight against poverty, illiteracy, and underdevelopment. The struggle, they say, goes on. . . . We are not blinded by the moral reparation of national independence; nor are we fed by it. The wealth of the imperial countries is our wealth too. . . . Europe is literally the creation of the Third World. The wealth which smothers her is that which was stolen from the underdeveloped peoples.[1]

Fanon gave voice to radicals attacking imperialism and struggling for liberation.

As countries gained independence, some writers looked beyond wholesale rejection of the industrialized powers. They, too, were anti-imperialist, but they were often also activists and cultural nationalists who celebrated the histories and cultures of their peoples. Many did not hesitate to criticize their own leaders or fight oppression and corruption.

**Reading Frantz Fanon** Kwame Ture (born Stokely Carmichael), a prominent civil rights activist born in Trinidad and raised in the United States, reads Frantz Fanon's *Black Skin, White Masks*.
(John Haynes/Bridgeman Images)

The Nigerian writer Chinua Achebe (chee-NOO-ah ah-CHAY-beh) (1930–2013) sought to restore his people's self-confidence by reinterpreting the past. For Achebe, the "writer in a new nation" had first to embrace the "fundamental theme" that Africans had their own culture before the Europeans came and that it was the duty of writers to help Africans reclaim their past. In his 1958 novel *Things Fall Apart*, Achebe brings to life the men and women of an Ibo village at the beginning of the twentieth century, with all their virtues and frailties. Woven into the story are the proverbs and wisdom of a sophisticated people and the beauty of a vanishing world:

> [The white man] says that our customs are bad; and our own brothers who have taken up his religion also say that our customs are bad. How do you think we can fight when our own brothers have turned against us? The white man is very clever. He came quietly and peaceably with his religion. We were amused at his foolishness and allowed him to stay. Now he has won our brothers, and our clan can no longer act like one. He has put a knife on the things that held us together and we have fallen apart.[2]

In later novels Achebe portrayed the postindependence disillusionment of many writers and intellectuals, which reflected trends in many developing nations in the 1960s and 1970s. He developed a sharp critique of rulers who seemed increasingly estranged from national realities and corrupted by Western luxury.

Novelist V. S. Naipaul, born in Trinidad in 1932 of Indian parents, also castigated governments in the developing countries for corruption, ineptitude, and self-deception. Another of Naipaul's recurring themes is the poignant loneliness and homelessness of people uprooted by colonialism and Western expansion.

For peoples emerging from colonial domination or confronting the poverty and social exclusion that was commonplace outside of industrialized nations, the postwar challenge of liberation was not simply political and economic, but also cultural and spiritual. The middle decades of the twentieth century saw a broad awakening of voices among peoples who had been rendered voiceless by their marginalization.

## Nation Building in South Asia and the Middle East

**How did religion and the legacies of colonialism affect the formation of new nations in South Asia and the Middle East after World War II?**

The three South Asian countries created through independence from Britain and subsequent partition — India, Pakistan, and Bangladesh — reflected the dominant themes of cultural and **economic nationalism** that characterized the end of colonialism: they tried to promote development through substitution of imports with domestic manufacturing and state control of key industries. However, ethnic and religious rivalries complicated state formation and economic development.

Throughout the vast *umma* (world of Islam), nationalism became a powerful force after 1945, stressing modernization and the end of subordination to Western nations. The nationalists who guided the formation of modern states in the Arab world struggled to balance Cold War pressures from the United States and the Soviet Union, as well as the tension between secularism and Islam. At the heart of this world, Jewish nationalists founded the state of Israel following the Second World War. The Zionist claim to a homeland came into sharp, and often violent, conflict with the rights and claims of the Palestinian people displaced by the creation of Israel.

## Independence in India, Pakistan, and Bangladesh

World War II accelerated the drive toward Indian independence begun by Mohandas Gandhi (see "Gandhi's Resistance Campaign in India" in Chapter 29). In 1942 Gandhi called on the British to "quit India" and threatened another civil disobedience campaign. He and the other Indian National Congress Party leaders were soon arrested and were jailed for much of the war. India's wartime support for Britain was substantial but not always enthusiastic, and the cause of independence gained momentum.

The Congress Party's rival was the **Muslim League**, led by lawyer Muhammad Ali Jinnah (1876–1948). Jinnah feared that India's Hindu majority would dominate national power at the expense of Muslims. He proposed the creation of two separate countries divided along religious lines:

> The Hindus and Muslims have two different religions, philosophies, social customs, literatures. They neither inter-marry, nor dine together, and indeed, they belong to two different civilizations which are based mainly on conflicting ideas and conceptions. . . . To yoke together two such nations under a single State, one as a numerical minority and the other as majority, must lead to growing discontent and final destruction of any fabric that may be so built up for the government of such a State.[3]

Gandhi disagreed with Jinnah's two-nation theory, which he believed would lead to ethnic sectarianism rather than collaboration.

Britain agreed to independence for India after 1945, but conflicts between Hindu and Muslim nationalists led to murderous clashes in 1946. When it became clear that Jinnah and the Muslim League would accept nothing less than an independent state of Pakistan, the British government hastily mediated a partition that created a predominantly Hindu nation and a predominantly Muslim nation. In 1947 India and Pakistan gained independence from Britain (Map 31.2).

Violence and mass expulsions followed independence. Perhaps a hundred thousand Hindus and Muslims were slaughtered, and an estimated 5 million became refugees. "What is there to celebrate?" exclaimed Gandhi in reference to independence, "I see nothing but rivers of blood."[4] Gandhi labored to ease tensions between Hindus and Muslims, but in the aftermath of riots in January 1948, he was killed by a Hindu gunman who resented what he saw as Gandhi's appeasement of Muslims.

After the ordeal of independence, relations between India and Pakistan remained tense. Fighting over the disputed area of Kashmir, a strategically important northwestern border state with a Muslim majority annexed by India, lasted until 1949 and recurred in later decades through both military conflict and popular unrest.

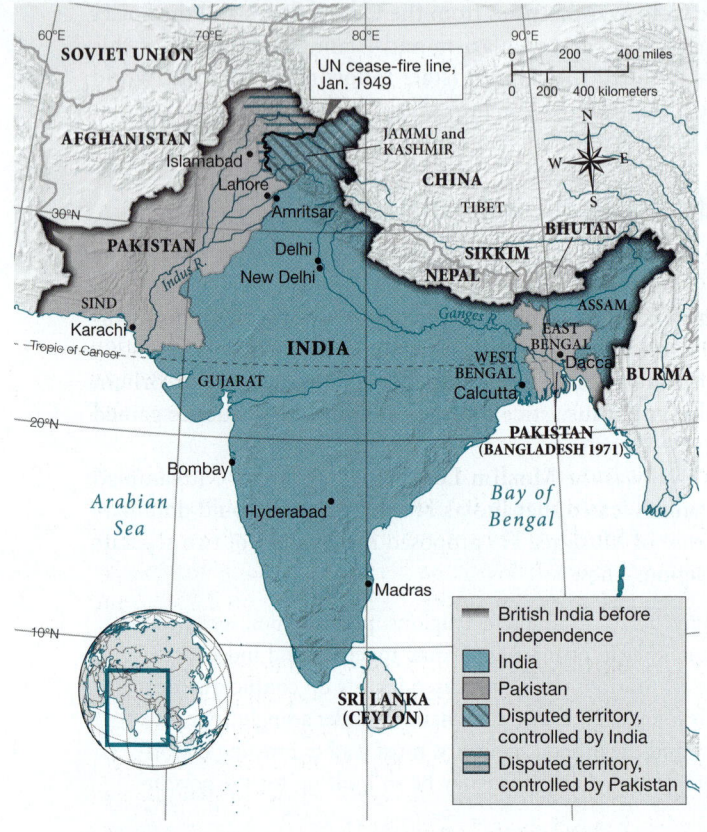

**MAP 31.2 The Partition of British India, 1947** Violence and fighting were most intense where there were large Hindu and Muslim minorities—in Kashmir, the Punjab, and Bengal. The tragic result of partition, which occurred repeatedly throughout the world in the twentieth century, was a forced exchange of populations and greater homogeneity on both sides of the border.

In India, Jawaharlal Nehru (1889–1964) and the Indian National Congress Party ruled for a generation and introduced major social reforms. Hindu women gained legal equality, including the right to vote, to seek divorce, and to marry outside their castes. The constitution abolished the untouchable caste. In practice, less discriminatory attitudes toward women and untouchables evolved slowly—especially in rural villages, where 85 percent of the people lived.

The Congress Party pursued state-driven economic development, but population growth of about 2.4 percent per year consumed much of the increased output of economic expansion. The relocation of millions during the partition of India and Pakistan exacerbated poverty. The Congress Party maintained neutrality in the Cold War, distancing itself from both the United States and the Soviet Union. Instead India became one of the leading voices in the Non-Aligned Nations Movement.

At independence, Pakistan was divided between eastern and western provinces separated by more than a thousand miles of Indian territory, as well as by language, ethnic background, and social custom. The Bengalis of East Pakistan constituted a majority of Pakistan's population as a whole, but were neglected by the central government, which remained in the hands of West Pakistan's elite after Jinnah's death. In 1971 the Bengalis revolted and won their independence as the new nation of Bangladesh after a violent civil war. Bangladesh, a secular parliamentary democracy, struggled to find political and economic stability amid famines that resulted from monsoon floods, tornadoes, and cyclones in the vast, low-lying, and intensely farmed Ganges Delta.

## Arab Socialism in the Middle East

In the postwar period, new Arab states in the Middle East emerged from colonial rule. For centuries the region had been dominated by the Ottoman Empire. After the First World War, France and Britain claimed protectorates in the former Ottoman territories; Britain already claimed Egypt as a protectorate, and France controlled Algeria. The new nations embraced **Arab socialism**, a modernizing, secular project of nation building aimed at state-sponsored economic development, a strong military, and Pan-Arab unity.

Socialism held particular significance for women in Middle Eastern societies because it cast aside religious restrictions on women's education, occupations, public activities, and fashions. In countries like Egypt and Iraq, the openness of education and access to professions enjoyed by urban, typically affluent women symbolized an embrace of modernity, although senior posts in government, the professions, and business were still dominated by men.

In 1952 army officers overthrew Egypt's monarchy and expelled the British military force that occupied the country. The movement's leader, Gamal Abdel Nasser (1918–1970), built a nationalist regime aimed at eradicating the vestiges of colonialism. Applying socialist principles, Nasser pursued the secularization of Egyptian society, created an extensive social welfare network, redistributed rural lands, and promoted industrialization.

Nasser's National Charter called for the nationalization of transportation, mining, dams, banks, utilities, insurance, and heavy industry. In the countryside the size of landholdings was limited and estates were broken up. As Nasser declared, "When we started this revolution, we wanted to put an end to exploitation. Hence our struggle to put capital at the service of man, and to put land at the service of man, instead of leaving man at the service of the feudalist who owns the land."[5]

In 1956 Nasser took a symbolic and strategic step toward national sovereignty when he ordered the army to take control of the Suez Canal, still held by Britain and France. In response, a coalition of British, French, and Israeli forces invaded to retake the canal, while the Soviet Union offered support to Egypt. To prevent Soviet intervention and a Soviet-Egyptian alliance, the United States negotiated a cease-fire that granted Egypt control of the canal. Nasser's other main economic accomplishment was the Aswan Dam on the Nile River, which generated electricity for industrialization in northern Egypt while allowing southern Egypt to control flooding and increase agricultural production. Nasser negotiated the funding and technical expertise for the dam with both the United States and the Soviet Union, eventually settling on Soviet aid. The Suez crisis and the Aswan Dam showed how a nationalist leader like Nasser could successfully play the superpowers against each other.

Military officers in other Arab countries emulated Nasser's nationalism and socialist developmentalism. In Syria and Iraq these nationalists formed the Pan-Arab socialist Ba'ath Party. For members of national Ba'ath parties, Egypt was a model for developing a single-party state that implemented nationalist and development aspirations. Syria briefly merged with Egypt from 1958 until 1961, forming the United Arab Republic. However, officers who resented Nasser's control of Syria revolted against Egypt and established a separate Syrian government dominated by the Ba'ath Party. In Iraq the Ba'ath Party helped overthrow the British-backed mon-archy in 1958, leading to Ba'ath Party rule that ended when a U.S. military invasion toppled Saddam Hussein in 2003.

## The Arab-Israeli Conflict

Before the Second World War, Arab nationalists were loosely united in their oppo-sition to the colonial powers and to Jewish migration to Palestine. In the aftermath of war, Palestinians and new Arab states emerging from British and French domina-tion opposed Jewish settlement in Palestine (see "Arab-Jewish Tensions in Palestine" in Chapter 29). The British government announced its intention to withdraw from Palestine in 1948. The difficult problem of a Jewish homeland was placed in the hands of the United Nations, which passed a plan to partition Palestine into two separate states—one Arab and one Jewish (Map 31.3). The Jews accepted, and the Arabs rejected, the partition of Palestine.

## MAP 31.3   The Middle East After 1947

The partition of Palestine by the United Nations resulted in the creation in 1948 of Israel, which faced repeated conflicts with rival Arab states.

By early 1948 an undeclared civil war raged in Palestine. When the British mandate ended on May 14, 1948, the Jews proclaimed the state of Israel. Arab countries attacked the new state, but Israeli forces drove off the invaders and conquered more territory. Roughly nine hundred thousand Palestinian refugees fled or were expelled from old Palestine. The war left an enormous legacy of Arab bitterness toward Israel and its political allies, Great Britain and the United States. In 1964 a union of Palestinian refugee groups opposed to Israel and seeking a Palestinian state joined together, under the leadership of Yasir Arafat (1929–2004), to form the **Palestine Liberation Organization (PLO)**.

Nationalist leaders in neighboring Syria and Egypt cultivated political support at home through opposition to Israel and threats to crush it militarily. This tension repeatedly erupted into war. On June 1, 1967, when Syrian and Egyptian armies massed on Israel's borders, the Israeli government went to war, launching air strikes that destroyed most of the Egyptian, Syrian, and Jordanian air forces. Over the next five days Israeli armies defeated Egyptian, Syrian, Jordanian, and Palestinian forces and took control of the Sinai Peninsula and the Gaza Strip from Egypt, the West Bank and East Jerusalem from Jordan, and the Golan Heights from Syria. In the Six-Day War (also known as the 1967 Arab-Israeli War), Israel proved itself to be the pre-eminent military force in the region, and it expanded the territory under its control threefold.

After the war Israel began to build large Jewish settlements in the Gaza Strip and the West Bank, home to millions of Palestinians. On November 22, 1967, the UN Security Council adopted Resolution 242, which contained a "land for peace" formula by which Israel was called upon to withdraw from the occupied territories, and in return the Arab states were to withdraw all claims to Israeli territory, cease hostilities, and recognize the sovereignty of the Israeli state. The tension between rival territorial claims persisted.

# Revolution and Resurgence in East and Southeast Asia

**How did the Cold War shape reconstruction, revolution, and decolonization in East and Southeast Asia?**

In Asia Japan's defeat ended the Second World War, but other conflicts continued. Peoples under European colonial rule intensified their struggle for independence, and in China Nationalist and Communist armies that had cooperated against the Japanese invaders now confronted each other in a renewed civil war. In 1949 Communist forces under Mao Zedong triumphed and established the People's Republic of China. The Communist victory in China shaped the nature of Japan's reconstruction, as its U.S. occupiers determined that an industrially and economically strong Japan would serve as a counterweight to Mao. U.S. fear of the spread of communism also drew the country into conflicts in Korea and Vietnam, intensifying the stakes in the decolonization struggle across East and Southeast Asia.

## The Communist Victory in China

When Japan surrendered to the Allies in August 1945, Communists and Nationalists both rushed to seize evacuated territory. Having put aside their hostilities during the war, they resumed their conflict once the war ended. By 1948 the Nationalist

**MAP 31.4**

**Decolonization in Asia**
After the Second World War, countries colonized by Britain, France, the Netherlands, Japan, Australia, and the United States gained their independence. In cases such as Vietnam and Indonesia, independence came through armed struggles against colonizers who were reluctant to leave.

forces had disintegrated before the better-led, more determined Communists. The following year Nationalist leader Jiang Jieshi and 2 million mainland Chinese fled to Taiwan, and in October 1949 Mao Zedong proclaimed the People's Republic of China (Map 31.4).

Communism triumphed in China for many reasons. Mao Zedong and the Communists had avoided pitched battles and concentrated on winning peasant support and forming a broad anti-Japanese coalition. By reducing rents and promising land redistribution, they emerged in peasant eyes as China's true patriots.

Between 1949 and 1954 the Communists consolidated their rule. They seized the vast landholdings of a minority of landlords and rich peasants and redistributed the land to 300 million poor peasants. Meanwhile, as Mao admitted in 1957, mass arrests led to the summary execution of eight hundred thousand "class enemies"; the true figure is probably much higher. Millions more were deported to forced-labor camps.

Mao and the party looked to the Soviet Union for inspiration in the early 1950s. China adopted collective agriculture and Soviet-style five-year plans to promote industrialization, while the Soviet Union provided economic aid and built factories. In the cultural and intellectual realms, too, the Chinese followed the Soviet example. Basic civil and political rights were abolished. Temples and churches were closed. The Chinese enthusiastically promoted Soviet Marxist ideas concerning women and the family. Full equality, work outside the home, and state-supported child care became primary goals.

In 1958 China broke from the Marxist-Leninist course of development and began to go its own way. Mao proclaimed a **Great Leap Forward** in which industrial growth would be based on small-scale backyard workshops and steel mills run by peasants living in gigantic self-contained communes. The plan led to economic disaster, as land in the countryside went untilled when peasants turned to industrial production. As many as 30 million people died in famines that swept the country in 1960–1961. When Soviet premier Nikita Khrushchev criticized Chinese policy in 1960, Mao condemned him and his Soviet colleagues as detestable "modern revisionists." Khrushchev cut off aid, splitting the Communist world apart.

Mao lost influence in the party after the Great Leap Forward fiasco and the Sino-Soviet split, but in 1965 he staged a dramatic comeback, launching the **Great Proletarian Cultural Revolution**. He sought to purge the party and to recapture the revolutionary fervor of the guerrilla struggle. The army and the nation's young people responded enthusiastically, organizing themselves into radical cadres called Red Guards. Students denounced their teachers and practiced rebellion in the name of revolution. Mao's thoughts, through his speeches and writings, were collected in the *Little Red Book*, which became scripture to the Red Guards. Here the young Red Guards learned the underlying maxim of Mao's revolution: "Every communist must grasp the truth, 'Political power grows out of the barrel of a gun.'"[6]

The Red Guards sought to erase all traces of "feudal" and "bourgeois" culture and thought. Ancient monuments and countless works of art, antiques, and books were destroyed. Party officials, professors, and intellectuals were exiled to remote villages to purify themselves with heavy labor. Universities were shut down for years. Thousands of people died, many of them executed, and millions more were sent to rural forced-labor camps. The Red Guards attracted enormous worldwide attention and served as an extreme model for the student rebellions in the West in the late 1960s.

## Conflict in Korea

The departure of Japanese troops in 1945 brought an end to a half century of colonial rule in Korea. But decolonization came with military occupation of southern Korea by the United States and northern Korea by the Soviet Union. Each occupying force organized a government in its region. The Soviet army chose Kim Il Sung (kim ILL sung), who had a history of fighting Japanese imperialism, to lead the north, while U.S. occupiers chose right-wing nationalist Syngman Rhee (sing-man reeh) to lead the south.

The leaders of the north and south seemed unlikely to yield power to each other, given the deepening ideological and political divisions between them. The Communist triumph in China in 1949 hardened these divisions and made the United States less willing to find a political compromise that included the Communist north. In 1950, Kim secured Stalin's and Mao's backing for an invasion of the south to unify Korea. President Truman sent U.S. troops to lead a UN coalition force to stop what he interpreted as a coordinated Communist effort to dominate Asia.

The Korean War (1950–1953) ended in a stalemate with little more than symbolic gains for either side. North Korea conquered most of the peninsula, but the South Korean, American, and UN troops repelled their foes north to the Chinese border. At that point China intervened and pushed the South Koreans and Americans back south. In 1953 a fragile truce was negotiated, and the fighting stopped. The United States had extended its policy of containing communism to Asia, but it drew back from invading Communist China and possibly provoking nuclear war. For Koreans the end of the Second World War did not bring independence in ways that had been imagined or desired: U.S. and Soviet military occupation led to the first major conflict of the Cold War, followed by a right-wing dictatorship in the south and a Communist dictatorship in the north.

## Japan's American Reconstruction

When American occupation forces landed in the Tokyo-Yokohama area after Japan's surrender in August 1945, they found only smokestacks and large steel safes standing amid miles of rubble in what had been the heart of industrial Japan. Japan, like Germany, was formally occupied by all the Allies, but real power resided in American hands. U.S. general Douglas MacArthur exercised almost absolute authority. MacArthur and the Americans had a revolutionary plan for defeated Japan, introducing reforms designed to make Japan a democratic society along American lines.

Japan's reconstruction began with demilitarization and a purge of officials involved in the war effort. The American-dictated constitution of 1946 allowed the emperor to remain the "symbol of the State." Real power resided in the Japanese Diet, whose members were popularly elected. A bill of rights granted basic civil liberties and freed all political prisoners, including Communists. Article 9 of the new constitution abolished the Japanese armed forces and renounced war. The American occupation left Japan's powerful bureaucracy largely intact and used it to implement fundamental social and economic reforms. U.S. occupation administrators strengthened the Japanese labor movement, introduced American-style antitrust laws, and granted Japanese women full legal equality with men, a reform that extended far beyond the legal rights of women in the United States. The occupation also imposed land reform that strengthened small independent farmers.

America's efforts to remake Japan in its own image were powerful but short-lived. As Mao's forces prevailed in China, American leaders began to see Japan as a potential

**Baseball in Japan** Though baseball arrived in Japan in the late nineteenth century, it increased in popularity during U.S. occupation. This photo from 1950 shows children in their baseball uniforms, with a U.S. Jeep in the background. (Courtesy CSU Archives/ Everett Collection)

ally, not as an object of social reform. The American command began purging left-ists and rehabilitating prewar nationalists. The Japanese prime minister during much of the occupation and early post-occupation period was Shigeru Yoshida. A former diplomat with a facility for negotiating with Western nations, Yoshida was the ideal leader in Western eyes for postwar Japan. He channeled all available resources to the rebuild-ing of Japan's industrial infrastructure, while he left the military defense of the country to the American occupying forces.

The occupation ended in 1952 with a treaty that restored Japan's indepen-dence and a role for Japan as the chief Asian ally of the United States in its efforts to contain the spread of communism. Japan's industry provided matériel used by the U.S. armed forces in Korea and Vietnam, and a Security Treaty provided territory for U.S. military installations, particularly the island of Okinawa.

## The Vietnam War

French Indochina experienced a bitter struggle for independence. In 1945 as Japanese forces evacuated, nationalist leader Ho Chi Minh (1890–1969) declared an independent Democratic Republic of Vietnam. The French government refused to recognize the new government and moved forcefully to reimpose imperial rule. With U.S. financial and military support, French forces recaptured southern and central Vietnam in a protracted war. Finally, after the Democratic Republic of Vietnam won a decisive victory in Dien Bien Phu in 1954, France withdrew and recognized Vietnamese independence. Laos and Cambodia became separate states, and Vietnam was temporarily divided into separately governed northern and southern regions pending elections to select a single unified government within two years.

Communist leaders had led the resistance against Japan and successfully ended French colonialism. Recognizing that most South Vietnamese would vote for reuni-fication under Communist rule, the U.S. government organized and financed a gov-ernment in South Vietnam and rejected elections that would reunify the country. Opponents of the government of South Vietnam, known as the Viet Cong, organized a guerrilla war against what they saw as an illegitimate government, which in turn received rapidly increasing economic and military support from the United States.

By the time the Democratic Republic of Vietnam came to the aid of the Viet Cong in 1959, Vietnam was again engulfed in war, with another powerful foreign nation involved in the fighting. Cold War fears and U.S. commitment to the ideology of containment drove U.S. involvement in Vietnam. U.S. president Lyndon Johnson greatly expanded America's role in the Vietnam conflict, seeking to "escalate" the war sufficiently to break the will of the North Vietnamese and their southern allies with-out resorting to "overkill," which might risk war with the entire Communist bloc.

South Vietnam received massive U.S. military aid, and at the war's peak over a half million of American forces joined in combat. The U.S. government also enlisted the support of allies; the greatest support came from South Korea, which sent over three hundred thousand troops. The United States bombed North Vietnam with ever-greater intensity, but it did not invade North Vietnam or launch a naval block-ade of its ports.

While most Americans saw the war as a legitimate defense against commu-nism, feelings about U.S. involvement were more complex in South Vietnam.

Many supported the Democratic Republic as the author of Vietnamese independence. In addition, U.S. tactics took a steep toll on civilian populations, while South Vietnamese leaders were notoriously corrupt and dealt harshly with religious and ethnic minorities in the highly diverse country.

By the late 1960s growing numbers of critics in the United States and around the world denounced American involvement in the conflict. The north's Tet Offensive in January 1968, which took over several South Vietnamese cities, shook Americans' confidence. Within months President Johnson announced he would not stand for re-election and called for negotiations with North Vietnam.

Elected in 1968, President Richard Nixon sought to disengage America from Vietnam. But to strengthen his negotiating position, he intensified aerial bombardment of northern cities and began to secretly bomb neighboring Cambodia and Laos. Nixon reached a peace agreement with North Vietnam in 1973, and the remaining American forces withdrew in 1975. Soon after, the South Vietnamese government surrendered, and the country was reunified as the Socialist Republic of Vietnam.

After more than thirty-five years of battle, the Communists turned to a nation-building process that had been delayed by decades of war against colonial rule and the U.S. effort to force a political and economic model on the country as part of its doctrine of containment. Millions of Vietnamese civilians faced reprisals for aligning with the United States, including Hmong (ha-MUHNG) and Degar peoples, such as the Mnong (MUH-nong), and other ethnic minorities. They first fled to refugee camps elsewhere in Southeast Asia and later settled as refugees in the United States.

The war toll was staggering. Three million people in Vietnam lost their lives to war between the declaration of independence in 1945 and reunification in 1976. Casualties included 58,000 U.S. and 16,000 South Korean troops. U.S. armed forces dropped 6 million tons of bombs on Vietnam, Cambodia, and Laos—nearly three times the amount used by the United States in the Second World War. In addition, the United States sprayed 19 million gallons of herbicide in Vietnam, mainly Agent Orange, which contained highly toxic dioxin and caused enduring health problems for millions of Vietnamese people and tens of thousands of U.S. troops. Defoliants, as well as unexploded bombs and the chemical remains of exploded bombs, remained a lasting environmental catastrophe.

# Decolonization in Africa

### What factors influenced decolonization in Africa after World War II?

By 1964 most of Africa had gained independence (Map 31.5). Many nationalist leaders saw socialism as the best way to sever colonial ties and erase exploitation. But colonial legacies hampered these efforts: new nations inherited inefficient colonial bureaucracies, economic systems that privileged the export of commodities, and colonial educational systems intended to train administrators of empire. The range of actions available to new leaders was narrowed by former colonizers' efforts to retain their economic influence and by the political and ideological divisions of the Cold War.

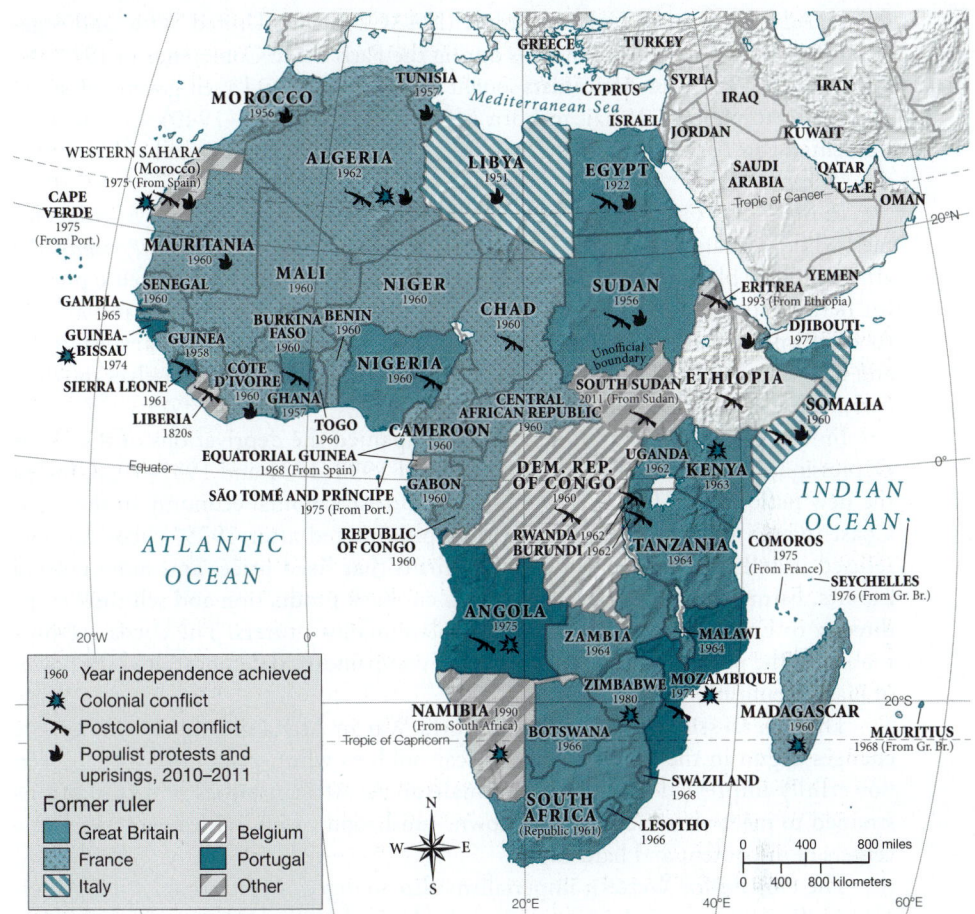

**MAP 31.5** **Decolonization in Africa, 1947 to the Present**
Most African territories achieved statehood by the mid-1960s, as European empires passed away, unlamented.

## The Growth of African Nationalism

African nationalism resembled similar movements in Asia and the Middle East in its reaction against colonialism, but it developed in a more difficult context. Colonial powers had created territorial boundaries that did not fit historical patterns or ethnic divisions. These divisions complicated the development of political—as distinct from cultural—nationalism. Was a modern national state based on ethnic or clan loyalties? Was it to be a continent-wide union? Would the multiethnic territories carved out by European empires become the new African nations? Newly independent peoples would have to confront these questions.

The first nationalist impetus came from the United States and the Caribbean. The most renowned participant in this "black nationalism" was W. E. B. Du Bois (1868–1963). Du Bois (doo-BOISS) was a cofounder of the National Association for the Advancement of Colored People (NAACP) in the United States and organized Pan-African congresses in Paris during the Paris Peace Conference in 1919 and in Brussels in 1921. **Pan-Africanists** sought black solidarity and a self-governing union of all African peoples. Jamaican-born Marcus Garvey (1887–1940) was the most influential Pan-Africanist, rallying young, educated Africans to his call of "Africa for the Africans."

In the 1920s a surge of anticolonial nationalism swept French and British colonies, while African intellectuals in Europe formulated and articulated *négritude*, the affirmation of blackness and black creativity. This westernized African elite pressed for better access to government jobs, steps toward self-government, and an end to discrimination. They claimed the right to speak for ordinary Africans and denounced government-supported chiefs for subordinating themselves to white colonial leaders.

In West Africa, mass protests that accompanied the deprivations of the Great Depression, in particular the **cocoa holdups** of 1930–1931 and 1937–1938, fueled the new nationalism. Cocoa dominated the British colonial economy in the Gold Coast (which became Ghana). As prices plummeted after 1929, cocoa farmers refused to sell their beans to the British firms that fixed prices and monopolized exports. Farmers organized cooperatives to cut back production and sell their crops directly to European and American chocolate manufacturers. The cocoa holdups mobilized the population against the foreign companies and demonstrated the power of mass organization and protest.

The repercussions of the Second World War in Africa greatly accelerated the changes begun in the 1930s. Many African soldiers who served in India had been powerfully impressed by Indian nationalism. As African mines and plantations strained to meet wartime demands, towns mushroomed into cities, which became centers of discontent and hardship.

The climate for Western imperialism also changed. Most notably, the principle of self-government was written into the United Nations charter. The question became not *whether* but *when* colonies would become independent. Colonial powers were in no rush. But new leaders emerged and formed part of a small elite that had been educated in Europe or the United States and were influenced by Western thought, including socialism and communism. Coming from humbler social origins than previous generations of leaders, they included former schoolteachers, union leaders, government clerks, lawyers, and poets.

Postwar African nationalists pragmatically accepted prevailing colonial boundaries to avoid border disputes and achieve freedom as soon as possible. Sensing a loss of power, traditional rulers sometimes became the new leaders' worst political enemies. Skillfully, the new leaders channeled postwar hope and discontent into support for mass political organizations that offset this traditional authority. These organizations staged gigantic protests and became political parties.

## Ghana Shows the Way

The most charismatic of this generation of African leaders was Kwame Nkrumah (KWA-may ihn-CROO-mah) (1909–1972). Nkrumah studied in the United States, where he was influenced by European socialists and Marcus Garvey. He returned after the Second World War and entered politics. Under his leadership the Gold Coast—which he renamed "Ghana"—became the first sub-Saharan state to emerge from colonialism.

Nkrumah built a radical party that appealed particularly to modern groups such as veterans, merchant women, union members, and cocoa farmers. He and his party injected the enthusiasm of religious revivals into their rallies and propaganda as they called for "Self-Government Now." Rejecting halfway measures, Nkrumah and his Convention People's Party staged strikes and protests.

After he was arrested in 1950, the "Deliverer of Ghana" campaigned from jail and saw his party win a smashing victory in the 1951 national elections. He was released from prison to head the transitional government, declaring independence in 1957. After Ghana's breakthrough, independence for other African colonies followed. The main problem in some colonies was white settlers, not the colonial officials: wherever white settlers were numerous, as in Algeria, Kenya, and Rhodesia, they fought to preserve their privileged position.

## Countries Emerging from French Rule

Decolonization took a different course in French-speaking Africa. Two colonial wars, in Vietnam and the North African colony of Algeria, shaped France's attitude toward its sub-Saharan African colonies.

Even more than Vietnam, France attempted to retain Algeria, as it was home to a large French settler population, known to Algerians as pieds-noirs (black feet) because the settlers wore black shoes instead of sandals. In 1954 Algeria's **National Liberation Front** (FLN) began a war for independence. In the ensuing struggle with the French colonial police and armed forces, over 500,000 Algerians died and millions more were displaced. After the FLN won and created an independent Algerian state in 1962, an estimated 900,000 of the 1.25 million Europeans and indigenous Jews fled.

The war in Algeria and Indochina's military victory divided France and undermined its political stability. As a result, it was difficult for France to respond to nationalists in its other African colonies until Charles de Gaulle returned to power in 1958. Seeking to maximize France's influence over the future independent nations, de Gaulle devised a divide-and-rule strategy. He divided the French West Africa and French Equatorial Africa federations into thirteen separate governments, thus creating a "French commonwealth." Plebiscites were called in each territory to ratify the new arrangement. An affirmative vote meant continued ties with France; a negative vote signified immediate independence and a complete break with France.

De Gaulle's gamble was shrewd. The educated black elite—as personified by the influential poet-politician Léopold Sédar Senghor (LAY-o-pold SAY-dar SEHN-gohr) (1906–2001), who led Senegal's government—identified with France and dreaded an abrupt separation. In keeping with its goal of assimilation, the French government extended limited suffrage to colonial elites, and about forty Africans held French parliamentary seats after 1946. These factors moderated French African leaders' pursuit of independence.

In Guinea, however, a young nationalist named Sékou Touré (SAY-koo too-RAY) (1922–1984) led his people to overwhelmingly reject the new constitution in

1958. Inspired by Ghana's Nkrumah, Touré laid it out to de Gaulle face-to-face: "We have one prime and essential need: our dignity. But there is no dignity without freedom. . . . We prefer freedom in poverty to opulence in slavery."[7]

Weaker European nations such as Belgium and Portugal responded to decolonization in ways that were more destabilizing. Portugal's dictatorship fought to keep its colonies, such as Angola and Mozambique, by intensifying white settlement and repression of nationalist groups. Belgium, which had discouraged the development of an educated elite in the Congo, abruptly granted independence in 1959, leaving in place a weak government. Independence resulted in violent ethnic conflict and foreign intervention. The United States backed a dictatorship by Mobutu Sese Seko (muh-BOO-too SEH-seh SEH-koh), who renamed the country Zaire. Poverty deepened as the tremendous wealth generated from mining went into the hands of foreign companies and Mobutu's family and cronies.

# Populist and Revolutionary Pathways in Latin America

## Why did populism emerge as such a powerful political force in Latin America?

In the decades after the Second World War, Latin American nations struggled to find a political balance that integrated long-excluded groups such as women, workers, and peasants. Populist politicians built a base of support among the urban and rural poor. They often combined charisma with promises of social change, particularly through national economic development that would create more and better job opportunities. In many cases, the conservative reaction against populists led the armed forces to seize power. Revolutionary leader Fidel Castro carved an alternative path in Cuba. Castro went beyond the reforms advocated by populists and sought an outright revolutionary transformation of Cuban society.

## Economic Nationalism in Mexico

In the decades following the Mexican Revolution, a durable political and economic formula emerged under the Institutional Revolutionary Party (PRI), which dominated public life while adhering to the social goals demanded by the movements that had fought in the revolution, especially the redistribution of land. By the end of the Second World War, Mexico had embraced economic nationalism, especially through control of the oil industry.

As before the revolution, Mexicans faced a curtailed democracy, though in this case the government was controlled by a single party rather than a single individual. The PRI controlled every major political office as well as networks of patronage. The party was also an omnipresent intermediary between business and labor. Mexico's economy grew consistently through the 1970s, in what was termed an "economic miracle." This was a time of rapid urbanization, with people leaving rural areas for jobs in factories or for lower-paying service jobs, such as maids and janitors. Economic nationalism softened some of the edges of economic change that Mexicans had experienced in the liberal era, but social inequities remained.

The upper and middle classes reaped the lion's share of the benefits of this economic growth.

A housing and civic complex in the Tlatelolco (tlah-tehl-OL-koh) district of Mexico City symbolized both the promise of the Mexican economic miracle and also the limits to democracy in Mexico. In the 1960s the Mexican government built dozens of modernist apartment buildings and government ministries. Their centerpiece was the Plaza of the Three Cultures, which contained ruins from the Aztec Empire, a colonial Spanish church, and the contemporary nation reflected in modernist architecture. It was in Tlatelolco where government forces silenced political dissent in advance of the 1968 Olympics by opening fire on a student march.

## Populism in Argentina and Brazil

Argentina and Brazil's postwar economic development was shaped by populist politicians who championed economic nationalism. These politicians sought support from millions of people who gained the right to vote for the first time as universal suffrage spread through Latin America. Universal male suffrage was achieved in Argentina in 1912 and in Mexico in 1917. Women gained the right to vote across Latin America in the decades that followed, beginning with Ecuador in 1929 and Brazil in 1932. To appeal to these millions of new voters, populist candidates promised schools and hospitals, higher wages, and nationalist projects that would create more industrial jobs.

At the turn of the century Argentina's economy prospered through its liberal export boom, but industrialization followed only haltingly and the economy faltered. Populist Juan Perón, an army colonel, was elected president in 1946 with the support of Argentina's unions. Juan Perón was charismatic, but his wife, known as Evita, was even more so and played a vital role in promoting Perón. Once in power, Perón embarked on an ambitious scheme to transform Argentina's economy: The government would purchase all the country's agricultural exports in order to negotiate their sale abroad at a higher price. Perón would then reinvest the profits in industry and raise worker wages to stimulate demand.

Perón's scheme worked in the immediate postwar period, when European agricultural production had not yet recovered from the war. But as commodity prices declined, Perón reduced government payments to farmers, who ceased to bring their harvests to market. Argentina never returned to the high rates of economic growth it had enjoyed at the beginning of the century, and many blamed Perón for distorting the economy for his own political gain. Others saw Perón's efforts as halting a worse decline: Argentina's economy had long been dependent on Britain, and as Britain's capacity to import declined, so did Argentina's fortunes.

Despite these economic setbacks, Perón initially remained highly popular, buoyed by the public appeals made by Evita. After Evita died of cancer in 1952, much of the magic slipped away. Amid the stagnating economy even Perón's union support wavered, and he responded harshly to press criticism. In 1955 the armed forces deposed and exiled Perón. For the next three years the military ruled Argentina and conducted a process of "de-Peronization," banning Peronist organizations and forbidding mention of his name. But Perón remained the most popular politician in the country. Presidential candidates could not win without discreetly securing the exiled Perón's endorsement.

In Brazil, reacting against the economic and political liberalism through which coffee planters dominated the country, the armed forces installed Getúlio Vargas as president in 1930. Vargas initiated democratic reforms but veered into a nationalist dictatorship known as the "New State" (1937–1945), inspired by European fascism. Despite his harsh treatment of opponents, he was popular with workers and was elected in 1950 to a new term as president, now reinvented as a populist who promised nationalist economic reforms. The armed forces and conservatives mistrusted Vargas's appeals to workers and organized to depose him in 1954. Before they could act, Vargas killed himself.

The Vargas era saw rapid industrialization, the legalization of labor unions, and the creation of a minimum wage. Juscelino Kubitschek, elected in 1955, continued to build upon Vargas's populism and nationalism. Between 1956 and 1960 Kubitschek's government borrowed heavily from abroad to promote industrialization, especially in steel and automotive manufacturing, and build the futuristic new capital of Brasília in the midst of a wilderness. Kubitschek's slogan was "Fifty Years' Progress in Five."

In 1961 populist João Goulart became Brazil's president. Goulart sought deeper reforms, including the redistribution of land and limits on the profits multinational corporations could take out of the country. In 1964 the armed forces, backed by the United States, deposed Goulart and held on to power for the next twenty-one years.

## Communist Revolution in Cuba

Cuba remained practically an American colony until the 1930s, when a series of rulers with socialist and Communist leanings seized and lost power. Cuba's political institutions were weak and its politicians notoriously corrupt. In March 1952 Fulgencio Batista (1901–1973) staged a coup with American support and instituted an authoritarian regime that favored wealthy Cubans and U.S. businesses.

The Cuban Revolution (1953–1959) brought Fidel Castro (1927–2016) to power through an armed insurgency that used guerrilla tactics crafted by Argentine

**Revolutionaries in Cuba** Che Guevara (left) and Fidel Castro (right), whose successful revolution in Cuba inspired armed movements across Latin America. (United Archives GmbH/Bridgeman Images)

revolutionary Ernesto "Che" Guevara. Castro pursued deep economic reforms such as land redistribution and rent caps to help the urban poor. Because Castro's nationalization of utilities and industries as well as land reform came at the expense of U.S. businesses, U.S. president John F. Kennedy staged an invasion of Cuba to topple Castro. When the invasion force of Cuban exiles landed at the Bay of Pigs, soldiers commanded by Castro repelled it, turning the invasion into an embarrassment for the United States.

Castro had not come to power as a Communist: his main aim had been to regain control of Cuba's economy and politics from the United States. But U.S. efforts to overthrow him and to starve the Cuban economy drove him to declare himself a Marxist-Leninist and form an alliance with the Soviet Union, which agreed to place nuclear missiles in Cuba to protect against another U.S. invasion. Kennedy demanded the missiles be removed. The military and diplomatic brinksmanship of the 1962 Cuban missile crisis ensued until the Soviet Union relented and removed the missiles. In 1963 the United States placed a complete commercial embargo on Cuba that remains in place, although diplomatic relations were restored in 2015.

Though Castro relied on Soviet military and economic support, Cuba retained a vision that differed from the rest of the Soviet bloc. Castro was committed to spreading revolution to the rest of Latin America, and Guevara participated in armed struggles in the Congo and Bolivia before being assassinated by U.S.-trained forces in 1967. Within Cuba activists swept into the countryside and taught literacy. Medical attention and education became free and widely accessible. The Cuban Revolution inspired young radicals across Latin America to believe in the possibility of swift revolution and brisk reforms to combat historic inequalities. But these reforms were achieved at great cost and through the suppression of political dissent. As Castro declared in 1961, "Inside of the revolution anything, outside the revolution, nothing."[8]

# The Limits of Postwar Prosperity

### Why did the world face growing social unrest in the 1960s?

In the 1950s and 1960s the United States and the Soviet Union, as well as both western and eastern Europe, rebounded economically from the combined strains of the Great Depression and the Second World War. The postwar return of prosperity increased living standards but did not resolve underlying tensions and conflicts.

## The Soviet Union Struggles to Move Beyond Stalin

The Cold War provided Stalin with the opportunity to revive many of the harshest aspects of the repression citizens of the Soviet Union had experienced in the 1930s, such as purges of soldiers and civilian officials and the revival of forced-labor camps. Stalin reasserted control of the government and society by reintroducing five-year plans to cope with the enormous task of reconstruction. He exported this system to eastern Europe. Rigid indoctrination, attacks on religion, and a lack of civil liberties became facts of life in the region's one-party states. Only Yugoslavia's Josip Tito (1892–1980), the popular resistance leader and Communist Party chief, could resist Soviet domination successfully because there was no Russian army in Yugoslavia.

After Stalin died in 1953, his successor Nikita Khrushchev (CROO-shehv) (1894–1971) realized that reforms were necessary because of widespread fear and hatred of Stalin's political terrorism. Khrushchev and the reformers in his administration curbed the secret police and gradually closed many forced-labor camps. Change was also necessary for economic reasons. Agriculture struggled, and shortages of consumer goods discouraged hard work. Moreover, Stalin's foreign policy had provoked a strong Western alliance, isolating the Soviet Union.

Khrushchev denounced Stalin and his crimes in a "secret speech" delivered to a closed session of the Twentieth Party Congress in 1956:

> It is clear that . . . Stalin showed in a whole series of cases his intolerance, his brutality, and his abuse of power. Instead of proving his political correctness and mobilizing the masses, he often chose the path of repression and physical annihilation, not only against actual enemies, but also against individuals who had not committed any crimes against the party and the Soviet Government.[9]

The liberalization of the Soviet Union — labeled de-Stalinization in the West — was genuine. Khrushchev declared that "peaceful coexistence" with capitalism was possible. The government shifted some economic resources to production of consumer goods, improving standards of living throughout the booming 1960s. De-Stalinization opened new space for creative work and for expressing dissent. The writer Aleksandr Solzhenitsyn (1918–2008) created a sensation when his *One Day in the Life of Ivan Denisovich* was published in the Soviet Union in 1962. Solzhenitsyn's novel portrayed life in a Stalinist concentration camp in grim detail and was a damning indictment of the Stalinist past.

De-Stalinization stimulated rebelliousness in the eastern European satellites. Poland won greater autonomy in 1956 after extensive protests forced the Soviets to allow a new Communist government. Led by students and workers, the people of Budapest, Hungary, installed a liberal Communist reformer as their new chief in October 1956. But the rebellion was short-lived. After the government promised open elections and renounced Hungary's military alliance with Moscow, the Soviet army invaded and crushed the revolution, killing thousands. When the West did not come to Hungary's aid, many eastern European reformers concluded that their best hope was to strive for incremental gains rather than broad change.

In August 1961 the East German government began construction of a twenty-seven-mile wall between East and West Berlin. It also built a ninety-mile-long barrier between the three allied sectors of West Berlin and East Germany, thereby completely cutting off West Berlin. Officially the wall was called the "Anti-Fascist Protection Wall." In reality the Berlin Wall prevented East Germans from "voting with their feet" by defecting to the West.

By late 1962 opponents had come to see Khrushchev's policies as a dangerous threat to party authority. Moreover, Khrushchev did not succeed in alleviating tensions with the West. The hard line taken by Khrushchev and Kennedy during the Cuban missile crisis put the superpowers on the brink of war until Khrushchev backed down and removed the missiles. Two years later, Communist Party leaders removed him. After Leonid Brezhnev (1906–1982) and his supporters took over in 1964, they stopped further liberalization and launched an arms buildup, determined not to repeat Khrushchev's humiliation by the United States.

## Postwar Challenges in Western Europe and the United States

In 1945 much of western Europe was devastated by the war, and it faced mass unemployment, shortages of food and fuel, and the dislocation of millions of people. But in the decades that followed, western Europe experienced a dramatic recovery. Democratic governments thrived in an atmosphere of broadening civil liberties. Progressive Catholics and their Christian Democratic political parties were particularly influential. Socialists and Communists active in the resistance against Hitler returned with renewed prestige. In the immediate postwar years welfare measures such as family stipends, health insurance, and expanded public housing were enacted throughout much of Europe.

An immediate result of the Cold War was the partition between a Soviet-controlled German Democratic Republic (East Germany) and a Federal Republic of Germany (West Germany) that had been occupied by the United States, Britain, and France. With the support of the United States, which wanted to turn an economically resurgent West Germany into a bulwark against Soviet expansion, Chancellor Konrad Adenauer (1881–1967) brought Germany firmly into the Western capitalist camp. He also initiated dialogues with leaders of Europe's Jewish community and with Israel to encourage a reconciliation following the Holocaust. As Germany recovered from the war, it became Europe's leading economic power, a member of NATO, and an architect of efforts at European unity.

Amid the destruction and uncertainty brought by two world wars caused by Europeans and fought in Europe, many Europeans believed that only unity could forestall future European conflicts. The first steps toward economic unity were taken through close cooperation over Marshall Plan aid. These were followed by the creation in 1952 of a Coal and Steel Community, made up of France, West Germany, Italy, Belgium, the Netherlands, and Luxembourg. In 1957 these nations formed the European Economic Community, popularly known as the **Common Market**. The treaty's goal was to eliminate trade barriers between them to create a single market almost as large as that of the United States.

Migrant laborers, mainly from southern Italy, North Africa, Turkey, Greece, and Yugoslavia, also shaped western European societies and drove their economic recovery. Tens of millions of migrant workers made it possible for western European economies to continue to grow beyond their postwar labor capacity. This was especially important in Germany, where they filled gaps left by the wartime loss of a large proportion of the adult male population. Governments at first labeled the migrants as "guest workers" to signal their temporary status, though in practice many remained in their new homes. As their communities became more settled, migrants faced a backlash from majority populations, and they resisted their treatment as second-class citizens.

In the United States the postwar era was also shaped by economic recovery and social pressures. The Second World War ended the Great Depression in the United States, bringing about an economic boom that increased living standards dramatically. By the end of the war, the United States had the strongest economy and held an advantage over its past commercial rivals: its industry and infrastructure had not been damaged by war. After the war, U.S. manufactured goods saturated markets around the world that had previously been dominated by Britain, France, and Germany.

Postwar America experienced a social revolution as well: after a long struggle African Americans began to experience major victories against the deeply entrenched system of segregation and discrimination. This civil rights movement advanced on several fronts, none more prominent than legal victories that ended the statutory segregation of schools. African American civil rights activists challenged inequality by using Gandhian methods of nonviolent resistance: as civil rights leader Martin Luther King, Jr. (1929–1968), said, "Christ furnished the spirit and motivation, while Gandhi furnished the method." He told the white power structure, "We will not hate you, but we will not obey your evil laws."[10]

## The World in 1968

In 1968 pressures for social change boiled over into protests worldwide. The preceding two decades offered an example of how much people could change as decolonization swept much of the world. Revolutionary struggles stretched from Cuba to the remaining colonies in Africa and the war in Southeast Asia. The architecture of white supremacism and racial segregation was being dismantled in the United States. Young protesters drew upon recent history to appreciate how much could be achieved and looked at their world to see how much more was needed. Around the world, streets and squares filled with protesters.

In Czechoslovakia the "Prague Spring"—a brief period of liberal reform and loosening of political controls—unfolded as reformers in the Czechoslovakian Communist Party gained a majority and replaced a long-time Stalinist leader with Alexander Dubček (DOOB-chehk), whose new government launched dramatic reforms. Dubček and his allies called for "socialism with a human face," rolling back many of the strictures imposed by Stalin. He restored freedom of speech and freedom of the press. Communist leaders in the Soviet Union and other eastern European states feared they would face similar demands for reform from their own citizens. Protests against the excesses of Communist rule erupted in Poland and Yugoslavia.

In France students went on strike over poor university conditions. When the government responded with harsh punishments, larger and more radical student protests erupted. Labor unions called a general strike. The strikes captured the anxieties of the generation that had been raised in postwar Europe. For many of them, their governments' postwar socialist reforms were incomplete and the time was now ripe for more far-ranging change — if not outright revolution. Similar student movements erupted across western Europe.

In Latin America students rose in protest as well. In Argentina students and factory workers in the industrial city of Córdoba went on strike against a military dictatorship that had held power since 1966, taking control of the city in an event known as the Cordobazo. In Brazil a national student strike challenged the military dictatorship that had been in power since 1964. In Mexico City, where the 1968 Olympic games would be held, students used the international visibility of the event to protest the heavy-handed ruling PRI Party. The Latin American students challenging their regimes were motivated by the example offered by revolutionary Cuba, which they saw as a model of swift social transformation.

The ongoing U.S. military intervention in Vietnam met with growing opposition worldwide. In Japan protesters denounced what they saw as the complicity of their government and businesses in the U.S. military intervention in Vietnam, and they challenged the Security Treaty that bound Japan and the United States. As the continuation of the war depended increasingly on military drafts, protests against the Vietnam War and against the draft erupted on college campuses across the United States.

In the United States the antiwar movement reflected increased popular mobilization: civil rights marches in the South now extended to protests against discrimination and police violence in cities like Boston and Chicago. Protesters around the world were aware of each other and felt empowered by the sense that they were participating in a worldwide movement against the abuses of the established order. Their actions echoed Che Guevara's call for "two, three or many Vietnams" of resistance against imperialism.

In 1968 it seemed that social movements worldwide were on the verge of opening the floodgates to a wave of radical change, but the opposite was more true. Protesters and reformers faced violent reactions from the powerful political and economic groups they challenged. Conservatives reacted against more than the protests of 1968: they sought to slow or sometimes reverse the dramatic changes that had taken place in the postwar era.

Around the world, protests were followed by violent crackdowns such as the Soviet deployment of tanks in Czechoslovakia in October 1968, which crushed the Prague Spring, unseated Dubček, and led to harsh persecutions of the Prague Spring's supporters. In Mexico, Argentina, and Brazil, military and paramilitary groups launched violent campaigns against protesting students and workers, such as the Mexican government's shooting of protesters in Tlatelolco before the Olympics. In the United States assassins killed Martin Luther King, Jr., and other civil rights leaders. Around the world, revolutionary violence and peaceful protest were met with increasingly violent repression.

# Chapter Summary

The Second World War was followed by an era of rebuilding, a term that had different meanings for different peoples. In Europe, the Soviet Union, and Japan, rebuilding literally meant clearing the rubble from wartime devastation and restoring what had been destroyed. In Germany and Japan in particular, rebuilding meant charting political and economic paths different from the ones that nationalist fervor had forged.

For the United States and the Soviet Union, rebuilding involved developing a military and ideological complex with which to confront each other in the Cold War. In the Soviet Union it also meant finding ways to reform the system of political terror and coercion through which Stalin had ruled, while in the United States it meant struggling to overcome the structures of white supremacism and other forms of racial discrimination.

In Asia, Africa, and the Middle East, rebuilding meant dismantling European colonialism to establish independent states. This required replacing not just colonial institutions but also colonial mentalities, patterns of production, and forms of education, and developing ways of relating that were not based on terms dictated by colonizers. Intellectuals and artists strove to decolonize minds as politicians worked to decolonize the state in a process that proved slow and difficult. In Latin America rebuilding meant overcoming patterns of social exclusion that were legacies of colonialism and neocolonialism. It also meant finding the means to industrialize, overcoming the dependency and underdevelopment diagnosed by Latin American intellectuals and social scientists.

The decades after 1945 showed how much was possible through mass movements, advancing industrialization, and political self-determination. But the balance of these years also showed how much more work remained to overcome poverty, underdevelopment, and neocolonialism.

## NOTES

1. Frantz Fanon, *The Wretched of the Earth*, trans. Constance Farrington (New York: Grove Press, 1968), pp. 43, 93–94, 97, 102.
2. Chinua Achebe, *Things Fall Apart* (London: Heinemann, 2000), pp. 124–125.
3. Syed Sharifuddin Pirzada, ed., *Foundations of Pakistan: All-India Muslim League Documents*, vol. 2: *1924–1947* (Karachi: National Publishing House, 1970), p. 338.
4. Quoted in K. Bhata, *The Ordeal of Nationhood: A Social Study of India Since Independence, 1947–1970* (New York: Atheneum, 1971), p. 9.
5. Cited in Sami Hanna and George Gardner, *Arab Socialism: A Documentary Survey* (Leiden: Brill, 1969), p. 106.
6. Mao Zedong, *Quotations from Chairman Mao Tsetung* (Peking: Foreign Language Press, 1972), p. 61.
7. Quoted in R. Hallett, *Africa Since 1875: A Modern History* (Ann Arbor: University of Michigan Press, 1974), pp. 378–379.
8. Quoted in Samuel Farber, *Cuba Since the Revolution of 1959: A Critical Assessment* (Chicago: Haymarket Books, 2011), p. 22.

9.  *Congressional Record: Proceedings and Debates of the 84th Congress, 2nd Session* (May 22, 1956–June 11, 1956), C11, Part 7 (June 4, 1956), pp. 9389–9403.
10. Regarding Gandhi's methods: see M. L. King, Jr., *Stride Toward Freedom: The Montgomery Story* (New York: Perennial Library, 1964), p. 67. Regarding evil laws: quoted in S. E. Morison et al., *A Concise History of the American Republic* (New York: Oxford University Press), p. 697.

## MAKE CONNECTIONS  LOOK AHEAD

The great transformations experienced by peoples around the world following the Second World War can best be compared to the age of revolution in the late eighteenth and early nineteenth centuries (see Chapter 22). In both eras peoples rose up to undertake the political, economic, social, and cultural transformation of their societies. In both eras, history seemed to accelerate, driven by events that had impacts across the globe. As in the age of revolution, which saw the independence of the United States and most of Spanish America as well as the Haitian and French Revolutions, people swept aside old notions of authority tied to kings and empires. In Asia the Chinese Revolution and the independence of India and Pakistan marked the increasing pace of liberation movements that dismantled European colonialism and ushered in new political ideologies and economic systems.

Liberation movements spanning the globe sought not only to end imperial domination and remove social boundaries imposed by white racism, but also to make deeper changes in how peoples perceived themselves and their societies. As radical and new as these ideas were, they nonetheless owed much to the Enlightenment ideals about liberal individual rights that were promoted by the ideologues of the French and American Revolutions.

Though the social revolutions in countries like China and Cuba and the independence movements across Africa, Asia, and the Middle East brought unprecedented deep and fast changes, they were only the first steps in remaking societies that had been created by centuries of colonialism. Uprooting the legacies of colonialism — in the form of poverty, continued domination of economies by foreign powers, limited industrialization, and weak states — remained a daunting challenge that societies continued to face in the future.

# Chapter 31 Review

## IDENTIFY KEY TERMS

**Identify and explain the significance of each item below.**

Cold War (p. 821)
denazification (p. 821)
Truman Doctrine (p. 822)
Marshall Plan (p. 822)
NATO (p. 822)
dependency theory (p. 825)
modernization theory (p. 826)
import substitution industrialization (ISI) (p. 826)
liberation theology (p. 826)
economic nationalism (p. 828)

Muslim League (p. 829)
Arab socialism (p. 831)
Palestine Liberation Organization (PLO) (p. 833)
Great Leap Forward (p. 835)
Great Proletarian Cultural Revolution (p. 835)
Pan-Africanists (p. 840)
cocoa holdups (p. 840)
National Liberation Front (p. 841)
Common Market (p. 847)

## REVIEW THE MAIN IDEAS

**Answer the focus questions from each section of the chapter.**

1. How did the Cold War and decolonization shape the postwar world? (p. 821)

2. How did religion and the legacies of colonialism affect the formation of new nations in South Asia and the Middle East after World War II? (p. 828)

3. How did the Cold War shape reconstruction, revolution, and decolonization in East and Southeast Asia? (p. 833)

4. What factors influenced decolonization in Africa after World War II? (p. 838)

5. Why did populism emerge as such a powerful political force in Latin America? (p. 842)

6. Why did the world face growing social unrest in the 1960s? (p. 845)

## MAKE COMPARISONS AND CONNECTIONS

**Analyze the larger developments and continuities within and across chapters.**

1. What changes in the postwar world had their roots in developments that predated the war? How did the Second World War (Chapter 30) itself accelerate or spur changes in the postwar era?

2. What effect did the Cold War have on the process of decolonization?

3. How might the postwar era be compared to the age of revolution (Chapter 22)?

## CHRONOLOGY

| | |
|---|---|
| **1920s** | • Anticolonial nationalism sweeps Western-educated Africans in French and British colonies |
| **1930–1931; 1937–1938** | • Cocoa holdups in the Gold Coast |
| **1945** | • United Nations established |
| **1946–1955** | • Populist Juan Perón leads Argentina |
| **1947** | • Independence of India |
| **1947–1975** | • Decolonization in Africa, Asia, and Middle East |
| **1948** | • Marshall Plan enacted |
| **1948** | • Creation of Israel |
| **1949** | • Formation of NATO |
| **1949** | • Chinese Revolution |
| **1950–1953** | • Korean War |
| **1953–1959** | • Cuban Revolution |
| **1953–1964** | • Khrushchev implements de-Stalinization in the Soviet Union |
| **1956** | • Soviet invasion of Hungary |
| **1956** | • Nasser nationalizes Suez Canal |
| **1957** | • Formation of Common Market |
| **1957** | • Ghana gains independence from colonial rule, marking the beginning of a rapid wave of decolonization in Africa |
| **1959–1975** | • War in Vietnam |
| **1961** | • East German government builds Berlin Wall |
| **1962** | • Cuban missile crisis |
| **1965** | • Great Proletarian Cultural Revolution in China |
| **1967** | • Six-Day War in Israel |

# 32

# Liberalization and Liberation

## 1968–2000s

**IN THE 1970S TWO CURRENTS RAN AGAINST EACH OTHER IN MUCH OF** the world. The radicalism of liberation in decolonization, revolutions, and mass social movements continued. Women's movements achieved important successes in pressing for reproductive rights and equity in education, employment, and compensation, both in the West and in nationalist regimes around the world. Gay rights movements emerged. Dramatic years of decolonization in Africa and civil rights mobilization in the United States led to new efforts to organize around shared black experiences and demands for equity.

But alongside this current ran a different one whose influence was not easily apparent in the early 1970s but was undeniable by the 1990s: liberalization. Liberal political and economic ideology experienced a resurgence. After the Second World War, the United States had championed liberal economic policies and global free trade, even if this objective ran against the desires of other countries to protect and promote their own industrialization and economic development. In the last decades of the century, the U.S. drive for global liberalization of trade gained momentum, while opposition movements in the Eastern bloc and in Latin America pursued human rights and political liberalization.

# Oil Shocks and Liberalization

## What were the short-term and long-term consequences of the OPEC oil embargo?

In 1973 war erupted again between Israel and its neighbors Egypt and Syria. The conflict became known both as the Yom Kippur War and the Ramadan War because it coincided with the Jewish religious holiday of atonement and the Muslim month of fasting. Armed with advanced weapons from the Soviet Union, Egypt and Syria came close to defeating Israel before the U.S. government airlifted sophisticated arms to Israel. Israel counterattacked, reaching the outskirts of both Cairo and Damascus before the fighting ended.

Middle Eastern oil-exporting countries retaliated against the United States and other countries that had aided Israel by imposing an embargo on oil. The war and the oil embargo had regional and global consequences. In the Middle East the high stakes of the war prompted political settlements that fell short of resolving the territorial and political conflict between Israel and Palestine. The oil embargo unleashed a series of crises that would reshape political regimes and national economies.

## The OPEC Oil Embargo

In 1960 oil-exporting countries formed a cartel called the **Organization of the Petroleum Exporting Countries (OPEC)** to coordinate production and raise prices. They aimed to increase national revenue to support economic development. Until the early 1970s OPEC had failed to control the market for oil. But in 1973 OPEC countries agreed to an embargo, withholding oil sales to the United States and western Europe in response to their wartime support for Israel.

Since oil is a commodity that is traded globally, it remained available in Europe and the United States. But the embargo disrupted the market and caused panic. The price of oil increased almost overnight from $3 to $12 per barrel, quadrupling energy costs. OPEC's ability to disrupt the world economy, and the U.S. government's powerlessness to reverse the disruption, suggested a new world order. Some countries began to question their alignment with the United States and built closer relations with OPEC countries. Brazil halted exports to Israel, while promoting arms sales and engineering services to Libya and Iraq. Brazil's foreign minister told U.S. secretary of state Henry Kissinger, "If you could supply us with a million barrels of oil a day, perhaps this shift would not be so abrupt."[1]

Oil prices remained high and peaked again in the second oil shock of 1979, which resulted from the Iranian Revolution that brought religious leaders to power. OPEC countries such as Saudi Arabia deposited their profits in international banks, particularly in the United States, which reinvested these deposits as loans that governments around the world used to finance development. This money was known as **petrodollars**. In this economic cycle, consumers around the world paid higher prices for fuel, which generated profits for oil exporters, who invested the profits in large banks. In turn, these banks loaned this capital out to foreign governments. Many industrializing countries faced both high energy costs and increasing debts amassed through petrodollar loans.

In the United States, as economic stagnation and inflation combined in what was dubbed stagflation and the 1979 second oil shock also fueled inflation, the Federal Reserve Bank raised its main interest rate to 20 percent. Increased interest rates in the United States made it more expensive to borrow money, which slowed economic activity and led to an economic recession. The recession diminished consumer demand for goods, which reduced inflation. But the United States was not the only country to experience this recession: countries that exported to the United States faced reduced demand for their goods, and countries that borrowed from U.S. banks found that the interest on their debts increased as well. In industrializing nations the rapid increase in interest on their heavy debts became a crippling burden, triggering a global crisis. Countries facing soaring debts and interest rates became dependent on U.S. assistance to restructure unsustainable loans, allowing the U.S. government to dictate terms that imposed neoliberal free-market reforms.

Beginning in the 1980s neoliberal policies increasingly shaped the world economy. **Neoliberalism** promoted free-market policies and the free circulation of capital across national borders. Debtor countries needed to continue to borrow in order to pay the interest on the debts they held, and their ability to secure loans now depended on their adherence to a set of liberal principles known as the **Washington Consensus**: policies that restricted public spending, lowered import barriers, privatized state enterprises, and deregulated markets.

The forces unleashed by the OPEC oil embargo of 1973 at first tipped the scale in favor of less industrialized nations, but by the 1980s the scale had swung back as debt and liberalization returned power to the most economically powerful countries, in particular the United States. The experience of two oil-producing countries — Mexico and Nigeria — reflected the boom-and-bust economy of the oil shocks as well as their far-reaching social and political consequences.

## Mexico Under the PRI

By the 1970s Mexico's Institutional Revolutionary Party (PRI) had been in power since the revolution. PRI candidates held nearly every public office, and the PRI controlled both labor unions and federations of businessmen. More than a party, it was a vast system of patronage. It was also the party of land reform, universal public education, industrialization, and state ownership of the country's oil reserves. Mexico's road from economic nationalism to the liberal reforms of the 1970s and 1980s is also the story of the PRI.

In the aftermath of the 1968 Tlatelolco massacre, the PRI chose and elected as president populist Luis Echeverría, who sought to reclaim the mantle of revolutionary reform by nationalizing utilities and increasing social spending. He and his successor, José López Portillo, embarked on development projects financed through projected future earnings of the state oil monopoly PEMEX. Amid the decline of oil prices during the global recession, in 1982 the Mexican government stopped payments on its foreign debt, nationalized banks, and steeply devalued the peso.

The PRI was further undermined by its inept and corrupt response to a devastating earthquake that struck Mexico City in 1986. Two years later, the PRI faced its first real presidential election challenge. Cuauhtémoc (kwow-TAY-mokh) Cárdenas, son of populist Lázaro Cárdenas and named after the last Aztec ruler, ran against PRI candidate Carlos Salinas de Gortari. On election night, as the vote counting favored Cárdenas, the government declared that the computers tabulating the votes had crashed and declared Salinas the winner. The PRI-controlled congress ordered the ballots burned afterward.

As Mexican leaders found themselves hemmed in by the debt crisis, they were compelled to embrace the Washington Consensus, which meant restricted spending, opening of trade borders, and privatization. They abandoned the economic nationalism that had driven development and negotiated a free-trade agreement with the United States and Canada, the North American Free Trade Agreement (NAFTA), which went into effect in 1994.

## Nigeria, Africa's Giant

Nigeria's boom-and-bust oil economy deepened the challenges of nation building after independence. Britain imposed the name *Nigeria* on a region of many ancient kingdoms and hundreds of ethnic groups (see Map 31.5). After independence from Britain in 1960, Nigeria's key constitutional question was the relationship between the central government and its ethnically distinct regions. Under its federal system, each region had a dominant ethnic group and a corresponding political party. Postindependence ethnic rivalries intensified, especially during the 1967 Biafran war in which the Igbo ethnic group in southeastern Nigeria fought unsuccessfully to form a separate nation. The war lasted three years and resulted in famine that left millions dead.

The wealth generated by oil exports in the 1970s had contradictory effects on Nigerian society. On one hand, a succession of military leaders who held power after a 1966 coup grew increasingly corrupt throughout the 1970s. When the dictator General Murtala Muhammad (1938–1976) sought to eradicate corruption, fellow officers assassinated him. On the other hand, oil wealth allowed the country to rebuild after the Biafran war. By the mid-1970s Nigeria had the largest middle and professional classes on the continent outside of South Africa. But Nigeria's oil boom in the 1970s resembled Mexico's experience: the expectation of future riches led to growing indebtedness, and when global demand and oil prices collapsed amid the global recession of the early 1980s, Nigeria faced a debt crisis.

Oil wealth allowed Nigeria to develop an innovative approach to its ethnic divisions: the construction of a modernist new capital, Abuja. Located in the center of the country at the confluence of major regional and ethnic boundaries,

Abuja symbolized equal representation in government. Its urban planning reflected both the reality of ethnic divisions and the objective of integration: residential areas were divided by ethnicity, but shopping and services were located between them to encourage commingling.

Nigeria's oil boom propped up a succession of military dictators who held power until the 1998 death of General Sani Abacha. Nigeria adopted a new constitution in 1999, held free elections, and re-established civilian rule. Elections in 2007 marked the first civilian-to-civilian transfer of power. But ethnic tensions remained. Violence by the fundamentalist Islamic group Boko Haram has left thousands dead in the predominantly Muslim northern Nigerian states. Much of the violence can be attributed to conflicts between Muslims and non-Muslim groups in northern Nigerian states that resent the introduction of shari'a (Islamic law).

## The Camp David Accords and the Israeli-Palestinian Conflict

After the 1973 war, the United States intensified efforts to mediate a resolution to conflicts in the Middle East. Peacemaking efforts by U.S. president Jimmy Carter led to the 1978 Camp David Accords, which established diplomatic and trade relations between Israel and its neighbors Egypt and Jordan. In the agreement, Egypt gained the return of the Sinai Peninsula from Israel.

Egypt's president Anwar Sadat (1918–1981) was condemned by some Middle Eastern leaders for his part in the agreement, and in 1981 he was assassinated by religious radicals. Sadat's successor, Hosni Mubarak, maintained the peace with Israel and mediated between Israel and the Arab world. In return for helping to stabilize the region, the United States gave Egypt billions of dollars for development and humanitarian and military aid. Domestically, this aid failed to yield economic development, and Mubarak ruled with an increasingly dictatorial hand.

With the prospect of border wars between Israel and its neighbors diminished, political attention turned to the conflict between Israel and Palestinian nationalist organizations. Tensions between Syria and Israel shifted from their border into Lebanon, where Syria backed the militia Hezbollah, or Party of God. Hezbollah condemned the 1978 and 1982 Israeli invasions of Lebanon that targeted the Palestine Liberation Organization's control of southern Lebanon, and one of its stated objectives was the destruction of the state of Israel.

In 1987 young Palestinians in the occupied territories of the Gaza Strip and the West Bank began the **intifada**, a prolonged campaign of civil disobedience against Israeli soldiers. Inspired increasingly by Islamic fundamentalists, the Palestinian uprising eventually posed a serious challenge not only to Israel but also to the secular Palestine Liberation Organization (PLO), long led from abroad by Yasir Arafat. The result was an agreement in 1993 between Israel and the PLO. Israel agreed to recognize the PLO and start a peace process that granted Palestinian self-rule in Gaza and called for self-rule throughout the West Bank in five years. In return, Arafat renounced armed struggle and abandoned the demand that Israel must withdraw from all land occupied in the 1967 war.

The peace process increasingly divided Israel. In 1995 a right-wing Jewish extremist assassinated Prime Minister Yitzhak Rabin. In the years that followed,

**Israel's Wall of Separation** This wall, shown under construction in 2006, blocks off a Palestinian refugee camp in Arab East Jerusalem, limiting the camp inhabitants' access to the city they call home. (Awad Awad/AFP via Getty Images)

extremists opposed to a Palestinian state and opposed to Israel deepened political polarization and fear, dimming the immediate prospects for a political settlement between Israel and Palestine.

In the first decades of the twenty-first century, a second intifada began and Israel took measures to claim and defend territory by building a wall separating Israel from the West Bank, much of it built on Palestinian territory, and by increasing Jewish settlement with Israeli military backing in the West Bank. Following the 2004 death of Arafat, Hamas, a Sunni Muslim party, gained significant support in the Gaza Strip and the West Bank for its militant opposition to Israel and its investments in social welfare. In 2010, under the combined impact of the conflict and economic blockade by Israel, the majority of the 1.5 million citizens of Gaza lived below the United Nations–defined poverty line.

## Revolution and War in Iran and Iraq

In oil-rich Iran foreign powers competed for political influence in the decades after the Second World War, and the influence of the United States in particular helped trigger a revolutionary backlash. In 1953 Iran's prime minister, Muhammad Mossadegh (MOH-sah-dehk) (1882–1967), tried to nationalize the British-owned Anglo-Iranian Oil Company, forcing the pro-Western shah Muhammad Reza Pahlavi (r. 1941–1979) to flee to Europe. Mossadegh's victory was short-lived. Army officers, with the help of the American CIA, restored the shah to his throne.

Pahlavi set out to build a powerful modern nation to ensure his rule, and Iran's gigantic oil revenues provided the necessary cash. The shah pursued land reform, secular education, and increased power for the central government. Modernization was accompanied by corruption and dictatorship. The result was a violent reaction against secular values: an Islamic revolution in 1979 aimed at infusing Islamic principles into all aspects of personal and public life. Led by the cleric Ayatollah Ruholla Khomeini, the fundamentalists deposed the shah and tried to build their vision of an Islamic state.

Iran's revolution frightened its neighbors. Iraq, especially, feared that Iran—a nation of Shi'ite (SHEE-ight) Muslims—would succeed in getting Iraq's Shi'ite majority to revolt against its Sunni leaders (Map 32.1). In September 1980 Iraq's ruler, Ba'ath Party leader Saddam Hussein (1937–2006), attacked Iran. With their enormous oil revenues and powerful armed forces, Iran and Iraq—Persians and Arabs, Islamists and nationalists—clashed in an eight-year conflict that killed hundreds of thousands of soldiers on both sides before ending in a modest victory for Iran in 1988.

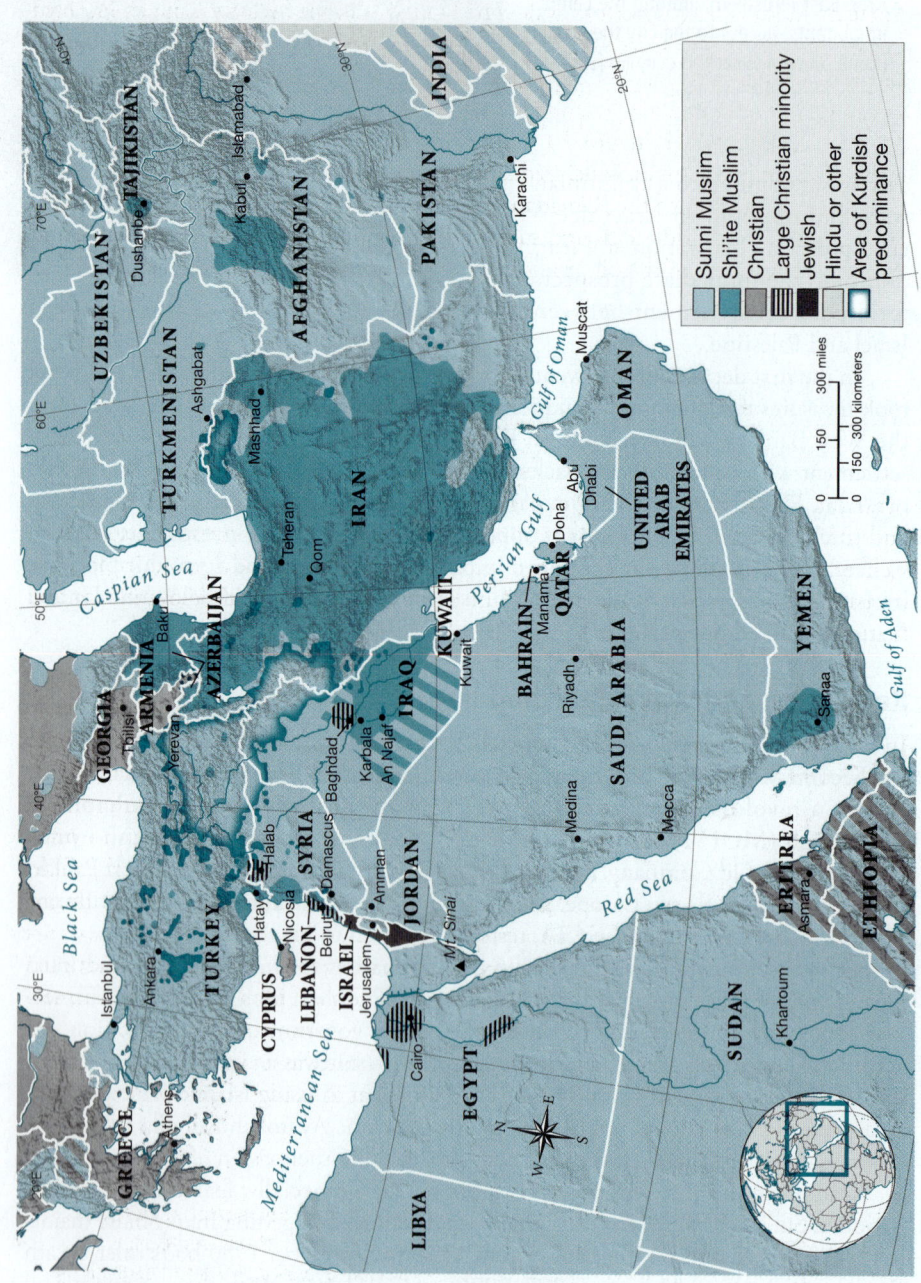

**Legend**

- Sunni Muslim
- Shi'ite Muslim
- Christian
- Large Christian minority
- Jewish
- Hindu or other
- Area of Kurdish predominance

**Scale:** 0   150   300 miles / 0   150   300 kilometers

In 1990, saddled with the costs of war, Hussein commanded an invasion of oil-rich Kuwait and proclaimed its annexation to Iraq. An American-led, United Nations–sanctioned military coalition, which included forces from Egypt, Syria, and Saudi Arabia, expelled Hussein's troops from Kuwait. The United Nations Security Council imposed economic sanctions to force Iraq to destroy its stockpiles of chemical and biological weapons. Alleging that Iraq still had such weapons, the United States led an invasion of Iraq in 2003 that overthrew Saddam Hussein's regime. The invasion led to the Second Persian Gulf War, which involved a lengthy U.S. occupation and a violent insurgency against U.S. military forces, which remained in Iraq until 2011.

In the decades since the Ramadan/Yom Kippur War and the oil embargo, political conflict in the Middle East and surrounding regions, as well as the economic and strategic significance of the oil produced there, continued to shape the world.

# Latin America: Dictatorship, Debt, and Democratization

### What effect did the Cold War and the debt crisis have on Latin America?

After the Cuban Revolution in 1959, the United States financed and armed military dictatorships to suppress any dissent that might lead to communism and to secure U.S. influence in the region. Elected governments were toppled in military coups that brought right-wing military dictatorships to power with U.S. military and financial support.

## Civil Wars in Central America

El Salvador, Guatemala, and Nicaragua experienced the greatest violence in Latin America during the Cold War. In the second half of the twentieth century reformers in Latin America sought economic development that was less dependent on the United States and U.S. corporations. Peasants and urban workers began to press for political rights and improved living standards. Through the lens of the Cold War, Central American conservatives and the U.S. government saw these reformers as Communists who should be suppressed. In turn, many workers and peasants radicalized and formed Marxist revolutionary movements. These tensions erupted into civil wars in which U.S. support for factions intensified the toll on Central American societies.

In Guatemala, after reformist president Jacobo Arbenz was deposed in 1954 by a military coup organized by the CIA, subsequent leaders backed by the U.S.

< **MAP 32.1**  **Abrahamic Religions in the Middle East and Surrounding Regions**
Islam, Judaism, and Christianity, which all trace their origins back to the patriarch Abraham, have significant populations in the Middle East. Since the 1979 Iranian revolution, Shi'ites throughout the region have become more vocal in their demands for equality and power. One of the largest stateless ethnic groups, the Kurds, who follow various religions, has become a major player in the politics of the region, especially in Iraq and Turkey, where the Kurdish communities seek independence.

**Genocide in Guatemala's Civil War** The United Nations declared the systematic killing of indigenous Guatemalans during the country's civil war an act of genocide. In recent years investigators have worked to identify victims of the government's violence, such as six people who disappeared in 1982, whose remains have been returned to their community for burial. (Reuters/Newscom)

government violently suppressed peasant movements, killing over two hundred thousand mostly indigenous people. In 2013 former dictator José Efraín Ríos Montt was convicted of genocide against Maya communities, though the Guatemalan Constitutional Court annulled the conviction.

El Salvador and Nicaragua, too, faced civil war. In 1979 the Sandinista movement overthrew dictator Anastasio Somoza Debayle in Nicaragua. The Sandinistas looked to Communist Cuba for inspiration, but they were undermined by a U.S.-trained and financed insurgent army called the Contras. In Latin American countries under dictatorship or experiencing civil war, much violence against civilians was conducted by **death squads**, informal groups connected to the government and usually comprising police and soldiers who assassinated the government's political opponents. In 1980, a death squad killed El Salvador archbishop Oscar Romero while he was leading Mass because he had denounced the death squads' violence.

U.S. policies that encouraged one faction to fight against the other deepened political instability and repression and intensified these civil wars. Acting independently of the United States, Costa Rican president Oscar Arias mediated peace talks in 1986 among the warring factions in Nicaragua, El Salvador, and Guatemala. The peace talks ended the wars and initiated open elections in each country, with former armed rivals competing instead at the ballot box. Peace did not bring prosperity:

violence, poverty, and corruption shaped the decades that followed, prompting many Central Americans to seek refuge in Mexico and the United States.

## Boom and Bust in Chile

In the 1960s Chilean voters pushed for greater social reforms, culminating in the election of the Marxist candidate Salvador Allende (ah-YEHN-day) as president in 1970. Allende redistributed land and nationalized foreign businesses, including the country's vast copper mines, drawing intense opposition from conservative Chileans, foreign businesses, and the U.S. government. Allende used mining revenue to pay for social welfare programs in housing, education, and health care. In response, U.S. president Richard Nixon organized an "invisible blockade" to disrupt the Chilean economy by withholding economic aid and quietly instructing U.S. companies not to trade with or invest in Chile. Nixon instructed his task force to "make [Chile's] economy scream."[2]

In 1973 Chile's armed forces deposed Allende, who killed himself when the military stormed the presidential palace. A **junta**, or council of commanders of the branches of the armed forces, took power. Its leader, General Augusto Pinochet (peen-oh-CHEHT) (1915–2006), instituted radical reforms, giving neoliberal economists a free hand to conduct what they called "shock treatment" to remake Chile as a free-market economy. Schools, health care, pensions, and public services were turned over to private companies. Land was concentrated into the hands of large agricultural corporations. The U.S. government lavished Pinochet with economic aid.

The reforms created a boom-and-bust cycle in which Chile became especially vulnerable to global economic changes. At its peak, Chile's economy grew at 8 percent per year. The costs of the reforms were just as intense. Income inequality soared: a handful of Chileans tied to big business conglomerates and banks made fortunes, while workers faced job loss and an increasing cost of living. In 1975 the implementation of reforms that cut social programs and caused mass unemployment left half of the country's children malnourished.

Under Pinochet, thousands of Chileans disappeared, and tens of thousands were tortured. These abuses brought international condemnation and resistance within Chile. Women who had lost relatives gathered under the protection of the Catholic Church and embroidered quilts known as *arpilleras*, rendering images of their missing relatives or experiences with repression. Catholic leaders used the church's privileged position to investigate human rights abuses, uncovering mass graves that served as proof of the dictatorship's violence.

Amid the excesses of Pinochet's dictatorship, opponents and even some allies looked for ways to curb his power and find the path for redemocratization. After a 1982 economic crisis, businessmen joined opposition groups to press for liberalization. These groups formed a coalition called Concertación, which proposed a return to democracy that maintained the major elements of free-market reforms. Concertación called on Chileans to vote "NO" in a 1988 plebiscite on whether Pinochet would remain in power. The "NO" vote won, and Chile held its first democratic elections in two decades.

The opposition alliance in Chile resembled many other alliances around the world that sought transitions from authoritarian rule: political opponents who advocated for human rights joined forces with business groups that sought markets in order to produce a democratic transition that combined free-market principles and support for human rights.

## The Dirty War in Argentina

After it deposed populist Juan Perón in 1955, the Argentine military intervened repeatedly in politics for decades. By 1973 the armed forces conceded that their efforts to erase Perón's legacy had failed. They allowed Perón to return, and he was again elected president, with his wife Isabelita, a political novice, as vice president. Soon after the election, Juan Perón died. Isabelita Perón, the first woman to become president in Latin America, faced daunting circumstances: Marxist groups such as the Montoneros waged a guerrilla war against the regime, while the armed forces and death squads waged war on them.

In 1976 a military junta took power and announced a Process of National Reorganization. Influenced by French military theorists who had been stung by their defeats in guerrilla wars in Vietnam and Algeria, the generals waged a "dirty war," seeking to kill and "disappear" people whom they considered a destructive "cancer" on the nation. Perhaps thirty thousand Argentines perished at the hands of the armed forces during the dirty war.

Mothers whose children had been "disappeared" began marching in front of the presidential palace at the Plaza de Mayo holding pictures of their missing children and carrying signs reading "Where are they?" An organization of the Mothers of the Plaza de Mayo was soon joined by the Grandmothers, who demanded the whereabouts of children born to women who gave birth in detention and disappeared. These children had been placed with adoptive families tied to the police or armed forces.

In 1982, emboldened by its success in eradicating its opposition, the Argentine junta occupied the Falkland Islands off its southern coast. Known in Argentina as the Malvinas, the islands were home to a small British settlement. Britain resisted the invasion, and the war resulted in a humiliating defeat for the Argentine junta. The discredited junta abruptly called for elections, and a civilian president took office in 1983.

The new president, Raúl Alfonsín, faced a debt crisis similar to Mexico's. He also struggled to prosecute the crimes committed by the junta. The conviction of junta leaders created a backlash in the armed forces: mid-ranking officers revolted out of fear that they, too, would face trial. Trapped by the economic and political crises, Alfonsín left office early. His successor, Carlos Menem, tried a different approach, pardoning the junta members and conducting free-market reforms such as privatization of businesses and utilities.

As the capacity to attract foreign investment through privatization ran out by the end of the century, Argentina faced economic crisis again. In 2001, amid a run on banks and a collapse of the Argentine peso, the country had five different presidents in a single month. Eventually, the economy stabilized during the presidency of Néstor Kirchner, who was succeeded by his wife, Cristina Fernández de Kirchner. Néstor Kirchner, who died in 2010 while Cristina Fernández de Kirchner was president, prosecuted those responsible for violence during the dirty war again, achieving convictions of not just the junta leaders but also members of the armed forces and police who perpetrated human rights violations.

## Development and Dictatorship in Brazil

Brazil's military dictatorship, in power since 1964, began with liberal reforms but moved to a nationalist project of industrialization and development that resembled some of the prescriptions of dependency theorists: increased state control, restrictions on imports, and heavy investments in infrastructure. They initially achieved high annual growth rates that peaked at 14 percent in 1972. This growth depended on cheap imported oil and harsh political repression. When the oil embargo threatened growth, the generals borrowed heavily to subsidize fuel costs and conducted costly alternative energy projects to substitute oil with hydroelectric dams and ethanol made from sugarcane.

The Brazilian cycle of borrowing petrodollars to subsidize oil imports and development projects was ruinous: by the end of the 1970s Brazil had the largest foreign debt in the developing world. When the second oil shock hit in 1979 and the U.S. government raised interest rates, making Brazil's dollar-dominated debt more expensive to manage, the country entered what became known as a "lost decade" of recession and inflation. Many workers earned less in 1989 than they had in 1980.

The economic crisis set the tone for a transition to democracy: as the generals made painful cuts to public services and as Brazilians faced soaring inflation and recession, the public overwhelmingly turned against military rule and supported redemocratization. Under military rule, the foreign debt had climbed from $3.2 billion to $95 billion. Inflation peaked at 3,375 percent per year before being tamed by the introduction of a new currency linked to the U.S. dollar, coupled with high interest rates.

As in Chile, Brazil's transition to democracy was shaped by liberalization. Business groups uneasy with the dictatorship's borrowing and central planning joined forces with human rights advocates. The debt left behind by Brazil's military leaders drove liberal economic reforms. To sustain its debt payments, the Brazilian government reduced public spending, privatized state enterprises, reduced protections for domestic industry, and kept interest rates high to control inflation. Inflation remained low, but Brazilians faced a high cost of living, and high interest rates suppressed economic growth, maintaining one of the most extreme gaps between rich and poor in the world.

# Gender, Race, and Liberation

### How did social movements advocate for human rights?

South American military dictatorships reinforced old patterns of gender and racial discrimination. Women were legally and economically marginalized in Chile as Pinochet's regime institutionalized views held by the armed forces and conservative Catholics. Racial and ethnic minorities also suffered: in Brazil black activists and intellectuals were targeted for repression, while indigenous communities paid the costs of state efforts to develop the Amazon. As regimes embraced conservative morality to justify their rule, the imposition of these norms often fell hardest on gay Argentines, Brazilians, and Chileans. But people who disproportionately felt the brunt of authoritarianism also became leading actors in the movements for democracy.

In a 1970s and 1980s world shaped by dictatorship, armed conflict, and pressures for liberalization, movements for the equality and integration of minority and marginalized peoples gained ground. As in Latin American political transitions, social movements focused on a widening spectrum of human rights began to change laws, norms, and cultures in relation to gender, sexuality, and race.

## Gay Liberation

In the years after the Second World War, people who were gay, lesbian, or transgender continued to endure legal sanctions and public hostility. Lesbian, gay, and transgender liberation movements emerged to challenge laws that criminalized homosexuality and transgender minorities, to gain effective human rights protections, and to openly live their gender identity. In the United States, the 1969 Stonewall uprising began when thousands of people protested against police harassment in New York. The uprising was followed in 1970 by the first gay pride marches in cities across the United States.

In Europe, some countries decriminalized homosexuality in the early decades of the twentieth century, but authoritarian regimes such as Stalin's Soviet Union, Nazi Germany, and Fascist governments in Italy, Portugal, and Spain intensified repression of homosexuality. In the decades after the Second World War, countries began to roll back laws regulating sexuality, including West Germany in 1957 and Britain in 1967. Forty years later, Britain's "Turing law" granted pardons to people convicted under indecency statutes. The law was named after Alan Turing, a famed mathematician, wartime codebreaker, and computing pioneer who was driven to suicide in 1954 after he was convicted for indecency and forced to undergo medical treatments.

European imperial powers imposed legal frameworks upon colonial peoples that regulated sexuality in the patterns of their colonizers. Postcolonial societies retained and sometimes expanded colonial legal restrictions, particularly in countries where Islam played a strong political role. Countries that continued to criminalize same-sex relationships—even imposing the death penalty in some cases—were concentrated in South Asia, the Middle East, and Africa.

In East Asia, authoritarian regimes in China, Korea, and Taiwan restricted sexuality. But movements for democracy in South Korea and Taiwan, along with the process of industrialization and urbanization in China and Japan, created new spaces to advocate for gay rights. In the last decades of the twentieth century, laws criminalizing homosexuality were gradually overturned. In Mongolia, Taiwan, and South Korea, laws began to allow transgender people to change the sex on their documents.

The impact of 1970s and 1980s lesbian, gay, and transgender activism, like that of other social movements, was remarkable but uneven. Even in countries that saw the greatest legal and cultural changes, violence and hostility persisted. Still, beginning in the 1990s, human rights bodies of the United Nations began considering laws criminalizing homosexuality to be a violation of human rights.

## Second-Wave and Third World Feminism

Gay liberation movements drew inspiration from **second-wave feminism**, also known as the women's liberation movement. Second-wave feminism was a movement for the full equality of women in law, labor, social and family relations, and reproductive rights. It was "second wave" because unlike older movements, which focused on specific legal changes, particularly the right to vote, it emphasized full equality and emancipation.

Second-wave feminism challenged inequalities and the conventions that sustained them on many fronts, recognizing that "the personal is political." One concern was reproductive rights, including the right to make choices about birth control and abortion, which were also foundational to women's rights in families. Another was equality of opportunity and pay in education and in employment.

As movements confronted these questions, their actions brought scrutiny to the structures and values that stood in the way of equality and emancipation, including homophobia, racism, misogyny, and patriarchal values in the family and the workplace. Audre Lorde, a daughter of Caribbean immigrants to New York who wrote about the intersection of gender, sexuality, race, and class, compared men's power in society and in families to that of slaveholders:

> Those of us who stand outside of the circle of this society's definition of acceptable women; those of us who have been forged in the crucibles of difference — those of us who are poor, who are lesbians, who are Black, who are older — know that *survival is not an academic skill*. . . . It is learning how to take our differences and make them strengths. *For the master's tools will never dismantle the master's house.* They may allow us temporarily to beat him at his own game, but they will never enable us to bring about genuine change.[3]

Feminists of Lorde's generation produced an intellectual critique of gender and sexuality akin to the critique that Frantz Fanon and an earlier generation of thinkers had brought to colonialism.

Third world feminism emerged as an alternative to, and sometimes a criticism of, second-wave feminism. The movement, which emerged from Latin America, Africa, the Middle East, and South Asia, identified poverty as a decisive force in many women's lives. Third world feminists formed alliances with other groups opposed to authoritarian regimes and critiqued capitalism, neocolonialism, and dependency as forces that had a disproportionate impact on the lives of women.

The United Nations 1975 International Women's Year Conference held in Mexico City became a forum for defining feminist goals for women's equality in a global context. Delegates focused on the legal and religious barriers women faced, but also on the global structures highlighted by third world feminists. The resolution drafted by conference delegates highlighted the impacts of colonialism and forms of discrimination like apartheid, and it emphasized that "under-development imposes upon women a double burden of exploitation" through which gender inequalities were compounded by poverty.[4] Following the conference, annual March 8 International Women's Day commemorations created opportunities to press for women's rights and for the larger social changes these rights depended on. The 1978 Women's Day March in Chile, for instance, marked the first mass protest against the Pinochet dictatorship.

## Pan-Africanism, Black Power, and the African Diaspora

The end of colonialism and segregation did not mean the end of inequality, exploitation, or racism. In the decades following decolonization in Africa and the dismantling of the system of racial segregation in the United States, social movements continued to struggle against the remaining white-minority governments holding power in southern Africa. But peoples in Africa and of African descent in the world formed new ways of organizing and advocating for equality.

In the United States, the Black Power movement of the 1960s and 1970s formed a radical response to racism, especially in regions outside the segregated South where prejudice and discrimination were still prevalent. The movement emphasized gaining pride and solidarity through political and community organizing, and its appeal extended beyond the United States. In the Caribbean and Latin America, it appealed to youth frustrated with what they saw as the accommodation of earlier generations to colonialism and discrimination. The movement became an especially powerful force in Trinidad and Tobago, Jamaica, Bermuda, and Barbados.

The Black Power movement was also inspired by the Pan-African movement championed by Marcus Garvey and C. L. R. James, which in the early and middle decades of the century had proposed that the challenges Africans and peoples of African descent experienced were best faced through a transnational approach sustained by international networks. In Latin America and the Caribbean, the Black Power movement created pathways for confronting problems that drew upon the experiences of people of African descent in other places, particularly the United States. Similar pathways opened in music (especially soul, reggae, and later hip-hop), literature, dance, cinema, and theater.

What emerged was a renewed understanding that although the experiences of Africans and those of African descent in the world were in many respects different, there was also a shared experience and the potential for shared lessons and approaches. This experience of a global African diaspora suggested new ways of interpreting and responding to challenges that, however local, fit larger patterns, including disparities in policing, unequal access to housing, lack of equity in access to education and employment, and lack of equity in community and environmental health.

# Resistance to White Rule in Southern Africa

**How did white-minority rule end in southern Africa?**

The racially segregated system of apartheid in South Africa existed in a region of white-minority rule that included Portuguese Angola and Mozambique, the government of Ian Smith in Rhodesia, and South African control of the former German colony of Namibia. Wars of independence in Angola and Mozambique eroded the buffer of neighboring white-minority governments around South Africa, and domestic and foreign pressure brought a political transition to majority rule in Namibia and South Africa in the 1990s.

## Portuguese Decolonization and Rhodesia

At the end of World War II Portugal was the poorest country in western Europe and was ruled by a dictatorship, but it still claimed an immense overseas empire that included Angola, Mozambique, Guinea-Bissau, and Cape Verde. Since the 1920s Portuguese dictator António Salazar (1889–1970) had relied on forced labor in Angola's diamond mines to finance his regime. To alleviate poverty in Portugal, Salazar also promoted colonial settlement in Angola and Mozambique, where the white population rose from seventy thousand in 1940 to over five hundred thousand in 1970.

Salazar resisted decolonization, insisting that Portuguese territories were "overseas provinces," whose status was akin to Alaska and Hawaii's relationship to the United States. Given Portugal's refusal to negotiate independence, nationalists resorted to armed insurrections. By the early 1970s independence movements in seven colonies were simultaneously fighting guerrilla wars against the Portuguese army and colonial militias. Demoralized Portuguese officers overthrew Portugal's government in 1974. Guinea-Bissau and Cape Verde became independent that same year, and Angola and Mozambique a year later. The nationalist movements that took power were all Marxist, their radicalism a product of their long struggle against oppression, inequality, and lack of access to their countries' resources.

The end of colonialism in Angola and Mozambique shifted the political landscape of southern Africa. Mozambique helped rebels fighting white-minority rule in Rhodesia, while the South African government saw independent Angola as a threat to apartheid and to its control over Namibia. The bloc of white-minority rule had been shattered. But after more than a decade of fighting for independence, neither Angola nor Mozambique would soon find peace.

The new government of Mozambique faced a guerrilla movement financed by Rhodesia. As Angola became independent, it faced immediate invasions from Zaire (encouraged by the United States) and South Africa. The new president of Angola, Agostinho Neto (nay-TOH) (1922–1978), requested military aid from Cuba, which airlifted troops that repelled both invasions and kept the regime in place. Until the late 1980s tens of thousands of Cuban troops confronted the South African and mercenary armies to defend the government of Angola.

In the British colony of Rhodesia white settlers, a small minority of the population, declared independence on their own to avoid sharing power with the black majority. In 1965 they established a white-minority government under farmer and politician Ian Smith. The new Rhodesian state faced international condemnation for segregating black citizens, including the first economic sanctions imposed by the United Nations. The Rhodesian army and police dealt violently with black political activists who challenged white rule.

The Zimbabwe African People's Union (ZAPU) fought a guerrilla war against Rhodesia's white regime. Rebuffed by the United States and Britain, ZAPU turned to China and the Soviet Union for support. When Mozambique gained independence in 1975, its government allowed ZAPU and other guerrilla groups to use neighboring Mozambican territory as a staging ground to launch attacks on Rhodesia, making it impossible for Ian Smith's government to endure.

Open elections were negotiated, and these were easily won in 1979 by ZAPU leader Robert Mugabe. The following year, the Mugabe government renamed the newly independent country Zimbabwe after an ancient city-state that predated colonial rule. Bob Marley and the Wailers took part in the independence day festivities, performing their recently released song "Zimbabwe," which began "Every man gotta right/to decide his own destiny."

## South Africa Under Apartheid

In 1948 the ruling South African National Party created a segregationist system of racial discrimination known as **apartheid**, meaning "apartness" or "separation." The population was legally divided into racial groups: whites, blacks, Asians, and racially mixed "coloureds." Good jobs in the cities were reserved for whites, who lived in luxurious modern central neighborhoods. Blacks were restricted to precarious outlying townships plagued by poverty, crime, and mistreatment from white policemen.

In the 1950s black South Africans and their allies mounted peaceful protests. A turning point came in 1960, when police in the township of Sharpeville fired at demonstrators and killed sixty-nine black protesters. The main black political organization — the **African National Congress (ANC)** — was outlawed but continued in exile. Other ANC members, led by a young lawyer, Nelson Mandela (1918–2013), stayed in South Africa to mount armed resistance. In 1962 Mandela was captured, tried for treason, and sentenced to life imprisonment.

In the 1970s the South African government fell into the hands of "securocrats," military and intelligence officers who adopted a policy known as the "total strategy," directing the state's resources into policing apartheid and dominating South Africa's neighbors by force. At the United Nations, African leaders denounced the South African government, and activists in countries around the world pressured their governments to impose economic sanctions against the South African regime. South Africa's white leaders responded with cosmetic reforms in 1984 to improve their international standing. The 3 million coloureds and the 1 million South Africans of Asian descent gained limited parliamentary representation, but no provision was made for any representation of the country's 22 million blacks.

The reforms provoked a backlash. In the segregated townships young black militants took to the streets, clashing with white security forces; these protests left five thousand dead and fifty thousand jailed without charges between 1985 and 1989.

**The Sharpeville Massacre** In March 1960, South Africans flee the area around the Sharpeville police station, where police opened fire on protesters demonstrating against the apartheid policy of requiring blacks to carry pass books to restrict their movements. (World History Archive/Ann Ronan Collection/AGE-FOTOSTOCK)

Across the Angolan border, South African troops fought escalating conflicts with Angolan, ANC, and Cuban forces. Mounting casualties and defeat in major battles shook white South Africans' confidence in their system of domination.

Isolated politically, besieged by economic sanctions, and defeated on the battlefield, South African president Frederik W. de Klerk opened a dialogue with ANC leaders in 1989. He lifted the state of emergency imposed in 1985, legalized the ANC, and freed Mandela in February 1990. Mandela suspended the ANC's armed struggle and negotiated a 1991 agreement with de Klerk calling for universal suffrage and an end to apartheid legislation, which meant black-majority rule.

In May 1994 Mandela was elected president of South Africa by an overwhelming majority. Heading the new "government of national unity," which included de Klerk as vice president, Mandela along with the South African people set about building a multiracial democracy. The government established a Truth and Reconciliation Commission modeled on the commission impaneled in Chile to investigate abuses under Pinochet. The commission let black victims speak out, and it offered white perpetrators amnesty in return for fully confessing their crimes. Seeking to avoid white flight and to sustain the economy built through South Africa's industrialization, Mandela repudiated his Marxist beliefs and reassured domestic and foreign investors of his commitment to liberalization.

## Political Change in Africa Since 1990

Democracy's rise in South Africa was part of a trend toward elected civilian rule that swept through sub-Saharan Africa after 1990. The end of the Cold War that followed the breakup of the Soviet Union in 1990 transformed Africa's relations with Russia and the United States. Both superpowers had treated Africa as a Cold War battleground, and both had given large-scale military and financial aid to their allies to undermine rivals. Communism's collapse in Europe brought an abrupt end to Communist aid to Russia's African clients. Since the world was no longer divided between allies of the United States and of the Soviet Union, U.S. support for pro-Western dictators, no matter how corrupt or repressive, declined as well. But the decrease in support for dictators left a power vacuum in which ethnic conflicts intensified, with often-disastrous results. For instance, in the early 1990s the United States cut off decades of support for the anticommunist General Mobutu Sese Seko (1930–1997), who seized power in 1965 in Zaire (the former Belgian Congo, renamed the Democratic Republic of the Congo in 1997) and looted the country. Opposition groups toppled the dying tyrant in 1997. The Second Congo War, a civil war that began in 1998 and was followed by further conflicts, left more than 5 million dead over the next decades, making it the world's deadliest conflict since World War II.

The agreement by national independence leaders across the continent to respect colonial borders prevented one kind of violence, but resulted in another. In countries whose national boundaries had been created by colonial powers irrespective of historic divisions, political parties were often based on ethnicity and kinship. The armed forces, too, were often dominated by a single ethnic group.

At times, ethnic tensions became violent, such as the genocide carried out by ethnic Tutsis against Hutus in Burundi in 1972 and 1993, and by Hutus against Tutsi and Twa peoples in Rwanda in 1994, which left hundreds of thousands dead.

In Kenya disputes about the legitimacy of the 2007 re-election of Mwai Kibaki left hundreds dead before the National Accord and Reconciliation Act in 2008 ended the violence. A test of the alternative to preserving national boundaries came amid efforts to ease tensions that had created famine and hardship in Sudan. In 2011, 98 percent of the electorate in southern Sudan voted to break away and form a new country, South Sudan. The early promise of peace after separation was challenged by increased ethnic and political violence in South Sudan.

Amid these conflicts, political and economic reform occurred in other African nations where years of mismanagement and repression had delegitimized one-party rule. Above all, the strength of the democratic opposition rested on a growing class of educated urban Africans. Postindependence governments expanded opportunities in education, especially higher education. In Cameroon, for example, the number of students graduating from the national university jumped from 213 in 1961 to 10,000 in 1982 and 41,000 in 1992.[5] The growing middle class of educated professionals chafed at the ostentatious privilege of tiny closed elites and pressed for political reforms that would democratize social and economic opportunities. Thus after 1990 sub-Saharan Africa accompanied the global trend toward liberalization and human rights.

# Growth and Development in Asia

**How have East and South Asian nations pursued economic development, and how have political regimes shaped those efforts?**

China, Japan, and the countries that became known as the "Asian Tigers" (South Korea, Taiwan, Hong Kong, and Singapore) experienced fantastic economic growth in the last decades of the twentieth century. The Chinese Communist Party managed a transition in which it maintained tight political control amid liberalization and economic growth. Japan's economy stagnated in the 1990s and struggled to recover amid growing competition from its neighbors. In South Asia tensions between India and Pakistan persisted.

## Japan's Economic Miracle and the Emergence of the "Asian Tigers"

Japan's postwar economic recovery, like Germany's, proceeded slowly at first. But during the Korean War, the Japanese economy took off and grew with spectacular speed. Between 1950 and 1970 Japan's economic growth averaged a breathtaking 10 percent a year. By 1978 Japan had the second-largest economy in the world. In 1986 Japan's average per capita income exceeded that of the United States for the first time.

Japan's emergence as an economic superpower fascinated outsiders. Many Asians and Africans looked to Japan for the secrets of successful modernization, but some of Japan's Asian neighbors again feared Japanese exploitation. In the 1970s and 1980s some Americans and Europeans bitterly accused **"Japan, Inc."** of an unfair alliance between government and business and urged their own governments to retaliate.

In Japan's system of managed capitalism, the government protected its industry from foreign competition, decided which industries were important, and then made loans and encouraged mergers to create powerful firms in those industries.

The government rewarded large corporations and encouraged them to develop extensive industrial and financial activities. Workers were hired for life, and employees' social lives revolved around the company. Discrimination against women remained severe: their wages and job security were strikingly inferior to men's.

In the 1990s Japan's economy stagnated amid the bursting of a speculative bubble that crippled banks and led to record postwar unemployment as the country faced competition from industrializing neighbors in Asia. In the twenty-first century the return to growth remained elusive as Japan faced a decades-long crisis of deflation, a reduction of the value of goods and services that saps profits and increases debt burdens.

Japan's competition in Asia was intensified by the "Asian Tigers" — South Korea, Taiwan, Hong Kong, and Singapore — so named for their rapid economic development. In the early postwar years, South Korea and Taiwan were underdeveloped agrarian countries. They also had suffered from Japanese imperialism and from destructive civil wars with Communist foes. They pursued development through a similar series of reforms. First, land reform allowed small farmers to become competitive producers as well as consumers. Second, governments stimulated business through lending, import barriers, and control of labor. Third, the state favored specific industries it termed "national champions," helping them grow and develop export markets. These firms were often in the hands of powerful clans — known as *zaibatsu* (zy-BAHT-soo) in Japan and *chaebol* (CHEY-bowl) in South Korea — which became even more economically and politically powerful.

Finally, South Korea's Park Chung Hee maintained stability at the expense of democracy. Park, who seized power in a 1963 military coup, governed through various kinds of dictatorial rule, even deposing his own government in order to impose a more authoritarian one. Park was assassinated in 1979, and an even more authoritarian regime was established. In the late 1980s, however, young protesters mounted a series of challenges to the regime and pressured it to yield to a democratic transition. They were known as the "386 Generation," named for the processor that powered the era's personal computers.

In Singapore, Lee Kwan Yew (1923–2015), the prime minister who shepherded the island's independence from Britain in 1965 and held power until 1990, also pursued a modernization project that came at the cost of political dissent. This project

**Protesting Dictatorship in South Korea** In the 1980s, South Korean university students led protests against the country's military dictatorship. When students were killed by the police in Gwangju in 1980, widespread protests erupted. This vigil mourned some of the hundreds of protesters killed by the army during the uprising. (François Locon/Gamma-Rapho via Getty Images)

made Singapore into an affluent banking and trade center linking markets in East Asia, the Middle East, Europe, and the United States.

In 1949, after Jiang Jieshi had fled to Taiwan with his Nationalist troops and around 2 million refugees, he re-established the Republic of China (ROC) in exile. Over the next fifty years Taiwan created one of the world's most industrialized economies, becoming a leader in electronic manufacturing and design. Mainland China continued to claim Taiwan, considering it part of "One China." Hong Kong, which was returned to Chinese control by Britain in 1997, became a Special Administrative Region (SAR), as did the former Portuguese colony Macau, under a "one country, two systems" formula of partial autonomy.

## China's Economic Resurgence

Amid the Cultural Revolution of 1965–1969, Chairman Mao and the Red Guards mobilized the masses, shook up the Communist Party, and created greater social equality. But the Cultural Revolution also created chaos and a general crisis of confidence, especially in the cities. Intellectuals, technicians, and purged party officials launched a counterattack on the radicals and regained much of their influence by 1969. This shift opened the door to a limited but lasting reconciliation between China and the United States in 1972.

In the years following Mao's death in 1976, Chinese leader Deng Xiaoping (shee-ow-ping) (1904–1997) and his supporters initiated the "Four Modernizations": agriculture, industry, science and technology, and national defense. China's 800 million peasants experienced the greatest change from what Deng called China's "second revolution." Rigid collectivization had failed to provide the country with adequate food. Deng allowed peasants to farm in small family units rather than in large collectives and to "dare to be rich" by producing crops of their choice. Peasants responded enthusiastically, increasing food production by more than 50 percent by 1984.

The successful use of free markets in agriculture encouraged further experimentation. Foreign capitalists were allowed to open factories in southern China and to export their products around the world. Private enterprise was permitted in cities, where snack shops and other small businesses sprang up. China's Communist Party also drew on the business talent of "overseas" Chinese in Hong Kong and Taiwan who understood world markets and sought cheap labor. The Chinese economy grew rapidly between 1978 and 1987, and per capita income doubled in those years. Most large-scale industry remained state owned, however, and cultural change proceeded slowly.

Economic change was not accompanied by greater political openness. As Mao's health had declined, pressures for democratization had grown. After his death, the People's Congress ratified a new constitution in 1978 that granted "Four Big Rights" and that protected freedom of speech and political debate. This opening gave rise to popular political mobilization and debate, particularly in the form of the Democracy Wall Movement, in which citizens, first in Beijing and later in other cities, put up posters calling for political reforms. But the movement was suppressed in 1980. A new constitution enacted in 1982 removed references to the Four Big Rights, emphasizing instead economic development and reinforcing the political primacy of the Communist Party.

As the worldwide movement for political liberalization gained momentum, the government of China maintained restrictions on demonstrations and slowed economic reform. Inflation soared to more than 30 percent a year. The economic reversal, the continued lack of political freedom, and the conviction that Chinese society was becoming more corrupt led idealistic university students to spearhead demonstrations in 1989.

More than a million people streamed into Beijing's central **Tiananmen Square** in support of the students' demands. The government declared martial law and ordered the army to clear the students. Masses of courageous citizens blocked the soldiers' entry into the city for two weeks, but in the early hours of June 4, 1989, tanks rolled into Tiananmen Square. At least seven hundred students died as a wave of repression, arrests, and executions descended on China. As communism fell in eastern Europe and the Soviet Union broke apart, China's rulers felt vindicated. They believed their action had preserved Communist power, prevented chaos, and demonstrated the limits of reform. People in China were not alone in pressing for democratization—popular protest met with repression in other Communist or military regimes.

China became a socialist market economy, ruled by the Communist Party but with a mix of state and private enterprise. In 2001 China joined the World Trade Organization, completing its immersion in the liberal global economy. From 1978, when Deng Xiaoping began economic reforms, through 2019, the Chinese economy grew at an average annual rate of over 9 percent, and foreign trade at an average of 14 percent. Average per capita income in China doubled every ten years, and in March 2011 China replaced Japan as the world's second-largest economy, surpassed only by the United States. As China's economy became one of the world's leading economic engines, its growth fueled global trade of commodities imported to China and manufactured goods exported around the world.

## Development Versus Democracy in India and Pakistan

Jawaharlal Nehru's daughter, Indira Gandhi (no relation to Mohandas Gandhi) (1917–1984), became prime minister of India in 1966 and dominated Indian political life for a generation. In 1975, amid economic disruptions following the oil embargo and growing political opposition, she subverted parliamentary democracy and proclaimed a state of emergency. Gandhi applied her expanded powers by quelling labor unrest, and jailing political opponents. She also initiated a mass sterilization campaign to reduce population growth. More than 7 million men were forcibly sterilized in 1976. Many believed that Gandhi's emergency measures marked the end of liberal democracy, but in 1977 Gandhi called for free elections. She suffered a spectacular electoral defeat, but would later return to office.

Separatist ethnic nationalism plagued Indira Gandhi's last years in office. India remained a patchwork of religions, languages, and peoples, always threatening to further divide the country along ethnic or religious lines. Most notable were the 15 million Sikhs of the Punjab in northern India (see Map 31.2), with their own religion, distinctive culture, and aspirations for greater autonomy for the Punjab. By 1984 some Sikh radicals fought for independence. Gandhi cracked down and was assassinated by Sikhs in retaliation. Violence followed as Hindu mobs slaughtered over a thousand Sikhs throughout India.

One of Indira Gandhi's sons, Rajiv Gandhi, was elected prime minister in 1984. Rajiv Gandhi departed from his mother's and the Congress Party's socialism and prepared the way for Finance Minister Manmohan Singh to introduce liberal market reforms that brought new investment and Western technology and that led to accelerating economic growth and deepening social inequalities.

Though the Congress Party held power in India almost continuously after 1947, in the 1990s Hindu nationalists increasingly challenged the party's grip on power. These nationalists argued that India was based, above all, on Hindu culture and religion and that these values had been undermined by the Western secularism of the Congress Party and the influence of India's Muslims. The Hindu nationalist party, known as the BJP, gained power in 1998. The new government immediately tested nuclear devices, asserting its vision of a militant Hindu nationalism. Promising to accelerate economic growth, BJP candidate Narendra Modi became prime minister after a sweeping electoral victory in 2014. Under Modi, economic change has been slow but nationalist policies have targeted religious minorities, such as the Muslim population of Kashmir, which in 2019 lost protections established in the 1950 constitution.

When Pakistan announced in 1998 that it had developed nuclear weapons, relations between Pakistan and India worsened. In 2001 the two nuclear powers seemed poised for conflict until intense diplomatic pressure brought them back from the brink of nuclear war. In 2005 both countries agreed to open business and trade relations and to try to negotiate a peaceful solution to the Kashmir dispute (see "Independence in India, Pakistan, and Bangladesh" in Chapter 31). Tensions again increased in 2008 when a Pakistan-based terrorist organization carried out a widely televised shooting and bombing attack across Mumbai, India's largest city, killing 164 and wounding over 300.

In the decades following the separation of Bangladesh, Pakistan alternated between civilian and military rule. General Muhammad Zia-ul-Haq, who ruled from 1977 to 1988, drew Pakistan into a close alliance with the United States that netted military and economic assistance. Relations with the United States chilled as Pakistan pursued its nuclear weapons program. In Afghanistan, west of Pakistan, Soviet military occupation lasted from 1979 to 1989. Civil war followed the Soviet withdrawal, and in 1996 a fundamentalist Muslim group, the Taliban, seized power. The Taliban's leadership allowed the terrorist organization al-Qaeda to base its operations in Afghanistan. It was from Afghanistan that al-Qaeda conducted acts of terrorism like the attack on the U.S. World Trade Center and the Pentagon in 2001. Following that attack, the United States invaded Afghanistan, driving the Taliban from power.

When the United States invaded Afghanistan in 2001, Pakistani dictator General Pervez Musharraf (b. 1943) renewed the alliance with the United States, and Pakistan received billions of dollars in U.S. military aid. But U.S. combat against the Taliban and al-Qaeda drove militants into regions of northwest Pakistan, where they undermined the government's already tenuous control. Cooperation between Pakistan and the United States in the war was strained when U.S. Special Forces killed al-Qaeda leader Osama bin Laden on May 1, 2011. He had been hiding for years in a compound several hundred yards away from a major Pakistani military academy outside of the capital, Islamabad.

In 2007 Musharraf attempted to reshape the country's Supreme Court by replacing the chief justice with one of his close allies, bringing about calls for his impeachment. Benazir Bhutto (1953–2007), who became the first female elected head of a Muslim state when she was elected prime minister in 1988, returned from exile to challenge Musharraf's increasingly repressive military rule. She was assassinated while campaigning. After being defeated at the polls in 2008, Musharraf resigned and went into exile in London.

# The End of the Cold War

## How did decolonization and the end of the Cold War change Europe?

In the late 1960s and early 1970s the United States and the Soviet Union pursued a relaxation of Cold War tensions that became known as **détente** (day-TAHNT). But détente stalled when Brezhnev's Soviet Union invaded Afghanistan to save an unpopular Marxist regime.

The United States reacted with alarm to the spread of Soviet influence. Ronald Reagan (U.S. pres. 1981–1989) sought to halt the spread of Soviet influence, much like predecessors John F. Kennedy and Harry Truman had. But as Reagan and conservative allies in Europe rekindled the Cold War, the Soviet Union began reforms that culminated in the release of control over eastern Europe and the dismantling of the Soviet Union and its Communist state.

## The Limits of Reform in the Soviet Union and Eastern Europe

After their 1968 intervention in Czechoslovakia, Soviet leaders worked to restore order and stability. Free expression and open protest disappeared throughout their satellite nations.

A rising standard of living helped ensure stability as well. Beneath this appearance of stability, however, the Soviet Union underwent a social revolution. The urban population expanded rapidly. The number of highly trained professionals increased fourfold between 1960 and 1985. The education that created expertise helped foster the growth of Soviet public opinion about questions ranging from pollution to urban transportation.

When Mikhail Gorbachev (b. 1931) became premier in 1985, he set out to reform the Soviet system with policies he called democratic socialism. The first set of reforms was intended to transform and restructure the economy. **Perestroika** permitted freer prices, more autonomy for state enterprises, and the establishment of some profit-seeking private cooperatives. A more far-reaching campaign of openness, or **glasnost**, introduced in 1985, allowed significant new space for public debate by increasing transparency and allowing a more open media.

Democratization under Gorbachev led to the first free elections in the Soviet Union since 1917. Gorbachev and the party remained in control, but an independent minority was elected in 1989 to a revitalized Congress of People's Deputies. Democratization encouraged demands for greater autonomy from non-Russian minorities, especially in the Baltic region and in the Caucasus.

Finally, Gorbachev brought "new political thinking" to foreign affairs. He withdrew Soviet troops from Afghanistan in 1989 and sought to reduce Cold War tensions. Gorbachev pledged to respect the political choices of eastern Europe's peoples. Soon after, a wave of peaceful revolutions swept across eastern Europe, overturning Communist regimes.

**Albanians**
**Bulgarians**
**Croatians**
**Hungarians**
**Macedonians**
**Montenegrins**

**Bosnians or
Sandzak Muslims**
**Serbs**
**Slovenes**
**No majority present**

**Former Yugoslavia**
**Yugoslavia in 1991**
**1991** Date of independence
**Bosnia-Herzegovina**
Autonomous region
boundaries
Federation of Bosnia and
Herzegovina, 1994
**Bosnian Serb Republic, 1992**

AUSTRIA

SLOVAKIA

Vienna

Bratislava

*Danube R.*

Budapest

HUNGARY

ROMANIA

Ljubljana

**SLOVENIA**
1991

Zagreb

**CROATIA**
1991

VOJVODINA

Novi Sad

Belgrade

**SERBIA**
2006

Banja
Luka

**BOSNIA**
1992

Sarajevo

**HERZEGOVINA**

MONTENEGRO
2006

Podgorica

KOSOVO
2008

Priština

MACEDONIA
1991

Skopje

Tiranë

ALBANIA

BULGARIA

Sofia

GREECE

TURKEY

*Adriatic Sea*

ITALY

Rome

25°E

20°E

15°E

45°N

0        50        100 miles

0    50    100 kilometers

N  E  S  W

Poland led the way. In August 1980 strikes grew into a working-class revolt. Led by Lech Wałęsa (lehk vah-LEHN-suh) (b. 1943), workers organized the independent trade union **Solidarity**. Communist leaders responded by imposing martial law in December 1981 and arresting Solidarity's leaders. By 1988 labor unrest and inflation had brought Poland to the brink of economic collapse, pressuring Poland's Communist Party leaders into legalizing Solidarity and allowing free elections in 1989 for some seats in the Polish parliament. Solidarity won every contested seat. A month later Solidarity member Tadeusz Mazowiecki (mah-zoh-VYEHT-skee) (1927–2013) was sworn in as the first noncommunist prime minister in eastern Europe in a generation.

Czechoslovakia and Romania reflected different paths to reform: Czechoslovakia's Velvet Revolution led to the peaceful ouster of Communist leaders amid massive street protests led by students and intellectuals. But in Romania the revolution was violent. Communist dictator Nicolae Ceauşescu (chow-SHEHS-koo) (1918–1989) unleashed his security forces on protesters, sparking an armed uprising. After Ceauşescu's forces were defeated, he and his wife were captured and executed by a military court.

Amid the transformation of eastern Europe, Germany reunified. Reunification began with the millions of East Germans who flooded across their country's borders to reach West Germany (see Map 31.1). As neighboring countries liberalized, East Germany's leaders gave in to public pressure and opened the Berlin Wall in November 1989, before being swept aside. An "Alliance for Germany" won general elections and negotiated an economic union with West Germany.

West German chancellor Helmut Kohl reassured American, Soviet, and European leaders that a reunified Germany would have peaceful intentions. Within the year, East and West Germany merged into a single nation under West Germany's constitution and laws.

Many people in eastern Europe faced wrenching hardships in the process of liberalization as economies were restructured and the state infrastructure of social welfare crumbled. But the greatest postcommunist tragedy was in Yugoslavia, whose federation of republics and regions had been held together under Josip Tito's Communist rule. After Tito's death in 1980, rising territorial and ethnic tensions were intensified by economic decline.

After Yugoslavia split into seven separate countries, Serbian president Slobodan Milošević (SLOH-buh-dayn muh-LOH-suh-vihch) (1941–2006) attempted to grab land from other republics to create a "greater Serbia." His ambitions led to civil wars that between 1991 and 2001 engulfed Kosovo, Slovenia, Croatia, and Bosnia-Herzegovina (Map 32.2). The ensuing "ethnic cleansing" killed thousands of civilians in an attempt to change the ethnic compositions of regions, and with them, borders. In 1999 Serbian aggression prompted NATO air strikes, led by the United States, against the Serbian capital of Belgrade as well as against Serbian military forces until Milošević relented. Milošević was voted out of office in 2000. The new Serbian

< **MAP 32.2**  **The Breakup of Yugoslavia**

Yugoslavia had the most ethnically diverse population in eastern Europe. The Republic of Croatia had substantial Serbian and Muslim minorities, and Bosnia-Herzegovina had large Muslim, Serbian, and Croatian populations, none of which had a majority. In June 1991 Serbia's brutal effort to seize territory and unite all Serbs in a single state brought a tragic civil war to the region.

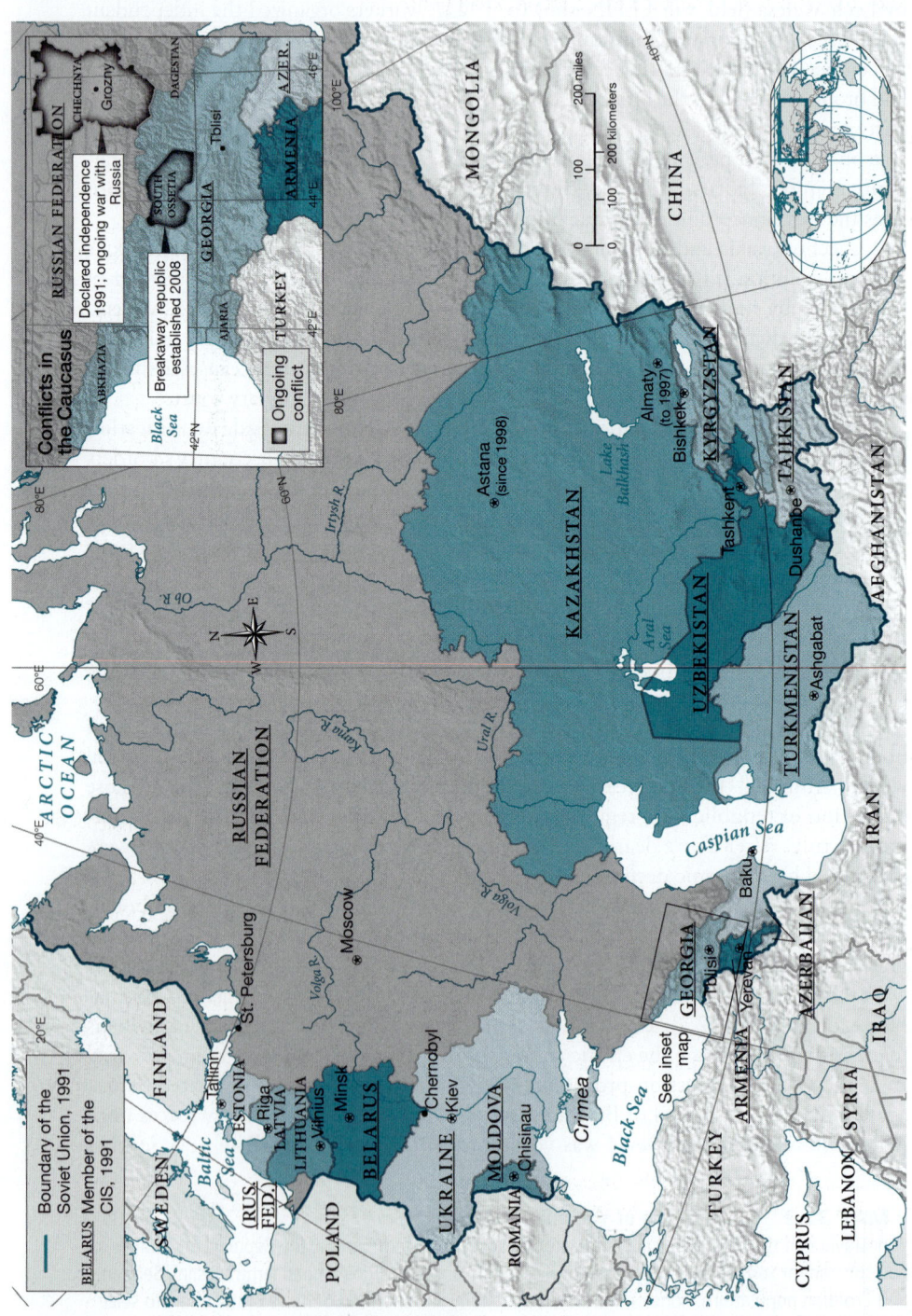

government extradited him to a United Nations war crimes tribunal in the Nether-lands to stand trial, where he was charged with genocide.

## Recasting Russia Without Communism

In February 1990 the Soviet Communist Party was defeated in local elections throughout the country, eroding Gorbachev's power and strengthening his rival, Boris Yeltsin (1931–2007), the former mayor of Moscow. As leader of the Russian parliament, Yeltsin announced that Russia would declare its independence from the Soviet Union. In 1991, hardliners committed to preserving a Communist Soviet Union attempted a coup against Gorbachev. Their effort failed, and Yeltsin became a popular hero for publicly resisting the coup.

In the aftermath of the attempted takeover, an anticommunist backlash swept the Soviet Union. Yeltsin and his liberal allies declared Russia independent and withdrew from the Soviet Union. All the other Soviet republics followed suit. Gorbachev agreed to their independence, and the Soviet Union ceased to exist on December 25, 1991 (Map 32.3). The newly independent post-Soviet republics faced challenges, including the need to quickly build new political systems and the urgency of economic reforms meant to open socialist economies to free-market principles. Liberal reforms doomed much of Russia's industry, and its economy depended increasingly on oil and natural gas exports. Despite its weakened economy, Russia retained the world's second-largest nuclear arsenal, as well as a powerful vote (and veto) in the United Nations Security Council.

As Yeltsin presided over newly independent Russia, he opted for breakneck lib-eralization. This shock treatment, which followed methods similar to radical free-market policies in Chile and other parts of Latin America, freed prices on most goods and launched a rapid privatization of industry. Prices soared and production col-lapsed. State industrial monopolies became private monopolies that cut production and raised prices in order to maximize profits. The quality of public services and health care declined to the point that the average male life expectancy dropped from sixty-nine years in 1991 to fifty-nine years in 2007.

The election of Yeltsin's handpicked successor, President Vladimir Putin (b. 1952), in 2000 ushered in a new era of "managed democracy." Putin's stress on national-ism, public order, and economic reform was popular, even as he became increasingly authoritarian. Significant restrictions were placed on media freedoms, regional elections were abolished, and the distinction between judicial and executive authority collapsed. Putin consolidated the power and authority of the state around himself and his closest advisers, closing off the development of democratic pluralism and an independent legal system in Russia.

**< MAP 32.3   Russia and the Successor States**
After the attempt in August 1991 to depose Gorbachev failed, an anticommunist revolution swept the Soviet Union. Led by Russia and Boris Yeltsin, the republics that formed the Soviet Union declared their sovereignty and independence. Eleven of the fifteen republics then formed a loose confederation called the Commonwealth of Independent States, but the integrated economy of the Soviet Union dissolved into separate national economies, each with its own goals and policies.

Putin's illiberal tendencies were also evident in his brutal military campaign against Chechnya (CHEHCH-nyuh), a tiny republic of 1 million Muslims in southern Russia (see Map 32.3, inset) that in 1991 declared its independence. Up to two hundred thousand Chechen civilians are estimated to have been killed between 1994 and 2011. Many more became refugees. Chechen resistance to Russian domination continued, often in the form of attacks such as a suicide bombing at Moscow's airport in 2011 that killed scores of travelers.

In the aftermath of the dissolution of the Soviet Union, political and ethnic divisions threatened peace and stability among the post-Soviet republics. In 2014 pro-Western protesters in Ukraine toppled a president who refused to sign agreements with the European Union. In the aftermath of the uprising, Russian forces occupied the Ukrainian province of Crimea along the Black Sea and backed secessionist movements in ethnically Russian regions of Ukraine. Russia's seizure of Crimea undermined the terms under which the Soviet Union had dissolved into separate republics, provoking unease among other new states such as the Baltic republics.

## Integration and Reform in Europe

Germany and France continued to lead the push for European unity, building on integration efforts in the 1940s and 1950s established through NATO and the Common Market. French president François Mitterrand (1916–1996) and German chancellor Helmut Kohl (b. 1930) pursued the economic integration of European Community members, and in 1993 the European Community rechristened itself the **European Union (EU)**. The European Union, a political and economic body, allowed for the free movement of people and goods among twelve member countries; created a common currency, the euro, introduced in 2002; and formed a European Parliament that established regulations and pooled infrastructure and education investments.

The creation of the European Union resolved diverse challenges for different parts of Europe. It created a logic for a unified Germany integrated with Europe. For eastern Europe it provided a blueprint for reforming economies and institutions in countries transitioning away from Soviet models. For western Europe it created an economic alternative after the loss of colonies in Africa and Asia. For five centuries overseas empires had not only provided the engine for economic development at home but also shaped international relations as well as intellectual currents ranging from abolitionism to scientific racism and even Marxism. Empires had provided raw materials and markets that fueled industrialization. For different reasons but for the first time since before the French Revolution, almost all of Europe now followed the same general political model.

European leaders embraced a neoliberal, free-market vision of capitalism. The most radical economic changes had been implemented in the 1980s by Margaret Thatcher (1925–2013) in Britain, who drew inspiration from Pinochet's Chile. Other governments also introduced austerity measures to slow the growth of public spending and the welfare state. Many individuals suffered under the impact of these reductions in public spending and social welfare. Harder times meant that more women entered or remained in the workforce after they married.

The success of the euro encouraged the EU to accelerate plans for an ambitious enlargement to the east. On May 1, 2004, the EU started admitting eastern

European countries and by 2009 had adopted a common constitution. In 2017 the European Union had twenty-eight member states, including most of eastern Europe, and a population of nearly 500 million. As it grew, the EU faced questions about the limits of its expansion and the meaning of European unity and identity. If the EU expanded to include eastern Europe and some former Soviet republics, how could Turkey, a secular nation with a Muslim majority, be denied its long-standing request for membership? Turkey had been a member of NATO since 1952 and had labored to meet membership requirements (Map 32.4).

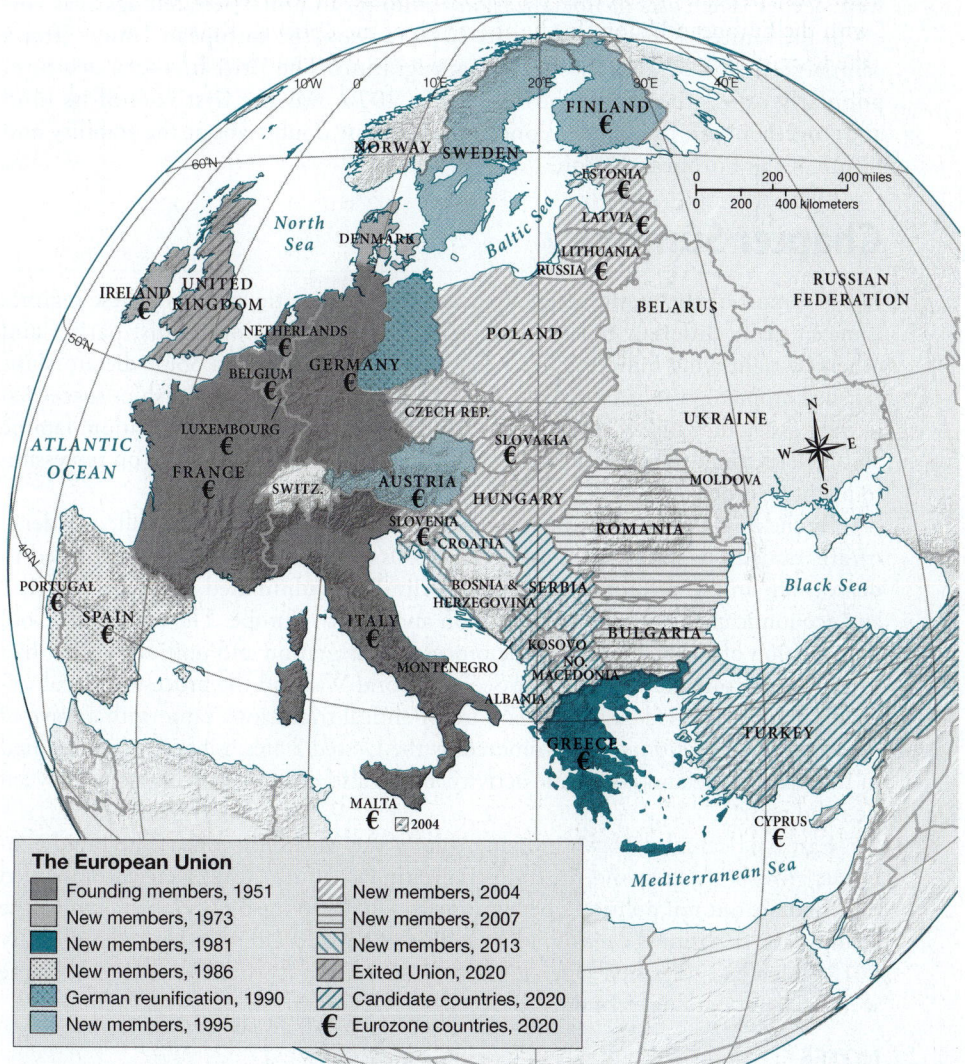

**MAP 32.4   The European Union, 2020**
No longer divided by ideological competition and the Cold War, much of today's Europe banded together in a European Union that has become strained by economic and migration pressures.

In 2008, economic crisis tested the European Union. Countries that had adopted the euro currency had to meet stringent fiscal standards and imposed deep budget cuts. The resulting reductions in health care and social benefits hit ordinary citizens hard. National governments could no longer expand their own monetary supplies to promote recovery, and governments were forced to slash budgets to meet debt obligations. Austerity brought ruinous economic conditions that crippled Greece, prompting its near-departure from the Eurozone in 2015.

The consequences of liberalization in Europe resembled the consequences elsewhere: economic growth was greater, but economic hardship and dislocation were deeper. The costs of liberalization to European unity were felt again as voters in the United Kingdom chose in 2016 to leave the European Union after a campaign fueled by anxieties about immigration. The British voters' decision, popularly called Brexit and carried out in 2020, was the first vote of its kind and, together with the Greek economic crisis, cast doubts about the stability and future of the European Union.

## Chapter Summary

In 1976 most of the world was governed by undemocratic regimes. These regimes came in many different types: some were controlled by Communist parties and others by right-wing military officers loyal to the United States. Some dictatorships pursued utopian projects to remake nations. Even when such dictatorships succeeded in their goals, they did so at enormous costs, measured in debt and inflation, famine and malnutrition, the tattering of public institutions, and the reliance on repression to maintain order.

By the mid-1980s dictatorships around the world had begun to fall, and democratic transitions followed. During the 1980s most of Latin America returned to democracy, and in 1989 the fall of the Berlin Wall culminated a wave of political and economic change in the Soviet Union and eastern Europe. The end of the Cold War division of Europe accelerated a process of integration and unification that had its roots in reconstruction after the Second World War and the process of decolonization that dismantled European empires. Political transitions came with a wave of economic liberalization, often promoted by the United States. Liberalization resulted in increased trade and economic activity, but it also created growing gaps between rich and poor.

East Asia came to play a growing role in the world economy. The rapid economic growth of Japan and the industrialization of South Korea were accompanied by economic but not political liberalization in China. In the 1970s Japan became the second-largest national economy by GDP in the world after the United States. By 2010 China had surpassed Japan amid projections that it would soon emerge as the world's largest national economy.

## NOTES

1. *Jornal do Brasil*, March 14, 1976, quoted in Roberto Jorge Ramalho Cavalcanti, "O presidente Ernesto Geisel e o estabelecimento do retorno à democracia ao Brasil pós Regime Militar de 1964," *Governo e Politica*, November 7, 2010, https://www.webartigos.com/artigos/artigo-o-presidente-ernesto-geisel-e-o-estabelecimento-do-retorno-a-democracia-ao-brasil-pos-regime-militar-de-1964/51497/.

2. CIA Director Richard Helms, notes on Nixon's plan for Chile, September 15, 1970, accessed October 14, 2012, http://www2 .gwu.edu/~nsarchiv/NSAEBB/NSAEBB8/docs/doc26.pdf.

3. Audre Lorde, *Sister Outsider: Essays and Speeches* (Trumansburg, N.Y.: Crossing Press, 1984), p. 112.

4. Report of the World Conference of the International Women's Year, Mexico City, 1975, https://digitallibrary .un.org/record/586225.

5. D. Birmingham and P. Martin, eds., *History of Central Africa: The Contemporary Years Since 1960* (London: Routledge, 1998), p. 59.

## MAKE CONNECTIONS  LOOK AHEAD

The experiences of people living under authoritarian regimes varied greatly. Many supported the regimes from which they drew privileges or found a reassuring sense of order. Others avoided political questions and stayed out of trouble. But even they were affected by authoritarianism: censorship and propaganda meant that official pronouncements lacked credibility, so rumors, some true and others wild, became their basic currency of exchange.

Many, however, resisted the regimes. For some, a closed political system meant that the only tools available were armed resistance. Guerrilla movements against authoritarian regimes were common, though the imbalance in their resources meant they mostly met with violent ends at the hands of security forces. Another form of resistance proved more effective: nonviolent, and ostensibly nonpolitical, resistance was harder for regimes to repress. Mothers asking for the whereabouts of missing children or quilting the scenes of their grief in Argentina and Chile, or workers organizing an independent union in Poland, found ways to challenge their regimes.

The most successful resistance was often opposition that was not explicitly ideological, such as the defense of human rights, or the establishment of the rule of law that would restrict a regime's arbitrary power. These pressures had a similar effect when applied to right-wing or socialist dictatorships alike: they were liberalizing. As dictatorships in Latin America, East Asia, and eastern Europe moved toward multiparty democracy, and as the Soviet bloc disintegrated, those countries shared a historical moment in which liberal economic and political reforms swept the world.

## Chapter 32 Review

### IDENTIFY KEY TERMS

**Identify and explain the significance of each item below.**

Organization of the Petroleum
    Exporting Countries (OPEC) (p. 855)
petrodollars (p. 856)
neoliberalism (p. 856)
Washington Consensus (p. 856)
intifada (p. 858)
death squads (p. 862)
junta (p. 863)
second-wave feminism (p. 866)
apartheid (p. 870)

African National Congress (ANC)
    (p. 870)
"Japan, Inc." (p. 872)
Tiananmen Square (p. 875)
détente (p. 877)
perestroika (p. 877)
glasnost (p. 877)
Solidarity (p. 879)
European Union (EU) (p. 882)

### REVIEW THE MAIN IDEAS

**Answer the focus questions from each section of the chapter.**

1. What were the short-term and long-term consequences of the OPEC oil embargo? (p. 855)
2. What effect did the Cold War and the debt crisis have on Latin America? (p. 861)
3. How did social movements advocate for human rights? (p. 865)
4. How did white-minority rule end in southern Africa? (p. 868)
5. How have East and South Asian nations pursued economic development, and how have political regimes shaped those efforts? (p. 872)
6. How did decolonization and the end of the Cold War change Europe? (p. 877)

### MAKE COMPARISONS AND CONNECTIONS

**Analyze the larger developments and continuities within and across chapters.**

1. How did transitions to democracy and free markets around the world draw on earlier ideologies (Chapters 22, 24, 29)?
2. How did the impact of oil shocks resemble previous economic crises?
3. What similarities do you see among social movements that advocated for democracy and for majority rule around the world?
4. How did historical factors contribute to the formation of the European Union? How have recent events challenged European unity?

## CHRONOLOGY

**1973**        • Yom Kippur War / Ramadan War triggers OPEC oil embargo

**1975**        • Independence from Portugal of Angola and Mozambique ends European
                  colonial rule in Africa

**1978**        • Deng Xiaoping initiates economic reforms in China

**1979**        • Islamic revolution in Iran leads to second oil shock

**1980**        • Segregationist white-minority government in Rhodesia replaced by majority
                  rule; country renamed Zimbabwe

**1980–1988**   • Iran-Iraq War

**1982**        • Falklands (or Malvinas) War leads to collapse of Argentina's military junta

**1982**        • Mexico defaults on loan payments, triggering debt crisis

**1983–1991**   • Transitions to democracy in the Soviet Union, eastern Europe, Latin America,
                  South America

**1985**        • Glasnost leads to greater freedom of speech and expression in the
                  Soviet Union

**1987**        • Palestinian intifada

**1988**        • The "NO" vote wins the Chilean plebiscite ousting dictator Pinochet

**1989**        • Tiananmen Square protests in China

**1990–1991**   • Persian Gulf War

**1991**        • Congress Party in India embraces Western capitalist reforms

**1991–2001**   • Civil war in Yugoslavia

**1993**        • Formation of the European Union

**1997**        • First civilian-to-civilian transfer of political power in Nigeria

**2003–2011**   • Second Persian Gulf War

**2007**        • Hamas seizes control of Gaza Strip from Palestinian Authority

**2009–2014**   • Popular uprisings and protests across the Middle East

# 33

# The Contemporary World in Historical Perspective

**THE APPROACHES TO THE HISTORY OF WORLD SOCIETIES IN THE** preceding chapters give us critical tools for interpreting the contemporary world. Through this lens, we can understand contemporary events and debates as rooted in history, and we can interpret them using the same approaches we use to study the past.

Since the end of the Cold War, many nations have undergone transitions from dictatorship to democracy, and a growing number of nations have pursued free trade. The intensified movement of people, goods, and capital has produced uneven outcomes and triggered nationalist reactions in many parts of the world. In other regions, political conflicts remain and poverty and marginalization continue to be widespread.

The contemporary world is also facing a threat in the form of global warming. Throughout the history of world societies, humans have had the ability to shape, adapt, and transform the problems they confront. This ability is being tested again by the acceleration of global warming and its impacts on world societies.

# The Neoliberal World and Its Limits

## What tensions have resulted from the rise of neoliberalism?

At the turn of the twenty-first century, neoliberalism had become the dominant political and economic philosophy. Throughout the world, societies transitioned to free-market economics and multiparty electoral systems. This was especially true among countries of the former Soviet bloc transitioning from socialism, but it was also the case of countries in Africa and Latin America emerging from dictatorship and countries in East Asia undergoing rapid economic growth.

But neoliberalism also meant changes for western Europe and the United States, even though they already engaged in liberal practices. In these countries, business regulations and social welfare practices that had protected communities gave way to the neoliberal logic of free markets and public policies that would sustain them: the promotion of economic growth became the state's primary means of generating social welfare. Long championed by political parties on the right, this approach also became embraced by parties on the left, which gradually moved away from universal public education, labor rights, or redistributive tax policies.

But the costs of neoliberalism became increasingly apparent. Though neoliberal policies increased economic growth, that growth was unevenly distributed and produced rapidly growing social inequalities. The possibilities for social mobility also decreased. A diagnosis made about liberalism a half century earlier by dependency theorists applied well to this pattern. These theorists argued that trade between wealthy developed countries and poorer countries was an unequal exchange that further increased the wealth of developed countries relative to poorer countries, trapping the latter in underdevelopment. Neoliberal economies were also vulnerable to sharp economic shifts such as the 2008 Great Recession, which left 34 million people unemployed worldwide.[1]

The interconnectedness of people and places in the age of neoliberalism presented other risks, such as the rapid spread of epidemic diseases like H1N1 in 2011. In 2020, within six months of its first human infection, the COVID-19 pandemic led to the shutting of schools and businesses worldwide. These economic effects were compounded by the disruption of globalized supply chains. But the main effects were on people's lives and health, and felt worst in large urban centers where it transmitted easily. Neoliberal policies that weakened social safety nets and increased social inequalities deepened the pandemic's toll.

Another limitation was that neoliberalism treated people as economic individuals, especially as consumers. Though this concept produced a kind of equality, it did little to overcome gender, ethnic, or racial marginalization or systemic challenges that affected whole communities, such as gang violence in Central America or environmental degradation in the oil-producing Niger Delta. As a result, the rise of neoliberalism has been accompanied by evolving social activism.

Finally, neoliberalism created a common economic and political approach after the end of the Cold War. But this did not reduce regional conflicts. And neoliberalism has been met by an increasingly conservative religious reaction. Whereas earlier religious opposition to secular modernizing had mainly occurred in national contexts, by the twenty-first century it too was increasingly global in its goals and actions.

## Al-Qaeda and Afghanistan

In the Middle East and Central Asia, conflicts that had involved the superpowers continued beyond the Cold War. The 1979 Soviet invasion of Afghanistan, as well as the Iranian revolution, which was followed by the Iran-Iraq War, led to enduring political conflict.

In Afghanistan rebel groups supported by the United States fought the Soviet armed forces occupying the country and forced a humiliating Soviet withdrawal in 1989. In 1996, after years of civil war, a puritanical Islamic movement called the Taliban took power. The Taliban pursued a radical religious transformation of Afghan society, in particular by imposing harsh restrictions on women. The Taliban government also provided safe haven in Afghanistan for a terrorist organization called al-Qaeda (al-KIGH-duh). In the 1990s, led by Osama bin Laden (1957–2011), al-Qaeda attacked U.S. diplomatic and military targets in Africa and the Middle East.

On September 11, 2001, al-Qaeda militants hijacked four passenger planes in the United States. They flew two of them into the World Trade Center buildings in New York City and a third into the Pentagon in Washington, D.C. A fourth, believed to be targeting the White House or the U.S. Capitol, crashed into a field in Pennsylvania. These terrorist attacks killed almost three thousand people. Though the U.S. government had repeatedly attacked al-Qaeda in the 1990s, it had failed to destroy it. Now the U.S. government demanded that the Taliban government in Afghanistan surrender the al-Qaeda leadership it hosted. When the Taliban refused, the United States formed a military coalition including NATO members as well as Russia, Pakistan, and rebel groups in Afghanistan. The coalition mounted an invasion, deposed the Taliban, and pursued al-Qaeda.

After the U.S.-led coalition deposed the Taliban in 2001 and installed a new government, it faced a protracted guerrilla war against Taliban forces that controlled rural areas. The Taliban drew upon Afghanistan's long experience in resisting foreign military incursions such as the Soviet and earlier British invasions. The conflict in Afghanistan spread to Pakistan, where some members of al-Qaeda found refuge, and acts of terrorism increased around the world in the years following the invasion of Afghanistan.

The United States and allied governments devastated al-Qaeda's leadership, but groups in the Middle East and Africa continued to act under al-Qaeda's name. These actions included bombings in 2004 and 2005 that killed 191 in Madrid and 56 in London. A suicide bomber who may have had links to al-Qaeda has also been blamed for the 2007 assassination of Pakistani presidential candidate Benazir Bhutto.

In the decade following the conclusion of the Persian Gulf War (1990–1991), Iraq faced international economic sanctions along with constant political and military pressure from the United States to surrender its chemical and biological weapons stockpiles. After the U.S. invasion of Afghanistan, U.S. president George W. Bush accused Iraq of rebuilding its nuclear, chemical, and biological weapons programs. The U.S. government also falsely implied that there were connections between Iraq and al-Qaeda. In 2002 UN inspectors determined that Iraq's chemical and biological weapons had been destroyed. Most countries argued for continued weapons monitoring, and France threatened to veto any resolution authorizing an invasion of Iraq. Rather than risk this veto, the United States and Britain claimed that earlier Security Council resolutions provided sufficient authorization and invaded Iraq in 2003.

A coalition of U.S.-led forces defeated the Iraqi military, and in the power vacuum that ensued, armed groups representing all three main factions in Iraq—Sunni Muslims, Shi'ite Muslims, and Kurds—carried out daily attacks on Iraqi military and police, government officials, religious leaders, and civilians. Estimates of Iraqi deaths since the beginning of the war in 2003 and the U.S. withdrawal in 2011 ranged from 100,000 to over 1 million. Though the U.S. military occupation ended in 2011, the violence continued. Though the connection between al-Qaeda and the government of Saddam Hussein implied by President Bush did not exist, the violent environment of postwar Iraq became a place where militant groups that identified with al-Qaeda proliferated.

The most powerful of these groups called itself the Islamic State (commonly known as ISIS). ISIS took advantage of the political vacuum created by the U.S. invasion of Iraq and the Syrian civil war to establish a radical Islamic regime that briefly spanned regions of the two countries and controlled several major cities. It used a sophisticated Internet footprint to recruit disaffected youth around the world to join its ranks, prompting attacks in 2015 and 2016 by individuals claiming to act in ISIS's name in the United States, France, Turkey, and Bangladesh.

## Conflict and Change in the Middle East

When he initiated the Iraq War, U.S. president George W. Bush argued that the war would create a wave of democratic change across the Middle East. Years later, U.S. president Barack Obama, addressing students in Egypt, called for democratic change for a region that had been ruled by dictators ever since independence. Both U.S. presidents spoke to a historic current of dissent against authoritarian rule. But when opposition groups challenged their regimes, the cultural, ideological, and political differences between them proved to be pronounced. Religious conservatives, students, professional classes, the armed forces, and ethnic minorities often found themselves at odds with one another.

In December 2010 demonstrations broke out in Tunisia against the twenty-three-year authoritarian rule of President Zine Ben Ali, leading to his downfall in January 2011. This populist revolt soon spread across North Africa and the Middle East, including to the streets of Cairo and other cities in Egypt as Egyptians of all ages united in revolt against Mubarak's dictatorial rule. After three weeks of growing demonstrations, Mubarak stepped down as president in 2011 and was arrested soon after. Libya also witnessed an uprising against its dictatorial leader of forty-two years, Muammar Gaddafi. Gaddafi was deposed and killed amid European and U.S. air strikes. That same year, a lengthy and intense civil war erupted in Syria, pitting opponents of ruler Bashar al-Assad against an army equipped and trained to oppose Israel. Russia, Iran, the United States, and Turkey became involved in the Syrian conflict.

The "Arab Spring" uprisings that swept the Middle East shook a political order that had rested in the hands of the armed forces and pursued secular, nationalist objectives. The deposed leaders were the ideological descendants of Nasser, though

**Arab Spring Movements**
A lawyer faces security forces in Tunisia, where protesters challenged the authoritarian regime of Zine Ben Ali, beginning a wave of protests known as the "Arab Spring." (Fethi Belaid/AFP via Getty Images)

their regimes had come to rely more on force than on modernizing social reform. The reaction against these regimes was often religious and culturally conservative. Among the countries where regimes were brought down by Arab Spring protesters, Egypt alone reversed course, returning to rule by the secular armed forces under the leadership of General Abdel Fattah el-Sisi.

In 2013, Iran experienced protests that echoed the Arab Spring. "Green revolution" protesters not only chafed at the cultural, political, and economic restrictions that many Iranians faced, but also showed distaste for the confrontational foreign policy through which the regime engaged in brinkmanship over developing nuclear weapons. Opposition groups came together to support the election of Hassan Rouhani, a centrist cleric who promised civil rights reforms. In 2015 Rouhani reached an agreement with a group of world powers led by the United States to freeze the country's nuclear program in return for the lifting of economic sanctions that had sapped Iran's economy.

## Right-Wing Nationalism Re-emerges

The consequences of the war in Iraq were felt throughout the Middle East, sharpening political, religious, and ideological tensions. But the conflict also created a crisis of confidence in the United States and Great Britain, the two countries that had led the march to war. Worse than the failure to find the weapons that justified the war was the mismanagement of the postwar occupation and reconstruction, which imposed a harsh toll on Iraq and upon the members of the occupying coalition's armed forces. The United States and Great Britain looked very different in the aftermath of the war than they did before.

The war led to a crisis of political credibility that, combined with other social tensions and compounded by the Great Recession, led to the rise of right-wing nationalism. People in both Great Britain and the United States joined a growing global reaction against neoliberalism and the inability of political leaders to address its consequences, such as increases in economic inequality and insecurity. This reaction also included nativism and xenophobia, as people who felt stuck economically resented newcomers who were in many cases also victims of globalization or of conflicts such as the Iraq War.

This new right-wing nationalism bore many similarities to the nationalism of the early decades of the twentieth century: it scapegoated outsiders and minorities, and it questioned and undermined traditional institutions such as legislative bodies, courts, universities, and the press. It also resembled earlier nationalism in its global reach. Nationalists rose to power in countries as diverse as Brazil, India, Turkey,

Israel, Thailand, and the Philippines. The new nationalism became especially power-ful in Russia and eastern Europe, notably Hungary.

Under socialism, people in eastern European countries had enjoyed rights to social welfare and economic redistribution, but they were denied democratic rights and liberal freedoms. The postsocialist period brought increasing political freedom, but also rising income inequality. The new regimes drew on nationalist ideas about victimization at the hands of foreigners. In the process, they produced less social welfare and fewer democratic freedoms. Viktor Orbán of Hungary exemplified the nationalist turn. In his youth he advocated for political and economic liberalization, but as prime minister he became increasingly xenophobic while eroding the demo-cratic and constitutional guarantees that helped him to power.

As in the past, the new right-wing nationalism was a political instrument used by a generation of charismatic or iconoclastic leaders—political figures who culti-vated a dedicated base of followers and governed by visibly and deliberately breaking norms. Paradoxically, the new right seized issues that had been abandoned by left-wing parties when they embraced neoliberalism, such as the protection of industrial employment, and in Europe, of health-care and pension systems.

The new right-wing leaders governed through the scapegoating of minorities. U.S. president Donald Trump's racial discourse and harsh policies toward immigrants and refugees made him typical of the cohort of right-wing nationalists that emerged around the world. These policies placed him alongside India's prime minister Narendra Modi, whose political project is based on intensifying Hindu nationalism through steps such as lifting the protections put in place for the Muslim majority in the province of Kash-mir, a region disputed with Pakistan. Brazilian president Jair Bolsonaro built his polit-ical project on nostalgia for Brazil's military dictatorship and on homophobic remarks, which formed the sharp edge of an attempt to assert traditional gender norms in a country that had made strides in defining LGBTQ rights as human rights.

Britain's vote to leave the European Union reflected both the crisis of neoliberal lead-ership and the social divisions it unleashed. At the beginning of the century, global capital flowed into London, which experienced a real estate boom. At the same time, growing numbers of migrants from poorer countries in eastern Europe, particularly Poland and the Baltic states, settled in Britain after those countries joined the European Union and no longer faced migration restrictions. People in poorer regions of Britain felt left behind as the liberalized circulation of capital and people took place around them.

British prime minister David Cameron believed he could easily defuse these pres-sures within his governing Conservative Party by holding a public referendum on leav-ing the European Union. The referendum compressed a range of complex questions about Britain's political organization, economic model, system of trade, migration pol-icy, and social welfare system into a yes-or-no vote. The referendum question, "Should the United Kingdom remain a member of the European Union or leave the European Union?" was written by political leaders who never imagined it would pass, while pro-ponents of Brexit had few concrete notions for how to execute the break.

The manner in which Brexit voters repudiated the economic and social frame-work created by the European Union, and the failure of a succession of British gov-ernments to develop a framework to carry out Brexit, raised important questions about both neoliberalism and right-wing nationalism. What happens when the promises of the new nationalists fail to improve the lives of people already failed by neoliberalism? And what political, economic, and social alternatives can address the inequality and marginalization that characterize both nationalism and neoliberalism? As Britain exited the European Union in 2020, these questions remained unresolved.

# Global Circulation and Exchange

**How have migration and the circulation of capital and technology continued to shape the world?**

Much of the history in this textbook is driven by the circulation of people, sometimes over great distances. Migration continues to be one of the great engines of history, though its experience exposes one of the major contradictions regarding liberalization: governments have pressed for the free circulation of goods and capital, but they have often sought to limit the movement of people across borders.

## Migration

National immigration policies vary considerably. In Europe the process of integration has meant that European Union member countries permit the free movement of citizens from other EU nations. But restrictions on migration from outside of the EU have increased even as barriers to trade and investment have fallen.

The border between the United States and Mexico reflects many of the challenges of contemporary migration. Long before a border existed between the United States and Mexico, migrants circulated throughout North America. But as the United States conquered land that had belonged to Mexico in the nineteenth century (see "Mexico and the United States" in Chapter 27), it began to restrict the movement of migrants across the new border. At the beginning of the twenty-first century the U.S. government began building a wall at its border with Mexico, further restricting the circulation of people even as the United States and Mexico implemented a free-trade agreement that made it easier for goods and capital to cross that border.

A migratory circuit is a connection created between two regions that results in a greater circulation of people. Circuits of migration are shaped by many forces. Pursuit of economic opportunity and flight from persecution are the major factors that drive international migration. Historical connections, such as the spaces shared by indigenous and Latino peoples on both sides of the U.S.-Mexico border, are another such force. Another is the intensification of trade, which reshapes national economies and the connections between them. Yet another is U.S. military intervention: countries that are the sites of conflict spurred by or involving the United States are reshaped in ways that often create migrant and refugee circuits connected to the United States. For example, since the 1960s millions of people, first from South Korea and then from Vietnam, Cambodia, and Laos, have found legal refuge in the United States.

Migrants usually become ethnic, religious, or linguistic minorities in the countries where they settle, and they commonly face discrimination. Sometimes this discrimination is expressed in violence and oppression, such as that experienced by contemporary Zimbabwean workers in South Africa. In many cases, restrictions on immigration have increased in countries where national economic growth has slowed. For instance, as Japanese industry boomed in the 1980s, the country welcomed

**Migrant Labor and Global Industry** The Homi Danchi public housing complex outside of Toyota City, Japan, is home to over five thousand Brazilian and Peruvian workers, mainly descendants of immigrants from Japan, working in auto parts manufacturing and food production. (Jerry Dávila)

descendants of Japanese emigrants who had settled in South America in the first half of the century. Because these migrants were culturally and linguistically different from natives, Japanese citizens considered them *dekasegi*, or "temporary guest workers," who had no right to citizenship despite their ancestry. Then, as manufacturing and economic growth stagnated in the 1990s, this migration to Japan dwindled.

The experience of immigration following U.S. military intervention in Central America, the Caribbean, and Southeast Asia forms a pattern into which future immigration from the Middle East may well fit. In 2015 the European Union became the setting of a new migration crisis as over 1 million refugees fled armed conflicts and poverty in Africa and the Middle East.[2] The largest contingent was refugees from Syria's civil war. The refugees faced a succession of challenges ranging from perilous crossings of the Mediterranean, in which thousands perished, to the hostility of peoples and governments, particularly in eastern Europe, where countries like Hungary had once welcomed East Germans fleeing communism but now blocked the transit of refugees. Countries began building fences and re-establishing border controls to limit the movement of refugees.

## Urbanization

Cities in Africa, Asia, and Latin America expanded at an astonishing pace after 1945. Many doubled or even tripled in size in a single decade (Table 33.1). In 1950 there were only eight cities with 5 million or more inhabitants, and only two were in developing countries. By 2018 there were forty-eight cities with populations between 5 and 10 million, and another thirty-three, known as **megacities** with populations above 10 million. Of these thirty-three megacities, twenty-seven are outside of the United States and Europe and are located mainly in South Asia and East Asia.

What has caused this urban explosion? More than half of all urban growth comes from rural migration. Manufacturing jobs in the developing nations have been concentrated in their major cities. Even when industrial jobs have been scarce, migrants have streamed to cities, seeking any type of employment. As large landowners have found it more profitable to produce export crops, their increasingly mechanized operations have reduced the need for agricultural laborers. Ethnic or political unrest in the countryside can also send migrants into cities.

Most of the growing numbers of urban poor earn precarious livings in an **informal economy** made up of petty traders and unskilled labor. In the informal

| TABLE 33.1 | URBAN POPULATION AS A PERCENTAGE OF TOTAL POPULATION IN THE WORLD AND IN EIGHT MAJOR AREAS, 1925–2025 | | | | |
|---|---|---|---|---|---|
| Area | 1925 | 1950 | 1975 | 2000 | 2025 (EST.) |
| World Total | 21% | 28% | 39% | 50% | 63% |
| North America | 54 | 64 | 77 | 86 | 93 |
| Europe | 48 | 55 | 67 | 79 | 88 |
| Soviet Union | 18 | 39 | 61 | 76 | 87 |
| East Asia | 10 | 15 | 30 | 46 | 63 |
| Latin America | 25 | 41 | 60 | 74 | 85 |
| Africa | 8 | 13 | 24 | 37 | 54 |

Note: Little more than one-fifth of the world's population was urban in 1925. In 2000 the total urban proportion in the world was about 50 percent. According to United Nations experts, the proportion should reach two-thirds by about 2025. The most rapid urban growth will occur in Africa and Asia, where the move to cities is still in its early stages.

economy, which echoes early preindustrial markets, regular salaried jobs are rare and highly prized, and a complex world of tiny, unregulated businesses and service occupations predominates. Peddlers and pushcart operators hawk their wares, and sweatshops and home-based workers manufacture cheap goods for popular consumption. These workers typically lack job security, unemployment insurance, and pensions.

After 1945 large-scale urban migration profoundly affected traditional family patterns in developing countries, just as it had during the Industrial Revolution. Particularly in Africa and Asia, the great majority of migrants to cities were young men seeking temporary or seasonal work. For rural women, the consequences of male out-migration to cities were mixed. Asian and African women found themselves heads of households, faced with added burdens in managing the farm and sustaining families. African and Asian village women became unprecedentedly self-reliant and began to assert greater rights.

In Latin America migration patterns differed: whole families generally migrated, often to squatter settlements. These families frequently belonged to the class of landless laborers, which was generally larger in Latin America than in Africa and Asia. Migration was also more likely to be permanent. Another difference was that single women were as likely as single men to move to the cities, in part because women were in high demand as domestic servants. Some women also left to escape male-dominated villages where they faced narrow social and economic opportunities.

**The Informal Economy**
Merchant women selling vegetables in Pisac, Peru. (Juergen Ritterbach/AGE Fotostock)

In cities the concentration of wealth in few hands has resulted in unequal consumption, education, and employment. The gap between rich and poor around the world can be measured both between the city and the countryside, and within cities (Map 33.1). Wealthy city dwellers in developing countries often have more in common with each other than with the poorer urban and rural people in their own country. As a result, the elites have often favored globalization that connects them with wealthier nations.

## Multinational Corporations

A striking feature of global interdependence beginning in the early 1950s was the rapid emergence of **multinational corporations**, or multinationals, which are business firms that operate in a number of different countries and tend to adopt a global rather than a national perspective. Their rise was partly due to the revival of capitalism after the Second World War, increasingly free international economic relations, and the worldwide drive for rapid industrialization. Multinationals treated the world as one big market, coordinating complex activities across political boundaries and escaping political controls and national policies.

The impact of multinational corporations, especially on less industrialized countries, has been mixed. The presence of multinationals helped spread the products and values of consumer society to elites in the developing world. Critics considered this part of the process of neocolonialism, whereby local elites abandoned their nation's interests and contributed to continued foreign domination.

Multinational corporations are among the main beneficiaries of economic liberalism: growing openness of national markets and economic integration allow corporations to move goods, capital, and technology more fluidly and more intensely. But the growing interconnectedness of world markets comes with costs. In particular, it has meant increased economic volatility, as exemplified by the banking crisis that swept the United States and Europe into the Great Recession in 2008.

The large size of many multinational corporations is due to changes in the ways people in the world communicate or process information. The first communications revolution began in the nineteenth century with the invention of the telegraph, the telephone, motion pictures, and improvements in the circulation of newspapers and mail. The invention of these and other communications technologies between 1875 and 1900 prepared the way for a twentieth-century era of mass communications. New information-processing technologies began with the development of adding and calculating machines and culminated in the development of the first computers during the Second World War. As computing and communications technologies converged, they created the "information age."

The global availability and affordability of radios and television sets in the 1950s introduced a second communications revolution. The transistor radio reached the most isolated hamlets of the world. Governments embraced radio broadcasting as a means to project their power, disseminate propaganda, and broaden education. Though initially less common, television use expanded into nearly every country during the 1960s and 1970s, even if there was only one television in a village.

Governments recognized the power of the visual image to promote their ideologies or leaders, and a state television network became a source of national pride. The television transmission towers that rose up in the 1960s became monuments

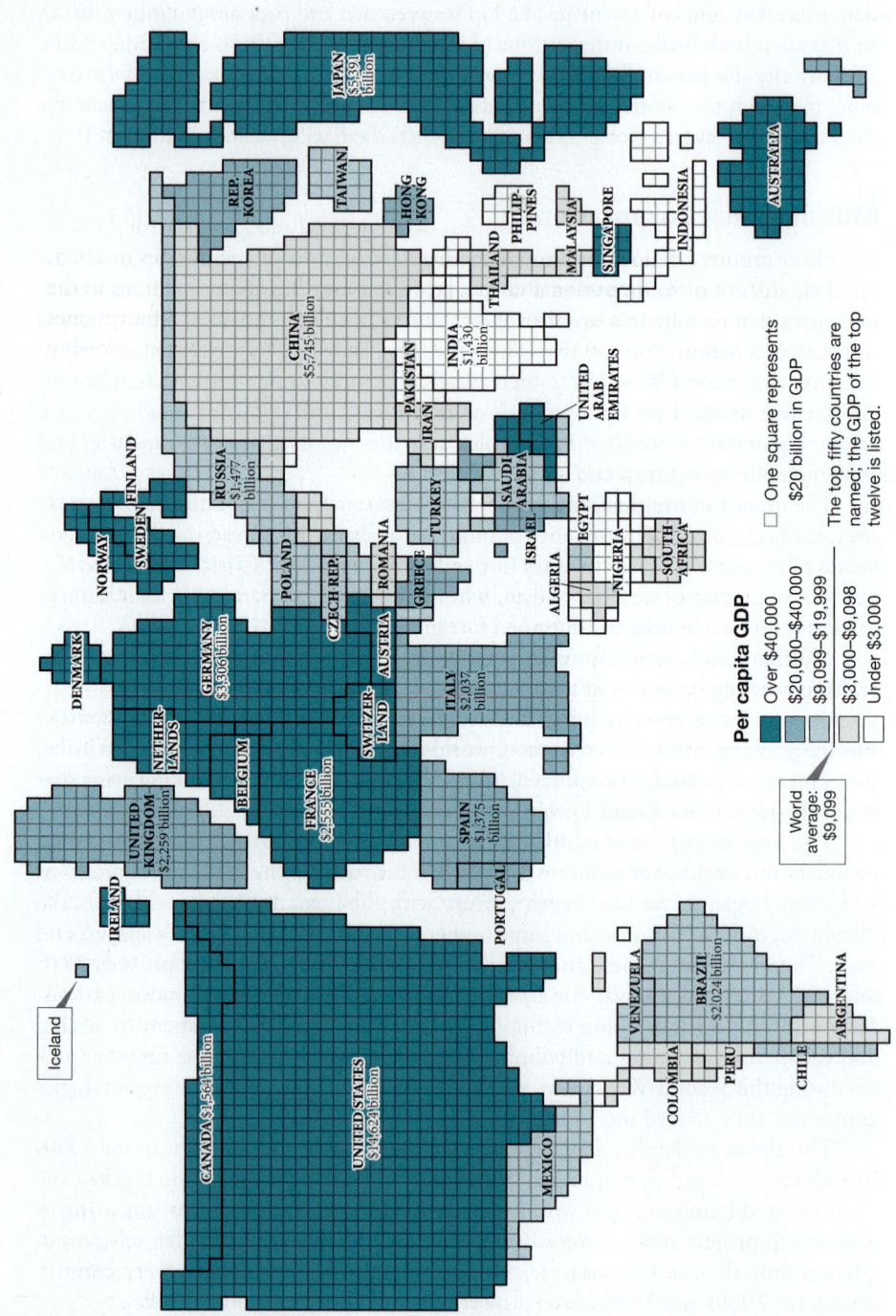

JAPAN
$5,591
billion

AUSTRALIA

TAIWAN

REP.
KOREA

HONG
KONG

THAILAND

PHILIP-
PINES

MALAYSIA

SINGAPORE

INDONESIA

CHINA
$5,745 billion

PAKISTAN

INDIA
$1,430
billion

IRAN

UNITED ARAB
EMIRATES

FINLAND

RUSSIA
$1,477
billion

SAUDI
ARABIA

EGYPT

NORWAY

SWEDEN

POLAND

TURKEY

ISRAEL

SOUTH
AFRICA

DENMARK

CZECH REP.

ROMANIA

GREECE

ALGERIA

NIGERIA

GERMANY
$3,306 billion

AUSTRIA

ITALY
$2,037
billion

NETHER-
LANDS

SWITZER-
LAND

BELGIUM

FRANCE
$2,555 billion

SPAIN
$1,375
billion

UNITED
KINGDOM
$2,259 billion

PORTUGAL

IRELAND

Iceland

VENEZUELA

BRAZIL
$2,024 billion

ARGENTINA

COLOMBIA

PERU

CHILE

CANADA $1,564 billion

UNITED STATES
$14,624 billion

MEXICO

**Per capita GDP**

☐ One square represents
   $20 billion in GDP

The top fifty countries are
named; the GDP of the top
twelve is listed.

Over $40,000
$20,000–$40,000
$9,099–$19,999
$3,000–$9,098
Under $3,000

World
average:
$9,099

to modernity and development. Around the world, governments controlled the introduction of color television to symbolize progress. The Argentine military junta introduced color broadcasting to the nation for the 1978 soccer World Cup, transmitting games that took place within earshot of the notorious detention center where it waged its "dirty war." Television also became a powerful disseminator of culture: U.S. television programming reached around the world, Mexican television programs dominated Spanish-speaking regions, and Brazilian soap operas gained loyal followers from Angola to the Soviet Union.

The third, and perhaps greatest, communications revolution began with the first personal computers in 1976, followed by the introduction of cell phones in 1985. The rapid diffusion of computing and cellular technology has allowed nations in the developing world to bypass investment in traditional telephone lines. Smartphones have become the most common instruments for connecting to the Internet, allowing people in poorer and rural regions of the world to communicate and access information digitally without a computer or physical network.

Internet access has made global access to information and communications seemingly infinite. Meanwhile, authoritarian governments have realized that the Internet and social media platforms like Facebook and Twitter pose a threat to their power and control. The governments of China and North Korea, for example, restrict information that travels in and out of their countries over the Internet, while the governments of the United States and other nations have invested heavily in monitoring that information. Even as expanding means of communication through cell phones, computers, and their networks have made censorship more difficult to enforce, they have made it even harder to keep information or communications private.

The intensity of innovation in communications and information technology created new multinational giants. The success of these technology companies and the proliferation of computer, smartphone, and Internet use are remarkable changes, but they also deepen socioeconomic inequalities between and within countries. For instance, when Windows XP was released in 2001, a Nigerian cocoa laborer would have had to save her or his entire year's earnings to buy the Home Edition.[3] The unevenness of both the production and consumption of computer technology has resulted in a **digital divide**, a gap in access to Internet, computer, and telecommunications resources. This gap is the greatest between nations like the United States, western European countries, and Japan and nations in Africa and South and Southeast Asia. The digital divide also exists between the wealthy and poor, as well as between urban and rural areas within countries. As the Internet becomes more integral to business, education, and government, communities with no or limited access face growing disadvantages.

**< MAP 33.1   The Global Distribution of Wealth, ca. 2010**
This size-comparison map, arranged according to global wealth distribution, vividly illustrates the gap in wealth between the Northern and Southern Hemispheres. The two small island nations of Japan and the United Kingdom have more wealth than all the nations of the Southern Hemisphere combined, although wealth creation in India and Brazil has advanced significantly. The wealthiest countries are also the most highly urbanized. As market capitalism expands in China, Vietnam, and other Asian countries and in Latin America and Africa, the relative-size ratios on the map will continue to change and evolve. Tiny Iceland, whose GDP is less than $20 billion, nevertheless has one of the highest per capita GDPs in the world.

# Social Movements

## What challenges did social reformers address at the turn of the twenty-first century?

Just as nineteenth-century social reformers embraced the cause of ending slavery, modern social reformers have sought to end global inequality, racism, and sexism and to expand human rights. Social movements played a critical role in the victory of the democratic movements in Latin America and Europe and the end of the apartheid system in South Africa.

The 1977 Nestlé boycott exemplified the kinds of success such movements could achieve, as well as their limitations. Critics charged that the Swiss company's marketing of powdered baby formula in poor countries or regions with little access to clean water posed a risk to children. Activists called on consumers around the world to boycott Nestlé products.

At first, Nestlé dismissed the boycott and sought to discredit the movement. The president of the company's Brazilian division declared that "the US Nestlé Co has advised me that their research indicates that this [boycott] is actually an indirect attack on the free world's economic system." Condemnation of Nestlé mounted. In a 1978 hearing, U.S. senator Ted Kennedy asked a Nestlé executive: "Can a product which requires clean water, good sanitation, adequate family income and a literate parent to follow printed instructions be properly and safely used in areas where water is contaminated, sewage runs in the streets, poverty is severe and illiteracy is high?"[4]

In 1981 the UN World Health Organization responded to the campaign by developing a set of voluntary standards regulating the marketing of infant formula in countries where access to clean water was precarious. Nestlé agreed to follow the standards. The movement succeeded, but its success raised questions. Multinational corporations operated beyond the reach of single governments and often in regions with weak regulatory or investigatory structures. As a result, it was hard to hold them accountable when their conduct was unethical. At the same time, social movements and nongovernmental organizations also acted outside the realm of public accountability.

## Children: The Right to Childhood

In 1989 the United Nations adopted the Convention on the Rights of the Child, which spells out a number of rights that are due every child. These include human rights and economic, social, and cultural rights. The convention addresses the reality that globally a billion children live in poverty—one in every two children in the world—and that children make up half the world's refugees. It also focuses on the problems of child labor and exploitation, sexual violence and trafficking, police abuse of street children, HIV/AIDS orphans, lack of access to education, and lack of access to adequate health care. The convention has been ratified by more countries than any other human rights treaty—196 countries as of 2017. The only United Nations member nation that has not ratified it is the United States.

The rights of children are in part the rights to health and to education. Medical advances have made diseases that afflict children more treatable, making public health access rather than science the determining factor in many children's lives. The medical revolution began in the late nineteenth century with the development of the germ theory of disease (see "Improving the Urban Environment" in Chapter 24) and continued rapidly after World War II. Scientists discovered vaccines for many of the deadliest diseases. The Salk polio vaccine, developed in 1952, was followed by the first oral polio vaccine (1962) and vaccines for measles (1964), mumps (1967), rubella (1970), chicken pox (1974), hepatitis B (1981), and human papillomavirus (2006). According to the UN World Health Organization, medical advances reduced deaths from smallpox, cholera, and plague by more than 95 percent worldwide between 1951 and 1966.

Children became increasingly likely to survive their early years, although infant and juvenile mortality remained far higher in poor countries than in rich ones. By 1980 the average inhabitant of the developing countries could expect to live about fifty-four years, although life expectancy at birth varied from forty to sixty-four years depending on the country. In industrialized countries, life expectancy at birth averaged seventy-one years.

Between 1980 and 2000 the number of children under the age of five dying annually of diarrhea dropped by 60 percent because of the global distribution of a cheap sugar-salt solution mixed in water. Still, over 1.5 million children worldwide continue to die each year from diarrhea, primarily in poorer nations. Deaths worldwide from HIV/AIDS, malaria, and tuberculosis are concentrated in the world's poorest regions, while tuberculosis remains the leading killer of women worldwide.

As the twenty-first century began, nearly a billion people — mostly women denied equitable access to education — were illiterate. Increasing economic globalization has put pressure on all governments to improve literacy rates and educational opportunities; the result has been reduced gender inequalities in education. While the percentage of illiterate adults in 2010 who were women was 64 percent, the percentage of girls among illiterate children was 60 percent, with the greatest gains in literacy occurring in South Asia and the Middle East.

In the 1990s Mexico pioneered a new approach to combating poverty that has been implemented in a growing number of countries. Conditional cash transfer, or CCT, provides a stipend to families who meet certain goals, such as keeping their children in school. This approach addresses poverty directly while enlisting families to work toward its long-term solution by increasing education levels, which will broaden opportunities for new generations. Mexico's Oportunidades (Opportunities) CCT was followed by Brazil's Bolsa Família (Family Scholarship) and by similar projects in many other countries in Latin America. Versions of the program have been introduced across Asia and the Middle East, including in Bangladesh, where a CCT program promotes the education of girls.

## Women's Right to Equality

Continuing work begun during the 1975 "Year of the Woman," the 1995 United Nations Fourth World Conference on Women, held in Beijing, China, called on the world community to take action in twelve areas of critical concern to women: poverty, access to education and training, access to health care, violence against women, women and war, economic inequality with men, political inequality with men, creation of institutions for women's advancement, lack of respect for women's rights, stereotyping of women, gender inequalities and the environment, and violation of girl children's rights.[5] These are concerns that all women share, although degrees of inequality vary greatly from one country to another.

The **feminization of poverty**, the disproportionate number of women living in extreme poverty, applies to even the wealthiest countries, where two out of every three poor adults are women. There are many causes for this. Because women are primarily responsible for child care in many cultures, they have less time and opportunity for work. Male labor migration also increases the number of households headed by women and thus the number of families living in poverty. Job restrictions, discrimination, and limited access to education reduce women's employment options to the informal economy. Finally, the poorest women usually suffer most from government policies, usually legislated by men, that restrict their access to reproductive health care and family planning.

Women have made gains in the workplace; in the early 2000s they made up 38 percent of the nonfarm-sector global workforce, as compared to 35 percent in 1990. But segregated labor markets remain the rule, with higher-paying jobs reserved for men. In the farm sector, women produce more than half of all the food and up to 80 percent of the subsistence crops grown in Africa. Because this is informal labor and often unpaid, these women laborers are denied access to loans, and many cannot own the land they farm.

Beyond the labor market, women also began in the 1960s to experience more control over pregnancy and childbirth decisions, particularly following the introduction of the birth control pill in the early 1960s. In the early twenty-first century, more than half of the world's couples practiced some form of birth control, up from one in eight just forty years earlier. Birth control and abortion were most accepted in North America, Protestant regions in Europe, the Soviet Union, and East Asia.

Social class continues to be a major divider of women's opportunities. Over the course of the twentieth century, women from more affluent backgrounds experienced far greater gains in access to education, employment, and political representation than women in poverty did. In the aftermath of decolonization and state formation, women emerged as heads of state in Bangladesh, India, Israel, and Pakistan. A wave of democratic political transitions in the 1980s yielded women heads of state in the Philippines and Nicaragua. In the years following democratic transitions, the same occurred in Panama, Chile, Argentina, Brazil, Indonesia, and Liberia.

## LGBTQ Challenges

Soon after it emerged, the global gay rights movement faced a historic crisis when members of its community were besieged by the AIDS epidemic. Since the epidemic first impacted gay and transgender communities, whose sexuality and identity remained the subject of entrenched prejudice, policymakers and public health officials often approached AIDS with moral judgment rather than with seriousness and sophistication. That response hampered prevention and treatment, contributing to many deaths. This crisis, which involved both a disease and public attitudes, required an organized response from the LGBTQ movement.

In the United States, the organization ACT UP promoted a campaign for AIDS research that created a powerful symbol to represent the AIDS crisis, using the words "Silence = Death" beneath a pink triangle. A journalist who wrote about AIDS described his reaction to the ACT UP symbol in the 1980s:

> When I first saw the [ACT UP] poster, I didn't really know what it was. . . . I recognized the triangle as the symbol of homosexual victimization by the Nazis, but this triangle pointed up. Did it suggest supremacy? And the phrase itself,

with its diabolical math, lodged in my imagination. Did it suggest conspiracy? Because of the word "death" I supposed it was about AIDS; had I noticed the tiny type at the bottom, which for a time included the instruction "Turn anger, fear, grief into action," perhaps I would have been sure.[6]

Around the world, approaches to prevention and treatment depended on public attitudes and public health capacity. In 2018 the World Health Organization calculated that 38 million persons globally were infected with HIV, the virus that causes AIDS, and that AIDS was the world's fourth-leading cause of death, claiming 770,000 lives per year. In Africa, the continent hardest hit by HIV/AIDS, it is predominantly spread through heterosexual sex. Widespread disease and poverty are also significant factors: people already suffering from other illnesses such as malaria or tuberculosis are less resistant to HIV and have less access to health care for treatment. About 61 percent of all persons who die from AIDS and 68 percent of those currently infected with HIV live in sub-Saharan Africa, though the death rate has decreased nearly 40 percent since 2010 because of the increased availability of drugs that suppress HIV/AIDS known as antiretroviral therapies (Map 33.2).

Another factor contributing to the spread of AIDS in Africa is political instability, particularly in the corridor running from Uganda to South Africa. This region was the scene of conflicts that resulted in massive numbers of refugees and a breakdown in healthcare services. The people in Uganda, Rwanda, Burundi, Zaire/Congo, Angola, Zimbabwe, Mozambique, and South Africa have been decimated by HIV/AIDS. South Africa has the largest number of HIV/AIDS cases in the world. In 2018 around 13 percent of the South African population, about 7.7 million people, was living with HIV/AIDS.

A counterpoint was Brazil, where the response to the AIDS epidemic was a successful result of its redemocratization process. The new constitution approved in 1988 determined that health was a right and established a national public health system. As the epidemic spread in the 1990s, public health officials made costly new medical treatments free for all patients in Brazil, and they threatened to declare a national emergency and break the patents on drugs to force pharmaceutical companies to allow the government to manufacture and freely distribute generic versions. Coupled with extensive public health education campaigns, the measures led to infection and survival rates similar to those of the United States, Japan, and western Europe. Partly in response to the Brazilian threat to break the patents, since 2001 antiretroviral therapies that are widely available in the West have been dispensed freely to many of those infected in Africa and Asia.

By the 1990s gay rights activists had broadened their efforts to challenge discrimination in employment, education, and public life. In 1995 Canada became the first country to allow same-sex marriage. In the ensuing years many European countries followed suit. But the legalization of same-sex marriage was not only a Western achievement: by 2013 Argentina, South Africa, Ecuador, and Uruguay had legalized same-sex marriage, while many other nations provided legal protections for families that stopped shy of marriage. Argentina led the way in legal support for transgender people and made sexual reassignment surgery a legal right in 2012. In 2014 the U.S. Supreme Court invalidated state laws and constitutional amendments barring same-sex marriage.

The movement toward recognition of same-sex marriage reflects the connection between liberalization and human rights: beyond dignifying discriminated groups,

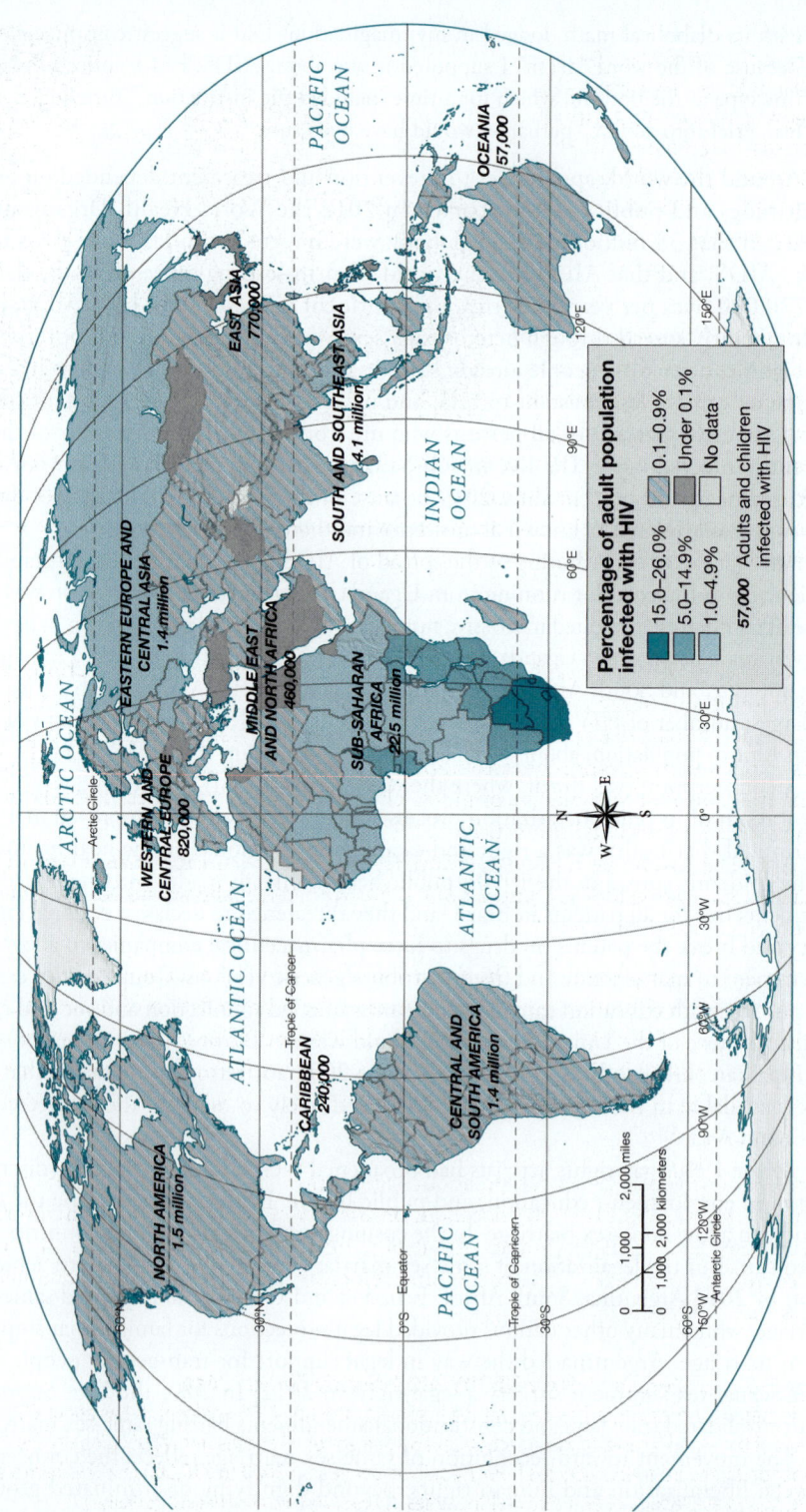

ARCTIC OCEAN

PACIFIC OCEAN

OCEANIA
57,000

EAST ASIA
770,000

SOUTH AND SOUTHEAST ASIA
4.1 million

INDIAN OCEAN

EASTERN EUROPE AND CENTRAL ASIA
1.4 million

MIDDLE EAST AND NORTH AFRICA
460,000

SUB-SAHARAN AFRICA
22.5 million

WESTERN AND CENTRAL EUROPE
820,000

ATLANTIC OCEAN

CARIBBEAN
240,000

CENTRAL AND SOUTH AMERICA
1.4 million

NORTH AMERICA
1.5 million

Tropic of Cancer

Equator

Tropic of Capricorn

PACIFIC OCEAN

Arctic Circle

Antarctic Circle

0   1,000   2,000 miles

0   1,000  2,000 kilometers

**Percentage of adult population infected with HIV**

15.0–26.0%

5.0–14.9%

1.0–4.9%

0.1–0.9%

Under 0.1%

No data

57,000  Adults and children infected with HIV

**Equal Marriage in Argentina** José Maria Di Bella, right, and his partner, Alex Freyre, celebrate Latin America's first same-sex marriage, which occurred in Tierra del Fuego, Argentina, in 2009. (Marcos Brindicci/ Reuters/Newscom)

marriage rights give same-sex families legal equality to manage property rights and financial activities, such as the ability to inherit a home or jointly purchase insurance. However, human rights successes in Latin America, Europe, and parts of Asia have contrasted with lesbian, gay, or transgender experiences in many other regions of the world, where religious strictures against same-sex relationships can include imprisonment or death.

## Environmentalism

The modern environmental movement began with concerns about pollution, rapid consumption of energy and food supplies, global deforestation, and threats to wildlife. By the 1970s citizens had begun joining together in nongovernmental organizations to pursue preservation or restoration of natural environments. By the end of the twentieth century, the challenge of global climate change figured prominently in the agenda for environmental protection.

American biologist and writer Rachel Carson was an early proponent of the environmental health movement. In *Silent Spring* (1962), she warned of the dangers of pesticides and pollution:

> Along with the possibility of the extinction of mankind by nuclear war, the central problem of our age has therefore become the contamination of man's total environment with such substances of incredible potential for harm — substances that accumulate in the tissues of plants and animals and even penetrate the germ cells to shatter or alter the very material of heredity upon which the shape of the future depends.[7]

Carson and others were concerned about the harmful effects of chemicals, radiation, pollution, waste, and urban development on the environment and on human health. Environmentalists like Carson acted out of concern that all living things were connected and that damage to one part of an ecological system could have consequences across that ecosystem.

**< MAP 33.2   People Living with HIV/AIDS Worldwide, ca. 2010**
As this map illustrates, Africa has been hit the hardest by the HIV/AIDS epidemic. It has about 68 percent of the world's cases of HIV infection and 61 percent of all deaths from AIDS. Globally the number of deaths from HIV/AIDS fell from 1.4 million per year in 2000 to 770,000 in 2018 thanks to the increased availability of antiretroviral therapies. (Source: Data from World Health Organization.)

The environmental movement is actually several different movements, each with its own agenda. Some movements focus on the preservation of animal, plant, and marine diversity as well as the ecosystems those populations depend upon; others focus on clean water and air, or the management of waste; and others focus on practices such as environmental racism, by which the costs of environmental degradation or of contamination are concentrated in poor and minority communities. Taken together, they are actions directed at mitigating, preventing, or reversing other human actions. In particular, the environmental movement is concerned with the unintended—and unevenly distributed—consequences of development.

# Global Climate Change

**What do historical perspectives bring to our understanding of climate change?**

History shapes our understanding of climate change by giving us data and methods to examine its causes, context, and consequences. Experiences with both past climate change and the effects of human transformations of the environment provide ways of interpreting their impacts. In addition, this history helps us understand that those impacts are experienced unevenly.

## Causes of Global Warming and Responses to It

**Global warming** is caused by carbon emissions, particularly from industry, electricity production and transportation, cattle ranching, and deforestation. These emissions form greenhouse gases that trap heat in the atmosphere, producing warmer air and surface temperatures and, in particular, warmer oceans, since oceans capture most of the additional heat produced. This warming causes **climate change**, the patterns of changes in climate that can range from drought and heat to heavier rainfall or even colder weather, as well as severe weather. Climate change is especially influenced by the warming of oceans, which disrupts long-standing weather patterns.

Over the past century, global temperatures have accelerated rapidly and have risen 1.5 degrees Fahrenheit due to population growth and rising demands for energy and transportation. Since 1950 the world's population has increased from 2.5 billion people to over 7 billion, multiplying the consumption of fossil fuels, food, and industrial goods. The goal identified by scientists and pursued by countries through international agreements is to keep the total warming of the atmosphere below 3.6 degrees Fahrenheit to prevent a continuous cycle of warming. Meeting these goals would demand significant reductions in the emissions produced by industrialized and industrializing countries, modifications to patterns of farming and ranching, the widespread use of new technologies, and efforts at energy efficiency.

The United Nations Framework Convention on Climate Change that was established in 1992 set the groundwork for a series of agreements between nations to limit greenhouse gas emissions. The first agreement was the 1997 Kyoto Protocol to reduce emissions of carbon dioxide and other gases, which has been ratified by 132 countries but not the United States. The U.S. government did sign on to the 2015 Paris Climate Agreement, which set targets for keeping the change in average global temperatures to below 3.6 degrees. The largest reductions in greenhouse gas emissions would be made in China, followed by the United States. In 2017, U.S. president Trump initiated steps to withdraw from the Paris Agreement effective in 2020.

If societies succeed at keeping the change of temperature below 3.6 degrees, this action would prevent the most catastrophic consequences of global warming. Still, the effects of the increase in temperatures is already being felt, and the further increases that are already inevitable will cause further changes to climate.

## Historical Experiences with Climate and Environmental Change

Almost all of the history in this book took place in a period of stable global temperatures. The major exception was the Little Ice Age that affected Asia, Europe, and North America beginning in the thirteenth century and lasting until the mid-nineteenth century. Climate stability shaped the opportunities, constraints, and choices that are the substance of this volume. These included patterns of settlement and social organization; farming, herding, and hunting; and connections between world regions through religion, trade, and migration.

As a recent period of climate change, the Little Ice Age offers insight into the kinds of social stresses a changing climate can cause. Some regions, such as northern Europe, China, and Southeast Asia, became cooler and wetter. This change shortened growing seasons and triggered crop failures. Other areas, such as the Ottoman Mediterranean countries and North America, faced a series of droughts that sometimes lasted for decades.

The onset of these extremes had similar consequences, starting with famine. Some areas of settlement were abandoned altogether. In other cases, the impoverishment of peasants and farmers led to the concentration of lands in the hands of the nobility. Political and trade networks withered. Populations stressed by famine were also more susceptible to diseases such as the plague epidemic, which stretched from Asia to Europe.

Other climate problems have been the result of human transformation of physical environments, such as farming and settlement of the plains of North and South America or the steppes of Soviet Central Asia, where soil erosion and the disruption of native vegetation caused the desertification and dust bowls of the early twentieth century. Similarly, the early Industrial Revolution had immediate and far-reaching environmental consequences (see "Environmental Impacts of Industrialization" in Chapter 23). The intensive use of coal in the nineteenth and early twentieth centuries blanketed British cities with toxic and sometimes lethal smoke while producing acid rain and contaminating cities and their surroundings with heavy metals such as mercury and lead, which were unlocked and dispersed from coal as it was burned.

## Automobility

The Industrial Revolution had a dramatic impact on transportation, reshaping lives and societies. Railroads remade human and natural landscapes around the world and changed how people, commodities, information, and states could circulate and connect. Their influence was felt in diverse ways: remote regions were connected to global markets, the imposition of railroad time regulated clocks around the world, mail services intensified, and whistle-stop tours for political campaigns became possible. The spread of railroads was followed by steam shipping, road transportation, and air travel. Within this transportation revolution, the automobile was especially consequential.

Automobility—the uses of automobiles—spread swiftly in the twentieth century. By 1922 there were 12.5 million cars in the world, 10.5 million of which were in the United States. The changes shaped by automobility were first and most extensively experienced in the United States. The development of highways redirected regional and

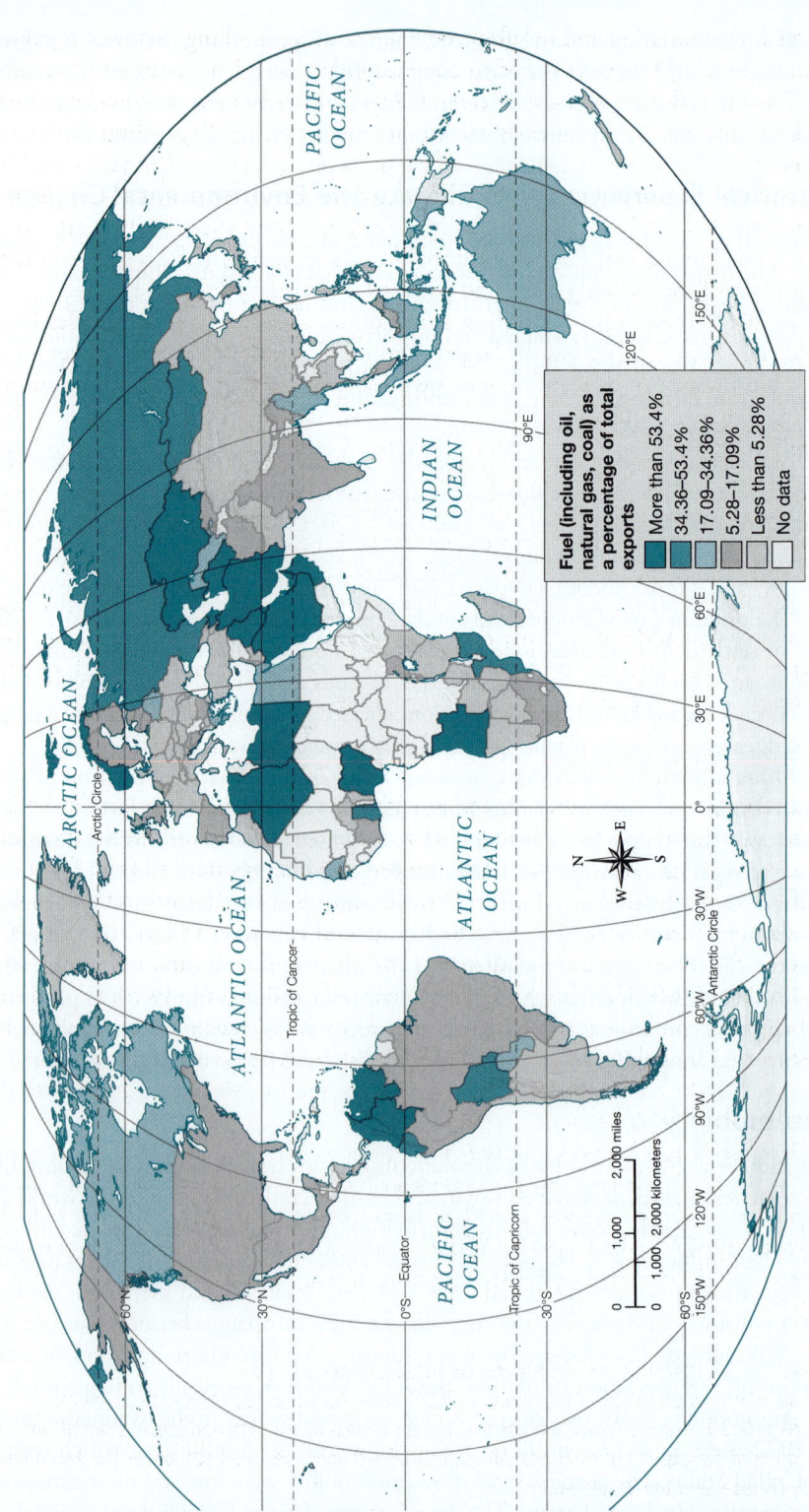

Fuel (including oil, natural gas, coal) as a percentage of total exports

More than 53.4%
34.36–53.4%
17.09–34.36%
5.28–17.09%
Less than 5.28%
No data

national transportation and redefined cities by creating far-flung networks of suburbs not just linked by roadways but often designed to be dependent on car transportation.

The manufacture and use of cars, which came to be seen worldwide as a hallmark of modernity, have greatly affected climate change. Expanding production beyond the United States, Europe, and Japan, countries such as China, India, Mexico, and South Korea invested heavily in automobile production. New planned cities such as Brazil's Brasília and Nigeria's Abuja were specifically designed for automobile circulation. Global automobile manufacturing drove industrialization, the growth of the working class, and patterns of consumption and leisure.

In 2015, there were 1.2 billion automobiles and commercial vehicles in the world. The United States has the largest number of automobiles, with 1.8 per household. But the rate of new automobile ownership is growing the fastest in countries such as China and India. As in the United States, around the world owning an automobile is one of the most desirable goals for families. As a result, the number of motor vehicles is projected to reach 2 billion as soon as 2030.[8]

The number of motor vehicles has significant consequences for the concentration of greenhouse gases. Approximately 16 percent of global and 29 percent of U.S. carbon emissions come from road transportation. The fastest growth of carbon emissions is from automobiles.[9] Thus any effort to significantly reduce carbon emissions must address not only the current impact of motor vehicles on the concentration of greenhouse gases, but also the rate of automobility expansion, while meeting the growing demands of transportation around the world.

## Global Energy Reliance

Some scholars call the period beginning with the Industrial Revolution the "hydrocarbon age" because of the growing reliance on carbon-based fossil fuels such as coal, oil, and natural gas. The impact of the concentrated energy released from fossil fuels is difficult to overstate: it has driven industrialization, transformed transportation, remade warfare, and shaped the experiences of world societies in myriad other ways.

Global economies are structured around the production and consumption of fossil fuels (Figure 33.1). Virtually all global trade and most industry rely on fuel. Global food supplies are increasingly sustained by industrialized farming, especially in Argentina, Brazil, Canada, and the United States, but increasingly also in Africa and Asia. Daily life for most of the world's population would be unrecognizable without the use of fossil fuels.

Fuel exports and imports illustrate the significance of fossil fuels to national economies. In 2018, 13 percent of the global trade in goods was composed of fossil fuel exports (Map 33.3). Fuel constitutes nearly all of the exports of Iraq, Libya, and Venezuela. For many countries in Central Asia, the Middle East, and Africa, it constitutes half or more of exports. The economies of many other countries rely on fuel imports.

< **MAP 33.3   Fuel as a Percentage of Total Exports, 2018**
Oil, natural gas, and coal are a large part of global trade. For some countries such as Angola, Iraq, Nigeria, and Venezuela, oil and gas account for almost all exports. And fuel is a significant proportion of the exports of countries with industrialized and diversified economies like Australia, Brazil, Canada, and the United States.

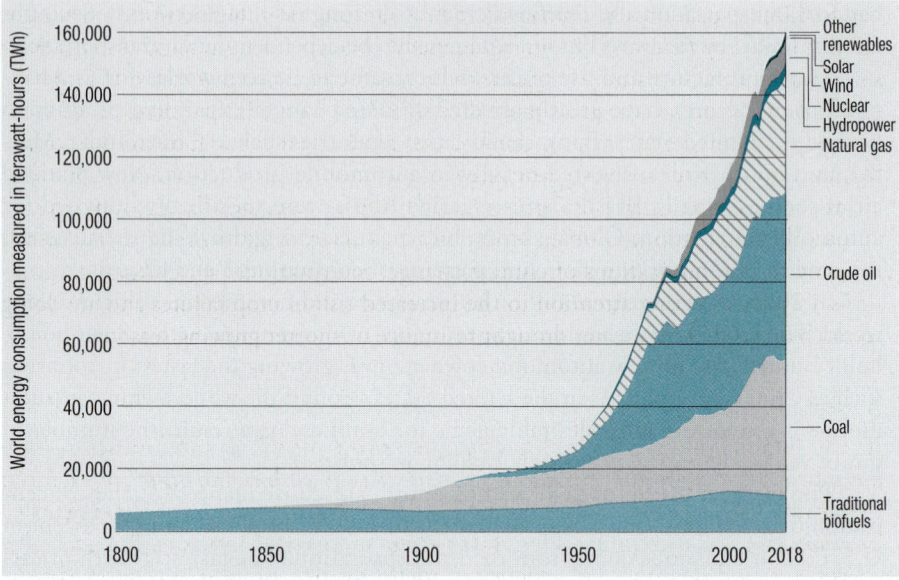

**FIGURE 33.1   World Energy Consumption, 1800–2018**
The growth in world energy consumption, which closely matches the concentration of greenhouse gases in the atmosphere, has increased dramatically since the Second World War. Energy that is not derived from hydrocarbons accounts for only a small percentage of the world's consumption.

Fossil fuels play such a significant role in the world that reducing them enough to combat global warming would create a much different world from the one we experience today. It would change how fuel is used, how it is produced or traded, and how it affects cultural, social, and political patterns. The differences would be felt more acutely in countries that rely on the production of fossil fuels than in countries that consume them the most.

## Intensified Agriculture and the Green Revolution

As the world's population grew in the second half of the twentieth century, food production strained to keep pace, prompting a greater emphasis on rural development and agricultural sciences. The **green revolution** began when crop scientists began to develop genetically engineered and hybridized seeds to suit particular growing conditions. A major breakthrough came in Mexico in the 1950s when an American-led team developed new strains of wheat that enabled farmers to double their yields, though the plants required greater amounts of fertilizer and water for irrigation.

A similar innovation in Asia introduced a new strain of rice that allowed farmers to plant two to four crops a year rather than one. New strains of soybeans created the possibility for growing multiple crops per year in tropical regions. As they applied green revolution technologies, many Asian countries experienced rapid increases in grain production. Farmers in India increased production more than 60 percent in fifteen years.

The green revolution offered new hope to industrializing nations. Though its benefits often flowed to large landowners and export farms that could invest in irrigation and fertilizer, experiences in China and other Asian countries showed that even peasant families with tiny farms could gain substantially. Indeed, the green revolution's greatest successes occurred in Asian countries with broad-based peasant ownership of land.

Farming is one of the areas most directly affected by climate change. The technologies and practices that drove the green revolution contributed to climate change by intensifying mechanized agriculture and the use of chemical fertilizers, but they are also affected by climate change. As in the Little Ice Age, farming and ranching are vulnerable to shifts toward dryer, wetter, hotter, cooler, or simply less stable weather. Attuned to the implications of climate change, multinational agricultural corporations are now directing attention to the increased risk of crop failures and are doing research on seeds with greater drought resistance or shorter growing seasons.

## Impacts of Climate Change

As the habitats for organisms that carry diseases — such as mosquitoes — have expanded due to warming conditions, climate change has become a growing factor in the spread of disease. Changes in rainfall also play a role because areas that experience increasing rain have more standing water where mosquitoes incubate. Paradoxically, areas beset by drought also experience an intensification of mosquito-borne disease because in dry periods people tend to store water, which becomes a breeding ground for mosquitoes. In Africa, Asia, the Pacific, and the Americas, these factors have intensified mosquito-borne diseases such as malaria, dengue, chikungunya, and Zika.

The impacts of climate change will be fall hardest upon poorer regions of the world, for several reasons. Poorer nations are less able to adapt, and their governing capacity will be more taxed by economic, social, and weather stress. Many poorer countries are paradoxically also fuel-exporting countries, so efforts to mitigate climate change by using alternative energy could bring negative consequences without corresponding benefits, particularly since technologies such as solar and wind power are concentrated in wealthier countries. The effects of climate change on farming are felt disproportionately in tropical regions of Africa, Latin America, and South and Southeast Asia, which face drought as well as limitations on the types of crops that can be cultivated in hotter conditions.

One of the most recognized climate scientists has said that "climate change will have a bigger impact on your family and friends and all of humanity than the Internet has had."[10] Our understanding of patterns of historical climate and environmental change suggests that this will be true.

# Chapter Summary

The twenty-first century has witnessed new versions of historic challenges. The end of the Cold War confrontation between superpowers has resulted in a world in which regional tensions endure and sometimes become international conflicts. Despite the dominance of neoliberalism, discontent has grown over unevenly distributed costs and benefits. The growing inequalities and increasing interconnectedness of the contemporary world shaped the speed and impact of the COVID-19 pandemic. Rising inequalities also led to the global emergence of right-wing nationalism. A new generation of politicians build their appeal by scapegoating migrants and ethnic minorities, blaming them for the consequences of neoliberalism.

By the second decade of the new century, the scale of the challenge presented by global climate change and its stakes for populations worldwide became clear. But the political and technological pathways for slowing global warming were less clear, particularly given the resistance of many political leaders in the country that produces the largest amount of greenhouse gases, the United States, to face the problem. In the 1980s, LGBTQ activists confronted a similar intransigence among public officials reluctant to respond to the HIV/AIDS epidemic. The strategies of such social movements offer a road map for addressing the political obstacles to action on climate.

## NOTES

1. International Labour Office, *Global Employment Trends: January 2010* (Geneva: ILO, 2010), pp. 8–9, 39.
2. United Nations High Commissioner for Human Rights (UN Refugee Agency), "Europe Situation," updated January 24, 2017, http://www.unhcr.org/europe-emergency.html.
3. James Gockowski and S. Oduwole, *Labor Practices in the Cocoa Sector of Southwest Nigeria with a Focus on the Role of Children* (Ibadan, Nigeria: International Institute of Tropical Agriculture, 2003), p. 23.
4. Quoted in Judith Richter, *Holding Corporations Accountable: Corporate Conduct, International Codes, and Citizen Action* (London: Zed Books, 2002), p. 55; Simon Robinson, "Nestlé Baby Milk Substitute and International Marketing: A Case History," in *Case Histories in Business Ethics*, ed. Chris Megone and Simon Robinson (New York: Routledge, 2002), p. 141.
5. United Nations, "Critical Areas of Concern," *Report of the Fourth World Conference on Women* (New York: United Nations Department for Policy Coordination and Sustainable Development, 1995), chap. 1, annex II; chap. 3, pp. 41–44, http://www.un.org/esa/gopher-data/conf/fwcw/off/a--20.en. See also Population Reference Bureau, *Women of Our World 2005* (Washington, D.C.: Population Reference Bureau, 2005), for the latest data and ten-year follow-up to the Beijing meeting.
6. Jesse Green, "When Political Art Mattered," *New York Times*, December 7, 2003, https://www.nytimes.com/2003/12/07/magazine/when-political-art-mattered.html.
7. Rachel Carson, *Silent Spring* (1962; repr., New York: Houghton Mifflin, 2002), p. 8.
8. Michael Gross, "A Planet with Two Billion Cars," *Current Biology* 26 (April 2016): R307–R318; Daniel Sperling and Deborah Gordon, "Two Billion Cars: Transforming a Culture," *TR News* 259 (November 2008): 3–9.
9. World Health Organization, *Health in the Green Economy: Health Co-benefits of Climate Change Mitigation—Transport Sector* (Geneva: WHO, 2011), p. 13; Environmental Protection Agency, *Inventory of U.S. Greenhouse Emissions and Sinks, 1990–2017* (Washington, D.C.: EPA, 2019), pp. 2–23.
10. Joseph Romm, *Climate Change: What Everyone Needs to Know* (Oxford: Oxford University Press, 2016), p. xiv.

## MAKE CONNECTIONS   LOOK AHEAD

The present shapes the ways we ask questions about the past. Understanding of the past also shapes our questions about the present and the future. Our history of world societies shows that the forces that shape the world we live in have deep roots. Globalization reaches back for centuries. Current armed conflicts are based on historic tensions often rooted in ethnic differences or legacies of colonialism. The gaps between rich and poor countries, and between the rich and poor within countries, have sometimes been diminished by advances in science and technology or by reforms in social policy. But science, technology, and public policy also deepen those inequalities, as reflected by uneven industrialization and the digital divide.

Our relationship with the past is one of continuity and change. The study of history allows us to frame questions about complex, competing, and often-contradictory experiences. Asking these questions sharpens our focus on not only the past but also the present. We are shaped by history. But we also make it.

# Chapter 33 Review

## IDENTIFY KEY TERMS

**Identify and explain the significance of each item below.**

megacities (p. 895)

informal economy (p. 895)

multinational corporations (p. 897)

digital divide (p. 899)

feminization of poverty (p. 902)

global warming (p. 906)

climate change (p. 906)

green revolution (p. 910)

## REVIEW THE MAIN IDEAS

**Answer the focus questions from each section of the chapter.**

1. What tensions have resulted from the rise of neoliberalism? (p. 889)

2. How have migration and the circulation of capital and technology continued to shape the world? (p. 894)

3. What challenges did social reformers address at the turn of the twenty-first century? (p. 900)

4. What do historical perspectives bring to our understanding of climate change? (p. 906)

## MAKE COMPARISONS AND CONNECTIONS

**Analyze the larger developments and continuities within and across chapters.**

1. Why hasn't the end of the Cold War been followed by an easing of regional conflicts?

2. How do socioeconomic inequalities in the twenty-first-century world resemble the gaps between rich and poor in earlier eras?

3. How do contemporary technological and scientific developments reflect historical change and continuity?

## CHRONOLOGY

| | |
|---|---|
| **1950s** | • Beginning of green revolution |
| **1957–1975** | • Decolonization (Chs. 31, 32) |
| **1959–1975** | • Vietnam War (Ch. 31) |
| **1962** | • Cuban missile crisis (Ch. 31) |
| **1965** | • Great Proletarian Cultural Revolution in China (Ch. 31) |
| **1967** | • Six-Day War between Israel, Egypt, Syria, and Jordan (Ch. 31) |
| **1970** | • Treaty on the Non-Proliferation of Nuclear Weapons |
| **1978** | • Deng Xiaoping initiates economic reforms in China (Ch. 32) |
| **1987** | • Palestinian intifada (Ch. 32) |
| **1989–1991** | • Fall of communism in the Soviet Union and eastern Europe (Ch. 32) |
| **1993** | • Formation of the European Union (Ch. 32) |
| **1994** | • Nelson Mandela elected president of South Africa (Ch. 32) |
| **1994** | • North American Free Trade Agreement (Ch. 32) |
| **1994** | • Zapatista Army for National Liberation insurrection in Chiapas, Mexico |
| **1997** | • Kyoto Protocol on global warming |
| **2000–2010** | • Second warmest decade on record |
| **2001** | • Al-Qaeda attacks on World Trade Center and U.S. Pentagon |
| **2001** | • U.S. invasion and occupation of Afghanistan |
| **2003–2011** | • Second Persian Gulf War (Ch. 32) |
| **2010** | • China becomes the world's second largest economy |
| **2010–2020** | • Warmest decade on record |
| **2011** | • Civil war in Syria begins (Ch. 32) |
| **2015** | • Iran freezes its nuclear program |
| **2016** | • Paris Climate Accord |
| **2016** | • Zika epidemic spreads through Latin America and the Caribbean |
| **2020** | • Britain leaves the European Union |
| **2020** | • COVID-19 pandemic spreads globally |

# Glossary

**absolutism** A political system common to early modern Europe in which monarchs claimed exclusive power to make and enforce laws, without checks by other institutions; this system was limited in practice by the need to maintain legitimacy and compromise with elites. (Ch. 18)

**African National Congress (ANC)** The main black nationalist organization in South Africa, led by Nelson Mandela. (Ch. 32)

**Afrikaners** Descendants of the Dutch settlers in the Cape Colony in southern Africa. (Ch. 25)

**age-grade systems** Among the societies of Senegambia, groups of teenage males and females whom the society initiated into adulthood at the same time. (Ch. 20)

**alternate residence system** Arrangement in which Japanese lords were required to live in Edo every other year and left their wives and sons there as hostages to the Tokugawa Shogunate. (Ch. 21)

**anarcho-syndicalism** A version of anarchism that advocated placing power in the hands of workers' unions. (Ch. 27)

**Antifederalists** Opponents of the American Constitution who felt it diminished individual rights and accorded too much power to the federal government at the expense of the states. (Ch. 22)

**apartheid** The system of racial segregation and discrimination that was supported by the Afrikaner government in South Africa. (Ch. 32)

**Arab socialism** A secular and nationalist project in the Middle East aimed at economic development and a strong military. (Ch. 31)

**Aztec Empire** An alliance between the Mexica people and their conquered allies, with its capital in Tenochtitlan (now Mexico City), that rose in size and power in the fifteenth century and possessed a sophisticated society and culture, with advanced mathematics, astronomy, and engineering. (Ch. 16)

**Balfour Declaration** A 1917 statement by British foreign secretary Arthur Balfour that supported the idea of a Jewish homeland in Palestine. (Ch. 29)

**banners** Units of the Manchu army, composed of soldiers, their families, and slaves. (Ch. 21)

**Berlin Conference** A meeting of European leaders held in 1884–1885 to lay down basic rules for imperialist competition in sub-Saharan Africa. (Ch. 25)

**Bill of Rights of 1689** A bill passed by Parliament and accepted by William and Mary that limited the powers of British monarchs and affirmed those of Parliament. (Ch. 18)

**Black Shirts** A private army under Mussolini in Italy that destroyed Socialist newspapers, union halls, and local Socialist Party headquarters, eventually pushing Socialists out of the city governments of northern Italy. (Ch. 30)

**blitzkrieg** "Lightning war" using planes, tanks, and trucks, first used by Hitler to crush Poland in four weeks. (Ch. 30)

**Bolsheviks** The "majority group"; this was Lenin's camp of the Russian party of Marxist socialism. (Ch. 28)

**bourgeoisie** The well-educated, prosperous, middle-class groups. (Ch. 24)

**Boxers** A Chinese secret society that blamed the country's ills on foreigners, especially missionaries, and rose in rebellion in 1900. (Ch. 26)

**bride wealth** In early modern Southeast Asia, a sum of money the groom paid the bride or her family at the time of marriage. This practice contrasted with the dowry in China, India, and Europe, which the husband controlled. (Ch. 16)

**captaincies** A system established by the Portuguese in Brazil in the 1530s, whereby hereditary grants of land were given to nobles and loyal officials who bore the costs of settling and administering their territories. (Ch. 16)

**caravel** A small, maneuverable, three-masted sailing ship developed by the Portuguese in the fifteenth century that gave them a distinct advantage in exploration and trade. (Ch. 16)

**caudillismo** In Latin America, government by people who rule through personal charisma and the support of armed followers. (Ch. 27)

**chattel** An item of personal property; a term used in reference to enslaved people that conveys the idea that they are subhuman, like animals, and therefore may be treated like animals. (Ch. 20)

**Circum-Caribbean** The region encompassing the Antilles as well as the lands that bound the Caribbean Sea in Central America and northern South America. (Ch. 27)

**civil service examinations** A highly competitive series of written tests held at the prefecture, province, and capital levels in China to select men to become officials. (Ch. 21)

**class-consciousness** An individual's sense of class differentiation, a term introduced by Karl Marx. (Ch. 23)

**climate change** The patterns of changes in climate caused by global warming, which can range from drought and heat to heavier rainfall or even colder weather. (Ch. 33)

**cocoa holdups** Mass protests in Africa's Gold Coast in the 1930s by producers of cocoa who refused to sell their beans to British firms and instead sold them directly to European and American chocolate manufacturers. (Ch. 31)

**Cold War** The post–World War II conflict between the United States and the Soviet Union. (Ch. 31)

**collectivization** Stalin's forcible consolidation, beginning in 1929, of individual peasant farms in the Soviet Union into large, state-controlled enterprises. (Ch. 30)

**Columbian exchange** The exchange of animals, plants, and diseases between the Old and the New Worlds. (Ch. 16)

**Combination Acts** English laws passed in 1799 that outlawed unions and strikes, favoring capitalist business owners over skilled artisans. Bitterly resented and widely disregarded by many craft guilds, the acts were repealed by Parliament in 1824. (Ch. 23)

**Common Market** The European Economic Community created in 1957. (Ch. 31)

**concubine** An enslaved woman whose primary role was to have sexual relations with the male slave owner. (Ch. 17)

**Congress of Vienna** A meeting of the Quadruple Alliance (Russia, Prussia, Austria, Great Britain) and France held in 1814–1815 to fashion a general peace settlement after the defeat of Napoleonic France. (Ch. 24)

**conquistador** Spanish for "conqueror"; a Spanish soldier-explorer, such as Hernán Cortés or Francisco Pizarro, who sought to conquer the New World for the Spanish Crown. (Ch. 16)

**conservatism** A political philosophy that stressed retaining traditional values and institutions, including hereditary monarchy and a strong landowning aristocracy. (Ch. 24)

**constitutionalism** A form of government in which power is limited by law and balanced between the authority and power of the government, on the one hand, and the rights and liberties of the subject or citizen, on the other; it includes constitutional monarchies and republics. (Ch. 18)

**Continental System** A blockade imposed by Napoleon in which no ship coming from Britain or its colonies was permitted to dock at any port controlled by the French. (Ch. 22)

**Copernican hypothesis** The idea that the sun, not the earth, was the center of the universe. (Ch. 19)

**Coptic Christianity** Orthodox form of Christianity from Egypt practiced in Ethiopia. (Ch. 20)

**Cossacks** Free groups and outlaw armies living on the borders of Russian territory from the fourteenth century onward. In the mid-sixteenth century they formed an alliance with the Russian state. (Ch. 18)

**cottage industry** Manufacturing with hand tools in peasant cottages and work sheds, a form of economic activity that became important in eighteenth-century Europe. (Ch. 19)

**cowrie shells** Imported from the Maldives, they served as the medium of exchange in West Africa. (Ch. 20)

**Creoles** People of European descent born in the Americas. (Ch. 19)

**Crystal Palace** The location of the Great Exhibition in 1851 in London, an architectural masterpiece made entirely of glass and iron. (Ch. 23)

**daimyo** Regional lords in Japan, many of whom were self-made men. (Ch. 21)

**Dawes Plan** The product of the 1924 World War I reparations commission, accepted by Germany, France, and Britain, that reduced Germany's yearly reparations, made payment dependent on German economic prosperity, and granted Germany large loans from the United States to promote recovery. (Ch. 28)

**death squads** Informal groups usually composed of police and soldiers who assassinate political opponents of the government. (Ch. 32)

**Declaration of Independence** The 1776 document in which the American colonies declared independence from Great Britain and recast traditional English rights as universal human rights. (Ch. 22)

**deism** Belief in a distant, noninterventionist deity, shared by many Enlightenment thinkers. (Ch. 19)

**denazification** The process of removing Nazi Party figures from roles of public authority and dismantling Nazi laws and institutions in postwar Germany. (Ch. 31)

**dependency theory** The belief, formulated in Latin America in the mid-twentieth century, that development in some areas of the world locks other nations into underdevelopment. (Ch. 31)

**détente** The progressive relaxation of Cold War tensions between the United States and the Soviet Union in the late 1960s and early 1970s. (Ch. 32)

**devshirme** A process whereby the sultan's agents took Christian youths to be trained as soldiers or civil servants. (Ch. 17)

**digital divide** The gap between rich and poor regions and populations in levels of access to computing, the Internet, and telecommunications. (Ch. 33)

**divine right of kings** The belief propagated by absolutist monarchs in Europe that they derived their power from God and were only answerable to him. (Ch. 18)

**Dreyfus affair** A divisive case in which Alfred Dreyfus, a Jewish captain in the French army, was falsely accused and convicted of treason. The Catholic Church sided with the anti-Semites against Dreyfus; after Dreyfus was declared innocent, the French government severed all ties between the state and the church. (Ch. 24)

**economic liberalism** The theory, associated with Adam Smith, that the pursuit of individual self-interest in a competitive market would lead to rising prosperity and greater social equality, rendering government intervention unnecessary and undesirable. (Ch. 19)

**economic nationalism** The effort to promote development through substitution of imports with domestic manufacturing and state control of key industries. (Ch. 31)

**empiricism** A theory of inductive reasoning that calls for acquiring evidence through observation and experimentation rather than reason and speculation. (Ch. 19)

**Enabling Act** An act pushed through the Reichstag by the Nazis in 1933 that gave Hitler absolute dictatorial power for four years. (Ch. 30)

**enclosure** The controversial process of fencing off common land to create privately owned fields; increased agricultural production at the cost of reducing poor farmers' access to land. (Ch. 19)

**encomienda system** A system whereby the Spanish Crown granted the conquerors the right to forcibly employ groups of indigenous people as laborers and to demand tribute payments from them in exchange for providing food, shelter, and instruction in the Christian faith. (Ch. 16)

**enlightened absolutism** Term coined by historians to describe the rule of eighteenth-century monarchs who, without renouncing their own absolute authority, took up the call to reform their governments in accordance with the rational and humane principles of the Enlightenment. (Ch. 19)

**Enlightenment** An intellectual and cultural movement in late-seventeenth- and eighteenth-century Europe and the wider world that used rational and critical thinking to debate issues such as political sovereignty, religious tolerance, gender roles, and racial difference. (Ch. 19)

**Estates General** Traditional representative body of the three estates of France that met in 1789 in response to imminent state bankruptcy. (Ch. 22)

**European Union (EU)** An economic and political alliance of twelve European nations formed in 1993 that has since grown to include twenty-eight European nations. (Ch. 32)

**Europe first policy** The military strategy, set forth by Churchill and adopted by Roosevelt, that called for the defeat of Hitler in Europe before the United States launched an all-out strike against Japan in the Pacific. (Ch. 30)

**evolution** The idea, developed by Charles Darwin, that all life had gradually evolved from a common origin through a process of natural selection. (Ch. 24)

**existentialism** The name given to a highly diverse and even contradictory philosophy that stresses the meaninglessness of existence and the search for moral values in a world of terror and uncertainty. (Ch. 28)

**extraterritoriality** The legal principle that exempts individuals from local law, applicable in China because of the agreements reached after China's loss in the Opium War. (Ch. 26)

**Factory Act of 1833** English law that led to a sharp decline in the employment of children by limiting the hours that children over age nine could work and banning employment of children younger than nine. (Ch. 23)

**fascism** A movement characterized by extreme, often expansionist nationalism, anti-socialism, a dynamic and violent leader, and glorification of war and the military. (Ch. 30)

**feminization of poverty** The issue that those living in extreme poverty are disproportionately women. (Ch. 33)

**fiscal-military state** A state form that emerged in seventeenth-century Europe in which an increasingly centralized and bureaucratic state harnessed domestic resources to maintain a large army for internal order and to compete for territory within Europe and overseas. (Ch. 18)

**five-year plan** Launched by Stalin in 1928 and termed the "revolution from above," its goal was to modernize the Soviet Union and generate a Communist society with new attitudes, new loyalties, and a new socialist humanity. (Ch. 30)

**free womb laws** Laws passed across the nineteenth-century Americas that instituted a gradual form of abolition through which children born to slaves gained their freedom. (Ch. 27)

**functionalism** The principle that buildings, like industrial products, should serve the purpose for which they were made as well as possible. (Ch. 28)

**general will** A concept associated with Rousseau, referring to the common interests of all the people, who have displaced the monarch as the holder of sovereign power. (Ch. 19)

**germ theory** The idea that disease is caused by the spread of living organisms that can be controlled. (Ch. 24)

**Girondists** A moderate group that fought for control of the French National Convention in 1793. (Ch. 22)

**glasnost** Soviet premier Mikhail Gorbachev's popular campaign for government transparency and more open media. (Ch. 32)

**global warming** The consensus view of an overwhelming majority of the world's scientists that hydrocarbons produced through the burning of fossil fuels have caused a greenhouse effect that has increased global temperatures over time. (Ch. 33)

**Grand Empire** The empire over which Napoleon and his allies ruled, encompassing virtually all of Europe except Great Britain. (Ch. 22)

**Great Leap Forward** Mao Zedong's acceleration of Chinese development in which industrial growth was to be based on small-scale backyard workshops run by peasants living in gigantic self-contained communes. (Ch. 31)

**great migration** The mass movement of people from Europe in the nineteenth century; one reason that the West's impact on the world was so powerful and complex. (Ch. 25)

**Great Mutiny / Great Revolt** The terms used by the British and the Indians, respectively, to describe the last armed resistance to British rule in India, which occurred in 1857. (Ch. 26)

**Great Proletarian Cultural Revolution** A movement launched in 1965 by Mao Zedong that attempted to recapture the revolutionary fervor of his guerrilla struggle. (Ch. 31)

**great white walls** Discriminatory laws passed by Americans and Australians to keep Asians from settling in their countries in the 1880s. (Ch. 25)

**green revolution** Beginning in the 1950s, the increase in food production stemming from the introduction of high-yielding wheat, hybrid seeds, and other advancements. (Ch. 33)

**gunboat diplomacy** The imposition of treaties and agreements under threat of military violence, such as the opening of Japan to trade after Commodore Perry's demands. (Ch. 26)

**Haskalah** A Jewish Enlightenment movement led by Prussian philosopher Moses Mendelssohn. (Ch. 19)

**Holocaust** The attempted systematic extermination of all European Jews and other "undesirables" by the Nazi state during World War II. (Ch. 30)

**id, ego, superego** Freudian terms for the primitive, irrational unconscious (id), the rationalizing conscious that mediates what a person can do (ego), and the ingrained moral values that specify what a person should do (superego). (Ch. 28)

**import substitution industrialization (ISI)** The use of trade barriers to keep certain foreign products out of one's country so that domestic industry can emerge and produce the same goods. (Ch. 31)

**Inca Empire** The vast and sophisticated Peruvian empire centered at the capital city of Cuzco that was at its peak in the fifteenth century but weakened by civil war at the time of the Spanish arrival. (Ch. 16)

**indentured laborers** Laborers who agreed to a term of employment, specified in a contract. (Ch. 26)

**Indian Civil Service** The bureaucracy that administered the government of India. Entry into its elite ranks was through examinations that Indians were eligible to take, but these tests were offered only in England. (Ch. 26)

**Indian National Congress** A political association formed in 1885 that worked for Indian self-government. (Ch. 26)

**Industrial Revolution** A term first coined in 1799 to describe the burst of major inventions and economic expansion that began in Britain in the late eighteenth century. (Ch. 23)

**informal economy** An economy with few salaried jobs and an abundance of tiny, unregulated businesses such as peddlers and pushcart operators. (Ch. 33)

**intifada** Beginning in 1987, a prolonged campaign of civil disobedience by Palestinian youth against Israeli soldiers; the Arabic word *intifada* means "shaking off." (Ch. 32)

**iron law of wages** Theory proposed by English economist David Ricardo suggesting that the pressure of population growth prevents wages from rising above the subsistence level. (Ch. 23)

**Jacobin club** A political club during the French Revolution to which many of the deputies of the Legislative Assembly belonged. (Ch. 22)

**janissaries** Turkish for "new soldiers"; they formed the elite army corps. (Ch. 17)

**"Japan, Inc."** A nickname from the 1970s and 1980s used to describe what some considered the unfair relationship between Japan's business world and government. (Ch. 32)

**Java War** The 1825–1830 war between the Dutch government and the Javanese, fought over the extension of Dutch control of the island. (Ch. 26)

**Jesuits** Members of the Society of Jesus, founded by Ignatius Loyola in 1540, whose goal was the spread of the Roman Catholic faith through schools and missionary activity. (Ch. 18)

**jihad** Religious war waged by Muslim scholars and religious leaders against both animist rulers and Islamic states that they deemed corrupt. (Ch. 25)

**junta** A government headed by a council of commanders of the branches of the armed forces. (Ch. 32)

**kibbutz** A Jewish collective farm, first established by Zionists in Palestine, on which each member shared equally in the work, rewards, and defense. (Ch. 29)

**laissez faire** A doctrine of economic liberalism advocating unrestricted private enterprise and no government interference in the economy. (Ch. 24)

**Lateran Agreement** A 1929 agreement in which Mussolini in Italy recognized the Vatican as an independent state and agreed to give the church heavy financial support in return for the pope's public support. (Ch. 30)

**latifundios** Vast landed estates in Latin America. (Ch. 27)

**law of universal gravitation** Newton's law that all objects are attracted to one another and that the force of attraction is proportional to the object's quantity of matter and inversely proportional to the square of the distance between them. (Ch. 19)

**League of Nations** A permanent international organization established during the 1919 Paris Peace Conference to protect member states from aggression and avert future wars. (Ch. 28)

**Lerdo Law** An 1856 Mexican law that barred corporate landholdings. (Ch. 27)

**liberalism** A philosophy whose principal ideas were equality and liberty; liberals demanded representative government and equality before the law as well as such individual freedoms as freedom of the press, freedom of speech, freedom of assembly, and freedom from arbitrary arrest. (Ch. 24)

**liberation theology** A movement within the Catholic Church to support the poor in situations of exploitation that emerged with particular force in Latin America in the 1960s. (Ch. 31)

**Long March** The 6,000-mile retreat of the Chinese Communist army in 1934 to a remote region on the northwestern border of China, during which tens of thousands lost their lives. (Ch. 29)

**Lucknow Pact** A 1916 alliance between the Hindus leading the Indian National Congress Party and the Muslim League. (Ch. 29)

**Luddites** Group of handicraft workers who attacked factories in northern England in 1811 and after, smashing the new machines that they believed were putting them out of work. (Ch. 23)

**Majlis** The national assembly established by the despotic shah of Iran in 1906. (Ch. 29)

**mandate system** A system established by the League of Nations whereby certain territories were transferred from the control of one country to another following World War I. (Ch. 28)

**manifest destiny** The doctrine that the United States should absorb the territory spanning from the original Atlantic states to the Pacific Ocean. (Ch. 27)

**March Revolution** The first phase of the Russian Revolution of 1917, in which unplanned uprisings led to the abdication of the tsar and the establishment of a provisional democratic government that was then overthrown in November by Lenin and the Bolsheviks. (Ch. 28)

**Marshall Plan** A 1948 American plan for providing economic aid to Europe to help it rebuild after World War II. (Ch. 31)

**May Fourth Movement** A Chinese nationalist movement against foreign imperialists and warlord rule; it began as a 1919 student protest against the decision of the Paris Peace Conference to leave the Shandong Peninsula in the hands of Japan. (Ch. 29)

**megacities** Cities with populations of 10 million people or more. (Ch. 33)

**Meiji Restoration** The 1867 ousting of the Tokugawa Shogunate that "restored" the power of the Japanese emperors. (Ch. 26)

*Mein Kampf* Adolf Hitler's autobiography, published in 1925, which also contains Hitler's political ideology. (Ch. 28)

**mercantilism** A system of economic regulations aimed at increasing the power of the state that was derived from the belief that a nation's international power was based on its wealth, specifically its supply of gold and silver. (Ch. 18)

**Middle Passage** Enslaved Africans' horrific voyage across the Atlantic to the Americas, under appalling and often deadly conditions. (Ch. 20)

**migration chain** The movement of peoples in which one strong individual blazes the way and others follow. (Ch. 25)

**militarism** The glorification of the military as the supreme ideal of the state with all other interests subordinate to it. (Ch. 28)

**Mines Act of 1842** English law prohibiting underground work for all women and girls as well as for boys under ten. (Ch. 23)

**Ming Dynasty** The Chinese dynasty in power from 1368 to 1644; it marked a period of vibrant urban culture. (Ch. 21)

**modernism** A variety of cultural movements at the end of the nineteenth century and beginning of the twentieth that rebelled against traditional forms and conventions of the past. (Ch. 28)

**modernization** The changes that enable a country to compete effectively with the leading countries at a given time. (Ch. 24)

**modernization theory** The belief, held in countries such as the United States in the mid-twentieth century, that all countries evolved in a linear progression from traditional to mature. (Ch. 31)

**Monroe Doctrine** An 1823 proclamation that established a U.S. sphere of influence over the Americas by opposing European imperialism on the continent. (Ch. 27)

**moral economy** The early modern European view that community needs predominated over competition and profit and that necessary goods should thus be sold at a fair price. (Ch. 18)

**Mountain** Led by Robespierre, the French National Convention's radical faction, which led the Convention in 1793. (Ch. 22)

**Mughal** A term used to refer to the Muslim empire of India, which was the largest, wealthiest, and most populous of the Islamic empires of the early modern world. (Ch. 17)

**multinational corporations** Business firms that operate in a number of different countries and tend to adopt a global rather than a national perspective. (Ch. 33)

**Muslim League** Political party founded in 1906 in colonial India that advocated for a separate Muslim homeland after independence. (Ch. 31)

**Napoleonic Code** French civil code promulgated in 1804 that reasserted the 1789 principles of the equality of all male citizens before the law and the absolute security of wealth and private property. (Ch. 22)

**National Assembly** French representative assembly formed in 1789 by the delegates of the third estate and some members of the clergy, the first estate. (Ch. 22)

**nationalism** The idea that each people had its own spirit and its own cultural unity, which manifested itself especially in a common language and history and could serve as the basis for an independent political state. (Ch. 24)

**National Liberation Front** The anticolonial movement in Algeria, which began a war against the French in 1954 and won independence in 1962. (Ch. 31)

**NATO** The North Atlantic Treaty Organization, an anti-Soviet military alliance of Western nations, formed in 1949. (Ch. 31)

**Navigation Acts** Mid-seventeenth-century English mercantilist laws that greatly restricted other countries' rights to trade with England and its colonies. (Ch. 18)

**Nazism** A movement born of extreme nationalism and racism and dominated by Adolf Hitler from 1933 until the end of World War II in 1945. (Ch. 30)

**neocolonialism** The establishment of political and economic influence over regions after they have ceased to be formal colonies. (Ch. 27)

**neoliberalism** A return beginning in the 1980s to policies intended to promote free markets and the free circulation of capital across national borders. (Ch. 32)

**New Culture Movement** An intellectual revolution beginning in 1916 that attacked traditional Chinese, particularly Confucian, culture and promoted Western ideas of science, democracy, and individualism. (Ch. 29)

**New Deal** Franklin Delano Roosevelt's plan to reform capitalism in the United States through forceful government intervention in the economy. (Ch. 30)

**New Economic Policy (NEP)** Lenin's 1921 policy re-establishing limited economic freedom in the Soviet Union in an attempt to rebuild agriculture and industry in the face of economic disintegration. (Ch. 30)

**New Imperialism** The late-nineteenth-century drive by European countries to create vast political empires abroad. (Ch. 25)

**New Order** Hitler's program, based on the guiding principle of racial imperialism, which gave preferential treatment to the Nordic peoples above "inferior" Latin peoples and, at the bottom, "subhuman" Slavs and Jews. (Ch. 30)

**Nguyen Dynasty** The last Vietnamese ruling house, which lasted from 1802 to 1945. (Ch. 26)

**1911 Revolution** The uprising that brought China's monarchy to an end. (Ch. 26)

**Nō theater** A type of Japanese theater performed on a bare stage by one or two actors wearing brilliant brocade robes, one actor wearing a mask. The performers conveyed emotions and ideas as much through gestures, stances, and dress as through words. (Ch. 21)

**oba** The title of the king of Benin. (Ch. 20)

**October Manifesto** The result of a great general strike in Russia in October 1905, it granted full civil rights and promised a popularly elected Duma (parliament) with real legislative power. (Ch. 24)

**oligarchs** In Latin America, the small number of individuals and families that had monopolized political power and economic resources since the colonial era. (Ch. 27)

**Opium War** The 1839–1842 war between the British and the Chinese over limitations on trade and the importation of opium into China. (Ch. 26)

**Organization of the Petroleum Exporting Countries (OPEC)** A cartel formed in 1960 by oil-exporting countries designed to coordinate oil production and raise prices, giving those countries greater capacity for economic development and greater leverage in world affairs. (Ch. 32)

**Ottomans** Ruling house of the Turkish empire that lasted from 1299 to 1922. (Ch. 17)

**Palestine Liberation Organization (PLO)** Created in 1964, a loose union of Palestinian refugee groups opposed to Israel and united in the goal of establishing a Palestinian state. (Ch. 31)

**palm oil** A West African tropical product often used to make soap; the British encouraged its cultivation as an alternative to the slave trade. (Ch. 25)

**Pan-Africanists** People who, through a movement beginning in 1919, sought black solidarity and envisioned a vast self-governing union of all African peoples. (Ch. 31)

**peninsulares** A term for natives of Spain and Portugal. (Ch. 22)

**perestroika** Economic restructuring and reform implemented by Soviet premier Mikhail Gorbachev that permitted an easing of government price controls on some goods, more independence for state enterprises, and the establishment of profit-seeking private cooperatives. (Ch. 32)

**Permanent Mandates Commission** A commission created by the League of Nations to oversee the developed nations' fulfillment of their international responsibility toward their mandates. (Ch. 29)

**petrodollars** The global recirculation by international banks of profits from the higher price of oil following the 1973 OPEC oil embargo. (Ch. 32)

**Petrograd Soviet** A counter-government to the 1917 Russian provisional government, this organization was a huge, fluctuating mass meeting of two to three thousand workers, soldiers, and socialist intellectuals. (Ch. 28)

**philosophes** A group of French intellectuals who proclaimed that they were bringing the light of knowledge to their fellow humans. (Ch. 19)

**Plan de Ayala** Document written by Zapatistas during the Mexican Revolution that demanded the government return all land, forests, and waters taken from rural communities. (Ch. 27)

**Popular Front** A party formed in 1936 in France that encouraged unions and launched a far-reaching New Deal–inspired program of social reform. (Ch. 30)

**Porfiriato** The regime of Porfirio Díaz, who presided in Mexico from 1876 to 1880 and again from 1884 to 1911. (Ch. 27)

**proletariat** The Marxist term for the working class of modern industrialized society. (Ch. 24)

**protectorate** An autonomous state or territory partly controlled and protected by a stronger outside power. (Ch. 25)

**Protestant Reformation** A religious reform movement that began in the early sixteenth century and split the Western Christian Church. (Ch. 18)

**Ptolemy's *Geography*** A second-century work translated into Latin around 1410 that synthesized the classical knowledge of geography and introduced latitude and longitude markings. (Ch. 16)

**public sphere** An idealized intellectual space that emerged in Europe during the Enlightenment. Here, the public came together to discuss important social, economic, and political issues. (Ch. 19)

**Puritans** Members of a sixteenth- and seventeenth-century reform movement within the Church of England that advocated purifying it of Roman Catholic elements, such as bishops, elaborate ceremonials, and wedding rings. (Ch. 18)

**Qing Dynasty** The dynasty founded by the Manchus that ruled China from 1644 to 1911. (Ch. 21)

**Qizilbash** Nomadic tribesmen who supplied the early Safavid state with military troops in exchange for grazing rights. (Ch. 17)

**quinine** An agent that proved effective in controlling attacks of malaria, which had previously decimated Europeans in the tropics. (Ch. 25)

**Reign of Terror** The period from 1793 to 1794, during which Robespierre's Committee of Public Safety tried and executed thousands suspected of political crimes, and a new revolutionary culture was imposed. (Ch. 22)

**republicanism** A form of government in which there is no monarch and power rests in the hands of the people as exercised through elected representatives. (Ch. 18)

**revisionism** An effort by various socialists to update Marxist doctrines to reflect the realities of the time. (Ch. 24)

***Rocket*** The name given to George Stephenson's effective locomotive that was first tested in 1829 on the Liverpool and Manchester Railway and reached a maximum speed of 35 miles per hour. (Ch. 23)

**Romanticism** A movement in art, literature, and music characterized by a belief in emotional exuberance, unrestrained imagination, and spontaneity in both art and personal life. (Ch. 24)

**Roosevelt Corollary** A corollary to the Monroe Doctrine stating that the United States would correct what it saw as "chronic wrongdoing" in neighboring countries. (Ch. 27)

**Russo-Japanese War** The 1904–1905 war between Russia and Japan fought over imperial influence and territory in northeast China (Manchuria). (Ch. 26)

**Safavid** The dynasty that ruled all of Persia and other regions from 1501 to 1722; its state religion was Shi'ism. (Ch. 17)

**salons** Regular social gatherings held by talented and rich Parisian women in their homes, where philosophes and their followers met to discuss literature, science, and philosophy. (Ch. 19)

**sans-culottes** The laboring poor of Paris, so called because the men wore trousers instead of the knee breeches of the wealthy; the term came to refer to the militant radicals of the city. (Ch. 22)

**satyagraha** Loosely translated as "soul force," which Gandhi believed was the means of striving for truth and social justice through love, suffering, and conversion of the oppressor. (Ch. 29)

**second-wave feminism** A movement for the full equality of women in law, labor, social and family relations, and reproductive rights. (Ch. 32)

**sensationalism** An idea, espoused by John Locke, that all human ideas and thoughts are produced as a result of sensory impressions. (Ch. 19)

**separate spheres** A gender division of labor with the wife at home as mother and homemaker and the husband as wage earner. (Ch. 23)

**sepoys** The native Indian troops who were trained as infantrymen. (Ch. 17)

**settler colonialism** The practice of displacing indigenous or pre-existing populations and creating culturally, economically, and demographically distinct societies in their place. (Ch. 27)

**shah** Persian word for "king." (Ch. 17)

**shore trading** A process for trading goods in which European ships sent boats ashore or invited African dealers to bring traders and slaves out to the ships. (Ch. 20)

**Social Darwinism** The application of the theory of biological evolution to human affairs, it sees the human race as driven to ever-greater specialization and progress by an unending economic struggle that determines the survival of the fittest. (Ch. 24)

**socialism** A radical political doctrine that opposed individualism and that advocated cooperation and a sense of community; key ideas were economic planning, greater economic equality, and state regulation of property. (Ch. 24)

**Sokoto caliphate** Founded in 1809 by Uthman dan Fodio, this African state was based on Islamic history and law. (Ch. 25)

**Solidarity** Led by Lech Wałęsa, an independent Polish trade union organized in 1980 that worked for the rights of workers and political reform. (Ch. 32)

**sorting** A collection or batch of British goods that would be traded for a slave or for a quantity of gold, ivory, or dyewood. (Ch. 20)

**spinning jenny** A simple, inexpensive, hand-powered spinning machine created by James Hargreaves about 1765. (Ch. 23)

**steam engines** A breakthrough invention by Thomas Savery in 1698 and Thomas Newcomen in 1705 that burned coal to produce steam, which was then used to operate a pump; the early models were superseded by James Watt's more efficient steam engine, patented in 1769. (Ch. 23)

**sultan** An Arabic word used by the Ottomans to describe a supreme political and military ruler. (Ch. 17)

**Swahili** Meaning "People of the Coast," the term used for the people living along the East African coast and on nearby islands. (Ch. 20)

**Sykes-Picot Agreement** The 1916 secret agreement between Britain and France that divided up the Arab lands of Lebanon, Syria, southern Turkey, Palestine, Jordan, and Iraq. (Ch. 29)

**Taghaza** A settlement in the western Sahara, the site of the main salt-mining center. (Ch. 20)

**Taiping Rebellion** A massive rebellion by believers in the religious teachings of Hong Xiuquan, begun in 1851 and not suppressed until 1864. (Ch. 26)

**Tanzimat** A set of radical reforms designed to remake the Ottoman Empire on a western European model. (Ch. 25)

**tariff protection** A government's way of supporting and aiding its own economy by laying high taxes on imported goods from other countries, as when the French responded to the flood of cheaper British goods in their country by imposing high tariffs on some imported products. (Ch. 23)

**Thermidorian reaction** A reaction in 1794 to the violence of the Reign of Terror, resulting in the execution of Robespierre and the loosening of economic controls. (Ch. 22)

**Thirty Years' War** A large-scale conflict extending from 1618 to 1648 that pitted Protestants against Catholics in central Europe, but also involved dynastic interests, notably of Spain and France. (Ch. 18)

**Tiananmen Square** The site of a Chinese student revolt in 1989 at which Communists imposed martial law and arrested, injured, or killed hundreds of students. (Ch. 32)

**Tokugawa Shogunate** The Japanese government in Edo founded by Tokugawa Ieyasu. It lasted from 1603 to 1867. (Ch. 21)

**totalitarianism** A radical dictatorship that exercises complete political power and control over all aspects of society and seeks to mobilize the masses for action. (Ch. 30)

**total war** Practiced by countries fighting in World War I, a war in which the government plans and controls all aspects of economic and social life in order to make the greatest possible military effort. (Ch. 28)

**Treaty of Guadalupe Hidalgo** The 1848 treaty between the United States and Mexico in which Mexico ceded large tracts of land to the United States. (Ch. 27)

**Treaty of Lausanne** The 1923 treaty that ended the Turkish war and recognized the territorial integrity of a truly independent Turkey. (Ch. 29)

**Treaty of Paris** The 1763 peace treaty that ended the Seven Years' War, according vast French territories in North America and India to Britain and Louisiana to Spain. (Ch. 22)

**Treaty of Tordesillas** The 1494 agreement giving Spain everything west of an imaginary line drawn down the Atlantic and giving Portugal everything to the east. (Ch. 16)

**Treaty of Versailles** The 1919 peace settlement that ended World War I; it declared Germany responsible for the war, limited Germany's army to one hundred thousand men, and forced Germany to pay huge reparations. (Ch. 28)

**trench warfare** Fighting behind rows of trenches, mines, and barbed wire; used in World War I with a staggering cost in lives and minimal gains in territory. (Ch. 28)

**Triple Entente** The alliance of Great Britain, France, and Russia in the First World War. (Ch. 28)

**Truman Doctrine** The 1945 American policy of preventing the spread of Communist rule. (Ch. 31)

**Tuareg** Major branch of the nomadic Berber peoples who controlled the north-south trans-Saharan trade in salt. (Ch. 20)

**ulama** Religious scholars who interpret the Qur'an and the Sunna, the deeds and sayings of Muhammad. (Ch. 17)

**Valladolid debate** A debate organized by Spanish king Charles I in 1550 in the city of Valladolid that pitted defenders of Spanish conquest and forcible conversion against critics of these practices. (Ch. 16)

**viceroyalties** The name for the four administrative units of Spanish possessions in the Americas: New Spain, Peru, New Granada, and La Plata. (Ch. 16)

**viziers** Chief assistants to caliphs. (Ch. 17)

**War Communism** The application of the total-war concept to a civil conflict; the Bolsheviks seized grain from peasants, introduced rationing, nationalized all banks and industry, and required everyone to work. (Ch. 28)

**Washington Consensus** Policies restricting public spending, lowering import barriers, privatizing state enterprises, and deregulating markets in response to the 1980s debt crisis in Latin America. (Ch. 32)

**water frame** A spinning machine created by Richard Arkwright that had a capacity of several hundred spindles and used waterpower; it therefore required a larger and more specialized mill — a factory. (Ch. 23)

**white man's burden** The idea that Europeans could and should civilize more primitive nonwhite peoples and that imperialism would eventually provide nonwhites with modern achievements and higher standards of living. (Ch. 25)

**Young Turks** Fervent patriots who seized power in the revolution of 1908, forcing the conservative sultan to implement reforms; they helped pave the way for the birth of modern secular Turkey. (Ch. 25)

**zaibatsu** Giant conglomerate firms established in Japan beginning in the Meiji period and lasting until the end of World War II. (Ch. 29)

**Zionism** The movement toward Jewish political nationhood started by Theodor Herzl. (Ch. 24)

# Index

# About the Authors

**Merry E. Wiesner-Hanks** (Ph.D., University of Wisconsin–Madison) is Distinguished Professor of History, emerita, at the University of Wisconsin–Milwaukee. She is the long-time Senior Editor of the *Sixteenth Century Journal* and the author or editor of more than thirty books, including *A Concise History of the World.* From 2017 to 2019 she served as the president of the World History Association.

**Patricia Buckley Ebrey** (Ph.D., Columbia University) is Professor of History at the University of Washington in Seattle. Editor of the *Journal of Chinese History,* she is the author or editor of some twenty books, including *The Cambridge Illustrated History of China* and *Chinese Civilization: A Sourcebook,* as well as more specialized books on Song Dynasty China. In 2014 she was awarded the American Historical Association's Award for Scholarly Distinction and in 2020 the Association for Asian Studies Award for Outstanding Contributions to Asian Studies.

**Roger B. Beck** (Ph.D., Indiana University) is Distinguished Professor of History, emeritus, at Eastern Illinois University, where he taught African and world history. His publications include *The History of South Africa;* a translation of P. J. van der Merwe's *The Migrant Farmer in the History of the Cape Colony, 1657–1842;* and more than a hundred articles, book chapters, and reviews. In 2018 he received the Pioneer in World History award from the World History Association, its highest honor.

**Jerry Dávila** (Ph.D., Brown University) is Jorge Paulo Lemann Chair in Brazilian History at the University of Illinois and directs the Illinois Global Institute. He is the author of *Dictatorship in South America; Hotel Trópico: Brazil and the Challenge of African Decolonization,* winner of the Latin Studies Association Brazil Section Book Prize; and *Diploma of Whiteness: Race and Social Policy in Brazil, 1917–1945.* He has served as president of the Conference on Latin American History.

**Clare Haru Crowston** (Ph.D., Cornell University) is Associate Dean of Humanities and Interdisciplinary Programs and Professor of History at the University of Illinois at Urbana-Champaign. She is the author of *Credit, Fashion, Sex: Economies of Regard in Old Regime France* and *Fabricating Women: The Seamstresses of Old Regime France, 1675–1791,* which won the Berkshire and Hagley Prizes. She edited two special issues of the *Journal of Women's History,* has published numerous journal articles and reviews, and is a past president of the Society for French Historical Studies.

**John P. McKay** (Ph.D., University of California, Berkeley) is professor emeritus at the University of Illinois. He has written or edited numerous works, including the Herbert Baxter Adams Prize–winning book *Pioneers for Profit: Foreign Entrepreneurship and Russian Industrialization, 1885–1913.*